JOSEPH ROARK

His Life and Times

JOSEPH ROARK

His Life and Times

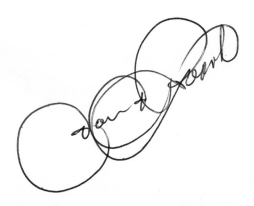

John J. Roark

First Printing, Summer 2001

For Reba Wilson,
who made it all possible.

Contents

Preface

My interest in family history was slow in coming. The focus of my initial interest was limited to my paternal grandfather and was primarily the result of the stories I had heard my father tell of him. This interest in my namesake, John W. Roark, 1841-1928, centered around the fact that he had been a Confederate soldier during the Civil War, and my fascination with that conflict endeared him to me. His stories about the war related by my father and others of his family, all of whom were born during the decade following the war, plus my own involvement in military service, made my grandfather a natural hero for me. Primarily in hopes of gaining more information on him in the geographical area of his early years, I attended my first Roark-Conner family reunion (my paternal grandmother was a Conner) in Hamilton County, Tennessee, in July 1961. There it was that I initially saw the home place of Joseph Roark, my hero's father, and learned of him for the first time. I was not immediately enamored with him–he had not served in the military at any time during his life; he had fought in no battles nor had he been involved in any major conflicts or political events. He was merely a farmer who had come south from upper Tennessee to homestead government land in the southeast part of the state–hardly the type of individual about whom books are written or exciting stories told. I thus catalogued Joseph Roark in remote memory cells and continued my limited and narrow focus on his son.

Thirty years passed before I learned of the availability of the Joseph Roark papers, which had been carefully preserved, in turn, by his youngest son, William, by his youngest grandson, Grover Roark, by Laura Roark Shropshire, eldest daughter of William, and most recently by Laura's daughter, Reba Shropshire Wilson. The preserved papers were catalogued by the Roark-Conner Association in 1996 and were subsequently filed in the Chattanooga-Hamilton County Bicentennial Library. They later were made readily available to the public through microfilming by the Tennessee State Library and Archives. In examining his papers, one is impressed with the careful preservation of records by Joseph Roark. He served as administrator of the estate of his father-in-law, Samuel Carr, and preserved records from that estate dating as far back as 1795. It is obvious that Joseph's objective in maintaining his records was not historical preservation but rather a careful documentation of financial transactions. The papers of Joseph Roark contain little correspondence, probably because few letters were written in a period when writing skills were limited and when paper was in short supply on the frontier of development. Letters that must have been written were not preserved by Joseph Roark in his papers, because he obviously considered them of much less importance than promissory notes, payment receipts, and legal documents. Nevertheless, the complete collection of his papers includes a richness of detail that, when integrated with historical events of the period, tells a marvelous story. Could that story be told in a definitive biography of Joseph Roark? What would it be like to get to know an ancestor from the first half of the nineteenth century through a biography like those written on celebrities, war heroes, and political statesmen? Could such a biography be written on Joseph Roark that would tell of his ambitions, hopes, disappointments, joys and sorrows, strengths and weaknesses? After some deliberation, I was determined to attempt such a biography.

In analyzing and evaluating each of the almost one thousand documents in the Joseph Roark papers and in putting together this biography on his life, I began to feel a sense of comradeship with my great-grandfather. I began to feel as if I knew him personally and could reasonably anticipate what he would do in response to various situations. Character traits were identified in him, his father and his grandfather, which I can, today, relate to myself and many other descendants.

Joseph Roark aggressively pursued the independent lifestyle of self-sufficiency so prevalent on the American frontier following the Revolutionary War and spent most of his life in a sparsely developed rural area isolated from the mainstream of America's development. But no one lives in isolation–each person is influenced by the times in which he or she lives. To fully understand and appreciate Joseph Roark, a person must have an understanding of the environment in which he lived. Thus this biography became a "life and times" work so that, hopefully, the reader could walk in Joseph's shoes with a cursory understanding of the issues he confronted and decisions he faced. In 1861, for example, he was forced to choose between his country and the newly formed Confederacy. His decision placed him in the minority in East Tennessee, separated him from his siblings in the northern part of the state, and resulted in his financial ruin. A study of his life is thus incomplete if the reader does not gain an understanding of the times and issues that impacted his life. For the historical parallel to Joseph's life that the reader may feel provides limited benefit to a biography, I apologize for its wordiness but hope that a serious reading will show its purpose and benefit.

The primary source of information in this work was, of course, the catalogued papers of the Joseph Roark collection. Endnotes have been used extensively to document each item. Documents from the Joseph Roark papers can be readily identified in the notes by the collection catalogue number, e.g., 1-1-1-492. Documents from the collection have been quoted verbatim in the text with the original punctuation and, much to the consternation of my spell checker, the grammar and spelling used by the original writer. Joseph and his contemporaries were not strict grammarians, and creative spelling was used to convey the desired message. While some documents have been edited slightly to permit easier reading and better understanding, the large majority have been included just as they were written.

For historical references, I have relied extensively on the *History of Tennessee* in four volumes by Folmsbee, Corlew, and Mitchell, and the publications of the East Tennessee Historical Society. Of particular benefit was *War at Every Door* by Noel C. Fisher on violence in East Tennessee during and following the Civil War, and the Ph.D. dissertation of Dr. Charles F. Bryan at the University of Tennessee, The Civil War in East Tennessee: A Social, Political, and Economic Study. Special thanks should be extended to Ms. Clara Swann, head of the Local History and Genealogy Section of the Chattanooga-Hamilton County Bicentennial Library, for her help and support. Materials and support staff of the Library of Virginia in Richmond and the Tennessee State Library and Archives in Nashville and the extensive collection of materials of the Genealogy section of the Dallas Public Library were particularly helpful.

Many people graciously helped in supplying data on the several related families that were followed in this work. Anne Moore of Danville, Arkansas, was particularly helpful in providing needed information on Mary Talley Smith, Benjamin F. Talley, and Andrew Jackson Talley, children of Josephs daughter Elizabeth, all of whom relocated to Arkansas with their father. Don Thompson of Tulsa, Oklahoma, was an encyclopedia of knowledge on Mary Ann Roark Scott and Robert Beane Scott. Fran Marlow of Citrus Heights, California, a great-granddaughter of Margaret Roark Swafford, was helpful with the family of the Swaffords. Russell Webb of Oakville, Connecticut, and Faye and R.V. Thompson of Richardson, Texas, descendants of Jane Webb, provided key information on Jane Clingan Webb and her family. Kathryn Conner of Dayton, Tennessee, was helpful on Sarah Roark Webb and Bill Webb. Darwin and Joyce Roark Lane and David Roark, descendants of James P. Roark, spent considerable time and effort with me in estimating and locating the land holdings of James. Edgar Roark of Georgetown, Tennessee, provided copies of information on John Roark, brother of Joseph. Becky Campbell of Crofton, Maryland, a descendant of Timothy Roark Jr., supplied a copy of the Timothy Jr. family Bible, pictures, and other data on that family. Steve Roark of Tazewell, Tennessee, was helpful with Claiborne County information. Of particular help was Ina Mae Sandefur of Kokomo, Indiana, in sharing information and pictures and in brainstorming on the Elizabeth Roark Ellison and the Mary Ann Roark Lambert families in Claiborne County. On Jeremiah Roark, much information was needed and it was graciously supplied by Sondra Martin and Merriam White of Kansas City, Missouri; Janis Ragar of Sedalia, Missouri; and Thelma Johnson of Cookeville, Tennessee, all descendants of Jeremiah. Linzey Estridge of Big Stone Gap, Virginia, a descendant of James and Lucy Eastridge, provided a copy of the Eastridge family Bible and was a true friend in supporting my research. In Tazewell, Virginia, Pat Surface and the Tazewell County Historical Society were invaluable in the search for information on James Roark in Baptist Valley. Marleita Carmichael of Hixson, Tennessee, the current owner and restorer of the Joseph Roark home place, provided valuable information on its history. Howard Scott of Cleveland, Tennessee, was a right arm in his knowledge of historical farming methods and of people and places in the old Salem Community area of Hamilton County. And, of course, Reba Wilson was there to correct, advise, and encourage at all times.

To the kind and supportive professionals at Brown Books Publishing Group, I am indebted for their criticism, creative suggestions, and careful editing, plus their unlimited patience and encouragement. These include: Milli Brown, President; Kathryn Grant, Editorial Director; Suzanna Brown, Creative Director; Laura Gloege, editor; Chesle Blair, book designer; and Abbey Rosenbaum, proofreader/ copy editor.

There are others, I'm sure, that I have unknowingly omitted. To them, I humbly apologize and ask their forgiveness for not mentioning their names. Also, if mistakes have been made in the history of any of the families of Timothy Roark and Joseph Roark, I claim those errors as my own and hold harmless all those wonderful people who were so helpful.

This, then, is the objective story of Joseph Roark and the times in which he lived. I can only hope that the reader will share in some small measure the respect and admiration of Joseph Roark that I have gained through this effort and maybe will be encouraged, even motivated, to diligently pursue family history and develop a biography of another staunch pioneer who passed the torch to this generation.

John J. Roark
Dallas, Texas
December 29, 2000

Chapter 1

Independence Day 1813

Independence Day fell on Sunday in 1813 and commemorated the thirty-seventh anniversary of the signing of the Declaration of Independence. The July 4th celebrations that year throughout the country–in the cities, in the rural areas, and on the western frontier–were somewhat muted and less dramatic than in past years due to the oppressive war then under way with England. Self-imposed embargoes and later naval blockades by British ships of war had seriously restricted the American economy and had placed financial burdens on the New England merchants, the Southern planters, and the frontier farmers. The economic conditions impacted the holiday festivities on this Independence Day. Traditional holiday events were held in some local communities, but international circumstances discouraged universal celebration and extended activities.

In Tennessee and western Claiborne County, which lies adjacent to the southern border of Virginia, the frontier farmers followed the events of what history has named the War of 1812 through public meetings in the county seat of Tazewell. The war, with its military setbacks, and depressed economic conditions were of more concern than celebrations. Independence Day in 1813 was observed as it had been in the past, but ominous war clouds over the country diminished the enthusiasm for activities in this and other rural areas. On this particular Independence Day, Timothy Roark and his wife Sarah, at their farm home on the Powell River located just six miles from the Cumberland Gap into Kentucky, celebrated not the nation's anniversary, but the birth of their new son born early that Sunday morning. They named him Joseph. Both his mother and the country into which he was born, the United States of America, were thirty-seven.

Joseph's mother had grown up with the new republic. She had been five years old when the Revolutionary War ended at Yorktown, eleven when the Constitutional Convention met in Philadelphia, and thirteen when Washington was inaugurated as the first president. She remembered little of the war and had never known government under the British Crown. Her generation was the first to grow up with the personal liberties guaranteed under a republic. Probably educated to a degree higher than most of her contemporaries, she would spend her early life on the western frontier of Virginia and her middle and later years among the ridges and mountains of Claiborne County, Tennessee. Because of her life on the frontier and in the rural areas of Virginia and Tennessee, she probably was able to see little difference between the British parliamentary system and the evolving government of the new nation. Governments have little impact on frontier life and, in that era, had little effect on rural areas. Her generation had little opportunity to fully enjoy the "blessings of liberty" and to reap the benefits of a free market economy. For her son Joseph, however, born on that fourth day of July 1813, it would be different.

Joseph Roark and his generation represented the first to be born in a new century, after the war for independence, following the struggle for governmental organization and stability, and during the efforts of the republic to take a position in the world of nations. Joseph and his contemporaries would experience the new republic's manifest destiny in westward expansion, would understand more fully the benefits of political and economic freedom than had their parents, would suffer the devastation of a terrible civil war, and would later struggle to rebuild following the deep personal losses of that war. During his life, Joseph would understand the benefits of economic freedom in a rural, frontier enterprise. He would accumulate land, create new business endeavors, understand the rural system of economics, raise a family, participate and lead in the local development of churches and schools, and enjoy the fruits of his labor. This is his story. It is not atypical of those of his generation and generally is representative of the lives of the first native-born sons of the new republic who lived during its first one hundred years. Joseph's story begins with a brief history of the United States of America from its declaration of independence to his birth on its thirty-seventh anniversary.

The time span covering the thirty-seven years between 1776 and 1813 has been defined by some historians as an era unto itself. For the new nation, struggling to establish its governmental traditions, overcome its wartime indebtedness, and bind the original thirteen colonies and five new states into a "united" government, the era was one of trial and struggle. It was a time in which crisis followed crisis, full of anxiety, self-doubt, foreboding, internal and external hostility, instability, and confusion.[1] The country had struggled to envision an image of itself and a national character, to become independent of British traditions, products, and currency, and to become, on its own, an accepted member of the world of nations.

The vote by the Continental Congress on July 2, 1776, was unanimously cast in favor of the motion that "these united colonies are and of a right ought to be free and independent states, that they are absolved from all allegiance to the British Crown, and that all political connection between them and the state of Great Britain is and ought to be totally dissolved." Following the approval and acceptance of the Declaration on the evening of the fourth, with signatures affixed by the president and secretary of the Congress, the new nation would experience significant crises which would later be remembered as "historical events."

For five trying and disappointing years the new nation had fought the armies and navies of the most powerful nation in the world to secure the "inalienable rights" endowed by their Creator. Held together primarily by the tenacity and financial support of Gen. George Washington through the trials and defeats at Long Island, Harlem Heights, and White Plains, the surrender of West Point, the devastation of the Continental army by smallpox, and the suffering at Valley Forge, the new nation had struggled to survive. In October 1781, the American Revolution had ended with the defeat of General Cornwallis by Washington at Yorktown, although the British would continue to hold and occupy New York City until November 1783.

Just twenty-six years before Joseph Roark was born, a constitutional convention met to "establish a more perfect union" and in the summer of 1787 had proposed a written constitution for the United States of America. The new constitution had been ratified by the required ninth state (New Hampshire) in June 1788, and on April 30, 1789, George Washington was inaugurated as the first president in a brief, simple ceremony in New York City. From his experience as the former commander of the Continental army during the Revolutionary War and as the president of the Constitutional Convention, Washington had solid qualifications for the office of president. Honest, straightforward, prudent, and admired by the country overall, he had seen the need for the Union and had believed in its possibilities. Washington had seen the wisdom in a strong central government capable of uniting the states, promoting peace and industry, and dealing firmly with foreign governments. To the comfort of Joseph's father and mother and average citizens like them, Washington had provided the prestige and dignity needed for the new government and the leadership to guide the country's growth during its first eight years.

The Constitution had provided for the admission of new states, and the Congress had set the criteria to admit a new state when a territory numbered sixty thousand inhabitants. Under these requirements, Vermont had been admitted as the fourteenth state in 1791, Kentucky as the fifteenth in 1792, and Tennessee, the adopted state of Joseph's father, as the sixteenth on June 1, 1796. By the time Joseph Roark was born in 1813, two other states had been admitted–Ohio in 1803 as the seventeenth state and Louisiana in 1812 as the eighteenth.

In the four years of his first administration, Washington and the nation had been troubled by Indian wars in the northwest in what would become the state of Ohio. Motivated by selfish interests, Canadian fur traders had supplied the Indian tribes with weapons and had encouraged the tribes to make war against white settlements, contrary to treaties executed in 1784 and 1785. In August 1794, Gen. "Mad Anthony" Wayne had defeated the Indian tribes at a British outpost on the Maumee River, and the following summer a treaty had been signed at Fort Granville that had opened up the area north of the Ohio River for settlement without the danger of Indian aggression. The victory by Wayne, at a time when Joseph's father was considering a move into the Tennessee frontier, had significantly reduced the risk of Indian raids in western Virginia, Kentucky, and the Claiborne County area of northern Tennessee.

The seat of the federal government, by prior agreement and compromise among the states, was to be located first in New York, then in Philadelphia, and finally within a ten-mile square tract provided by Virginia and Maryland on the Potomac River. In 1800, the Congress had held its first session in the Federal City, which had been christened as Washington in the District of Columbia. By Independence Day 1813, the Federal City had a population slightly greater than 8,000. The President's Mansion had been completed and was then occupied by its third resident. The Capitol building consisted only of the Congress House, which was later to become the House of Representatives' side of the ultimate Capitol. The Treasury Department was then housed in its newly completed Treasury Building, while other departments of the executive branch occupied privately owned buildings.

Four presidents had held office by the time the nation celebrated its thirty-seventh birthday. John Adams (1797-1801) had been the first president to reside in the executive mansion and was succeeded by Thomas Jefferson (1801-1809). James Madison took office in 1809 and in November 1812 was re-elected for a second term. The nation had been saddened on December 14, 1799, when George Washington died after a brief illness at his home at Mount Vernon. His death had been mourned throughout the country.

Following Jefferson's inaugural as president in March 1801, the U.S. Military Academy had been opened at West Point on the Hudson River in New York. In December 1803, the nation had taken possession of Louisiana from the French, and in 1804, Jefferson had commissioned the expedition of Captains Meriwether Lewis and William Clark to explore the new territory and the northwest. In September 1806, Lewis and Clark had returned to St. Louis after an absence of two and one-half years. Joseph's mother would have read to her husband and family from the available newspapers of the adventures of the men in the "Corps of Discovery."

Through 1811, relations between the U.S. and Great Britain had continued to deteriorate. The governor of the northwest Indian Territory, William Henry Harrison, had charged the British with supplying the Indian Chief Tecumseh with guns and ammunition to use against American settlers in what is now Indiana and Illinois. In the battle of Tippecanoe in November 1811, Harrison had routed the Tecumseh forces and the battle had given support to the War Hawks in Congress for a punitive war with Great Britain for supplying the Indians with weapons, for the seizing of American ships, and for the impressment of American sailors. The British actions had led to war.

By Independence Day 1813, the new nation had grown in its thirty-seven years from a population of just over three million in 1776 to over eight million.[2] America in 1813 was primarily rural in character and was becoming more so as the newly opened areas in Tennessee, Kentucky, and Ohio provided cheap land for the new populations.

The household size of American families just after 1800 averaged close to six persons–greater than the average size of English households, which was well under five persons per household.[3] By 1813, the country's population was still predominately rural with only seven percent of the population living in urban areas with greater than 2,500 population.[4] When Joseph Roark was born, the five major cities in America were New York with a population of 96,373, Philadelphia with 53,722, Baltimore with 35,583, Boston with 33,250, and Charleston, South Carolina, with 24,711.[5]

Immigration had continued to expand the population of the United States. It has been estimated that roughly 200,000 immigrants entered the country in its first thirty-seven years. By 1830, when immigration records were first kept, the number of immigrants averaged around 8,000 per year with the majority coming from England and Ireland. The British government as early as 1773 had become concerned with the magnitude of emigration to the Colonies and the loss of skilled workmen from the British industrial work force. Since England had no reason to encourage the industrialization of the United States after the Revolutionary War, a bill was introduced in Parliament in November 1773 to restrict the emigration of skilled artisans and industrial workers to the Colonies.[6] Still, immigrants continued to seek the freedoms and available lands of the U.S. and, by various means, gained transport to the new country.

Even with the immigration and natural growth of the new nation, it still faced shortages of skilled ironworkers, shipbuilders, and clothes makers. Indentured servants were sought for terms of four to seven years for unskilled workers and even convicts seeking to learn a trade. By 1813, the available land west of the Allegheny Mountains was a significant attraction to those who had become free of indenture to leave the tidewater areas and to gain the independence of a "landowner" and farmer.[7]

Available land had also encouraged speculation on the frontier by numbers of successful businessmen who had survived the Revolutionary War. Large tracts were available for purchase from Revolutionary War veterans who had received land grants from the individual states and a grateful nation. Following the adoption of the new Constitution, states had ceded their western lands to the United States. In 1784, Virginia had relinquished her western lands to the national government.[8] Similarly, in the North Carolina Act of 1783, that state had relinquished to speculation four million acres in what was to become Tennessee.[9] The door had thus been opened for Joseph Roark's father to obtain land in Tennessee.

An enormous western area had thus become available to settlement just prior to the turn of the century. Land was in abundance, waiting to be cleared, waiting to appreciate in value, and waiting for sale by speculators to farmers who would be the first actual users of the land. Soldiers' land warrants were bought for five cents on the dollar, and respectable tidewater businessmen made fortunes on land they had never seen. Land had been the chief speculative enterprise in the first thirty-seven years of the United States.[10] By 1813, most of the land in Claiborne County,

Tennessee, had been acquired by farmers either through homestead grants by the state or through purchase from speculators or land brokers.

Land speculation and development quickly outpaced the construction of roads and other internal improvements. By 1800, the young republic desperately needed roads. The vast stretches of land far from the ocean, separated from rivers that could provide waterborne transportation, could not be developed and inhabited without roads. There had not been a soundly paved road in the country when the federal government was set up in 1789. The few existing roads, if they could be called that, wound their way through uncleared land with heavily wooded areas bordering the pathway. By 1808, the national government had taken an interest in providing roadways and in 1810 had begun the construction of the Cumberland Road to extend from western Virginia to the Ohio River. In the more removed areas of southwestern Virginia and northern Tennessee, roadways prior to 1813 had been cut through the rugged mountainous terrain by local labor with landowners being required to provide the manpower for construction. Bridges were nonexistent with creek and river crossings made by fording the stream if possible or by ferry if an enterprising local resident had seen enough traffic to initiate ferry service.

While the Appalachian mountain range restricted expansion by the new nation, development beyond the mountains was accelerated after Fulton's demonstration of the steamboat on the Hudson River in 1807. By 1813, steamboats with stern paddle wheels were making the trip upstream from New Orleans to Pittsburgh via the Mississippi and Ohio Rivers. But the steamboat did not solve the nation's transportation problems. Its usefulness was limited to rivers, lakes, and protected bays along the Atlantic coast. On the major rivers, keelboats and flatboats provided more service than steamboats to move bulk cargo downstream.[11] River travel was, however, of little benefit to the mountainous country of northeast Tennessee and Claiborne County. Railroads were then still decades away, and even stagecoach travel up the Shenandoah Valley in western Virginia would not be available until nearly 1820.

By 1813, the new republic had expanded the system of postal service. At the beginning of the federal government in 1789, the main postal route extended from Maine to Georgia, serving fifty post offices. The postal route to Pittsburgh had just been opened in 1813, and that town on the Ohio River had become the most western post office. Postal service was expensive, with the cost of a letter from New York to Savannah, Georgia, being thirty-four cents. With a concern about the loyalty of the new settlers west of the Appalachians, the federal government after 1790, recognizing the benefit of better communications, pushed postal service into the more remote regions. The post office in the wilderness areas most often had been a settler's cabin and later was a corner in the local tavern or general store.[12]

Churches continued to play a large role in the culture of the United States in 1813. The Revolution and the concept and organization of American government had been led by men of what has been called "moderate enlightenment"–men who believed that the universe is orderly and can be understood by rational inquiry.[13] Men like Jefferson and Adams had stressed the concern that the new nation have no government-sponsored religion and that the United States not become involved in the religious wars that had plagued Europe for centuries. Jefferson, a deist, had praised the Baptists for their focus on religious liberty, their refusal of government funds, and their adherence to separation of church and state. Orthodox churches, with their strong Calvinistic belief, had dominated the religious culture in the new country until shortly after 1800, at which time the "great revival" in evangelical Christianity blossomed in the United States. The great revival was characterized by "camp meetings" in rural areas in which thousands would attend week-long evangelistic services. The camp meetings, and the revival in general, "emphasized emotion, a deeply felt commitment, and the religion of the heart, and it explicitly or implicitly jettisoned Calvinist belief in predestination in favor of a salvation open to all who would reach for it."[14] The great revival and camp meeting culture were to have a significant influence on the family of Joseph Roark.

Along with the spiritual development of the new nation, education was also sought for the betterment of the individual and the nation as a whole. James Madison had argued that "a people who mean to be their own governors must arm themselves with power which knowledge gives." Education therefore could not be limited to a privileged few but, as was recognized by the founding fathers, it had to become the possession of the masses. The basis of the new republican government required emphasis on the public responsibility for the instruction of young people.[15]

For a rural people in 1813 and by the standards of their time, Americans were basically literate, exceeding the literacy of most of the nations of western Europe. This did not mean, however, that Americans were highly qualified readers. Many of them, with their limited formal education, read slowly and haltingly. Large numbers of seemingly literate Americans probably read only the Bible, religious tracts, and newspapers.[16] By 1810, more than 22 million copies of 376 newspapers had been circulated annually in the United States, a larger circulation than anywhere else in the world. Recognizing the importance of the flow of information in a republic, the post office subsidized the distribution of newspapers through the mail, enabling people in remote areas to obtain papers from the major cities.[17]

In 1813, Americans were a heterogeneous people. Even in the first census in 1790, diversity of the backgrounds of the people in the new nation was obvious. The largest group by national origin was the men and women of English descent located in New England and the Chesapeake Bay area, and the Quakers in Pennsylvania. Second, making up almost twenty percent of the population, were those of the Celtic regions of Great Britain–the Scotch-Irish from Ulster, the southern Irish, the Scottish, and the Welsh–generally distributed south and west of the New England states. In eastern Pennsylvania, Maryland, and New Jersey were the Germans, and in the Hudson Valley of New York were the Dutch.[18]

In spite of their heterogeneous character, the American public by 1813 had begun to develop a homogeneous society and common heritage. This may best be illustrated by the holidays commonly celebrated throughout the country. Considered by Europeans to have few holidays because the American calendar was not filled with saints days, feasts, and fasts, Americans commonly celebrated only three holidays: Thanksgiving, although it primarily was limited to New England in 1813, Christmas, and Independence Day, which after the turn of the century had become the holiday most universally celebrated in the United States.[19]

The Fourth of July was the holiday of midsummer when weather generally permitted assemblage of large numbers of people to celebrate a common heritage.[20] Within a few years after the Declaration in 1776, Independence Day was singled out as "the great day" on which to celebrate the national origin.[21] By 1789, it was already a sacred place on the American calendar and, as a national festival of remembrance, was widespread after 1800.[22]

While the type of festival planned for Independence Day varied from place to place, the celebration generally had similar characteristics throughout the country. Fireworks, militia parades, dinners, recitals of the Declaration of Independence, and formal speeches were generally part of each local celebration. It was a day of coming together in local communities, county seats, and urban areas and offered an opportunity for much bombast and self-congratulation. It was also, however, a formal occasion for giving thanks for the republic, thinking about the state of affairs and, in a sense, a time for patriotic rededication to the nation's democratic principles. On Independence Day 1813, in Tazewell, Tennessee, county seat of Claiborne County, the traditional celebration joined men, women, and families in a time together. The day of festivities was spent at home, however, by the parents of Joseph Roark as they celebrated the birth of their new son.

The new baby was oblivious to the disharmony that blanketed the nation on its thirty-seventh birthday. The War of 1812, by Independence Day 1813, had become a divisive factor for the various parts of the country. Begun in June 1812 by the Congress at the recommendation of President James Madison, the war had sought to redress the impressment of American seamen by the British navy and the violation of U.S. territorial waters. Great Britain had been in a war with Napoleon and France since 1803 but, following the British naval victory at Trafalgar in 1805, the British fleets had been free to tighten their control over the naval commerce between the U.S. and France and to otherwise restrict American trade. Thomas Jefferson, as Madison's predecessor, had tried to defend American rights by an embargo in 1807 that was to prohibit foreign ships from trading in American ports. More than hurting the British, it had completely disrupted the U.S. economy. Southern planters in the U.S. supported the war with England while the New England merchants actively opposed it because of the lost trade with France. All sections of the U.S., including the western frontier of Claiborne County, suffered financially because of the war, and the attitude of each section toward the war seriously divided the country.

The early months of the war had seen major naval victories by the U.S., principally due more to Great Britain's concentration on Napoleon than on the naval strength of the United States. By early 1813, the British had established a tight blockade of the American coast and attempts to run the blockade had resulted in the loss of several U.S. ships. American attempts to invade Canada had been frustrated when the U.S. detachment under Gen. James Winchester was defeated south of Detroit and over 500 Americans were massacred by Indians supporting the British. By July 1813, "Mr. Madison's War" was at low tide from the American point of view, and the administration was being severely criticized for the conduct of the war.

To President Madison, Independence Day in 1813 was not for him a celebration in the President's Mansion. He had been sick since June 16 and word had spread that the President was critically ill with bilious fever. Madison conducted no government business for over three weeks, during which time the war was at its low point for the United States. Two days before the Fourth of July, Dolley Madison wrote her friend Edward Coles that she had nursed her husband day and night for over three weeks and only recently had seen some improvement. By July 7, the President was to resume only the most urgent matters of government business.[23]

At his home at Monticello, Thomas Jefferson celebrated Independence Day in 1813 in his usual routine of letter writing. He had begun writing a response to a letter from former President John Adams that he had received and had read "with infinite delight."[24] The two signers of the Declaration of Independence had only recently begun a correspondence following their estrangement in 1800 when Adams was defeated for re-election by Jefferson. Their common friend, Benjamin Rush of Philadelphia, had worked diligently to bring the two old friends back together and had succeeded only shortly before his death in April 1813. On May 27, 1813, Jefferson had written Adams about Rush: "Another of our friends of seventy-six is gone, my dear sir, another of the co-signers of the independence of our country. . . . I believe we are under half a dozen at present; I mean the signers of the Declaration. Yourself, Gerry, Carroll and myself are all I know to be living."[25]

John Adams lived with his wife, Abigail, at Peacefield, their home in Quincy, Massachusetts. He had expressed his concern about the health of President Madison for whom he had a great respect. Earlier in the spring Adams had received word of the appointment by Madison of his son John Quincy Adams as one of the peace negotiators with Great Britain.[26] John Adams spent the anniversary of the Declaration of Independence at home engulfed with concern about the health of his daughter Nabby (Mrs. Abigail Adams Smith) who was terribly ill with cancer and who would die at Peacefield the following month.[27] Nevertheless, Adams had by now begun again his correspondence with Jefferson. It was to continue for another thirteen years. By strange coincidence, both died on Joseph Roark's thirteenth birthday,

July 4, 1826, the fiftieth anniversary of their signing of the Declaration of Independence.

At his home at the Hermitage near Nashville, Andrew Jackson celebrated Independence Day 1813 following his return from the expedition to Natchez on the Mississippi. Having been commissioned a major general of militia in February 1802, Jackson had been ordered in November 1812 to muster 1,500 volunteers and move them to Natchez for possible use in protection of New Orleans or in defense of West Florida against the Creek Indians. General Jackson had assembled 2,000 volunteers in January 1813, and by March had moved them successfully to Natchez only to receive on March 15, 1813, orders from the secretary of war to return home since the "causes of embodying and marching to New Orleans the corps under your command having ceased to exist." Jackson had returned his troops to Nashville by June 1813, having pledged his own credit to pay the cost of transporting the sick of his unit.[28] On the return trip from Natchez to Nashville, Jackson's troops expressed the opinion that their commander was "tough as hickory." He was admired by his troops as a commander and they soon added the prefix "old" to their chosen nickname for him, thereby giving Jackson his everlasting nickname, "Old Hickory."[29] Only eight months were to pass after Joseph Roark was born before Jackson would defeat the Creek Indians at the Battle of Horseshoe Bend and eighteen months before Jackson would gain the admiration of the country for his defeat of the British at New Orleans January 8, 1815. He would remain a hero to the people of Tennessee throughout the life of Joseph Roark.[30]

At his father's home in Columbia, Tennessee, seventeen-year-old James K. Polk celebrated the Fourth of July in 1813 at local festivities and prepared for enrollment within the next few days as a student in the Presbyterian Academy in Maury. Small for his age and sickly, Jim Polk had been taken by his father, Sam Polk, on surveying trips in the wilderness to improve Jim's physical strength. In April 1813, at his father's house, Jim Polk had helped his father entertain Gen. Andrew Jackson on his return from the Natchez expedition. Jim had also been in the crowd that day when Columbia welcomed home its returning militia from General Jackson's command.[31] Twenty-seven years later, as governor of Tennessee, James K. Polk would sign land grants to Joseph Roark in southeast Tennessee.

In Raleigh, North Carolina, another future governor of Tennessee and president of the U.S. was but four years old on July 4, 1813. Andrew Johnson and his brother, William, six years older than himself, would have little cause to join in the Independence Day celebration. Their father had died in January the year before and their mother was forced to earn a living for herself and her two sons as a "washerwoman." Mary McDonough Johnson, uneducated and without family support, tried to feed and clothe her two boys in the ravishing throes of "grinding poverty." Within nine years, Mary was to find a means to provide for Andrew's upkeep by apprenticing him to a tailor in Raleigh. It was to be the trade that would later carry him over the mountains to Greeneville, Tennessee, and involve him in the politics of East Tennessee.[32]

Not far from what had been the home of Joseph's grandfather, in Wythe County, Virginia, William Gannaway Brownlow was eagerly awaiting his eighth birthday on August 29. The oldest of five children, William Brownlow would lose both parents to illness within three years, imbuing him with bitterness, hatred, and vengeance. Much later, as the reconstruction governor of Tennessee following the Civil War, he would bring all his venom and wrath against Joseph Roark and other former supporters of the Southern Confederacy.[33]

In Missouri, on that Independence Day in 1813, at his home southwest of St. Louis, Daniel Boone, then eighty years old, was still mourning the death of his wife, Rebecca. In the late winter of 1812-1813, Boone and Rebecca had returned to their cabin located on the farm of their son Nathan where they had lived for seven years and had spent more time together than at any time during their marriage. Rebecca, who had hardly been sick a day in her life, had been working together with Boone in the pleasant work of sugar-making in the sugar grove during the warm early days of spring when she became ill. After a week of suffering, Rebecca died on March 18, 1813, and was buried on a grassy knoll overlooking the Missouri River. On Independence Day 1813, Daniel Boone still grieved for her and his "inexpressible loss" in what had been the "saddest affliction of his life."[34]

Three hundred miles south of where Joseph Roark was born in Claiborne County–in Rhea County, Tennessee, on the Tennessee River across from present-day Dayton–two men who much later would significantly influence the life of Joseph Roark were, during the 1813 Independence Day celebration, negotiating the sale and purchase of two slaves. William Blythe and Samuel Carr would consummate the transaction and record the sale on July 10, 1813.[35]

So, on July 4, 1813, Joseph Roark was born during a period of troublesome and uncertain times for the United States. Within thirteen months of his birth, the British would capture Washington, D.C., and burn the Capitol and President's Mansion. Within fourteen months, Francis Scott Key would pen the Star Spangled Banner while watching the bombardment of Fort McHenry near Baltimore, and days later, the nation's spirits would be lifted by the American naval victory on Lake Champlain. After the Treaty of Ghent ended the War of 1812 on December 24, 1814, Andrew Jackson would bring glory and pride to the new nation at the Battle of New Orleans. The nation would be at peace once more. The economic and personal stress of war would fade. In retrospect, the summer of 1813 was an exciting time in which to be born. The nation would soon experience an expansive growth, and new opportunities would be available to a growing population. But all that was unforeseen on the Fourth of July 1813 by people living among the ridges and valleys of Claiborne County, Tennessee, and in the humble home into which Joseph Roark was born.

Chapter 2

Ancestry–James Roark
Southwestern Virginia Pioneer

The ancestry of Joseph Roark was Scotch-Irish,[1] and the history of his forefathers was closely linked to the settlement of the area west of the Blue Ridge in Virginia by Scotch-Irish pioneers. The best evidence available to researchers today suggests that Joseph Roark descended from Scotch-Irish settlers who immigrated to the American Colonies in the first wave of Scotch-Irish immigrants, between 1717 and 1720. Probably under the name of "Ororke" or some similar old-world spelling, the Roarks landed at Philadelphia with the majority of Scotch-Irish emigrants and moved westward toward the Appalachian range. Turned southward by the mountain barrier, the family was in the lower Shenandoah Valley and on the western frontier of Virginia by the 1730s. During the next twenty years, the family was part of the southern migration of Scotch-Irish settlers and, by 1750, was in the middle Shenandoah Valley. In late 1772 or early 1773, James Roark, who was of the third generation of Roarks to push forward the American frontier and who would later be the grandfather of Joseph Roark, moved with other pioneers further west into the unsettled area of the Clinch River Valley in southwest Virginia. Four subsequent generations of Roarks were to move to frontier homesteads or sparsely settled areas in search of richer lands and better opportunities. What kind of people were these Scotch-Irish settlers and what were the circumstances that consistently motivated them to move with their families to the fringe of civilization? Any attempt to grasp a history of the family and to understand the characteristics that were to be passed to later generations must begin with the history of the Scotch-Irish and their role in the colonization of the New World and the settlement of the American frontier.

The Scotch-Irish as an identifiable segment of society came into being as a result of the English problem with the Irish. For almost five centuries between 1138 and 1603, the Irish had been a thorn in the side of the British Crown and royal politicians. Characteristics common to the Irish throughout the centuries were poverty, clan rule, illiteracy, primitiveness, and hatred of the English. With the establishment of the Church of England in Ireland, the Catholic faith of the Irish contributed to the friction between the Irish and the English conquerors. The Reformation had not come to Ireland, and Jesuits in Ireland actively resisted the spread of Protestantism. In order to assume some control over the Irish and reduce the cost of a military force maintained in Ireland for that purpose, England's Queen Elizabeth in 1560 conceived the idea of transplanting hundreds of Englishmen to form a colony in the subdivided Irish "kingdoms." These colonies, however, failed miserably because of the fierce resistance of the Irish and the reluctance of the English to assume the hard work of colonization amid murderous Irish raids. All of Ireland was troublesome, but the biggest problem for Queen Elizabeth lay in Ireland's northern kingdom of Ulster. In 1603, in the last year of her life, Queen Elizabeth saw her armies devastate the Irish in the nine counties of Ulster, destroying crops, cattle, and the homes of the native Irish. The removal of the population to the south, to prevent friction with any English settlers, opened Ulster to a new scheme of colonization.

Queen Elizabeth's successor, James I of England, formerly James VI of Scotland, was enthusiastic in creating colonies. In 1606, he had approved the colony named for him at Jamestown in Virginia, and some months later King James and his advisors conceived the idea of a similar colony in Ulster. This colony would "plant" Protestant farmers not only from England but also from the lowlands of Scotland. Land grants for Ulster farms, then, were provided to the Scots along with farm implements to ensure successful crops and weapons by which to protect themselves. Eager to escape the poverty of Scotland and the oppression of English rule, the lowlanders traveled by boat across the twenty miles that separated Ulster from Scotland, and by 1610 the "plantation of Ulster" was well under way.

While Englishmen were involved in the colony, it was the Scots who made the colony a successful endeavor. The poverty of Ireland was indeed a step down from the comforts of England and, as at Jamestown in America, colonization was difficult for the English gentry. The poverty of Scotland, however, had better prepared the Scots for assuming the hardships in Ireland. As a result, the Scots enthusiastically welcomed the opportunity in Ulster. The Scots brought with them their Presbyterian ministers, thereby quickly reestablishing their sense of community around their dearest institution, the church. The Scots, then, much more quickly than the English, established a new home in northern Ireland.

The plantation of Ulster was economically successful for over a century. By the early 1700s, Ulster had established an enterprising export of woolen goods and linen products to England, the European continent, and the American Colonies. Manufacturing supplanted farming as the primary economy in Ulster. During the century of growth and success of the Scots in Ulster, the Irish lived nearby and thousands of Irish Catholics were subtenants on the Scottish farms. While their faith separated the Irish from the Protestant Scots, both had much in common in that both had known poverty and the lack of social distinction. Both Scots and Irish had been designated barbarians by the English. With the intermixing of the two cultures, inter-marriage was perhaps inevitable; however, the extent to which intermarriage occurred between the Protestant Scots and the Catholic Irish is questionable. The Scotch-Irish, as they came to be known in the American Colonies, were predomi-nately Scottish in ancestry and Presbyterian in religious faith.

The century of prosperity of the Ulster plantation came to an abrupt end within a brief period at the beginning of the eighteenth century. It was the success of the plantation which became its biggest problem and resulted in the migration of its pop-ulation to the American Colonies. The English Parliament had grown alarmed at the competition of Ulster's manufactured goods with that of English products. In 1699, Parliament passed the Woolens Act, which restricted the exportation of woolen cloth from Ulster. Shortly thereafter, an economic downturn in the linen industry further devastated the Ulster economy. Adding to the misery was the suffering caused by Ulster landlords, many of whom were absentee landlords in England, drastically raising rents as leases expired on Ulster lands.

Two other factors added to the impetus for emigration. First was a period of disastrous crops for the farmers that resulted from six years of drought beginning in 1714. The farmers faced ruined crops and the linen manufacturers suffered from an insufficient supply of flax. Second, as the final straw, in the second year of the rein of Queen Anne of England (1703), Parliament passed an act requiring all office holders in Ulster to take the sacraments of the established Anglican church. Presbyterian ministers were almost universally put out of their pulpits in Ulster and were threatened with legal prosecution for conducting weddings and funerals out-side the Church of England. The first major emigration from Ulster to America thus began in 1714 as the result of a combination of restriction against exporting woolen goods, economic depression, racked rents, drought, and religious persecution. In a single generation then, an attitude of optimism was replaced with one of pes-simism. Opportunities in America beckoned.[2]

The opportunity of choice for the Scotch-Irish in their first immigration to America was the New England Colonies. At least ten ships from Ulster arrived in New England between 1714 and 1716; however, the reception to the Scotch-Irish there was not favorable. The immigration of the Scotch-Irish to New England was from the first viewed with anxiety and distrust by the leading people there. Even ministers in New England expressed concern about the Scotch-Irish immigrants. Because of the reception in New England and its subsequent report back to Ulster, later ships carrying immigrants to America from Ulster turned toward Philadelphia as their destination.[3]

More than five thousand Scotch-Irish immigrated to America in 1717. William Penn had advertised the availability of cheap land and religious freedom in his Pennsylvania colony and the Scotch-Irish were eager for new opportunities. After the first immigration, reports were sent back to Ulster that were highly favorable. In

Ireland and Northern Ireland showing the Traditional Provinces and Counties in Ulster, home of Joseph Roark's ancestors

Penn's colony, land was fertile and available at a cheap price, authorities accepted the newcomers, and there was no religious persecution. The favorable reports resulted in five great waves of Scotch-Irish emigration: 1717-18, 1725-29, 1740-41, 1754-55, and 1771-75. By the time of the American Revolution, over 200,000 had migrated from Ulster to the American Colonies with over 90% of the number arriving in America through the port at Philadelphia.[4]

A word should be said about the difficulties of the journey across the Atlantic for the Ulster emigrants. A speedy trip was hoped for by all emigrants undertaking the trip and was enthusiastically promised by the agents arranging passage on all ships. The actual journey, however, was neither speedy nor comfortable. The average trip length under the most favorable conditions in the 1720s lasted between eight and ten weeks. Comforts for the passengers simply did not exist. During the eighteenth century, there were no laws regulating the number of passengers that could be carried on an oceangoing vessel, and ship owners tried to crowd on board as many paying passengers as possible. Passengers were massed on deck and below. Sometimes for days or even weeks the emigrants were required to remain below deck because of bad weather. There, in crowded conditions, they cooked their food, performed their daily functions, slept or tried to sleep, sang and wept, suffered under and obeyed the petty tyrants in their midst, rejoiced for the newly born and mourned for the dead. Disease thrived in the crowded conditions and added to the discomfort of the passengers. The shipowner was to provide provisions for the passengers during the trip; however, the passengers were not fed on a princely scale and provisions could, and often did, run low when the journey was extended by squalls and other bad weather. The immigrants arrived at their destination more often than not cold and hungry, possibly having lost a loved one or friend to disease and death on the journey, and doubtless with failing confidence that the future held much hope for better conditions.[5]

William Penn had also recruited heavily on the European continent and his efforts had resulted in the migration of large populations from west Germany to Pennsylvania, arriving at Philadelphia prior to or at generally the same time as the first wave of Scotch-Irish were disembarking. German and Scotch-Irish settlers moved past the Quaker settlements in and around Philadelphia and migrated westward along the Great Valley of Pennsylvania to compete for available land. Both were eager to get to the frontier, which was then only thirty to forty miles west of Philadelphia, and neither the Germans nor the Scotch-Irish were able to purchase the more expensive lands from the Quakers. There was minimal conflict between the Germans and Scotch-Irish even though the religious cultures and social heritages were significantly different. The difference between the two cultures was recognized by local inhabitants. "The settlement of five families from Ireland gives me more trouble than fifty of any other people," wrote James Logan, the Pennsylvania agent of William Penn in 1730.[6] The Scotch-Irish were wild and independent, yet they were to learn much from their German fellow immigrants. Since the Scotch-Irish came from Ulster lands that had been denuded of forests and the Germans had emigrated from the thick woods of west Germany, the Scotch-Irish settlers were to learn from the Germans the important art of building cabins from logs. Both Germans and Scotch-Irish followed the same migration pattern into western Pennsylvania before the Scotch-Irish turned south to migrate into the Shenandoah Valley of Virginia.

The two cultures integrated in the move westward even though their temperamental traits were so divergent. The contemporary writers of the period quickly recognized the difference between the two peoples.

It was usual to expect Germans to be orderly, industrious, carefully frugal; they rarely had trouble with Indians; if they interested themselves at all in politics, it was usually on the local level. Scotch-Irish, by contrast, were regarded as quick-tempered, impetuous, inclined to work by fits and starts, reckless, too much given to drinking. No contemporary observer praised them as model farmers. Their interest in politics on the Provincial level was soon to become active, even tempestuous; and their fame as Indian fighters was to become almost as notable as their reputation for causing trouble with the Indians.[7]

The early movement of the Scotch-Irish in Pennsylvania followed the river valleys. One band of immigrants moved up the Delaware River, and by 1720 the Scotch-Irish settlers were arriving in Bucks County. The primary Scotch-Irish path westward, however, was the Susquehanna River. From Lancaster County, Pennsylvania, the Scotch-Irish moved into the interior along the east bank of the Susquehanna, settling near creeks for water to operate mills and to meet other household needs. As they moved west into Cumberland County, the Scotch-Irish immigrants encountered the Appalachian Mountains, which presented a barrier to further settlement to the west. From Cumberland County the migration trail turned south to the Cumberland Valley, across the Potomac River, and into Virginia, following a path of least resistance between the Blue Ridge on the east and the Appalachian chain on the west.[8] By 1730, settlement had begun in the Shenandoah Valley.

While Pennsylvania was almost completely settled by Quakers and German and Scotch-Irish immigrants within fifty years of its formation, Virginia remained a tidewater colony for over one hundred and twenty-five years after the Jamestown settlement. The western region of Virginia, including the fertile valley of the Shenandoah, was practically empty until the second quarter of the eighteenth century. It was not until 1730 that the Governor of Virginia opened the Shenandoah Valley by granting large tracts to individual entrepreneurs. In 1732, a grant of forty thousand acres to John and Isaac Van Meter was purchased by Joist Hite, a German who brought in the first families, many of them Scotch-Irish, to the Shenandoah Valley.[9] The objective of the Virginia governor in opening the valley was less than altruistic–it was to use the Scotch-Irish settlers as a buffer and protection against the Indians on the western frontier of the colony. To further encourage settlement in pursuit of his objective, the governor openly permitted the erection of churches that dissented with the establishment church in Virginia, the Church of England. Presbyterians, Methodists, and particularly Baptists who had been persecuted in the colony for their resistance to taxes collected in support of the Anglican church, found welcomed opportunity on the western frontier of Virginia. By 1750, the lower valley of the Shenandoah was populated with Scotch-Irish, thereby fulfilling the policy objective of the governor:

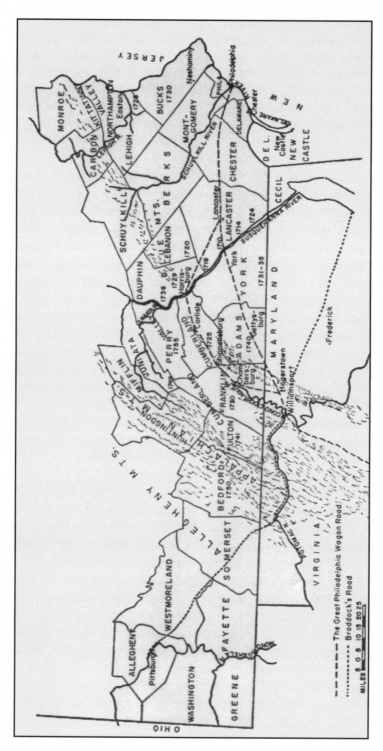

Southern Pennsylvania and Northern Virginia showing the Great Philadelphia Wagon Road and the probable route of Joseph Roark's ancestors from Philadelphia to the Shenandoah Valley in Virginia

In the adoption of this policy the government of the Colony of Virginia was actuated by selfish motives; they little dreamed that they were thus giving a foothold to a vigorous people who were destined to play a strong part in the future history of their country.[10]

The Scotch-Irish on the northwest Virginia frontier, including the ancestors of Joseph Roark, had arrived in the lower Shenandoah Valley by the 1730s. Bryan Roark (ca. 1690-1760), probably a direct ancestor of Joseph, was first mentioned in the court records of Frederick County in northern Virginia on May 14, 1743. The court records on Bryan consistently used what would become the traditional spelling of the family name–"Roark." No record remains that Bryan Roark owned land in Frederick County. Also in Frederick County during the same period was Timothy Ororke Sr. (1700-1768), who had by then not "Americanized" the old Scotch-Irish spelling of the family name. Probably a nephew or cousin of Bryan Roark, Timothy Ororke Sr. owned over 400 acres in the Shenandoah Valley which, at his death in 1768, was left to his widow and his son Philemon. Philemon lived on the homestead after his mother's death for several years with his siblings and settled permanently in the area of present-day Shenandoah County. The families of Bryan Roark and Timothy Ororke Sr. were then to settle different areas of the valley and in different ways. Contrary to the stability and permanent settlement of the family of Timothy Ororke Sr., Bryan Roark's family was to push the frontier farther up the Shenandoah Valley. His son Timothy (ca.1715-1780), who was referred to in Frederick County as Timothy Roark Jr., doubtless to distinguish him from the older Timothy Ororke Sr., and who gave reason for Timothy Ororke to be referred to as "Senior," left Frederick County in the late 1750s to move with other Scotch-Irish settlers farther up the valley. Such was the consistent pattern of Scotch-Irish migration–those that had sufficient land settled and remained in a location while those without land moved with their families to the frontier to find an area in which to settle and farm. By 1770, Timothy Roark Jr.* was in Botetourt County near Christiansburg in present-day Montgomery County.[11]

As they filled the lower Shenandoah Valley, and for that matter wherever they went, the Scotch-Irish stressed education for their children. Schools were almost certain to follow churches as the first institutions to be embraced in the frontier community. The Reformation in Scotland had stressed the idea to each citizen that education was the mark of a man. This ingrained belief of the Scotch-Irish in particular resulted in schools being formed in every community that could possibly afford them. Any such school was decidedly elementary, teaching reading, writing, arithmetic, and the Bible. If a school could not be formed, a subscription arrangement was set in place with an educated indentured servant or available "schoolmaster" to teach the local children. The entire community contributed proportionally by number of children to be trained to the support of the teacher whose curriculum was similar to that of any organized school.[12]

---

*For identification, the son of Bryan Roark is consistently referred to herein as Timothy Roark Jr. although the "Junior" is not technically correct.

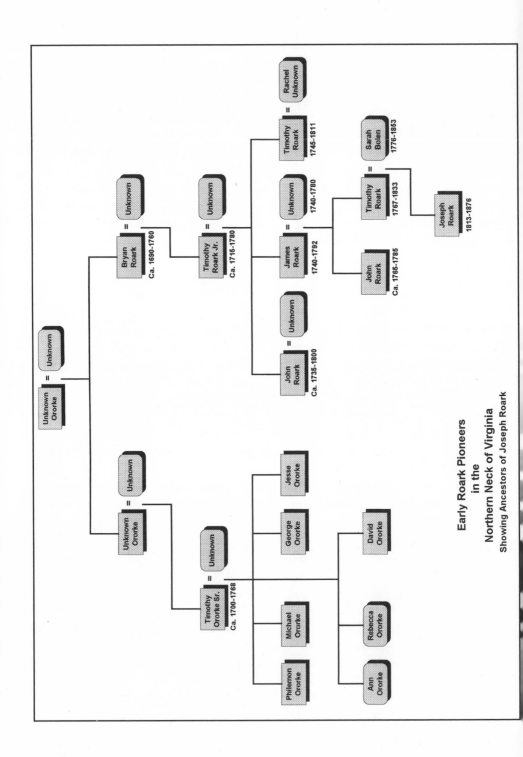

**Early Roark Pioneers
in the
Northern Neck of Virginia**
Showing Ancestors of Joseph Roark

This emphasis on education was evident in the Ororkes and Roarks during this early period in the development of the Shenandoah Valley. On January 22, 1766, Timothy Ororke Sr. was one of twelve men in Frederick County to sign an agreement with Joseph Goare to teach the children of the local community. In the agreement, Goare contracted to "teach their said children, if committed to my care, according to their capacities in reading, writing, and arithmetic and all other Christian principles in my power." The twelve Scotch-Irish citizens agreed to pay at the rate of one pound and three shillings per pupil and bound themselves for a total payment of fifty pounds to guarantee the contract. Timothy Ororke Sr. paid for two of the nineteen "scholars" registered for the school.[13]

The churches that preceded the schools in the early settlement of the Shenandoah Valley were primarily of one Protestant denomination. The Scotch-Irish that migrated to America in the first half of the eighteenth century were predominantly Presbyterian in religious faith. The Presbyterian Church had been the peculiar institution of the Scotch-Irish in Ulster and had represented their proud tradition of opposing kings and tyrants in Scotland. The John Knox heritage remained strong in the staunch pioneers in the Scotch-Irish immigration; however, as all institutions will do, the Presbyterian church was to be influenced and changed by time and events. A cursory study of the church in the Colonies and early days of the Republic illustrates the transition in the faith of the Scotch-Irish settlers.

The Presbyterian church in America in the early eighteenth century faced unique problems. First, few Presbyterian ministers immigrated to America with the thousands of Scotch-Irish who left Ulster for the Colonies. Only a few instances are recorded where a minister immigrated to the Colonies with his flock. As a result, religion among the immigrants suffered a setback since few congregations could prosper without a minister. "Without the influence of a church, and in the daily exigencies of conquering a wilderness, moral sensibilities might easily become dulled; life was hard and sometimes cruel; determination to succeed could result in bickering and ill will; hard drinking and coarse manners found little check."[14]

Second, the Presbyterian church faced difficulty in securing and training ministers from within the faithful in America. The church demanded that the Presbyterian minister be thoroughly trained in Hebrew, Greek, and Latin, as well as in the holy scriptures. Schools for Presbyterian ministers were founded in America, the first being in Bucks County in eastern Pennsylvania in 1726, but such schools could offer little hope of meeting the pulpit needs of the migrating Scotch-Irish populations.

Third, the Scotch-Irish were scattered over many miles of rough frontier. To encourage an educated minister, trained in either Scotland, Ulster, or the small American schools, to serve among the desperately poor and sparse pioneers was a difficult task for the church. The pioneer settlers could ill afford to support a minister on a fixed salary. Any minister then would be required to support himself as a farmer or merchant to survive, and this, of course, did not fit the mold of the educated Presbyterian minister. Thus the Presbyterian church in America struggled to meet the needs of its faithful as the Scotch-Irish continued to migrate along the American frontier.

While the Presbyterians found it difficult to succeed among the pioneer community, the Baptists easily moved to the forefront among the Scotch-Irish. The Baptists had no requirement like that of the Presbyterians that a minister must be educated and trained. To the Baptists the gospel was simple and uncomplicated and could easily be understood and accepted by everyone. While the Presbyterians were requiring their ministers to spend six years or more in preparing for the ministry, the individual Baptist congregations, which could be formed without the approval of a presbytery, could accept as minister any man who felt the call. Baptist ministers, many of whom could barely read or write but who knew much of the scriptures by memory, came from the ranks of the people. They could support themselves since they had come from self-sufficient families; they required little financial support from their congregation; and they could relate to the daily hardships faced by their parishioners. The Baptist church thus experienced significant growth among the Scotch-Irish pioneers.

The Methodist church also made inroads among the Virginia frontier settlements. With John and Charles Wesley encouraging change in the Church of England, and under the influence of their associate George Whitefield, who traveled extensively in the American Colonies, the Methodist church was a major instigator in the "great awakening" that swept through the Colonies and to the frontier. Creatively, the Methodists devised the "circuit rider ministry." The traveling minister, rather than serving a single and fixed congregation, was to ride hundreds of miles each month to visit pioneer families, strengthening their faith, marrying their young couples, and burying their dead. The demanding rigors of such an itinerary required that the minister primarily be both young and strong. Most Methodist circuit riders were men in their twenties or early thirties who had little guidance from preachers of greater maturity or seasoning.[15] The Methodist church in America paralleled the Baptist approach of plain talk, direct evangelism, and simple gospel.

As the numbers of Baptists and Methodists grew among the Scotch-Irish, the Presbyterians were less dominant. By the time of the Revolution, the total number of Baptist and Methodist ministers, when combined within all the Colonies, was only slightly lower than the total of Presbyterian ministers; however, the total membership of Baptist and Methodist churches on the Virginia frontier largely outnumbered all other faiths.[16] The Baptist and Methodist churches became the faith of the common folk. Their growth was not viewed with favor by the established churches within the Colonies, and their characteristics were evaluated, along with the Quakers and Presbyterians, by an Anglican minister in 1760:

> The Baptists are obstinate, illiterate, and grossly ignorant, the Methodists ignorant, censorious, and uncharitable, the Quakers rigid, but the Presbyterians are pretty moderate except here and there a bigot or rigid Calvinist.[17]

It is unclear when the ancestors of Joseph Roark made the transition from the Presbyterian faith to the Baptist. In all probability the switch occurred gradually over time when, on the frontier, the Ororkes and the Roarks were separated from their traditional faith. At some point they accepted the frontier gospel of the Baptists. By 1773, the grandfather of Joseph Roark, maybe if not a Baptist himself, had most certainly located in a frontier community predominantly of the Baptist persuasion.[18]

As the lower Shenandoah Valley filled with settlers and land was no longer readily available, the Scotch-Irish, and the Roarks, pushed up the valley toward southwest Virginia. Entrepreneurs and influential land speculators received sizeable land grants in the 1740s, and the lands that were later to be occupied by the Roarks in southwest Virginia and northeast Tennessee were first explored and surveyed. One of the earliest and most influential men in the upper Valley of Virginia was Col. James Patton, who had come from Ulster in 1736. In 1745, Patton secured a grant from the Governor and Council of Virginia for one hundred and twenty thousand acres of land west of the Blue Ridge.[19] In 1748, Colonel Patton and Dr. Thomas Walker surveyed valuable tracts within the grant, many of which covered lands on the waters of the Clinch and Holston Rivers. On July 12, 1749, Patton and Walker, with forty-four others, formed the Loyal Land Company and received a grant from the Governor and Council of Virginia for 800,000 acres of land extending westward of the Blue Ridge. The Loyal Land Company was allotted four years to locate the land, identify tracts therein, and file the individual surveys with the Council of Virginia.

On December 12, 1749, Dr. Thomas Walker and four others of the Loyal Land Company began a fact-finding expedition to the southwest in order to locate the most valuable lands under the Loyal grant. By April 12, 1750, Walker's party reached the Powell River in what is now Claiborne County, Tennessee, and the next day crossed through Cumberland Gap, which Walker named in honor of the Duke of Cumberland, son of George II of England. Walker kept an extensive journal of his trip which, by its descriptions of the fertile lands, encouraged settlement on the "western waters" of Virginia. Settlement was further encouraged in November 1753 when the House of Burgesses of Virginia passed an act which exempted Protestants settling on lands west of the Blue Ridge from all county taxes and parish levies for a period of fifteen years.[20] This encouragement by the Crown was primarily for the purpose of competing with the French, who were claiming the area west of the Appalachian Mountains and who, by 1753, had sent soldiers to notify the British traders to vacate the territory.

*The Shenandoah Valley of Virginia, with present-day counties, showing the
Great Philadelphia Wagon Road and the probable route of Joseph Roark's ancestors
in their migration up the Valley*

Doubtless, this encouragement by the Crown significantly influenced the future
plans of the Roarks in the Shenandoah Valley. The opportunity for new land encour-
aged Timothy Roark Jr. (ca. 1715-1780) to move his family in the late 1750s up the
Shenandoah Valley to present-day Montgomery County, east of the New River.
Evidence suggests Timothy brought with him his three sons, John, James, and
Timothy.[21] John Roark (ca. 1735-1800), the eldest, had, as a young man in Frederick
County, been a chain carrier in a survey for the O'Neal tract in 1752.[22] John Roark
moved south up the Shenandoah Valley, probably with his father, and by 1754 was in
Augusta County (prior to the creation of Fincastle County). John is noted in the

Augusta County court records in 1754 and again in 1759.[23] Timothy Roark (1745-1811), the youngest son, doubtless was with the family in the New River area but is not mentioned in court records until he occupied his land grant on Elk Creek in present-day Grayson County. James Roark (ca. 1740-1792), the middle son would be the grandfather of Joseph Roark, is judged to have been born about 1740. He would have been thirteen when the Crown began encouraging settlers and doubtless heard of the opportunities for cheap land in the Appalachians and started to plan for his own farm and homestead. For the next few years he would remain with his father's family east of the New River and wait with other future pioneers for the frontier to open. It would be almost twenty years before his opportunity would come to move west. During those twenty years he would mature, become part of the militia with others of his age, marry, and begin his family. His move west would wait for the termination of the Indian wars that were to engross the attention of the Virginia frontier for the next decade.

The year 1754 saw the beginning of the French-Indian War, which in all its fury was to last nine terrible years. Very few settlers had occupied lands beyond the Blue Ridge in the upper end of the Shenandoah Valley when the war began, and these few were forced by the circumstances to move back east of the New River. The French-Indian War, and its terrible Indian raids incited by the French, basically terminated all new settlement in southwest Virginia and transactions of the Loyal Land Company. Few, if any, settlers remained in the vicinity of the Clinch and Holston Rivers during the conflict. The area west of the New River remained unsettled until the war was successfully terminated with the Peace of Paris, signed February 10, 1763. Under the treaty, France relinquished all of Canada and all claims to territory east of the Mississippi. The French were no longer an obstruction to western expansion, but in October 1763 the British Crown erected a new barrier to settlement. The Crown reserved for the Indian tribes all lands west of the divide beyond which waters flowed not to the Atlantic Ocean but to the Mississippi. The Crown issued the Proclamation of 1763, which ordered that the crest of the Appalachians was the furthest west that settlement would be permitted. Indians living west of the Proclamation Line under the protection of the colony were not to be molested or disturbed in possession of their lands. Their territories were to be neither ceded nor purchased by the English but were reserved for the Indians for hunting. All persons living beyond the Proclamation Line were ordered to move east of the divide.[24]

Sometime in the early 1760s, James Roark, with brothers Timothy and John, made application with the Loyal Land Company for specific land grants within the company's 800,000 acres. Each brother was successful in purchasing, or agreeing to purchase, a tract on the frontier for future settlement and occupancy. James Roark received a grant and was promised title to a tract of sixty-three acres "on the waters of Beaver Creek, a branch of the Holston [River]." When finally surveyed in February 1774, the tract was located in Fincastle County, which at that time covered all of southwest Virginia. Its location would most likely be in present-day Washington County.[25]

James' brother Timothy received a grant of 110 acres "lying on both sides of Beaver Dam Fork on the waters of Elk Creek a branch of the New River." Timothy's tract lay to the south of the family home in Botetourt County and was located in what is now Grayson County.[26] John Roark's tract of ninety-three acres was apparently near the tract of James as it was also on "the waters of Beaver Creek, a branch of the Holston."[27] Since the Holston River, in its upper reaches, divides into three major forks, the tracts of the two brothers are difficult to locate with any exactness. James, Timothy, and John Roark would be forced to wait on a clear title from the Loyal Land Company and peace negotiations with the Indians before attempting to settle the tracts.

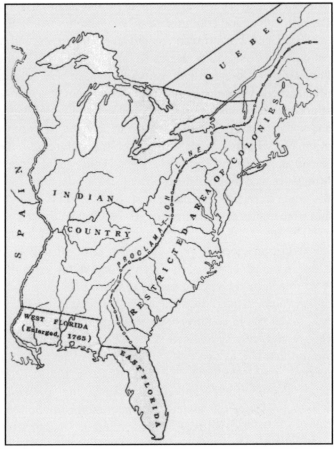

The Proclamation Line of 1763 issued by the British Crown to restrict the Colonies and create a barrier between the Colonies and the Indian Tribes

In spite of the Proclamation of 1763, most of the former settlers who had been forced to move east as a result of the French-Indian War soon thereafter returned to their lands. Settlers who had taken up lands under Loyal Land Company grants were promised by the company that each settler's land title would be confirmed irrespective of the Proclamation. From 1763 until the Revolutionary War, long hunters, surveyors and squatters continued to ignore the King's orders regarding the limits of settlement west of the Proclamation Line, while great numbers of immigrants waited impatiently east of the Blue Ridge for an opportunity to legally occupy new lands on the western waters. A few settlers, however, risked the wrath of the British Crown and moved into southwest Virginia in violation of the Proclamation. In 1766, men by the name of Carr and Butler, although long hunters, decided to stay and settle on the

Clinch River. Carr and Butler built a cabin at a place later known as the "Crab Orchard," about three miles west of the present town of Tazewell, Virginia.[28]

New challenges faced the settlers who ignored the Proclamation Line. The primary challenge was the mountain range itself. In the decades preceding the Proclamation, settlers had gradually moved the frontier to the southwest in the Shenandoah Valley, and each new farm carved out of the wilderness was only a short distance from the previous settlement. The new settler was not totally isolated, and soon other settlers would move the frontier farther to the southwest. The Indians gradually withdrew as the Scotch-Irish moved across the Blue Ridge and up the Shenandoah Valley. By 1763, the Indians had moved west of the Appalachian Mountains and the frontier had reached the mountain range. No longer could a settler move a short distance to carve out his plot; after 1763 he had to cross the mountains, leaving behind a hundred miles to separate him from civilization.

> The slow and apparently inexorable advance of the frontier had come to a halt at the foot of the mountains. The former cabin-by-cabin and mile-by-mile advance was no longer possible. Among the forested heights were only rocky and isolated creek bottoms in which a first settler would be defenselessly exposed. For the generation before 1763 the frontier instead of moving westward had skirted the mountains and pushed southward down the Valley of Virginia. But by now this slack had been taken up. There was no more wild free land to be had for the taking. There were only the mountains. And beyond them the vengefully waiting Indians.[29]

Both Indians and settlers were displeased with the Proclamation of 1763 and its results. Both peoples violated the Proclamation at will. The Shawnees continued "a war of merciless extermination against the western frontier settlements."[30] New settlers violating the Proclamation were constantly in fear of murderous Indian raids. The British government recognized that the Proclamation Line of 1763 was unworkable and directed in 1768 that Sir William Johnson negotiate a new treaty with the Indians. Johnson and his congress of negotiators, which included Dr. Thomas Walker of the Loyal Land Company, successfully negotiated a treaty on November 5, 1768, with six tribes including the Shawnees, Delawares, and Mingos. Concurrently, John Stewart, Superintendent of Indian Affairs for the Colonies, executed a treaty with the Cherokees along the Tennessee River. Under both treaties, the Indians conveyed to the British Crown extensive lands west of the Appalachian Mountains. Dr. Walker, of course, was primarily interested in extinguishing the Indian title to all 800,000 acres of the Loyal Land Company so that development of the land grants in southwest Virginia could occur at the earliest possible date.[31]

Following the treaties in the winter of 1768 and early 1769, large numbers of settlers moved into southwest Virginia. Scotch-Irish settlers who had remained east of the New River took renewed interest in the availability of land and made forays into and west of the Appalachians in search of possible farm sites. The Indians remained at peace although individual raids on settlers still occurred. Settlement was aided in 1769 when the Cherokees entered into a war with the Chickasaws, thereby diverting the interest of Cherokees from raiding new white settlements.

The upper Clinch Valley remained popular in the eyes of the long hunters, the most renowned of whom was Daniel Boone. In 1760, Boone and his wife lived in North Carolina on the Yadkin River, and in his long hunts, he had ventured into southwest Virginia as far as the Holston and Clinch Rivers. While serving as a teamster in Braddock's army in 1755, Boone had heard tales about good hunting and rich lands in Kentucky. By 1764, he had wanted to move closer to Kentucky and suggested to his wife that they move to the Blue Ridge in Virginia. But Rebecca, with four children, would not agree. Still, Boone would hunt on the Clinch River for extended periods. Boone was in the Clinch Valley in the winter of 1767-68, and hunted the valley to the headwaters of the Clinch before moving to the Big Sandy River and then into Kentucky. Boone was to return many times to the Clinch Valley and later would make it his home for a brief period.[32]

In 1771, following the creation of Botetourt County, James Roark was involved in a dispute with Thomas Evans and petitioned the court for a judgement against Evans. The cause for the action against Evans is unknown. The petition was filed in February, but court action was postponed until April 18, 1772:

James Rorke	Petitioner
against	
Thomas Evans	Defendant

This day came the parties by their attorneys and the defendant having been duly summoned and served with a copy of the petition as per current [law] and the petitioner having proved his demand to be just. Therefore it is commanded by the Court that judgement be given for the petitioner against the defendant for four pounds ten shillings current money besides his costs by him expended and the said defendant in mercy judged.[33]

Interestingly, when James Roark moved west to the Clinch River Valley the following year with several other families from Botetourt County, Thomas Evans remained east of the New River. He was still living in that area in 1790.[34]

The settlements, as they began to occur, demanded government structures under which courthouses could be located closer to the new populations. In response to this need, the House of Burgesses of Virginia passed an act creating Botetourt County on January 31, 1770. The new county would replace Augusta County as the county to encompass all lands in southwest Virginia west of the New River.[35]

As settlements occurred and new counties were organized, circumstances dictated that a protective force of militia be organized. Officers were immediately appointed in the new counties to take charge of military affairs. The military laws required that each male between the ages of eighteen and fifty be registered with the captain of the militia in their local neighborhood. Members of the militia were required to report periodically for muster and to maintain contact with the local captain. On the western boundary, the militia members were used to patrol the frontier and were required to report for duty at any time of an Indian scare.[36]

The militia structure served another function in addition to its responsibility for protection against the Indians. The Colony of Virginia used the militia structure as a mechanism for collection of taxes in the sparsely settled counties on the frontier, and tax collectors used militia lists as tax rolls for land taxes and personal property taxes. Statutes declared that "all male persons of the age of sixteen years and upwards, and all Negroes, mulatto, and Indian women of the same age . . . shall be and are hereby declared to be tithable, and chargeable for defraying the public county, and parish levies, of this colony and dominion . . ."[37] Lists of tithables to be taxed were thus maintained on an annual basis for the frontier counties.

In 1772, James Roark was listed among the tithables in Capt. James Thompson's militia company, then in Botetourt County, and in what is now Montgomery County, Virginia. Probably centrally located among the members of his company, Thompson lived on Back Creek on the New River and west of Blacksburg and Christiansburg. The list of tithables for Captain Thompson's Company was prepared in response to a 1772 court order by Botetourt County. The list was signed by Stephen Trigg, who resided at Dunkard Bottom (now Claytor Lake) near the New River. The list contained a total of seventy names.[38] At the time of his membership in Thompson's Company, James Roark was about the age of thirty-two, and his family probably consisted of his wife and four children, all younger than ten years.

It was during this period in 1772 and 1773 that excitement began to build for settlements in southwest Virginia, Tennessee, and Kentucky. Daniel Boone had spent the winter of 1771-72 in what is now Kentucky and Tennessee, and by the fall of 1772, Boone had returned with skins and glowing reports of rich lands. Boone's reports generated considerable interest in Kentucky by the seaboard colonies. Typical of most investors in the tidewater area who believed that Virginia might soon grant patents for the area west of the New River, George Washington arranged for ten thousand acres to be marked off for him in the western portion of the Virginia Colony.[39] Following the cessation of hostilities in the French-Indian War and the diminution of Indian raids west of New River, the lands along the Holston and Clinch Rivers slowly opened to settlement, in many instances to those tithables in Captain Thompson's Company.

The 1772 list of tithables with James Roark in Thompson's Company included men who later would be instrumental in settling southwest Virginia and in leading the controversy with the British Crown that was to result in the Revolutionary War with England. Captain James Thompson served on the county court of Botetourt County and was later to serve in a similar office in Fincastle County and still later was to fight in the Revolution at the decisive victory over the British at Kings Mountain.[40] William Christian was later to serve as a colonel under General Washington and was even later to represent Washington County in the Virginia Senate.[41] Stephen Trigg, brother-in-law to William Christian, would later serve in the Virginia House of Burgesses.[42] David Crouch would emerge as a large land holder, accumulating over 1000 acres just west of the New River and north of Goose Creek.[43] James Roark would later sell his farm to David Crouch and, in 1785, he and Crouch would serve on juries together.[44] Several others on the list of tithables were close associates of James Roark and would later settle close to him in the Clinch Valley. Jacob Harman would settle on the Bluestone River east of present-day Tazewell, Virginia. In 1774, shortly after his

---

Capt. James Thompson's Company, 1772

James Allison	Samuel McGeehee
John Allsup	James Moonee
John Bradshaw	Joseph Martin
James Boylestone	John Madison
Josiah Baker	Joseph Montgomery, Senior
John Blackmore	James Montgomery, Senior
Richard Brindley	John Norris
William Cicil	James Newell, Senior
William Cleary	John Norris
Samuel Cicil	Samuel Pepper
Robert Carr	James Patton
Dale Carter	Thomas Patton
Samuel Cobun	Alexander Page
William Christian	Hugh Patrick
Samuel Cloyd	George Pearis
John Cloyd	Samuel Piercifull
David Crouch	George Parks
John Draper	Jeremiah Patrick
Ephraim Drake	James Roarke
John Denton	Benjamin Ray
Henry Dooley	Michael Riziner
Joseph Edgington	Samuel Shannon
Joseph Grey	James Skaggs
Charles Gorden	William Stewart
John Gorden	John Taylor
Henry Grub	Stephen Trigg
Jacob Harman	William Thompson
Joseph How	James Thompson
Addam Hance	James Walker
Daniel Johnson	Samuel Walker
Samuel Ingram	John Wigal
William Longley	Peter Wyley
William Lockart	Addam Waggoner
Robert Miller	William West
Joseph Maires	Samuel Woodfin

Source: Glimpses of Wythe County, Virginia, Volume 2, by Mary B. Kegley, Pictorial Histories Publishing Co., Charleston, West Virginia, Page 154.

move west, Harman, through fear of Indian raids, would move his family back to the New River settlements.[45] James Skaggs was to settle in 1773 in Baptist Valley near the Clinch River, and with his family were the first Baptists in the valley and later Tazewell County.[46] Another on the list of tithables, John Taylor, would leave the New River settlements shortly after the Thompson list was compiled in 1772 and move to the North Fork of the Clinch. He was to become a major in the militia and would submit the "official report" of the catastrophe that was to befall James Roark and his family.[47] Samuel Walker on Thompson's list would settle in what became Tazewell County and was to become a member of the first county court of Tazewell County when it was organized in May 1800. He and William Peery were to be the first Presbyterians in the county.[48] Much later, Walker would be one of five men who were appointed by the court to settle the estate of James Roark.[49] Samuel Cecil and his son, William, were also among the list of Thompson's tithables and both would be neighbors of James Roark in the Clinch Valley. Joseph Martin and John Bradshaw were two others on the list who settled on the upper headwaters of the Clinch.[50]

Tragic circumstances surrounded one of James Roark's associates in the militia. John Draper had been an early settler in the Valley of Virginia, having settled shortly after 1750 with his family at Draper's Meadow east of the New River and close to the present town of Blacksburg. John Draper had been away from the settlement on July 8, 1755, when the village was plundered by a group of Shawnees from far beyond the Ohio. All persons at the settlement were either killed or captured, including Col. James Patton, the early pioneer, who was quickly slain in the attack. Draper's wife, Betty, had been captured, broke her arm in an attempt to escape, and was forced to endure unspeakable hardships including seeing her child brutally slain. John Draper had searched diligently for his wife for over six years and, after learning of her location from an old Indian, had paid the substantial reward demanded for her return. Draper and his wife again lived briefly at Draper's Meadow before moving to the area of Captain Thompson's Company in 1765. Betty Draper died in 1774; however, John Draper remained active in the militia and served at the Battle of Point Pleasant in 1774.[51] Within eight years from the time they were listed together on Thompson's roster, James Roark and John Draper would have much in common in family tragedy.

Sometime in 1772, James Roark left his home east of the New River for an inspection tour with other men to stake out individual claims in the Clinch Valley. Although some of the richer lands had been claimed by the time James made his move, prime tracts were still available to be claimed. Documentation of land titles by field surveys was, at that time, fifteen years away, and occupying a tract plus providing improvements to the tract was the prime evidence of ownership. Ownership established by an earlier claimant could be purchased, and the tract would then be assigned to the buyer through some written document that, in most instances, was not recorded in the official deed records. In 1773, James purchased the claim of John Peery, whom he had known in Botetourt County, for a tract in Baptist Valley that was later surveyed to contain 130 acres.[52] He apparently also claimed other acreage and began the construction of his cabin and the cultivation for crops that would support his family. John Peery retained his claim to other lands and settled about four miles east of the Roarks on the Clinch. He operated a distillery, and in 1781, he died in the battle at Guilford Court House in North Carolina during the Revolutionary War.[53]

His move to the frontier meant James Roark was to leave his family home, his parents, and his brothers, both of whom by then had families and would soon relocate. James and his family more than likely moved with the Harmans, Cecils, Taylors, and others, to the valley of the Clinch River in early March 1773 before winter thaws and spring rains made travel even more difficult. The Clinch River runs northeast to southwest and has its headwaters approximately sixty miles west of the settlements on the New River. The route followed by the settlers had previously been used by Indian hunting parties and, much earlier, by herds of buffalo. From the settlements, the caravan traveled west along the north bank of the New River to ford the river at the shallows located across from the present town of Ripplemead, about a mile below the mouth of Walker's Creek. After crossing the river, the settlers moved south along Walker's Creek to Kimberling Creek and followed that stream southwest to its source at the base of Wolf Creek Mountain. To this point in the journey west, James Roark and the other settlers had moved in valleys along rivers and creeks. At Wolf Creek Mountain, however, the party had to leave the valleys where travel had been relatively easy and had to begin the most difficult part of the trip, that of crossing the divide through what has since been known as "the Wilderness." This portion of the settlers' route is now part of the Jefferson National Forest. After crossing the ridge, the group passed through Rocky Gap to the Clear Fork of Wolf Creek, which the party followed to the headwaters of the Clinch near the location of the present town of Tazewell. From there it followed the river five miles downstream and up the ridge to the Baptist Valley. In the difficult journey of over two weeks, with a wagon filled with all the family's earthly possessions, James Roark had traveled just over eighty-five miles.[54]

The Baptist Valley is a small valley of fertile soil and flat terrain roughly one-half mile wide between two ridges. The valley itself runs parallel to the Clinch River one and one-half miles northwest at an elevation of two hundred feet above the river. The valley was so named because of the "number of persons belonging to the Baptist denomination of Christians who settled in it."[55] It is approximately ten miles long and covers an area of over 3,000 acres. The north boundary of the valley, "Sandy Ridge," serves as the divide between the waters of the Clinch and the watershed of the Dry Fork of the Sandy River. James Roark's tract was located about midway in Baptist Valley at a gap in the south boundary, "River Ridge." His tract of 130 acres occupied the Tennessee Valley Divide, which separates the watersheds of the Tennessee and Ohio Rivers. Water from the south portion of the Roark tract flowed south to the Clinch and into the Tennessee while runoff from the northern portion of the tract flowed north into the Dry Fork, then the Tug Fork of the Sandy River, and

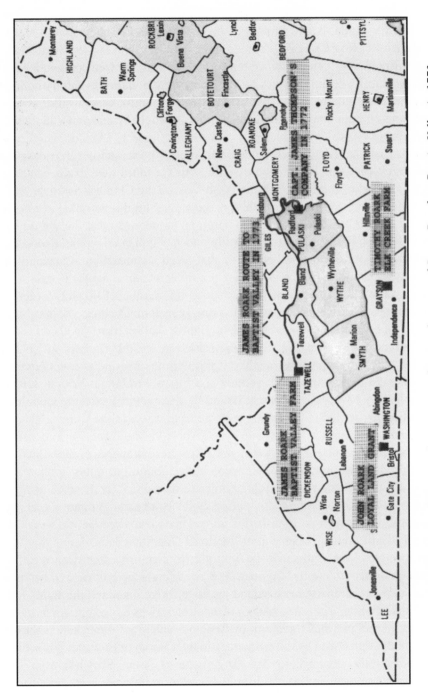

Southwest Virginia, with present-day counties, showing the route of James Roark to Baptist Valley in 1773

ultimately into the Ohio near present-day Huntington, West Virginia. The trail north through Sandy Ridge, connecting Baptist Valley with present-day McDowell County, West Virginia, is now known as the Dry Fork Road. The gap in both ridges is still known as "Roark's Gap."

James Roark also gained ownership to another tract located three miles southwest of the Baptist farm. Whether he filed an original claim or purchased a prior claim is unclear in the records. This second tract was approximately 100 acres and lay along and on both banks of the Clinch River. It would be known to the family as the "river farm."

East of Baptist Valley, seven miles from James Roark, and north of the current town of Tazewell, John Taylor would settle with his family on Cavitt Creek. Two miles east of Taylor at the head of the north fork of the Clinch River near Wittens Mills was the home of Jesse Evans. Evans moved his family with that of his father to the head of the Clinch from Amherst, Virginia, in the same year that James Roark moved to Baptist Valley. The Evans family and the family of James Roark would share similar misfortunes. Another family that faced a similar fate was that of John Henry who moved into Thompson Valley six miles south of James Roark in 1773 and lived in the vicinity of Plum Creek.[56] In 1773, William Patterson settled on a tract adjacent to that of James Roark. The same year, John Deskins, Thomas Masten, and James and Charles Skaggs settled in Baptist Valley near the Roark cabin.[57] Earlier settlers were Thomas Witten, who settled near Crab Orchard in 1771, and after 1774, with the help of his neighbors and with his son-in-law John Greenup,[58] built Wittens Fort. William Cecil, another son-in-law to Thomas Witten, settled in Baptist Valley in 1774 under a patent issued by the authority of King George III.[59] Absalom Looney settled in a valley east of the headwaters of the Clinch, which valley was later named and is to this date called Abb's Valley. Jacob Harman, with his brothers, Matthias and Henry, settled on one of the head branches of the Clinch. Also in 1771, Joseph Martin settled in Thompson Valley about four miles south of James Roark, and John Bradshaw settled three miles to the west.[60] Of those that settled in the Clinch River Valley during this period, John Bradshaw, William Cecil, Jacob Harman, Joseph Martin, and John Taylor, all had been listed with James Roark in the company of Capt. James Thompson in Botetourt County in 1772.

These Scotch-Irish settlers of the Virginia frontier were significantly different from the colonists of tidewater Virginia and even different from those who had moved from the tidewater area to the east side of the Blue Ridge. They were different in both ancestry and religion. The early settlers of tidewater Virginia were English by birth, steeped in the culture and traditions of England, and were close adherents to the Christian faith as practiced by the aristocracy in the Church of England. The settlers of southwest Virginia, contrary to the early colonists, were Scotch-Irish by birth, Presbyterians, Baptists, and Methodists in Christian faith, and were fresh from the persecutions by the British Crown in Ulster of northern Ireland. As the Scotch-Irish

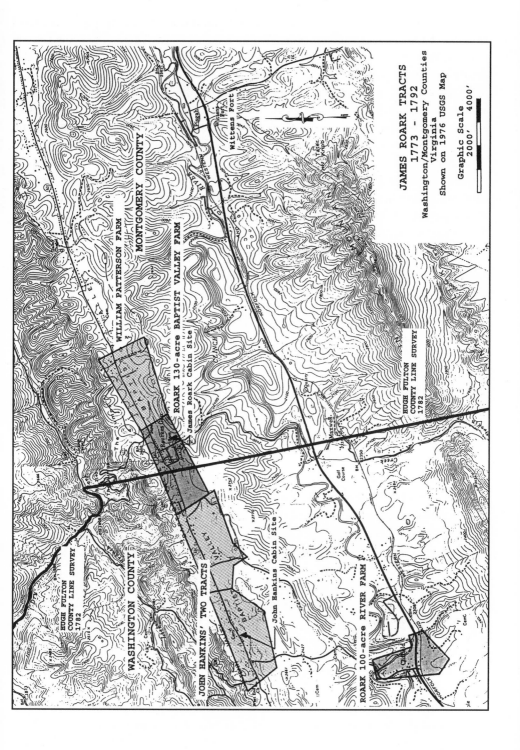

JAMES ROARK TRACTS
1773 - 1792
Washington/Montgomery Counties
Virginia
Shown on 1976 USGS Map

Graphic Scale
2000'   4000'

MONTGOMERY COUNTY

WILLIAM PATTERSON FARM

ROARK 130-acre BAPTIST VALLEY FARM

James Roark Cabin Site

HUGH FULTON
COUNTY LINE SURVEY
1782

WASHINGTON COUNTY

JOHN HANKINS' TWO TRACTS

John Hankins Cabin Site

HUGH FULTON
COUNTY LINE SURVEY
1782

ROARK 100-acre RIVER FARM

settled in the Valley of Virginia during the eighteenth century, they were adamant adherents of religious freedom and had begun to speak against the political oppression of Parliament and King George III. Historians have long recognized the role of the Scotch-Irish in the era leading to the Revolution. "The first voice raised in America to destroy all connection with Great Britain came from the Scotch-Irish Presbyterians."[61]

The Scotch-Irish were noted for their religious faith but also for their aggressive toughness and tenacity. "It may have been true that the Scotch-Irish kept the Sabbath and everything else they could lay their hands on. It may also have been true that, when they reached America, the Scotch-Irish fell on their knees and worshipped God and then fell on the Indians. But if their outlook was narrow and harsh—and it was, surely, at least partly due to land-hunger and the natural instinct of self-preservation—was it not mainly due to a harsh background?"[62] As the Scotch-Irish moved into the frontier along the Clinch River in 1771-73, they were a significantly different class of people than those of nobility who had first settled in Virginia at Jamestown in 1607:

> They had no wealthy corporate body, like the London Company, to give them supplies of food and clothing, arms and ammunition, and houses to dwell in, nor soldiers of a royal government to protect them from attacks of the hostile natives. Nor were they of an indolent, vagrant class, like those first settlers at Jamestown, who were listed as "gentlemen," but who died from starvation because they were too lazy or too proud to work. They found no fertile fields on banks of noble rivers and splendid bays, already prepared for cultivation, and which they could wrest by fraud or by force from the simple hospitable natives. But these glorious pioneers of the Clinch Valley were real men and women, with great hearts, strong and willing hands, and inspired with a resolute purpose to do all they could, with the means they had, to secure for themselves and their descendants the political and religious freedom that had been denied them or their fathers in the "Old Country." In perseverance, in self-command, in forethought, in heroism, in all the virtues that conduce to success in life, [these pioneers] have never been surpassed.[63]

Following the restoration of peace in 1763 after the French-Indian War, the Loyal Land Company had petitioned the Governor and the Council to permit the Company to honor the grants it had issued in 1749. Favorable consideration of the Loyal Company petition, and the indication that the petition, if approved, would permit the Land Company to confirm titles to settlers' land, resulted in new settlements on the Clinch River in 1772 and 1773. On December 16, 1773, the Governor and Council acted on the Loyal petition and made an order that:

> . . .those settlers who resided on any tract before last October, and continue to do so having cleared some part thereof, whereby their intention to reside is manifested; and that every settler shall have fifty acres at least, and also for every three acres of cleared land fifty acres more . . .[64]

In February 1774, just at the end of his first year in Baptist Valley, James Roark received word that his grant of sixty-three acres from the Loyal Land Company had been surveyed and filed in the grant records of the Colony.[65] The grant to his brother John had been surveyed on the same date. Both tracts were located on Beaver Creek on the Holston River approximately fifty miles southwest of Baptist Valley. Available records give no indication that James Roark ever attempted to occupy his sixty-three acres in Washington County. He obviously had made the decision to remain in Baptist Valley and make it his homestead. Evidence suggests, however, that his brother John did settle on his ninety-three acres and probably made it his home.[66] Nothing available today indicates that James was ever to see John again after they left their family home on the New River.

James' other brother Timothy received in December 1774 the survey of his 110-acre grant from the Loyal Company. Since his tract was only a few miles west of the New River and closer to the settled areas of southwest Virginia, Timothy occupied his tract probably before 1773.[67] He was to make it his homestead and remain there for the rest of his life, expanding his lands to over 400 acres.[68] Some evidence suggests that Timothy moved his parents to the Elk Creek area and supported his mother after her husband's death.[69] James Roark was to return from his frontier farm to visit Timothy and their mother and probably lived for a time on Elk Creek. The children of James and Timothy appear to have remained close into their adult years.

When James Roark and the first company of settlers moved to the Clinch Valley, the Indians were at peace with the Virginia pioneers and would remain so for the next two to three years. The upper Clinch settlements were then on the extreme line of outposts occupied by white men beyond the New River. Unfortunately, the settlements along the upper Clinch were directly in line with the three favorite warpath trails used by the Shawnees to come from the northwest to hunt or to raid the settlements. The primary trail used by the Shawnees was along the Sandy River from the Ohio to the Tug Fork and Dry Fork of the Sandy to Sandy Ridge and over the ridge through Roark's Gap.[70] At the time of the initial settlements, the pioneers, although at peace with the Indians, erected forts at central points–Wittens Fort at Crab Orchard, Bowen Fort at Maiden Spring, and Wynn's Fort at Locust Hill. Further down the Clinch Valley, forty miles to the southwest, was the fort at Castlewood, supported by over twenty families.

It was to Castlewood, southwest of Baptist Valley, that Daniel Boone would return in his move to the Clinch Valley in 1773. As settlement was occurring in Baptist Valley and James Roark was establishing his home and family on the upper reaches of the Clinch, Daniel Boone, forty miles away, was planning an attempt to settle Kentucky. With William Russell, a well-known tobacco farmer and Indian trader, Boone planned to gather families from North Carolina and Virginia who would be interested in settling Kentucky lands. Boone moved his family to Russell's home at Castlewood on the Clinch in August 1773. Here, some forty to fifty people were to rendezvous for a move into Kentucky that began September 25, 1773.[71] Because Russell was renowned in southwest Virginia, James Roark knew of the expedition and was familiar with many of the families.

Boone's expedition was to end in tragedy when on October 9, his son James and a small group of six men following the main party with supplies were killed by the Shawnees on the Powell River approximately forty-five miles below Castlewood and less than thirty miles northeast of Cumberland Gap. The expedition was postponed and Boone returned the group to Castlewood where the families slowly drifted back to their homes in Virginia and North Carolina. Boone and his family remained on the Clinch River in a cabin owned by an associate of William Russell, and he supported his family during the winter of 1773-74 by hunting in the upper Clinch Valley. It is quite probable that during that somber winter in the life of Boone that James Roark made his acquaintance.[72]

The attack on the Boone and Russell expedition into Kentucky was to signal the beginning of Indian resistance to settlements west of the Appalachians. To aid the new settlements, Fincastle County was created from Botetourt County by the House of Burgesses in December 1772, and in January 1773, three of James Roark's associates from Thompson's 1772 company of militia–William Christian, James Thompson, and Stephen Trigg–were named to the county court. By the fall of 1773, Indian attacks occurred so frequently that it was apparent a general uprising was in the making. The Shawnees, with Mingos and Cherokees participating, were involved in the murder of eleven people in 1773 in Fincastle County alone.[73] The Indian attacks were fomented by murderous attacks of barbarous white men, chief of whom was Michael Cresap, who in April 1774 murdered and scalped friendly Shawnees near present-day Wheeling, West Virginia. The best element of settlers, however, including those in the Clinch Valley, were reluctant to engage in a war with the Indians, recognizing that a significant number of the much-maligned Indians were still at peace with the white settlers and wanted to maintain peaceful relations with them.[74] With the Cresap outrage, the conditions on the frontier in 1774 continued to deteriorate, and early 1774 saw an exodus of frightened frontier families from the Clinch Valley, many returning to settlements on the New River and others to the forts along the valley.

Settlers on the frontier, like James Roark, recognized their exposure to Indian raids and dreaded the savagery of an all-out war with the Indians in which the settlers would be on the "front lines."

> To the settler the principal theater of war was his own clearing. He could never know when howling savages might not burst from the woods enclosing it to burn his home, axe his children, disembowel his wife. If he was near he fell beside them and his fears for them which so long haunted him were over. If he was at a little distance he was confronted with the dreadful choice of returning to share their fate or seeking his own safety in flight alone. If for a time Indian attack passed him by to strike his neighbors this

but made his dread more harrowing for the postponement made it ever more likely that the next would not spare him.[75]

Following the initial Indian reprisals, caution and preservation of peace would have been the better option, but such was not the case when Lord Dunmore, Governor of Colonial Virginia, took steps to pursue the Indians in what history has named "Dunmore's War." An army was assembled under Colonel William Christian and moved to the Clinch Valley in the first military expedition to that area. Moving to the northwest, Christian's army passed through Baptist Valley and Roark's Gap to the Dry Fork and the headwaters of the Tug River. Whether James Roark participated in the expedition is unknown. It is unlikely, with the multiple excursions by the Shawnees into the valley, that men would feel comfortable in leaving their families alone. The men of the upper Clinch Valley were primarily involved in the defense of their own homes and settlements, although many did much volunteer scouting for the army.[76] Following the move of his army through the upper Clinch Valley, Christian was directed to participate in a coordinated attack on the Indians with an army from the Ohio. The coordinated effort resulted in the defeat of the Shawnees, Delawares, and Mingos in the Battle of Point Pleasant in October 1774.

While Christian's army was marching to the Ohio Valley and the settlements on the Clinch were left to their own defense, small bands of Shawnees and Mingos invaded the Clinch Valley and areas to the east in murderous raids upon the settlers. The first raid in the valley occurred September 8, 1774, when a band of twelve to fifteen Indians murdered the John Henry family in Thompson Valley. Henry's farm was located six miles from James Roark's cabin and three miles from Wittens Fort. John Bradshaw, who lived nearby, discovered the attack and left immediately to spread the alarm in Thompsons Valley. After capturing other victims, the Indians returned north through Roark's Gap following the Dry Fork to the Tug River to the Ohio.[77] During this raid and the others that followed, James Roark undoubtedly had his family at Wittens Fort with other families from the Clinch.[78]

The period of Dunmore's War in 1774 was a particularly trying but eventful time for the settlers in the Clinch Valley. Anxiety was intense as the settlers struggled to protect their families and at the same time tried to make a crop and preserve it from the fires set during Indian raids. The crops were of utmost importance since the settler's family was dependent upon the grain for subsistence during the following year. Also in 1774, tensions were mounting between the Colonies and Great Britain, and in the spring, Lord Dunmore dissolved the Virginia House of Burgesses after it expressed sympathy for the colonial struggle in New England. In September 1774, the first Continental Congress was held in Philadelphia, and events began to move rapidly toward armed conflict with Great Britain. Indian raids continued even after the Battle of Point Pleasant and both powder and lead became scarce. Supplies of both to the settlers were limited as the revolutionary forces quickly moved to confiscate all available war materials. The Revolutionary War would result in additional hardships for the settlers in the Clinch Valley.

Following the Battle of Point Pleasant, a treaty was made by Lord Dunmore with the Ohio Indians in which the Indian tribes agreed to discontinue all raids upon settler's homes. For a time, settlers in the Clinch Valley felt more comfortable in their endeavor to provide for their families and to successfully farm their fields. In early 1775, Daniel Boone again left the Clinch Valley in a second attempt to move families into Kentucky. Boone's move across the Powell River, through Cumberland Gap, and into Kentucky was to benefit those settlers remaining along the Clinch River in that Boone's settlement

> . . . erected on the western frontier a strong barrier against the Western Indians. It was of great value to the Clinch settlements, because it largely diverted the attention of the Western tribes from this region, and relieved our pioneer ancestors from hostile invasions by large bands of the red men. But it did not relieve the inhabitants on the headwaters of the Clinch and Bluestone rivers from frequent bloody attacks by small scalping parties. The Sandy River Valley still remained an open way by which the Indians could approach undetected the Clinch and Bluestone settlements.[79]

Following the treaty after Dunmore's War, James Roark returned his family to their home in Baptist Valley, less anxious than before but still aware of isolated Indian attacks.

Outside the valleys of southwest Virginia, events moved rapidly toward increased conflict with King George III and the British Empire. The Continental Congress adjourned in October 1774 after passing resolutions stating the grievances of the Colonies against the Crown. Closer to the Clinch, a meeting was held in January 1775 of the freeholders of Fincastle County in support of the Continental Congress resolutions. It is unknown whether James Roark participated in the meeting or how many Fincastle citizens attended; however, the attendance from the Clinch Valley was sufficiently adequate for the area to be represented by two men on a committee to draft what history has named "the Fincastle Resolutions." Colonel William Christian chaired the committee and guided the drafting of the resolutions which closed with a declaration that clearly illustrated the spirit of the backwoodsmen of Fincastle County and the Clinch Valley–"These are our real, though unpolished, sentiments of liberty and loyalty, and in them we are resolved to live and die."[80]

By April 1775, James Roark and his family had been on the Baptist Valley farm for two years. His oldest son was ten when, on April 17, the minutemen of Lexington and Concord took up arms against the British and the Revolutionary War was under way. For over six years the war would have a devastating impact on the frontier in southwest Virginia, and the James Roark family would not be spared from the agonies of the conflict. The brief respite from Indian wars following the Battle of Point Pleasant in 1774 was quick to fade as new antagonists arrived on the scene to incite the Indians against the frontier settlements.

As soon as the war began, the British Ministry initiated a policy of enlisting the Indians against the frontier settlements of the Colonies. Numerous British agents were sent to organize the northern tribes–the Shawnees, Wyandots, Mingos, and Iroquois–and to fully equip the Indians with supplies from the British arsenals in Canada. Agents of the Royal government were also at work among the southern tribes–the Creeks, Cherokees, Choctaws, and Chickasaws–which took up arms against the Colonies. The siding by the Cherokees with the British was much later to rob that tribe of sympathy in actions by the American government. Throughout the western frontier, the savagery of the Indian raids during the Revolutionary War made life most difficult for the American pioneer. British agents bought and paid for American scalps brought into the British headquarters in Detroit. The English and the Indians were engaged in a realistic effort to exterminate the border pioneers, to push back the frontier, and to expel the settlers from the Appalachians. On the Virginia frontier the panic was tremendous.

> The people fled into the already existing forts, or hastily built others; where there were but two or three families in a place, they merely gathered into block-houses–stout log-cabins two stories high, with loop-holed walls, and the upper story projecting a little over the lower. The savages, well armed with weapons supplied them from the British arsenals on the Great Lakes, spread over the country; and there ensued all the horrors incident to a war waged as relentlessly against the most helpless non-combatants as against the soldiers in the field. Block-houses were surprised and burned; bodies of militia were ambushed and destroyed. The settlers were shot down as they sat by their hearthstones in the evening, or plowed the ground during the day; the lurking Indians crept up and killed them while they still-hunted the deer, or while they lay in wait for the elk beside the well-beaten game trails.[81]

To afford themselves more protection from the Indian raids, settlers along the Clinch, Holston, and New Rivers petitioned the newly created General Assembly of the Virginia Commonwealth to create new counties along the frontier. In December 1776, the General Assembly provided for the division of Fincastle County into Kentucky County on the west, Washington County in the middle, and Montgomery County on the east. Fincastle County ceased to exist. Interestingly, the dividing line between Montgomery County and Washington County passed through the Baptist Valley farm of James Roark. The exact county line would not be established until 1782, and then the boundary survey would mention James Roark's farm.[82]

As the Revolutionary War progressed and the Continental Army was assembled to fight the British along the coast, the frontier was defended only by the militia organized in the local counties. James Roark's associate from Thompson's Company in 1772, William Christian, now a colonel in the Continental Army, returned to the Clinch Valley, along with others, to assist in the defense of their homes against the combined attacks by the Indians and their British supporters.[83] Without the military outposts previously manned by the British army before the war, the entire frontier of Virginia along the Ohio River was left wide open to invasion by the Indians. The valley of the Sandy River, fed by waters immediately north of Baptist Valley, was left unguarded. The upper Clinch Valley and Bluestone settlements were left exposed to the Shawnees and other northern tribes. Throughout the Revolution, settlers along the Clinch River and Baptist Valley were left to defend themselves by their own exertions and bravery.[84]

> From the fall of 1775 to the close of the Revolutionary War, the settlers in this part of Virginia were compelled to occupy their forts from early spring until late in the fall, as their settlements were constantly visited by bands of Cherokee and Shawnee Indians sent upon them by the British agents, but the settlements enjoyed perfect freedom from the Indians from the first appearance of winter until the return of spring. During this interval of time the Indians were deterred from making raids into the settlements, by the great danger of detection in consequence of the nakedness of the trees, by the danger of being traced by their tracks in the snow, and by suffering produced by exposure to cold while traveling and lying in wait. The settlers took advantage of this immunity from attacks by the Indians, cleared their lands, built their houses and made every possible preparation for their crops during the coming season.[85]

The strain on the frontier family in southwest Virginia during the Revolutionary War was overwhelming. The strategy of battle, the movement of troops, the logistics of supporting an army, and bravery in combat were not the determinants of success in the war on the frontier. There the issue was decided by the determination of the individual settler and his family to endure the strain.

> The young men and bachelors who constituted a majority of the males on the border could come and go. They tended to swarm westward when times were good and to drift eastward again when dangers multiplied. But the genuine settler, the man of family, had to stay put. He could never fall asleep without first holding his breath to listen to the night noises without. His first need upon arising was to peer from the cabin's loopholes into his familiar dooryard and his next warily to comb the fringes of the surrounding forest. Weeks and months might pass without any alarm in his immediate neighborhood but the mutter of distant thunder was always in his ears and he could never know that his own roof might not be the target of the next bolt.
>
> This apprehension that he must daily feel was a dreadful fear. The misfortune hanging over him and over his women and children was death by butchery, accompanied by outrage unspeakable and without parallel. Yet he could not keep his family in the shelter of the nearest stockade. To feed

them he had to work his farm and for this he needed their assistance. So he kept on, cultivating his corn and clearing another acre or two around his cabin, taking care, usually, to have his rifle always within reach and his senses strained to catch the first indication of danger.

The average Indian raid so closely followed the pattern set by its forerunners and its successors that these visitations were like the same nightmare, endlessly repeated. Indians occasionally lurked among the settlements singly or in pairs, watching for the opportunity to steal a horse or snatch a scalp, but the ordinary raiding party was made up of a dozen to twenty warriors. They might spring upon the most outlying cabin along the fringe of the frontier or they might penetrate deep into the settlements where people were less likely to be on guard. If on foot they took expert care to keep out of sight and to leave few tracks that might attract the notice of a chance hunter. If mounted, they traveled fast to keep ahead of the spreading alarm. Having found a place inviting attack, they crept closer, studying the ground and the behavior of the inhabitants.

A favored time to strike was just after dawn when people first emerged to deal with early morning duties but any time when surprise could be achieved was acceptable. The first rush was accompanied by a sudden din of gunshots, whistles, rattles, and the screeching whoop of the war cry, a pandemonium calculated to paralyze the victims with terror. If surprise were as planned, the adult male defenders, their positions marked in advance, were shot down or struck down in the first few seconds.

The farmstead then lay at the mercy of Indian caprice. Their next concern was loot and the premises, however poor, were ransacked for anything that was not too heavy to carry off. . . . After selecting the better horses to take with them, the livestock was butchered. The Indian had a particular aversion to cows, for their possession meant the settler had milk for his children and thus was prepared to stay. The cabin and out-buildings were set afire if they had not been fired as an adjunct to the first assault.[86]

The Virginia government gave little attention to the exposed settlements along the Clinch until July 1779, at which time it requested recommendations from Gen. Andrew Lewis and Col. William Fleming on proper outposts and assignment of troops to defend the western frontier. Lewis and Fleming recommended to Governor Thomas Jefferson a series of five outposts manned by 250 men along the Ohio, one of which was to be at the mouth of the Big Sandy River. Unfortunately, the outposts were not established. "If the recommendations of Lewis and Fleming had been adopted and promptly carried out, there would have been no subsequent incursions made by the Indians to the Clinch Valley; and a number of precious lives would have been saved from the tomahawks and scalping knives of the savages."[87]

During the time of the Indian raids along the Clinch, James Roark doubtless remained with his family, serving in the militia as necessary to provide for a common defense. In addition to the defense of the forts, the militia along the frontier was used in great measure as spies against the Indians. It is highly probable that James Roark served at times as an Indian spy for the militia.[88] While their families were at the fort, the spies

> . . . were employed to hang upon the great trails leading into the settlements from the Ohio. Upon discovering the least sign of Indians, they hurried into the settlements and warned the people to hasten to the forts or stations, as the case might be. They received extra wages for their services, for they were both laborious and important, and also fraught with danger. For such office the very best men were chosen . . . They always went two together, and frequently remained out several weeks upon a scout. Great caution was necessary to prevent the Indians from discovering them, hence their beds were usually of leaves, in some thicket commanding a view of the war-path. Wet or dry, day or night, these men were ever on the lookout.[89]

The families along the Clinch settled into an annual routine as a result of the British-incited Indian raids during the war. During the winter months, from October through March, the family would be in their cabin as the snow and lack of foliage minimized the possibility of an Indian raid. Summers would be divided between the cabin and the fort–farming the land where possible and hurrying to the fort at the first word from the spies that a raid was imminent. Summer to the James Roark family meant frequent moves to Wittens Fort at Crab Orchard, two and one-half miles from the homestead, a distance that was covered quickly when the warning of an Indian raid was received. The sensitivity of the frontier family to Indian raids is described by Joseph Doddridge, whose father settled in the Washington County area in 1773:

> I well remember that, when a little boy, the family was sometimes waked up in the dead of night, by an express with a report that the Indians were at hand. The express came softly to the door, or back window, and by a gentle tapping waked the family. This was easily done, as an habitual fear made us ever watchful and sensible to the slightest alarm. The whole family were instantly in motion. My father seized his gun and other implements of war. My stepmother waked up and dressed the children as well as she could, and being the oldest of the children, I had to take my share of the burdens to be carried to the fort. There was no possibility of getting a horse in the night to aid us in removing to the fort. Besides the little children, we caught up what articles of clothing and provision we could get hold of in the dark, for we durst not light a candle or even stir the fire. All this was done with the utmost dispatch, and the silence of death. The greatest care was taken not to awaken the youngest child. To the rest it was enough to say *Indian* and not a whimper was heard afterward. Thus it often happened that the whole number of families belonging to a fort who were in the evening at their homes, were all in their little fortress before the dawn of the next morning. In the course of the succeeding day, their household furniture was brought in by parties of men under arms.[90]

In the summer of 1779, Indians attacked the home of Jesse Evans, seven miles east of the Roark farm in Baptist Valley. Evans lived close to Wittens Mills immediately east of the present city of Tazewell and within two miles of Maj. John Taylor, an associate of James Roark in Capt. James Thompson's Company in 1772. The Indians attacked during the day while Evans was plowing. Mrs. Evans resisted the attack, but four children of the family were killed. The Evans' daughter Mary, age four, was found early the next day wandering in a daze. Her scalp had been torn from her skull and was hanging over her face, which was smeared with blood. The little girl recovered and lived to adulthood; however, her father and mother became disenchanted with life in the Clinch Valley and moved back east.[91]

By March 1780, James Roark's family consisted of himself, his wife, his two oldest sons, John, aged about fourteen or fifteen and Timothy, aged between twelve and thirteen. Both boys were named for brothers of their father. Seven younger children, aged between twelve and less than a year, completed the family. The family had been in their homestead cabin since the preceding November, and plans were being made to begin work on cultivation for the crops as soon as the winter lifted. On Saturday, March 18, there was a heavy snow on the ground, and James took his two oldest sons, John and Timothy, to hunt for game since corn was scarce for the family and for the rest of the valley.[92] James doubtless was not uncomfortable leaving his family alone since Indian raids were not expected that early in the year and, too, the heavy snow on the ground had greatly discouraged Indians from raiding in the past. Unfortunately this day was an exception to the experience of the settlers. Probably late in the morning of that fateful Saturday, as the mother was preparing lunch for her family, a child's scream shattered the cabin's warmth, tomahawks split the entry door and, as in the worst of nightmares, Indians were suddenly in the cabin. Roark's wife and children were murdered in cold blood and then scalped by the Shawnees who had come south along the Big Sandy. A stark and somber report on the attack was supplied by Maj. John Taylor, Roark's old associate in Thompson's Company, to Col. William Preston, County Lieutenant of Montgomery County. The report was as follows:

> Sir:
>
> The 18th Instant the Indians was In this Neighborhood and Fell in at James Roark's where they Scalped seven of his Children And his wife. They are all Dead only one Girl. They took Seven Head of Horses Five of which was the property of Wm. Patterson. This part of yr. County is In a scene of Confusion And I can make no doubt but the Country will Break up without they Can Get Some Assistance. I am as yet Living at home but Captain Maxwell's Compy are Chiefly Gathered together in Small Parties. Corn is very Scarce Here but if a few good men could be raised I think they Could be found, Sir if you have resigned yr Commission Pray let the County Lieut. Have this Letter or a few lines from yr. self which I think will Answer a better end. I expected a few lines from you By Capt Moor

but Dont hear of any My family is In Health As I hope yours and I am Sir yr. Most Hum Srt.

Jno Taylor

Head Clinch 23rd March 1780

C B the Murder was Committed In seven Miles of here.[93]

The report mentions that one girl survived the attack; however, later records do not identify her. It can be safely assumed that she died soon after the attack making a total of eight members of James Roark's family killed that dreadful Saturday morning. One can only imagine the horror and shock of James on his return in finding the mutilated bodies of his wife and children. Hopes and dreams vanish quickly and lives are shattered beyond reconstruction in such events. James lost his life companion and, with her name lost to history, she was buried with her children in unmarked graves on a snow-covered ridge in Baptist Valley.

James remained in the Clinch Valley with his two sons for just over two years. He may have found the grief too great to continue to live in his cabin on the 130 acres in Baptist Valley and, as a result, moved to his 100-acre tract along the Clinch River south of Roark's Gap.[94] The river farm had significant outcropping of rock and was far less fertile than the rich soils in Baptist Valley. The Clinch River did, however, provide water to support more livestock. After building a new cabin on that portion of the river farm that lay on the north side of the river,[95] Roark cultivated the little fertile land on the farm and added cattle and horses.[96] Creating a new life for himself and his sons was Herculean; however, it appears that in the two years following the massacre, James struggled to cope with his loss and to provide his two sons with a home. Doubtless the neighboring families of John Deskins, John Hankins, and William Patterson were supportive.[97]

Roark's two sons matured quickly under the circumstances. Maturity came early in the life of almost every adolescent boy on the Virginia frontier, but with the sudden, horrible death of their mother and siblings, John and Timothy were forced to quickly adjust to complete self-sufficiency. Limited evidence suggests that John and his father were embittered by the massacre more so than Timothy and even sought revenge against the Shawnees and other Indian tribes. Bickley, in his history of Tazewell County written in 1852, mentions that:

> From this time forward [after the massacre], the Roarks became the deadly enemies of the Indians, and sought them, even beyond the limits of the county. Mr. Roark and one of his sons (John), were afterward killed in a battle, fought at what was then known as the Station bottom, within the present limits of Floyd County, Kentucky.[98]

Bickley is in error in many of his facts and no record of a battle at Station bottom (Harman Station) has been found. Available evidence seems to indicate that Bickley was at least partially in error on the death of James. No later record of his son John has been located indicating he may have died an early death as Bickley has stated.

Report from Major John Taylor, March 23, 1780, to Col. William Preston, providing the details of the James Roark family massacre.

Family tradition strongly suggests that James' son Timothy was captured by the Shawnees and remained with them anywhere from two to twelve years. The variety of sources reporting his capture gives credibility to the story.[99] Timothy's capture could have occurred at the time of the massacre since he was not specifically named as the other son with James on that Saturday; however, no historical records have surfaced that document his capture. Histories of the period, however, are rife with such captures and, while it could have occurred at the massacre, Timothy's capture more than likely took place during his time on the river farm. Later events in Timothy's life, i.e., the birth date for his first child, and his age at the time of his death suggest that he was between twelve and thirteen in 1780, was with his father at the time of the massacre, and was captured by the Shawnees at a later date. The details of Timothy's capture by the Shawnees and his later escape must be accepted as tradition without definite confirmation by fact. No records have been found on Timothy before 1787.[100]

Roark's Gap, Tazewell County, Virginia, looking south toward the Clinch River from the location of the James Roark Cabin.

In 1779, the Assembly of Virginia had passed a law setting up a Commission for Washington and Montgomery Counties to rule on land claims in both counties. The purpose of the Commission was to review all claims and provide a clear title to deserving owners. Clear title was to be based on the year the claimant occupied the land and the time he made improvements to it. These improvements generally consisted of building a family cabin and beginning cultivation for crops. In the summer of 1781, James Roark began the effort to obtain clear title to his 130-acre tract in Baptist Valley and appeared before the commissioners. On August 15, 1781, James received title for 150 acres (unsurveyed) in the form of a certificate that read:

> We the commissioners for the district of Washington and Montgomery Counties do certify that James Roark assignee of John Pearie [Peery] is entitled to one hundred & fifty acres of land in Washington County lying on the waters of the North fork of Clinch [River] & on the north side to include the improvements he having provided to the Court that he was entitled to the same by actual improvements made in the year 1773.
>
> As witness our hands this 15th day of August 1781.
>
> Test,   Jos. Cabell
> James Reid, Clk.   Harry Innis   Commers.
>   H. Cabell[101]

The Revolutionary War ended in October 1781 with the surrender of Cornwallis at Yorktown just months after James Roark received title to his Baptist Valley farm; however, Indian raids continued for several years in the Clinch Valley. In September 1784, a party of Shawnees, traveling by way of the Sandy River, raided homesteads at the head of the Clinch and in Abb's Valley to the east. As late as September 1786, a Shawnee raid occurred again in Abb's Valley. Raids continued in the area after 1786 but became much less frequent, with one of the last raids being made on the lower Clinch River in April 1794.[102]

The boundary between Montgomery and Washington counties had been ill-defined in 1776 at the time of creation of the counties and, in the early spring of 1782, both counties employed Hugh Fulton to survey the county line. On May 6, 1782, Fulton presented his survey which read, in part:

> Thence from said knob [Morris' Knob] north crossing the spurs of the same, and Paint Lick Mountain, the north fork of the Clinch by John Hines' plantation, and over the river ridge by James Roark's in the Baptist Valley . . .[103]

With the new county line drawn by Fulton, James Roark's 130 acres in Baptist Valley was to be partially in both Washington and Montgomery counties[104] while his 100-acre tract on the Clinch was to remain in Washington County.

In the spring of 1782, before or about the time of Fulton's survey, James Roark left the Clinch Valley. It appears that he began to devote more time to hunting than to farming as bitterness from the murder of his wife and family engulfed him. As his two remaining sons matured, and considering even that son Timothy was captured by the Indians sometime within the first two years following the massacre, James began to dwell on his loss and quite possibly did become, as Bickley suggests, the bitter pursuer of the hated Shawnees. In his wanderings, he sought the comfort of family and for a year lived near or with his brother Timothy and possibly his mother in southern Montgomery County on Elk Creek (now Grayson County).[105] He was forty-two years old at the time. During his stay on Elk Creek, James became a member of the local militia, and on September 6, 1782, he was listed with his brother Timothy as a member of Captain Charles Morgan's Company.[106]

Evidence suggests that it was emotionally impossible for James to return to his cabin on the 130 acres in Baptist Valley. Apparently the memories were much too great to overcome and maybe, we just do not know, his son John had been killed and son Timothy captured within two years following the massacre. Hence, whatever the circumstances, James decided to sell the homestead tract. Since he now had clear title to the tract, he returned to Baptist Valley in early 1783 to have the tract surveyed. The survey for the 130 acres was completed by the end of April 1783, and Roark sold his interest in the tract to his old friend from the James Thompson militia company, David Crouch, signing his certificate of title as follows:

> I do hereby assign the within Certificate to David Crouch for value rec'd this 30th April, 1783.

his
James X Roark
mark[107]

Following the sale of the Baptist Valley farm, James neither purchased nor claimed any land other than the 100-acre tract on the Clinch, and there is no record that he spent any time on the river farm after 1786.[108] James established a residence in the east portion of Baptist Valley and later was in Montgomery County either in Baptist Valley or with his brother on Elk Creek. While his exact residence in the period between 1783 and 1787 is difficult to pinpoint, there is evidence that he spent time both at his brother's place on Elk Creek and at his residence in northern Montgomery County. It is clear that he had difficulty in resuming again the life of a farmer and establishing a permanent residence. He did respond to public notices and requirements. On July 26, 1785, James served on a jury for Montgomery County at the courthouse which was then located in the old county seat of Fincastle County at the Lead Mines on the New River. Serving on the jury with him was David Crouch who had purchased James' Baptist Valley farm. The jury ruled in favor of the plaintiff, Archibald Reaugh, that the defendant, Robert Sayers, had not paid an unspecified debt. The following day, July 27th, James again served on a jury that ruled in favor of the plaintiff. In that case the Buchanan Executors, and the defendant, James McDaniel, were ordered to pay an unspecified debt plus interest.[109]

The settlements in southwest Virginia increased in number following a decline in Indian raids after the Revolutionary War. As the number of settlers increased so did the demands for additional counties and courthouses. Petitions were submitted to the Virginia Legislature in 1785 for a new county within Washington County, and on January 6, 1786, Russell County was created from the upper portion of Washington County north of Clinch Mountain. As a result of the legislative action, the 100-acre tract of James Roark was afterwards located in Russell County.[110] The 130-acre tract James sold to David Crouch was, after January 1786, located in both Montgomery County and Russell County.[111]

By 1787, James Roark had returned to the southern part of Montgomery County and was with his brother Timothy on Elk Creek. It is an interesting exercise to compare the fortunes of life between James and his brother Timothy as they both approached their middle-age years and as delegates met in Philadelphia during that summer in 1787 to draft the U.S. Constitution. By 1787, Timothy had acquired 400 acres along Elk Creek and lived there with his wife Rachel.[112] His livestock consisted of eight horses and eleven head of cattle.[113] His farmlands were very profitable and were able to support Timothy and his four sons, William, Charles, Timothy Junior, and Moses, and his three daughters, Rebecca, Mary, and Sarah. William appears to have been the oldest; however, he suffered some malady that prevented him from supporting himself. The other three sons established their homes and supported their families on their father's four hundred acres. Moses was the youngest son, and in 1787, still lived at home with his parents. Timothy was obviously a successful farmer and enjoyed seeing his children grow to maturity to support themselves on the fruits of his labors.[114]

James, on the other hand, had seen little financial success and by 1787 owned only his horse and an abandoned farm on the Clinch River.[115] His family life had been destroyed by the massacre and he now lived alone. Perhaps his oldest son John had, by 1787, also been killed by Indians. His younger and surviving son, Timothy, had been captured by the Shawnees and, after many months in captivity, had only recently returned to his father. Doubtless, James gained support both morally and financially from his brother, and it was during these visits to Elk Creek and the time spent there that James and son Timothy grew close to the nieces, nephews, and cousins in the Elk Creek area. As son Timothy matured, he was to establish his home in the Clinch Valley but remained close to his Elk Creek cousins. By 1787, Timothy was in Baptist Valley, farming as a tenant on the 130-acre homestead place now owned by David Crouch.[116]

During his time on Elk Creek, James Roark was active in the militia, probably because it was a requirement to serve and also since he had the time to devote to drill activities without competition from family affairs. With his experience in the militia and on the frontier, Roark was made a constable in Captain Enoch Osborn's Company on October 3, 1787.[117] He was forty-seven years old at the time.[118] Interestingly, his son Timothy, in 1787, was in Capt. James Maxwell's Company in Montgomery County, James Roark's old unit in the Clinch Valley.[119]

James was to remain in the Elk Creek area until late 1788 at which time he, too, returned to Baptist Valley. He left his brother's place late that year and on December 2, 1788, was replaced by Joseph Fields as constable in the local militia.[120] In March 1789, as George Washington was taking the oath as first president of the United States, James Roark was in Baptist Valley seeking to reestablish a residence near his son Timothy.

In September 1789, James Roark was in legal action in Russell County at Lebanon against Obadiah Payne. Roark, probably represented by an attorney, was the defendant in a complaint brought by Payne.[121] Nothing is known of the issue involved, but it probably had to do with Roark's 100-acre river farm and possibly Payne as a tenant farmer. Obadiah Payne was a tithable in Russell County from 1787 through 1790 but owned no property so he probably made his living as a tenant farmer.[122] The case was continued until June 1790 at which time James Roark, as defendant, pleaded "general issue and cause continued." A deposition from Charles Miller was ordered.[123] Miller [or Millard] was also a tithable without land holdings in Russell County in 1787, 1788, and 1789.[124] The case was dismissed in September 1790.[125] After 1790, Payne and Miller were no longer listed as tithables in Russell County.

On December 1, 1789, the Virginia General Assembly responded to a petition for a new county in the northern portion of Montgomery and passed a statute creating Wythe County on May 1, 1790, after which time Baptist Valley became part of Wythe County. In the last inventory of personal property by Montgomery County in Baptist Valley, James Roark's taxable personal property was appraised on February 23, 1790.

He had only his horse.[126] Wythe County was to be his place of residence at his death.

James Roark died July 21, 1792.[127] The circumstances of his death are unclear, and Bickley could be correct in stating that James was killed by Indians in Kentucky. He would have been in his early fifties at his death, somewhat young to die of natural causes although that would certainly have not been considered terribly unusual. The place of his burial is unknown, but it probably was next to his wife somewhere in Baptist Valley. His son Timothy, still unmarried but living nearby, was the only family present at the burial.

The settlement of the estate of James Roark extended for over nine years and was not finally resolved until September 1801. Apparently there were claims against the estate and probably some title issues dealing with the 100-acre river farm. Following Roark's death in 1792, the river farm was listed on the Russell County tax records under "James Roark Estate."[128] It appears that, to protect his father's title in the river farm, Timothy employed John Greenup as an attorney-in-fact not only to clear all claims against the farm but also to serve as administrator of the estate.[129]

Two appraisals of the estate, exclusive of the river farm, were returned to the Wythe County Court in July 1794. The first appraisal was by James Whitten [Witten] and Thomas Whitten [Witten] Junior and listed:

> 107 pounds of grey dear skins
> 2 pounds of red dear skins
> Three small firs and one other
> for a total value of five pounds, ten shillings, and two and one-half pence.[130]

A second appraisal, listing household items common to a widower's estate, was made by James Maxwell, Thomas Witten Junior, and John George, and was returned to court on Tuesday, July 8, 1794. This appraisal was in the amount of thirteen pounds, nineteen shillings, and ten pence. It included:

> 2 Coats
> 1 pair Britches
> 1 Shirt and pair Breeches
> 1 Case Razors
> 1 Auger & hammer
> 1 Blacksmith's Rasp
> 2 Saddles
> 1 Gun Lock
> 1 Hat
> 1 Frying pan
> 1 Rifle gun, shot pouch & powderhorn
> 3 Small fur skins
> 1 pair Spurs
> 6 horse shoes & nails

1 Carpenters Rule
1 pair Silver knee buckles[131]

The estate was finally settled on September 8, 1801, and was recorded in the records of Wythe County as follows:

> To the Worshipful Court of Wythe
> Agreeable to an order to us directed we have settled with John Greenup,
> Administrator of Jas. Roark Dec'd, and stated as followeth–
> The Amount of James Roark estate   21 pounds, 3 shillings, 10 pence
> The Amount of Debts against the estate of
> the sd Roark   24 pounds, 18 shillings, 8 1/2 pence
> Given under our hands this 14th day of January 1801
>
> Wm. George
John Thompson
Arch'd Thompson
>
> At a Court held for the County of Wythe the 8th day of September 1801,
> This Settlement of the Estate of James Roark Dec'd with John Greenup the
> Adm. thereof to Court and ordered to be recorded.
> Teste
> Robert Crockett CWC[132]

It is unclear whether William George and the Thompsons were the claimants against the estate or were named by the Court to settle the issues between unnamed claimants and the administrator, John Greenup. In any event, it appears that the claimants received the total value of the estate, excluding land, as a settlement for the debts that exceeded the value of the estate. In the estate settlement of James Roark, his son Timothy received title to the 100-acre river farm. During the nine years it had taken to settle the estate, Timothy had, on January 16, 1797, repurchased from David Crouch the family homestead farm of 130 acres in Baptist Valley.[133]

Chapter 3

Ancestry–Timothy Roark
Tennessee Pioneer Farmer

The father of Joseph Roark was born about 1767, probably in present-day Montgomery County, Virginia, east of the New River.[1] Timothy Roark was, to the best of our knowledge, the second son of James Roark. He was six years old when his father and mother and the four children had moved to the Clinch River and settled in Baptist Valley. As a young boy, the excitement of a two-week migration to a new and unsettled area would have been indelibly planted in his memory.

In Baptist Valley, Timothy and his older brother, John, learned to hunt and fish and to survive on the frontier. By age twelve he had his own rifle and shot pouch. Hunting squirrels, turkeys, and raccoons soon made him an expert in the use of his rifle and, with that expertise, he was able to take on the responsibility of part-time soldier. "Each well-grown boy at the age of twelve on the Virginia frontier was expected to become a fort soldier and was assigned a port hole at the local fort."[2] No doubt Timothy was assigned a port hole at Wittens Fort, a position he would assume at any time the local families would gather at the fort to defend themselves during Indian raids.

As a young boy on the frontier, Timothy, along with his brother John and others of their age, assumed many of the ways of the Indians. The clothes of the men on the frontier often were more Indian than civilized.

> The hunting shirt was universally worn. This was a kind of loose frock, reaching half way down the thighs, with large sleeves, open before, and so wide as to lap over a foot or more when belted. The cape was large, and sometimes handsomely fringed with a revelled piece of cloth of a different color from that of the hunting shirt itself. The bosom of this dress served as a wallet to hold a chunk of bread, cakes, jirk, tow for wiping the barrel of the rifle, or any other necessary for the hunter or warrior. The belt which was always tied behind answered several purposes, besides that of holding the dress together. In cold weather the mittens, and sometimes the bullet-bag occupied the front part of it. To the right side was suspended the

tomahawk and to the left the scalping knife in its leathern sheath. The hunting shirt was generally made of linsey, sometimes of coarse linen, and a few of dressed deer skins. These last were very cold and uncomfortable in wet weather. The shirt and jacket were of the common fashion. A pair of drawers or breeches and leggins, were the dress of the thighs and legs, a pair of mocassons [sic] answered for the feet much better than shoes. They were made of dressed deer skin. They were mostly made of a single piece with a gathering seam along the top of the foot, and another from the bottom of the heel, without gathers as high as the ankle joint or a little higher. Flaps were left on each side to reach some distance up the legs. They were nicely adapted to the ankles, and lower part of the leg, by throngs of deer skin, so that no dust, gravel, or snow could get within the mocasson [sic]. The mocassons [sic] in ordinary use cost but a few hours labor to make them. This was done by an instrument denominated by a mocasson awl, which was made of the backspring of an old clapknife. This awl with its buckshorn handle was an appendage of every shot pouch strap, together with a roll of buckskin for mending the mocassons. This was the labor of almost every evening. They were sewed together and patched with deer skin thongs, or whangs as they were commonly called.

In cold weather the mocassons were well stuffed with deer hair, or dry leaves, so as to keep the feet comfortably warm; but in wet weather it was usually said that wearing them was "a decent way of going barefooted," and such was the fact, owing to the spongy texture of the leather of which they were made.

In the latter years of the indian [sic] war our young men became more enamoured of the indian dress throughout, with the exception of the matchcoat. The drawers were laid aside and the leggins made longer, so as to reach the upper part of the thigh. The indian breech clout was adopted. This was a piece of linen or cloth nearly a yard long, and eight or nine inches broad. This passed under the belt before and behind leaving the ends for flaps hanging before and behind over the belt. These flaps were sometimes ornamented with some coarse kind of embroidery work. To the same belts which secured the breech clout, strings which supported the long leggins were attached. When this belt as was often the case passed over the hunting shirt the upper part of the thighs and part of the hips were naked.

The young warrior instead of being abashed by this nudity was proud of his indian like dress. In some few instances I have seen them go into places of public worship in this dress. Their appearance however did not add much to the devotion of the young ladies.[3]

The Indian clothing was easy to make and made use of the materials that were available to the frontier family. In a sense, it was in the fashion of "making do" so common to the frontier. Self-reliance was, by necessity, the focus of the family struggling to survive without the benefit and availability of manufactured goods. Timothy Roark thus grew to be self-reliant at an early age and gained an independence that was to be needed in the eventful days that lay ahead.

Timothy was almost thirteen on that Saturday in March 1780 and had been hunting with his father and brother when his mother and the rest of the family were massacred in their cabin by the Shawnees. With his father and brother, Timothy assisted in the burial of his mother and the children and in removing from the cabin the grim vestiges of the gruesome murder which would be forever in the far reaches of his memory.

Timothy and John moved with their father to the river farm following the massacre and attempted to start a new life. A new cabin had to be built and new lands had to be cultivated. The hard work was good therapy but it was a difficult time for a thirteen-year-old boy, now without a mother and younger brothers and sisters. Both Timothy and his brother were also forced to take on household duties such as cooking, mending, and cleaning. Defense against Indian attacks also required continued vigilance. Bitterness against the Shawnees and other Indian tribes was to be expected and, unfortunately, Timothy's relationship with the Shawnees did not end with his mother's murder. Indian raids continued and the Revolutionary War dragged on throughout the Atlantic coast as well as along the frontier.

By Timothy's second summer on the river farm, conditions in the Revolutionary War had turned favorable for the American forces. Early in 1781, the British army had been maneuvered to the Virginia coast along the James River, and General Washington moved swiftly to surround the British army under Cornwallis at Yorktown. By August 30, the French fleet under DeGrasse had arrived to seal the blockade. On October 19, 1781, as Timothy Roark, his father, and brother labored on the river farm, Cornwallis surrendered and, for all practical purposes, the Revolutionary War was over. It had lasted seven long years.

The Revolutionary War had actually been three wars fought in different locations and with different styles of warfare in each. All three were of almost equal importance. First, the land war, given the most attention in published history, had been fought by American and British armies along the tidewater area of the Atlantic coast with British forces occupying first Boston, then New York, Philadelphia, and other coastal cities. Major land battles had been fought near the coast at Bunker Hill, Trenton, Princeton, Monmouth, and finally Yorktown. The second war was a naval war and had been fought along the coast as the British used its superior navy to blockade ports and to move the British army to occupy New York, Charleston, and Savannah. The third war of the Revolution had been fought not near the Atlantic seaboard but rather on the American frontier and had involved almost continuous combat between the Indians and the frontier militia. On the frontier, the English plan had always been the same:

It was to ravage the screen of scattered western settlements until their necessary abandonment had opened the way for the descent of hordes of savages upon the less hardy inhabitants east of the mountains and thereby to
provoke such widespread terror as must once and for all discourage the
rebellion. The resolution with which the frontier people clung to their
clearings and stockades, year after year against odds which appeared even
more hopeless, frustrated this design. Their desperate resistance was a
service to the national cause that played no inconsiderable part of the
nation's final victory.[4]

The land war had been punitive to tidewater cities during their occupation by the
British army but, for most of the cities, the war came and went. Boston was evacu-
ated by the British just nine months after Bunker Hill, and Philadelphia was abandoned by Clinton's army less than a year after it had been occupied. For periods of
time, many of the tidewater areas suffered as both American and British armies
moved up and down the coast, but all areas experienced times of relief and comfort
as the armies moved on. But, for the entire seven years of the war, the frontier people had no such intervals of peace. For them, there were

no such intervals, no relief from danger, no surcease from dread. For them
the day that passed without an attack was nevertheless always a day when
an attack might be but an hour away. Theirs was to remain a conflict in
which victory was beyond the reach of valor. The enemy was not a ponderous army of disciplined and uniformed soldiers commanded by civilized officers, but packs of painted savages, capable of springing at any
moment from the wilderness to burn a homestead and butcher a family and
then of disappearing again as suddenly into the wilderness. This enemy's
method of waging war was as fearful as his terrifying antics and macabre
appearance. His favorite weapons were surprise, ambush, mutilation, the
war whoop, the knife, the hatchet, and the burning stake. As the years of
such a war rolled on, they were to impose on these Americans of the frontier a strain more nearly unendurable than any to which any other people
have ever been subjected.[5]

The war on the American frontier during the Revolution was no insignificant
conflict. More Americans were killed in action in the frontier area of the war than in
all of the major battles of the Revolution combined. It was a distressing war to the
frontier participants. Women and children in their homes were in as much danger as
the soldier in the field. Year after year and conflict after conflict appeared to bring
neither victory nor defeat appreciably nearer. It was an inglorious war, one not understood by the participants for its reason or its objective.[6] Unfortunately for Timothy
Roark, his father, and his brother, the war did not end with the surrender at Yorktown.
For them and many others like them on the American frontier, the war was savagely
to continue for another thirteen years without respite. Timothy Roark was to personally feel the brunt of this continuing conflict. The Indians, principally the

Shawnees, then without British support, intensified their efforts to protect Indian lands. After Yorktown, the threat of further English war effort had ended. The American army was quickly disbanded, Washington resigned his commission to the Congress in Annapolis, and, for the tidewater area, the war was over. The leaders of the American army were exhausted, Congress and the people were tired of war, and there was little or no interest in a military campaign to protect the frontier from the Indian raids which continued. For the American frontier, "the war ground on. To the settler at the time there was no apparent sign that this was a war he was predestined to win. In fact the Indians won every major battle–until the last one."[7]

While supplied by the British and Tory traders, the Indians had developed an appreciation of a concerted effort among several tribes. Long after the Treaty of Paris had been accepted by the British and American delegations on September 3, 1783, and the British forces had abandoned their forts along the Great Lakes, the Indian raids were to continue. Frontier counties requested military aid now that the war was over. With little thought given to the welfare of the frontier families and their continued war with the Indians, the American Congress met, with barely a quorum, on January 14, 1784, to ratify the peace treaty but not to provide military assistance to the frontier.

The most difficult and savage of all the Indian tribes were the Shawnees. Joined by the Delaware, Miami, Wyandot, and Mingo tribes, the Shawnees led a concerted effort to stop the westward advance of the white man on the frontier. The early frontier settlers had, like the Indians, been well schooled in the woodland way of life and competed directly with the Shawnees for game and survival in the wilderness. It has been observed that the American frontier conflict with the Indians came not because they were so alien to each other but precisely because they were so much alike. British agents at the time noted that early on there would have been little conflict if the settlers had "pursued agriculture alone" and not continuously hunted game in the wilderness.[8] Originally having lived east of the mountains in what is now Pennsylvania, the Shawnees had been forced westward to the Ohio Valley by the advance of the frontier. By 1781, the Shawnees had settled in present-day Ohio, south of Lake Erie and west of Fort Pitt, the westernmost fort of the American forces. They had fought with the Cherokees to the south and, prior to the settlements in southwestern Virginia, had continuously used a well-worn path west of the Clinch Valley to make war with the Cherokees. Later, with the movement of the white man into southwestern Virginia and Kentucky, the Shawnees were determined to fight, with or without their tribal allies, to halt the westward advances. Their murderous raids would continue long after the Revolutionary War until their defeat at the Battle of Fallen Timbers in 1795 and the treaty at Fort Greenville with Gen. "Mad Anthony" Wayne. The Shawnees would, however, continue to resist white settlement in the Ohio Valley until 1813 when their vanishing hopes were dashed with the death of their last famous chief, Tecumseh, in the Battle of Thames north of Detroit.[9]

It was in the summer or early fall of 1781, almost eighteen months following the massacre, that Timothy himself was captured by the hated Indians. Details of his capture or any recorded history of his time with the Indians has not been found. His capture is strongly supported by both family tradition and independent references.[10] In all probability, Timothy was taken by Shawnees and was probably captured while he was hunting alone as no records or stories have been preserved of a similar capture of either John or his father or of fights with Indians involving all three. In any event, Timothy's life on the frontier, and even his dress in Indian style, served him well in surviving his capture. While no description of his life among the Indians is available, history has provided accounts of some of the many other captives by the Indians during the period.

The size of the Shawnee bands raiding the western frontier of Pennsylvania and Virginia ranged from ten to twenty in number. Motives for the heinous raids seem to have been primarily in response to the British purchase of scalps in an organized and deliberate effort to exterminate the American western pioneers and to push the frontier back to the east. Most Indian tribes, however, took prisoners in addition to scalps and apparently were compensated by the British for prisoners as well as scalps. The small bands of Indians in a general pattern would kill and scalp older adults and young children, as traveling with either or both as captives would be difficult and slow. The execution might be by tomahawk, knife or gunshot, but the Indians had a peculiarly perverse weakness for swinging infants by their heels to pop their skulls against a tree.[11] Young adults and those in their adolescent years were most often taken captive with the idea of using them as captive labor and even adopting them as members of an Indian family. Once an Indian raid was completed and prisoners taken, the Indian band had to move rapidly lest they be overtaken by a responding body of the frontier militia.

For the prisoners the first twenty to thirty days of captivity were the most severe as they involved continuous travel to the British forts along the Great Lakes. Food and provisions were scarce even for the Indians, and the prisoners often were required to go for days without food and with little water. Mrs. Archibald Clendenin, following her capture and the murder of her husband near Greenbriar, Virginia, in 1763, told of how the Indians traveled by placing the prisoners between two groups of Indians, almost in single file and moving the group very rapidly.[12] During the first few nights of captivity, when escape would have been most likely, the prisoners were secured in the most inhuman manner. Abner Gilbert, who was captured at the age of fourteen with a group on the Pennsylvania frontier on April 4, 1780, later described the first few nights of captivity:

> It may furnish information to some to mention the method the Indians generally use to secure their prisoners. They cut down a sapling as large as a man's thigh, and therein cut notches, in which they fix [the prisoner's] legs, and over this they place a pole, crossing the pole on each side with stakes

drove [sic] in the ground, and in the crotches of the stakes they place other poles or riders, effectually confining the prisoners on their backs; besides which they put a strap round their necks which they fasten to a tree. In this manner the night passed. Their [the prisoner's] beds were hemlock branches strewed on the ground and blankets for a covering, which was an indulgence scarcely to have been expected from savages. It may reasonably be expected, that in this melancholy situation, sleep was a stranger to [our] eyelids.[13]

As the raiding party continued its rapid pace and fatigue took its toll on the prisoners, chances of their escape decreased and the captives were given more freedom at night. Food supply remained a problem for both Indians and captives, and accounts that remain tell of times where the raiding party halted for the Indians to seek game for food. Gilbert tells that the only food was venison since the Indians carried no corn or flour.[14]

On the third or fourth day of their captivity the prisoners experienced the Indian culture of coloring the skin. Each prisoner was painted according to the Indian custom. Some of the captives were painted red with mixtures of berry juice and Indian paints while other prisoners were painted black with smut. Those painted black were considered to have little value and were generally slated for ill treatment and most likely an early death at the hands of the Indians. These were generally older prisoners but also included those who had proven to be weak during the days on the trail. Those prisoners painted red were the young adults who had value as farm laborers when the Indians would reach their village near the Great Lakes.[15]

As the raiding party moved away from the American settlements more time was devoted by the Indians to hunting and to providing themselves and the prisoners with a variety of meat. When friendly Indian villages were reached, turnips and potatoes were to be had along with wild turkey and fish. During the meals on the trail, the Indians ate separately, and after eating, let the prisoners eat by the fire from the provisions that remained.[16]

During the first few days on the trail, prisoners were sometimes able to escape before fatigue caused them to lose hope and while they still knew the country and the direction to safety. These early escapes were rare; however, they did at times occur. Mrs. Francis Scott was captured by a band of Delawares and Mingos in Washington County, Virginia, on June 29, 1785, and was taken by the raiding band north along the Clinch and Sandy rivers. After eleven days on the trail, security conditions were relaxed while the Indians hunted for game, and Mrs. Scott was able to escape from the older Indian left to guard her. After wandering for over thirty days, surviving on the juice of cane stalks and on sassafras leaves, Mrs. Scott found her way to the New Garden settlement on the Clinch River.[17] Although these early escapes were difficult and risky to the prisoner, they doubtless were considered by all captives. However, as fatigue, quickened by anxiety, overcame the prisoners, and as the small convoy reached areas far from their homes, escape could not be seriously considered.

In most instances, the captives and the raiding band of Indians were on the trail up to thirty days before they reached the British forts near Niagara or other locations on the Great Lakes. During this period, the prisoners were pushed and often dragged as the party moved as rapidly as possible over rough terrain. Travel was especially hard on women or other prisoners not accustomed to extended travel and outdoor conditions.

> All suffered during the rigors of the march back to the Indian country when to fail to keep pace meant the tomahawk. Their initial reception was also painful. To the Indian captor a live prisoner, even if only a child or a woman, was more convincing evidence even than a scalp of his prowess in war and every care was taken for a while to view the prisoner as an enemy. During this period of boasting and vainglory captives were insulted, humiliated, beaten, and made to feel that death by torment was imminent.[18]

It would have been during this period of his captivity that Timothy Roark would have been most grateful for his outdoor lifestyle plus his Indian dress and training.

As the party neared their destination and home on the Great Lakes, it more frequently passed through villages of various tribes. In almost every village, Indian women would come from the huts and strike each prisoner a blow across the face. Several prisoners reported that Indian women and children would collect rocks and sticks to throw at the prisoners as they passed through the villages.[19]

Upon reaching the British forts, the prisoners were displayed and paraded before the British officers. The prisoners remained, however, under the control of the Indians and were not released to the British who had little use for additional prisoners to feed and maintain. Abner Gilbert told of being interrogated by a British colonel in the presence of his Indian captors after which the colonel released him to the Indians and paid them for their captives. The Indians' "pay" was a belt of wampum made of New England shells and glass beads strung together on leather throngs. Thus, in this particular manner, the Indians were rewarded for their inhuman acts against the frontier populations.[20]

Individual prisoners, particularly those in their adolescent years, were quite often adopted by Indian families. Abigail Dodson related her adoption rite by a family of the Seneca tribe. In a formal ceremony that was unintelligible to her, she was required to sit close to a young Indian man while the eldest chieftain repeated an adoption ritual. Mrs. Dodson was concerned that it was a marriage vow to the Indian man but was relieved when she was taken away with her new adoptive family leaving behind the young Indian.[21] Abner Gilbert was adopted by a family of the Cayuga nation and moved with the family as they settled near the Niagara fort, to be dependent on provisions from the British until a corn crop could be harvested.[22]

With their individual families, the captives were assigned mundane tasks which ranged from cutting wood, planting and harvesting corn, and protecting the crop by constructing and maintaining a rudimentary fence. At one period, much to his chagrin and boredom, Abner Gilbert was assigned the task of gathering hickory nuts.[23] With the adoption by families and the assignment of responsibilities, however, the captives enjoyed more freedom of movement and flexibility in schedule. Escape was now out of the question, therefore prisoners were able to mingle with other Indian families or seek solitude in the forest. Thomas Peart, captured in 1780 at the same time as Abner Gilbert, told of meeting a white woman who had been taken captive and who had married into an Indian family. The woman had in her possession a New Testament which Peart borrowed. Peart recorded that he would retire "into the woods and enjoy [myself] in reading and meditating upon the instruction couched in it."[24]

All captives spoke of the filth and deplorable sanitary conditions that were customary with the Indians. Abner Gilbert spoke of a supper of hominy which the Indians made by pounding available corn into a mush. The Indians ate first and when they finished eating "they wiped the spoon on the soal of their mockasons [sic] and gave it to the captives. Hunger alone could prevail on anyone to eat after such filth and nastiness."[25] Thomas Peart had particular difficulty with the living conditions of his adoptive family:

> The Indian manner of life is remarkably dirty and lousy; and although they themselves disregard their filth, yet it was extremely mortifying to the prisoners to be deprived of the advantages of cleanliness. . . . Their provisions [of food], notwithstanding it was a season of great plenty, was often deer guts, dried with the dung, and all boiled together, which they consider strong and wholesome food. They never throw away any part of the game they take.[26]

Later, Peart spoke of conditions when food was scarce and prisoners and Indians alike were reduced to digging roots for food. During this period of want "one of the Indians killed a fine elk, which was a long wished for and delightful supply; but as the weather was very warm, and they had no salt, it soon became putrid and filled with maggots, which they, notwithstanding, [ate] without reserve."[27]

These were some of the hardships and deprivations that Timothy Roark doubtlessly endured during his captivity. How much he later spoke in detail of his captivity is unknown, but most likely in later years he shared some of his experiences with his family and his son Joseph. Unfortunately no family member recorded the details of this very trying period in the life of Timothy Roark.

When and how Timothy secured his release from the Shawnees is unknown. Many captives of the Indians gained their freedom through a ransom paid by members of their family. In Timothy's case this was unlikely, considering his father's poor financial condition and personal instability at the time. Family tradition is that he escaped by stealing a canoe, taking with him two white women who were also captives.[28] If the escape story is true, Timothy probably traveled to a nearby fort and received assistance from the British who were then abandoning their Great Lakes outposts following execution of the peace treaty. Some help from the British would have been necessary since transportation back to southwest Virginia would otherwise have been extremely difficult. Other captives also received assistance from the British. With the Revolutionary War then over, Abner Gilbert had used the opportunity of assistance by the British to end his captivity and return to civilization. He was assisted by the British, the treaty having been signed, and with their help returned to his home after an absence of three years.[29] Similarly, Thomas Peart was released by the Indians through the help of a British colonel at Fort Niagara. His adoptive family, after a conference with the British, finally consented to give him up although they expressed some regret "at parting with their own flesh and blood." Peart later expressed the thought "that flesh and blood did not bind hard on his side."[30] Timothy Roark may have had a similar experience in his release and return. Most likely he was given new clothes by the British and provided transportation by ship to Philadelphia or some other port on the Atlantic coast.

Timothy Roark was a captive of the Shawnees somewhere between two and four years, most likely between 1782 and 1786.[31] Upon his return from captivity, Timothy probably returned first to Baptist Valley, learned that his father was in southern Montgomery County with Timothy's uncle on Elk Creek, and went to Elk Creek for a reunion with his father and his uncle's family. There he embraced his father again and took great pleasure in company with his uncle Timothy, his aunt Rachel, and cousins William, Charles, Timothy, Moses, Rebecca, Mary, and Sarah. The son, nephew, and cousin that had been lost was now found and, with his return, the family rejoiced. Now began a new life for him among his own people and near his family.

Nothing has been recorded of any difficulties Timothy may have encountered in adjusting again to a civilized way of life. Many of the estimated one thousand white captives taken by the Indians to the Great Lakes area did not adjust to life again at home and ran off to the Indian country.[32] Stories have been preserved of former captives, many of them young, that preferred the Indian life and who returned to their adoptive family.[33] No evidence suggests that Timothy ever wanted to return to Indian lands, and doubtless he was gratified for his freedom when he found his way again to southwest Virginia in 1786.

After a period of adjustment to civilized society, Timothy was encouraged by his father to approach David Crouch about farming, on a tenant basis, their old homestead place in Baptist Valley. Timothy met with Crouch, who had maintained a friendship with Timothy's father and reached an agreement to farm the 130 acres. Soon thereafter, then, Timothy returned to Baptist Valley and began life as a farmer. Just over a year later, in the fall of 1788, his father would also return to northern Montgomery County to remain there until his death in 1792.

Interestingly, one of the first problems Timothy faced after his return was with the tax collector. Living on and farming the old homestead farm in Baptist Valley, he also had livestock on the river farm. With the creation of Russell County out of Washington County in 1786, the river farm and that portion of the homestead place previously in Washington County were then located in Russell County. In developing a personal property tax roll for the newly created county, the tax collector had listed Timothy for personal property as a resident in Russell County while the tax collector for Montgomery County also listed him for taxes as a resident of that county. The Russell County tax list had assessed Timothy for two head of livestock (the tax list did not differentiate between horses and cattle) which were considered personal property in the county of residence. Timothy protested his assessment in two counties and won his argument. The record that survives shows his name crossed out on the 1787 Russell County tax list.[34]

Timothy Roark lived alone on the Baptist Valley farm between 1787 and 1796, during which time he raised crops on the 130-acre Crouch tract and maintained cattle on the river farm. While most men his age were married and needed a wife not only for companionship but also for household support, Timothy lived these years without a wife. His experience with the Indians had taught him self-reliance. He was probably comfortable as a bachelor and enjoyed the solitude following the anxiety and turmoil of his captivity. In 1790, he was included on the Montgomery County Personal Property Tax List in Baptist Valley. His personal property consisted of one horse. No record is available of the livestock on the river farm at that period. His neighbors in 1790 included James Maxwell, William Cecil, James Witten, John Greenup, Thomas Witten Sr., Thomas Witten Jr., and Timothy's father, James Roark.[35]

In addition to his adjustment to civilization, Timothy also found it necessary to assist his father who continued to struggle following the murder of his wife and family almost a decade before and the probable death of his son John. Timothy and his father were doubtless close as both struggled to adjust, but records seem to indicate that they lived separately albeit in close proximity in Baptist Valley.[36] Timothy's father had never fully recovered from the massacre and may have spent his last years in retaliation against the Shawnees. Timothy provided what support and comfort he could. The tragic life of James Roark ended in July 1792, and Timothy buried the last member of his immediate family. He was now alone.

Following his father's death, Timothy employed John Greenup as an attorney to settle all claims against the James Roark estate but primarily to secure a clear title to the 100-acre river farm. Appraisers of the estate were appointed by the court and inventories were taken of the limited possessions owned by Timothy's father. Nine years were to pass before the estate was finally settled.

Timothy continued to live alone and farm the 130-acre Crouch tract in Baptist Valley that had been the Roark family homestead. On the national scene, the United States gained in stability under the new Constitution that had been adopted in 1788.

The new government with George Washington as president had taken office in March 1789. By the time of the death of James Roark in July 1792, two new states had been added to the Union–Vermont in 1791 and Kentucky in 1792. Indian wars continued in the northwest above the Ohio River from 1790 to 1795, but peace was reached by the summer of 1795 following the victory at Fallen Timbers by Gen. "Mad Anthony" Wayne. As a result, Indian troubles subsided in western Virginia and Kentucky.

In 1792, George Washington had been re-elected as president; however, the United States faced problems of neutrality in European wars as the French revolution brought a reign of terror with the murder of King Louis XVI and gave rise to the military career of Napoleon Bonaparte. These international affairs were probably of little interest to Timothy Roark, who was more interested in the tax policies of the new national government and the Commonwealth of Virginia. He doubtlessly followed with interest the rebellion against the whiskey tax in western Pennsylvania in the summer of 1794 and the use of the Virginia Militia to suppress the uprising. Timothy also noted events in North Carolina, which had ceded its western lands to Congress in 1790 giving rise to the Southwest Territory. By 1796, the State of Tennessee had been formed from that Southwest Territory and had been admitted as the sixteenth state in the Union. Timothy began to consider the opportunities of available land grants in the new state.

Others were, at that time, beginning to see opportunities in the Clinch Valley. These included Timothy's cousins from the Elk Creek area. Shortly before Timothy's return to civilization, his father, in moving from Baptist Valley to Elk Creek, had taken word to Timothy's uncle that tracts near the river farm in Washington County (prior to the creation of Russell County in 1786) were available for purchase. This was of interest to James Ramey, who had married Timothy's cousin Mary and was living near his father-in-law, Timothy Roark, on Elk Creek.[37] Ramey returned with James Roark to Washington County and purchased 100 acres near Roark's river farm. Shortly thereafter, James Ramey and Mary moved to the Clinch Valley and began farming.[38] The Rameys expanded their land holdings in 1792 when Ramey received a grant from the Commonwealth, signed by Governor Henry Lee, for 296 acres.[39] Sometime before, Timothy's other cousin Sarah, sister of Mary Ramey, had left her father's home on Elk Creek in southern Montgomery County to live with the Rameys on the Clinch River. By 1790, Sarah had married a Deskins, neighbor to the Rameys, and a descendant of one of the early pioneer families. Soon Sarah and Deskins had a son named John Deskins.[40] Timothy doubtless was close to his cousins as no other family was available to him. But this was soon to change, as in 1795 Timothy was to make the acquaintance of Sarah Bolen.

Sarah Bolen was the daughter of Joseph Bolen[41] and was nineteen years old when she met Timothy Roark in 1795. Timothy was twenty-nine. Little is known of Sarah's father before 1782. On February 1 of that year, he was listed on the Personal

Property Tax List of Montgomery County, Virginia, east of the New River. He was taxed for one horse. Joseph Bolen (spelled *Bowling* on the tax list) was listed close to a John Bowling, a William Bowling, and a John Bowling Jr. which could have been his father (John) and his brothers.[42] By 1795, Joseph Bolen had moved his family to Wythe County, and in November 1796 he signed the petition to create Tazewell County out of Wythe County.[43] It was while she was living in Wythe County with her father that Sarah heard about the bachelor farmer in Baptist Valley who had spent some time with the Indians and still lived alone.

Sarah Bolen was educated beyond the norm of women of her generation. She could read and write well and signed her name in good penmanship rather than the "X" used by most women and many men. We know little of her family but do know that she had a sister named Lucy with whom she was particularly close. Lucy was seven years younger than Sarah but the sisters were to remain close throughout their adult lives.[44]

How Timothy and Sarah met is unrecorded, but as Timothy recovered financially from his Indian captivity and accumulated some resources, he no doubt became an eligible bachelor of some renown. After an extended courtship, Timothy and Sarah were married in late 1796. He was thirty and she was twenty.[45]

Timothy was, at the time of his marriage, a tenant farmer on the land owned by David Crouch. Since the 130 acres had been owned by his father, Timothy doubtless had an interest in purchasing the old home place from Crouch. He probably had been negotiating with Crouch for some time for purchase of the tract and found that Crouch was also interested in selling the tract since he did not live in Baptist Valley or in close proximity to the farm. Following his marriage, Timothy decided to actively pursue the purchase, and on January 16, 1797, he bought the 130 acres from Crouch for one hundred pounds cash.[46] Witnesses to the deed were Samuel, William, and Zachariah Cecil. Samuel Cecil was a brother-in-law to Thomas Witten of Wittens Fort and was an early settler in the Clinch Valley. William and Zachariah were his sons.[47] Timothy Roark and William Cecil were to be closely associated during the next few years.

That Timothy had been a successful farmer since his return from his time with the Indians is evidenced by the fact that he had accumulated one hundred pounds and was able to pay cash for the farm. He probably received little or no help from his new father-in-law for, as years passed, Joseph Bolen would look to Timothy and Sarah for financial help and support. Within a year of his marriage to Sarah, it appears that Timothy moved his father-in-law to the river farm on the Clinch River. Joseph Bolen was to live there between 1797 and 1799, close enough to frequently visit his daughter and his new son-in-law.[48]

With Sarah settled in the old Roark homestead and with her father's family nearby, Sarah and Timothy were eager to begin their family. The first born was not long in arriving. Their first child was a boy born October 9, 1798, whom they named

James, after Timothy's father. Timothy was thirty-two when his first child was born.

Timothy's success as a farmer continued, and his hard work was reflected in the value of his farm. After his purchase of the 130 acres in Baptist Valley, Timothy appeared on the land tax list of Wythe County in 1798, 1799, and 1800. In each of the three years, his 130 acres were taxed on a value of $0.50 per acre for a total value of $65. The relative value of his farm and its crop production capacity can be evaluated from the land tax list. The highest appraised value per acre for all tax listings during the three years was $0.66 per acre for fifty acres owned by a Robert Steel. Similarly, tracts of 100 acres belonging to James and John Peery were taxed at the rate of $0.60 per acre. By far, however, most of the land listed on the tax record between 1798 and 1800 ranged in value from $0.17 to $0.33 per acre.[49] Thus Timothy's tract ranked high in value and, no doubt, was considered an above average, productive farm.

As early as 1796, a movement was under way to secure the designation of a new county that would serve the western area of Wythe County and the eastern portion of Russell County. The first petition was circulated and submitted to the legislature on November 30 of that year. Since the legislature did not act on the petition, other petitions were submitted in December 1797 and 1798. The 1798 petition included the names of Timothy Roark and his father-in-law, Joseph Bolen. Other names on the 1798 petition included John Deskins, neighbor to Timothy's river farm; Embly Millard, who was to be a future relative of Timothy Roark by marriage; John Greenup, who was then assisting Timothy with the settlement of the James Roark estate; Samuel and William Cecil; Kinsey Cecil, who was to own a farm next to Timothy's in Baptist Valley; Thomas Witten of Wittens Fort; Archibald Thompson and William George, both of whom were to witness the estate settlement of James Roark in 1801; John Hankins, a long time neighbor of James Roark in Baptist Valley; and James Maxwell, commander of the Russell County militia.[50]

The legislature still did not act favorably on the local petitions, and another petition was circulated and submitted in December 1799. The list of persons signatory to the petition followed very closely that of the 1798 petition. This time the legislature acted favorably on the petition, and the act passed by the General Assembly called for a new county to be created as of the first of May 1800. The new county was named Tazewell in honor of Henry Tazewell, who was a member of the U.S. Senate from Virginia when the act was passed creating the county.[51] Now for the first time since before Washington and Montgomery counties were created from Fincastle County in 1776, Timothy's 130-acre Baptist Valley farm and his 100-acre river farm would lie within the same county.

Timothy continued to maintain a close relationship with his cousins from the Elk Creek area. Mary and James Ramey prospered on their 396 acres on the Clinch River. Timothy's other cousin, Sarah Roark Deskins, apparently left Deskins and married Isaac Brewer to whom a son, Isaac Junior, was born. By the time Timothy's first son was born in 1798, Sarah had divorced Isaac Brewer and on October 7, 1800, Sarah was to marry Embly Millard in Tazewell County.[52] Millard was of German descent and a Revolutionary War veteran. By 1805, Embly and Sarah would relocate to Logan County (now West Virginia) where they would raise a large family. From his local cousins, Timothy learned that his namesake uncle on Elk Creek (in Grayson County since 1793) was doing well, that his daughter Rebecca was unmarried and living at home, and his sons Charles, Moses, and Timothy Jr. were farming on their father's place.[53]

Timothy's own family continued to grow, and on May 18, 1800, Sarah gave birth to their second son.[54] Timothy named him John after his father's brother and after Timothy's own brother who had died an early death at the hands of the Indians.[55]

After the organization of Tazewell County and the first meeting of the court in July 1800, the first grand jury of the new county was convened in November. Timothy Roark was one of eighteen selected for this jury, which included William Cecil, John Peery, James and William Witten, with Andrew Thompson as foreman of the jury.[56] The grand jury met at the newly constructed courthouse located at the county seat selected by the court as the present-day Tazewell.[57]

As a property owner in Tazewell County, Timothy Roark was subject to call for jury duty and his name frequently came up for that community service. He served again on a grand jury empaneled March 3, 1801,[58] and again on the grand jury for August 3, 1801.[59] In October 1802, Timothy was again named to the grand jury in Tazewell. One case brought before the grand jury during the October term was a charge against James Cecil for not keeping a road in good repair. James Cecil was a brother to William Cecil and a son of Samuel Cecil, both of whom had witnessed Timothy Roark's purchase of his Baptist Valley farm. James Cecil owned 200 acres near Roark's 100-acre river farm and had been designated by the county as overseer of a nearby road. Apparently Cecil had not maintained the road in a satisfactory condition, particularly that portion at the "upper end by Widow Wallace's fence" which could not be traveled. The grand jury minutes indicate that James Cecil was known by Timothy Roark who probably removed himself from the grand jury on this case and served as a character witness for Cecil.[60]

The day following the October 1802 grand jury service by Timothy, he himself was involved in an action against him by William Cecil in Chancery Court.[61] Details of the disagreement are not available; however, the case was dismissed by the court the same day. Apparently, however, the issue was not fully settled as Cecil was back in court against Roark on March 10, 1803. "By consent of both parties," the case was referred to Wellington George, John I. Trigg, William Neil, and Hezikiah Whitt who were to serve as an ad hoc committee with the judgement of the committee "to be the judgement of the court."[62] No further details are available.

Timothy's father-in-law, Joseph Bolen, continued to live on the river farm in 1798 and 1799 and was listed on the Russell County personal property tax list for those two years.[63] It appears that in late 1799 Joseph Bolen lived for a time with Timothy and Sarah, probably in preparation for a move south to Tennessee. During this brief period, Joseph signed the petition in December 1799 as a resident of Wythe County to create the new county of Tazewell.[64] Sometime in 1800, Joseph Bolen decided on a move to the new state of Tennessee and relocated his family, including Sarah's sister, Lucy, to an area between the Clinch and Powell Rivers in Grainger County, Tennessee.[65]

By September 1801, Timothy had received word from Wytheville that the James Roark estate had been settled by the Wythe County Court, which had maintained jurisdiction of the estate that had been in the court since 1792. Under the settlement, Timothy received title to the 100-acre river farm. John Greenup had served as administrator for the estate and apparently remained a close friend of Timothy Roark. Shortly after the estate settlement, Greenup moved with his family, including sons Thomas and Christopher, to Kentucky where the family became active in state politics. In 1804, Christopher was to be elected governor of Kentucky for a four-year term. Greenup County of Kentucky on the Ohio River was later named for Christopher Greenup.[66]

Timothy Roark continued to add livestock on his two farms. He was listed on the personal property tax list of Tazewell County in August 1801 as owning one horse.[67] By April 1802, Timothy was appraised on the personal property tax list as owning three horses.[68] Timothy's land holdings continued to be the 130-acre Baptist Valley farm and the 100-acre river farm, and he was taxed on both farms under the land tax appraisals in 1802 for Tazewell County.[69] At some point Timothy purchased a land warrant for 50 acres in Tazewell County, for on November 21, 1802, he transferred the warrant to Thomas Barrett.[70] The location of the 50-acre tract is unknown and no record exists that Timothy ever occupied the tract.

In June 1801, Timothy and Sarah received word that Joseph Bolen had purchased a farm in Tennessee in the northern portion of Grainger County on the Powell River.[71] Bolen had purchased 123 acres on May 25, 1801, from David Hodgson, also of Grainger County. Hodgson had purchased 253 acres in December 1797 from Robert King and continued to live on the 130-acre tract north of Bolen after the sale to him.[72] Shortly after receiving word that her father had purchased the farm and was settled in Tennessee, Sarah received word that her sister, Lucy, was to marry James Eastridge. Eastridge was, as Lucy explained, originally from South Carolina but now lived in Grainger County. He was five years older than Lucy.[73] Joseph Bolen signed permission to the county clerk September 13, 1801, for the marriage license to be issued[74] and, in accordance with the Tennessee statutes, both Joseph Bolen and James Eastridge, jointly and severally, posted on October 16, 1801, a marriage bond to the governor of Tennessee, Archibald Roan.[75] The wedding doubtless took place during the third week of October 1801.

At the time of Lucy's wedding, Timothy's father-in-law was settled and involved in the community, but was also having difficulties. After Claiborne County was created October 29, 1801, from Grainger and Hawkins counties, Bolen was to serve as a juror on the first Monday in September 1802. With the county yet without a courthouse, the court and the jury met "at the house of John Hunt Sr. on the Kentucky Road."[76] Troubles began for Bolen shortly thereafter as he was charged with disturbing the peace.[77] This was the first of several instances in which Bolen's propensity for fighting was recorded. It is both unfair and perhaps unwise to judge a person's character and personality by the few court records in which he might be listed. Yet in the records pertaining to Joseph Bolen, one can safely draw the conclusion that Bolen was hot-tempered and could easily be provoked into a scrap. At least five court records between 1799 and 1808 remain in which Joseph Bolen was charged with assault and battery or similar offenses.[78]

In late November or early December 1802, Sarah and Timothy received word that Bolen was being held by the court pending bond on a charge of disturbing the peace. Apparently Bolen had filed a charge of trespassing against David Hodgson, from whom he had purchased his 123-acre farm, and soon thereafter had threatened violence toward Hodgson and perhaps had attacked him physically. Hodgson had, in turn, charged Bolen with assault and battery, and Bolen was jailed. At the immediate insistence of his wife, Timothy Roark made a hurried trip to Tazewell, Tennessee, and, with his brother-in-law James Eastridge, got Bolen out of jail, each posting a peace warrant in the amount of $250 that Bolen "would behave himself toward all good citizens and especially David Hodgson during the term of one year."[79] The amount of the peace warrants required of Roark and Eastridge gives an indication of the seriousness of the charge against Bolen and his reputation before the court. The relative value of $500 on the Tennessee frontier in 1802 should be considered. With good cultivated farm land valued at $1.00 per acre, a peace warrant in the amount of $500, if surrendered, would be equivalent of giving up a working farm of approximately 500 acres, a size sufficient to support at least five families on the frontier. Obviously, the court had lost patience with Joseph Bolen and intended for him "to behave himself."

Doubtless, Sarah was concerned about the explosive and combative nature of her father and she began to support Timothy when he spoke of land opportunities in Tennessee. Whatever the influence of his wife, Timothy began to seriously consider a move to the Tennessee frontier in Claiborne County. From all appearances, Timothy and his family were happy and very comfortable in Baptist Valley, yet the advantages of almost free land in Tennessee and the close proximity of Sarah's father and sister made it worthwhile to consider a move. Also, Sarah was convinced that her father's problems were not at an end and only she and Lucy together could provide a positive influence on him. It may have been, too, that Joseph Bolen was not in good financial shape and needed cash for his 123-acre farm. Would Timothy and Sarah consider buying him out? Shortly after the first of the year in 1803, Timothy made a decision to move south and began to seek buyers for his two farms in Tazewell County.

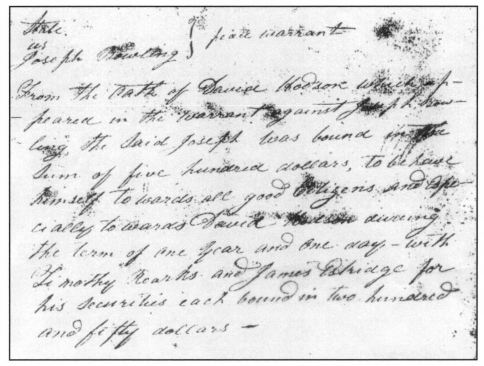

County Court Minutes of Claiborne County, Tennessee, for December 1802, at which time Joseph Bowling (Bolen), father-in-law of Timothy Roark, was placed under a peace warrant "to behave himself towards all good citizens and especially towards David Hodson (Hodgson)." Sons-in-law James Eastridge and Timothy Roark posted the required $500 bond.

By April 1803, Timothy had found buyers for the Baptist Valley farm. Thomas Bruster agreed to buy roughly the eastern one-half of the farm (66.5 acres) for 100 pounds, and William Witten was to purchase the western remainder of the farm for 150 pounds. The two tracts were surveyed and Timothy and Sarah executed deeds to Bruster and Witten. Both deeds were recorded April 14, 1803.[80] The deeds were signed with an "X" by Timothy as "his mark" while Sarah signed her name in full–"Sarah Roark."

Both Bruster and Witten had served with Timothy Roark on the first grand jury in November 1800, and both had been in the Tazewell area for some time.[81] Bruster and Witten had signed the first petition in October 1796 to create Tazewell County from Wythe and Russell counties.[82] William Witten was the son of Thomas Witten of Wittens Fort and was a brother-in-law to John Greenup.[83] Two years following his purchase from Roark, Witten, with his brother-in-law Greenup, were to give land for the Pisgah Methodist Church near Wittens Fort–the first meeting house of Methodist churches in Tazewell County.[84] Later William Witten would move south from Virginia settling in Sequatchie Valley in southeast Tennessee.[85]

On the same date that he sold the Baptist Valley farm, Timothy sold the river farm to William Cecil for thirty-four pounds.[86] Cecil and Timothy Roark had been associated in various ways in Tazewell County for several years. Unfortunately the transaction with Cecil would be clouded and Timothy would again in 1824 claim title to the tract (which surveyed in 1803 for 90 acres rather than 100 acres). Timothy would again have clear title to the tract in 1833 after purchasing Cecil's claim of title. Although not recorded in the deed, there apparently was a note to be paid by Cecil or perhaps some restriction that was violated by Cecil which would result in the later title dispute.

On the Baptist Valley farm, it is interesting to note that Timothy was able to sell the 130 acres for two and one-half times what he paid for the farm only six years before. He had made a significant profit, but in so doing he was selling what had been a large part of his life. One wonders the emotions felt by Timothy as he left the farm he had first seen when he was six years old, the cabin where he had experienced the shock of his mother's death and the family massacre, the homestead farm he had purchased on which to settle his new bride six years before, and the home where his two sons had been born. Timothy had been raised in Baptist Valley and had participated in its agonies during the Indian raids and the Revolutionary War. In 1803, at the age of thirty-seven with a wife expecting her third child in six months and with two sons ages five and three, he was leaving to begin a new life on the mountainous frontier of northeast Tennessee.

It would take Timothy and his family over two weeks to make the journey and to move the family possessions the 150 miles from Baptist Valley to Claiborne County in Tennessee. They would follow the Clinch River to the southwest, keeping to the west of the ridge known as Clinch Mountain. On the third day, the family reached Castlewood where Daniel Boone had spent the winter following the death of his son and the abortive migration to Kentucky in 1773. There Timothy explained to his two sons, James and John, that his father had met and known Boone, who by 1803, was already a legendary figure. Timothy also related to his family that he had been just over six years old, almost the same age as his own son James, when his father's family had made the move to Baptist Valley from east of the New River. No doubt the move to Tennessee was as exciting to Timothy's sons as the trip to Baptist Valley had been to him.

One day south of Castlewood, the family reached Fort Blackmore and there spent the night close to the fort. Here the Clinch Valley narrowed with high ridges, Copper Ridge on the east and Big Ridge on the west, confining the crude trail and making further travel along the Clinch difficult. From Fort Blackmore then, Timothy and his family would move due west to follow Stony Creek to Valley Creek and Stock Creek to intersect with the North Fork of the Clinch, east of Powell Mountain. Near the present-day Stickleyville, Timothy would take the family to the west over Wallen Ridge, which was over one hundred feet above the adjacent valley, into the Powell

River valley where travel was much easier. On this route Timothy and the family were following the trail used by Daniel Boone to take pioneers into Kentucky.[87] Timothy probably explained this to the boys as they made campfire each night.

After crossing the Powell River, Timothy passed near the current town of Jonesville until he reached the ridge known as Cumberland Mountain that separates Virginia from Kentucky. Here the family turned more to the southwest and follow the ridge to Cumberland Gap. Along the east side of Cumberland Mountain the trail improved as it had been the route followed by many families moving into Kentucky. When they reached Cumberland Gap, Timothy pointed out to his family the route through the gap that had been used by numerous pioneer families like themselves to move westward into Kentucky and then along the Cumberland River to Nashville and middle Tennessee. Just east of Cumberland Gap, Timothy and his family crossed from Virginia into Tennessee and reached the Kentucky Road that ran from southeast to northwest through Claiborne County. It was the Kentucky Road from Cumberland Gap through the county seat of Tazewell and further east across the Clinch River that served to carry settlers from the Carolinas to Kentucky.[88] Moving east along the Kentucky Road, Timothy and his family reached the Powell River where he doubtless asked at Roddyes Ferry for directions to the Joseph Bolen place.[89] From there, Timothy took the road that followed along the north side of the Powell River–the Bolen place was about seven miles up the river.

Timothy and his family followed the river road as directed, and after two and one-half miles they forded Indian Creek. At five miles, the family forded Little Creek, and as they passed what would later be known as Bussell Ford just south of Little Creek, they noticed the steep bluffs on the west side of the river. Unknown then to Timothy and his family, they were close to what was to be their homestead and where Timothy and Sarah would live out their lives. On top of the bluffs, Timothy was later to homestead over 350 acres. A mile farther on, just before they reached a sharp bend in the river now known as Ellison Bend, the family would pass through the eastern edge of the 150-acre tract that Timothy's son John was later to settle and claim. The family had no way, of course, to foresee these later events, and their attention was then focused on the excitement of reaching their destination, then only minutes away.

As Timothy and family rounded Ellison Bend and moved again in a northern direction, they passed the steep ridge around which the Powell River meanders to form Ellison Bend. On the northwest side of the river the topography became more rolling with gentle slopes to the river, which was now wider and moved with a much slower current. The Joseph Bolen cabin was near the road a short distance from the river, and one can only imagine the excitement of Sarah and the boys as the team was halted in front of the cabin and father/grandfather emerged. Sarah was united with her father and the next day her sister, Lucy, would come for a visit. A happy family gathering resulted.

Joseph Bolen's 123-acre farm had almost a mile of riverfront on the Powell River. Across the river to the southeast, steep bluffs over 200 feet high rose above the gentle waters of the Powell. To the northwest the land rose just over two hundred feet in the fifteen hundred feet between the river and Bolen's north property line. When Bolen had purchased his farm from David Hodgson in 1801, both men had agreed on a "conditional line" separating Bolen from Hodgson's 130 acres to the north. This conditional line would continue to be referenced in deed records through 1839. Following his sale to Bolen in 1801, Hodgson had sold his 130 acres to Amos Johnson on September 6, 1802. The conditional line had apparently become a source of disagreement between Bolen and Hodgson shortly after Hodgson's sale to Johnson and most likely was the cause of the Bolen-Hodgson fracas in November 1802. By Timothy's arrival in early May 1803, Hodgson had sold out to Amos Johnson and had left the county. Bolen was then temporarily at peace with his neighbors.[90]

Although by 1803, the American frontier had pushed its way into Kentucky as far as Louisville and into middle Tennessee surrounding Nashville, the Claiborne County area was still very much a frontier environment. True, the Cumberland Gap had seen hundreds of settlers pass through its environs to settle in Kentucky and Tennessee. Also, the Kentucky Road through Claiborne County to Cumberland Gap had provided a wagon-road route for other hundreds from the Carolinas. Between 1790 and 1800 the population of Tennessee had increased threefold from thirty-five thousand to more than one hundred thousand;[91] however, among the steep ridges and narrow valleys in Claiborne County, north and south of the Kentucky Road, little settlement had occurred by 1803. The areas adjoining the Powell and Clinch Rivers were still very much a part of the American frontier.

This frontier had developed its own society that was peculiar unto itself. It had been affected by the topography in which north-south ridges limited east-west travel, by an almost constant conflict with the Indians until 1795, and by limited contact with the Atlantic seaboard. By 1792, a postal route had been established between Rogersville to the east in Hawkins County and Richmond, Virginia. By 1803, mail would arrive every two weeks at Rogersville to be forwarded to the west along the Kentucky Road through Cumberland Gap and beyond.[92] Outside the infrequent mail delivery, the challenge to the frontier farmer of Claiborne County was that of isolation and physical prowess.

By the middle of May 1803, Timothy, Sarah, and the two boys were settled in the home of Sarah's father. Sarah had made the trip in good condition and had not experienced any difficulty in her pregnancy. Primarily because of the financial condition Joseph Bolen was in, Timothy began immediately to make arrangements to purchase Bolen's farm. By the first week in June the purchase had been arranged, and on June 15, 1803, Timothy bought the 123 acres for eighty pounds.[93] The best evidence suggests that Timothy and Sarah were to build their own cabin a short distance from the river and were to make this their home for the next four years. Bolen continued to live

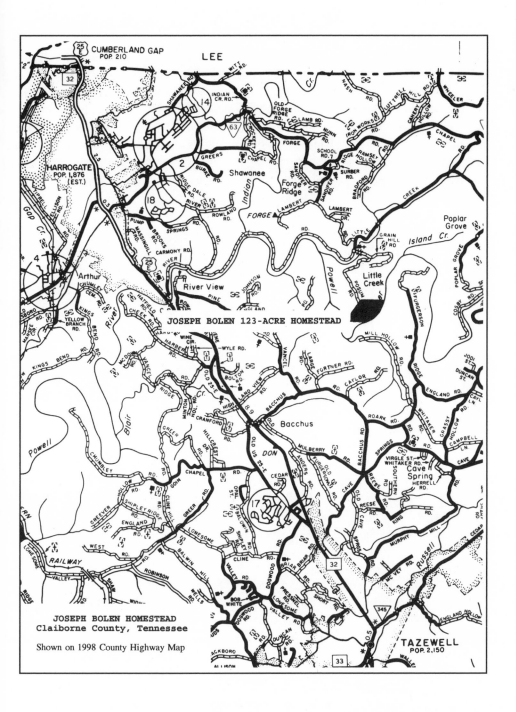

JOSEPH BOLEN HOMESTEAD
Claiborne County, Tennessee

Shown on 1998 County Highway Map

in his cabin near the river.

His father-in-law doubtless was a help to Timothy in his initial efforts at farming in Claiborne County. By October 1803, Timothy had harvested the corn crop planted by Bolen the previous April. On October 6, Timothy and Sarah were blessed with their third child and first daughter. They named her Nancy, probably either after Timothy's mother or Sarah's mother, neither of whom was still living. At Nancy's birth, Timothy was thirty-seven and Sarah was twenty-seven.

The building of roads and their maintenance for wagon travel was a major problem for the early settlers of Claiborne County. The steep ridges and the heavy annual

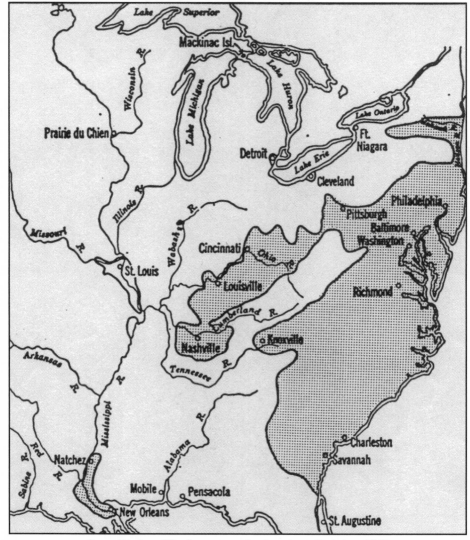

Outer Limits of Settlement on the American Frontier–1803.

rainfall demanded constant attention to roads that had been constructed with great difficulty along the ridge lines and down the steep grades to individual settlements in the creek and river valleys. Within a year of its creation, the Claiborne County Court had passed an ordinance requiring all able-bodied males twenty-one years old and over living along a particular road to furnish five days labor each year to main-

Site of Joseph Bolen homestead in Claiborne County, Tennessee, looking northeast from the Powell River. Cabin site was most likely to the left of the later-day barn. The Powell River runs between the barn and the hills in the background.

tain the road. A man could be excused from this duty only if he was physically unable to work; however, later courts were to require a doctor's certificate before excusing anyone.[94] The same month that he sold his farm to his son-in-law, Joseph Bolen was named by the Claiborne County Court to serve as a "hand" under Christopher Damron to maintain the Kentucky Road between Blair's Creek and Roddyes Ferry on the Powell River. James Eastridge, Lucy's husband, was also one of the fourteen named to serve as the road crew for maintenance of the approximately three miles of roadway.[95] The previous December, Bolen had been named by the County Court to a committee to lay out a road along Powell River from the south to Cumberland Gap.[96] By September 1805, Timothy Roark had been in Claiborne County long enough to also be named to

Powell River in Claiborne, County, looking southwest from the Joseph Bolen homestead tract.

work on roads in the county. In that month he was named to work under Harmon Evans as one of ten road hands. In June 1806, Roark was again named to a road crew, this time under John Belcher.[97]

Joseph Bolen continued to get into arguments and scraps and to have problems with the court. On March 9, 1804, Bolen was in court to defend himself against an unspecified charge by Pleasant Miller and Thomas Gray. The court found in favor of Miller and Gray, and Bolen was assessed damages in the amount of $32.50. At the same time that he was defending himself against Miller and Gray, Bolen was, however, also named to several juries during the March 1804 term of the County Court.[98]

Timothy's family continued to grow. On December 4, 1805, his second daughter was born. The proud parents named her Sarah after her mother. Timothy and Sarah by then had four children. James, the oldest, had just celebrated his seventh birthday.[99]

In March 1806, Timothy undertook to collect some debts owed him in Russell County, Virginia, probably from tenant farmers or laborers on the river farm before the creation of Tazewell County. The defendant in the case, which was pursued by an attorney on behalf of Roark since no records indicate that Timothy made a return trip to Russell County, was Mark Hart. William Akerd and Samuel Kirk were also included with Hart as defendants, with Kirk pledged to pay the debt if the court found in Roark's favor or "would render his body in execution of the same."[100] The case was heard before the court in March, June, September, and December 1806, with Roark's attorney claiming that debts due his client amounted to $75.45 with six percent interest per annum. In December, the court held that the claim by Roark as plaintiff be dismissed and costs and damages assessed as follows: Clerk $0.64, Attorney $5.00, Court Costs $5.64, and Damages to Plaintiff $5.84. Roark's attorney appealed.[101]

Also in 1806, as he sought to collect debts due him in Russell County, Timothy began to add cattle to his holdings. The minutes of the Claiborne County Court for November 24, 1806, note the following action: "Timothy Roarks [sic] came into the Court and recorded the ear mark of his stock with a crop and a slit in the left ear."[102] The year also opened opportunities for Timothy to acquire lands under a new statute passed by the Tennessee legislature. For the first time in its ten-year history, the State of Tennessee took control of the granting of public lands within the state. The new law would permit citizens of Tennessee to acquire public lands and ended the conflict with North Carolina over the right to issue warrants and land grants.

The public lands in Tennessee had a complex history that had begun in the late 1770s with passage by the North Carolina legislature of several statutes dealing with grants in its western reserve (now Tennessee). In 1777, North Carolina created Washington County, covering what is now Tennessee, and offered the sale of public lands there at the price of fifty shillings for every one hundred acres. In 1780, however, North Carolina rescinded the act permitting land sales and passed an act to set aside lands in its western reserve to pay North Carolina soldiers who had served in the Continental Army by granting lands for their military service. The area reserved for military land grants was officially established by North Carolina in 1782 and covered the Cumberland River Valley in upper middle Tennessee. The reservation land had previously been purchased by Richard Henderson of the Transylvania Land Company from the Cherokees. His purchase was disallowed by the North Carolina legislature, which compensated Henderson by giving him 200,000 acres in the Powell River Valley in what is now Claiborne County, Tennessee. The large grant was surveyed into tracts of 6,500 acres on the Powell River, making it easier for these smaller tracts to be sold and exchanged.[103] Many of the land transactions in Claiborne County in the fifty years following Tennessee's admission as a state were connected with the exchanged land titles of the Henderson Grant.[104]

North Carolina continued to sell lands and issue grants in its western reserve until 1790, at which time it ceded the lands in the western reserve to the United States with the reservation that all military grants plus all other entries and warrants would be honored. Between 1790 and 1796, the area ceded by North Carolina was officially known as the "Territory of the United States South of the River Ohio," but it was usually referred to as the "southwest territory." During this period to 1796, all entries and warrants by North Carolina were honored by the U.S. government, which itself granted no additional warrants. After Tennessee became a state in 1796, it was prevented from selling any of its public lands because of outstanding claims by holders of North Carolina entries and warrants. Revolutionary War veterans continued to come forward to claim grants which had been poorly described but yet which would preempt settlement by Tennessee citizens. To add to the confusion, North Carolina continued to issue warrants in the area even after Tennessee had become a state. Land titles in Claiborne County and other areas were thus very complicated and, even with new settlers entering the state almost daily, Tennessee could issue no public land grants for the first ten years of its statehood. During these ten years, however, settlers like Timothy Roark continued to move into northeast Tennessee. They, of course, wanted land–that was the reason they had come–but speculators and others held title to most of the more fertile lands in the river bottoms. An incoming settler like Timothy Roark could not be sure, as he chose a location, whether a speculator or Revolutionary War veteran might not have already entered a claim on the tract. For the first three years that he was in Tennessee, Timothy Roark anxiously awaited the resolution of issues between the states of Tennessee and North Carolina and the availability of public lands in Claiborne County.

In April 1806, with the U.S. government as arbitrator, the disputes between the two states were settled, and the Tennessee legislature passed an act that encouraged settlement in spite of the land title confusion. The Tennessee statute set up "occupant grants" for settlers who had occupied land prior to May 1, 1806, and gave preference of title to such occupant. The settler in an occupant grant was limited to 200 acres and was required to make improvements to the tract. Corners and boundaries of the occupant tracts were to be designated by marking trees. Should a settler destroy any marked trees "that were corners or lines of any ancient boundary, such person or persons shall forfeit all rights and preference by this act given."[105]

The 1806 Act by the Tennessee legislature established six surveying districts for the state and designated entry takers to receive entries from individual occupants. Surveyors were named for each district and an oath of office was prescribed for the surveyor. Claiborne County was in the Fifth Surveyor District and the district surveyor was to maintain his office in Knoxville.[106] Procedures were specified in the Act by which the occupant in the Fifth District would make his entry at Knoxville, how the entry taker would record it, by when the tract would be surveyed by the district surveyor, and the manner in which the warrant for the tract would be issued.[107] Public lands in Claiborne County were thus opened to settlement and claim. Timothy Roark moved quickly to locate an available tract.

It was unfortunate for the settlers and land claimants after 1806 that the few flat and fertile areas within Claiborne County by the time of the 1806 statute had already been claimed. The Richard Henderson grant had acquired the rich, fertile lands of the Powell Valley lying south of the Kentucky Road. Available lands along the Powell River north of the Kentucky Road were marked by steep ridges and dead-end hollows, with little cultivatable land remaining. Nevertheless, Timothy Roark and his brother-in-law, James Eastridge, located tracts near the Powell River on which they would stake their claims. Doubtless Roark and Eastridge had scouted the area prior to 1806 and had tentatively identified parcels on which no claim had previously been filed. With the effective date of the statute, Eastridge settled on 150 acres north of the Powell River adjacent to Little Creek. Timothy Roark marked off 350 acres south of the Powell River adjacent to the mouth of Little Creek. Both men set out in late 1806 to establish their homesteads on their newly acquired tracts. Their wives, sisters Lucy Eastridge and Sarah Roark, would live within a mile of each other but would be separated by the Powell River.

Interestingly, neither Roark nor Eastridge submitted an entry at Knoxville for his claim. Perhaps it was because each was comfortable that he had a legitimate claim as a result of his occupancy and because submitting an entry at Knoxville required a three- to four-day trip. Perhaps also it was because Timothy had correctly estimated the size of his claim at more than 200 acres and decided not to assume the risk that a survey would document a larger-than-permitted claim. Nevertheless, both Roark and Eastridge settled on their claims and began the arduous task of clearing the land and providing lodging for their families. By mid to late 1807, both families were settled in their new homesteads.

Timothy's homestead tract of 350 acres was located in a bend of the Powell River opposite Little Creek. The tract had an unusual "panhandle" on the north end as it wrapped around the tract owned by Aaron Cox. Although almost fifty percent of the

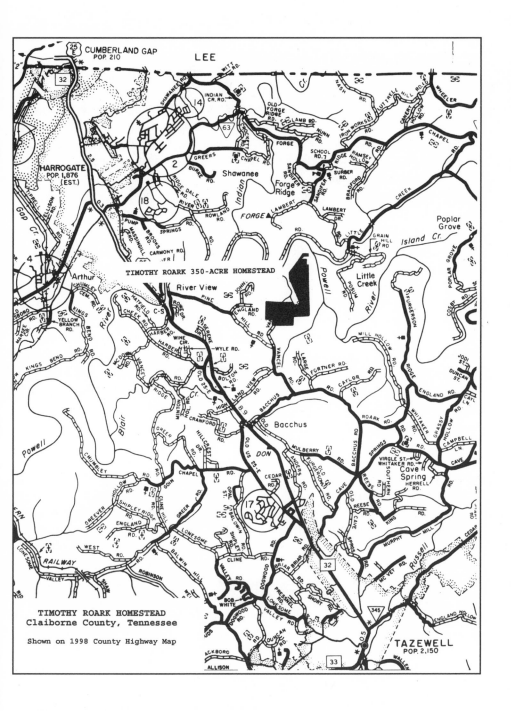

TIMOTHY ROARK HOMESTEAD
Claiborne County, Tennessee

Shown on 1998 County Highway Map

land was generally flat and the soil fertile, access to the tract was difficult. Timothy's grant did not take him to the Powell River, which was separated from his land by a steep bluff that fell approximately 300 feet to the river. Access to the tract was gained by a rough trail that followed a steep ridge, isolating Timothy's pioneer farm from neighbors and peddlers alike.[108] Thus isolated and distant to travelers, Timothy's homestead was again on the frontier. The southern portion of the farm gently sloped upward toward the south from the cabin location to a point approximately fifty feet above the cultivated area of the farm. From this high point on the tract, the Cumberland Gap, six miles away, could be seen. The north, east, and west boundaries of the farm all sloped to the Powell River, which was approximately one hundred feet wide and three to six feet deep in the area.

His new frontier farm required hard work to clear the land, remove the tree stumps, and cultivate the area suitable for crops. That first autumn was given totally to getting the land ready for crops to be planted in the spring to follow. With little or no labor available for hire, Timothy could only look to his two sons–James 9, and John 7–for their help with the difficult work of clearing the land. The autumn passed quickly, and Timothy and Sarah celebrated Christmas day 1807 with Sarah's giving birth on Christmas day to their third son, whom they named William. Timothy was forty-one and Sarah was thirty-one.[109]

Sarah's father continued to have his problems. In August 1808, he was again charged by the court, doubtless on assault and battery. Bolen was arrested by Aaron Davis, constable, who "delivered" Bolen to the court "on a peace warrant in discharge of himself as security."[110] Bolen thus either spent some minimum time in jail or posted a bond in whatever amount was dictated by the court.

In 1808, a year after his move to his public land claim, Timothy Roark placed his 123-acre farm for sale. In mid 1809, he found a buyer for the 123 acres in Amos Johnson, who owned the adjoining farm to the north. Closing on the sale was set for early July with the purchase price being $240. Probably at the convenience of both parties, the county clerk, Walter Evans, agreed to open the courthouse on July 4th since both Roark and Johnson would be coming into Tazewell for the Independence Day celebration. The sale was closed on July 4, 1809. Walter Evans himself attested to the signatures.[111]

Following Timothy's sale of the 123-acre farm, Joseph Bolen continued to live in his cabin on the river on a twenty-acre parcel which, by a surveying flaw, had not been included in the survey for the 123 acres. While it is clear that David Hodgson had originally owned all of the land along the river and that he intended to sell the full river frontage to Bolen, the recorded survey for the deed called for a straight line between Bolen's northeast corner and his southwest corner rather than following the meanders of the river. Thus when Timothy sold the 123 acres to Amos Johnson in 1809, the legal description for previous survey was used again and the approximately twenty acres along the river was omitted from the sale. Apparently Johnson

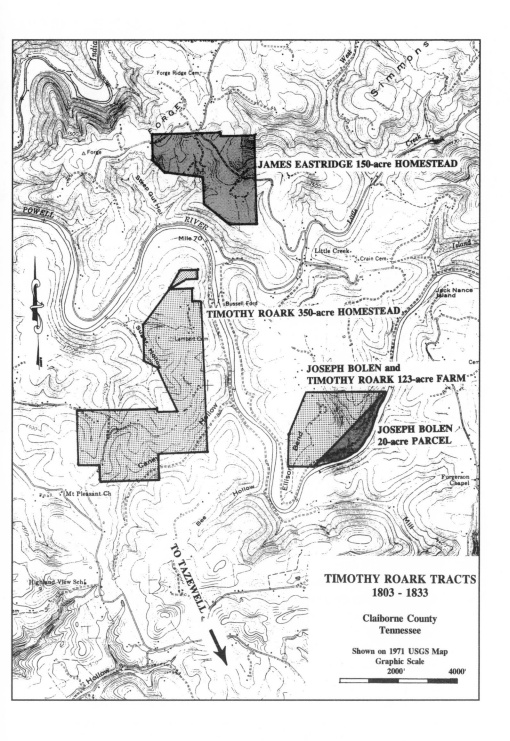

JAMES EASTRIDGE 150-acre HOMESTEAD

TIMOTHY ROARK 350-acre HOMESTEAD

JOSEPH BOLEN and
TIMOTHY ROARK 123-acre FARM

JOSEPH BOLEN
20-acre PARCEL

TO TAZEWELL

TIMOTHY ROARK TRACTS
1803 - 1833

Claiborne County
Tennessee

Shown on 1971 USGS Map
Graphic Scale
2000'   4000'

was satisfied with his purchase, and since David Hodgson was no longer present to argue the land issues again with Bolen, Sarah's father continued to occupy the small parcel along the river.[112]

As Timothy was settling in his new place, he received word in March 1810 from his attorney in Russell County, Virginia, that his appeal was again before the court in Lebanon. William Welch Jr. now represented both Mark Hart and Samuel Kirk and pledged their security for the debt in the amount of $75.00. Roark's attorney reported that Welch had agreed to settle in an amount of $6.12, and the amount had been supported by the court. Thus Timothy's claim of debts of over $75.00 was settled for $6.12, much of which doubtless went to his attorney.[113]

Life on Timothy's new pioneer farm was difficult as the land had to be cleared, a cabin had to be raised, and a barn provided for the livestock. Timothy was assisted by his brother-in-law, James Eastridge, and to some extent by his own sons James and John, who were now twelve and ten. By 1810, Sarah was pregnant again and, on December 10, a daughter was born.[114] They named her Elizabeth after Sarah's sister, Lucy. Timothy and Sarah were now the parents of three boys and three girls.

In late June 1811, Timothy received word that his namesake uncle on Elk Creek in Grayson County, Virginia, had died. At the time of his death, Timothy's handicapped son William and his daughter Rebecca were living at home with their mother. His other three sons, Charles, Moses, and Timothy Jr., all were married and still farmed their father's farm. James and Mary Ramey, the deceased Timothy's daughter and son-in-law who had purchased a farm near the Roark river farm in Russell County, Virginia, had sold out to a David Hansen in 1798 and, at the time of her father's death, were living in Scott County, Virginia.[115] The remaining daughter, Sarah Millard, who was close to her cousin Timothy in Tazewell County, Virginia, lived with her husband in Logan County, Virginia (now West Virginia). Timothy's uncle had left a will, which was probated in the July Court of Grayson County. The bulk of his estate was left to sons Charles, Moses, and Timothy Jr., who were to provide for their brother William. From the estate, the three sons were to each pay $100 to the three daughters, Mary Ramey, Sarah Millard, and Rebecca Roark, and were to make the payment to the girls within five years.[116] Unfortunately, there was to be a dispute over the estate, and after her mother's death in 1817, Rebecca was to file suit against her three brothers charging that she had not received her $100 from their father's will. The lawsuit was to result in a redistribution of items from the estate totaling $160.75. Rebecca was to receive a cow, cowbell, five sheep, pewter dishes, a stone jug, and a tin bucket, all for a total value of $28.00.[117] There is no record that Timothy maintained contact with his cousins or was to ever to see them again.

Sometime before 1813, Sarah's father died. The exact date of the death of Joseph Bolen is unknown, but records indicate that he was deceased by May 1813. In that month the county court found in favor of a claim against Bolen by the firm of King and Beatty in the amount of $8.08 and ordered the sale of a tract owned by

Bolen "in Powell Valley where John Henderson now lives."[118] The sheriff's sale for the claim against Bolen was the twenty-acre tract occupied by Bolen since he had originally purchased the 123 acres from Hodgson in 1801. By 1813, John Henderson had purchased and was living on the 123 acres and thus his name appeared to identify and locate the tract ordered sold by the court. The court in its judgement noted that Bolen owned no other land or property. Thus with little or no property, Joseph Bolen died, ending the somewhat troubled life of Timothy's father-in-law. In all likelihood, Joseph Bolen was the first to be buried in a small plot Timothy set aside as a cemetery southwest of his homestead. The cemetery overlooked Cumberland Gap six miles to the west.

Sarah was pregnant again in 1813 and was expecting the birth by midyear. She and Timothy had been married for sixteen years and had been on their pioneer farm for six years. The family was settled in primitive but comfortable frontier style. A new baby would bring joy, but a new birth was hardly exciting to parents of six children. The latest child was a boy. They would name him Joseph after his recently departed maternal grandfather.[119]

Chapter 4

The East Tennessee Frontier Farm
1813

The primitive frontier farm where Joseph Roark was born was nestled among the steep ridges of Claiborne County in east Tennessee less than ten miles from the Tennessee-Virginia state line. Claiborne County sits squarely astride the Appalachian chain of mountains, which runs northeast to southwest. The mountain range, small in height compared to the Rocky Mountains, nevertheless was the barrier that restrained the western expansion of the original thirteen colonies. While of sufficient elevation to impede development, the mountains of Claiborne County were not so high or expansive as to be unpenetrable, and occasional gaps in the mountain range such as the historic Cumberland Gap provided access to the flat and richer lands of Kentucky. The range of mountains through Claiborne County served as the continental shelf dividing surface water flow between the Atlantic Ocean and the Mississippi River. East of Claiborne County, low-lying valleys carry water eastward to the Atlantic Ocean, while west of the Appalachian range water finds its way to the Gulf of Mexico.

The general elevation of the mountain crests in the area is approximately 2,500 feet above sea level, with the highest elevation being 3,100 feet. The mountain ridges were difficult to cross in the late eighteenth century, and settlers moving east to west were forced to move laterally in a southerly direction to find and scale mountain passes or gaps. The modern-day traveler can identify in the current road system the same restricted patterns of travel through the Appalachians. The Powell and Clinch Rivers flow between the mountain ridges and provide water to the narrow fertile valleys of alkaline soil. Settlers starting in Virginia found it easier to move southwesterly along the rivers into Tennessee than to ascend the mountain range through the difficult mountain gaps for a westerly move into Kentucky.

Years before the settlers arrived, trappers and hunters came down the Clinch River in search of game and pelts. Prior to 1750, adventurers from southwest Virginia hunted in the area of what was later Claiborne County and developed a lucrative trading business with the Indians for furs to satisfy the demands of colonial agents for

London and Paris fur merchants. Little or no settlement occurred in the area until the end of the French-Indian War in 1763. Daniel Boone hunted the area in what was later Claiborne County from his home in North Carolina prior to his move to Virginia and later to Kentucky. Boone and others like him were referred to as "long hunters" since they hunted for months at a time without returning to their homes. Long hunters and trappers provided the major activity by white men in the area until hostilities ended in the Revolutionary War.[1] Boone and other long hunters of the era initially sought meat and hides to feed and clothe their families; however, the effort quickly became economic in nature as deer skins and furs became valuable for sale or trade. Boone was a third-generation American and his grandfather, like most emigrants to America, had come from Europe without hunting experience because in most European countries hunting had been reserved for the nobility. Boone and his father, like the Ororkes and Roarks and many others, developed on their own the Indian knowledge and skill for hunting.[2] The abundant game in the valley of the Powell River in the area that later was Claiborne County attracted Daniel Boone to the area as early as the 1760s.

The common style of land development in northeast Tennessee, as had been the case on the frontier in early colonial times, was that the first arrival–after the hunters and trappers–a restless and temporary pioneer. He was poor, alone, seeking free or very cheap land and, more often than not, was not interested in land title or ownership–just a place to "squat" for a brief period. Often the squatter was shiftless, but he cleared a very small plot of land, planted a limited crop of corn, grazed hogs in the nearby woods, killed wild game for meat and skins and, after a brief period, moved on again to repeat the process. After these men, came the steady farmers, like Timothy Roark, who would have a proper title to their land, who would laboriously clear their land and build respectable cabins, all with the idea in mind of a permanent residence on their own land.

By the time Joseph's father settled in the Claiborne County area, the long hunters and squatters had moved westward in the excitement of new adventures and in the interest of finding other places to temporarily locate. By the end of the eighteenth century, few long hunters remained on the frontier of east Tennessee and, after 1800, that area of Tennessee was the domain of the farmer who raised his crops on a small farm sandwiched among the mountainous ridges. Away from the economic and class restrictions placed upon them within the original thirteen colonies but also separated from the conveniences of the tidewater area, the farmers between the Powell and Clinch Rivers, many of whom were still first- and second-generation Americans, loved the land and enjoyed the newly gained freedoms of the republic. In these early days of the United States, at least nine out of every ten Americans made their livelihood by working the land. Proud, independent, and self-confident, farmers glorified country life and considered it the most noble and honorable way of making a living. "Those who labor in the earth are the chosen people of God" was the expressed opinion of Thomas Jefferson, the talented and intellectual president who never lost his love for the land. "Farmers are," he said, "the most vigorous, the most independent, the most valuable citizens."[3]

The early farmer along the Powell River was a "frontier farmer" in the truest sense. He differed from his predecessors–the long hunters and the squatters–in that he came to stay and to make his living from his new land. The frontier farmer could be identified by several unique characteristics. First, of course, he was on the frontier where few, if any, public services or conveniences were available. Counties, if they had been formed and designated, were large in geographical area, with the county seat and its courthouse of land title records often several days' journey away. Merchants consisted of traveling peddlers with the rare general store located only in the county seat. Second, the frontier farmer was the first pioneer to bring his family to the unsettled area on the frontier. Long hunters and squatters had previously operated alone or in very small groups of restless, wandering men. Contrary to his predecessor's lifestyle, the frontier farmer was a family man, interested in stability and dedicated to making a living for his family on his own plot of ground. Third, the frontier farmer was the first to clear the land, remove trees, cultivate the soil, and make his living from raising crops and livestock rather than trapping and trading in furs from the wild game in the area. Last, the frontier farmer was self-sufficient in a manner related to those who preceded him on the frontier. He accepted the challenge to provide for his family with what they could do on their own without support from government, society, or manufacturers of goods.

In the early days of settlement when Joseph's father moved to Claiborne County, the population density was low, less than six persons per square mile. The absence of almost any transportation system made isolation an accepted fact for the frontier farm family and demanded a self-sufficiency which cannot be appreciated by later generations. In shelter, food, and even clothing, the farmstead had to be self-providing. In a rare economic survey of the period, principally done at the direction of Secretary of Treasury Alexander Hamilton, the making of clothing by the farm family was recognized, and it was reported that a "vast scene of household manufacturing" was evident in the agricultural environment and through it "two-thirds, three-fourths, and even four-fifths of all the clothing of the inhabitants are made by themselves."[4] The frontier farmer was, by necessity, self-sufficient since he enjoyed little financial credit beyond that he might gain in the original purchase of his land and the seed for his first crop.[5] Nevertheless, the farmer felt pride in his self-sufficiency as he and his family struggled against the day-to-day challenges to their survival.

The typical frontier farmer in the northeast region of Tennessee in the late eighteenth and early nineteenth centuries could purchase between two hundred and four hundred acres on which he could expect to raise crops sufficient to support himself and his family. He had to expect an outlay of several hundred dollars–the first cost of the land, the expense of clearing it, digging a well, buying and planting seed for his first wheat and corn crop, constructing fences for his livestock, and building his house and barn. The available valley lands in northeast Tennessee filled quickly with farmers who were considered to be "of a better class of farmers." Land for these dedicated farmers was primarily available only on the frontier since the older states in the Union could no longer afford large land grants to speculators and veterans. The public land was sold in small tracts, generally less than one hundred fifty acres. Thus land on the frontier could be purchased by farmers who were interested in cultivating the land for their livelihood and who had little interest in land speculation.[6] During these early years of developing his homestead, the farmer and his family faced the risk of devastating weather conditions, calamitous destruction of crops, bad harvests, poor health, and economic depression, which could destroy the demand for his limited marketable crop.

Of the farmer's production, corn was the staple crop. Since it was grown on almost every farm in the sixteen states in 1800, corn was grown primarily for the consumption of the farm family and its livestock, primarily hogs, and little market demand for corn existed beyond the boundary of the farmer's own fence line.[7] Wheat was a major crop in Virginia and east Tennessee but, like corn, little wheat was exported beyond the local community. Wheat crops in the Appalachia area by 1800 had suffered severely from the Hessian fly, which attacked wheat with vigor and spread rapidly. At the urging of Thomas Jefferson, who feared the extinction of wheat in the U.S., the American Philosophical Society undertook scientific studies that resulted in the development of new varieties of wheat, especially the yellow-headed wheat, resistant to the Hessian fly.[8] It was probably yellow-headed wheat which Timothy Roark raised on his Powell River farm.

Other crops of early Tennessee farmers included rye, which was used for distillation among the Scotch-Irish and for bread among the Germans. Oats were popular among the Scotch-Irish farmers although the oats grown in Claiborne County were of a poor quality. Scotch-Irish farmers grew them for horse feed and for the daily breakfast staple of oatmeal.[9] After 1790, cotton farming had begun to expand westward from Virginia and Carolina's tidewater area. Similarly, tobacco replaced indigo, rice, and sugar as the major export from the new republic.[10] It is doubtful, however, that Joseph's father raised either cotton or tobacco on his farm since poor or non-existent means of transportation would have hampered his getting such a product to market.

Cultivating the soil for the crops was difficult for the frontier farmer and was achieved primarily by the sweat and strain of human exertion. Land was initially cleared by burning. Each year the burning was repeated in March to remove the dead grass from the fields so as to reveal the new green grass to the livestock. Generally, trees to be removed were belted by an axe-cut, a notched section that stopped the nutrients transmitted by the bark. After the trees were dead, they were cut into logs, piled, and burned. The frontier farmer would also attempt to burn out the stumps, but generally stump removal was accomplished only by difficult hand labor devoted to digging out the stumps. Canebrakes were removed by chopping down the cane with an axe and by digging out the roots with a pickaxe or mattock. Following this work in canebrakes, very little other effort was needed to fully cultivate the area previously covered with the cane. Areas other than canebrakes were often cultivated by hand labor with a hoe and pickaxe, although plowing was the most common means of cultivation. Because the soil was rich and virginal, deep plowing was unnecessary.[11] While oxen were the work animals of the northern part of the U.S., they had been replaced by horses in Virginia and areas south. Mules were becoming popular as farm animals after 1800, but their special breeding requirements limited their extensive use by the small farmer. Doubtless, Joseph's father cultivated his land using plows pulled by horses that were also used for personal transportation.

Plows used by farmers in 1800 differed little from those used in medieval Europe and even earlier times. The common Carey plow was made entirely of wood except for the iron coulter on the wooden moldboard for cutting the soil. Strong arms were needed to hold the plow in the ground and, even with such an implement, an acre was a good day of plowing. The farmer's other tools were few in number and consisted of a spike-tooth harrow, sledge, hoe, pickaxe, and an iron-plated shovel. Few such farm implements were made in quantity before 1810, and initial manufacture before then was accomplished by a local blacksmith. Wooden parts, when broken, were cut, shaped, and replaced by the farmer himself. Harvesting was done by the backbreaking work of the sickle, and the farmer often sized his planting area in the spring by what he could cut in the late summer days by his own efforts.[12]

The farmer's livestock in 1800 were lean and rangy. Because of the availability of wild game for meat, cattle were rarely raised for beef but instead provided milk and butter for home consumption. Each farm had from one to three cows for that purpose. Hogs were generally found on every farm and "hog-killing time" provided fresh meat for a few weeks. Most of the pork, however, had to be cured for future use, smoked, dried, and hung in the smokehouse. Sheep were raised for wool but required protection from the wolf and wildcat. The horse, however, remained the farmer's greatest asset in livestock, for the horse provided a means to cultivate the soil as well as transportation for the farmer and his family to infrequent community meetings, church services, and camp-meetings.

However important his crops and his livestock were to the frontier farmer, his primary concern had to be that of providing housing for his family. He was neither successful nor happy until he had provided shelter for his wife and children. The initial dwellings were constructed of logs from timber cut from the farmer's own land. Such a log dwelling could easily be finished by a half-dozen men in three or four days. The cost was negligible and the raising was a community social event enlivened by music, dancing, and a tub of whiskey. The farmer would apply the roof himself through the use of homemade shingles which he would have previously shaved from local timber at the rate of almost a thousand per day. Thanks to the invention of a nail-making machine, nails were no longer rare and costly, and by 1810 could be purchased through local merchants.[13] The farmer worked quickly upon his arrival to construct lodging for his family, but it was a rare frontier farmer who devoted much detail to the architecture of his cabin. Housing was small and simple in design. The universal symbol of the frontier farmer's first major victory in his struggle against the elements arrayed against him was the erection of his cabin.

The houses of the frontier farmers in east Tennessee by the early 1800s were primarily of log construction. The logs were squared off into timbers and notches were cut in the logs to meet at corners. Logs were then stacked on top of one another until the walls of the cabin were complete. Log construction was not an English nor a Scotch-Irish building tradition and had not made its appearance in the first settlements in New England or on Chesapeake Bay. It was the Germans who settled in Pennsylvania that were responsible for the log construction methods adopted by most frontier farmers. The German log-construction technique was taken up by the many Scotch-Irish settlers who passed through eastern Pennsylvania on their way south and west. The farm cabins were constructed by farmers who had made themselves proficient in woodworking, who prepared the logs to be ready for raising with help of the community, and who thus built their cabins using the quickest and least laborious method possible. Cabins constructed in this way became the houses that were often occupied by two or more generations of the same family.[14]

The first cabin of the frontier farmer was seldom larger than twenty feet square, in which the family cooked, ate, lived, and slept. In the single room cabin, the family ate around the fireplace at the end of the cabin farthest away from the door. The beds of the family were in another corner and opposite them was the space for sitting and entertaining, furnished with rough-cut chairs and possibly a clock if the family was able to afford one. Given the size of the families and the limited space of their home, the household of most frontier farmers learned to live in close quarters. Their living space expanded and contracted both during daily activities and by the season. As night fell, particularly during the long winters, the meagerness of light available from candles or oil lamps drew the members of the family closer together or sent them to bed. Family members learned from early childhood how to move in small spaces, how to adjust for the presence of several people close to the same source of light and heat, and how to carry on many different activities in close proximity to other family members.[15]

When Timothy Roark raised his family in northeast Tennessee, the concept of a family member, even the parents, having one's own room, or even one's own bed, would have been a strange and almost unbelievable idea. Children and other adults living in the same household slept together in a single room or hall or loft, although the sexes were usually separated if there was enough room. Even where separate bed chambers were possible, the space was rarely heated and was furnished for no other activity but sleeping or storage. Often even the kitchen area in the cabin was used for sleeping at night. The coveted place in winter for one's bed or pallet was at the hearth near the fireplace.[16]

Furniture in the frontier farmer's cabin was simple and limited. Most often the chairs and tables were made by the farmer himself with the most simple tools. If the cabin had a loft for sleeping, a rough-cut ladder provided the access by the children to their sleeping area. Bed frames were also handmade of rough-hewn lumber with rawhide or rope support for the occupant.[17] The mattress would have been a loose tick or case filled with straw. Cold in winter and hot in summer, the straw tick was a far cry from the luxury of sleeping on a feather bed or cotton mattress. A rich prize in any frontier home would have been a chest of drawers which would have been carried with great effort into the frontier country. Such a piece of furniture might well have been the only tangible link to the girlhood home of the woman now serving as the matron of the frontier cabin.[18]

Winters in the frontier farmer's cabin in the Tennessee mountains were especially harsh and severe. A single fire warmed most of the household during the long winter months, but lofts and secondary rooms, if they existed, were never heated at all. Although the huge fireplace consumed enormous quantities of wood, the roaring fire provided little warmth in the drafty, completely uninsulated cabin. On bitterly cold days, the fire warmed only a space close to it, causing family members to rotate positions in order to maintain some evenness of heat, yet with little comfort.

Often the fireplace also provided what light that was available for reading or other such activities. The frontier farmer probably saw by firelight alone as candles were expensive and oil lamps were beyond the limited financial resources of the farmer. For the elderly and others with poor eyesight, the visual world within the frontier cabin was shadowy at best. Readers, and doubtless they were few in number, had to strain to see the written word and sometimes set their book or newspaper on fire by holding the reading material too close to the fire. During the winter day in the frontier cabin, the farmer and his family depended on direct sunlight entering through a window or open door. The family read, sewed, and did other close work close to the window and moved their chairs during the day to follow the sun's rays throughout the house.

Window coverings and curtains were rare in most cabins of frontier farmers. Floors were equally bare, as rugs were beyond the reach of most families. Often, however, bear skins and deer skins provided some little additional cover and warmth on the otherwise barren floor. Most walls were also bare and only one in ten families had a painting, print, or engraving. Usually only looking glasses or a framed mirror broke the expanse of barren walls. Most families possessed only one such mirror; few families had more than one. The rarity of the framed mirror made them prized possessions, to be displayed prominently in that part of the cabin where guests were to be seated. The mirror was not only necessary for good grooming–the family had sufficient difficulty in looking presentable in any circumstance but would have found it impossible without a mirror–but also added scarce light to the cabin by reflecting back what little light was available. Few frontier farm homes had pictures for cabin walls, and the families with pictures had bought them from peddlers–engravings of statesmen like George Washington and Napoleon Bonaparte. Landscapes and scenes of social work were scarce indeed and rarely graced the walls of the frontier farmer's cabin.[19]

Inundated with the daily demands of routine farm tasks, the farmer and his spouse struggled to provide for the family and had little time or occasion for improved appearance. Similarly, outside the house, the frontier farmer devoted little time or energy to beautification. The log house was most often faced away from the roadway and no grassy lawns or fenced front yard greeted the visitor. The unenclosed spaces between the house and road were trampled and bare with a sprinkling of straggling, uncut weeds. Bits of wood, timber, boards, chips, broken farm implements, and discarded containers were to be seen around the farmhouse with pigs snorting about in a sort of confusion.[20]

From the outside, the appearance of the log cabin of the frontier farmer was gray or brown with neglect. Cracks between the logs were filled with mud, and the logs often showed peeling strips of bark. The proximity of the barnyard, the inevitable mud during rainy periods, open fireplaces with ashes dispersed nearby, and dirt roads insuring dust from any rare passerby meant that the frontier farm homestead was inevitably dusty and dirty. Without window screens, the open windows and doors provided ready access to flies, and in summer, the homes were filled with flies and flyspecks. Dogs and cats had the run of most frontier farmhouses and were considered assets to protect against rats, mice, and other smaller animals of the wild. They did, however, add to the confusion surrounding the unkempt farmhouse.

Women in the frontier farm household played an important part in the success of the family as a unit. They clothed and fed all members of the family. All the garments worn by the frontier farm family were made by the women in the family. Fabrics produced by the family–woolens, linen, and "towcloth" made from flax and the combinations of the three–were the source of the clothing for the pioneer American farmers in 1800. Wool and flax were processed laboriously by hand through pounding for softening, then combed into fibers for spinning. Different spinning wheels were used for spinning flax and wool. In the laborious task of spinning, mother and daughter developed a skill in simultaneously and gracefully guiding the yarn and governing the spinning wheel. Most families wove their own cloth; however, looms were more rare than spinning wheels on the frontier, and some farm families had to depend on their neighbors with looms to do the weaving. From the cloth, clothes for the family were cut and sewn by hand. Girls in the family learned from their mother the craft of the needle–sewing straight seams, darning socks, and stitching waistbands. Sewing and stitching was an endless task for the women in the household as the family grew and levied more demands for clothes and oft-needed repairs.

As Joseph Roark grew up in East Tennessee, the technology used in cooking by the women of the family differed little from that of previous generations. As they cooked over the fireplace, the women used heavy iron pots and kettles that sat directly on the coals or were hung by an iron frame over the hearth. The cook inevitably did heavy lifting and stooping in front of of the huge fire in the fireplace. In many households, the bread was baked in the ashes, fireplace ovens being a generation or two in the future. Wooden trays, trenchers, and dressed boards were often used in place of dishes. Most kitchens on the frontier farm were equipped with the homing block or the handmill that was so necessary in the preparation of corn for the meals of the farm family.[21]

> In these American kitchens . . . everything came in the rough, and had to be reduced to a useable form in the household. Women needed to know the crafts of salting, pickling and smoking meat to preserve it, of making wheat or rye bread, johnnycake or hominy, of stewing, roasting and frying. Salt, sugar, spices and coffee had to be taken in bulk form, ground and pounded. Housewives hauled water, killed chickens, set their children to search for eggs in the barnyard and harvested vegetables from the garden or root cellar.[22]

Salt was the most important provision necessary for the frontier farm cabin. It was used extensively for preserving meats as well as for seasoning. While saline springs existed in some nearby areas, Timothy Roark and other frontier farmers could not devote the time away from crops and other farm tasks to work the salt springs. Salt was obtained from merchants who purchased it in bulk from the salt wells and mines in Virginia. Because of the heavy demand for salt by the farmers, merchants advertised it for sale at a cheap price in order to attract customers to their places of business at the county seat settlements.[23]

Another daily activity of the matron of the household was the making of butter and, in some homes, cheese. After separating the cream from the milk following its delivery from the barn by one of the older boys of the house, the women would vigorously churn the cream to "bring the butter." Butter was then worked by hand into the proper butter molds, then wrapped in cloth and placed in the well or springhouse to be kept cool until ready to be placed on the table at meals.

On washdays–usually one a month in most farm households–women would rise long before sunup to scrub and pound clothes in nearby streams or in pots of heated water if the family was fortunate to possess such containers. After repeated washing with homemade soft soap and rinsing in fresh water, the clothes were spread to dry or hung from low limbs of nearby trees. Washday was a day of unpleasant and tiring work for the farmer's wife, who was expected to also prepare the meals and perform her routine tasks. Repetition was the constancy of women's work in the same dull round of chores–cooking, clearing away, washing, sewing, mending. It was a daily sequence of time-consuming, physically demanding, and constantly repeated tasks.

Children in the home of the frontier farmer learned what they knew from the home–by working with their parents in the daily work tasks. Apprenticeship was in the home, and work skills were gained by "following after" the parents and imitating their efforts. Here they learned the most important things in their life. Exposure outside the family was limited; however, occasionally an opportunity would be available for a farmer's son to learn other occupational skills by clerking in the store of a local merchant or by following the practitioner of some profession. Particularly fortunate were those farm children whose parents, or one parent, could read and write and who were willing to see that the knowledge was passed to their children.

Opportunity for even a very limited education was available to very few in the Appalachian mountain area of Virginia and Tennessee. In moving to the frontier regions with his family, the farmer basically surrendered the opportunity of providing his children with what would be classified today as an elementary education. A frontier farmer's son in the early 1800s found it even more difficult to learn to read and to write than had his father and grandfather years before.[24] The opportunity of apprenticeship available one or two generations before in the settled areas of the New World, and thus the gaining of some literate skills, were beyond the reach of the frontier farmer's son in the isolation of the mountainous frontier of Claiborne County in Tennessee. The Appalachian mountain area was particularly illiterate as overall conditions reflected the tough financial status of the rural homestead and the concomitant emphasis on survival rather than education.[25]

The new republic had, by 1800, begun to stress the responsibility of the government, state and local, to provide a free public education for all children. Leaders in the new nation strongly felt that public education would provide a unique American culture distinctly different from that in Europe where education was available only to the socially elite; however, formal education in the U.S. was limited to private and parochial schools in the urban areas. When the republican government assumed responsibility for free public education, the transition was slow and difficult. Education was stressed by governmental leaders but was not ready to be funded by the taxpayers in general. Of the sixteen states in the Union in 1800, only seven had included public education in their constitutions and, as late as 1810, no states were providing funding for public schools.[26]

In Claiborne County, during Joseph Roark's early years there, tax-supported schools rarely existed. The public consensus was in favor of placing the responsibility on parents alone for the education of their children. Any schools that were provided were underwritten by a small group of local farmers who assessed themselves for the expense of a school and a schoolmaster.[27] Even in those rare instances in which a schoolmaster was available, attendance at a school was limited to the winter months after harvest and before the planting season. Nowhere was school attendance mandatory and even the little schooling provided was limited to the young men of the family. The frontier farmer, in general, wanted his sons to be able to read, write, and "figure," but the daughters were not schooled and were expected to remain in the home of the parents until marriage and later in the home of her husband.

By 1800, in parts of the U.S. other than the Appalachian Mountain country of Claiborne County, most American children between the ages of five and fifteen attended school a few weeks or up to a couple of months each year. In the backwoods communities of the frontier, illiteracy was common and many families made no effort to educate their children. It has been estimated that as many as three-fourths of American males of the period could read and considerably fewer could write. In the backcountry, however, illiteracy was much higher.

Any schooling available outside the home was provided primarily by itinerant schoolmasters–generally unmarried men who made their services available to groups of farmers. Tuition charges by the schoolmaster were modest and included room and board in the home of a farmer with space available. If a schoolhouse was somehow provided, it was generally poorly constructed and located on a piece of ground that was considered unproductive and worthless.

Books and other reading materials were expensive and scarce and were only purchased to fill a specific need. Newspapers were particularly scarce on the frontier. Bibles were often the only printed material available to farm children on which to practice their reading skills. Hymn books, if they were available in local worship services, also provided exposure to the printed word. If peddlers or merchants stocked any books, the selection would have been limited to the Bible and various almanacs which provided information on planting of crops and treatment of illnesses. Such books, when owned by the frontier family, were prized possessions and readily became heirlooms for family treasure.

Religion was an important part of the life of the frontier farmer and his family. On the Tennessee frontier, Timothy Roark and his neighbors in Claiborne County were part of the movement to meet the spiritual needs of the less educated on the western frontier. On the fertile rivervalley farms nestled among the forested ridges of the area, the frontier people and the itinerant preachers of the day struggled awkwardly but earnestly with the age-old question of man–his moral relationship to the world around him and his future life in the hereafter of eternity. Religion was to play a significant role in the life of Joseph Roark and an equally important role in the lives of his children and his descendants. So significant were the embracing religious beliefs to be in the lives of Timothy Roark, his son Joseph, and later families, some attention must be paid here to the religious atmosphere at the time of Joseph's early years.

Historians have identified two periods of religious fervor in America. The first was termed by some as the "First Great Awakening" which extended generally from 1730 to 1760. In this period, religious thought moved away from predestination and the strict demands of Calvinistic theology toward a recognition that the love of God is available to all men and women. Led by Jonathan Edwards, a brilliant theologian who graduated from Yale at the age of seventeen, the revival began with Edwards' teachings while pastor of the church at Northampton, Massachusetts. Stressing the importance of a religious conversion experience, Edwards preached the fear of death and judgement but held up to his congregations a forgiving and loving God. Stressing that refusal to accept God's forgiveness was due to the stubborn choice of the individual, Edwards preached that the gates of Heaven beckoned and that "Christ has flung the door of mercy wide open and stands in the door calling and crying with a loud voice to poor sinners." The refreshing theology of a loving God drew thousands into the churches of the Colonies and encouraged the independent faith of the individual. The First Great Awakening "made the thirteen colonies into a cohesive unit," gave them a sense of unique nationality, and "inspired them with the belief that they were, and of a right ought to be, a free and independent people."[28]

The second period of extensive growth in religion in America has been named by some as the "Second Great Awakening, 1800-1830"[29] or by others as the "Great Revival in the West, 1797-1805."[30] Both refer to the period following the American Revolution in which fundamentalist faith was greatly expanded among the frontier farms west of the Appalachian Mountains. Led principally by Methodists and Baptists but also to some extent by Presbyterians, the movement expounded the Christian faith to meet the needs of the "plain-folk." The term "plain-folk" has been used by some writers to describe "the great mass of ante-bellum Southern farmers and townspeople who were neither rich nor starving" but which were considered to be the backbone of the new American frontier culture following the revolutionary period.[31] Referred to herein as the Great Revival, this religious awakening came to the frontier just as Timothy Roark was establishing his homestead in Tennessee and raising his family in the isolated frontier cabin on the Powell River. It would be embraced by Timothy and his family and would provide a common family culture for generations to come.

Prior to the Revolution, church membership was generally centered in three main denominations: the Congregational Church in New England, the Presbyterian Church in the middle states, and the Episcopal Church in the south. Some Catholics were located in Maryland and other middle colonies, but shortly after the Revolution there were only thirty Catholic churches in America. Baptists, Methodists, and other religious sects could be identified in all states following the Revolution but were looked down upon by upper-class citizens. These sects and denominations catered to the poorer classes in the social structure or to a particular nationality and immigrant group.

All churches and denominations had suffered during the Revolution. Prior to the Revolution, the larger denominations were guaranteed state support, which had been the traditional and statutory rule in England and Scotland. The separation of church and state in the new republic halted the flow of tax-derived funds to the churches and ceased support of the clergy from state-collected taxes. All three major denominations were thus forced to depend upon voluntary financial support from their attending members. This was particularly true of the Episcopal Church, which not only received its budget requirements from the state but also its supply of ministers from England. When the Revolution came, most Episcopal ministers sided with the King and became unpopular Tories. At the successful conclusion of the Revolution, most of the Virginia Episcopal parishes were without clergy. With the enthusiasm engendered by the refreshing birth of individual freedom guaranteed by the new republic, interest in religion faded in favor of financial gain. A spirit of rationalism spread in both the United States and Great Britain.[32]

With the opening of new lands in what was to become Tennessee, Kentucky, and Ohio, the migration of farmers to the western frontier began. The immigrants to the area west of the Appalachians brought their religious faith and churches with them to their new homes. It was not, however, the major denominations which furnished the majority of immigrants that poured into the new territory but rather representatives of the various other faiths and sects. It was not the established church with its affluent members who furnished settlers for the new lands. As had been the case in the early emigration from Great Britain to America, the comfortable, wealthy, and well-established did not, and normally do not, choose to relocate. It was the Baptists, Methodists, and Presbyterians, fleeing persecution and hard times, who primarily made up the numbers of emigrants leaving the tidewater states and moving into the western frontier. Of these three denominations, the Presbyterian Church was best represented in the move into southwest Virginia, Kentucky, and Tennessee by the Scotch-Irish from Pennsylvania. The first Presbyterian immigration into Tennessee followed the Holston River into eastern Tennessee in about 1780 and for many years was the leading denomination in that area. The growth of the Presbyterian Church on the frontier was limited, however, by its emphasis on and strict requirement for a well-educated and trained clergy. The Methodists and Baptists, however, were not constrained by such an emphasis on an educated clergy and found their preachers many times within the local churches themselves. The move of these two denominations into the western frontier marked a major beginning of the Great Revival.[33]

The Great Revival first made its appearance west of the Appalachians in Tennessee and Kentucky and was found first among the Presbyterian community. It soon spread to the Baptists and Methodists along a frontier that was constituted by a turbulence of a constantly changing population, an uncontrolled sense of individual freedom, and an aggressive and independent spirit. The Great Revival was fostered and encouraged by young ministers, many of them not well educated, who saw the need for religion on the frontier and were dedicated to their faith to the extent they were willing to endure the hardships of the frontier to strengthen the faith of the frontier farmer. They "labored diligently to preach the gospel, to awaken the people to the sinfulness of careless indifference to their own spiritual welfare and that of their neighbors."[34] Like Timothy Roark, most neighboring farmers were Scotch-Irish who maintained the religious traditions of John Knox, and were conscious that they had fallen short of the strict Presbyterian standards. Strong, courageous, adventuresome, and ambitious, the frontier farmer saw the need for a practical and emotionally satisfying faith to meet the demands of a harsh and unforgiving frontier life. As a result, the Great Revival swept like a prairie wildfire into the western frontier of Tennessee and Kentucky.

The loneliness of the frontier farm cabin, particularly among the women who were not involved in the limited commerce and business intercourse of the day, encouraged the involvement of the family in religious gatherings. Methodists circuit riders in the tradition of Francis Asbury were greeted warmly as they brought encouragement, human contact, and a civilizing influence to the raw frontier. The family on the typically isolated river farm thirsted for human companionship and readily responded to the influence of the Great Revival as strict Presbyterianism gave way to the more emotional approach of the less-educated Methodist and Baptist preachers of the day. Preaching in a straightforward, masculine style, the Methodist and Baptist preachers brought the revival message to the frontier in a fashion that was warmly accepted by the plain-folk of the frontier. The Baptist Church was definitely a frontier organization that ministered to the plain-folk. Preachers were drawn from the ranks of the congregation, and the congregations themselves were comprised initially of frontier farmers who had immigrated from more settled areas. "Further, the Baptists drew much strength from gathering in the unchurched and dissatisfied members from other churches, particularly Presbyterians. So close were the Baptists to the feelings and thoughts of the plain-folk that many frontier Presbyterians chose to become Baptists either in masse . . . or as individuals seeking religious satisfaction."[35]

In a manner that would be continued through the life of Timothy Roark and that of his son Joseph, the frontier churches–Baptists and Methodists as well as Presbyterians–developed and enforced church discipline. Disciples were focused not on theological issues that had concerned the major denominations during the days before the Revolution, but rather were concentrating on governing the social conduct of church members. Churches of the period have later been referred to as "frontier moral courts."[36] More democratic than their fellow Christians in the Methodist and Presbyterian churches, Baptists generally established a series of "gospel steps" to be taken in disciplining a member who had violated the established code of social behavior.

> First, offender and offended attempted to settle their differences in a face-to-face confrontation; second, the parties called on the assistance of several witnesses; and finally, if these two steps produced no settlement, the matter was brought before the whole congregation. Although the pastor served as moderator, the entire membership was allowed to participate in the proceedings, and the accused was expelled only on unanimous vote of

all present; in some associations, however, a two-thirds majority was considered sufficient. The chief public offenses were drunkenness, cursing, and fighting, with private complaints including wife-beating and child neglect. Civil issues within the churches' jurisdiction included repudiation of contracts, abuse of another's livestock, and fraud.[37]

Church buildings were few, and meeting places were limited to routine weekly congregational association. The fervor of the Great Revival resulted in the unique phenomenon of the day–the camp-meeting. After 1800, the camp-meeting became a regular feature of the Methodists and Baptists and overcame the lack of buildings in which to meet. Camp-meetings, as great open-air revivals, took worship to the outdoors to large congregations, most of which had traveled some distance and camped nearby. "No other American gathering was more notorious, or more spectacular" than the rural area camp-meeting.[38] As the fundamentalism of Baptists and Methodists spread westward in the U.S., outdoor revivals became commonplace. But they were the largest and most influential in the Appalachian area of Virginia, Tennessee, and Kentucky. Camp-meetings in Claiborne County were perhaps some of the most exciting and influential events for the young family of Timothy Roark. These camp-meetings were, in retrospect, so important in the cultural development of Timothy's family that special attention should be devoted to their description.

A "large" camp-meeting consisted of a congregation of several thousand and was both a religious revival and a major social gathering. Families ate and slept in their wagons or small tents or in the open air. While the younger members of families enjoyed the play, new adventures, and general excitement of camping beyond their family cabin, adults visited in the camp during the morning and spent the afternoon in prayer-meeting tents in preparation for the outdoor preaching which began at dusk. Under the glow of lamps hung on tree branches and by the flickering light of campfires, preachers expounded the gospel from a crudely constructed rostrum. "The voice of the revivalists–men who could reach an audience of thousands without amplification–and the massed singing and shouting of the crowd generated powerful tides of emotion."[39]

The camp-meetings were very much a part of the Great Revival and represented, for many, the religious experience of the Tennessee frontier. Their importance and the atmosphere they created has been discussed in studies of the Great Revival period.

> Soon camp-meetings came to be a regular feature of the revival and were to be met with wherever it spread. These meetings usually began on Thursday, or Friday, and continued until the following Tuesday. People living thirty, sixty, and even one hundred miles away attended. There was preaching every day with the administration of the Holy Sacrament on Sunday. Provisions and bedding were brought from home by those who purposed remaining on the ground. The wagons were stationed at a convenient distance, near wood

and water. Improvised tents and rude huts, hastily constructed, supplemented the covered wagons and afforded the necessary shelter. The numbers attending increased to such an extent that the meeting-house could not accommodate the crowds, and stands were erected in the grove near by in order that several ministers might preach at the same time. As the excitement increased, the singing, praying, and exhortation were kept up in various parts of the grounds night and day. There was no regularity about the life. Many seemed unconscious about the need for food and sleep.[40]

Music played a large role in the regular services of the day–both at camp-meetings and at local church services. Sunday itself was not a day of silence but a time for extended group singing by church congregations. Central to the Protestant churches from their early days in Europe in the sixteenth century, singing also was exceptionally strong in the backwoods Tennessee countryside. The process by which illiterate or partially literate farm families participated in group singing was "lining out." Used also when the number of hymn books was severely limited, "lining out" required the minister or leader read each line of the hymn before it was sung by the group.

Written texts and tunes were the ultimate basis of Protestant congregational singing, but many congregations were only partially literate, and hymn books were expensive and usually far fewer than the number of singers. The actual "practice of music" in most American churches remained oral, and without instrumental accompaniment. Worshipers sang a handful of tunes from memory, and fitted a wide variety of psalm and hymn texts to the music. They memorized some of the most familiar, often sung words as well, but well into the nineteenth century American congregations continued in the practice of "lining out." . . . When a thousand or more singers were assembled for a camp-meeting, the lined-out music could be shattering; the grandson of the famous revivalist Francis Asbury remembered that "the immediate din was tremendous; at a hundred yards it was beautiful, and at a distance of half a mile it was magnificent." But whether outsiders overheard it with pleasure or pain, lining out was not intended for them. It was purely participatory music, aimed at no audience outside its own performers, members of a congregation wholly engaged in worship.[41]

Religion thus was an important part of the life of the frontier farmer and his family, particularly as it related to his social behavior and the social intercourse of his family in the local community. However important the social aspects of the frontier religion might have been, its primary focus was religious rather than social. Persons did not join a Baptist or Methodist church in those days on the frontier to gain social status in a community and certainly were not motivated to join to have their social conduct regulated.

Most people joined for religious reasons, especially out of a desire for salvation and a life to come, and the religious belief system also contributed to the resolution of tensions and instabilities in plain-folk life.

Frontier religious belief provided, on the one hand, a set of alternative goals, since those of the dominant society were essentially unattainable to most frontier farmers. More importantly, the religious beliefs constituted a new view of the world, offering the believer a different way of looking at himself and those around him.[42]

Weddings were closely related to church activities and most marriages were performed by the local pastor–if the sparse congregation were fortunate to have one–or by an itinerant minister if he were the most available. A wedding marked the beginning of a new family and the separation of a daughter from her parents and family. Most couples on the Appalachian frontier were married in the home of the bride in a simple yet solemn ceremony. Family, kin, and neighbors crowded into the "parlor" of the bride's home, most standing against the walls as chairs were limited in number. The bride and groom, dressed in their best homespun broadcloth, faced the minister. Following a reading from New Testament scripture, the preacher joined the couple's hands and led them through a simple exchange of vows.

It was traditional for the bride's family to invite the entire neighborhood from local farms to the wedding. The wedding was most often followed by a "covered dish" with visiting families bringing their special recipe. After the ceremony and bride's meal, there were games for the young people and visiting by the adults. All but the nearest neighbors were invited to spend the night, though bedrooms and sleeping accommodations were severely limited. Often, with bedrooms crowded, the guests would spend the night talking with no time devoted to sleep.

Women on the Appalachian frontier usually married in their middle to late teens. Most often they chose to marry in the spring months of March and April before the planting season or in the fall months of November and December after the annual harvest. Wedding dates generally avoided the months of heavy farm work between May and October. Most of the frontier farm couples "married and then settled into their new homes to begin the work that would structure the rest of their lives together."[43] The honeymoon, if there was one, consisted of visiting nearby relatives and friends then returning to the home of the bride's parents until a home of their own could be constructed. No extended travel was part of the honeymoon. Most couples had little choice other than to return immediately to their farm chores and then begin their lifetime of work together.

In the tradition of childbearing on the Appalachian frontier, children began to arrive within the first year of marriage and were to follow thereafter at a spacing of eighteen to twenty-four months. As the young wife's time of delivery approached, the accepted procedure was to "call the women together" and to summon the midwife who would, with the women kin and neighbors, direct the delivery. Menfolk of the household, including the expectant father, were required to remain outside the room and usually outside the house altogether until called. The mother-to-be was expected to give birth at home, in the company of other women. "In most American households around 1800, children were born in a warm and crowded room, usually the parents' bedchamber. A circle of women surrounded the expectant mother, talking to her in low tones or encouraging her as she groaned in labor."[44] The skill of midwives varied. Most had no formal training, having learned their art from older practitioners. Although most childbirth ended successfully for both mother and child, many were exhausting and traumatic experiences which weakened the mother for months. After the birth, the ideal called for the mother to be confined for a month of bedrest without responsibility for household chores. Most new mothers, however, did not enjoy the luxury of a month of rest and returned to their household chores and responsibilities within a few days. While childbearing was to change during the lifetime of Joseph Roark and doctors would replace midwives before the latter part of the nineteenth century, Joseph's mother, nevertheless, gave birth to her family on the Appalachian frontier by "calling the women together."

Perhaps the most significant difference between the early nineteenth century and the present age was the unhealthiness of daily life in that day and this. Poorer diet and less-than-protective housing worked then against a long and healthy life. In the warmer climate of the southern part of the U.S., food was more difficult to preserve from contamination. Mosquitos and parasitic diseases like the hookworm attack the shoeless. Health was a constant concern of the frontier farm family. Letters from that period consistently include a statement of the health of the writer–"I am well at present"–plus an expression of wishing for the good health for the receiver–"I trust this finds you in good health." Death more evenly impacted adults of all ages than it does today. People in their twenties, thirties, and forties recognized death as a serious possibility to cut short their life. Most adults could name at least one sister, brother, or other close relative who had died in the early years of adulthood. Widows and orphans were commonly encountered; marriages were broken primarily by death and not by divorce; and children frequently had to face the death of one or both parents before reaching maturity.

Death was more likely to visit a household during the hot summer months of August and September as malaria and intestinal infections took their toll. Infections posed the most serious threat to health and life itself. Typhoid fever, bacterial dysentery, and viral pneumonia as well as influenza took the lives of men and women in their prime of life. Accidents were a constant threat to the men of the family in their work with cultivation equipment and farm animals. An open wound or injury could quickly lead to tetanus, gangrene, or blood poisoning. Farmers on the frontier escaped the contagious diseases such as small pox, yellow fever, and cholera which plagued the urban areas. Similarly, the modern causes of death in an industrial society such as stroke, heart disease, and cancer were relatively unknown to the frontier farmer, maybe perhaps because individuals died earlier from the diseases of the day and were spared those that usually come later in life.

The most prevalent of the diseases that could take the life of a frontier family member was tuberculosis or, "consumption" as it was called at the time. One-fourth of the deaths in the middle U.S. was attributable to the frightful mortality of the disease. Probably no single disease accounted for more deaths in the period up to the Civil War.[45] A debilitating disease, tuberculosis attacked young and middle-age adults and slowly caused the death of the infected by the agonizing destruction of the lungs. Like typhoid fever, tuberculosis caught entire families in its grip and slowly caused the death of one family member after another as the infection was passed unknowingly from one person to the next.

When illness struck, the farm family members turned first to their own resources or to lay healers in the extended family or neighborhood. Rural America, out of reach of doctors, was full of persons who practiced with herbs, treating illness with preparations from their own garden. Many Appalachian farmers used guidance from the almanacs not only to plant their crops but to dose themselves with herbal remedies. Others remained wholly within the realm of folk medicine.[46] In reality, there was little difference between the practice of medicine by the nearest doctor and the remedies suggested by family and neighborhood healers. In general, the frontier farmer took his doses of herbs and roots and waited for God's will to unfold.

When treatment failed, death was inevitable. It was a common occurrence on the farmer's frontier and was experienced in the home as a part of everyday living. Family members did not die in hospitals or nursing homes but in the family bedroom with family members at the bedside. Men and boys injured in accidents were carried to the house "on a plank."[47] Neighbors came to help and participate in the funeral ceremony. They "laid out" the body, washing it, trimming the hair, and shaving the men. The body was dressed in its shroud–a long white cotton garment with open back and long sleeves. Corpses were not embalmed and funerals could not be delayed. If a carpenter was available, he was quickly employed to make a coffin. If a carpenter was not available, the body was wrapped in a blanket for burial.

If a coffin was made, the body and coffin were placed in the best front room of the house. The coffin remained open and family members and friends "sat up" with the corpse around the clock until the funeral. The funeral service was held in the home–church services were rarely held for funerals–graveside services often provided the official and formal funeral service. Before the burial, mourners gathered at the house, often full and overflowing, heard a few words of comfort, and formed a procession to the grave site. Before horse-drawn wagons were available to the community, the coffin was carried on the shoulders of the pall bearers, often stopping to rest, to the grave site.

Cemeteries were most often family plots on a hilltop near the road abutting the family farm. Later generations would combine to use the burial plot, often fencing it and caring for the grounds. In the early years of the Tennessee frontier, formal grave markers of granite or other stone simply were not available. Graves were marked at the head with a "field stone,"–a flat piece of sandstone–obviously with the intent of replacing it when granite markers were available and could be afforded by the family. Upkeep of the family plots varied with the actual frontier conditions, and local cemeteries often fell into disrepair as well-meaning families struggled to make a living and were forced by conditions to leave the family cemetery in a rustic state.

Life on the frontier farm west of the Appalachian mountains in the late eighteenth century and the first decades of the nineteenth century thus demanded a toughness and a quality of strength and endurance from those staunch plain-folk who struggled to provide for their family by working the soil. Little but hard work and the spirit of community was known by the individual born in that period and raised under the circumstances of the times. Life offered little but demanded much. The young men could dream dreams but could see little beyond the same lifestyle as their fathers. At best, young people could envision their own small farm in the future, a cabin that they would build with their own hands, and a family that they would raise to follow in their footsteps with similar values and morals. They would find strength in their faith and relied heavily on their church to provide both a promise of life after death and a community of fellowship in this life. Beyond that, life would be simple, and if one were to escape major illness or serious accident, one could hope for the support and care of family in the later years of declining health. These were the times in which Joseph Roark was born that Sunday morning in July 1813.

Chapter 5

Early Years and Adolescence
1813-1832

Joseph Roark was born on Sunday, July 4, 1813, into an already large family of six children, with a father just over forty-six and a mother of thirty-seven years. Joseph, like most of those of his generation, was born at home–in the rustic twenty-foot by twenty-foot log cabin so typical of the frontier in northeast Tennessee. His mother was grateful to give birth during the summer months–the last three children had each been born in December–when the older children could be outdoors and not crowded in the cabin. During each of the previous three births in the dead of winter, Timothy had taken the older children across the Powell River to spend a day and night with Sarah's sister, Lucy. By noon on the Sunday of Joseph's birth, the new baby had arrived and the children could be invited back into the house to see their new baby brother.

The six children greeted the new addition to the family. James, the oldest son was almost fifteen, John was thirteen, Nancy ten, Sarah (they called her "Sary" to distinguish her from her mother) was almost seven and a half, William five and a half, and Elizabeth two and a half. James and John had already witnessed a similar event four times before, so at Joseph's birth they doubtless showed little interest in their new brother and chose to remain outside and enjoy the one day of the week in which farm chores were kept to a minimum. Nancy and Sary helped with the new baby, and Sarah was assisted by several of the neighboring women including her sister Lucy. With the demands of a large family, Sarah had but a short time to recuperate from the birth and soon was back at work managing the family home. Within a few days, she would take her quill pen and log the birth of Joseph Roark into the family Bible.

Joseph was the seventh child in a family that would ultimately consist of twelve children. As a child he was seldom alone. If he spent time by himself, it was in the nearby woods or along the banks of the Powell River. At night–every night–he would move within the limited space assigned to him in the small family cabin. His early and formative years were spent closely with other family members, developing his personality while constantly surrounded by brothers and sisters within their small living quarters. Playmates were family members and only later would he move in larger circles to make friends with cousins and children from neighboring farms. Joseph was almost three when his brother Jeremiah was born April 7, 1816. Jeremiah, or Jerry as the family would call him, would be the family member closest to Joseph and the two would share their early years together. By the time Joseph was three and at an age to begin to identify with individual family members, brothers James and John were eighteen and sixteen and were viewed with respect, almost as father figures by the much younger Joseph. William, almost six years senior to Joseph, probably considered himself too mature to play with someone as young as Joseph. Sisters were around to be tolerated, and Nancy, as the eldest sister, would be close at hand to attend to hurts and bruises, but younger Jerry was to be his closest family companion.

Education for Joseph and the rest of the children was provided in the home. Both Timothy and Sarah stressed the importance of the children's ability to read and write. Sarah assumed the responsibility of instructing the children, particularly the boys, in the rudiments of reading by recognizing letters and words and of writing by carefully practicing letter forms and practical words. Reading for all the children was practiced from the family Bible and perhaps from the one or two other books the family possessed. Spelling was phonic in character—no strict rules for spelling were stressed. Mathematics was emphasized for Joseph and the other boys in detail sufficient to transact basic agrarian business. The girls of the family learned from Sarah not only to read and write but also to manage household duties such as cooking, spinning, sewing, and mending.

Timothy stressed the need for the boys to learn basic mathematics and to write in support of common business transactions. With little cash available on the frontier, business was transacted through the use and exchange of promissory notes. To succeed, even on a frontier farm, a man had to be able to write promissory notes, calculate interest, determine land area, and conduct simple business. Timothy impressed upon his sons the importance of keeping and maintaining all financial records and business notations. Reclaimed promissory notes were to be carefully preserved for possible use as receipts and future credit references. This emphasis on record preservation was not to be lost on Joseph.

Each boy of the family was encouraged to maintain a copy book in which to note events, business transactions, and other records. Copy books were homemade and space within the copy book was carefully preserved—not wasted on frivolous doodling. The copy book of Joseph's older brother James has survived and provides an example of similar copy books kept by each boy in the family. James' copy book was made by tying together loose pages of available legal-size, tablet paper and binding the booklet in homespun linen. James Roark made his first notes in his copy book in January 1818, when he was nineteen, and in it recorded personal notes and his early business deals. James also used his copy book to practice his writing skills in the production of promissory notes. The following fictitious promissory note was repeated several times in his copy book as James Roark labored to hone his writing skills:

> We or either of us promise to pay or cause to be paid unto Reed McGrew or assigns the just some of ten dollars which may be discharged in one hundred cut of good bar iron it being for value received of him. Witness my hand and seal January 13, 1818
>
> Attest: John Noproof   Signed: Samuel Stayhere (Seal)
>   Saul Fearfull   (Seal)[1]

Outside the small world of Joseph Roark on the Tennessee frontier, significant national events swiftly occurred following his birth. Joseph was just over one year old when the British burned the Capitol and president's home in Washington, D.C. One month later, as the British bombarded Fort McHenry near Baltimore, Francis Scott Key was to pen what later became the national anthem. Joseph was just over one and a half when Andrew Jackson defeated the British at New Orleans and ended the fighting in the War of 1812. Internationally, just two weeks before Joseph's second birthday, Napoleon Bonaparte was defeated near Waterloo, a small town in Belgium, and empire wars in Europe subsided. In the national elections in November 1816, James Monroe of Virginia was elected president, and when Joseph was five his parents read that Congress had recently adopted a national flag for the U.S. with thirteen red and white stripes with a blue square containing a white star for each state of the Union.

The family of Joseph's mother and father continued to grow. On April 7, 1819, exactly three years after Jerry was born, Sarah gave birth to another son whom they named Timothy Junior. Two years later, October 22, 1821, yet another son, David, was born. Unfortunately, David died soon after his birth and was buried in the small family plot southwest of the home place.[2]

Joseph and his brothers and sisters were close to their cousins, the children of James and Lucy Eastridge, whose ages closely matched their own. James and Lucy Eastridge would parent eleven children. Mary "Polly" was their first child, born April 27, 1801, and just three years younger than Sarah's eldest, James. Shortly before Timothy and Sarah Roark had lost their son David in 1821, James and Lucy Eastridge had lost a daughter, Elizabeth, who died July 19, 1820, after living only six weeks. At that time the family of James and Lucy consisted of Polly 19, Ezekiah "Squire" 17, Lawson 14, Aleon 11, Jeremiah 8, John 6, and Isaac 3.[3] The cousins provided to Joseph Roark an expanded world beyond the immediate family. He and his brothers and sisters enjoyed times together with their cousins and competed with them in the childhood games so familiar to children raised on a farm. Joseph's brother James noted in his copy book the names of Polly Eastridge and Squire Eastridge, and in one instance James noted, "Polly Eastridge–I can beet [sic] you."[4] The sons of James Eastridge were frequently mentioned as sworn chainers in the surveyor's books of

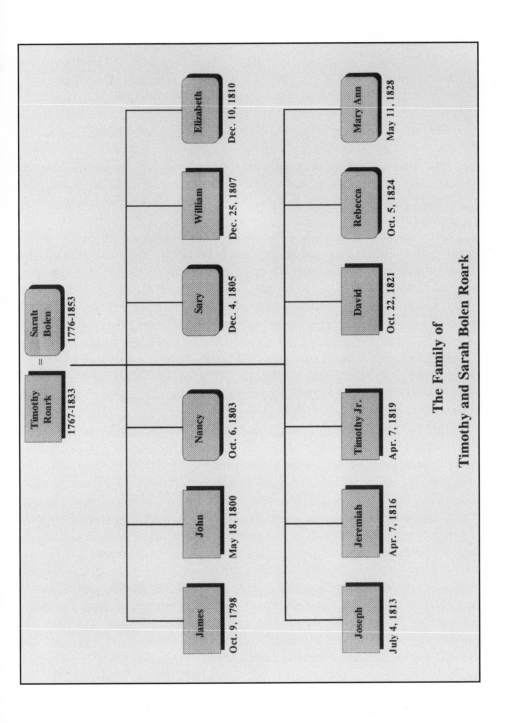

The Family of
Timothy and Sarah Bolen Roark

Claiborne County as Eastridge expanded his land holdings and help was needed by the county surveyor to assist in the boundary survey. At some time, the exact date is uncertain, James Eastridge purchased the fifty acres to the north of Timothy Roark's homestead, between Timothy and the Powell River. Eastridge was later to give this tract to his son-in-law James Ferguson, following his marriage to Polly Eastridge.[5]

From the best evidence available, it appears that Joseph's sister Sary was the first of the family to marry and leave the homestead. Sometime in late 1821 or early 1822, Sary married Larkin Ferguson.[6] Sary was just over sixteen; Larkin was older, probably over twenty-five. He had settled in Claiborne County in 1816, purchasing from John Dobbs a sixteen-acre tract on the road between the Powell River and Mulberry Gap.[7] Later, Larkin had purchased another tract of an estimated eighty acres.[8] More than likely Larkin had met Sary through her brother James, who had sold iron to him.

Before Joseph was six, his oldest brother James began working for William Sayers, a local farmer who owned land north of Little Creek near Forge Ridge.[9] Sayers operated an iron forge, and James mentioned in his copy book the sale of iron from the Sayers forge. Sayers also had two daughters, Nancy and Polly. Nancy Sayers is mentioned several times by James Roark in his copy book, indicating that perhaps there was an interest in the Sayers family beyond simple employment. After James had worked for him for a few months, Sayers apparently expanded his business endeavors since James Roark noted in his copy book that February 19, 1821, he "commenced stilling for William Sayors [sic]." Subsequent pages note the names of John Deen, William Fielder, Jack Gibson, John Sellers, and others with each name followed by the quantity of whiskey delivered to him.

Although he was learning a "trade," James, like his father and grandfather before him, yearned to find available land to claim for his own. Business opportunities outside of farming were limited on the frontier, and the number of children in the large families of that era hindered any chance of an inheritance sufficient in size to remain on the family farm. True, public land was still available in Claiborne County, but most of what was then unclaimed lay on ridges or in hollows and could not be cultivated for satisfactory farm produce. To the south, however, opportunity beckoned. The Cherokee lands recently acquired by the Calhoun Treaty of February 27, 1819, lay south of Rhea County and west of the Tennessee River in the newly created Hamilton County. Several families and young friends of James had already moved south or were talking of relocating. Jeremiah Bowling, a hunting partner of James and perhaps also a cousin from his mother's family, had frequently discussed with James the opportunities in Rhea and Hamilton Counties.[10] Additionally, Larkin and Sary Ferguson wanted to seek opportunities of available land in southern Tennessee and expressed a desire to go south with James. So in 1822, James Roark made the decision—he would go south with his sister and brother-in-law and Jeremiah Bowling to investigate the availability of land. James was twenty-four; Sary was seventeen.

When Joseph was nine, James told his parents that he was leaving home and was to seek opportunities along the Tennessee River in the southern part of the state. He and Sary were the first of the family to leave the homeplace in Claiborne County and doubtless Joseph regretted their departure. Joseph admired and looked up to James and watched with pride as his brother bid the family farewell in a manly way. Before James left, he had his mother copy from the family Bible into his copy book a record of the family births. This record would remain close to him for the rest of his life, and he would later add in his own handwriting the names and birth dates of other children of his parents. Much later, James would add to his copy book the names and birth dates of his own children.[11]

At the time that James was leaving home, Joseph's brother John was courting Margaret Gross, and in late 1823 or early 1824, John became the second of Timothy Roark's family to marry. Margaret Gross was the daughter of John Gross and granddaughter of William Gross of Hawkins County. Margaret was born April 18, 1806, and was seventeen or eighteen when she married.[12] Records indicate that her father had died before her marriage or died shortly thereafter. Her brother, Lewis, and sisters, Mary and Nancy, also lived in Claiborne County. Margaret and Lewis were to remain close and Lewis was later to move with John and Margaret to southeast Tennessee. At the death of her grandfather, William Gross, four years after her marriage, Margaret was to receive $15.00 as her part of his estate.[13] After their marriage, John Roark built a cabin on 150 acres of public land on the Powell River immediately east of the Timothy Roark home place.[14] John and Margaret's first child was a daughter, Mary Ann, born February 1, 1825.[15]

Since 1809 Timothy Roark and his family had lived on his homestead of 350 acres, but by 1823, Timothy still had not filed with the state to record his claim. In 1821, the Tennessee State Legislature, in an attempt to determine the magnitude of outstanding North Carolina and Tennessee land warrants, passed "an act to limit the time for the satisfaction of land warrants and certificates" and set the date of May 1, 1823, as the deadline for entering claims on public lands within the State of Tennessee but outside the military reservation.[16] Following the "inventory" provided by the Act of 1821, the legislature moved to set guidelines by which settlers could gain title to public lands on which they had established their homestead. In 1823, the Tennessee Legislature passed an act specifying a procedure for receiving entries on available public lands.[17] The enterer was limited to not less than fifty acres unless boundaries forced his entry to be less than fifty acres. Also the entry could not be for more than 160 acres. Anyone interested in entering a parcel had to provide the property description, in writing, to the Entry Taker for each county, "setting forth the nearest water courses, mountains, or remarkable places . . . on at least a quarter of a sheet of paper." Enterers were given three months in which to register their claims and were charged 12-1/2 cents per acre. After the three months elapsed, the then current settler would lose his preference and the parcel was subject to entry by others.

Under the statute, the Entry Taker was to copy the description of the entry, take the money required to cover the charge for the entry, and forward a copy of the entry to the elected county surveyor. The county surveyor was to survey the parcel within ninety days and return "a fair plat thereof, on not less than a half sheet of paper." Completed surveys were to be submitted to the register's office in Knoxville every six months, at which time the register was to forward the surveyed entries to the Tennessee Secretary of State for issuance of the individual grants.

With the knowledge of the new statute, Joseph's father carefully deliberated on his plans to enter the homestead parcel. Realizing, by his rough calculation, that his homestead tract seriously exceeded the upper limit of 160 acres, Joseph's father decided to enter only the fifty acres then under cultivation and on which the family cabin was located. Doubtless, Joseph's father discussed his land strategy with the family. Under the strategy planned by Timothy, he would take the risk that his remaining 300 acres would not be claimed. He would gamble that after the three months had passed for the initial entries, the State would reduce the entry charge below the then current 12-1/2 cents per acre. Joseph listened intensely to his father's strategy—he would use it himself in years to come.

James Eastridge, Joseph's uncle, used a different strategy. He decided to file an entry for his entire 150 acres, to pay the 12-1/2 cents per acre, and not to take the risk of a competing entry as Joseph's father had done. Eastridge's entry was filed April 29, 1824, and was designated Entry Number 30 in Claiborne County. The tract was surveyed June 15, 1824, by Walter Evans, County Surveyor, who used Joseph's cousins, Ezekiah and Lawson Eastridge, as chain carriers.[18]

Following the lead of his brother-in-law, Timothy Roark wrote out the description of the fifty acres that he chose to claim and filed his entry September 20, 1824. It was designated Entry Number 136. Walter Evans surveyed the tract March 6, 1825, using Joseph's brother William and John Friar as chain carriers. The survey read as follows:

> State of Tennessee, Claiborne County
> By Virtue on an Entry of No. 136 dated the 20th day of September 1824
> I have surveyed fifty acres of land for Timothy Roark on the waters of Powell River, including his improvement on the south side of the river about opposite the mouth of Little Creek,
> Beginning on a poplar on the southwest side of the improvement on the side of the river hill, Running thence East forty-three poles to a small white walnut,
> North one hundred poles (crossing the drane of a spring on a steep hillside) to a maple,
> West sixteen poles to a gum,
> North twenty-six poles to a small hicory and sourwood,

West fifty-one poles to a black oak & poplar,
South one hundred and twenty-six poles to a small sasafras and
[illegible] white oak,
East twenty-four poles crossing a spring branch to the Beginning.

Surveyed the 6th day of March 1825

Walter Evans, Surveyor
for Claiborne County

Recorded
the 13th day
of July 1825[19]

Ninety-eight entries were received in Claiborne County within the first three months following the first entry April 5, 1824, and within twelve months the ninety-eight entries at 12-1/2 cents per acre had been surveyed by Walter Evans. All ninety-eight surveys were later taken by Evans on his first trip to Knoxville to deposit them with the register for East Tennessee. The names of these first enterers reflect the influence of the Old Testament in the selection of given names. Men with names of Gideon Wright, Azariah Watson, Obediah Fields, Samuel Hamilton, Jacob Pike, Zechariah McCubbin, and Jeremiah Fields were listed as enterers in those first surveys conducted by Evans.

By the end of 1825, a significant number of entries had been submitted within the state and the Tennessee State Legislature, in a move to increase the development of public lands, reduced the charge for parcel entries to one cent per acre. On May 9, 1826, Walter Evans, County Surveyor for Claiborne County, noted in his official surveyor book that all surveys for entries at 12-1/2 cents per acre, approximately 200 in number, had been completed. He noted that "the following plats are made on entries made at one cent per acre."[20] The strategy of Joseph's father had paid off, and January 16, 1826, Timothy Roark filed Entry Number 203 at one cent per acre for 150 acres, still not the entirety of his claim but less than the maximum 160 acres that was allowed under an entry. Walter Evans surveyed the 150 acres June 2, 1826, using neighboring land owners Samuel Hamilton and Azariah Watson as chain bearers.[21] In late March 1827, Joseph's father received a grant signed by Tennessee Governor William Carroll for the 150 acres.[22]

After filing his first entry in September 1824, Joseph's father returned to Tazewell County, Virginia, on business. Sarah could not accompany Timothy on the trip since she was again pregnant, and Timothy delayed his trip until his fourth daughter, Rebecca, was born October 5, 1824. Before they had left Tazewell County in 1803, Timothy and Sarah had sold the ninety-acre river farm to William Cecil. Although the deed for that transaction noted that the tract was sold for thirty-four pounds, the receipt of which Timothy acknowledged, there evidently was some subsequent consideration

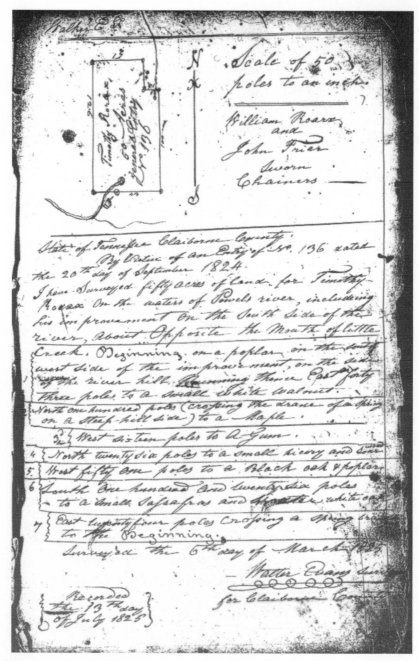

Boundary survey for the 50 acres of Land Grant Entry No. 136, March 6, 1825–the first of three entries submitted by Timothy Roark in Claiborne County. This entry was the location of the home place. The sworn chainers were William Roark, son of Timothy, and John Friar. Years later, the children of William Roark and John Friar would marry.

due from Cecil that apparently was unfulfilled. Joseph's father therefore returned to Tazewell County to again claim title to the tract. Although no record remains of a foreclosure by Timothy, he nevertheless again sold that portion of the tract–twenty acres that lay on the north side of the Clinch River–to Henry Creswell. The twenty acres contained the cabin that Joseph's grandfather and father had built following the massacre in 1780. In a deed "made the 20th day of October in the year of our Lord one thousand eight hundred and twenty-four between Timothy Roark of the County of Claiborne and State of Tennessee of the one part and Henry Creswell of the County of Tazewell and State of Virginia of the other part," Joseph's father sold the twenty acres for fifteen dollars. The deed was signed by Timothy Roark with his "X" and was attested by John Crockett, County Clerk of Tazewell County. It is interesting to note that although Sarah Roark had signed with Timothy the deed to William Cecil in 1803, she did not sign this deed to Creswell because she did not make the trip to Virginia. Apparently the husband had, in those days, the authority to convey community property. Unfortunately, Joseph's father would have additional title problems with the tract in later years.

Timothy and Sarah were to encounter sadness upon Timothy's return from Virginia in their second loss of a child. Rebecca died soon after her birth and was buried in the family plot southwest of the homestead.[23]

In 1826, when he was thirteen, Joseph Roark had his first opportunity to work for someone other than his father and receive wages for his labor. His uncle, James Eastridge, had filed a claim March 25, 1826, for twenty-five acres on both sides of the Powell River just west of the homestead tract of Joseph's father. The tract came up to be surveyed in July, and Walter Evans chose Joseph and his cousin Lawson Eastridge to be the chain bearers for the survey. The date of the survey was Saturday, July 29, just over three weeks after Joseph's thirteenth birthday.

The chain bearer's job was to drag a measuring chain between corners of the boundary survey and to accurately record the distance measured. The "chain" was a measuring device used extensively in land surveying and was made of

Location of the Timothy Roark homestead, Claiborne County, Tennessee, from picture taken in 1999 looking north toward the Powell River from the approximate south line of the 50-acre Entry No. 136.

wrought iron links eighteen inches long. The chain was sixty-six feet in length or the equivalent of four "poles" of sixteen and one-half feet each. So extensive was the use of the chain in land surveys and engineering that even today surveyors, with the graduated, 100-foot steel surveying tape, still refer to the measuring device as a "chain." By using the chain, surveyors noted call measurements in poles. Doubtless Joseph swelled with pride when chosen to be a chain bearer and was called upon to take the oath required of all "chainers." The 1806 statute by the state legislature required that:

> each chain carrier shall, before the principal or deputy surveyor, take an
> oath that he will truly and impartially measure every line, of which he is
> chain carrier, and render a true account thereof to his surveyor.[24]

Early that hot Saturday morning, Joseph listened intensely to the instructions given by Walter Evans and then proudly took the required oath. The survey was completed that same day and was placed of record, with Joseph's name as "sworn chainer" in the official county records.[25]

Surveying was not easy work. The surveyor and chainers had to locate the trees or other prominent features described in the entry as marking the corners of the tract and then had to scale the steep ridges, wade the shallow streams, and cross the rugged hollows to measure the "calls" of the survey. The chainers had to hack their way through the thick underbrush and maintain a straight line of measurement between the corners. Cane-brakes and creek bottoms were the habitat of the timber rattlesnake, copperhead, and water moccasin, and the chainers had to be continually alert. An account of the number of chains along a particular call could easily be confused, and often the chainers would have to repeat the measurement to record an accurate distance. Even experienced surveyors were often frustrated with the complexity of surveying and the difficulty in closing a complicated boundary survey. Walter Evans, in the county surveyor's official record book, recorded a comment preceding his certification of a particularly difficult survey of 220 acres for a Hugh Montgomery: "I wish I may have no more surveys like Montgomery's."[26]

In the same month that Joseph was serving as chain bearer on the Eastridge survey, his father received a letter from Henry Creswell offering to buy the remaining seventy acres of the Tazewell County river farm. Timothy Roark did not return to Tazewell County but rather made the deal by correspondence. A price of forty dollars was agreed to and a legal description and deed were drawn up. The deed was mailed to Joseph's father for execution, and on Monday, August 14, 1826, Timothy and Sarah Roark rode the thirty miles to Jonesville, county seat of Lee County, Virginia, to sign the deed before two justices of the peace in Lee County. Apparently Timothy had been advised to have the deed witnessed in a county office in Virginia rather than Tennessee and, for that reason, he and Sarah made the longer trip to Jonesville in lieu of the much shorter trip to their own county seat.[27] In any event,

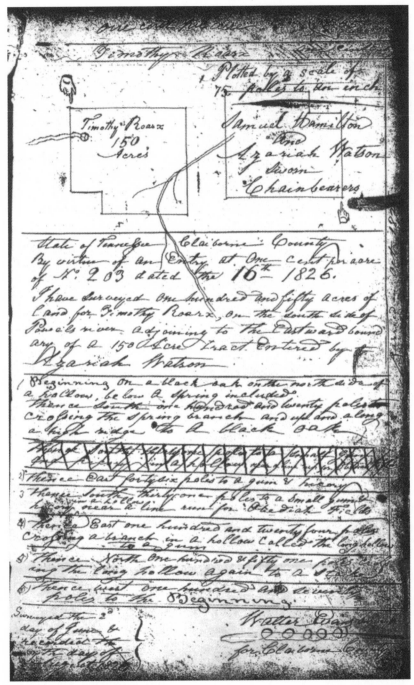

Boundary survey for the 150 acres of Land Grant Entry No. 203, June 2, 1826–
second of three entries submitted by Timothy Roark, located southwest of the first entry.

Joseph's father considered himself free of all real estate in Virginia. Unfortunately, this was not to be the case and, within four years, Timothy Roark was to employ an attorney in Tazewell County, Virginia, to clear the land title for Henry Creswell.[28]

Although communication was difficult and mail service slow, Joseph's parents maintained contact with Joseph's brother James, then in Rhea County. With the declaration by the U.S. Post Office in 1823 that rivers and other waterways were considered "post roads," mail service was provided to Rhea County via the Tennessee River before roads were available for postal routes.[29] James wrote that he had settled on the very southern edge of Rhea County very close to the line with Hamilton County. James found work and supported himself through the trade he had learned under William Sayers in Claiborne County–that of operating a still. His business consisted of producing and distributing the whiskey, keeping records in his copy book. He developed a market for his product and maintained a list of steady customers that he supplied on a regular basis. This gave him an opportunity to intermingle with the local farming community and expanded his contacts within the area. A regular customer on his distribution list was William Blythe, who operated a ferry across the Tennessee and Hiwassee Rivers at their confluence.[30] William Blythe was to have a significant impact on the life of Joseph's eldest brother and on Joseph Roark himself.

William Blythe was a well-to-do businessman and was influential within the local community. Blythe was eight years older than James Roark and was the fifth child of John and Martha Chastain Blythe of South Carolina. When he was nineteen, William Blythe married Nancy "Nannie" Fields, the daughter of prominent Cherokee Richard Fields.[31] Like some of the other white males in the region, Blythe cast his lot with the Cherokees and decided to rear his three children as Indians. Between 1815 and 1817, the Blythe family had begun the operation of the ferry across the Tennessee River just south of its confluence with the Hiwassee. In 1817, Blythe was one of nearly 160 men who applied for 640-acre reservations under the 1817 treaty with the Cherokees. His application, made "in the right of his wife," was approved, and the five-member family made their home on the "south side of the Tennessee River" near their ferry. Soon Blythe's Ferry had earned a reputation as "the most important crossing between Ross's Landing (Chattanooga) and Knoxville."[32]

William's brother Elijah and his sister Nancy's husband, Samuel Fry, were close associates of James Roark and were on his distribution list of steady customers. Of more importance, William Blythe had a younger sister by the name of Jerusha who would be mentioned frequently in James' letters to his parents in Claiborne County.

James wrote that after he arrived in Rhea County he became a member of the local militia and was assigned to Captain Jackson's Company. He wrote of two friends serving with him under Jackson, John Roddy and Samuel Fry.[33] He hunted frequently with Jeremiah Bowling and also did some work shucking corn for a

Zachariah Gibson. Also, James assisted Larkin and Sary Ferguson in "raising a house," in which he probably resided with the Fergusons for a period of time.[34] In a letter in the autumn of 1825, James wrote that he was married–to Jerusha Blythe. He had obtained the license on August 24th and on Thursday, September 1, 1825, he and Jerusha were married by Rev. Thomas Wall, a local minister.[35] James was twenty-seven at the time of his marriage. Jerusha was just shy of nineteen.

Joseph's brother John, at the time of his marriage to Margaret Gross, had built his cabin on 150 acres of public land and had marked the corners to stake his claim. On April 7, 1826, John entered the 150 acres, paid the one-cent-per-acre fee, and was assigned Entry Number 350. By late summer, Walter Evans got around to surveying the tract, and August 10, 1826, the tract was surveyed using Timothy Roark and Joseph's brother William as the chain carriers for the survey. John Roark's 150 acres was just 400 feet east of the Timothy Roark family homestead and was located on a steep ridge overlooking the Powell River. The tract boundary crossed the river

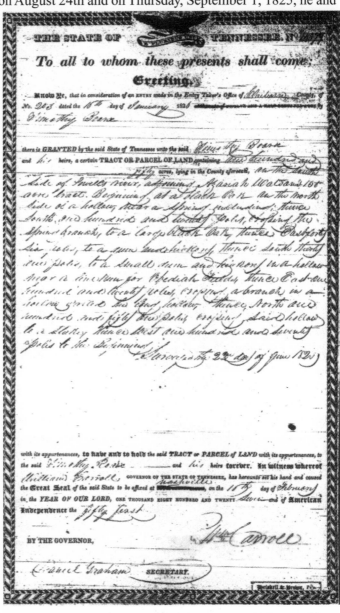

Land Grant to Timothy Roark, February 10, 1827, signed by Tennessee Governor William Carroll, for Entry No. 203 for 150 acres in Claiborne County.

and provided river frontage on both banks of the river. Little of the tract could be cultivated, probably not more than five to ten acres.[36]

From Rhea County, James wrote that Jerusha had given birth on October 23, 1826, to their first child, whom they named Timothy in honor of James' father.[37] James further wrote that he was assigned in 1827 to Captain Russell's Company of militia,[38] and that he was at that time attempting to buy land in order that he could support his family by farming rather than by operating a still. James later wrote that he had purchased 184 acres in Rhea County and that in 1828 he had been elected as captain of the militia company, no small honor for a man just thirty years old.[39] Serving under him in the militia company of fifty men were William Blythe, Samuel Fry, Jeremiah Bowling, Charles McDonald, and John Roddy.

Joseph was just over fifteen when his eldest sister Nancy married James Richardson and made plans to leave the homestead. Nancy was twenty-five when she married and, as the oldest sister, had been a second mother to Joseph. She had remained at the homestead much longer than most girls of that era, many of whom married in their late teens. But Nancy waited to marry and helped at home with the family as Joseph grew and matured. Nancy and James Richardson were married, probably at the homestead, on Sunday, July 15, 1828.[40] James was four years younger than Nancy and was born October 18, 1807,[41] the youngest of seven children of George W. Richardson and his wife, a Miss Weaver before her marriage. His parents had moved to Claiborne County in 1815 from Pennsylvania, settling near Blair's Creek, south of Timothy Roark. James and Nancy lived at the homestead with her parents for at least the first two years of their marriage. Their first child was born April 10, 1829–a boy whom they named George Washington Richardson after his paternal grandfather.[42]

Another wedding was held at the homestead in 1828 when Joseph's sister Elizabeth, at the age of seventeen, married Thomas Ellison. Ellison was the son of Robert and Elizabeth Ellison of Ohio[43] and had apparently come to Claiborne County in 1815 from Kentucky. Ellison was a farmer and a blacksmith and was thirty-three years old when he and Elizabeth were married. Following their marriage, Thomas and Elizabeth lived for five years near the rest of Elizabeth's family[44] before Ellison built his forge and cabin at Forge Ridge just north of the James Eastridge 150-acre homestead.[45] Their first child, Timothy, named after Elizabeth's father, was born in 1829.[46]

As Joseph saw his brothers James and John and sisters Nancy, Sary, and Elizabeth leave home, he and William were then the oldest children at the homestead. Joseph was closer to Jeremiah than to William, but all three boys enjoyed the additional space in the homestead available to them now that five of the family had left home. The family continued to grow, however, and on Sunday, May 11, 1828, a daughter, Mary Ann, was born to Timothy and Sarah. At the time of Mary Ann's birth, Timothy was sixty-two and Sarah was fifty-two. Mary Ann was to be their last.

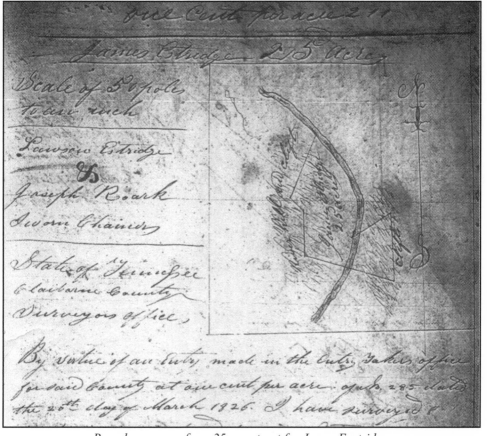

Boundary survey for a 25-acre tract for James Eastridge,
brother-in-law to Timothy Roark, July 29, 1826. The sworn chainers were cousins Lawson
Eastridge and Joseph Roark. Joseph had just celebrated his thirteenth birthday when he
was employed to serve as chainer under county surveyor Walter Evans.

In the summer of 1828, just over a month after Mary Ann's birth, Timothy and Sarah were to share in the sorrow of James and Lucy Eastridge when Sarah's sister and brother-in-law lost two of their children within a period of one week. Lucy had given birth to her last child, Louisay Jane, on March 1, 1828. Four months later, her fourth child, Aleon 17, and the sixth, John 14, were dead. Aleon died June 29, and John, July 5.[47] The cause of death is unknown. John Eastridge was only a year younger than Joseph Roark and Joseph had celebrated his fifteenth birthday only the day before he went to the home of his aunt and uncle to attend the brief service for his cousin.

At the encouragement of both parents but particularly his mother, Joseph continued his education at home. He doubtless practiced his writing in his copy book as his brother James had done and learned early the mechanics of writing promissory notes and other business documents. His father provided the understanding of basic mathematics necessary for agrarian business, and Joseph seemed to possess an innate business sense with an eye toward land acquisition and effective utilization. The few books and newspapers that were available and, of course, the Bible provided him opportunity to practice reading. In regard to his parent's participation in politics and community affairs, we have little information available and no way of knowing how Joseph, his father, and mother followed activities outside the confines of the ridges and valleys along the Powell. We do know, however, that his father was involved in community affairs, serving on juries in Tazewell when named,[48] and interacting within the farming community. A safe assumption would be that current events were discussed at home, and Joseph grew under the influence of debate on current issues then facing the frontier farmer and small landowner.

Opportunities for the small landowner abounded as democracy flourished in the years following the War of 1812. The country, including the more-or-less frontier area of Claiborne County, was young and growing, conscious of its increasing strength, and confident of the future. Thanks in many ways to U.S. Supreme Court decisions that were in harmony with the democratic trends of the times, the courts protected the small property owner. The opportunities for the acquisition of private property on a scale not seen in the world prior to Joseph's era were not then limited to a few, but were open to the individual choices of the many.

From the limited number of newspapers, and from the community gossip that Joseph and his father would have heard in their infrequent visits to Tazewell, Joseph would have learned in 1820, when he was seven, of the death of England's King George III, the despot of the revolutionary period. In early 1824, Joseph's father explained the reports of President Monroe's message to Congress on December 2, 1823, that was later to become the Monroe Doctrine. The United States, with its industrial growth and expanding frontiers, was to be independent of European interference. The community gossip in late 1824 was primarily devoted to the national election. Claiborne County, as well as all of Tennessee, expressed its disappointment and frustration in the election of John Quincy Adams as president over its own Andrew Jackson of Nashville. The citizens of Tennessee were, nevertheless, optimistic as Tennessee continued to provide additional land opportunities to settlers. Land was available, since by 1819, up to eight treaties with the Cherokees had opened lands surrendered by the Cherokee Nation. By the time Joseph was six years old, all of Tennessee had been cleared of Indian claims except the Cherokees in the southeastern corner of the state. Joseph doubtless heard at an early age of these opportunities and, like his father and grandfather before him, eagerly awaited the time when he would be old enough to seek his own fortune in the great western and southern expansion in the U.S.

The growth and expansion within the country was in full swing as Joseph entered his teenage years. From the time of his birth in 1813 until he was eight in

1821, six new states had entered the Union–Indiana, Mississippi, Illinois, Alabama, Maine, and Missouri. With the addition of Missouri under the Missouri Compromise, twenty-three states then made up the Union. Population growth within the new states was phenomenal for that time. Tennessee grew from a population of 261,727 in 1810, to 422,823 in 1820, and by 1830 had a population of 681,904. During the same twenty-year period, Kentucky grew by 70% to almost 700,000, Ohio grew by over 300% to 940,000, and Missouri, then the most western state in the Union, grew from just over 20,000 to 140,455[49] By 1820, Florida had been surrendered to the United States by Spain who acknowledged the existence of a Spanish-American ownership all the way to the Pacific. Opportunity abounded for the ambitious and courageous. Joseph Roark possessed both qualifications.

Unfortunately during Joseph's teenage years, small dark clouds began to appear on the horizon of the expanding nation. These dark clouds of slavery and sectionalism were to grow and would sweep over the country in violent storms of sectional conflict during Joseph's life. In the 1820s, in spite of the new democratic freedoms and the strong spirit of nationalism, a three-way struggle among North, South, and the West was in evidence. Political decisions on the national level were influenced by the perspectives of the northern manufacturer, of the southern plantation owner, and of the small western independent farmer. The sectional divisions were most obvious in the presidential race of 1824 in which Andrew Jackson, Henry Clay, William Crawford, and John Quincy Adams competed for the presidential office. The selection of Adams by the House of Representatives over Jackson, son of poor Scotch-Irish immigrants, resulted in charges of bargain and corruption. Sectionalism was born, and a two-party system was begun.

Slavery had existed in the southern states since the early days of the Colonies. With the growth of the cotton and tobacco industries, the demand for slave labor increased as large plantation owners sought to meet labor requirements by the importation of slaves. Abolition societies began in the north in the late 1820s, and slavery quickly became a national issue that influenced the admission of new states as attempts were made to balance the number of free and slave states. In 1821, under the Missouri Compromise, Missouri was admitted as a slave state while, as a compromise, slavery was prohibited north of a specified latitude. Slavery as a "peculiar and powerful interest" became a divisive national issue as Joseph Roark entered adulthood.

While sectionalism may have been an issue in Claiborne County following Andrew Jackson's defeat in 1824, slavery most certainly was not. The combination of small farms and large families in Claiborne County made slavery of little economic value. The family provided all the labor necessary for the small farm. Slavery was simply not an issue of any interest in the late 1820s to Joseph Roark or other members of his family and, when considered, probably conflicted with the freedom-loving, independent attitude of the Scotch-Irish who shunned the responsibility of large, management-intensive plantations. This was also generally true of the rest of Tennessee beyond Claiborne County. Even with the large cotton farms in West Tennessee, over 65 percent of the white population of Tennessee just prior to the Civil War owned no slaves.[50]

National issues had little effect on the strategy of Joseph's father in acquiring clear title to his homestead property. The two entries made in 1824 and 1826 covered 200 acres, and when the grants were received, the latest in 1827, Joseph's father had clear title to almost two-thirds of his homestead farm. In June 1828, Timothy Roark entered the remaining 150 acres, paid the fee of one cent per acre, and was assigned Entry Number 589. The survey by the county surveyor was completed within the required ninety days and tied all three parcels of the homestead together. Entry Number 136 for fifty acres lay in the northern portion of the farm, Entry Number 589 of 150 acres was generally in the center but wrapped around the initial entry to include a small panhandle to the north, and Entry Number 203 of 150 acres was at the extreme southwest corner of the homestead tract.[51] Joseph's father had successfully stayed within the statutory requirements in obtaining grants for the homestead parcels but yet had paid the minimum price when balanced against the risk of competing claimants. In following his father through the process of timing the submission of entries for public land, Joseph was gaining valuable insight and experience that was to serve him well in future years.

Unfortunately, Timothy Roark's sale of real estate in Tazewell County, Virginia, continued to present title issues and boundary problems. In January 1830, Timothy received word from Henry Creswell, who had purchased the river farm four years earlier, that the adjacent landowner, one William Deskins, had encroached on a portion of the river farm and had questioned in court Creswell's claim to the title for a portion of the tract. While the record is unclear as to whether Timothy returned to Tazewell County or employed an attorney to represent him, nevertheless, in February 1830, a suit against William Deskins was filed on Timothy's behalf in the Chancery Court of Tazewell County. On the day of the trial, the court rendered a judgement that the suit would be dismissed at the next term of the court since "the Plaintiff is not an inhabitant of this state [and] on the motion of the Defendant, by his attorney [that the case be dismissed] unless security for the payment of such costs and damages as may be awarded the Defendant be given by the Plaintiff." Since Timothy was out of state and the suit was in danger of being thrown out, Timothy's attorney approached Henry Creswell about providing the necessary security in lieu of Timothy. Creswell agreed, and the court record of the following day indicates that the Plaintiff "shall pay and satisfy all such costs as shall be awarded against him . . . or the said Henry Creswell shall do it for him."[52]

The case of "Timothy Roark, heir-at-law of James Roark versus William Deskins" was heard in the July term of the Chancery Court. The court records note:

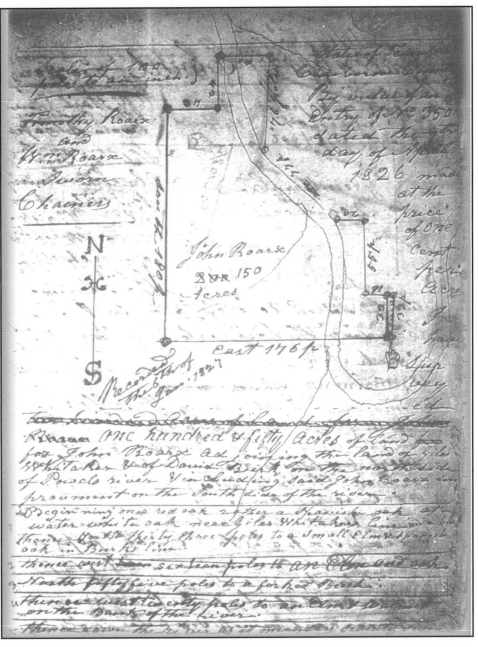

Boundary survey for 150 acres of Land Grant Entry No. 350, April 7, 1826, for John Roark, son of Timothy and Sarah Bolen Roark. The tract was located along the Powell River southeast of the Timothy Roark homestead. The sworn chainers, interestingly, were John's father and his brother William.

And on the motion of the Defendant it is ordered that the Surveyor of Tazewell County do go upon the land in controversy on the fifteenth day of November next if fair, if not, the next fair day, and survey and lay out the same as either party shall require and return three fair plats and reports thereof to court and that any one of the Justices of the said County do then and there meet him and examine and take the depositions of such witnesses as shall be produced by any of the parties which are to be returned with the said plats and reports and the Sheriff of said County is to attend the said survey and remove force if any shall be offered.[53]

Court records neither reflect the outcome of the survey nor contain any depositions that were taken. The case came before the Chancery Court again in the September 1831 term. In the interim, William Deskins had died and the suit was revived against John Deskins, heir-at-law of William Deskins. Under the decision of the court, a writ of fieri facias was awarded to Timothy Roark as plaintiff.[54] The writ of fieri facias is "in practice, a writ of execution commanding the sheriff to levy and collect the amount of the judgement stated."[55] Apparently, the court later ruled in favor of John Deskins or at least assigned court costs to Timothy Roark and/or Henry Creswell in the amount of $19.22. The court costs were paid to James William Witten, Deputy for John Cecil, Sheriff of Tazewell County, in September 1833.[56] Although it is not clear who actually paid the court costs, probability is quite strong that the costs to settle the title and boundary issues were paid by Henry Creswell. Unfortunately, the publicity surrounding the lawsuit against Deskins would result in other title issues being raised before Creswell was to pay the court costs involved in the Deskins matter.

In 1830, James Roark wrote from his home in Rhea County that his second son, John B., was born January 19, 1829,[57] and that he was elected again as a captain of militia in 1829.[58] After James' purchase of his farm land, he was eligible for jury duty and was called to serve on a jury three times in 1828 and twice in 1829. In one jury assignment in 1828, he wrote that he served on the grand jury in indicting Edward Templeton for disrupting a church service conducted by Ansolem Dearing. The grand jury found that Templeton "did wickedly and fatally bent to disrupt others desirous of devoting themselves to the service of the Deity" and "by loud words and gestures used and directed to a certain Ansolem Dearing . . . did disturb, interrupt, and annoy said Congregation."[59] James wrote that both Templeton and Dearing had served with him in 1824 in Captain Jackson's Company of militia.[60] James also wrote of the death of his brother-in-law, Larkin Ferguson, with whom he had come from Claiborne County. After Ferguson's death, the County Court appointed Sary as administratrix of the estate. Since such an appointment required a bond to insure accurate accounting of the estate, James and Jeremiah Bowling had posted a bond of $300 on Sary's behalf.[61] James wrote that Sary and her three young children, two daughters and one son, the eldest less than seven, were living with James and

Jerusha.[62] Sary was twenty-four when she became a widow.

When he was twenty, Joseph's brother William had a disagreement with one Evan Burk over some now unknown issue. For whatever the reason, William brought suit against Burk in early 1827. Apparently William, as plaintiff, softened his position when he appeared in court and withdrew his suit after some initial discussions with the defendant. The County Court on Tuesday, June 19, 1827, ordered the case dismissed but also ordered that William reimburse Burk for "his costs in this behalf expended for which execution may issue."[63] William, and perhaps also his younger brother Joseph, learned from the court's decision and gained experience with the court system.

Shortly thereafter, in early 1828, William left the homeplace when he married Nancy Cox. Nancy was the daughter of Aaron Cox and Polly Hill Cox, both natives of Stokes County, North Carolina.[64] Aaron Cox owned the land east of Timothy Roark between the Roark tract and the Powell River. Nancy was the second of six daughters of Aaron Cox who, for a wedding present, gave William and Nancy twenty-five acres of his tract along the Powell. Cox retained the south portion of his tract establishing a "conditional line" between the two properties.[65] William and Nancy developed their home on the twenty-five acres and began their family. Their son John was born in 1828 and daughter Cynthia in early 1830.[66]

Shortly before his eighteenth birthday, in the spring of 1831, Joseph told his parents that he planned to leave the homestead. Doubtless he had been encouraged by his brother James who had written the family about local agitation for removal of the Cherokees and the possibilities of available public lands in the southeast corner of the state. James had, directly and indirectly, offered to provide Joseph with a place to live until he could establish his own home and had written that work was readily available on the surrounding farms on Sale Creek in Rhea County. Joseph would travel south with his cousin, Ezekiah "Squire" Eastridge, who was ten years older than Joseph and who also saw opportunities in land in southeast Tennessee.[67] One day that spring of 1831, Joseph bid goodbye to his mother and father; the other members of the family at home: Jeremiah, his closest playmate in the childhood years, Timothy Jr., and Mary Ann, the baby, now almost three; Aunt Lucy and Uncle James Eastridge and his Eastridge cousins; his married brothers, John and William; and his married sisters Nancy Richardson and Elizabeth Ellison. The last farewells were to his parents. Joseph was not to see his father or mother again.

Joseph traveled by road to Knoxville. From Knoxville he and Ezekiah traveled down the Tennessee River to Washington, then the county seat of Rhea County, located on Washington Creek on the west side of the Tennessee River. Washington had been chosen as the county seat in 1808 after the creation of Rhea County, and by 1830, Washington had become an important river port. When Joseph first arrived in Washington, he saw the two-story frame courthouse, thirty feet square, built in 1809 at a cost of $936.25. He heard talk in the town that a new brick courthouse was planned to accommodate the growth of the county, which by the time Joseph arrived, had reached a population of over 8,000, only slightly smaller in number than Claiborne County. On the city square, Joseph also noticed the old county jail constructed of logs, with double walls filled in between with small stones. Adjacent to the old jail, Joseph saw the pillory and stocks used to punish recalcitrant prisoners.[68] The new jail, then in use, was a more substantial structure and contained a dungeon for the more difficult residents. Joseph was doubtless impressed with the Monmouth Presbyterian Church, the first church in Rhea County, that had its own building dedicated solely for worship.[69] The large church building was impressive to Joseph since he was unaccustomed to church buildings other than the brush arbors used in camp meetings in Claiborne County.

From Washington, Joseph traveled southwest, parallel to and east of Walden Ridge, a distance of just over fifteen miles passing over into Hamilton County after the first six miles. Asking directions as he went, Joseph located his brother's farm on Sale Creek approximately three and one-half miles west of the Tennessee River. Sale Creek, named by frontiersmen in 1779 following the "sale" of captured supplies previously furnished by British agents to the Cherokees to stimulate Cherokee warfare against the settlers,[70] rises west of its mouth on the Tennessee for just over three miles, then turns almost due north through the rest of its watershed. James Roark's farm lay on the west bank of Sale Creek in that section of the creek that runs north and south, probably near the present community of Graysville.[71] James had purchased the farm in 1827[72] when it was in Rhea County, but by the time Joseph arrived in 1831, county lines had been adjusted and his brother's farm was then in Hamilton County.[73] Joseph was greeted by James and Jerusha and their two children, Timothy, age 5, and John B., age 2, and by his sister Sary with her three children.

Joseph found work on adjacent farms, saved his money, met friends of James, became acquainted with Jerusha's family, and saw again his cousin Jeremiah Bowling. Through James and Jerusha, Joseph got to know Jerusha's brothers, William and Elijah, her sister-in-law Nancy Fields Blythe, and her sisters Elizabeth and Sarah. In addition to the Blythes, Joseph also became acquainted with a local family by the name of Carr, since living on the farm adjacent to that of James Roark was John Carr.[74] Carr was almost thirty and was the son of Samuel Carr, an active trader/merchant whose place was separated from John Carr's by the farm of George Washington Clingan. Of utmost importance was the fact that Samuel Carr had a daughter by the name of Juda Ann. Family tradition tells the story that Joseph Roark first met Juda Carr when they were both involved in gathering muscadine grapes growing wild in the Sale Creek area.[75] Certainly the location of the James Roark cabin adjacent to that of Juda's brother John provided ample opportunity for Joseph to know of Juda and to arrange an "accidental" meeting. At the time of their meeting, Juda was living with her parents, Samuel and Margaret Carr. As Samuel Carr was then soon to become the father-in-law of Joseph Roark, his life to that point, as we understand it today, should be discussed.

Samuel Carr was sixty-one when Joseph Roark first met him in 1831. Carr's wife, Margaret, was fifty-nine. Both were natives of Virginia[76] and apparently had met and married before leaving the Commonwealth. History has provided no record of Samuel's father or the area of Virginia in which he was raised. Samuel was a young boy during the Revolutionary War and was eleven when the Battle of Yorktown terminated the conflict with the British. The first recorded biographical information on Samuel Carr is that of a promissory note, dated August 20, 1795, when he was twenty-five, for one hundred dollars written in favor of Samuel by James Carr, probably a brother. On the reverse side of the promissory note is the multiplication table, neatly written and signed by Jean Carr followed by a "Table of Pence" equating the new U.S. Dollar to the British pound sterling.[77] It is unclear whether the tables were added before or after the promissory note, nor is the identity of Jean Carr known. More than likely Jean Carr was a sister to Samuel and James and had used the paper to practice her math in her schooling, and later James used the reverse side to record his promissory note for the one hundred dollars.

Evidence suggests that Samuel was raised in tidewater Virginia or at least east of the Blue Ridge. His father most likely was not of the landed gentry in the tidewater area, and Samuel was forced to pursue his fortune either on the Virginia frontier or elsewhere. He chose to relocate, as other Virginians were then doing, to Georgia which, following the end of the Revolutionary War, was seeking settlers for its western frontier. Georgia apparently offered a better opportunity than the Virginia frontier. From the limited data on Samuel Carr, it appears that he left Virginia around 1800, when he was thirty and Margaret twenty-eight.

Around 1800 or 1801, Samuel and his family, along with his brother James and wife Anne, left Virginia and sailed to Georgia, first to Savannah and then up the Savannah River to Augusta and Richmond County. By 1800, Georgia had grown to a population of 162,000 up from 82,000 in 1790. The western two-thirds of Georgia in 1800 was still in the hands of the Cherokee and Creek Indians, although treaties with the two nations had opened an area for settlement as far west as the Oconee River.[78] The Carr families spent some time in Augusta but their time of arrival and departure is obscure. Samuel Carr was not a farmer and apparently had little desire to own land or to farm. No record remains to evidence that Carr ever owned any land, even a city lot. He was a trader and made his living by buying and selling livestock, cotton, general merchandise, and, regrettably, even slaves. While in Augusta, Samuel Carr did some trading with a George Keith to whom Carr signed a promissory note on January 15, 1805, in the amount of twenty dollars "for value received." The note was to be paid within three days, indicating that Carr's trading was based on turning his merchandise within a short period of time, probably within a matter of days.[79] Merchandising like that engaged in by Samuel Carr was more important than manufacturing in the Georgia economy of the period as goods moved into

Savannah and were distributed through Augusta to the frontier.[80]

The best evidence suggests that Samuel Carr was in Augusta between 1802 and 1805.[81] In late 1805, Carr decided to move inland to the area of the Tennessee River in Tennessee. Between the Oconee and Tennessee Rivers, a distance of 200 miles, was the land of the Cherokee Nation. The Carrs' move was doubtless encouraged by the new federal road constructed from Augusta to the northwest corner of Georgia. Begun as a federal project, the project was completed in 1805 through state appropriations. Unopposed by the Cherokees, the new road encouraged the movement of settlers, like the Carrs, from Virginia and the Carolinas.[82]

By 1806, the Carrs had settled in what was to become Rhea County in Tennessee, but what was then Roane County. The land in which the Carrs settled was within the area reserved for the Cherokees in previous treaties. Nevertheless, the Tennessee Legislature had approved in 1801 the formation of Roane County, which included Cherokee lands. Carr settled his family near Sale Creek and began to merchandize goods brought from Augusta. Carr was to make repeated trips to Augusta for the apparent purpose of obtaining other merchandise to sell.

The family of Samuel and Margaret is difficult to reconstruct. From the best evidence available, it appears that the first three children—James, John, and Jane—were born while the Carrs were in Augusta, and the remaining four were born in Rhea County. The estimated order and years of birth of the Carr children are as follows:

James Carr	1800
John Carr	1802
Jane Carr Mahan	1804
Alfred Carr	1806
- Carr Medley	1808
Margaret Carr Brooks	1810
Juda Ann Carr Roark	1813[83]

Personal records of Samuel Carr preserved through the Carr and Roark families present a vague picture of the merchandising business conducted by Carr. In early 1807, Carr received a written receipt for funds paid to a Colleen Campbell for merchandise purchased probably in Augusta.[84] On October 18, 1807, Carr received a promissory note in payment in the "full sum or quantity of five hundred weight of merchantable cotton of the first quality."[85]

By 1808, the State of Tennessee, through a bill passed by its legislature October 29, 1807, had created Rhea County with the county seat at Washington. Within two years of the creation of Rhea County, Samuel Carr was to experience the court system of the new county. In January 1810, a Joseph Dunham filed suit against Carr in a civil case but one in which a bail was required of Carr. James Carr assisted his brother in providing the bail, but on January 25, 1810, the court ruled that Dunham was to recover from Samuel Carr "his costs in entering up and carrying into execution this judgement."[86] Unfortunately, tragedy was to strike the Carrs that same year when Samuel's brother James died in June. His widow, Anne, for reasons unknown to us today, did not seek Samuel's help with the estate settlement but rather requested Henry Airheart to serve as administrator. Since James died intestate, Airheart's expertise was probably required since Samuel had little experience in the settlement of estates. Samuel did assist by providing the necessary bond for Airheart.[87]

Following his brother's death, Samuel Carr continued his business in Rhea County. On June 9, 1809, he received payment of three dollars from Irby Holt through David Gilbreath in a three-way transaction in which Gilbreath owed Holt for care of his horse during the spring, and Holt owed Carr three dollars for merchandise received from him. In the transaction, Gilbreath was to pay Carr directly the sum of three dollars.[88] Carr also supported the local school system run by John Rawlings in 1811. Although public schools did not exist at that time and all private schools were supported by parents of enrolled students, it appears that the county officials assisted in collecting amounts due the local schoolteacher. On November 23, 1811, Samuel Carr made a partial payment on his contract with John Rawlings and received a receipt for $2.50 from the local constable, Abner Witt.[89] The school fee doubtless was applied to the schooling for one of Carr's children.

In late 1812, Carr again experienced the local court system as he was the defendant in a suit brought by Thomas Clark, a large landowner of over 600 acres in Rhea County.[90] The issue between Clark and Carr is not of record; however, Carr lost the case and was forced to pay court costs and possibly other punitive damages. Sheriff Miller Francis issued on January 12, 1813, a receipt to Carr for costs of the sheriff's office in the lawsuit.[91] It was a less than auspicious beginning for the year in which Carr's youngest daughter was born. A few short months after settlement of the lawsuit by Clark, Juda Ann Carr was born to Samuel and Margaret Carr. Juda Ann was to be their last child. Samuel was forty-three, Margaret forty-one, when Juda Ann was born.[92]

Carr continued to make his living by trading, and records seem to confirm that he made frequent trips to Augusta, Georgia, to obtain merchandise to sell or trade. In such a trip he made in 1813, Carr purchased two slaves he brought back to Rhea County to sell. Slaves were not an important element in the area of Rhea County in 1813 as cotton was not a major crop and other farm products did not justify the employment of slaves. Also, most families could not afford slaves and found it unthinkable to acquire other mouths to feed when feeding their own family required their full effort. Only the wealthy could afford the economy of slaves. In early July 1813, Carr approached William Blythe concerning the two slaves brought from Augusta, and on July 10, Blythe purchased the two women.[93] Carr made subsequent trips to Augusta either on business for himself or in the employ of others in Rhea

County. In March 1816, he made the trip at the request of William Low, and on April 18, after his return, he received $39.10 from Low for his "expenses at Augusta."[94] He returned to Augusta in 1819 to purchase goods for William Smith, landowner and farmer of 166 acres in Rhea County.[95] For this trip Carr was paid $75.00 on March 7, 1819, "in part pay for hawling [sic] a load from Augusta at the rate of seven dollars per hundred weight."[96]

Through to his trips to Augusta for contract purchases, Samuel Carr continued to support his family as a merchant and trader. In May 1814, he sold livestock to James Cannon for $176.00, which sale was recorded in the deed records of the county[97] and witnessed by James C. Mitchell, a farmer in Rhea County with 168 acres.[98] Carr apparently developed steady customers and accommodated his regulars in the manner typical of merchants in that day. In January 1819, he received, and no doubt accommodated, the following request:

> Mr. Samuel Carr
> Sir, you will please let this little boy have one bushel of salt and I will settle with you for it for I have promast to let him have a bushel before you came hoam.
>> this 27 day of Jan 1819
>> Limeen Geren[99]

Carr also developed trading relations with the Cherokees south of the Tennessee River in both Tennessee and Georgia. He apparently made many friends in the Cherokee Nation and was respected as an honest trader of goods and merchandise. The Cherokees dealt fairly with Carr on several occasions. In 1823, the Supreme Court of the Cherokee Nation ruled that "on a plea of debt, it is the opinion of the Court that Bushey Head pay unto Samuel Carr sixty-five dollars."[100]

Samuel Carr developed a close personal friendship with William Blythe. Evidence suggested both men supported each other in business ventures and responded to requests for personal favors. One letter which has been preserved illustrates this relationship:

> Mr. Boon Mays
> Dear sir, after my compliments, I will inform you that it is out of my power to come back as I expected but I want you to send me my papers and 50 weight of picked cotton by the bearer Samuel Carr and I will settle with you when I see you at the annuity and in so doing you will confer a lasting favor on your friend.
>> Wm. Blythe
> March 10th 1818[101]

Blythe was to be a supportive friend to Carr as well. In 1820, by which time the county lines had been adjusted and the Carrs were residing in Hamilton County in lieu of Rhea County, Samuel Carr was the loser in two judgements against him brought to court first by McCarty and McGrew and then by Chrispen and Shelton.

On July 18, 1820, to satisfy the judgements against Carr, Charles Gamble, sheriff of Hamilton County, sold to William Blythe in an apparent public auction "Samuel Carr's two-thirds of a parcel of wheat and rye and eight head of sheep." Apparently Blythe bought the wheat, rye, and sheep at market prices to help his friend Carr. Inasmuch as Carr kept the sheriff's public sale order in his papers would seem to indicate that, following the public sale, Blythe returned the wheat, rye, and sheep to Carr.[102]

Blythe's help to Carr was especially beneficial since Carr continued to be involved almost regularly with the local court system. In October 1814, he had been taken to court by Jacob Schultz and, in the judgement of the court, was to compensate Schultz for damages.[103] The settlement of the judgement was witnessed by Samuel B. Mitchell, taxpayer in Rhea County.[104] On May 3, 1819, Carr paid to his friend, Miller Francis, sheriff of Rhea County, the full amount of a judgement against Carr in a suit brought by Andrew Bayer.[105]

Carr was not always the defendant in court cases. In the summer of 1830, almost one year before he was to make the acquaintance of the young Joseph Roark, Carr brought suit against William Carr, assumed to be his nephew, in the county court of Hamilton County. The issue and even the judgement of the court in the lawsuit is unknown; nevertheless, Samuel Carr paid to the court on June 10, 1830, the sum of $1.00 as part payment of his share of the court costs.[106]

This then was the Samuel Carr who was to become the father-in-law of Joseph Roark. From all evidence available to us today, supported also by family tradition, the father of Juda Ann Carr and his son-in-law were to be close throughout the remainder of their adult lives.

The courtship between Joseph and Juda began in late 1831 or early 1832. By then, Joseph was eighteen. He was five feet eight inches tall, his hair was a dark auburn, and his complexion was dark, matching his hair. Perhaps his most striking feature was his clear, piercing grey eyes.[107] By late summer 1832, the marriage question had been asked and answered in the affirmative, the parental consent had been solicited and received, and the date had been set for the wedding. On Tuesday, August 28, 1832, Joseph rode north from Sale Creek to Washington in Rhea County to the store of Jonathan Wood. There he ordered what he considered necessary items for an appropriate wedding: a new coat and vest, silk scarf, new pair of shoes, a new saddle and bridle, and, for the comfort of his new wife-to-be, an umbrella. As the charge ticket was being completed, Joseph, evidently running through a final mental checklist of items needed, added a pair of saddlebags. The total charge on the ticket for all items was $22.15 but included a mistake of one dollar by Wood when the saddlebags were added. The correct charge was $23.15, but perhaps the mistake by Wood was intentional in order to financially help a young man in an expensive time of his life. On the reverse side of the charge ticket, Jonathan Wood recorded the necessary measurements for tailoring the new coat:

The length of the back	21 inches
The length of the tail	38 inches
From the senter [sic] of the back to the hand	36 inches
Round the elbow	14 inches
Round the hand	12 inches
Round the waist	35 inches
Balance measure	27 inches
Breast measure	38 inches[108]

Now well attired, Joseph accompanied Juda to the home of her parents, and there the couple were joined as man and wife on an autumn day in 1832.

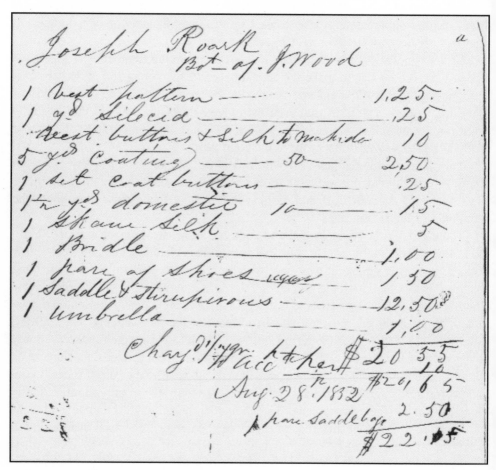

Joseph Roark's receipt, August 28, 1832, from merchant Jonathan Wood in Washington, Rhea County, for items purchased for his forthcoming wedding.

Chapter 6

Homestead and Family
1833-1839

Following their marriage, Joseph and Juda lived briefly with his brother James, and later built a small cabin near James and Jerusha. When Joseph had arrived from Claiborne County in 1831, James Roark was living with his family on his farm on the west side of Sale Creek near the Hamilton-Rhea County line. Just prior to Joseph's arrival, James had decided to move south to better land along Sale Creek near the present-day town by that name. In early 1831, James had begun negotiating with two local owners of large estates, Col. James Cozby and Charles McClung, to buy 200 acres on Sale Creek west of its mouth on the Tennessee. Colonel Cozby was a native of Virginia and a veteran of the Revolutionary War, serving under Gen. Lighthorse Harry Lee. He had migrated to Tennessee through North Carolina, living for a time in Knox and Rhea Counties before acquiring much land in Hamilton County.[1] McClung had purchased 3,800 acres in Hamilton County in 1819 from Stockley Donelson, prominent in Tennessee history, and in 1822, since Donelson had been unable to pay the taxes on a 10,000-acre grant in northern Hamilton County, McClung had, at a public auction, been able to purchase the 10,000 acres for the taxes due for a total investment of $122.65.[2] Unfortunately for James Roark, Colonel Cozby died February 13, 1831, before the sale could be consummated and James was forced to negotiate with McClung and the Cozby estate for the purchase. Since McClung lived in Knoxville at the time, he was represented by his attorney-in-fact, Daniel Henderson, son-in-law of Colonel Cozby. The Cozby estate was represented by Robert Cozby and William Smith, son and son-in-law, respectively, of Colonel Cozby, both of whom were administrators of the estate. During the subsequent negotiations, William Smith acknowledged that Colonel Cozby had, before his death, agreed to sell the 200 acres to James Roark for $200. Apparently, Colonel Cozby had also agreed for James Roark to occupy the land in 1831 (since Cozby and McClung had much land to sell and were courting buyers) and to begin construction of his cabin. This James had done in early 1831 although the sale was not closed until

August 4, 1834. The deed was witnessed by Samuel Igou and Alfred M. Rogers.[3]

While he was negotiating with Colonel Cozby and McClung in 1831 for the purchase of the 200-acre tract, James Roark approached his brother-in-law, William Blythe, about purchasing additional land from Cozby and McClung. Blythe was by that time a wealthy businessman, successful in farming and in his operation of ferries across both the Tennessee and Hiwassee Rivers. At James Roark's suggestion, Blythe successfully negotiated the purchase of another 200-acre tract from Cozby and McClung for $250. Again, the death of Colonel Cozby delayed the closing until August 4, 1834.[4]

James Roark also suggested to his brother-in-law that they try to purchase jointly even more land from Cozby and McClung. James had little money to put into a partnership to buy additional land, so Blythe agreed, if they could successfully negotiate a purchase from Cozby and McClung, to buy James' 110-acre farm on the west side of Sale Creek. Roark and Blythe were able to negotiate the purchase of another 250 acres but, again, the death of Colonel Cozby interrupted the transaction and the purchased was delayed. As in the case of the 200-acre tract, William Smith acknowledged the promised sale of 250 acres for a purchase price of $250. The sale was closed November 17, 1834. As he had agreed, William Blythe purchased James' 110-acre tract for $250 and the sale was closed November 11, 1834.[5] So with the help of his brother-in-law, James Roark had been able to pay his share of the joint purchase.

In 1831, James occupied the 200 acres of fertile crop land on the south bank of Sale Creek to which he was to gain title in August 1834. He also had access to the 250 acres on the north side of Sale Creek that he would own jointly with William Blythe in November 1834. While James' 200-acre tract on the south side of the creek was level and suitable for cultivation, his 250-acre tract jointly owned with Blythe and the 200-acre tract purchased by Blythe, both on the north side of Sale Creek, consisted of steep ridges and hollows. Since the land he now owned was more than he alone could farm, it was to this location near the big horseshoe bend on Sale Creek that James encouraged his brother Joseph to temporarily settle and build his cabin.

On January 1, 1833, within the first four months of his marriage, Joseph wrote his first promissory note. His first note was written to William Hutcheson in the amount of $6.81 and one-fourth cents, probably for seed corn, wheat, or other grain for the spring.[6] This was to be the first of many such promissory notes as cash was in short supply on what was then the Tennessee frontier, and promissory notes were used as a medium of exchange.

At the time Joseph Roark was establishing his household in Hamilton County in 1832, the county had grown to a population of over 2,300. Created by an act of the Tennessee Legislature in October 1819 from Rhea County, Hamilton County had been organized in 1820 with a population of 821 persons. The new county had been formed as a result of the Calhoun Treaty of February 1819 under which the Cherokees had surrendered their claim to all lands north of the Tennessee and Hiwassee Rivers. Hamilton County was thus formed on the north bank of the Tennessee,[7] south of Rhea County, and the area opened to white settlement. The new county had been named for Alexander Hamilton, secretary of the treasury under President George Washington. In creating the new county, the legislature had named three men, who would later be well known to Joseph Roark and his brothers, as commissioners to form a county government and select a county seat. The new commissioners were Charles Gamble, Robert Patterson, and William Lauderdale. Following formation of the county, Charles Gamble had been elected as the first sheriff of the county.[8]

First Promissory Note of Joseph Roark–January 1, 1833, for $6.81 [1/4].

At the creation of Hamilton County, its boundaries were established by the legislature as the Tennessee River on the southeast and on the northwest as the "height of the mountain" or Walden Ridge. The county was to extend between these two boundaries from the south line of Rhea County on the north, all the way south to the established state line between Tennessee and Georgia, a distance of approximately thirty-five miles. The first meeting of the commissioners court was held at the tavern of Hasten Poe at Poe's Cross Roads, now the town of Daisy. The commissioners chose for the county seat a location on the Tennessee River, approximately midway between the north and south boundaries of the county, on the farm of Asabel Rawlings. The location was given the name of "Hamilton County Courthouse" and Robert Patterson, Daniel Henderson, Jeremiah H. Jones, William McGill, James Riddle, and Cornelius Milliken had been named commissioners to plat the land and sell lots for the new county seat. The county seat would later be named Dallas in honor of Alexander James Dallas, secretary of the treasury under President James Madison.[9]

The farms of Joseph and James Roark were located in the northern portion of Hamilton County, less than three miles from the Rhea County line. At the time Joseph established his household, the economic center for the area was not in Hamilton County but continued to be Washington, then the county seat of Rhea County. In 1832, Washington had a population of about 400 and was the home of two doctors, two lawyers, two churches, five stores, two taverns, and two cotton gins.[10] Joseph had to travel the twelve miles to Washington to purchase those few items that could not be developed or manufactured on the farm.

Topographically, the dominant feature of Hamilton County within its boundaries of 1832 was Walden Ridge. As the southern extremity of the Appalachian chain of mountains, Walden Ridge is the shoulder of the Cumberland Plateau. Rising in rocky cliffs roughly parallel to and five miles west of the Tennessee River, Walden Ridge rises some 1,100 feet above the river valley floor and today still represents a significant barrier to westerly travel from the river. At the time of its creation, Hamilton County was roughly ten miles wide with half of this width being atop Walden Ridge. The area of the county within the river valley was defined by smaller ridges and hills which limited the amount of area suitable for cultivation. North of the location of the James Roark farm, Blackoak Ridge rises 300 feet above the valley floor and runs parallel to Walden Ridge three miles west of the river. Located along Sale Creek, however, the Roark farm was fertile, and a large portion was subject to cultivation. Other farms between the river and Walden Ridge were limited in areas of cultivation, and crops had to be raised in small, irregularly shaped tracts along creeks and branches. Across the Tennessee River on its south bank, within the lands reserved for the Cherokees, the land had fewer ridges and hills and more land was available for cultivation and crops. But in 1832, the white settlers were prohibited from moving into the area, and Cherokee law prohibited sale to anyone outside the tribe. Joseph decided to settle on Sale Creek and await events which might open the south bank of the Tennessee to settlement.

West of the river and on Walden Ridge, Joseph Roark hunted deer, wild turkeys, wild hogs, grouse, and water fowl. Although the demand for deer skins by the English and their trade by the Indians had earlier depleted the number of deer in the area, droves of deer were still available at the time that Joseph sought venison from the forest for his table. Trees making up the forests consisted of pines, varieties of oaks, hickories, and maples, plus cherry trees, walnut, beech, black locust, and dogwood. No doubt Joseph and Juda Ann enjoyed the fall color on Walden Ridge on crisp fall mornings the first year of their marriage.

In addition to the opportunity for cheap or even free land, the major attraction for settlement in the area was the potential provided by the Tennessee River. Water transportation for the movement of people and freight had been the cheapest and most efficient travel mode for centuries. All great cities of the world had been located on the coast or on major rivers. Such was also the case in the U.S. at the time Joseph Roark started his household. The western migration in the nation had to that time moved rapidly along navigable rivers and were now far to the west of Hamilton County. Settlements in large numbers had occurred along the Mississippi at Memphis and St. Louis; along the Cumberland at Nashville; and along the Ohio at Louisville, Cincinnati, and Pittsburgh. Those rivers provided transportation for crops through New Orleans to the markets of the world and, on the return route, steamboats brought needed merchandise, equipment, and goods to the settlements. Would not the Tennessee River provide the same economic advantage to farmers and merchants along its route as well?

Unfortunately, the Tennessee "of all the great rivers east of the Mississippi . . . has been the least friendly to civilization."[11] In fact, the valley of the Tennessee River was not, until the first half of the twentieth century, generally viewed as a single region but rather was divided into three separate sections. The upper region of the Tennessee and its tributaries flow through the mountainous areas of East Tennessee including Hamilton County. The middle section, from Chattanooga westward, serves Alabama and the deep cotton South. The lower reaches of the river as it makes the great bend and turns north to the Ohio flows through the flat lands of West Tennessee.[12] Prior to improvements made to the Tennessee in the twentieth century, profitable and continuous navigation on the river between Hamilton County and the Ohio and Mississippi Rivers was practically impossible due to obstacles in the Tennessee. The first of these obstacles encountered by boatmen from New Orleans was at Muscle Shoals in Alabama where the Tennessee falls more than three-and-one-half feet per mile over a distance of forty miles, thereby creating extensive rapids in which were located rocky islands, reefs, and bars. The second of the navigational barriers was the section of the river downstream from where it had centuries before cut its path through Walden Ridge, narrowing the river bed and creating rapid currents. Originally known as "the Narrows," this thirty-mile section consisted of numerous whirlpools. Early boatmen, trying to navigate the Tennessee, gave affectionate names to specific locations within the Narrows such as "the Suck, the Boiling Pot, the Skillet, and the Frying Pan." Later, the entire length of the Narrows would be referred to as the Suck and was a recognized barrier to navigation of the Tennessee. The "unfriendly river" thus had failed by the mid 1830s to provide the anticipated economic benefit to development and settlers along the banks of its upper reaches.

The Tennessee, the "river of the Cherokees" with its barriers to navigation, supported to a great extent the isolation of the Cherokee lands later to be settled by Joseph Roark and his brothers. The Cherokees were able to maintain their lands longer than the Shawnees, Iroquois, and other tribes primarily because of the isolation of their settlements along the Tennessee. The Cherokee country was, in the late eighteenth and nineteenth centuries, difficult to penetrate. Even today, with modern transportation, portions of the former Cherokee lands southeast of the Tennessee and south of the Hiwassee are not easily accessible.[13] Settlers of the area like Joseph Roark were doubtless disappointed in the reduced economic benefits of the Tennessee when compared to other major rivers in the U.S. Nevertheless, Joseph and his neighbors were to cherish the isolation and independence originally enjoyed by the Cherokees and later by other white settlers.

The Tennessee, fed by its supporting rivers such as the Clinch and Powell, on which the Roarks had made their homes for three generations, plus the Holston, French Broad, and the Little Tennessee, did provide limited water transportation between Hamilton County and Knoxville. This water transportation, in the days when Joseph Roark was living on his brother's place on Sale Creek, consisted of flatboats and keelboats. Flatboats were box-like in construction with a large bottom and were used for downstream travel only. Flatboats, as large as 20-by-100 feet, carried heavy loads but required as many as five men for steering. In seasons of high water, flatboats sometimes risked the trip through the Suck and Muscle Shoals to carry cargo all the way to New Orleans. Successful trips to New Orleans, however, were rare. Settlers used flatboats to move their family down the Tennessee and, upon arrival at their destination, often cannibalized the flatboat for timbers to build their first cabin.

For travel upstream, the keelboat was used. Slender, less than ten feet wide, and lengthy, between 30 and 70 feet long, the keelboat was moved upstream by manpower using a crew on each side of the boat to "pole" the craft against the current. Local keelboats operated in the early 1830s between Hamilton County and Knoxville in limited number. For obvious reasons, keelboats were not used for long stretches of the river, and none came upstream from below Hamilton County.

Steamboat travel was still in its infancy when Joseph Roark settled in Hamilton County. As early as 1828, in response to prize money offered by Knoxville, the steamboat "Atlas" became the first steamboat to travel from Paducah, Kentucky, up the Tennessee, arriving at Knoxville on March 3, after a struggle to master Muscle Shoals and the Suck. In spite of the success, or luck, of the Atlas, steamboat travel on the river above Hamilton County was slow to become economically feasible. The Atlas "was the first to make the trip [to Knoxville], got the money, and never went there again. She was a financial failure . . ."[14] It would be after Joseph Roark had moved to the south bank of the Tennessee before steamboats could guarantee travel north from Hamilton County to Knoxville.

While Joseph was content in early 1833 to farm his brother's land on Sale Creek, doubtless his aspirations were on the south side of the river in the Cherokee country. Joseph and James carefully followed the political activity under way in the early 1830s, particularly in Georgia, to relocate the Cherokees west of the Mississippi. Both Joseph and his brother were knowledgeable of the previous treaties with the Cherokees and could anticipate that the lands then occupied by the Cherokees would become available to white settlers. Beginning with the Treaty of Hopewell in 1785 and continuing through eight subsequent treaties to 1819, the Cherokees periodically had responded to political pressure and surrendered territory as the new U.S. nation grew and the frontier was expanded. By 1819, all of Tennessee had been cleared of Indian claims except the Cherokees in the southeastern corner of the state.

Because of their past involvement with the British, the Cherokees could gain little sympathy in their efforts to maintain lands granted to them under the various treaties. During the American Revolution, the Cherokees had chosen to support the British, a decision that proved to be disastrous as the American forces pushed the

British and the Cherokees out of North and South Carolina. After a smallpox epidemic among the Cherokees in 1739 had decimated their population, the Cherokees were to suffer further during the revolutionary period when another smallpox epidemic broke out in 1783. The Revolutionary War itself destroyed more than fifty Cherokee towns and villages.[15] Nevertheless, the Cherokees strove to relate to the new nation and its people. By 1820, the Cherokee Indians were well on the road toward the white man's culture. From the beginning of the century they had been steadily advancing in civilization. As far back as 1800, they had begun the manufacture of cotton cloth, and in 1820, there was scarcely a family in that part of the nation living east of the Mississippi "but what understood" the use of the card and the spinning wheel. Every Cherokee family had its farm under cultivation. The Cherokee territory was laid off in districts, with a council-house, a judge, and a marshal in each district. A national committee and council were the supreme authority in the Cherokee Nation. Schools were flourishing in all the villages. Printing presses were at work.[16]

The course of the Cherokee education and development was accelerated in the 1820s by the invention and acceptance of a syllabary by Sequoyah, son of a Cherokee woman and a white trader. This made possible the writing and printing of the Cherokee language, and a large number of the Indians learned to read and write in their own language. There was probably less illiteracy among the Cherokees than among the whites living in the same states.[17] Considerable credit for the advancement in education among the Cherokees can be attributed to the influence of Christian missions. Moravian, Presbyterian, Methodist, and Baptist churches established several mission schools. The most successful was the Brainerd mission that was established in 1817 on Chickamauga Creek near the later site of Chattanooga. With its advancement, the Cherokee Nation, with an estimated population of between 15,000 and 20,000 in 1820, produced men of property and influence such as John Ross, James Vann, Major Ridge, and Charles Hicks, all of whom were leaders in the Cherokee Nation.[18]

Serious agitation for removal of the Cherokees to the west began shortly before Joseph Roark had arrived in Hamilton County. In his first message to Congress in 1829 after his inauguration as president, Andrew Jackson had strongly urged removal of the Cherokees, and in May 1830, Congress passed a general removal act and appropriated $500,000 for that purpose. The major push for removal, however, came not from the U.S or from Tennessee but from Georgia where white citizens coveted the lands held by the Cherokees in northern Georgia. In December 1828, the Georgia legislature passed an act imposing the jurisdiction of the State of Georgia over Indian territory, even that area in northern Georgia granted by treaty to the Cherokees and in which the Cherokees had established their own government. The Georgia jurisdictional act went into effect in June 1830, and Joseph and James Roark followed with interest its appeal by the Cherokees to the U.S. Supreme Court. The Supreme Court, under Chief Justice John Marshall, declared the Georgia law unconstitutional; however, President Jackson refused to enforce the Court's decision. Georgia, encouraged by the action or lack thereof of the president, then passed other oppressive legislation against the Cherokees, had the Indian lands surveyed, and awarded land grants to white settlers by means of a lottery. Forced Cherokee relocation was rising to a crescendo. As Cherokees in Georgia were forced to move across the state line into Tennessee, Georgia pushed the Tennessee legislature to follow her example and extend the jurisdiction of Tennessee over the Indian lands south of the Tennessee. Approximately a year after Joseph's marriage, and after three previous failures to enact such legislation, the Tennessee legislature on November 8, 1833, passed the Indian jurisdictional act, less punitive, however, than that of Georgia.[19]

Immediately following signing of the jurisdictional act into law by the governor, the State of Tennessee issued instructions to Hamilton County to extend its boundaries to that prescribed under the new jurisdictional law, i.e., east to the White Oak Mountain and south to the Georgia line. The area of Hamilton County was thus almost doubled and the Commissioners Court given jurisdiction over part of the Cherokee lands south of the Tennessee. This did not open up the area to white settlement inasmuch as the 1833 law specifically stated: "nothing in this act contained, shall be construed to authorize any white man to settle within the limits of the lands in this State now within the occupancy of the Cherokee." In addition, "any entry or appropriation or any occupancy of any of the land" continued to be illegal.[20] Within lands of the Cherokee, laws passed by the Cherokee Nation before 1833 clearly stated that no Cherokee could sell land to any white without the consent of the National Cherokee Council. Individual members of the tribe were also forbidden to sign up for emigration to the west. Any Cherokee signing up for emigration was to lose all privileges as a Cherokee citizen. More importantly, any Cherokee who negotiated a land sale to a white settler was subject to the death penalty.[21] The issue was joined.

As Joseph waited for the situation to clear on the possibility of available grants within the Cherokee lands, word came from Claiborne County that his father continued to have title problems on the old river farm in Tazewell County, Virginia. In late 1832 or early 1833, Timothy had received word that William Cecil, the original buyer of the farm, was questioning the sale to Creswell and was threatening to cloud the title through legal action. To respond, Timothy had not attempted a trip back to Tazewell County because of his apparent ill health but rather negotiated with Cecil through an attorney whose name does not appear in the records. In March 1833, William Cecil agreed to sell his title claim on the river farm for thirty-one pounds, "in current money of this Commonwealth." Timothy and his attorney had agreed to settle in this fashion, and March 18, 1833, William Cecil executed what today would be referred to as a "quit claim deed" to Timothy Roark for thirty-one pounds. Under the deed, Timothy Roark was entitled to "hold, occupy, possess & enjoy the said tract or parcel of land and sue for & take all rents, fines & proffits [sic] thereof from &

after the first day of January one thousand eight hundred and seven until the present day & sale of the presents to & for his own use & benefit whereunto the Timothy Rorark [sic] has been unlawfully kept out of the use of said tract or parcel of land . . ."[22] Timothy Roark had thus cleared the title to the river farm for the benefit of Henry Creswell. It was to be Timothy's last property transaction.

It was in May 1833 that Joseph Roark and his brother James received word that their father Timothy Roark had died at the homestead in Claiborne County.[23] Their mother wrote that the funeral service was held at the homestead in the traditional manner and that the body was carried the roughly three hundred yards to the family cemetery southwest of the home place.[24] Sarah, now a widow at 57, was comforted by her children still at home, Jeremiah 17, Timothy Junior 14, and Mary Ann, and by her sister Lucy and brother-in-law James Eastridge. Also at the home place for the service were John and Margaret with their three daughters, Mary Ann 8, Sarah 6, and Elizabeth 4;[25] Nancy and husband James Richardson with children, George 4, and Sarah Jane 2; William and wife Nancy with John 5, and Cynthia 3; and Elizabeth and husband Thomas Ellison with their three sons, Timothy 4, John 3, and Jeremiah 1. James, Sary, and Joseph were the only three of the family that were not present.

Timothy Roark was 66 when he died. He had survived the Indian wars and the American Revolution and had lived to settle new lands during the formation of the new republic and its testing in the War of 1812. He farmed and raised his family during a period of great migration as pioneers moved through the Cumberland Gap, and he lived to see new settlements established in Kentucky and along the Cumberland in Tennessee. His grave in the family cemetery would overlook the Cumberland Gap as if it were providing a way for him to continue to monitor this great western migration.[26]

Family Burial Plot southwest of the Timothy Roark home place–place of burial of Timothy Roark. Cumberland Gap is in the background.

The will of Timothy Roark was submitted to the Claiborne County Court of Pleas for probate in June 1833.[27] The will had been witnessed by one Benjamin Carroll who testified, under oath, on the validity of the will. The Court of Pleas acted on the will probate during the court's regular session on Monday, June 17, 1833, and the court appointed Sarah Roark as administratrix of the estate. Sarah provided a bond to the court as security for settlement of the estate as was required by law dealing with estate settlements.[28] It was a testimony to the education and acumen of Sarah that she was considered qualified by the court to serve as administratrix, since most widows in that era did not possess the skills to read or write and were often passed over for settlement of estates in favor of the eldest son or even a friend of the family. Sarah completed the work necessary to settle the estate in accordance with her deceased husband's will and the settlement was returned to the court September 16, 1833, for recording.[29] The settlement was submitted to the court by Sarah's son John since he had to be in court that Monday to serve on jury duty.[30] The settlement apparently was simple–the widow was to receive all the homestead property which was to be divided equally among all surviving children at the time of her death. Accordingly, Sarah continued to live and farm at the homeplace with the help of her children remaining at home: Jeremiah, Timothy Jr., and Mary Ann.

Shortly after his father died, John Roark decided to move his family south to Hamilton County and join his brothers James and Joseph, with the thought that opportunities for land would be better than in Claiborne County. John had made a living for his family on his 150 acres on the Powell River and, in addition, he had submitted a claim March 18, 1831, receiving a grant for 75 acres on either side of Little Creek just upstream of its mouth at the Powell.[31] His land had not been very prosperous since he had less than ten acres in cultivation. He had, however, been active in the community, served on juries, and assisted the county in recommending new road locations. On Tuesday, March 16, 1830, John had served as chairman of the jury to try the case between Ralph G. Norvell as plaintiff and Isaac Vanbibber, defendant. The jury had found the defendant not guilty of the complaint filed against him, and the court ordered Norvell to reimburse the defendant "without delay" for court costs.[32] Three years later, December 17, 1833, John was again called to serve on a jury at the courthouse in Tazewell.[33] No record is available of the case or cases involved. John also assisted the county in serving under Hiram Johnson as overseer to work on a road "of the 3rd class" from Tazewell by Henderson Mill to Crockett's Iron Works. Designated by court order Monday, June 18, 1832, the men to work under Johnson in marking the road included John's brother William, his brother-in-law Lewis Gross, and his cousin Ezekiah "Squire" Eastridge.[34]

In the fall of 1833, after his limited crops were harvested, John put his 150 acres up for sale, and in the spring of the following year he joined his brothers James and Joseph in Hamilton County. As Joseph had done, John made his home with James and helped him on his farm on Sale Creek. On November 11, 1834, John witnessed the deed when James sold his 110 acres on the north reaches of Sale Creek to William Blythe.[35] By the next month, John had sold his 150 acres on the Powell River to Joseph Southern, a son of the Reverend Robert Southern, a local Baptist minister,[36] for $150. In December, John traveled to Claiborne County to execute the deed to Southern.[37] The deed was witnessed by Andrew Whitaker and Andrew's father, Reverend Rice Whitaker, also a local Baptist minister.[38] John Roark returned to Hamilton County to farm with his brother but was not to purchase land there for another ten years when he then would purchase a farm on the south side of the Tennessee, west of the present day Birchwood.

Shortly after his father's death in Claiborne County, Joseph was informed by Juda in May 1833 that she was pregnant, with the baby probably due after the first of the year. With a growing family, Joseph would need to establish a homestead and a farm of his own. For the first three years of his marriage, Joseph received help from his brother James, not only with land to farm but also in financial support as well. It appears that the two brothers had joint accounts with local merchants. On Tuesday, February 3, 1835, the two brothers settled their account to that date with Richard Waterhouse, merchant and landowner in the area who later would raise a company to fight in the Mexican War.[39] The receipt for the payment reads as follows:

> Rec'd of James and Joseph Roark Book Account with R. Waterhouse up to this Date Feb'y 3rd, 1835
>
> A. Decanian[40]

Apparently James also soon thereafter paid some bills for his younger brother. On Tuesday, July 16, 1835, James paid $2.75 to James W. Smith for Joseph. The receipt reads:

> Rec'd of Joseph Roark by the hand of James Roark, Two dollars and Seventy five Cents in full of his acpt. up to this day.
>
> Jas. W. Smith
> 16th July 1835[41]

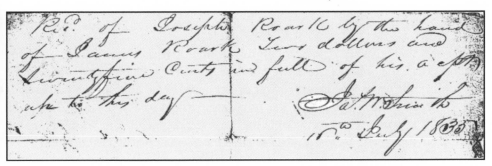

Receipt to James Roark for the settlement of the account of his brother, Joseph, with James W. Smith.

As Joseph brought in crops from his work on James' land on Sale Creek, he became more and more independent of James' help. On November 2, 1835, Joseph signed a promissory note to Lewis Patterson for $3.87 and a half cent. Lewis Patterson was the son of Robert Patterson, who was a veteran of the battle of King's Mountain in the Revolutionary War. Lewis Patterson had been born in Tennessee in 1796 and, by the time of his dealings with Joseph Roark, was an owner of extensive lands on the north side of the Tennessee. At the time he dealt with Joseph, he was serving as a ruling elder of the Mount Bethel Church south of Sale Creek (now the Soddy Presbyterian Church).[42] The promissory note, written by young Joseph Roark, reads:

> Dew Lewis Patterson three dollars and eighty seven and a half cents for
> value Rec of him witness my hand and seal
> > Nov the 2 1835
> > Joseph Roark[43]

Exactly three years after his very first promissory note, Joseph wrote a promissory note on Friday, January 1, 1836, to William and H. Hutcheson. The Hutchesons were merchants in the Sale Creek area who would later move their business south of the Tennessee. The promissory note reads:

> one day after date I promise to pay unto Wm & H. Hutchinson Three dollars fifty six & a quarter cts. for value Rec'd of them as witness my hand
> and seal the 1 day of Jan 1836
> > Joseph Roark[44]

In March 1836, Joseph purchased a coat from a local tailor in the Sale Creek area, J. Kelly. Was it a coat for his wife or for himself? The coat cost $4.00 and the receipt finally received from Kelly shows two payments of $0.50 each and finally a payment of $3.00:

> Joseph Rowark
> | | |
> |---|---|
> | 1836 March 23 | To J. Kelly |
> | To making coat | $4.00 |
> | Cr. by cash | .50 |
> | Cr. by cash | .50[45] |

Joseph also maintained an account in Washington, Rhea County, with merchant Thomas McCallie, who was to move his store from Washington to Chattanooga in 1838. McCallie was a veteran of the War of 1812, and at the time Joseph traded with him, McCallie was a colonel in the militia. He was to be a business leader in Chattanooga and a major contributor to the Presbyterian church.[46] In Washington, his clerk wrote the receipt to Joseph Roark when the account was made current:

> Washington, January 5, 1836
> Received of Joseph Roark two dollars twelve ½ cents in full of all accounts
> up to this date Thomas McCallie
> > by John A. Moore[47]

Joseph and Juda were blessed with their first child on Monday, January 20, 1834,[48] a girl whom they named Mary Ann. Their second child, Sarah Elizabeth, named for Joseph's mother, was born eleven months later on Wednesday, December 31, 1834.[49] It was in the summer of 1834, while Juda was pregnant with Sarah Elizabeth, that she raised a question with her husband—a question or request that might be considered strange since Joseph and Juda had each only recently celebrated their twenty-first birthdays and within months would have two baby girls less than a year old—could they consider taking in a seven-year-old girl and raising her to maturity? An explanation must have quickly followed. The little girl was Jeanette Clingan. Her parents, George Washington Clingan and Jeanette Cloyd Clingan, had lived in the Sale Creek area between John Carr and Juda's parents when Juda was growing up.[50] Unfortunately, both of Jeanette's parents had died within weeks of each other in 1830, the year before Joseph Roark had come south from Claiborne County. At the death of her parents, Jeanette, or Jane as she was called to differentiate her from her mother, was only three years old. She had gone to live with her uncle, Alexander Adam Clingan, who had assumed guardianship of Jane and four other minor children of George and Jeanette Clingan.[51] A.A. Clingan and Thomas K. Clingan were stepbrothers of George Clingan and had served as administrators of his estate upon his death.[52] After settlement of the estate, A.A. Clingan had moved his family, including Jane and her four siblings to the Cherokee territory near what would later become the town of Cleveland. After the formation of Bradley County, A.A. Clingan was elected the county's first sheriff. By the summer of 1834, Clingan had three children of his own plus his wife was then pregnant with their fourth child. Doubtless his cabin in the Cherokee territory was small and crowded with eight children and, perhaps for that reason, Clingan met with Juda personally to ask her consideration in taking the responsibility of raising young Jane Clingan, then seven.

The Clingans had apparently been close to the Carrs in the Sale Creek area. When John Carr had married Jane Land in April 1829, George W. Clingan had provided the required financial security.[53] Juda Carr had been seventeen when the Clingans died and doubtless had helped with the young children of the Clingan family during the period of sickness and death. Also, A.A. Clingan was related to James Roark by marriage having married Martha Blythe, a niece to James' wife, Jerusha. Clingan was to remain a close friend of the Carrs and Roarks and would be a help to Samuel and John Carr during the years they were to live in Bradley County.[54]

So Joseph and Juda took Jane Clingan into their home at what was perhaps a most inopportune time in their lives. Having been married only a short time, with a small cabin and two babies to care for, they nevertheless raised Jane as one of their own. Much later, their own children would consider Jane a close sister.[55]

As Joseph began his family, that of his brother James continued to grow. His third child, another son, whom they named William after his uncle in Claiborne

County, was born January 21, 1832. James' first daughter, Martha Jane, was born December 4, 1834.[56] By the time Joseph's brother John moved his family of five children to Hamilton County in the fall of 1834, the three brothers together had a total of nine children. With James' Martha Jane and Joseph's Sarah Elizabeth born in December, the total number of children was increased to eleven. The oldest of the cousins was John's daughter, Mary Ann, who was nine years old when her latest two cousins were born.

In addition to his brothers and their families, Joseph also lived close to Juda's brothers, John and James Carr, as well as Juda's parents. Samuel Carr continued to trade for a living with the farmers in both Hamilton and Rhea Counties. While Carr was neither to own land nor to farm for a living, he was sufficiently successful to help support members of his family during their adult years. In March 1831, Carr was to pay Clingen Fain of Hamilton County $6.00 on one occasion and $11.25 on another to bring current the accounts of two of his family.[57] Of all of Carr's children, his sons, John and James, seemed to require more than their share of help from their father. Neither could read nor write, and Samuel often sought the help of a family friend, J.D. Traynor, to guide his two sons in financial matters. Traynor's help would later prove to be expensive. On February 3, 1830, Traynor had drafted, in beautiful handwriting, a promissory note in the amount of $15.00 from John Mahan to John Carr. John Mahan signed with an "X" as "his mark." Traynor witnessed the "signature."[58] Again, on February 8, 1831, Traynor wrote and witnessed a promissory note for $1.50 from James Carr to William Powers for "value received." James Carr signed the note with an "X."[59]

Samuel Carr, while moderately successful, nevertheless continued to receive calls on notes that he had written or otherwise on debts that he owed. On the last day of the year in 1831, Carr received the following request:

> Mr. Samuel Carr
> Sir, please to pay Hubert Qualls seventy five cents and this shall be your receit for the same.
> this the 31 December 1831
>
> Gibson Witt[60]

Like many of his status and location, Samuel Carr began to see the opportunities within the Cherokee lands at such time as relocation was to occur. While he had little interest in farming, Carr understood the value of land and began to discuss the possibilities of obtaining Cherokee land with his sons John and James. The father could see opportunities of trading with new settlers in the area when white settlement occurred and, if a land grant were obtained, his sons could farm while Samuel traded. Like his son-in-law Joseph Roark, Samuel Carr was to follow closely the events leading up to the Cherokee relocation.

As the area waited on "resolution of the Cherokee issue," growth continued in Hamilton County. Mixed-blood Cherokees or whites who had intermarried with

Cherokees had, since the county's creation in 1819, taken a lead in opening stores along the Tennessee, as well as operating ferries across the river. James T. Gardenhire, son-in-law of the Cherokee leader Path Killer, who had fought under Andrew Jackson at the Battle of Horseshoe Bend, had begun operation of the Blue Springs Ferry across the Tennessee with the help of his father-in-law.[61] Since 1810, John Ross had operated a store on the south side of the Tennessee River. Referred to as Ross's Landing, it was later to become Chattanooga, and by 1836, was to be a military post, and a U.S. Post Office by 1837. John Ross was the son of Scot trader Daniel Ross, who had become a full-fledged member of the Cherokee Nation, and grandson of John McDonald, the first European to settle in the area of Hamilton County and marry into the Cherokee tribe.[62]

Another center of activity in the first decade of Hamilton County was the Hiwassee Garrison located four hundred yards of the north bank of the Tennessee opposite the mouth of the Hiwassee River.[63] Established in 1807 by Jonathan Meigs, special agent to the Cherokees appointed by President Thomas Jefferson, the Garrison remained the focal point of white-Cherokee relations. Meigs, a seasoned frontiersman and a colonel in the Revolutionary War, had a thorough knowledge of the Cherokees and possessed a keen sympathy of their problem with the U.S. government. During his twenty-two years of unselfish and dedicated work with the Cherokees, he guided the Indians in adopting improved methods of agriculture, hygiene, and government. Before his death in 1823, Meigs had distributed farm equipment to the Cherokees and had helped the Indian nation obtain blacksmiths, wheelmakers, and carpenters. He was also instrumental in seeing that "white intruders" were removed from Cherokee lands when they were identified. It was with Meigs that Cherokees, who had elected to become citizens of the U.S. under the 1817 treaty, registered to get their reservation of 640 acres with fee simple title in lands ceded to the United States. It was to Meigs that William Blythe had gone to register for his 640 acres on behalf of his wife Nancy Fields. In addition to helping the Cherokees, Meigs had adroitly counseled both white settlers and government officials.[64]

Early negotiations with the Cherokees before the formation of Hamilton County resulted in the development of the two major roadways through the Cherokee Nation, roadways that later were to impact white development within Cherokee lands and accelerate the Indian removal to the west. In 1805, the federal road in Georgia between Augusta and Spring Place (located just south of the Tennessee-Georgia line near present-day Dalton, Georgia) had been completed, and the Cherokees had agreed to a continuation of the road in two directions: one north connecting to Knoxville and the other west past Lookout Mountain connecting to Nashville. White settlers would later take advantage of these important roadways in gaining access to the Cherokee lands south of the Hiwassee.[65]

At the end of 1834, Joseph and Juda were proud parents of two girls. Joseph's farming operation with his brother was progressing, and opportunities could be seen for available land at such time as the federal government concluded negotiations with the Cherokees remaining in southeastern Tennessee. Railroads were a hot topic of conversation, and by 1835, over 1,098 miles of railroad were in operation in the U.S.[66] There was even talk of a possible railroad from Augusta to the middle of Georgia and possibly north to the Tennessee Valley.[67] Joseph and Juda could see an exciting future ahead as they adjusted to family life and children.

Beyond Hamilton County, as well as within, attentions in 1835 were focused on the Mexican territory of Texas to the southwest. There Stephen F. Austin, who had been born in Wythe County, Virginia, as a near neighbor to Joseph's grandfather, had been working since 1820 to colonize the territory. By early 1835, Austin and others had over 30,000 U.S. citizens as colonists in Texas. Storms were on the Texas horizon, however, as dictator Santa Anna had assumed total power in Mexico and had overthrown the Constitution of 1824 under which the colonization of Texas had begun. Trouble was brewing in early 1835 and hostilities were only days away. A former governor of Tennessee, Sam Houston, was then in Texas beginning to take on a mantle of leadership in the developing conflict. In Tennessee, Joseph was twenty-one years old with a wife and two baby daughters. The Texas situation was of interest to him but only as a distant land. His responsibilities and his future were at home in eastern Tennessee.

Also of interest to Joseph and other residents of the Sale Creek area were reports from the northeast that movements were under way to abolish slavery. In Boston on January 1, 1831, William Lloyd Garrison had begun publication of the *Liberator* as a beginning to the abolitionist movement. Following closely on the heels of Garrison's work, the New England Anti-Slavery Society had been formed in 1832, and on December 4, 1833, the American Anti-Slavery Society had been founded in Philadelphia. Joseph probably had little concern about the activities of the abolitionist movement since he neither owned slaves nor could see economic benefit in slavery. To him it was a nonissue since in eastern Tennessee the number of slaves was negligible in relation to the total population.[68] In fact, the Cherokees in southeast Tennessee held far more slaves in 1835 than did the white settlers in Hamilton County. With an almost equal population within Hamilton County compared to the Cherokees in southeast Tennessee, only 117 slaves were held by whites in Hamilton County[69] compared to 480 held by the Cherokees.[70]

Of little interest to Joseph Roark in 1835, but which would be of utmost importance to him in his later days was the concept of nullification and states' rights then being espoused by John C. Calhoun of South Carolina. Under Calhoun's concept, a state could protect its rights by declaring "null and void within the limit of the state" any federal law that the state felt violated its constitution. These and other sectional issues that would later divide the country were being debated outside of Hamilton County. Important as these issues were, they were not the focus of Joseph Roark's attention. His immediate thrust was toward obtaining land, building a modest cabin, and, above all, feeding his family.

Closer to home as Joseph waited for the Cherokee lands to open, the time between 1833 and 1835 was "a confusing and desperate period for the Cherokee people themselves."[71] U.S. policy toward the Cherokees and their relocation was modified almost annually. The State of Georgia continued a policy of harassment and aggressive encroachment. Through their various Indian agents, the U.S. government had first encouraged migration westward and had been successful in seeing some migration in small parties. The federal government ceased to encourage migration in small groups when it realized that such migration merely drained off the reservoir of those Indians who were supportive of relocation. This policy was shortly after reversed again, and the U.S. government appointed a "superintendent of removal for the Cherokee Nation," and in April 1832, the first removal party of about 500 Cherokee began its relocation. The U.S. government had also ceased paying the annuities to the Cherokee leaders that had been promised in the Calhoun Treaty of 1819 and insisted that the annuity payment be made directly to individual members of the Cherokee Nation, although the amount thus received would be as little as $0.15 per person.[72]

The Cherokee General Council under Principal Chief John Ross had met in July 1832 and voted heavily against removal. In the meantime, the Council had been encouraged by the Supreme Court's decision to overturn the Georgia jurisdictional law and hoped for President Jackson's enforcement of the decision. With Jackson's failure to act, the Council delayed any action on emigration since they had been led to hope for Henry Clay's election over Jackson in November 1832 and then more supportive policies for the Cherokees could possibly result.[73]

After Jackson's re-election, a Cherokee delegation under John Ross had journeyed to Washington in January 1833 for a two-month attempt to gain some support from the secretary of war and the president. The delegation had been offered little hope for a change in government policies, and in May 1833, the Cherokee General Council again voted to protest emigration.[74] Unfortunately, divisiveness began to work its way into the Cherokee unity and the U.S. government began to identify those individual Cherokees who favored migration under the terms of full compensation to each Cherokee for his property improvements. The Indian leader favoring relocation was John Ridge, a mixed-blood subchief, well educated in New England, and a man of considerable influence among the Cherokees. Ridge was supported by his father, Major Ridge, who had gained the title of "Major" while fighting under Andrew Jackson at the Battle of Horseshoe Bend, and by Elios Boudinot, also educated in New England and editor of the newspaper serving the Cherokee Nation, the *Cherokee Phoenix*. Divisions became apparent in the Cherokee Council meeting in October 1834 when threats resulted between representatives of the factions. Following the meeting, a member of the Ridge party, John Walker Jr., son-in-law to agent Jonathan Meigs, was killed as he returned home following the council meeting. The leaders of the Ridge party felt that they were in more danger from the Cherokees than from the whites. John Ridge sadly noted, "Our nation is crumbling into ruins."[75] In February 1835, two Cherokee delegations thus arrived in Washington, each claiming to represent the Cherokee Nation. The Ridge delegation negotiated for a relocation payment of $4.5 million plus 800,000 acres of western territory. The John Ross delegation argued for a relocation payment of $20 million, which was considered unreasonable by the U.S. government. A treaty was drafted along the lines negotiated with the Ridge delegation.[76]

In December, a notice was printed in the Cherokee language and circulated throughout the Cherokee Nation for the Cherokees to meet at New Echota in northern Georgia to conclude a treaty. The Cherokees assembled for council at New Echota on December 23, 1835, numbered only three to five hundred, hardly representative of the entire nation. The treaty was modified to include payment of $300,000 to Cherokees whose property had been damaged by white intruders and to permit an allocation of 160 acres for each Cherokee family head who desired to become a citizen of the U.S. and was qualified to become a useful member of society. The treaty was approved by the Cherokee Council assembled, and a committee was designated to travel to Washington to urge ratification of the modified treaty by the U.S. Senate.[77]

Following the presentation of the New Echota Treaty (as it was called) to the U.S. Senate, President Jackson signed a lengthy letter, dated March 16, 1835, addressed to the Cherokees and printed in newspapers, outlining the terms of the agreement. In his letter, Jackson stated:

> I have no motive, my friends, to deceive you. I am sincerely desirous to promote your welfare. Listen to me, therefore, while I tell you that you cannot remain where you now are . . .
>
> Think then of all these things. Shut your ears to bad counsels. Look at your condition as it now is, and then consider what it will be if you follow the advice I give you.
>
> Your friend, Andrew Jackson–Washington, March 16, 1835[78]

With the announcement of the treaty, even before its ratification by the Senate, great numbers of whites began to move into the Cherokee lands. Before the treaty, there had been encroachment into the Cherokee lands; however, such encroachment had been strongly discouraged by the U.S. Indian agents and removal had been enforced to a limited degree by the military forces available to the agents. But with the treaty announced, little effort was made to stem the flow into the Indian lands. On February 10, 1836, the Tennessee legislature authorized the organization of Bradley County east of Hamilton County in the Cherokee lands. John W. Ramsey of Bradley County later described the entry of whites into the area:

In 1832 my father, Edmund Ramsey, crossed the Hiwassee at the mouth of Mouse Creek and settled two or three miles from the river but in a few weeks was persuaded to move back across the Hiwassee. By the spring of 1834 the stream of emigration was set strongly into Bradley. Father then moved in again and settled near Flint Springs. By the summer of 1836 there were probably as many white men as Indians in the territory.[79]

At the time agreement was reached on the New Echota Treaty in 1835, the population of the Cherokee tribes within the state of Tennessee numbered 2,528.[80] The Cherokee area in Tennessee generally included the eastern half of Hamilton County and what later would become all of Bradley and Polk Counties. In Hamilton County, in the 1836 tax lists, a total of 262 white males over twenty-one years old were identified as residing within the Cherokee lands south of the Tennessee and Hiwassee Rivers. This provides an estimate, at an assumed average of six persons per household, of almost 1,600 people in Hamilton County south of the Tennessee. Included in the heads-of-household tax list were several who had married into the Cherokee tribe, including William Blythe and James T. Gardenhire. At the time of the 1836 Hamilton County tax list, Joseph Roark and brothers James and John, were listed together on James' 450 acres on Sale Creek in District 11.[81] Joseph did not make his move into the Cherokee lands until after news of the New Echota Treaty had been circulated.

South of the Tennessee and Hiwassee Rivers, confusion was rampant among the Indians. Throughout the Cherokee lands, it was the same–people were undecided about the future and what they should do about relocation. Should crops be planted, should houses be maintained, or should wagons be loaded for movement to the west?[82] Confusion bred indecision, and many Cherokees, puzzled by advice from the two factions in their leadership, decided to do nothing–to wait and hope for a better turn of events. Meanwhile, the U.S. Senate, in spite of opposition from John Ross and his supporters, ratified the New Echota Treaty on May 17, 1836, by a vote of just one over the required two-thirds majority. President Jackson signed the treaty on May 23, 1836. By the terms of the treaty, two years were allowed as the time within which the Cherokees would be required to relocate to areas west of the Mississippi.[83]

In early 1836, as Joseph began to make his plans to seek land grants across the river, he and Juda were saddened when their third child, and first son, died shortly after he was born. They had named him Timothy after his late grandfather.[84] He was buried in an unmarked grave, probably on a plot set apart on the James Roark land on Sale Creek. In losing her first son, Juda missed the comfort of her mother and father. Samuel Carr and Margaret had relocated in 1835 with sons James and John Carr to the Cherokee lands into what would be Bradley County. Their obvious intent was to locate a good tract, settle on it, and to be prepared to file for a land grant when procedures were established. For whatever reason, Samuel Carr was not to file for land in his own name. He was, however, to support his son John financially and to assist with legal matters in John's land grants. In anticipation of the grant, Samuel Carr, his wife, and sons John and James with their families, settled in the Cherokee lands. Carr's extended trade with the Indians doubtless was a significant benefit to Carr in moving early into the Cherokee area.[85]

As the news came to Hamilton County that the U.S. Senate had ratified the New Echota Treaty, word also came of events in Texas. The Alamo had fallen in March, and among the 183 men killed by the Mexican army was Davy Crockett, a former congressman from Tennessee who had earlier been mentioned as a possible presidential candidate. On April 21, after weeks of retreating with his small army across southeast Texas, Sam Houston had defeated Santa Anna's army at San Jacinto and proclaimed Texas' independence. President Andrew Jackson, who had been Houston's mentor since the Battle of Horseshoe Bend, was quick to recognize the new government in Texas.

As Joseph Roark followed these events, he was also keenly aware of the opposition of Principal Chief John Ross and many Cherokees with him, to the new treaty. Following the ratification of the treaty, Ross developed a vigorous campaign against the treaty, declaring it null and void, and railed against John Ridge and all others who had favored the treaty and relocation. Cherokee councils were held in which the actions of the U.S. government were denounced. The intent of the government to enforce the treaty was questioned and advice from the Indian agents was ignored.

Meanwhile, the State of Tennessee took action toward incorporating the Cherokee lands into the public lands of the state. On October 18, 1836, the legislature passed an act providing for the survey of land ceded by the Cherokees and creating a surveyor's district. The legislature named the new public land area "the Ocoee District." The act called for the naming of a surveyor general who was to establish a "basis line" from the main street in Calhoun, Tennessee, on the Hiwassee River "south twenty degrees west to the south boundary line of the State." From this basis line, the surveyor general was to layout townships of six miles square and was to include in the survey all islands in the Tennessee and Hiwassee Rivers. The Ocoee Act was quite specific on how the surveyor general was to mark the various townships and section lines in the survey. Even quarter sections were to have corners marked and identified. Under the Act, the sixteenth section of each township, "if fit for cultivation, and if not, then the section nearest thereto," was to be reserved for the use of schools in the township. The surveyor general was required by the Act to have his office in Cleveland, Bradley County.[86]

While the initial Ocoee Act did not indicate that the state planned to dispose of the lands through a public grants program nor when or how grants would be made, it was clear to all citizens of Hamilton County that the land would soon be available for settlement. In late 1836, Joseph Roark made trips across the Tennessee to conduct surveys of his own to locate good farm sites and probably to stake out a claim.

Doubtless Joseph knew many of the settlers who had moved into the Ocoee District area prior to its creation and, having observed his father's tactics in submitting claims for public lands in Claiborne County, realized that in all probability, priority would be given to occupants of the land when entries for land grants were to be received. Now that a treaty had been signed and a survey authorized by the state, he wanted to be an "occupant" and to establish an early claim.

The home site he selected was along Grasshopper Creek, approximately two-and-one-half miles southeast from its mouth on the Tennessee. Two miles to the southwest of Joseph's chosen home site was one of the first log structures erected by settlers in the Grasshopper Creek area–the Salem Baptist Church. Founded on May 23, 1835,[87] the church building was located on a slight rise overlooking the Tennessee River immediately north of "a free-flowing spring under a bluff."[88] Membership in 1836 included both white settlers and Cherokee families.[89] Joseph Roark was to be a part of this congregation during his life span, and the church was to have a significant impact on Joseph and his family.

In late 1836, clearly reading the government handwriting on the wall of the Cherokee Nation and seeing that relocation was inevitable, William Blythe, brother-in-law to James Roark and friend to Joseph Roark and Samuel Carr, began to liquidate his land holdings in anticipation of being part of the westward migration of the Cherokees. On October 25, 1836, just one week after the legislation creating the Ocoee District and authorizing its survey into public lands, Blythe sold two tracts on the north side of the Tennessee to William Clift for $1,900. The two tracts were the 110 acres that he had purchased from James Roark two years before and the 200 acres purchased from Cozby and McClung in August 1834.[90] The deed to Clift was witnessed by W.J. Able, Robert C. McKee, and John Roark. At the same time, Blythe apparently gave or sold to James Roark his half-ownership in the 250 acres purchased with James in 1834.[91] Clearly Blythe had decided to move west with his wife's people.

In mid 1836, Juda informed Joseph that she was again pregnant, expecting sometime the next March. Joseph realized that if he were to establish a claim in the Ocoee District and move his family there to establish his occupancy, he must begin construction soon. With two daughters less than three years old, Jane Clingan now almost nine, and a new baby expected in March, a substantial cabin would be required. In July 1836, one week after his twenty-third birthday, Joseph signed a promissory note to merchant Isaac Benson, doubtless for goods necessary for the new homestead. Benson had come to Rhea County with his parents when he was twenty. He operated a business with his partner, Joseph French, in Washington but owned a tract southwest of that town. In 1821, Benson sold his tract to William Smith, who would foster development of Smith's Cross Roads, later known as Dayton. A year after the date of Roark's note, Benson was named postmaster of Smith's Cross Roads.[92] Joseph Roark's promissory note read as follows:

One day after date I promis to pay Isaac Benson five dollars and seventy
sents for vallue rec'd. Witnys my hand and seal this 11 of July 1836

Joseph Roark[93]

On March 27, 1837, the third daughter was born to Joseph and Juda. They
named her Margaret, after Juda's mother. At a time when male children would desperately be needed to help in the cultivation of new farmland, Joseph had been
blessed with girls. Nevertheless, while Juda was caring for the new baby, Joseph
would be constructing their new home across the river. On March 1, 1837, just over
three weeks before Margaret was born, Joseph signed a promissory note in a sizable
amount to Thomas McCallie in Washington, Rhea County, apparently for household
needs and required construction tools/materials:

$17.36
One day after date I promise to pay Thomas McCallie Seventeen Dollars
thirty four cents–Value Rec'd March 1, 1837

Joseph Roark

Joseph was to pay the note at some later date plus $0.95 interest, reclaim the
note, and, as was his custom, cut out with his knife his signature from the note, thus
rendering it invalid for further transfer or exchange. The remainder of the note was
filed away for safekeeping.[94]

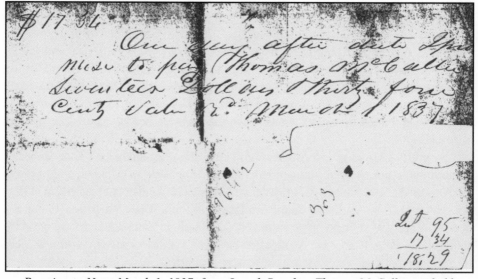

*Promissory Note, March 1, 1837, from Joseph Roark to Thomas McCallie, probably
for tools and materials for construction of the Roark cabin on Grasshopper Creek.*

By September 1837, Joseph Roark had completed work on his new home place
and moved his family to Grasshopper Creek on the south side of the Tennessee River.
The cabin was located on the south bank of the creek and, in the traditional fashion,

the construction was twenty feet by twenty feet with a large stone fireplace. The entry faced the west while the fireplace, which was used for heat and cooking, was on the east side of the cabin. Constructed of planed logs, in contrast with the cabins built in earlier years in which logs were neither planed nor had the bark removed, the homeplace cabin was weather-proofed by caulking between the planed logs with cemented material from the creek. The roof was constructed of homemade shingles shaved from local timber. The traditional outhouse completed the homeplace and was located to the east of the cabin. A barn would be constructed later and the home-place expanded as the family grew and space was needed. Into this cabin on Grasshopper Creek, Joseph moved Juda, Jane Clingan, and the three girls: Mary Ann 3, Sarah Elizabeth 2, and Margaret, six months. The family was in the cabin that was to be their home for the next forty years.[95] By the first of the year following their move into the homestead cabin, Juda was pregnant again. In the latter part of 1838, another girl was born, whom they named Jerusha after her aunt.[96]

In September 1837, doubtless in support of his move to Grasshopper Creek, Joseph signed another promissory note to Lewis Patterson of Sale Creek:

> Three dayes after date I promiz to pay Lewis Patterson ten dollars Sixty eight & three- fourth cent for Value Rec'd of him Wittness my hand and seal Sept 7th - 1837
>
> Joseph Roark[97]

On October 8th, Joseph made a payment of $4.12 on the Patterson note. No record remains as to the date the note was paid in full.

From crops raised on the farm on Sale Creek with his brother, Joseph was able to pay certain promissory notes and also to provide income for support of his family. On November 17, 1837, Joseph received a request from Mortimer Sams to pay William Clingan, a resident of Sale Creek:[98]

> Mr. Joseph Roark Sir, please pay William Clingan four bushels and three pecks of corn and this shall be your receipt for the same
>
> this 17th November 1837 Mortimer Sams[99]

The surveyor general for the Ocoee District was named in late 1836 and the land survey begun in the spring of 1837. John B. Tipton was named as surveyor general and he, in turn, selected his deputies to assist in the survey. The survey team consisted of John C. Kennedy, J. C. Tipton, Thomas H. Callaway, J.F. Cleveland, and John Hannah. The surveyor general, under the statute, was compensated for the survey on the basis of each mile of survey line laid out and marked: for each mile west of the basis line he was paid $2.50 per mile, and for each mile east of the basis line, because it was in more mountainous terrain, he was paid at the rate of $3.50 per mile. The survey crew received financial benefit beyond that paid based on the miles surveyed in that their work in the field made them knowledgeable of settled land and, more importantly, of unsettled land which could be claimed. Later, during the entry and land grant process, the names of the survey crew members frequently appeared on entries and grants for a large number of favorable tracts. The survey of the Ocoee District was completed in the late summer of 1838.[100]

As Joseph and his family were settling in their new homestead, the Tennessee legislature, on November 20, 1837, prescribed by statute the methods by which the public lands in the Ocoee District could be transferred to private ownership. The procedure for land grants in the statute specified that "every person or persons, except natives of the Cherokee Nation of Indians, who was or were in the actual possession of and residing upon any piece of vacant and unappropriated land . . . shall be entitled or priority of entry for one hundred and sixty acres of lands . . ." No person, however, was to be entitled to more than one such occupancy. Entries were classified as either "occupant" or "general entry" for non-occupants as claimants. The procedure specified that the occupant or claimant was to submit an entry to the entry taker with the location of the entry by section and township along with the prescribed sales price. An entry number was assigned and, following the issuance of a grant signed by the governor of Tennessee, the occupant or claimant would possess title to his tract. Since the new land law prescribed occupancy rights for those already in the Ocoee District, albeit illegal occupancy in many cases, Joseph Roark felt rewarded that he had occupied a homestead on Grasshopper Creek. The sales price for the public land was specified on a sliding scale beginning at $7.50 per acre. Occupants were given a priority right for three months after November 5, 1838, to submit an entry and purchase up to one quarter section (160 acres) at this price. Under the 1837 statute, all entries had to be submitted for a minimum of 160 acres. No smaller tract would be considered. After the three months allotted for occupants to file their entries, general enterers were allotted two months to file an entry at a sale price of $7.50 per acre. After five months, occupants were again given priority to submit entries for $5.00 per acre, and after two months, entries could be submitted by general enterers at the same price. In similar fashion after subsequent four-month periods, prices were reduced to $2.00 per acre, then $1.00, $0.50, $0.25, and $0.125. After twenty-nine months, the sales price was reduced to $0.01 per acre.[101]

There was a risk, of course, to an occupant enterer, and especially to a general enterer, in waiting to obtain his land at the cheaper price in that another settler could claim either his occupied land or his "held" tract and "take" the tract from under him. A few occupants declined to take this gamble and submitted their entry at the $7.50 per acre price for a total cost of $1,200 for a quarter section. Such was the case for Thomas Crutchfield who, having just sold the land for the town of Harrison[102] paid $7.50 per acre for his grant on Jolly's Island (later Hiwassee Island) and for other entries along the Tennessee.[103] Joseph Roark, however, chose to take the gamble. First, in all probability, he could not raise the $1,200 necessary to enter a full quarter section and, second, he had observed his father taking a similar gamble in submitting delayed entries in Claiborne County to obtain the lowest price. The lesson from his father was not lost on Joseph. He would wait the prescribed times to submit on his "occupant tract" and any other "general entry tract" to get the best price. Shrewdly, Joseph was to submit a total of ten entries, one as occupant and nine as general enterer, but in each case would wait until the price was reduced.

The act establishing the procedures for selling the land within the Ocoee District mandated that an entry taker's office be established in Cleveland, Bradley County, by the first Monday of November 1838. The act called for the election of the entry taker by the legislature and, following passage of the act, Luke Lea was elected to that office. Lea, then at the age of 55, had commanded a regiment under General Andrew Jackson during the Indian wars in Florida and against the Creek Indians in 1818. Prior to his election as entry taker, he had served in Congress for two terms between 1833 and 1837. A native of North Carolina and the son of a minister, Lea brought dignity to the office of entry taker and managed the sale of the public land in an evenhanded manner.[104]

Elsewhere in Hamilton County, in the summer of 1838, citizens at Ross's Landing met in the recently constructed log schoolhouse and agreed to change the name of the community to "Chattanooga"–Cherokee for Lookout Mountain. Growth had occurred at Ross's Landing following the establishment of a military post there in 1836. The Ross's Landing post office had been authorized March 22, 1837. In April 1838, the *Hamilton Gazette* published its first flyer announcing that the paper would begin weekly distribution in June. Subscriptions were priced at $3.00 per year. The announcement for the *Gazette* read as follows:

> With the view of contributing to the general interest of the citizens of, and circumjacent to Rosses' Landing, the subscriber proposes to incur the responsibility of publishing a newspaper, to be devoted to the discussion of General Intelligence among the people, of all the Commercial, Agricultural, and Internal Improvement advantages that are, or may hereafter connected with this place . . .

> Rosses' Landing is already at a point which a large portion of the produce and manufactures of East Tennessee are sold or deposited . . .

> As the location, or definite termination, of one or two Railroads from Georgia to Alabama, to the Tennessee river, is not yet decided, we shall gather and present such arguments in favor of this as an intersecting point . . .

> Thousands are looking with much solicitude to the Ocoee District–its growing importance, and its present and future prosperity, with the view of permanently locating on its fresh and fertile soil . . .

> . . . How far we may succeed in filling the expectations of our patrons, time will develop. We can only vouchsafe to devote our undivided attention to the "Gazette," and with it prosper or fail.
>
> F.A. Parham

May 15, 1838[105]

With the change in the name of the post office at Ross's Landing to Chattanooga on November 14, 1838, the name of the local paper would be changed to the *Chattanooga Gazette*.

By the summer of 1838, the deadline for the migration of the Cherokees had passed and, while a total of 2,103 Cherokees had moved to the Indian Territory,[106] almost fifteen thousand by government estimate, remained.[107] As Joseph Roark was beginning his first spring planting on Grasshopper Creek, Principal Chief John Ross was again in Washington protesting the 1835 treaty and asking the Congress to address the grievances of the Cherokee Nation. President Martin Van Buren, having taken office in March 1837, proposed a compromise by which the Cherokees would be allowed two more years to relocate. The compromise was vigorously opposed by the governor of Georgia and its congressional delegation. Following expiration of the deadline established in the treaty, Maj. Gen. Winfield Scott was ordered to assume command of troops already assigned to the garrison at Ross's Landing, to assemble other troops as needed including state militia, and "to put the Indians in motion to the West at the earliest moment possible."[108] General Scott, a veteran of the Black Hawk war and the campaign against the Seminoles, established his headquarters at New Echota in Georgia. John Ross rushed to meet him and again presented his argument against relocation. On May 10, 1838, General Scott sent his first proclamation to the Cherokees:

> *Cherokees!* The President of the United States has sent me, with a powerful army, to cause you, in obedience to the Treaty of 1835, to join that part of your people who are already established in property, on the other side of the Mississippi . . . The full moon of May is already on the wane, and before another shall have passed away, every Cherokee man, woman and child . . . must be in motion to join their brethren in the far West . . .
>
> I am come to carry out that determination. My troops already occupy many positions in this country that you are to abandon . . . Obey them when they tell you that you can remain no longer in this country. Soldiers are as kind hearted as brave, and the desire of every one of us is to execute our painful duty in mercy . . .
>
> Do not, I invite you, even wait for the close approach of the troops; but make such preparations for emigration as you can, and hasten to this place, the Ross' Landing, or to Gunter's Landing, where you all will be received in kindness by officers selected for that purpose . . .
>
> This is the address of a warrior to warriors. May his entreaties be kindly received, and may the God of both prosper the Americans and Cherokees, and preserve them long in peace and friendship with each other!
>
> Winfield Scott
> Cherokee Agency
> May 10, 1838

In Order 25, dated May 17, 1838, Scott provided direction to his troops in regard to the removal process. The order included:

> Every possible kindness, compatible with the necessity of removal, must, therefore, be shown by the troops, and, if in the ranks, a despicable individual should be found, capable of inflicting a wanton injury or insult on any Cherokee man, woman, or child, it is hereby made the special duty of the nearest good officer or man, instantly to interpose, and to seize and consign the guilty wretch to the severest penalty of the laws.

Scott was particularly concerned about treatment of the Indians by the Georgia troops under his command. As a officer who was especially attentive to detail, he was particularly watchful of the Georgia troops. He found, as a general rule, that the North Carolinians and Tennesseans were more "evenly disposed toward the Indians."[109]

On July 26, 1838, the *Hamilton Gazette* reported:

> Up to the time our paper goes to press, we have received no news of the termination of the conference between Gen. Scott and John Ross. It is supposed that an understanding will be brought about, which will give Ross an interest in, if not the whole removal of the Cherokees. We learn that many of the Indians are opposed to any arrangement being made with Ross–rather preferring to be removed by the whites for what reasons we are unable to divine.[110]

The same issue of the paper carried the following request for proposals:

> Sealed proposals will be received until the 15th day of August, 1838, to supply the Cherokee Indians emigrating from this place and other parts of the nation to the Cherokee Nation west of the Mississippi river, with rations to consist of one pound of fresh beef, or three fourths of a pound of salt pork or bacon & three fourths of a quart of Corn or Corn Meal, or one pound of flour to each person, and four quarts of salt to every one hundred rations, the price per ration must be specified, bacon or beef to be furnished as required. The above articles are to be of a good and wholesale quality . . .

> Bonds with good security will be required for the faithful performance of the contract. Endorsed proposals will be received through the Post Office at Calhoun, Tennessee, addressed to

JOHN PAGE
Capt & Disb'g Agent Cherokees[111]

As Joseph Roark harvested his first crops on Grasshopper Creek, several parties of Cherokees were moving west under the direction of the U.S. Army. The number moved by the summer of 1838 aggregated about 6,000.[112] Later the same year, contrary to the speculation of the *Gazette*, John Ross obtained the acquiescence of General Scott in a plan under which the remaining emigrants were to be moved at the direction of the Cherokee Council during the cool weather season. The last party of Cherokees began their march to the west on December 4, 1838.[113]

In Bradley County, Samuel Carr was again required to assist his son John in financial and legal matters. In late September or early October 1837, John Carr had been taken to court in Cleveland by William Hickman, who had won a judgement in the amount $27.50. Apparently John could not satisfy the judgement against him, so on October 11, 1837, Samuel Carr, with the help and apparent additional financial security of a James R. Finley, posted bond to satisfy the judgement:

> State of Tennessee, Bradley County
>
> Know all men by these presents That we Samuel Carr and James R. Finley are held and firmly bound unto William Hickman in the penal sum of twenty seven dollars and fifty cents, but to be void on condition, that the above bound Samuel Carr & James R. Finley doth, on the 26th day of October 1837, at the house of Samuel Carr doth deliver to John P. Angelly, Constable of said county, one sorrle [sic] mare taken as the property of Samuel Carr to satisfy a judgement that said Hickman received against John Carr before S.M. Taylor Esqr which was stayed by Samuel Carr that being the day and place of sale of said property, then the above to be void, otherwise to remain in force in law. Witness our hands and seals, this 11th day of October, 1837.
>
> Samuel Carr
> James R. Finley[114]

Within a week of posting the bond, Samuel Carr settled the judgement without surrendering the sorrel mare when he paid $14.00 to Constable Angelly for satisfaction of the judgement. Apparently John Carr was involved with a gentleman by the name of Jesse Poe in that the receipt for payment of the settlement notes that the judgement was against both Carr and Poe. Poe's involvement in the judgement is not clear. Three months after the settlement, Poe was one of nine members of the Cleveland City Commission that filed an entry for 320 acres in the Ocoee District on behalf of the City. The final settlement by Carr resulted in a receipt from the constable:

> Rec'd of Samuel Carr fourteen dollars the amount in full of a judgement and cost that William Hickman Recovered against John Carr and Jesse Poe Before S.M. Taylor Esqr Rec'd by me this 18th day of October 1837
>
> John P. Angelly
> Const.[115]

The times were not good financially for Samuel Carr. In late summer the year following his settlement of the Hickman judgement, Carr had purchased two pair of shoes from Stuart and Carmichael in Cleveland and charged them to his account. On October 23, a representative of the store visited Carr at his home and personally delivered a request for payment of $3.25:

Cleveland, Tennessee, Oct 23rd, 1838

> Samuel Carr for self and son
> To Stuart & Carmichael
> To 1 pr. Shoes at $1.50
> To 1 pr. do at $1.75

Mr. Carr Sir: Pay to the bearer this amount which is due and we need money and must cawl on our friends to collect as we are very much in need.

> Yours Respectfully
> Stuart & Carmichael[116]

The invoice was marked paid and left with Carr.

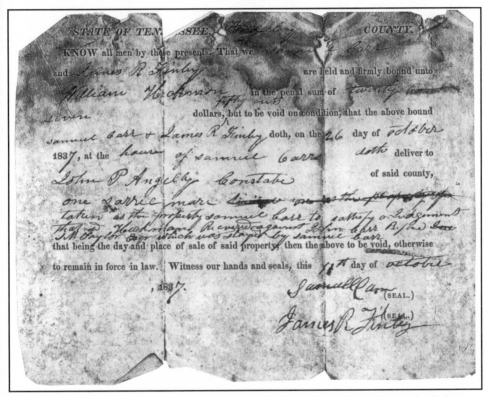

Bond, October 26, 1837, from Samuel Carr, father-in-law of Joseph Roark, pledg-ing a sorrel mare to guarantee payment of a judgement against John Carr, son of Samuel.

In early 1838, Joseph's brother James, seeing the near-term availability of cheap land in the Ocoee District, wisely decided to sell his two tracts on Sale Creek before land prices deteriorated. On March 7, 1838, James Roark executed a deed for the 200 acres of crop land on the south bank of Sale Creek. The deed was witnessed by John Roark and Hardy Hughes. The sale price was $500, two and one-half times what

James had paid for the tract four years earlier. The buyer was William Clift, who had also purchased the 310 acres from William Blythe in October 1836.[117] Clift had also purchased 10,000 acres in Hamilton County in 1836 from the McClung estate and was to be a major landowner in the county, being the first Hamilton County citizen to die a millionaire. Clift was commander of the local militia for many years, and later, at the beginning of the Civil War, he would declare himself for the Union and organize the Seventh Tennessee Federal Regiment.[118]

On August 27 of the same year, James Roark sold the 250 acres of ridge land on the north side of Sale Creek to Edward F. Wiley. Although Roark had jointly purchased the 250 acres with William Blythe, the sales deed was not executed by Blythe, indicating that Roark had in some way obtained full title to the tract. Nevertheless, he was able to make a significant profit on the tract as the sales price was $1,000, five times what Roark and Blythe had paid in 1834. The deed to Wiley was witnessed by George Hughes, John Pierce, and Fubliard Quarles.[119]

By mid 1838, word had spread that William Blythe had made the decision to remain dedicated to his family ties with the Cherokees and would move with them to the west. In a letter to his brother John Ross, who was then in negotiation with General Scott about the Cherokee relocation, Lewis Ross wrote that their friend William Blythe had divested himself of his holdings and was preparing to relocate to the west.

Appraisals had been made between August and October in 1836 on improvements made by individual Cherokees to determine the proper reimbursement by the U.S. government for their removal. Appraiser David Caldwell evaluated Blythe's property on September 27 and 28, and developed a total value of $16,174, which at the time would classify Blythe as very wealthy, by either white or Indian standards. In addition to two ferries, he owned more than 300 acres within the Ocoee District, all well fenced; twelve stables; more than 2,000 fruit trees: apple, peach, and cherry; a mill; cotton gin; several barns; and a blacksmith shop. The total appraisal had been increased by the supervising appraiser, John L. Young, who noted the following;

> It is clearly and decidedly the opinion of this agent that the above apple
> trees were valued too low [$6 per tree] . . . They are worth $10 each.
> J.L. Young

Blythe's home was described as a hewed log structure, two stories high, with a front porch and brick chimney and four fireplaces serving six rooms. The kitchen was a separate log building, weather-boarded, twenty feet square, with a stone chimney. Blythe's Ferry was appraised at $5000 based on a net income for the previous full year of $500.[120]

Sometime in late 1838 or early 1839, William Blythe accepted the government's appraisal and packed to move west. He bid farewell to his sister Jerusha and her husband, and to his friends in the lands that were no longer available to him, and left on his journey to present day Oklahoma. Ironically, one of the most heavily used routes on the Trail of Tears was across the Tennessee River at Blythe's Ferry. [121]

Following the sale of his two tracts on Sale Creek, James Roark moved his family to the south side of the Tennessee, north of his brother Joseph. For whatever reason, James chose not to submit an entry for Ocoee District land. On the contrary, James apparently purchased tracts in Sections 8, 10, and 15 of the Second Fractional Township, Range 3 West; however, deed records alone do not substantiate his purchases. The tract he purchased in Section 8 contained at least 130 acres and most likely was the fractional half-section immediately north of and adjacent to Joseph's Section 8 tract. His land holdings in Sections 10 and 15 lay along what would later be the Birchwood Pike and would contain by estimate 300 acres, more or less. [122] While both James and Joseph moved rather quickly into the Ocoee District, their brother John remained on Sale Creek and probably rented from Wiley after Wiley's purchase of James's 250-acre tract. It was to be several years before John would move across the river and purchase land near his brothers. [123]

Joseph Roark began 1838 by paying off the balance owed merchant Isaac Benson, receiving a receipt in return:

> Rec'd of Joseph Roark Sixteen Dollars and 43 ¾ cents in full of his acount
> to this Date 15th January 1838
>
> Isaac Benson[124]

Joseph, as was his disciplinary custom, filed the receipt in his papers for safe-keeping.

Later in January, Joseph signed a promissory note to Thomas McCallie in Washington, Rhea County:

> $13.18 One day after date, I promise to pay Thomas McCallie thirteen
> dollars & eighteen cents - value rec'd.
> Witnys my hand and seal this 26th January 1838
>
> Joseph Roark[125]

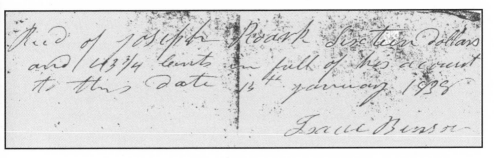

Receipt, January 15, 1838, from merchant Isaac Benson to Joseph Roark for settlement of his account in the amount of $16.43 ¾.

Within six months of the promissory note, McCallie was to move his store from Washington to Ross's Landing. On July 26, he would advertise in the *Hamilton Gazette* under the store name of McCallie and Long.[126]

In mid 1838, Joseph was to sell goods produced from his farm in the Ocoee District. He sold $6.75 worth of "upper leather" to Lewis Patterson, his friend from the Sale Creek area, receiving payment of $2.56 in cash. Joseph noted the payment received and preserved the record for collection of the rest of the note. [127]

Shortly thereafter, Joseph was to collect the remaining $4.19 from Patterson as credit in a promissory note:

> One day after date I promise to pay Lewis Patterson Three dollars and seventy five cents for value rec'd of him this the 30 July 1838
>
> Joseph Roark[128]

Joseph anxiously awaited legislation from the state government which would permit claims for land of less than 160 acres. Such legislation was being discussed and, if passed, it would permit Joseph to enter a claim on his homestead for 40 acres and pay the fee for an entry of that size rather than the 160 acres that was required as a minimum under the legislation that was in effect in 1838. But even if such legislation were to be passed and become law, Joseph still was faced with another problem. Part of his homestead parcel, when it was fitted within the grid network of the public land survey and into the prescribed corner of a section of the township, was occupied by a neighbor, Jesse Killian. Joseph could not file an entry claim as a general enterer on his homestead as long as Killian occupied a dwelling within the forty acres. Jesse and William Killian, assumed to be brothers,[129] had been in the Ocoee District lands since before 1836 and had been cooperative neighbors. The state statutes were clear in stating that an enterer could not dispossess a settler until the value of the improvements was paid by the enterer. If they could not agree on the value, two disinterested persons were to establish the value.[130] Joseph acted quickly in reaching agreement with Jesse Killian as to the value of his cabin and other improvements, paid the agreed amount probably with a promissory note, and received from Killian a bond guaranteeing the removal of his cabin by the first of the year. To convince the entry taker that the value was supported by two disinterested persons, Joseph had the bond witnessed by two nearby landowners:

> State of Tennessee, Hamilton County July the third-day ["second-day" had been scratched through and "third-day" written above] Jesse Killian doath bind himself in bond of two hundred and fifty dollars to give possession of his house and claim at January the 1st 1839 to Joseph Roark
>
>
> his
> Jesse X Killian
> mark
>
>
> Witness   Scott Johnson
>   Hiram Haney[131]

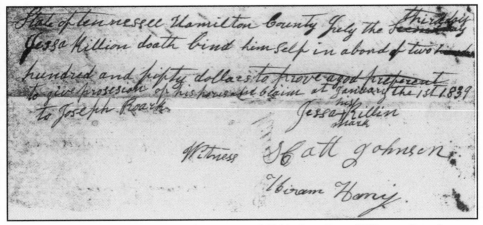

*Bond, January 1, 1839, in the amount of $250, from Jesse Killian to Joseph
Roark in which Killian agrees to surrender his house and claim on a tract in the Ocoee
District in order that Joseph can submit an entry for a land grant on the tract.*

Following the bond, Jesse Killian joined with his brother William and together
filed an entry for 80 acres adjoining the southeast corner of the Roark tract. William
Killian was to be a close friend and neighbor of Joseph Roark for the next forty
years. Much later, even after the death of both Joseph Roark and William Killian, the
two would be related through marriage of their adult children.[132]

In late 1838, at the age of twenty-five, Joseph Roark paid taxes for the first time.
He was assessed a per capita or poll tax of $0.50 by Hamilton County. His receipt
for payment of the tax was issued and signed by A.W. Rogers, Sheriff.[133]

The fall of 1838 also saw the removal of the remaining Cherokees. Assembling
at Rattlesnake Springs near the present-day Charleston, Tennessee, the remaining
thirteen thousand Cherokees departed in thirteen detachments under the leadership of
tribesmen designated by the Cherokee Nation. These last detachments moved west
along the Hiwassee, crossed the Tennessee on Blythe's Ferry, and traveled over
Walden Ridge to the western lands. John Ross and his family departed by steamboat.[134]

As the *Chattanooga Gazette* continued to promote the growth of Chattanooga,
Joseph Roark doubtless saw the benefits of a city at that location where roads inter-
sected the Tennessee River. A large community at that location would mean a

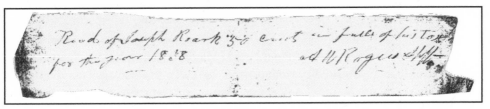

*Joseph Roark's receipt for his first poll tax paid in Hamilton County–issued by
sheriff A.W. Rogers in the amount of $0.50.*

stronger economy for Hamilton County as well as better local service such as improved mail delivery. In the summer of 1838, the *Gazette* had announced that mail would be delivered to Chattanooga three times a week in "four-horse post coaches from Jasper, Tennessee, and Spring Place, Georgia." From those points, mail from Chattanooga was to quickly go to Augusta, Georgia, and to the northwest to Nashville.[135] While Chattanooga was to become the focal point of activity in Hamilton County, the area around Grasshopper Creek would remain an isolated community, dependent on its own economy for survival.

As 1839 began, Joseph's father-in-law, Samuel Carr, continued to encounter financial difficulties. J.D. Traynor, ostensibly a friend, possibly an attorney but more than likely an associate who had advised Carr for over ten years, demanded immediate payment of $75.25 for past work and reimbursement for Carr's debts paid by Traynor to one William Grant. Traynor demanded that if Carr could not make payment in the full amount, he would be forced to mortgage his sorrel mare. Such was the case, and the mortgage, which was drafted and written by Traynor, was executed by Carr before witnesses and placed of record by Traynor at the Bradley County courthouse on the day following its execution. The mortgage was clear and self-explanatory:

> Samuel Carr
> from J.D. Traynor
> To Bal. of acct for 1837 & 38 - $45.45
>   Amt responsible to debts for
>   you   29.80
> $75.25
>
> State of Tennessee
> Bradley County I, Sam'l Carr of said county & state to serve the payment of the above sum of seventy five Dollars & twenty five Cents to John D. Traynor do pledge & mortgage to sd Traynor one sorrel mare four years old, sd Traynor takes her in his charge & if sd debt & cost that he is responsible for to Wm Grant of $29.80 & what I am indebted to him $45.45 is not paid or secured in thirty days from this time then sd Traynor may put up sd mare to public sale for ready money & sd amt. apply to the payment of sd claim. Witnys my hand and seal this 15th day of January 1839.
> Interlined before signed
> Witnys   Samuel Carr
> Samuel Lane, Daniel Lane[136]

The reason for the debt to William Grant, who was later to be a leading supporter of the Confederacy in Bradley County, is unclear. J.D. Traynor was later to be commissioned a captain in the Confederate Army and organized a company from Cleveland.[137] The resolved status of the sorrel mare is unknown.

For Joseph Roark, the new year of 1839 brought increased business activity, more promissory notes, and charge accounts in the agrarian economy. On January 9, 1839, Joseph brought his account up to date with William H. Mitchell of Sale Creek:

> Rec'd of Joseph Roark three dollars and 68 cents in full of his account with me up to this date January 9th 1839
>
> Wm. W. Mitchell[138]

Business in 1839 along Grasshopper Creek was still conducted north of the Tennessee River. Family shopping for Joseph's wife, Jane Clingan, and his four daughters, which, no doubt, was limited, was done with Isaac Benson of Benson and French in Washington, Rhea County. On February 11, Joseph received an invoice from Benson. The invoice is of particular interest because it was itemized and illustrates the items needed for Joseph's young family under frontier conditions:

> February 11, 1839
> Joseph Roark to Benson & French

15 doz Cotton thread .20	$3.00
2 ½ doz indig " .20	.50
1 doz pins and needles	.18 ¾
1 pound coperas	.12 ½
1 Comb	.12½
2 tuck combs .25	.50
3 yards flanel .62 ½	1.25
1 quart Botel Castor oil	1.00
by wife Balance for hankerchief	.25
1 yard Calico	.25
2 " " .40	.80
5 " " .30	1.50
Balance for Cap patron	.25
	$10.03 ¾

> Pleas pay the above acount
> to William Hickmon Jun. and oblige yours
> Isaac Benson
> 10.03 ¾[139]

Apparently Joseph could not pay the invoice at the time since a record of Joseph's account is noted on the reverse side of the invoice and shows two additional purchases in the amounts of $7.88 and $5.55. The next day, February 12, Joseph provided Benson with a promissory note, written in Joseph's own hand, in an amount that was probably to cover the first two of the above three amounts plus interest :

> one day after date I promis to pay Benson & French eighteen Dollars and 43 ¾ cnts value Rec'd witnys my hand and seal this 12th febuary 1839
>
> Joseph Roark[140]

Why would a merchant prefer a handwritten promissory note over a charge account debt since both represented a form of indebtedness? The answer obviously lies in the fact that in the frontier area of the Ocoee District and in most of Hamilton County in that era, the promissory note could be exchanged for other goods and services and served as a substitute for cash. The charge account was a debt unpaid while the promissory note pledged the good faith and credit of the issuer and could be traded by the holder as a medium of exchange. A letter that Joseph Roark received on October 2, 1839, from Wiley B. Skillern illustrates the utility of the promissory note:

> Mr. Joseph Roark, Sir you will please be so good to let Stephen Wallen have that Sixty five Dollar note which I let you have on William Clift, by so doing you will much oblige yours
> This 2 October 1839   Wiley B. Skillern[141]

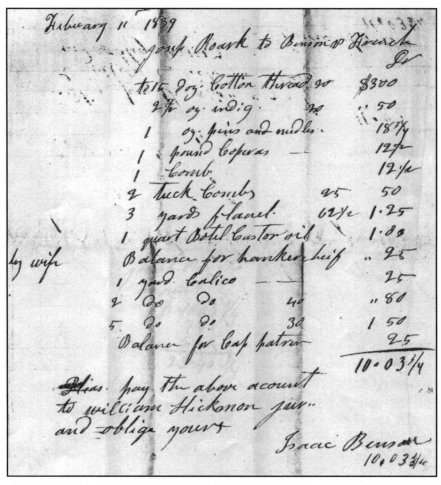

Itemized invoice from merchant Isaac Benson of the firm of Benson and French for purchases by Joseph Roark's family in February 1839.

Obviously William Clift, the future millionaire and Union Army colonel, had issued a promissory note in the amount of $65.00 to Skillern, who in payment to Joseph Roark for some goods or services, passed the note to him. It would appear that Skillern next needed to pay Stephen Wallen for some service and simultaneously needed to collect a like amount from Joseph, so Skillern, by letter to provide documentation and receipt, asked that the note pass to Wallen. Doubtless, other promissory notes, not available to us today, were involved in the transactions as a means of "making change." Thus with little cash in circulation and no banks or other credit mechanisms, the frontier community devised its own system of currency. Even the most casual reader will immediately note the importance of each individual fulfilling his obligation to make good on his promissory notes, even if it were presented for payment by a total stranger. No doubt some promissory notes were discounted and even rendered worthless by the poor credit of the signatory party. Quite simply, the individual who had even a slight reputation of defaulting on his promissory notes did not do much business in the local community.

Interestingly, each promissory note could be reduced in value by a partial payment on the note. Such partial payment was requested by the holder of the note if he needed cash in current bank notes and the issuer did not have the full amount available. Customarily, the partial cash payment received was recorded on the reverse side of the note, thus reducing its total value. Such was the case in July 1839 when Joseph Roark issued a promissory note in the amount of $20.00 to Jesse Killian probably as payment due Killian for removing his house and other possessions from Roark's homestead tract:

> one day after date I promis to pay Jesse Killian twenty dollars in current
> bank nots it being for value receved of him this the third day of July 1839.
>
> Joseph Roark

Ten days after the note was written, Joseph made a partial payment of nine dollars. Some time later, he was able to pay another one dollar on the note, and even later paid the remaining balance with interest. The notations on the reverse side of the original note reads as follows:

> I credit the within note nine dollars, this the 13th day of July 1839.
> Credit one dollar [no date given][142]

Joseph religiously followed throughout his life the habit of maintaining his redeemed notes in his business papers. Since the redeemed notes would still have value if circulated in the local community, Joseph cancelled the redeemed note by removing with his pocket knife his signature from the note. This was the equivalent of a later-day practice of stamping "paid" on a redeemed note.

Interestingly, Joseph had issued on July 3, 1839, another note to Jesse Killian for the same purpose, this time in the amount of $100.00. So, the day before his twenty-sixth birthday Joseph had committed to significant indebtedness. Additionally, he could also be facing in a few months a cash payment when he submitted his entries and paid the purchase price for Ocoee District tracts. The $100.00 promissory note and record of partial payments reads:

> On or before the first day October next I promise to pay Jesse Killian 1 hundred dollars in current Bank notes, it being for value recevd of him this the third July 1839
>
> Joseph Roark

On the reverse side of the note is written the payment record on the note:

> this the 29th July 1838 - to credit on the within note ten dollars
> credit 12 dollars Oct 1839
> Credit thirteen dollars this the 21st [The rest of the payment credits are missing as they were removed when Joseph at some later date cut his name from the note on the front side.][143]

In August, while he doubtless was struggling to repay the Killian note, Joseph issued a promissory note to a John Conner:

> Due John Conner thirteen dollars it being for value recevd of him this twenty first day of August 1839
>
> Joseph Roark[144]

A strong appreciation of the indebtedness of Joseph Roark during this period and his struggles to make good on his debts results from a review of his promissory note to Lewis Patterson of Sale Creek on November 1, 1839:

> Due Lewis Patterson three dollars seventy five cents for val Rec'd Wittness my hand and seal November 1, 1839
>
> Joseph Roark

As recorded on the reverse side of the note, it would be over three years before Joseph would make a payment on the note. Accompanied with numerous calculations, most probably of interest due, the single credit notation reads:

> Rec'd 10 of Feb 1843, $1.31 ¼[145]

The absence of Joseph's signature reflects that the note was ultimately paid, albeit sometime after the first partial payment. Lewis Patterson doubtless had little concern about getting his money and was patient with Joseph in redeeming the note.

In early December 1839, Joseph received the anticipated good news that the state legislature had passed an amendment to the Ocoee land statute on November 28 permitting entries for less than 160 acres. Entries for not less than forty acres could then be received provided the forty acres was located at a corner of a section or quarter section:

> That any person or persons wishing to enter less than a quarter section of land in said district, shall, from and after the passage of this act, be entitled to enter eighty acres in an oblong entirely across the quarter or fractional

quarter, or forty acres in a square in one corner of the quarter or fractional quarter, and in all cases beginning at one corner of the quarter or fractional quarter, with all the benefits, and under all the restrictions of this act and the act this act is intended to amend.[146]

The amendment also required the entry taker to develop a map of the Ocoee District of sufficient size and scale on which to note each enterer, the area of each entry, and the price paid for entries within the district. The map was to be available for inspection by all parties interested in acquiring land within the district. Apparently the legislature felt the process should be more open to the public and not give an unfair advantage to persons having inside knowledge on tract availability. Nevertheless, the amendment was what Joseph Roark had been waiting for. He began to ready his entry, writing out the tract description, and getting cash together to submit his entry after the first of the year.

On December 3, Joseph received a payment request from David McGill of Sale Creek:

> Mr. Joseph Roark sir please pay William Hickman the five dollars that you were to pay me for Cliftin and this shall be your reseipte for the same this third day of December 1839
>
> David McGill[147]

Joseph Roark and the McGills of Sale Creek were years later to be related through marriage.

As the year 1839 and the decade of the 1830s drew to a close and the promise of land grants within the Ocoee District began to approach reality for Joseph Roark and others like him, word was received of a gruesome event within the new home of the Cherokees in the west. At Honey Grove, in the northeastern corner of the Indian Territory, Major Ridge, his son John, and his nephew Elias Boudinot, all leaders in support of the New Echota Treaty in 1835, each had been murdered in cold blood on a June night in sight of his wife and family. The penalty of death to any Cherokee guilty of disposing of Cherokee lands had been enforced. Andrew Jackson, then ill at the Hermitage, simply shook his head when told of the murders.[148]

Chapter 7

Land Acquisition and Expansion
1840-1849

Joseph Roark eagerly began the new decade of the 1840s with his submission of entries for Ocoee District land. The homestead tract on Grasshopper Creek had to be protected with an official entry, although Joseph would not have title to the tract until a grant had been signed by the governor. Opportunity also existed for entries on other tracts which were unoccupied and could be claimed. Joseph moved quickly. On Wednesday, January 22, 1840, he made the trip by horseback to the entry taker's office in the new community of Cleveland and submitted three entries to Luke Lea. The first entry, designated as Entry Number 1654 by the recorder, was for a forty-acre tract on Grasshopper Creek located three quarters of a mile due east of the mouth of Grasshopper Creek on the Tennessee River. The tract was designated as the southwest quarter of the northwest quarter of Section 21, Fractional Township Two North, Range 3 West, of the Basis Line for the Ocoee District. Joseph submitted this entry as an "occupant enterer."[1] The second entry, which Joseph submitted as a "general enterer," was for forty acres upstream on Grasshopper Creek in Section 27 at a location that would become Joseph's homestead[2] It is unclear as to why Joseph submitted his one and only occupant entry for the first and northernmost tract rather than for what came to be the homestead tract. Was it because he had not cleared Jesse Killian's improvements from the homestead tract in Section 27, or was it simply because of confusion with the recorder and a mistake was made in the designation of the type of entry? The homestead tract was much better land than the downstream Section 21 tract and was certainly Joseph's ultimate choice for his homestead. No record remains that Joseph built a cabin on the downstream tract; however, it is quite possible that he did occupy the tract, build a cabin, and live there for a brief period. In any event, Joseph submitted the two entries, each for forty acres, and paid the statutory rate in effect thirteen months into the grant process– $1.00 per acre for a total of $40.00 for each of the two tracts. The homestead tract was designated as NW4, SW4, Section 27, FT2N, R3W.

The third entry was for a tract on the Tennessee River itself with river bottom land and the bluff overlooking the river. For this entry, Joseph paid the same $1.00-per-acre rate for 124 acres described as the FSW4, Section 8, FT2N, R3W.[3] The tract was described as "the fractional southwest one quarter" since, because of the area included in the river, the tract did not contain the 160 acres in a full quarter section of land. Similarly, and for the same reason of land occupied by the Tennessee, the township itself was designated as the "Fractional Township Two North" since it did not contain the full thirty-six square miles of a normal township.

On that Tuesday, then, in mid January 1840, Joseph invested a total of $204 in land in the Ocoee District. This did not, however, complete his land acquisition activities. He returned to the entry taker's office the following week, Thursday, January 30, probably after securing additional cash either through a loan or from collections on promissory notes, and submitted a fourth entry for forty acres in Section 21, a quarter-mile east of his very first entry. He again paid $40 for the tract as a general enterer.[4]

Prior to his twenty-seventh birthday, Joseph Roark was the owner (with full title to be granted within eighteen months) of 244 acres of good farmland. His four tracts were somewhat separated, and while his homestead tract was only 40 acres of the total, the tracts in Sections 8 and 21 had more than adequate water and good soil. No doubt he considered the riverfront tract in Section 8 a "real find" and a good investment. The property was located due west of the terminus of the present day Johnson Road and was among tracts claimed earlier at a much higher rate than the $1.00-per-acre paid by Joseph. The two fractional quarter sections immediately north of his tract, for example, were purchased separately by Francis Gamble and James Battson for $7.50 per acre. With good water available, the two tracts in Section 21 lay along Grasshopper Creek but with less land suitable for cultivation than the homestead tract. Landowners nearby the two tracts in Section 21 were Jacob Roler, William Grant, Hiram Haney, Goodman Scott, Hiram Cornwell, and to the west, the Chattanooga merchant Thomas McCallie.[5] All these neighbors to his original grants would be business associates of Joseph Roark throughout his life. With his 244 acres, Joseph had made a significant beginning as a landowner and farmer on the south bank of the Tennessee, but his land acquisitions were far from over. He would make the trip to the entry taker's office in Cleveland six more times during the next two years. In addition to submitting land grant entries, Joseph would also purchase other tracts on the free market.

As Joseph Roark began his acquisition of land, Hamilton County continued its growth. With the expansion of its boundaries on the south side of the Tennessee River and the migration into the Ocoee District, as well as growth in the Chattanooga area, the county had almost quadrupled its population over that of 1830. The census report of 1840 indicated an aggregate population of 8,175 persons, of which 584 were slaves and 93 were "free colored persons." The distribution of occupations

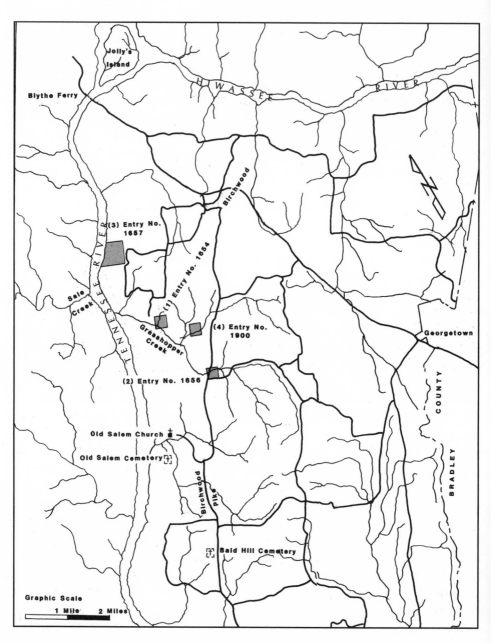

Tracts of land obtained by Joseph Roark through his first four Ocoee District Land Grants, January 22-30, 1840, for a total of 244 acres.

reported in the census is interesting. The large majority of heads of households listed "farmer" as their occupation. Only 30 listed "commerce," 192 listed "manufacturing" or "trades," and 40 were listed under "learned profession."[6] The predominance of farmers was even more significant on the south side of the Tennessee. With the high percentage of farmers, the age distribution is particularly interesting–Hamilton County was made up of young families. Of the white population, sixty percent were under twenty years of age and almost eighty percent were under thirty. Just eleven percent of the population was over forty years old.[7] It was the time of opportunity for young men like Joseph who were seeking their fortune in the fertile Tennessee Valley.

The expansion of Hamilton County south of the Tennessee to include a portion of the Ocoee District led to other changes beyond an enlarged population. With a large portion of the geographical area of Hamilton County now on the south side of the river, agitation developed to move the county seat from Dallas to a location that would serve the fertile farmlands and industrious farmers within the Ocoee District. The dynamics within the county were clearly south of the river. Also, rumors circulated that Georgia planned to build a railroad to connect to the Tennessee Valley. A county seat south of the Tennessee would be an attraction for a proposed railroad. In response to the local demands, the Tennessee legislature on January 3, 1840, authorized a referendum for the voters to choose between Dallas and a location south of the river "within one mile of the framed house lately occupied by Joseph Vann, a Cherokee Indian in said county."[8] Six commissioners were named to determine a specific location if voters favored a move of the county seat. Two of the commissioners were William Clift, who bought the James Roark tract on Sale Creek, and Jonathan Wood, the merchant in Washington who had outfitted Joseph for his wedding in 1832. Wood would move his business to Hamilton County south of the river and was to deal with Joseph for many years. The election for relocation carried, and the county seat was officially moved to Vannville. The commissioners chose a site near the mouth of Wolftever Creek and named the site for William Henry Harrison, hero of the battle of Tippecanoe and future president of the U.S. Having the county seat south of the river and just over twelve miles from his homestead cabin was to benefit Joseph Roark and add value to his land holdings.

Other commercial activities developed within the county. Demand for ferry travel across the Tennessee increased, and ferries originated by native Cherokees were acquired by local white citizens. Blythe's Ferry at the mouth of the Hiwassee was purchased by Charles Hutcheson following William Blythe's move to the Indian Territory. At Hutcheson's death in 1842, his widow married Burton Holman who would continue to operate the ferry under the Blythe name. Two miles south, the Doughty Ferry connected northern Hamilton County and southern Rhea County, its county seat then at Dayton, with the area south of the river near Joseph Roark's 124-acre river tract.[9] North of the new county seat of Harrison, Samuel Igou acquired the

Blue Springs Ferry from James T. Gardenhire, son-in-law to Cherokee Path Killer. The ferry became known as the Igou Ferry and the connecting roadway the "Igou Ferry Road."[10] Samuel Igou was one year younger than Joseph's brother James and had settled in Rhea County in 1824. He was an industrious businessman with unusual ability and was successful in several business ventures. In 1834, he had witnessed the deed from Charles McClung and the Cozby heirs when James Roark purchased his Sale Creek farm. Igou was to serve as brigadier general in the state militia and would be active in the political affairs of Hamilton County.[11]

In addition to the ferries, steamboat travel on the Tennessee between Hamilton County and Knoxville brought increased activity to landings on both sides of the river. Steamboats with such names as the *Holston, Harkaway, Reliance, Frankland,* and the *Huntsman* operated on the river along with others with popular feminine names such as the *Mollie Grant, Mary McKinney,* and the *Fanny Malone.*[12] While it was nowhere near the steamboat traffic on larger rivers such as the Mississippi or the Ohio, the steamers operating on the Tennessee nevertheless provided freight and passenger service along the river and, doubtless, some excitement to the pioneer families on the south side of the river.

Visionaries of the period were looking beyond the steamboat to the potential of the railroad. The state of Georgia, without significant rivers for transportation, had opted to spend large sums of money for railroads within the state and, in particular, for a line north to connect to the Tennessee River. Such a rail connection would take advantage of the steamboat traffic on the river and would provide an outlet, via the railroad, to the Atlantic coast. Georgia began discussion on the development of the Western and Atlantic Railroad through the center of the state, and the governor was instructed to learn if Tennessee would support an extension of the railroad to connect to the river. Joseph Roark doubtless participated in the local enthusiasm generated by such opportunities for railroad and steamboat interface.

Within the county, communities began to develop around churches and schools. Later, cities with strong economies would result from and be dependent on railroads, river travel, and major roadways; however, the initial communities in the agrarian economy would center on the church and, in most instances, the school that often was held in the church building. Schools were initially financed through local underwriting by parents on a per student basis, and in most cases, the schools operated for only three months out of the year. Teachers, mostly men, were employed on a contract basis and were paid partly in cash with the remainder to be paid "in good trade." By 1840, residents in Hamilton County were supporting five such schools with a total of 133 students. In 1841, schools were located at James McDonald's, Robert Patterson's, Clift's stillhouse, and near Archibald McCallie's.[13]

Churches were established early in the county. The Mount Bethel Presbyterian Church was organized in Soddy in December 1828. The Prairie Springs Methodist Church was organized and met near Dallas beginning in 1820. The Salem Baptist

Church on the south bank of the Tennessee provided the focal point of the Salem Community, and it would be the Salem Community that would be the home of Joseph Roark and, later, that of his brothers James and John. Records are nonexistent that would provide the size of the ill-defined Salem Community. Never organized or incorporated as a town or city, the Salem Community was not to enjoy the designation of a post office. Mail was later to be sent and received through various nearby communities with designated post offices. As the community grew and more young families established their farms south of the river, the center of the Salem Community moved away from the river to a location along what later became the Birchwood Pike. This roadway originally ran north from Harrison to the Hiwassee River and Blythe's Ferry. The new center of the Salem Community was strengthened in the late 1840s when the congregation of the Salem Baptist Church, following the fire that destroyed the meeting house, voted to move the church to a location along Grasshopper Creek. No records are available as to commercial establishments that operated within the Salem Community, although it is probable that Jonathan Wood owned and operated a store nearby, and later Joseph Roark was to build and operate a sawmill and gristmill. Other mills were also located within the community and served the local economy. By 1840 the growth and development of the Salem Community had begun and this small neighborhood would, for the next three quarters of a century, provide the social structure for the local farmers along Grasshopper Creek south of the Tennessee.

By early 1840, Joseph Roark had established his new homestead on the upper reaches of Grasshopper Creek. As the decade began, his family consisted of his wife and his four daughters: Mary Ann 6, Sarah Elizabeth 5, Margaret 3, and Jerusha 1. Also with them as part of the family was Jane Clingan, who was thirteen and now a big help with the girls. Juda had been expecting another child since the previous spring and shortly after the first of the year, on February 15, 1840, their hopes for a son were realized. They named their first son James after his uncle–Joseph's brother who had been so supportive of Joseph in his early days in Hamilton County. In a break with what seemed then to have been a family tradition, James was given a middle name. Unfortunately, only the middle initial survives. James A. Roark was to be the name of Joseph's eldest son.

At the beginning of the decade, Joseph's brother James, now almost 42, lived south of the Tennessee with Jerusha and their four children. His two oldest boys, Timothy 13, and John 11, were old enough to be of significant help on the farm. Son William 8, and daughter Martha 5, completed his family. Within a short period following his move to the south bank of the Tennessee, James was elected as the justice of the peace for the Salem Community and served in that capacity in 1840 and 1841.[14] Following his term as justice of the peace and probably because of his leadership experience in the militia, James was elected constable for the district that included the Salem Community.[15] He was to serve as constable for a period of two years.

In 1840, John Roark still lived with his family in the Sale Creek area. His family then consisted of seven children: Mary Ann 15, Sarah 13, Elizabeth 12, Nancy 9, Eliza 7, James W. 5, and Juda Ann 3. His wife was expecting another child, and within a few months John and Margaret welcomed their second son, William, in the late spring 1840. In March, John returned to Claiborne County to sell his remaining farm there–one hundred acres on Little Creek near its mouth on the Powell River. The buyer was Thomas Allison, who paid $60.00 for the farm. The deed was witnessed by Joab Cook and John's brother-in-law, James Richardson.[16]

No record remains that would indicate the level of contact between Joseph Roark, brothers James and John, and their mother and siblings that remained in Claiborne County. One cannot help but wonder as diligent as Joseph was in keeping receipts, promissory notes, and other records why no letters were preserved from his mother at the old home place. Although many of the siblings in Claiborne County were not prolific letter writers, we do know that his mother was well educated for her time and was capable of maintaining a correspondence with her three sons in Hamilton County. We can probably safely assume that such correspondence did take place and that Joseph, James, and John were kept informed of family events in Claiborne County, but for whatever reason, the letters were not preserved.

Early in 1840, either from letters from his mother or from John's trip to Claiborne County to sell his farm, Joseph learned that sister Nancy and husband James Richardson had not yet purchased a farm but now had a family of six children: George W. 11, Sarah Jane 9, Elizabeth 7, John 4, Mary Ann 2, and William 1. Also, Joseph's mother would have written that William and Nancy had purchased, in 1838, 50 acres on the Powell River from James Ferguson,[17] son-in-law to James Eastridge,[18] and with William's recent purchase of land from brother-in-law William Cox,[19] William Roark and Nancy now owned over 150 acres. He also was negotiating with Thomas McBroom to buy a large tract of over 415 acres. William was a hard-nosed businessman and had been quite successful in farming and in trading land. By mid 1840, he and Nancy had four children: John 12, Cynthia 10, James 7, and Eliza 5.

At the time, Joseph's sister Elizabeth and her husband Thomas Ellison had five children: Timothy 11, John 10, Jeremiah 8, Nancy 5, and George W. 2. As an aside, it is interesting to note that almost all of Joseph's siblings followed the family tradition of naming their children after grandparents and after uncles and aunts. The rare exception from such family names included George Washington and Andrew Jackson, both of which are understandable. In regard to Elizabeth and Thomas Ellison, Joseph's mother would have written that the blacksmith business of Ellison was going well, and that Ellison had approached her about buying the southwest 150 acres of the homestead tract. The tract produced little income as it was quite hilly, and Sarah was unable to farm it. The money would be helpful and, for that reason, she was seriously considering the sale to her son-in-law.

Joseph heard that his younger brother Jeremiah had, five years before in 1835, married Elizabeth Fultz,[20] whose father owned a large tract in the bend of the Powell River opposite Island Creek in Claiborne County.[21] Jeremiah was then farming for his father-in-law, and he and Elizabeth with their two children, John 4, and Sarah 1, were living on her father's land. Elizabeth was expecting their third child by midyear.[22]

Only Mary Ann was left at the homestead with Joseph's mother Sarah, when Timothy Jr. left to marry Mary Williams on March 12, 1840.[23] Mary Ann, 12, continued to be very close to her mother and was a significant help in maintaining the farm and the home place. Doubtless William, Jeremiah, and Timothy Jr., all of whom lived close by, assisted their mother in running the farm. Sarah was then sixty-four but apparently was in good health and had no intention of leaving the home place to live with some of her children.

On Grasshopper Creek, Joseph continued the development of his home place and farm. While he was waiting for his grant entry to be signed, Joseph purchased materials and equipment for his farm. Three days after his trip to Cleveland to submit his first three grant entries, Joseph crossed the Tennessee to the Sale Creek area to make a purchase from Dearson and McGill. For the purchase, Dearson and McGill accepted Joseph's promissory note:

> One day after date I promise to pay Dearson and McGill nineteen Dollars and fifty cents value Rec'd of them this the 25th of January 1840
>
> Joseph Roark[24]

By this time Joseph had made a sizeable investment in both time and money in his homestead and, through his crops, had accumulated sufficient income to meet cash demands on his charge accounts and promissory notes. On Saturday, February 29, 1840, Joseph was able to pay a $57.00 invoice in cash without relying on a promissory note:

> Received of Joseph Roark fifty seven Dollars in full of my acount with him this the twenty- ninth of February 1840
>
> Hardy Clifton[25]

With the promissory note system of business exchange, Joseph never knew when cash demands would be presented to him. On Friday, March 13, 1840, a gentleman by the name of Smith came to see Joseph at the homestead with this written message:

> Mr. Joseph Roark please to let heareby Smith have what you owe me and you will oblige your friend   March the 13th, 1840
>
> Hiram Haney[26]

Hiram Haney had a farm one and one-half miles due north of Joseph Roark and was a neighbor with whom Joseph was to have business dealings over the years. Oddly, the message did not say how much Joseph owed Haney. Apparently Joseph had quickly developed a reputation as an impeccable record keeper. Maybe Haney did not know the exact amount of the debt but he was apparently comfortable that Joseph did and the amount would be paid immediately as requested. The matter was closed–no further discussion nor receipt was necessary. Joseph was someone who could be trusted.

Another incident is illustrative. Just over a month after Haney's payment request, Joseph was forced to provide William Killian with a promissory note for value received. The promissory note was written in Joseph's handwriting:

> One day after date I promise to pay William Killian fifty-one dollars in current bank notes, it being for value Received of him this the twenty-ninth of April 1840
>
> Joseph Roark

Within thirty days Joseph made a payment of $32.50 on the promissory note and Killian acknowledged receipt, again in Joseph's handwriting, on the reverse side of the note:

> Received of the within note thirty-two dollars and fifty cents May the 26th 1840[27]

This particular note illustrates the importance placed on trust by the local community. Both the note and the receipt recorded on the reverse side were written by Joseph Roark in his handwriting–written by Joseph for only one reason–Killian could neither read nor write.[28] Yet he apparently trusted Roark to provide the correct content for both the promissory note and receipt. Honesty and trust were of primary importance within the frontier community.

Some comments should be made on the traditional promissory note. Many of the promissory notes written in the decades before the Civil War had at least four common features. First, most notes began with "one day after date I promise to pay . . . ." This clearly made the note redeemable almost immediately upon execution and gave it trading value without discounting as would be the case with a note to be paid in installments over an extended period. Any discounting of a promissory note was based on the credibility of the issuer. If that credibility were suspect, the holder could expect significant discounting of the note. Another term common to almost all promissory notes was "for value received of him" which made it clear that the note was not a loan with or without collateral but rather was payment for a commodity or service of value–value which had already been received and accepted by the issuer. Thus no claim could be made against redemption of the note because of unacceptable merchandise or inferior product. Also, many promissory notes contained a third feature in the form of a statement specifying how payment was to be made, e.g., "good bank notes" or "Alabama bank notes." Such bank notes were the closest commodity to the U.S. dollar bill as we know it today. Lastly, the fourth common feature of promissory notes was the acknowledgement and signature which most often read, "witness my hand and seal," followed by the signature.

This unique feature was a reference to the English tradition and the early American use of a seal along with the issuer's signature to support the authenticity of a note. A personal seal in the frontier Salem Community would have been a luxury and, of course, few existed. The "seal" on a promissory note was commonly fashioned onto a hand-drawn and small shaded circle that obviously had no significance, yet emulated a longstanding tradition of the times.

The requirement for promissory notes was a direct result of the absence of banks and the banking industry in general. Early U.S. presidents, including John Adams, Thomas Jefferson, and Andrew Jackson, opposed banking and particularly the issuance of paper money, preferring instead for the economy to be based on hard assets of gold and silver. Banking filled a need, however, in furnishing currency and credit to support trade. The first bank in Tennessee was the Nashville Bank, chartered in 1807, which was followed by the Bank of the State of Tennessee in Knoxville in 1811. One of the functions of the banks was the issuance of paper money or bank notes, the value of which were backed by "specie" of gold and silver coins and, of course, the credit of the bank itself. "Wild-cat banks" were guilty of having insufficient specie on hand which resulted in the issuance of unsound bank notes. Also, creditable banks were often forced to suspend specie payment during periods of financial panic, which obviously caused a depreciation in value of the bank notes.[29] Bank notes were available in limited supply to Joseph Roark and others in the Salem Community during the 1830s and 1840s from banks in Alabama and South Carolina, particularly the Farmers and Exchange Bank of Charleston. Tennessee banks issuing bank notes included the banks in McMinnville, Murfreesboro, Jefferson City, Shelbyville, the Union Bank of Tennessee and the Bank of Tennessee in Nashville, and the Farmers' Bank of Tennessee in Knoxville.[30] Merchants sought branch banks for the smaller towns and communities, but major banks resisted the dissipation of capital among areas where there was little trade. So the Salem Community, with no banks and few bank notes in circulation, some of which with questionable par value, devised its own system of promissory notes. Under this system, the redemption value of the promissory note was related almost solely to the credit and character of the issuing party. In most instances, the value of a poorly written promissory note issued by a man of known reliability in the community fluctuated less in value than did the printed bank notes pledging payment by engraved print.

Payment on promissory notes was, in addition to bank notes, also made in local commodities. Thirty days after his cash payment to William Killian, Roark executed a promissory note to A.A. Clingan with payment to be made in corn, obviously from a harvest anticipated months after the note was executed:

> On or before the first of November next I promise to pay A.A. Clingan one hundred seventy one bushels & a half of good sound corn to be delivered

at A.A. Clingan crib for value rec'd of him as witness my hand and seal this 24th June 1840

Joseph Roark[31]

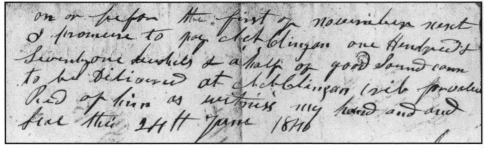

Joseph Roark promissory note, June 24, 1840, to A.A. Clingan for 171 ½ bushels of "good sound corn."

Alexander A. Clingan, the previous guardian of Jane Clingan, was the first sheriff of Bradley County, where he served 1837-1838 and 1840-1846. The "value received" from Clingan is not stated; however, Clingan was the officer to whom Joseph's father-in-law, Samuel Carr, made payments on legal issues and judgements. Was this a situation where Joseph was assisting his father-in-law again in payment of a debt in corn, or was this promissory note a receipt for an advance purchase of corn? We do not know the answer. In addition to serving as sheriff, Clingan also owned and operated a farm three miles northwest of Cleveland and would have legitimately needed corn for human consumption and for livestock feed. Clingan also had the family ties to Joseph through Clingan's niece, Jane, whom Joseph and Juda were raising, and to James Roark, through Martha Clingan's kinship to Jerusha. Joseph and James had a good relationship with Clingan; however, Samuel Carr would only have related to Clingan as sheriff in his official capacity for the collection of court judgements.

In late September, Joseph heard from his mother that she had sold the 150 acres from the homestead tract to her son-in-law Thomas Ellison, husband of Elizabeth. Ellison paid $200 for the southwest portion of the homestead for which Timothy Roark had made Entry Number 203 in 1826 and had received a grant for the tract in 1827.[32] Since Ellison's forge and home were on the north side of the Powell River and nowhere near the 150 acres, it is unclear as to whether he purchased the tract as an investment or as a courtesy to his mother-in-law to help her financially. For whatever reason, Ellison did not record the deed until almost eight years later just prior to his sale of the tract. When it was recorded, County Clerk Thomas J. Johnson required a witness to the deed executed by Sarah Roark. At the request of both Sarah Roark and Ellison, the eight-year-old deed was witnessed by Timothy Roark Jr., Peter Hazelwood, and Charles Bussell, an adjacent landowner to the north. Once the deed was recorded, Ellison sold the 150-acre tract plus 25 acres he had purchased in 1841 from James Carroll on the headwaters of Blair's Creek. Ellison's sale was to C.C. Smith of Claiborne County and John Netherland of Hawkins County for $400, and the deed was recorded April 8, 1848, one day after recording the deed from Sarah Roark.[33] Interestingly, John Netherland in 1859 would be the nominee of the Opposition Party (formerly the Whig Party) for governor of Tennessee to run against the Democratic incumbent, Isham Harris. Netherland would receive 47 percent of the statewide vote.[35] After her sale of the 150 acres to Ellison in 1840, Sarah Roark still owned more than 200 acres of the original homestead. Since Ellison had purchased both the 150 acres from the homestead and the 25 acres on nearby Blair's Creek, it could very well have been his intent to move his forge south of the river, closer to the Kentucky road northwest out of Tazewell. Nevertheless, less than two years were to pass following his sale to Smith and Netherland before Thomas Ellison and Elizabeth were to fall on hard times and encounter very unfortunate circumstances.

Late in 1840, Joseph Roark took steps to enlarge his land holdings. A neighbor to the southwest, Josiah Goforth, occupied 160 acres but owed Roark money for "value received." On the last day of 1840, to satisfy this debt, Goforth assigned his right and claim on the 160 acres to Joseph Roark. The assignment was drawn up by William F. McCormack, who owned land less than a mile south of Joseph but who, at the time, was the acting justice of the peace for that district of Hamilton County. Goforth executed the assignment and had it witnessed as evidenced by the signature of Isaac Smith and the mark of William Killian.[34] Following the assignment from Goforth, Joseph was still faced with the responsibility of filing an entry with the Ocoee Entry Taker and paying the required statutory purchase price for the Goforth tract. Since, under the Ocoee statute, the land prices in December 1840 were at $0.50 per acre, Joseph chose to wait until April 1842 to file the entry at which time land prices would be reduced to $0.01 per acre. Joseph then would be able to add a quarter section of good, fertile land near his homestead for a total cost of $1.60. The experience gained from his father in timing land entries in Claiborne County was serving him well.

The year 1841 opened with continued demands for cash and payments on promissory notes. Early in 1841, Joseph was presented with a payment requested by Thomas Gregory:

> Mr. Joseph Roark Sir, pleas pay the barer one dollar and twenty five cts and this shall bee your recept for the same
>
> Thomas Gregory[35]

Thomas Gregory was the youngest son of Revolutionary War veteran George Gregory whose widow had moved to Hamilton County in 1837.[36] Having come to Hamilton County with his mother and family, Gregory was a grant recipient in the Ocoee District.[37] Doubtless Joseph Roark was indebted to Gregory in some amount greater than $1.25 and would later use the above "receipt" to get credit for a payment on his debt.

In the spring of 1841, just after son James A. was a year old, Juda told the family that she was again pregnant, with the baby due in late summer. The addition would be their sixth living child, and on August 15, another son was born–John Wesley Roark–obviously named after both Joseph's brother John and the great Methodist minister whose influence had encouraged the Methodist circuit riders of the period. Two years later, on September 15, 1843, another son was born–William Marion–named after Joseph's brother in Claiborne County. With four girls and three boys in the family, plus Jane Clingan, a one-room cabin was no longer sufficient. Sometime during this period, Joseph enlarged the home place, adding a twenty foot by twenty foot room to the west of the main room with the large fireplace. The addition was of the same construction as the main room–planed logs with weatherproofed caulking and a roof of homemade shaved shingles. A loft was included with the addition to provide sleeping space for the children, particularly for the boys as they grew older.

On May 16, 1841, Joseph accepted from Britain Freeman a promissory note originally written by John W. Gamble. Along with the original note was a receipt discounting the note in the amount of a payment made by Gamble. The receipt illustrates the traditional system of using promissory notes as a medium of exchange yet noting discounts for payments received by any current note holder:

> Rec'd of John W. Gamble ten dollars in part of a note I hold on the said Gamble which I will read the said note for the saam this the 16 day of May 1841
>
> Britain Freeman[38]

The system of promissory notes was, of course, imperfect. Prompt payment was not always made to the note holder when payment demand was made. When such nonpayment occurred, the note writer had his credibility diminished, and for recourse, the note holder submitted the delinquent notes to the local sheriff or constable for collection. In late 1841, Joseph Roark had two such promissory notes from persons on the north side of the Tennessee–one on John Penny and Robert Bean to William Bean, which Joseph had taken as payment from William Bean on some debt, and a second note on Thomas Smith. The two notes were not paid when demand for payment was issued (probably over an extended delinquency period) so Joseph, to save a trip across the river, asked his brother John to deliver the two notes to the local constable James Gothard who was a large landowner north of the Tennessee.[39] The receipt from the constable was returned to Joseph:

> Received from Joseph Roark by the hand of John Roark too notes one on John Penny and Robert Bean to William Bean for fifteen dollars due 8 September 1841 one on Thomas Smith for five dollars twenty cents due

the 2 August witch I promise to collect or account for as an officer this 3 November 1841

James Gothard const.[40]

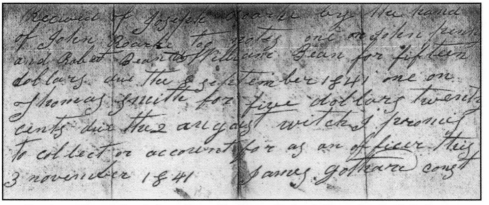

Receipt to Joseph Roark from Constable James Gothard, November 3, 1841, for two promissory notes submitted for collection.

The issuers of promissory notes went to significant lengths to preserve the trust and confidence in their notes. James T. Gardenhire, from south of the Salem Community, ran the following ad in the Chattanooga paper:

NOTICE

All persons are hereby forewarned from
trading for a note of hand given by myself
to Ezekiel Dunn, dated 3d January 1844,
for $140, due three months after date. Said
note was fraudulently obtained, and I am
determined not to pay it unless compelled by
law.

James T. Gardenhire
April 20th, 1844[41]

Joseph's father-in-law continued to have problems with meeting his financial obligations and with the courts. On the last day of May 1841, Joseph assisted by paying a debt of his mother-in-law to a local merchant. Apparently Alfred Hutcheson was demanding payment on a small purchase by Margaret Carr and it came to Joseph's attention. Probably unknown to Samuel Carr, Joseph stepped in, made the demanded payment, and received the following receipt:

Rec'd of Margaret Carr by the Hand of Joseph Roark amount $2.87 ½ it
being final acount with me May the 31 1841

Alfred Hutcheson[42]

Samuel Carr continued to have many of his debts and accounts submitted to the sheriff for collection. Such was the case in December 1841 when Sheriff A.A. Clingan called upon Carr for payment of a debt to M.F. Carle. Carr made the payment and subsequently received the following receipt:

> Received of Samuel Carr by A.A. Clingan Four Dollars in full of his account up to this date. Dec 29th 1841
>
> M.F. Carle[43]

While Samuel Carr was having his problems, it was a particularly troubling time for his son John, for in 1841 John Carr was to lose his forty-acre farm in Bradley County to the courts. On June 15, 1839, Elias and A.H. Pitner had taken John Carr to court on some issue and the matter was brought before Jesse Poe, justice of the peace in Bradley County. Poe had rendered a judgement against John Carr in the amount of $8.86; however, two years later, the judgement still had not been paid by Carr. On June 10, 1841, Justice Poe sent an order "To any lawful officer" of Bradley County, "you are hereby commanded that of the goods and chattels, lands and tenements of the said John Carr, if to be found, in your county, for the stay of execution you cause to be made the aforesaid sum of money with legal intrust on said judgement." Sheriff A.A. Clingan reported on June 12, 1841, that no goods and chattels of John Carr were to be found, and land owned by Carr consisted of forty acres, the SE4, SE4, Section 2, T2N, R1E in the Ocoee District. It was ordered by the court that the land "be sold to satisfy the Plaintiff's execution issued upon the Justice's judgement."[44] John Carr had lost his land for failure to pay a debt of $8.86.

Things were not gloomy, however, for Joseph Roark. On a sunny day in late March or early April 1841, Joseph received the final record of his first four Ocoee District land entries documenting his ownership. Four certificates, each signed by Tennessee Governor James K. Polk, named Joseph Roark and his heirs as the owner of the tracts on which entries had been submitted in January 1840. Joseph now had official title to his homestead and other acreage totaling 244 acres.[45] At age twenty-seven he was now an owner of land–a milestone in the life of a farmer. No doubt it was a red-letter day in the life of Joseph and Juda Roark as they celebrated the event together. Before the month of April was to end, however, Joseph would make another trip to the entry taker in Cleveland for the purpose of submitting yet another entry. Two more entries would follow in 1841.

Joseph Roark's land grant entry in April 1841 was for eighty acres immediately west of and adjacent to the homestead tract. It was level ground easily subject to cultivation and, although the statutory price was then at $0.50 per acre, Joseph felt it wise to make the entry rather than gamble on acquiring the tract at the next lowest price.[46] A month later, May 29, 1841, Joseph submitted another entry for forty acres downstream on Grasshopper Creek, close but not adjacent to his original occupant entry. A good tract with water frontage on the creek, it was also at the price of $0.50 per acre. Apparently Joseph felt there was competition for the tract and that it would not be available at a lower price.[47] In August, one week before his son John W. was born, Joseph made the trip to Cleveland to make entry for his third land grant of the year. This time the entry was submitted for forty acres at $0.25 per acre. The tract was located a quarter mile southwest of the homestead tract.[48]

Joseph continued in 1841 to make improvements to the homestead and to issue promissory notes for payment. On Friday, September 24, he signed a promissory note, payable on order, to Hiram Haney for $20.00 for lumber. On the reverse side of the note is written:

One inch plank   335 feet
3 quarter plank   275 feet[49]

One day later, Joseph issued a promissory note for $27.50 payable on October 1, 1841, to West Freeman, a landowner approximately a mile south of the homestead.[50]

On October 31, Joseph signed yet another promissory note to Thompson Crews and Company for $20.00 payable within twelve months "in current bank notes."[51] All three notes were returned to the financial papers of Joseph Roark with his signature neatly cut from each promissory note indicating full payment had been made as required.

In late fall 1841, Juda Roark received word that her sister Margaret planned to marry in December. Margaret was then in her early thirties and was late to marry. It is not clear where Margaret lived at the time, but we do know that she did not live with her parents. The best evidence suggests that Margaret went to live with her sister Jane Carr Mahan in Meigs County when her parents moved to Bradley County in 1835. It was there that she was to meet Leonard Brooks. Brooks was a widower with older children but with a young son, Zachariah, just over six years old. He was a responsible citizen with a good reputation in Meigs County. Somewhat older than Margaret–he was between fifty and sixty–he had obtained a quarter-section land grant north of the Hiwassee in 1825.[52] Brooks had played an active role in the formation of Meigs County and in 1836, after formation of the county, he and James Lillard had given fifty-one acres for creation of the county seat town of Decatur.[53] In 1838, Brooks had been elected to serve as one of five common school commissioners in District 2 of Meigs County.[54] He was a member of the Good Hope Baptist Church, and in September 1842, he was to be a delegate to the annual meeting of the Hiwassee United Baptist Association held in Bledsoe County.[55] Beyond his civic involvement, Brooks had twice taken on responsibilities as guardian for minor children of other families. In 1831, he had been named guardian of the six minor children of William and Sarah Buster and had raised them to maturity.[56] Just five years before his marriage to Margaret Carr, Brooks has assumed guardianship of the four minor children of Samuel Tillery and Brooks' sister, Irena Brooks Tillery.[57] Two of the Tillery children still lived with Brooks at the time of his marriage to Margaret. The wedding took place on Thursday, December 23, 1841, and the ceremony was performed by Reverend D.L. Godsey.[58] The marriage was to be short-lived but was to significantly impact the lives of Joseph and Juda Roark.

The Salem Community continued to grow as other farmers took up their grants in the Ocoee District and established homesteads within the area. The closest post office, however, had been established in Long Savannah in 1836 on Savannah Creek, approximately five miles south of Salem. The following year, a post office was established at Limestone (currently Georgetown) six miles east. Following the naming of Harrison as the county seat of Hamilton County, a post office was located there, first under the name of Vannville, then Harrison in 1841.[59] With the designation of a post office in these locations, merchants established stores and other business began to flourish; however, the Salem Community, without the postal designation, instead focused community life around the church and school.

A merchant who operated stores in both Harrison and Limestone was Jonathan Wood. He had been named in 1840 as one of the commissioners to locate, survey, and plat lots for the new county seat at Harrison[60] and was an enterprising business man who saw the retail possibilities in serving the Ocoee District farmers. Apparently Joseph Roark traded with Wood at both the Limestone and Harrison stores. In June 1840, Joseph opened an account with Wood who maintained a detailed record of each purchase made principally by Juda through her husband. By the end of December 1841, a significant list of items had been purchased:

Joseph Roark to Jon Wood
1840

June 6	for Wife to 1 pare of Shoes	1.75
	1 fine comb	.25
	1 tuck do. for Miss Killian	.37 ½
Aug 22	to 1 1/4 lbs sugar	.25
Oct 16	for Wife for Miss Elander Ferguson	
	to 3 yds callico 1/6	.75
	1 Blk Silk Scarf	.75
	3/4 yd fig'd muslin	.75
1841		
Apr 21st	for Wife to 2 side combs	.25
	1 tuck comb	.25
	3 Bowls	.50
	4 tin cups	.50
	21 yds callico 2/3	7.87 ½
	3/4 " Bobnet 3/9	.47
	3 " edgeing of C.	.37 ½
July 14	pr. order to merchandise	4.25
Aug 7	to 2 vials Bt. drops	.25
Sept 21st	for Wife to 1 pare of cards	1.00
	7 yds callico 2/6	2.91 ¼

	1/4 yd Bobnet 4/6	.18 ¾
	1 ribbon	.18 ¾
	2 paste boards 10	.20
	1 lb copras	.12 ½
Dec 30	for Wife to 2 tuck combs 2/3	.75
	2 lbs copras	.25
		$25.25[61]

Either Joseph was unaware of the purchases which had been made against the account or, for whatever reason, he had not seen fit to make a payment on the account, for on February 23, 1842, he received the following letter from Jonathan Wood:

Limestone the 23rd Feb 1842
Mr. Joseph Roark If you can send the amount of your act by my son you will much oblige me as I need money verry much–if you cannot please to close the act by note.

Respectfully yours
Jon Wood[62]

Without cash immediately available, Joseph chose to execute a promissory note and immediately–on the same day as the date on Wood's letter–Joseph delivered to the son of Jonathan Wood the following promissory note:

one day after date I promise to pay Jonathan Wood twenty five dollars seventy five cents for value rec'd of him witness my hand and seal this the 23 of February 1842

Joseph Roark   seal

Joseph returned to Harrison on August 2, 1842, to pay $10.00 on the note. Credit was noted by Wood on the reverse side of the promissory note:

Rec'd on the within at Harrison ten dollars in Alabama Bank note 2nd Aug 1842 for which I gave Roark a receipt[63]

In giving credit for the Alabama Bank Note, Wood expressed concern whether or not the bank note should be discounted. In giving Joseph Roark credit on his note, Wood also passed along the following receipt with the caveat on the Alabama Bank Note:

Rec'd of Joseph Roark ten dollars in Alabama Bank Notes which I promise to enter a credit for on a note I hold of his. If I cannot pass it at par value, I will return the same.

Jon Wood
2nd August 1842[64]

In some instances, therefore, on the Ocoee District frontier of development, promissory notes executed by trustworthy citizens had value equal to or better than

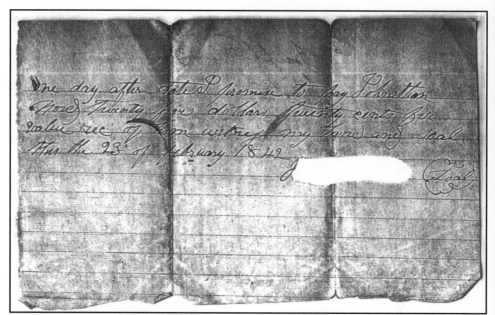

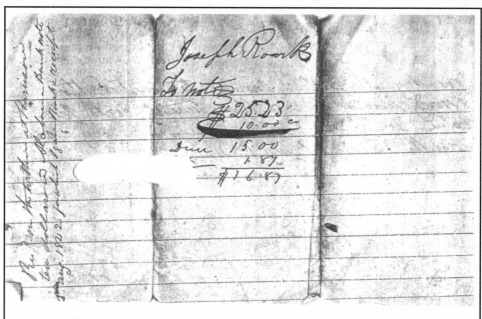

Front and reverse sides of a promissory note from Joseph Roark to merchant Jonathan Wood, February 23, 1842, with a credit given on the reverse side for $10 paid in an Alabama Bank note. Note that Joseph's signature has been removed indicating the note had been paid in full and returned to him.

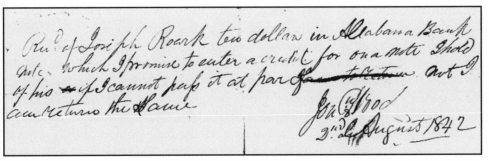

Receipt from Jonathan Wood to Joseph for the $10 Alabama Bank note promising to return the bank note if it cannot be "passed at par."

bank notes. The promissory note was ultimately paid in full and remains in the Joseph Roark papers with his signature neatly removed.

The items purchased from Wood included, it will be noted, a black silk scarf and material for a "Miss Elander Ferguson." It is interesting to consider that this could have been one of the daughters of Joseph's sister, Sary Ferguson. The two daughters of Sary would then have been between ten and fifteen years old. Could Joseph have assumed responsibility for raising one of the girls and, perhaps, the son of Sary? The 1840 census includes in the Joseph Roark household one male and one female, both between fifteen and twenty, who have not been identified. Could they be two of the three Ferguson children? It is an interesting thought, but only speculation.

Joseph continued to evaluate opportunities of acquiring additional land during the highly speculative early years of the Ocoee District "land rush." Land in the district was traded in three probable stages: (1) after a grant had been received and full title had been vested in the occupant; (2) before the grant was received but after the entry had been made; and (3) as Joseph had purchased from Goforth, before the entry when the claimant (or occupant if the claimant lived on the tract) possessed only a "right" to submit an entry. Some land speculators who had made early entries and paid the highest statutory price but had no interest in farming would sell the tract at the earliest date possible. Other speculators bought at much cheaper rates and could afford to hold the tract for a longer period and sell for a much bigger profit. Others, mostly farmers, bought with the intention of farming but for reasons of hardship, or perhaps the inability to farm their entire holdings, found it advantageous to sell all or a portion of their land in an unimproved state. Such probably was the case of West and Britain Freeman, brothers who had obtained adjoining grants of eighty acres two miles south of Joseph's homestead. On November 2, 1841, Joseph Roark purchased the eighty acres from West Freeman for $100.00. Freeman had obtained the tract under Grant No. 1939 for $1.00 per acre, which meant that he had a profit of $20.00 in the sale to Roark.[65] Three months later, Joseph was able to purchase the adjoining eighty acres from Britain Freeman for $50. In this instance, Britain Freeman had acquired the eighty acres in two grants, paying $0.50 per acre for the first entry of forty acres and $0.25 per for the second, thereby realizing a profit of $20.00 in his sale to Roark. The deed with Britain Freeman was executed February 16, 1842,[66] and was witnessed by two neighboring farmers with whom Joseph Roark was to develop a close personal friendship–Hiram Cornwell and M.H. Conner. Joseph held the two deeds until late in the year, probably to obtain some tax advantages, and then traveled to Harrison to record the deeds on Monday, November 28, 1842.

Joseph apparently paid cash to Britain Freeman for a portion of the purchase price and executed a promissory note for the remainder. One month after the deed was executed, Britain Freeman requested that a payment of $4.00 be made to his brother on the note:

> Mr. Joseph Roark Sir Please to pay West Freeman four dollars and I will credit your note for the same, this the 18 of March 1842
> Britain Freeman[67]

Unfortunately, Joseph Roark and Britain Freeman were to have a disagreement which was taken to the local justice of the peace Hiram Cornwell for resolution. Whether the issue involved the promissory note or the land purchase or both is unclear; however, regardless of the issue Joseph was the loser in the judgement. In late 1842, upon payment of the judgement, Joseph received a receipt:

> Received of Joseph Roark Ten dollars in pmt of a judgement that Britain Freeman obtained against him befor Esq. Cornwell Dec the 15th 1842
> Wm. C. Dyche[68]

In early January 1842, Joseph took his family to Harrison. While there, Juda bought some items for the oldest girls at the store of William H. Tibbs. The account charge ticket listed the items purchased:

Harrison

Joseph Rowark to Wm. H. Tibbs

Jan 16 1842	To	1 pr fine shoes 9/-		1.50
		1 do	6/-	1.00
		1 do	90	.90
		2 sets setting pins 5		.10
		1 fine comb		.20
		1 lot beads		.20
		1 cotton scarf		.20
		3 wool hats 4/6		2.25
				6.35[69]

Cash demands continued to be presented to Joseph–some large and significant, others quite small. In February 1842, Joseph received the following request for payment from Anderson Campbell,[70] who later was to be elected as a member of the Bradley County Court:

February the 25th 1842
Mr Joseph Roark Sir please to pay the bearer thirty seven and a half cents for that you owe me and this my order shall be your receipt for the same and oblige your friend

Anderson Campbell[71]

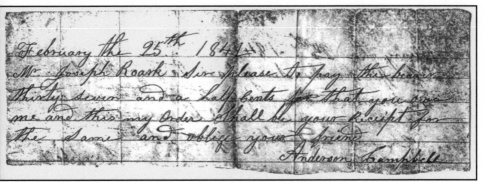

Request to Joseph from Anderson Campbell for payment of $0.37½.

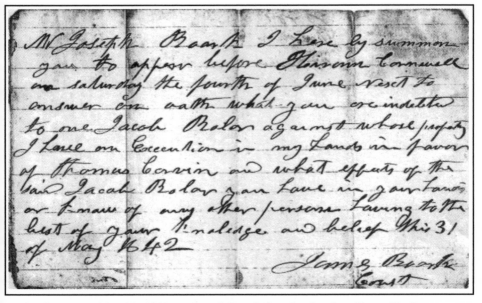

Summons, May 31, 1842, to Joseph Roark from his brother, Constable James Roark, to appear before Justice Hiram Cornwell in regard to a property settlement against Jacob Roler.

It was in 1842 that Joseph's brother James was elected constable to serve the district encompassing the Salem Community. The primary duty of the constable was to issue warrants and summons and to collect judgements rendered by the local justice of the peace. Neither a particularly desirable nor high-paying job, the office of constable was more of a public service. One of the cases for which James Roark was to issue a summons involved Thomas Colvin versus Jacob Roler, both landowners in the Ocoee District north of Grasshopper Creek. Apparently Colvin won a judgement against Roler in a significant amount, which required the liquidation of much of Roler's property, including debts owed to him that could be transferred to Colvin. One of the persons indebted to Roler was Joseph Roark, so on Tuesday, May 31, 1842, Joseph received a summons from his brother:

> Mr. Joseph Roark I hereby summon you to appear before Hiram Cornwell on Saturday the fourth of June next to answer on oath what you are indebted to one Jacob Roler against whose property I have on execution in my hands in favor of Thomas Colvin and what effects of the said Jacob Roler you have in your hands or know of any other persons having to the best of your knowledge and belief. This 31 of May 1842.
>
> James Roark
Const[72]

In a community like Salem, where the economy is built on trust and promissory notes, a sizeable judgement like the one against Jacob Roler resulted in significant cash demands that reverberated through the community. One of those indebted to Jacob Roler was Dr. John Hoyal. With the settlement of the judgement against Roler, Hoyal would be forced to pay to the court the amount owed to Roler. But Hoyal was owed $3.00 by Joseph Roark for medical services. To satisfy the court, then, in regard to his debt to Roler, Dr. Hoyal sent the following message to Joseph Roark:

> Mr. Joseph Roark   Dear sir please pay to Jacob Roler three dollars the amount of your account for medical services included up to this date
> 21st July 1842   John Hoyal[73]

Joseph Roark noted on the reverse side of the message his acceptance of the payment request and subsequently paid the three dollars to the court for payment, along with other assets of Roler, to Thomas Colvin.

Joseph Roark maintained a keen interest in additional land and clearly understood the opportunities open to those willing to take the risks in acquiring land and working to make the land productive. Even at the low prices for land provided in the Ocoee legislation, taxes could make acquisition unprofitable if the land was not made productive or sold quickly to another buyer. In early spring 1842, Joseph made the decision to acquire additional land, and on April 5, 1842, made the trip to Cleveland to file an entry for 160 acres southwest of the homestead. This entry was for the tract that Joseph had obtained in the assignment from Josiah Goforth.[74] While in Cleveland, he also filed, in a calculated move, an entry for 40 acres[75] between the homestead and the entry for the Goforth tract, thereby tying all three tracts together. Both tracts were acquired at the running statutory price of $0.01 per acre.

Joseph returned to Cleveland on May 19, 1842, to file his last entry for Ocoee land. On this visit he filed an entry for 80 acres west of the homestead.[76] This tract was adjacent to the tracts for which an entry had been submitted in April and gave Joseph a total of 400 acres in one block of land to serve as his homestead farm.

At the time of his last entry, Joseph was twenty-eight years old. Including his ten grants and his purchases from the Freemans, all twelve tracts located in the second fractional township, Joseph was the owner of 844 acres of good farm land. He had aggressively pursued the acquisitions, taken the risks inherent in real estate ownership, and exhibited the characteristics of ambition, hard work, and entrepreneurial spirit. Upon its acquisition, the land had to be made productive. Joseph had no desire to be a land dealer and thus support himself and his family by selling land. His obvious desire was to farm and make the land productive and profitable. Hard work lay ahead.

Joseph continued to provide additional income for his farming operation through the sale of hides. On June 7, 1842, he sold fifty-four pounds of dry hides to Jacob Goodner and received the following receipt:

> Rec'd of Joseph Rowarck 54 lbs of dry hides for Jacob Goodner, June 7th 1842
>
> Robert Morison for Jacob Goodner[77]

In Bradley County, troubles continued to hover over Samuel Carr and sons John and James. John Carr on June 4, 1841, had made as occupant enterer an entry for the 40 acres that he had occupied since 1837.[78] At the time of his entry, the statutory rate was $0.50 per acre but it appears that Carr did not have the required $20.00 for the entry application. The Ocoee District Register P.J.R. Edwards, apparently in good faith, let Carr submit his entry with an unsecured promise to pay the fee at a later date, perhaps with an additional fee as penalty. The grant was awarded, signed by the governor, and recorded in the Bradley County courthouse August 17, 1841. By the following April, John Carr still had not paid the statutory purchase price. Under the threat of possibly losing his home, John had to seek help from his father. On April 27, 1842, Samuel Carr paid Edwards $20.00 as "part payment" for the entry purchase with the penalty to be paid later. The amount of the penalty is not noted on any known record.[79]

In February 1843, Samuel Carr and his other son James were involved in judgements against them in the Bradley County court system. One judgement was in favor of John Mount and the other in favor of White, Stokely, and Smith, probably attorneys for Mount. The combined penalty for both judgements was $5.50. Rather than make the payment in person, Samuel Carr had his son John deliver the payment to the sheriff's office. A receipt for the penalty was issued February 4, 1843, by James Donohoe, deputy sheriff.[80]

Samuel Carr's other son Alfred, age twenty-eight in 1842, lived in the Salem Community of Hamilton County. Evidence is strong that Alfred Carr lived on land owned by Joseph Roark and assisted Roark in farming his extensive holdings.[81]

Alfred, too, in late 1842, was the recipient of a negative judgement before a justice of the peace. On November 10, 1842, Alfred paid $8.66 as a result of a judgement by Hiram Haney, justice of the peace, in favor of Alfred Hutcheson, a merchant in Meigs County south of the Hiwassee. The judgement was paid by Carr and a receipt obtained from Samuel Dunn, constable.[82]

Two of Juda's sisters now lived just across the Hiwassee in Meigs County. Jane Carr Mahan had lived alone since her husband's death in 1839. Jane continued to live close to Leonard and Margaret Brooks on forty acres she would occupy and farm for over fifteen years. The few details we have on Jane Mahan sketch a picture of a woman of strong character with little need of support.[83] Margaret by then had two girls since her marriage to Brooks. The older girl was named Matilda and the second Margaret had named Juda Ann after the little girl's aunt. Brooks remained active in the public affairs of Meigs County.

Late in 1842, Joseph was again presented with immediate cash demands. Two days after Christmas, Joseph received the following note:

> Mr. Joseph Roark   Sir please let M.H. Conner have five dollars and you will much obliged your friend
> December 27, 1842   E.M. Hall[84]

No information is readily available on E.M. Hall; however, Maximilian Haney Conner and Joseph Roark would be close associates in the Salem Community and in the Salem Baptist Church for over forty years. Close family ties were later to be established.

Less than two weeks later, Joseph was to receive another request from Hall, this time to pay five dollars to a Mr. [Thomas?] Gregory. Apparently Joseph was either extremely limited in the amount of cash on hand at the time or he did not consider it a matter of priority as $2.00 was all that was given to Gregory. Gregory noted on the reverse side of the request: "Rec'd of the within order two dollars, this 9th Jan'y 1843."[85]

As Joseph attempted to make his lands profitable, promissory notes payable to him were received for products sold or services rendered in his farming operation. From the records maintained by Joseph that are available to us today, it is much more difficult to establish his income stream than to tract his expenditures–for a simple reason–promissory notes issued by Joseph were for his expenses and were returned to him and maintained in his papers. On the other hand, promissory notes received by Joseph as income were returned to the issuer and could not be maintained in the Roark papers, thereby robbing us today of a true record of his finances. As a general rule, the only promissory notes maintained by Joseph, other than those written by him and returned when paid, were those that he was never able to redeem. These represented a total loss to him. Such was the promissory note from Mitchell R. Norman, unmistakably written by Joseph Roark in his style and handwriting, and signed by Norman:

> one day after date I promise to pay Joseph Roark five dollars and thirty two
> cents it being for value rec'd of him this the 16th day of January 1843
> Mitchell R. Norman   seal[86]

Other such unredeemed promissory notes were maintained by Joseph in his records. It should be noted, however, that the Joseph Roark papers do not contain a second unredeemed promissory note from Norman, nor do the papers contain two unredeemed notes from any one individual. As a business man, Joseph was not to continue to do business with those who did not meet their obligations.

In late October 1842, Joseph received word from his mother that the youngest of the family in Claiborne County, Mary Ann, was married on October 14 to James Jefferson Lambert.[87] Mary Ann was not quite fifteen when she married; her husband was eighteen.[88] They were to live at the homestead and help Sarah Roark with the farm. Mary Ann had been only three when Joseph left home and now she was married. Doubtless the news stirred some memories in the mind of Joseph. Did he think often of the family remaining in Claiborne County? It had been eleven years since he had left and, with the exception of James and John, he had seen none of the family during that time. Yet, it would be another fourteen years before he was to return to the home place.

Joseph was close to his brothers, James and John, and all three brothers appear to have been a strong support group for the families. Business was conducted among the brothers but always in the businesslike manner prescribed by Joseph in all his business transactions. The promissory note from Joseph to John Roark in early 1843 followed the same format as all other such transactions:

> one day after date I promise to pay John Roark fifteen dollars and fifty
> eight cents it being for value rec'd of him witness my hand and seal this the
> 11 February 1843
>
> Joseph Roark[89]

The families of all three brothers continued to grow and each brother struggled to provide the necessities for his family. In the week following his thirtieth birthday in 1843, Joseph returned to the store of Jonathan Wood. After domestic purchases totaled $5.43 1/4, Joseph paid cash in the amount of $1.70 and signed the ticket for a balance of $3.37, Wood writing off the 1/4 cents. The listed items illustrate the partial needs of a pioneer family of four girls and two boys all under ten, plus Jane Clingan who was then fifteen:

Jos Roark Bot of J Wood 8th July 1843

1 pare of cards	$1.00
¾ yds padding 3/	.37 ½
¾ " canvas 25	.08 ¾
1 dz buttons	.06 ¼
6 oz indigo	1.00
1 dz coat buttons	.25

2 skarves silk 6 ¼	.12 ½
patent thread	.12 ½
1 ½ yds domestic [?]	.18 ¾
3 yds black shirting 12 ½	.37 ½
3 " brown do	.50
4 small tin cups 6 ¼	.25
6 lbs coffee	1.00
	$5.43 ¼
credit by cash	1.70
	$3.73

Due J Wood for the above–three dollars seventy three cents[90]

Disagreements continued to occur and Joseph spent his share of time before the local justice of the peace in settling issues. Again, because Joseph maintained his records of receipts and payments, we know more about the judgements that went against him than those in which he prevailed. On Christmas Eve 1843, Joseph lost a judgement in favor of P.J. Riglea before Hiram Cornwell. Joseph duly preserved his receipt for payment of the "full amount" of the judgement. The issue nor the amount of the judgement was noted on the receipt.[91]

Joseph was attentive to detail in the purchases he made for his farming operation and doubtless checked carefully material he received and the amount paid for each item. This careful attention also led to disagreements that many times had to be settled before the justice of the peace. In one such instance, Joseph had purchased materials from the firm of Blair and Matthews, paying $13.00 as a portion of the account balance with that firm in March 1843.[92] By December 1844, however, there was disagreement between the two parties and the matter was taken before Hiram Cornwell as justice of the peace. The judgement went against Joseph and he paid the full cost and judgement to Constable Jonathan Belim on December 14, 1844.[93] Apparently Joseph did not hesitate to stand his ground when he thought himself to be in the right and readily took such issues to the appropriate court for resolution.

With the action by the state legislature in passing an act in 1838 that provided some direction for common schools in the state, emphasis was placed on starting schools in many of the local communities to serve the large number of children of school age. Initial legislation attempted to overcome the tendency to view common schools as "pauper schools" and put into operation a school system managed locally within each civil district of the counties.[94] Records do not exist that document action taken by the Salem Community to build and operate their school; however, some conclusions can be drawn from the fragmentary information available to us today. With the community of Harrison taking on new importance as the Hamilton county seat, and with the development of the road connecting Harrison with the post offices at Long Savannah and Limestone, the center of the Salem Community focused more along the Harrison Road (later the Birchwood Pike) than along the river and the Salem Church. The school that later would serve the Salem Community was located three hundred yards south of the Joseph Roark homestead on land included in his land grant. It appears to be a safe conclusion that Joseph made land available for the Salem school and was, in many instances, responsible for the construction and repair of the building. Initial construction on the building for the school appears to have occurred in 1840. Joseph paid $20.00 as a portion of his assessed cost of the building and received a receipt for the amount from William Killian on March 28, 1840.[95] A chimney was added to the school four years later and Joseph Roark took on the responsibility of constructing the chimney with local school monies. On March 13, 1844, Joseph received direction from J.A. Freeman, apparently a trustee of the local school commission, on disposition of the remaining public funds for the chimney:

> Mr. Joseph Roark Sir You will pleas to pay the barer three dollars the amount of the public money in your hands over and above what paid you for the Chimney and this will stand good between you and me March 13th 1844
>
> J.A. Freeman[96]

By 1847 it appears that William J. Rogers had been named trustee of the Salem school and was responsible for assessments and collection of school monies. Rogers was apparently a good choice since at the time he was clerk of the county court in Harrison. In July 1847, Rogers issued the following receipt to Joseph Roark:

> Rec'd of Joseph Rowark Two dollars and fifty cents being half the valuation of four head of hogs by him posted the 1st Jan 1847. This 27th July 1847
>
> Wm Rogers, Trustee[97]

The assessment against the hogs is not understood. Was this a special assessment on one form of livestock to fund schools or some other public improvement?

The Salem school was to serve the community for over three quarters of a century and would educate many of Joseph's family and descendants. He would be called upon from time to time to provide the maintenance and repair as needed. He later would provide land for relocation of the Salem Baptist Church so that church and school would be in the same proximity.

As the farm community grew and crops were produced by individual farmers, corn became an important commodity of exchange. Farmers would receive cash, service, or another commodity in advance of a forthcoming crop and would execute promissory notes for payment in corn. On June 13, 1844, Joseph Roark executed a promissory note with another Salem farmer (his name is unknown since Joseph removed both names when the promissory note was returned) to pay an obligation in corn:

> on the first day of November nexte we or either of us promis to pay William Hayes sixty bushels of good sound corn for value rec'd of him this

the 13th of June 1844

Joseph Roark
(Unknown Signatory)[98]

The day after the promissory note, Joseph received the following request from Morgan Potter:

> Mr. Joseph Roark please to pay Hannibal R. Brown seventeen bushels and a half of corn and to be paid next fall and in so doing you will oblige your friend June 14, 1844

his
Morgan X Potter
mark[99]

Similarly in 1846, Joseph received a payment "order" from D.L. Colvin:

> Mr. Joseph Rowark Sir you will pleas to except [accept] of this order and pay James Pithil eighty five bushels of good sound corn at your corn gatering [gathering] time this fall and oblige me this 28 August 1846
>
> D.L. Colvin

On the reverse side of the order was written:

> Lurell [middle name and commonly used name of D.L. Colvin?] accept[ed] eighty bushels of corn of the within order this the 28th day of August 1846

Joseph Roark[100]

In March 1844, Joseph's brother James made an additional purchase of land on the south side of the Tennessee when he and Archibald McCallie bought 160 acres from G.W. Dearing. The tract was located on both sides of Grasshopper Creek, less than one-half mile of its mouth at the river. The tract had previously been sold by Dearing to Daniel Rawlings for $500 in 1841; however, Rawlings did not make payment as required so the tract was sold at public auction by T.W. Spicer, trustee for Dearing. James Roark and McCallie submitted the "highest and best bid" of $353.00.[101] There is no evidence that James Roark lived on the 160 acres, and most likely, both men farmed the tract during the time they owned it.

The following year, in September 1845, Joseph's other brother John moved to the south side of the Tennessee when he purchased 118 acres on the river just north of the mouth of Grasshopper Creek. John Roark purchased the tract, previously owned at one time by Jacob Roler, from William J. Rogers on September 15, 1845, for $500. Here he established his home and was to remain there the rest of his life.[102] All three brothers were now part of the Salem Community.

Early in 1845, Juda gave birth to the couple's fourth son. They named him after the native-son hero of Tennessee, Andrew Jackson. Sorrowfully, the baby lived only a short time and was buried in an unmarked grave, most likely in the cemetery near the Salem Baptist Church. In September 1845 Juda Roark received tragic news from Meigs County. Both Leonard Brooks and her sister Margaret were dead.[103] Nothing is known about the cause of the deaths and only that Margaret died within a few days of Leonard.[104] Brooks' death was apparently sudden and he had made no provision for his three minor children: Zachariah, by his first wife, and Matilda, and the baby Juda Ann. Juda was particularly concerned about the welfare of her blood nieces and wanted to follow closely the court action to determine their guardians. In addition to Brooks' own children, there were the four Tillery children who were then left without a provider. On October 6, 1845, the Meigs County Court appointed Joshua Guinn and Harvey McKenzie as administrators of the Brooks estate.[105] Both Guinn and McKenzie were brothers-in-law to Leonard Brooks, having married, respectively, Elizabeth Brooks and Letitia Brooks.[106] An estate sale was held by Guinn and McKenzie on October 23, 1845; results were reported to the county court December 1, 1845;[107] and a final report on the estate was submitted to and approved by the Meigs County Court on October 21, 1847. Total value of the Brooks estate, excepting land, amounted to a sizable $1,071.77 1/4, after all expenses of the administrators, including $1.25 "for whiskey and paper," had been deducted.[108] At the time of his death, Leonard Brooks also was the owner of 560 acres which constituted his homestead.[109] Guinn and McKenzie and their families initially assumed responsibility for all the Brooks children until Caufield Tillery, an obvious relative, was named guardian of the Tillery children in February 1847.[110] It is unclear as to whether Guinn or McKenzie had primary responsibility of Zachariah, Matilda, and Juda Ann Brooks. Court action in Bradley County named Guinn as guardian in March 1848,[111] while Meigs County records indicate that McKenzie had guardian responsibilities.[112] Three years after the death of their father–until March 8, 1848–Matilda and Juda Ann Brooks were still cared for by the families of Guinn and McKenzie. Doubtless Juda Roark and Joseph expressed their concern to both Guinn and McKenzie, and offered their support and help. Guardianship of Zachariah Brooks was assumed by William Fairbanks of Saline County, Arkansas, in 1851. McKenzie passed through to Fairbanks Zachariah's share of the Brooks estate.[113]

Juda was also worried about her father, who continued to have his troubles in Bradley County. Much of the trouble came at the hands of J.D. Traynor, who had known the Carrs for over fifteen years and had assisted them in the past. In the mid 1840s, however, it was Traynor who represented several of the people who brought charges against the Carrs. On March 10, 1845, Samuel Carr was hit with a judgement awarded to Traynor in the amount of $12.00 before James Mitchell, local justice of the peace. Sheriff A.A. Clingan acknowledged payment of the judgement by Carr.[114] Also, in July 1845, Traynor again received a judgement against Samuel Carr before Justice Mitchell, this time for $20.00. A receipt to Carr for payment of the judgement was again issued by Sheriff Clingan.[115]

On January 12, 1846, Carr was to suffer two judgements before James E. Walker, justice of the peace, on the same day. First a judgement was awarded in favor again of J.D. Traynor for $2.00 plus an assessment of $6.17 to Carr for court costs. In the

Receipt from Sheriff A.A. Clingan, June 12, 1844, to Samuel Carr for payment of a judgement against Carr by Elijah Blythe.

second case, A. Ackinson was awarded $21.77 1/2 in his judgement against Carr. Receipts for payment of both judgements were signed by A.A. Clingan.[116]

The troubles of Samuel Carr were not limited to Bradley County. On June 12, 1844, Carr was assessed $13.57 for costs and a judgement in favor of Elijah Blythe rendered by the circuit court of Hamilton County. Collection of the judgement was made by Sheriff Clingan of Bradley County.[117]

Carr was also to suffer judgements against him in July 1845 brought by John W. Carver for $17.70,[118] and in September 1845 for $2.00 in favor of William Castillia. Both were in the court of James E. Walker.[119] Unfortunately for our understanding of the life of Samuel Carr, the issues resolved by James E. Walker in his court were not preserved.

It appears that Joseph Roark attempted to help the Carrs in that on May 15, 1845, he cosigned a promissory note with John Carr to E. Bates for $12.19 to be paid by December 1, 1845. The promissory note was attested by James Grigsby, constable in Bradley County, which indicates that the promissory note was probably to serve as a court-mandated payment. Apparently the note was not paid by Carr, and Joseph made the payment six weeks after the due date, removed his name from the note, filed it in his papers, and, quite probably, made a vow to himself under his breath.[120]

Evidence is strong that in 1846, John Carr moved his family from Bradley County to the Nashville area in Davidson County, probably leaving some time shortly after defaulting on the note with Joseph. Having lost his Ocoee District farm through the courts, John Carr sought better opportunities elsewhere. His parents remained in Bradley County in or near the James Carr home. Juda became so concerned about the well-being of her parents that she discussed with Joseph the possibility of building them a house near the homestead and close to Juda's brother Alfred, who could help with their parents. Joseph obviously concurred and after some persuasion by their daughter, Samuel and Margaret Carr agreed to move. By late 1846 or early 1847, they lived in the Salem Community in a house provided by their son-in-law. Juda then had her parents within two miles of her home. At the time of their move, Samuel Carr was seventy-seven. Margaret was seventy-five.[121]

Juda doubtless appreciated having her mother and father close at hand and no longer in Bradley County. Her father, however, continued to lose in judgements that were heard before the local justice of the peace, even in the Salem Community where the justices would be more favorably disposed toward the family. In November 1847, less than a year after he had moved from Bradley County, Samuel Carr appeared before Hiram Cornwell in a dispute with William F. McCormack. The receipt from McCormack documents the results:

> Recvd of Samuel Carr fifteen dollars and seventy cents in ful of a jude-
> ment that I obtained against him befor Hiram Cornwell Esq. cost exsepted
> this 22nd Nove 1847
>
> Wm F. McCormack[122]

Outside the Salem Community and at the national level, the primary interest of the nation was the annexation of Texas and a possible war with Mexico. James K. Polk, following his defeat for re-election as governor in 1841 and his defeat again for that office in 1843, took on a role as dark horse candidate as the presidential nominee of the Democratic party and was nominated by that party for the November 1844 election. Polk campaigned strongly for the annexation of Texas while the Whig candidate, Henry Clay, equivocated on the issue. On July 4, 1844, the Whigs of Hamilton County met at the grove surrounding the spring at Harrison for a round of patriotic speechmaking. In support of the national Whig platform, the local group passed twelve resolutions including one that supported annexation "when it shall be the will of the American people, and when it can be accomplished with safety to the Union, honor to our government, and justice to Mexico."[123] Such lack of a positive platform for annexation lost votes for the Whigs, and in a narrow race in which he did not carry Tennessee, Polk was elected president with a mandate for Texas annexation. During the last days of the Tyler administration, however, the lame duck president, reading the political winds, signed a congressional annexation resolution on March 1, 1845. Mexican protests against the annexation soon thereafter caused President Polk to send troops to the Rio Grande in early 1846. At the request of the president, Congress declared war on Mexico in May 1846. In the spirit of the times, three companies of infantry were organized in Hamilton County, one of which was recruited by Captain Richard Waterhouse of the Harrison area. William J. Rogers was a captain in the company.[124] At the conclusion of the war with Mexico in September 1847, and in fulfillment of the "manifest destiny" of the U.S. to reach from sea to sea, President Polk signed a treaty with Mexico whereby the U.S. added New Mexico, California, and Texas, which contributed land for five additional states. What seemed to be a time of glorious expansion for the U.S. would, in fact, accelerate the highly divisive issue of slavery—an issue which would become a storm that would roll over Joseph Roark and the peaceful community of Salem.

The addition of California upset the balance between the number of slave states and free states, and the nation was divided within three basic camps: abolitionists, moderates, and slavery advocates. Attempts were made to compromise on the issue of slavery and states rights; however, hard-liners on both sides rejected any moves toward resolution. The issue of slavery could not be avoided, and the country moved closer to armed conflict. Many concerned citizens, both Northerners and Southerners, including many in Hamilton County, had grave doubts about the safety of the Union.

Beyond the sectional conflicts endangering the country, the talk most common among all people, in cities as well as the most rural and remote areas, was the excitement surrounding the development of the railroad. Every U.S. city in the 1840s was seeking a commitment for rail service. The importance of the railroad became especially apparent in 1842 when a series of local short-line railroads began competing with the Erie Canal for service across the state of New York. By the mid 1840s, it had become common knowledge that canals like the Erie in New York and the Pennsylvania in that state could not compete with the transportation service provided by the railroad. East coast cities saw the railroads as a lifeline connecting to the Midwest to bring freight and passengers to the Atlantic coast rather than to New Orleans via the Ohio, Cumberland, and Mississippi Rivers. The Charleston and Hamburg Railroad operating west out of Charleston, South Carolina, was the first to carry passengers on a regular schedule and, for a time, was the longest railroad in the country.[125] There was talk of extending the line to Atlanta, Georgia, and even from there northward to the Tennessee Valley. States began to provide healthy subsidies plus grants for right-of-way to railroad companies to entice rail construction. The Georgia Railroad from Augusta to Atlanta, as an extension of the Charleston and Hamburg line, was completed in the fall of 1845, and rail service moved ever closer to Hamilton County on the Tennessee.[126] Hamilton County and particularly Chattanooga had been excited about rail service since 1836 when the state of Georgia had authorized the building of a railroad northward from the center of the state. This railroad, named the Western and Atlantic by its organizers, looked for a connection to the Tennessee River, and Chattanooga leaders lobbied for a terminal in their city. As a result of the national economic depression in 1837, all work was suspended on the Western and Atlantic through 1842 and leadership in Chattanooga was discouraged. One citizen wrote, "If Georgia fails to finish the road or make the appropriation for its completion all is flat in Chattanooga."[127] In addition to disappointments in railroad development, the hoped-for dynamics of the Tennessee for river travel were also faltering. The May 18, 1844, issue of the *Chattanooga Gazette* reported on the slow travel on the river:

RIVER LIST

Arrived

May 11 Joshua - Shipley from Sullivan county with iron and castings.

The River is very low, and trade corresponding dull.

> The above is the only trading boat at the landing.
> The steamer "Frankland" is above, and the "Huntsman"
> below. Neither can run without a tide.[128]

The U.S. in general was excited about new inventions that were reported in the papers including the *Chattanooga Gazette,* which Joseph Roark received through the mail at the Limestone post office. In 1843, Congress had appropriated $30,000 for Samuel F.B. Morse to build a telegraph line between Washington and Baltimore, and the first message was sent May 1, 1844. The impact of the telegraph on the country within the next ten years would have been far beyond even the wildest of imaginations in Hamilton County. In 1838, a company in Paterson, New Jersey, had begun manufacturing an invention of Samuel Colt–a repeating pistol in which six cylinders "revolved" to align with the barrel. Photography was finding its way to the American family in the use of the French "daguerreotype" process. In the late 1840s, a daguerreotype photographer visited Tazewell, Tennessee. The family of Sarah Bolen Roark insisted she pose for a photograph and an image was preserved.

While the anxiety of the country centered on sectional issues that were dividing the nation, the Salem Community focused on the day-to-day problems in an agrarian society. With his growing family, Joseph Roark had the need from time to time of medical assistance. While many ailments were addressed by home remedies, some had to have the attention of qualified doctors of the era. Joseph and Juda began to notice and feel some concern about the mental condition of their daughter Jerusha. A nervous disorder, mental anxieties, or perhaps epilepsy, caused Jerusha to have seizures. The seizures apparently were not severe in her early years but progressively got worse as she grew older. Joseph and Juda sought the help of the local physician, Dr. John L. Yarnell, on Jerusha's condition as well as on other day-to-day medical problems. In early 1846, Joseph paid his medical bill to Yarnell and received the following receipt:

> Received of Joseph Roark five dollars in full of his medical bill up to this
> date, Jan 14th 1846
>
> Yarnell & Edens[129]

Yarnell had a wide reputation among the pioneer settlers of the Ocoee District. Born in 1805, Yarnell had settled among the Cherokees prior to the Ocoee District and had married Jane Brown, daughter of Chief James Brown, one of the judges of the Cherokee Nation. Following Brown's removal with other Cherokees in 1838, Yarnell occupied Brown's Snow Hill farm on Long Savannah Creek five miles south of the Joseph Roark homestead.[130]

Joseph would not only seek medical advice from Yarnell, who operated his medical practice under the name of Yarnell and Edens, but would also have business dealings with Yarnell, particularly in the sale of corn. Sometime in the mid 1840s, Joseph was to receive a receipt from Yarnell which typifies the business relations with Yarnell. Sam Kennedy was Yarnell's farm manager, and it was he who delivered the following note from Yarnell addressed to "Mr. Joseph Rowark-At Home:"

> Mr. Joseph Rowark   Sir I send Mr. Kennedy over to see you to purchase
> some corn for me. Any contract he makes will be good in my name and I
> will abide the same.
>
> yours Respectfully
> J. L. Yarnell[131]

Joseph's brother James also had business dealings with Dr. Yarnell both in trade and in buying land. In December 1846, James executed a promissory note to Yarnell payable in treated pork.[132] In November 1847, James Roark was to buy another tract of land on the south side of the river, this time from Dr. Yarnell, Samuel Wilson, and Jacob Roler. The tract consisted of 140 acres of river frontage and was located south of and adjacent to the 124 acres Joseph Roark had obtained under Grant Number 1618 in 1840. The deed was witnessed by Joseph Roark and Merida Webb.[133] To pay for his purchase from Yarnell, Wilson, and Roler, James had, ten days before, sold his undivided interest in the tract purchased with Archibald McCallie to McCallie for $500. James had invested $187.50 in 1844 when he and McCallie together had purchased the tract for $375 three years before. This profit to James of 167% in three years gives an indication of the increase in land values within the Ocoee District and the Salem Community.

James Roark bought other land in the Salem Community following his purchase from Yarnell, Wilson, and Roler in 1847. Evidence suggests that he purchased at some later date approximately 300 acres in the NE4 and FNW4 of Section 8, FT2N, R3W, north and northeast of Joseph's river-bottom tract in Section 8. James was also to own 60 acres in the SW4, Section 10, and the 160 acres of the NW4, Section 15. At some point in time, probably before 1850, James Roark built his home in Section 15, immediately west of what would later be named the Birchwood Pike.[134]

Joseph continued to be active in land transactions. In 1844, he began to liquidate some land holdings to take advantage of inflated prices and to provide capital for his farm operation. On December 6, 1844, he sold to L.L. Ball for $300 the 160 acres that he had purchased from West and Britain Freeman in 1841-1842 for a total of $150, thereby realizing a profit of 100% in just under three years. The deed to Ball was witnessed by William F. McCormack and John L. McCormack.[135] Joseph also purchased additional land in 1846 to enlarge the homestead tract. In a deed dated March 17, 1846, Joseph purchased from Samuel Gamble fifty acres adjacent to and east of the homestead tract, south of Grasshopper Creek. The deed was witnessed by Hiram Cornwell and William Killian.[136]

In the spring of 1846, Juda gave birth to another girl whom they named Ruth. The family at home now consisted of Jane Clingan 19, Mary Ann 12, Sarah Elizabeth 11, Margaret 10, Jerusha 9, James 7, John 5, and William 3. Unfortunately Ruth was to live only a few months. The grieving parents buried her in the new Bald Hill Cemetery on the Harrison Road three miles south of the homestead.[137]

In the early fall of 1846, Juda and Joseph received one of those shocks that come only to parents and the magnitude of which can only be understood by parents. Their second daughter, Sarah Elizabeth, Elizabeth to her friends or Liz as she was known to the family, told her parents that she intended to marry within the next few days. Elizabeth was eleven at the time and would not celebrate her twelfth birthday until New Years Eve! Her husband to be was Joel A. Talley, 23, son of William H. Talley and Stacie Nicey Bryant, married in Rhea County in 1821. Joel had been the first of twelve children.[138] The thoughts and concerns of Juda and Joseph at the time can only be imagined. Nevertheless, a wedding was held in the home of the bride's parents, and Elizabeth and Joel A. Talley were pronounced man and wife. Whether or not neighbor William Killian, his son Henry who was Elizabeth's age, or others of the Killian family attended the wedding is unknown.

Following the marriage of Elizabeth and Joel, Joseph gave the young couple a farm of eighty acres and provided them a house to live in just south of Joseph's home place. This was a practice that Joseph was to follow with each of his children as they married and were ready to start their family. A unique feature of Joseph's land gift was that in no instance was a deed placed of record in the county courthouse. Doubtless a deed or some similar instrument was given to each of the children when the gift was made but no deed was ever recorded. Elizabeth and Joel, along with each of the other children when a gift of land was made, took the deed provided by Joseph to the county tax office to establish ownership in their name and their responsibility for taxes. The 80-acre tract provided to the Talley's consisted of the two 40-acre grants which Joseph had received through the Ocoee District, Grant Nos. 2131 and 3176. The farm was in Section 21 and was located adjacent to and west of the land grant of M.H. Conner.[139]

The year following her marriage, Elizabeth Talley gave birth to her first child whom they named Amanda.[140] The mother was twelve. Juda and Joseph were grandparents at age thirty-four.

Signature of Joseph Roark

As the Salem Community grew, Joseph sought and identified various business partnerships to take advantage of opportunities beyond farming. In the simplest of partnerships, Joseph and Hiram Cornwell jointly leased some of their land. Rent was to be paid by clearing the land, fencing it, and putting in a crop within a five-year period. On occasions, in renting cleared land, Cornwell and Joseph would provide cash, materials, and/or seed corn for a start-up farmer and then accept a promissory note for the rent. Interest was charged on the note and payment was made annually from a portion of the corn crop. An accounting for such an arrangement was provided by Cornwell in 1845-47, using the initials of the tenant for identification:

> H.L.D. our note $7.50, two years interest .90. Sixty bushels corn the rent
> for the year 1845 60 bushels out of which he is entitled to credit for nails
> to cover the house $2.00.
>
> Hiram Cornwell[141]

In another instance, Roark provided a house for the tenant to live on his tract in Section 28 west of the homestead and the tenant was to clear land on Cornwell's adjacent tract. Cornwell developed a lengthy contract (for that day) under which Duncan L. Colvin was to clear fifteen acres within five years, add a rail fence around the property, build a 16 by 18-foot house and "leave the same in good condition." The five-year lease could be extended if more than fifteen acres were cleared. The contract was signed by Cornwell and Colvin May 10, 1847, and was attested by Joseph Roark.[142] In this manner, Cornwell and Roark could more quickly put land into production and tenants would be available to support other business ventures of the landowners.

Sometime in the mid 1840s Joseph Roark joined with Archibald McCallie to create the McCallie and Roark sawmill. McCallie was twelve years older than Joseph, and it appears that their partnership was short-lived. McCallie's son, also named Archibald, would later marry a daughter of John Roark. The mill race for the sawmill was located along Grasshopper Creek, west of the home place.[143] Products from the sawmill were most likely traded for other commodities needed by the sawmill owners. Only those without a commodity to barter would infrequently pay cash or execute the traditional promissory note. For some service or commodity that he deemed valuable, Joseph would issue a promissory note to be paid in lumber. Such was the case on April 5, 1847, when Joseph issued a promissory note to Caswell Luttrell with payment to be made in specific cuts of lumber to be delivered at the "McCallie and Roark sawmill." The value of the note and lumber was noted on the reverse side of the note by Luttrell as $20.00.[144]

Joseph also worked with McCallie in selling bacon either on a partnership basis or with McCallie directing prospective buyers to Joseph as in the following request:

> Mr. Joseph Roark pls let the barer have Fifty pounds of Bacon and i will
> pay you for the same July 13th 1848
>
> Archibald McCallie[145]

Joseph also maintained a working partnership with his old friend from the Sale Creek area, Lewis Patterson, in which Joseph would sell leather for Patterson on the south side of the river. Working on a commission, Joseph received a load of leather from Patterson in 1848 and provided Patterson with a receipt:

> Received on commition [commission] of Lewis Patterrson fifty too dolars
> and sixty too cents worth of leather which I promice to sell or account for
> this the 4 day of October 1848
>
> Joseph Roark[146]

Beyond Joseph's business partnerships, other commercial ventures began to appear. In the mid 1840s, a community by the name of Birchwood began to develop four miles north of the Roark homestead. By 1854, a post office would be authorized for Birchwood, and it would be there rather than Long Savannah or Limestone that Joseph would receive his mail. At Birchwood, Joseph would purchase goods from Weir and Conner. A receipt was filed by Joseph in his papers when he brought his account with Weir and Conner up to date:

> Birchwood Feb 22, 1847
> Received of Mr. Roark $15.64 in full of acct at Weir and Conner
> Weir and Conner[147]

By 1847, the eldest daughter of Joseph's brother John, Mary Ann, had married John Cross and was living in the Salem Community. In December 1847, Cross requested Joseph to pay an obligation for him which Joseph was apparently willing to do:

> Mr. Joseph Roark Sir you will let D.K. Lykes have two dollars for me and
> I will see you in a few days and replace the same to you this 28 Decbr 1847
> John Cross[148]

In early summer of 1847, Jane Clingan told Joseph and Juda of her intentions to marry and leave the home place. Jane had been a member of the family for thirteen years and had been close to both Joseph and Juda as well as all the children. Her husband-to-be was Benjamin Webb, brother to Merida Webb and son of John Webb.[149] Benjamin was twenty-five at the time of his marriage and was well known in the community as a hard worker. Doubtless the marriage was solemnized at the home place since it had been Jane's home for most of her life and Joseph and Juda were parents to her.[150] Following their marriage, Jane and Benjamin were helped by Joseph, and Benjamin was employed for a time in the farm operation. Joseph apparently had significant trust in Benjamin and authorized him to make purchases for the farm from the local merchants.[151] Within seven years Benjamin would be able to buy his own farm.

As Joseph Roark's family grew, additional items and the consistent supply of "fine shoes" were needed to support the family. His account with W.H. Tibbs in 1847 lists the necessary items purchased:

> Joseph Roark with W.H. Tibbs

1847			
March 6	2 pr Cotton Cards	60	1.20
	2 1/2 yds calico	20	.50
	1 post board		.05
	wire		.02
	1 paper pins		.25
	1 pr candle molds		.20
	1 pad sack		.15

June 2	8 lb coffee		1.00
	1 set knives & forks		1.50
	1 pr fine shoes		1.00
	1 - pepper 25 1/2 spices 10		.35
1 pen knife	1 - good buttons	25	.62 ½
4 oz indigo			.50
10 yds blk silk		85	8.50
33 " calico		23	7.60
1 fine comb 13	1 fur hat 1.75		1.90
3 pr cotton hoes for 60 cts			.60

$25.98

1 set tea 40, 1 1/2 yds blk cambric,
1 pr shoes   1.65

$27.63[152]

The family grew rapidly in late 1847 and early 1848. In midyear, Juda gave birth to her sixth daughter, whom they named Nancy.[153] In addition to their new baby, two more children were added to the family. Juda had worked with Joshua Guinn after his designation as guardian of her sister's children, Matilda and Juda Ann Brooks, but apparently Guinn had transferred the guardianship to Harvey McKenzie. Juda must have felt that the children were being passed from family to family and needed a settled home. The issue was raised with McKenzie and discussions were held about the welfare of the children. Juda wanted to help raise the girls, and it was agreed that Joseph and Juda would take on that responsibility. So in mid 1848, in an already crowded household, Matilda 6, and Juda Ann 4, came to be part of the family. McKenzie was to be responsible for obtaining court approval of the guardianships, and within three years court records reflected the change. Ostensibly Joseph and Juda were to be allotted a portion of the Leonard Brooks estate to cover the expense of raising the girls; however, Joseph would later have to take legal action against McKenzie to obtain the estate inheritance for the two girls. Nevertheless, Matilda and Juda Ann were accepted by the other children as being part of the family. No record remains of any contention between the girls and the rest of the children. Unfortunately for Joseph and Juda, their relationship with the girls, especially Matilda, was not always to be pleasant.[154]

Joseph and Juda saw their oldest daughter, Mary Ann, married in January 1849, their second daughter to leave home. Probably in the front room of the home place, on a cold winter day, Mary Ann married Robert Beane Scott.[155] She had just turned fifteen. Scott was almost twenty. Robert Beane Scott was born April 18, 1829, in Hamilton County, the youngest child of Goodman Scott and Lydia Beane. His parents had been married in 1818 in Grainger County, Tennessee, his mother being the second wife of Goodman Scott.[156] Goodman Scott had obtained a grant for 80 acres in the Ocoee District in 1841 on Grasshopper Creek just a quarter mile north of the Joseph Roark homestead.[157] Records available to us today indicate that Robert Scott was a hard worker who provided well for his family. At some point in the next few years, he was to become a Baptist minister. As he had done for Elizabeth and Joel Talley, Joseph gave farm land to Mary Ann and Robert Scott soon after their marriage. The location and the size of the farm given to the Scotts cannot be determined since the deed was not recorded. Mary Ann was to maintain possession of the farm and would sell it to her brothers as part of the estate settlement following Joseph's death.

Mary Ann Roark, at age fifteen, in 1849 before her marriage to Robert Beane Scott .

As Joseph's farm operation continued to prosper, he was required to use fewer promissory notes, and when they were used, the amounts were significantly larger. Except solely for his convenience, Joseph had risen above the use of promissory notes for small amounts. The years 1848 and 1849 saw a reduced use of promissory notes and more receipts for cash payments. In early 1849, Joseph received a payment request from his neighbor Jesse Killian:

> Mr. Joseph Roark Sir Pleas to pay John Campbell 3 dollars and 25 centes
> that yew [you] yow [owe] me and yew will oblig yore friend
> Jesse Killion this 1st day of January 1849[158]

Joseph paid John Campbell the $3.25 requested and three days later settled his account with Killian. While Joseph had executed promissory notes to the Killians in 1840 as he was seeking to clear all encumbrances on his land entry, it is doubtful that the balance owed to Jesse Killian stemmed from those earlier promissory notes. Joseph simply would not have let a debt run that long. In any event, Joseph received a receipt from Killian that was attested to and probably written by Z. Martin, a local merchant in the area:[159]

> Ricivd of Joseph Roark twenty three dollars in full of his act with me this
> the 4th January 1849   his
> atiste   Jesse X Killian
> Z. Martin   mark[160]

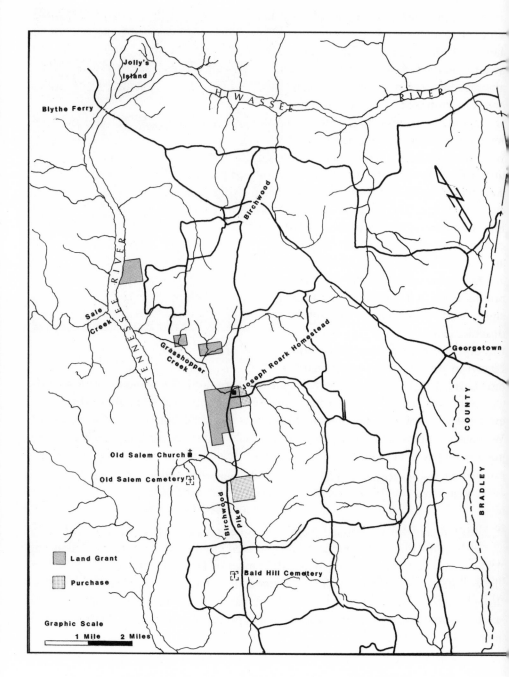

Land holdings of Joseph Roark in March 1849–734 acres.

In April 1849, Joseph had an opportunity to sell the river frontage he owned north of Grasshopper Creek in Section 8. He had filed an entry on the 124 acres in January 1840 and had paid the statutory price of $124. Now, nine years later he was able to sell the tract with no improvements to Pleasant Doughty for $612, a profit of almost 400%, discounting taxes and interest. The deed was executed April 13, 1849, and was witnessed by Hiram Cornwell.[161]

In spite of his obvious success, Joseph still chose to pay for his family purchases with a charge account and a periodic promissory note. On April 10, 1849, the same week he received $612 from his 124-acre land sale, Joseph issued a promissory note to Jonathan Wood to pay "on order" an amount of $17.02 for the current account balance including interest from January 1, 1849, to the date of the note. On the reverse side of the note, Wood had written: "Received on the within note from Joseph Roark–ninety six and ¼ cents, April 10, 1849."[162] Receiving hundreds of dollars in cash from land sales but making account payments in amounts as small as ninety-six and a fraction cents was Joseph's way of maintaining a strong cash position.

Similarly, a promissory note of the same period indicates Joseph's desire to use promissory notes and borrowed money rather than cash. On March 20, 1849, Joseph signed a promissory note to Merida Webb for $26.00, payable one day after the date of issue. On the reverse side of the note Webb had calculated the interest at 6% for two different periods, one for a year for $1.56 and one for nine months for $1.17. Elsewhere on the reverse side was noted: "Received on the within note 3 dollars, this the 1st of Sept 1850," followed by a calculation that, with interest and after the recent payment, the balance on the note was still $25.26.[163] Apparently Joseph's credit was extremely good within the community and few people called his promissory notes. With that being the case, Joseph saw little reason to use his cash. Exceptions to his pay-by-note rule were medical bills from Dr. Yarnell who either refused to accept promissory notes, which in all probability was unlikely, or Yarnell was a person that Joseph did not want to put off since he might be needed in emergencies. A somewhat large medical bill of $25.00 was paid in cash to Yarnell on August 24, 1849. The receipt was issued on behalf of Yarnell by R.H. Roddy.[164]

In addition to his trade with Jonathan Wood, Joseph also maintained an account with W.C. Hutcheson, probably in Birchwood, where Juda purchased much of the material needed for making clothes for the family. In September 1849, his account with Hutcheson showed the following purchases:

Joseph Roark Bot of W.C. Hutcheson Sept 11, 1849

14 yds calico	.16 2/3	
16 " do	.20	
3 " bond muslin	.30	
1 ½ " do	.50	
4 " lace	.18 3/4	
3 " black do	.06 1/4	

| 1 " ribbon | .20 |
| 2 ea bonnets | .87 1/2 each[165] |

As he did with promissory notes and receipts, Joseph faithfully kept all tax receipts in his papers. He had paid a poll tax of $0.50 per year in 1838 and 1839, but by 1842 when his land grants were on the tax rolls, he was paying an annual state and county tax of $2.50. His taxes increased very little during the decade of the 1840s and actually decreased to $2.15 in 1845 and 1846. In 1847, however, his taxes were up to $2.60. The tax receipt for 1849 gives only the acknowledgement of receipt and does not give the amount.[166]

Certainly in Joseph's eyes the times were good. With his land sales, his highly productive farm land, and his numerous business ventures serving him well, the future looked bright indeed. He was thirty-six and was far ahead of where his father had been at the same age. He obviously was happy with his wife and family, which now numbered eight at home including the Brooks girls. The future for the Ocoee District and Hamilton County was also bright. The *Chattanooga Gazette* and local citizens were excited about the proposed construction of the Western and Atlantic Railroad from Atlanta to Chattanooga. Construction had been delayed because of the necessity of a tunnel through Tunnel Hill south of Dalton, Georgia. Tracks had been laid on either side of the tunnel, and in early 1849, freight and passengers were hauled around the hill to connect with the rail service on the other side of Tunnel Hill.[167] The February 16, 1849, issue of the *Gazette* carried special articles on the progress of the W&A, reporting that the "sliding of the earth at the tunnel was much less consequence" than originally thought; however, "the waggon [sic] road is almost impassible from the tunnel to Dalton." A passenger schedule for the seven-hour trip between Dalton and Atlanta was published including all stops in between. Freight rates were quoted. Additionally, the *Gazette* reported that Virginia was considering a rail connection between the Tennessee line and Lynchburg, Virginia. Even river travel was encouraging–four steamers were working regular schedules between Knoxville and Decatur (Alabama) with "a good number of passengers on the boats."[168]

In late 1849, however, pessimism pervaded the U.S. as the nation struggled with the sectional issue of slavery and the balance of power between slave states and free states. In December 1849, Congress assembled for the first time since Zachary Taylor's inauguration and heard the president recommend the admittance of California and New Mexico to the Union without regard to their position on slavery. Southern extremists shouted against the proposal with anger and resentment. Chances for any kind of reconciliation looked slim. It was obvious to Joseph Roark and many others like him that the prosperity of Hamilton County would be in jeopardy if national issues were not resolved. Cool heads were in the minority against the radicals in both North and South. The fuse was getting shorter.

In Knoxville, as the decade drew to a close, William G. "Parson" Brownlow began publishing the *Knoxville Whig and Independent Journal* on May 19, 1849, and increased its circulation through vituperative language and wholesale abuse against Democrats, Catholics, Jews, Baptists, and abolitionists. In the February 19, 1849, issue of the *Chattanooga Gazette*, Joseph Roark had read the "Prospectus of the Knoxville Whig" to be published by Brownlow in May. In the prospectus, Brownlow said of himself:

> . . . the Editor will only say, that the paper will be conducted to suit *his own taste and inclination* [italics by Brownlow]–spurning the dictation of all men, utterly refusing to come under the control of any wing, or portion, of his own or any other party.[169]

Brownlow had been a Methodist circuit rider in East Tennessee for ten years between 1829 and 1839, fighting with Baptists and Presbyterians for the souls of men and women. Intense, bitter, and vengeful against all who opposed him, Brownlow's Bible either did not contain the "love chapter" of First Corinthians or it escaped his attention and interest altogether. Continuing as a licensed minister of the Methodist Church, he settled in Elizabethton, Tennessee, in 1839 and began publishing the *Elizabethton Whig*, later moving to Jonesboro and then to Knoxville. "Parson" Brownlow drew intense hatred and bitterness to himself wherever he went, and his tirade of abuse and venomous language in his newspaper earned him bitter enemies. In 1848, while in Jonesboro, Brownlow had suffered a physical beating from those whose hatred he had engendered and the clubbing he received affected him mentally and increased his hatred–hatred that later would be directed against all Confederate supporters.[170]

In the U.S. Congress in 1849, another East Tennessean, Andrew Johnson, was serving his third term as representative of the First Congressional District of Tennessee. Having left poverty in Raleigh, North Carolina, in 1824 as an apprenticed tailor, Johnson had continued his apprenticeship in Rutledge, Grainger County. He had been there, east of the Clinch River, as an eighteen-year-old tailor when Joseph Roark was serving as the thirteen-year-old chain carrier for the Eastridge survey in 1826. In 1827, Johnson had opened a tailor shop in Greeneville where involvement in local politics saw him elected mayor. After one term as state senator from 1841 to 1843, when Joseph Roark was establishing his homestead on Grasshopper Creek, Johnson was elected to the U.S. Congress. As Johnson began his third term, the congressional session was divided by increased tensions on the slavery issue. It was in this session of Congress that Johnson would get to know the single-term congressman from Illinois, Abraham Lincoln, who would later appoint Johnson military governor of Tennessee.[171]

Chapter 8

Prosperity With Dark Clouds
1850-1859

As the decade of the 1850s began, the nation was focused on the issue of slavery. The issue had increased in importance during the last twenty years until by 1850, it was the primary political topic in Congress and the individual state houses. Joseph Roark had followed the issue of slavery since his move to Hamilton County in 1831 and could not help but wonder why it was an issue at all. Slavery made no sense to him, nor to others like him, either from an economic or moral perspective. Joseph had been successful in acquiring land and bringing it into production through his own efforts. He, and he alone, had housed, fed, and clothed his family. He had prospered under a free market economy and believed in individual freedom and personal responsibility. To take on the inefficiency of bonded servants with limited motivation for work was beyond his comprehension. He knew less than ten slave holders and encountered few slaves as they made up less than seven percent of the total population of Hamilton County. Fewer than eighteen slaves were in the Salem Community in 1850.[1] Yet the issue of slavery gripped the Union. How had the "peculiar institution," as Abraham Lincoln would later term it, become such an important issue?

Joseph recognized that the South had come under the grip of slavery as a gradual process during the almost twenty years he had been in Hamilton County. Prior to that time, there had been leaders in all the southern states who had argued for the manumission of the slaves. Such men included Thomas Jefferson and Chief Justice John Marshall of Virginia, Congressman Henry Clay of Kentucky, Mississippi Governor William Chambers, and Georgia Governor William Crawford. In fact, the actual prohibition of slavery in Tennessee had barely failed in a vote for that purpose at the Tennessee constitutional convention in 1796. When Joseph Roark was a boy in Claiborne County, emancipation societies had been organized in six Tennessee counties with the stated objective of the "gradual abolition of slavery . . . by having laws passed declaring all those born after a fixed period, to be free at some reasonable age." By the late 1820s, twenty-five such societies existed in Tennessee.[2] Similar sentiments were expressed in other states, North and South. In 1832, the Virginia legislature had debated a bill for the gradual abolition of slavery and, although defeated, the bill had produced comments that slavery was "the greatest calamity which had ever befallen any portion of the human race."[3]

As Joseph Roark had observed, the southern states after 1831 began to harden their position on slavery because of the radical position taken by abolitionists. William Lloyd Garrison, the most radical of the abolitionists, first published the *Liberator* in 1831 and began the argument for the immediate and uncompensated freeing of all slaves. With such proposals to immediately free the slaves without thought toward their lack of education or training for a trade, the Southern position began to harden. Joseph noted that the abolitionists encouraged slave revolt and read that Garrison, while seeing a copy of the U.S. Constitution burned, called it "a covenant with death and an agreement with hell." Joseph could understand the concern of all southern states that such radicals might gain control of the government in Washington. "The attitude expressed by the Garrison group served to nullify efforts at emancipation and caused Southerners to develop a defense of slavery rather than consider it an evil which in due course must be eradicated."[4] Roark and the Salem Community noted that Tennessee, like many of the other southern states, was by 1850, defending slavery when earlier it had tried to eradicate the institution. Even William G. Brownlow, in his Whig newspaper, described himself as "a proslavery man who hated secession" and blamed the abolitionists for the desperate situation of 1850. In spite of the sentiments expressed in this statement, Brownlow regrettably was later to be the nemesis of all southern sympathizers while serving as the reconstruction governor of Tennessee.

Among the southern political leaders a form of paranoia developed. The northern states, with radicals like Garrison as self-appointed spokesmen, were viewed as out to destroy not only slavery but slave holders and the southern economy as well. To the southern states, a balance of power in the Congress was extremely important if they were to prevent such a radical reformation. The distribution of seats in the U.S. House of Representatives had already placed the North in control of that body because of the North's much greater population. The key was in the Senate in which the seats were then equally divided between slaves states and free states. Since the Missouri Compromise of 1820, as states were added to the Union, Congress had carefully added one slave state for every free state and thus maintained the balance in the Senate. Early in 1850, Joseph read in the *Chattanooga Gazette* that President Zachary Taylor was proposing, contrary to the Missouri Compromise, that California and New Mexico be added to the Union without regard to their position on slavery. It appeared that the balance of power was about to swing to the North. Soon, if nothing were done, the North and the radical abolitionists would control the U.S. Senate. The southern states sought ways to stem the tide and collectively agreed to send delegates to a meeting to discuss their precarious position. The meeting was scheduled for June 1850 in Nashville. The small landowner in Tennessee and other southern states could only await the outcome of such meetings and hope for a resolution. Thus Joseph Roark and others in the Salem Community saw an issue, that of slavery, in which they had little interest, take control of the country and even threaten the life of the Union itself. Joseph could only watch as events unfolded in Washington and Nashville.

Fortunately there were statesmen in the Congress. In January 1850, Henry Clay of Kentucky, "the great compromiser," again filled that leadership role and proposed what became known as the Compromise of 1850. Under Clay's proposal as finally adopted, California was to be admitted as a free state, New Mexico and Utah were to be admitted with no restrictions on slavery, the fugitive slave law was to be strengthened, and slave trade was to be abolished in the District of Columbia. The compromise plan was debated in Congress and throughout the country for almost nine months.

The Southern Convention, as the meeting in Nashville of the southern delegates was known, discussed at length the proposed compromise plan. In the June 14 issue of the *Chattanooga Gazette*, Joseph Roark read that in the meeting of the Convention on June 5, a resolution was submitted for consideration, "declaring that the spirit of the Convention was conciliatory, and desirous of preserving . . . the Union." On June 9, another resolution was submitted recommending that the old Missouri Compromise line be extended to the Pacific Ocean with all states to the north of the line be free states and all to the south be slave states.[5] Little was done by the delegates to the Southern Convention except to discuss such resolutions and to set another meeting of the convention following the adjournment of Congress later in the year.

The *Chattanooga Gazette* reported from Washington on the debate on Taylor's plan and the proposed compromise and announced that "the next Tuesday [June 18] the House will begin to vote on amendments to the Clay plan" as well as the President's proposal.[6] The illness and death of the president would, however, be a factor in the debate. At the death of President Taylor in July 1850, Vice President Millard Fillmore of New York assumed the office of president and gave his full support to the Clay compromise.

The Compromise of 1850 was approved by Congress in September in the form of five separate laws dealing with the major proposals under the Clay plan. The people of the South generally supported the new laws and the crisis atmosphere receded. The issue of slavery had not yet become the divisive issue with strength sufficient to rend the Union. Joseph Roark, the Salem Community, and the nation breathed a sigh of relief. Attentions could again be focused on productive matters. Exciting things were happening in the country and Hamilton County and, with the compromise now in the form of law, the economy could continue to grow in the Tennessee Valley.

The country was fascinated with the railroad, and speculation was rampant on its future impact. The total mileage of the rail system in the U.S. had almost quadrupled between 1840 and 1850 to over 9,000 miles. Rail lines had begun to connect what was then the northwest U.S.–Ohio, Indiana, Illinois, and Michigan–to the northeast coast. States offered public lands in large quantities to the railroads to support new lines and railroad officials became experts in "grantsmanship." Land grants to U.S. railroad companies in the twenty years following 1850 would cover more territory than France, England, Wales, and Scotland combined.[7] Railroad was king and cities eagerly competed for rail service. Now that the Compromise of 1850 was in place, the next ten years appeared to be a decade of prosperity and growth, not only for the railroads but the entire country as well.

In Hamilton County the excitement was contagious. Noted Chattanooga historian Dr. James Livingood describes the era as "the bustling decade of the 1850s."[8] On May 9, 1850, the Western and Atlantic Railroad (W&A) ran its first train over the 137-mile line from Atlanta, and entered downtown Chattanooga for the first time. Chattanooga entered a building boom and the *Gazette* exclaimed that "New buildings are springing up in Chattanooga as if by magic." The paper published the W&A train schedule for passenger trains to arrive at 5:00 P.M. and to depart at 7:00 A.M. daily except Sundays. The freight train arrived at 11:00 A.M. each day and departed at 1:00 P.M. Retail business was active, and the paper quoted Chattanooga market prices for corn at $0.50 a bushel, coffee at 0.12 per pound by the sack, butter at 0.10 per pound, and eggs at 0.50 per dozen. Under public notices, the *Gazette* included a notification from the executors of the estate of the late Thomas Crutchfield to all claimants and debtors to the estate to "come forward."[9] Twelve years before, in 1838, Crutchfield had purchased Jolly's Island (now Hiwassee Island) in its entirety under grant entries in the Ocoee District.

With the completion of the W&A, Chattanooga and the Tennessee River were connected to Atlanta and, via the Georgia Railroad and the Charleston and Hamburg, to the east coast. Freight from the steamers on the river could now be transferred to rail and shipped quickly to the markets on the Atlantic shore. Southbound freight from the river arrived in more volume than could be handled by the W&A, and freight accumulated in Chattanooga. Farm produce of corn, wheat, oats, bacon, flour, and whiskey from the upper Tennessee collected on the city wharf.[10] The rail shipment of freight from the Tennessee Valley had become a reality and Hamilton County rejoiced in its new rail connection. True, it then only linked Chattanooga to Atlanta with a connection to Charleston, but plans were underway for rail lines reaching northwest to Nashville and northeast to Knoxville and Virginia.

The availability of rail freight service to a larger market encouraged a significant change in the agricultural economy of the Salem Community. The change was gradual and probably was much less apparent to Joseph Roark and others of the community than it is in a historical perspective. With steamers on the river connecting with the east coast rail system, farmers in the Salem Community had access to the eastern markets and no longer were required to produce on their own farms all the necessities of life. New and better farm equipment was available. The cast iron plow replaced the old moldboard plow and permitted soil to be cultivated deeper. The McCormick reaper and other agricultural equipment permitted the farmer to produce far more than his family could consume. He had products to sell and the steamers and railroads gave him extensive markets in which to sell his products. The same markets were, in return, to furnish the farmer with commodities he previously had to make or build for himself. The days of the self-sufficient farmer were gradually disappearing. Times in general, however, changed much more slowly in the isolation of the Salem Community than in the environs of the fast growing town of Chattanooga.

The early 1850s brought new growth to Hamilton County and Chattanooga. The first bank in the city, the Bank of Chattanooga, opened its doors in 1853 and provided capital for the local area. Col. Josiah McNair Anderson and George Williams completed the Anderson Pike to the northwest, constructed under authority of the state, and opened up the Sequatchie Valley to the Chattanooga rail head. Lookout Mountain was opened to summer residents and even tourists when the old road to the summit was reconstructed and carriage service was furnished by a local livery stable. Coal and iron ore from the area opened the possibility of foundries in the manufacture of iron products.[11] While growth in Hamilton County was focused primarily within the city of Chattanooga, growth was slow in the Salem Community. A new community center evolved on Harrison Road at the Grasshopper Creek ford. The meeting house of the Salem Baptist Church burned in late 1849 or early 1850, and the congregation expressed the desire to locate the meeting house away from the river to a location that would have better access. A new meeting house was constructed on land owned by Joseph Roark adjacent to and north of Grasshopper Creek on the Harrison Road which would provide much greater access to the church.[12] No title to the land was transferred nor recorded. That was unnecessary. The church needed a meeting house on the Harrison Road; Joseph Roark owned the desired location and made the land available to the church. Formal dedication of the land and transfer of the title would come a quarter of a century later.

Other communities developed south of the Tennessee and Hiwassee Rivers. Originally known as Dixon Spring or Hutcheson Spring, the community of Birchwood had established its identity in the early 1850s. Located just south of the Hamilton-Meigs county line, Birchwood was near the northern terminus of the Harrison Road at the Bunker Hill Ferry across the Hiwassee. In time the Harrison Road would become known as the Birchwood Pike. On September 4, 1854, a post office was established at Birchwood and, since Joseph Roark's homestead was slightly closer to Birchwood than to Limestone, his official address then became Birchwood, Tennessee.

By 1850 Hamilton County had grown to a population of 10,075 residents, and the Salem Community had an estimated population of 975.[13] The community was growing and so were the business ventures of Joseph Roark. Joseph continued to buy and sell leather hides with Lewis Patterson of Sale Creek and, based on records in his papers, Joseph's business with Patterson increased in the early years of the 1850s. A note from Roark to Patterson acknowledging receipt of leather hides to sell typifies their transactions:

> Rec'd of Lewis Patterson nineteen hides of upper leather amounting to forty dollars & seventy nine centes also 164 [pounds] sole leather at 25 centes per lb making forty one dollars sole & upper leather all amounting to Eighty one dollars & seventy nine centes which leather I promis to sell and act for in good hides or cash–hides at 10 centes per lb   August 26 1851
>   Joseph Roark
> Sole lether way [weighed] 158 when Rec'd[14]

Both Patterson and Roark were careful to document transactions so as to minimize misunderstanding. The partnership was operated on a friendly but businesslike basis. The following receipt from Patterson illustrates their business relationship:

> Rec'd of Joseph Roark a note I gave him to hand to an offer on Abigah Harris $7.75 cents which note he has returned and I have lost the recpt I take of [illegible] So this is to show he has returned P note   May 5 1852
>   Lewis Patterson[15]

To account to Lewis Patterson for his commission, Joseph maintained a list of his leather sales. Sales to Merida Webb, Abner Smith, Joseph Smith, Benjamin Webb, and William Shipman were recorded.[16]

Business for the sawmill was also good. It is unclear whether the partnership in the sawmill with Archibald McCallie had been continued or whether by 1850 Joseph operated the mill as a sole proprietorship. Nevertheless, orders for lumber continued to increase. Orders specified the materials desired and the required dimensions. Typical lumber orders read: "400 ft of plank, 16 ft long, 6 in wide and 1 in thick; 8 ea joists 16 ft long, 3 in thick and 6 in wide; 1000 ft of weather boarding 16 ft long."[17] Lumber orders included scantling, flooring, weatherboarding, sealing, and lathing. In a note, obviously written hurriedly in 1850, Joseph recorded a lumber order from Jesse Eldridge:

> Jesse Eldridge wants 225 feet floring 10 ft long, 400 ft of sealing, 250 ft wether bording, 16 plank 9 ft long 1 in thick 8 by 10[18]

Apparently Joseph occasionally employed carpenters for home construction in order to sell lumber from the sawmill. One order, seemingly for the addition of a room to a local residence, reads as follows:

to frame & roof	30.00
to weatherboarding 300 ft	4.50

to flores 576	16.00
to sealing 1630 ft	40.75
to windows 3	6.00
to doors frame 3	3.75
to dooer sutters [shutters] 2 at 3.00, 1 at 2.75	8.75
to columes 3 at 1.50, 3 at 1.25	8.25
to mantel	3.00
to caseing poorsh [porch] plates	2.00
to partishion frame	1.00
	124.00[19]

No records remain of flour sales from the gristmill. Apparently Joseph ground his own corn but made little or no effort to establish an ongoing business around the gristmill.

In addition to his partnership operations, Joseph continued to buy and sell land within the Salem Community. In October 1850, Joseph was approached by Thomas McCallie, brother of Archibald, about buying Joseph's forty acres on the lower end

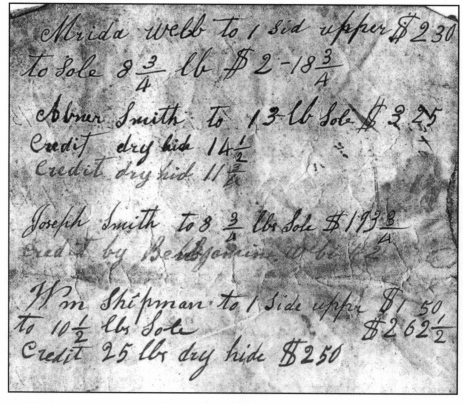

Joseph Roark's list of sales of leather under agreement with Lewis Patterson of Sale Creek.

of Grasshopper Creek. The tract was the forty acres on which Joseph had filed Entry No. 1654 as "occupant enterer" in January 1840. Joseph had not put the tract into cultivation and, although it was on the creek for a good source of water, it had no roadway access. The tract adjoined the 160 acres that Archibald McCallie and James Roark had jointly purchased in 1844 and in which James had sold his interest to McCallie in 1846. Since the tract had value to the McCallies but had limited value to Joseph, he sold the forty acres to Thomas McCallie on October 24, 1850, for $54. The deed was witnessed by Archibald McCallie and Robert McCallie.[20] Joseph had paid $40 for the tract in 1840, so the sale did not result in a significant profit; however, Joseph was able to dispose of a tract that had not been productive for him.

Two months later, Joseph used the monies from the McCallie sale to buy fifty acres from Hiram Cornwell. The Cornwell tract was located diagonally across the Birchwood Pike from Joseph's homestead and served as an extension of the homestead tract which, with this purchase, amounted to a total of 570 acres. The tract, for which Joseph paid Cornwell $150, was described as the SE4, NE4, and 10 acres of the NE4, NE4, of Section 28, FT2N, R3W. Cornwell had obtained the tract as a grant in the Ocoee District for which he had paid $0.50 per acre. The deed from Cornwell was witnessed by William F. McCormack and Joel A. Talley.[21]

As his partnership interests and his farming operations grew, Joseph continued to use promissory notes in his day-to-day business activities; however, by the 1850s Joseph used them less frequently but in larger amounts. In the first year of the new decade Joseph wrote promissory notes to George W. Gardenhire for $9.50,[22] to William F. McCormack for $60.00,[23] and to T. Rayl for $14.00,[24] with the purpose of each promissory note unstated. For whatever reason, Joseph seldom sent requests to other persons in the community asking payment of debts to him. Perhaps this was because he had sufficient cash to settle unanticipated cash demands without the necessity of requesting payment on an obligation to him. An exception to this occurred in October 1850 when Joseph asked Pleasant Doughty to settle a debt with Joseph's brother:

> Pleasant Doughty Sir Please to settle ten dollars to James Roark and oblige your friend   October 17, 1850
>
> > Joseph Roark[25]

In late February or early March 1850, Joseph and his brothers received a letter from their mother with distressing family news from Claiborne County. Thomas Ellison, Elizabeth's husband, had been charged with murder in Tazewell and found guilty by the court. It had happened on a night in January, at a store owned by Walter Buchanan in Tazewell. Apparently Buchanan's place was more of a local saloon than a store although groceries were sold to some extent. Men gathered there to drink, and by 1850, Buchanan's had developed a bad reputation for fights and rowdy behavior. Thomas Ellison had been at the bar that evening and gotten into an argument with

James McVey. McVey lived somewhat near Ellison within the same tax district, so the two men doubtless knew each other before the fight.[26] McVey owned little if any land and made his living as a tenant farmer.[27] He was described by persons in the community as "a very nice, gentlemanly looking young man but was inclined to be dissipated at times."[28]The argument had become heated and evolved into a fight, first with fists and then with knives. In the melee, McVey was killed. At the trial held in Tazewell, Ellison was found guilty of murder and was sentenced to ten years in the state penitentiary. He was incarcerated at Nashville on January 31, 1850.[29] McVey's wife was the former Nancy Killion who was left with several small children. She was to remarry four years later to Ira Scalf.[30] Thomas Ellison was to serve nine years of the ten-year sentence in the state penitentiary. As he was taken to prison, Elizabeth was left with eight children still at home, her two eldest having married. At home with their mother were Jeremiah 17, Nancy 15, George 13, William 11, Wiley 7, Elizabeth 6, Thomas Jr. 5, and Joseph less than a year old.[31] Within a year, Elizabeth would divorce Ellison during his prison term. Two years later she would marry Martin B. Nunn.[32]

At home in the Salem Community, Joseph and Juda had eight children still living at the homestead. Margaret was 13, Jerusha 12, James 10, John 8, William 6, Nancy 3, Matilda Brooks 7, and Juda Ann Brooks 5. Juda, already the mother of eight living children, was expecting again in 1851. Another daughter, Susannah, was born in mid 1851 and added to the crowded household. As their family grew, Joseph and Juda maintained a deep concern about the mental stability of their daughter Jerusha. She still had periodic seizures that disrupted the family routine. Dr. Yarnell had been unable to help, so Juda kept a watchful eye on her and provided loving care as the only expedient recourse of support and correction. The two oldest boys, James and John, were beginning to take on more responsibility for farming chores, leaving their father more time for his business activities.

The Brooks girls were treated very much as a part of the family. By early 1850, however, Joseph had not received from Harvey McKenzie any monies from the Brooks estate for support of Matilda and Juda Ann. Joseph and Juda had provided and cared for the two girls for over two years by that time and had continually sought from McKenzie the monies that were due. Under the statutes governing the settlement of estates, the monies received from the sale of personal property were to be distributed to all heirs including guardians for support of minor heirs of the estate. Land holdings of the estate were to be used for operating revenue or sold if necessary to provide funds for the support of minor heirs. The statutes were quite specific in requiring the administrator of an estate to report to the county court the details of all distribution of monies and particularly how minor children were to be supported.[33] Court records in Meigs County indicate that Harvey McKenzie and Joshua Guinn did report on the sale of the personal property in the required detail. Subsequent reporting by McKenzie and Guinn on distribution of funds to the Tillery minor children, to Zachariah Brooks, and to Matilda and Juda Ann, was

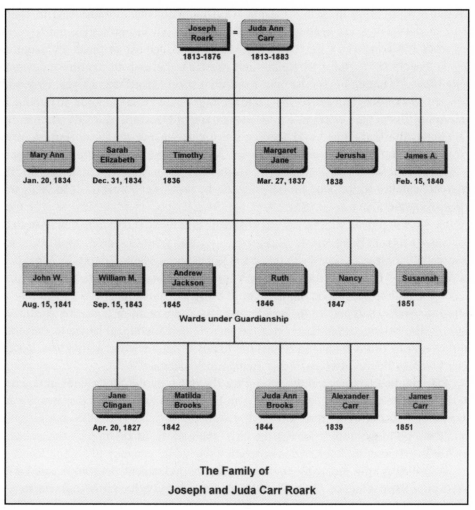

The Family of
Joseph and Juda Carr Roark

severely limited in scope and detail. The title to and income from the 560 acres owned by Leonard Brooks at his death is particularly difficult to follow. The year following his death, the tax records for Meigs County list the 560 acres under "Harvey McKenzie Administrator" while the following year in 1847, the tract was listed as the "Leonard Brooks Estate." Tax records in 1848 indicate disposal or transfer in title of a portion of the tract since only 160 acres was listed for "Leonard Brooks heirs." After 1848, however, no further tax listing for any portion of the Brooks estate is included in the tax records.[34]

Joseph Roark was not one to be put off and ignored. In late 1850 or early 1851, without an attorney, he sought help from William B. Russell, a judge for the Meigs County Circuit Court. In the spring of 1851, Joseph filed against McKenzie for monies due Matilda and Juda Ann as heirs of the Brooks estate. The process was obviously time consuming for Joseph, who doubtless made many trips to Meigs County and spent hours in court appearances. Following Joseph's presentation of the situation and facts, the Circuit Court rendered a judgement in favor of Joseph on September 3, 1851. Since McKenzie did not have the cash to pay the judgement, Judge Russell ordered lands be sold from the estate. Sheriff J.F. Zieglar issued the order of sale on September 15, 1852, and the highest and best bidder in an auction on December 27 "at the Courthouse door in the town of Decatur" paid $300 for the tract auctioned. While the tract sold was not the full 560 acres, the exact portion of the estate tract that was auctioned could not be identified from the records. Monies received from the sale were also to pay another judgement against McKenzie, so after court fees and commissions, Joseph was paid by the Court a total of $136.20 against a judgement in his favor of $362.63.[35]

Oddly, the court action by Joseph was against not only Harvey McKenzie but also his older brother, Benjamin F. McKenzie, as well. Why Benjamin McKenzie was involved is unclear. He had been taxed for 320 acres in Meigs County in 1844, prior to the death of Leonard Brooks, and was listed for the same acreage for subsequent years. It could be speculated that Benjamin McKenzie, who had been a justice of the peace between 1836 and 1846, was farming as a tenant all or a portion of the 560 acres of the Brooks estate farm since the sheriff "delivered legal notice to the tenant in possession" of the tract sold at auction. In any event, the court action was "Joseph Roark versus Harvey McKenzie and Benjamin McKenzie."

One might also question the reason for the delay by the McKenzies in payment of the estate share to Matilda and Juda Ann Brooks. Possibly the McKenzies felt that Joseph and Juda Roark were sufficiently well off to support the Brooks girls and would not go to the trouble to seek the girls' share of the estate through the courts. If such was the case, the McKenzies seriously misread the tenacity of Joseph Roark.

A few days after receiving payment under the judgement, Joseph received a letter from a Sam White in Meigs County (the signature on the letter unfortunately is located on a fold of the letter and the writer's name is almost illegible and could have been misread) with helpful advice on investing the monies received and on reporting an audit to the county court. Addressed to "Mr. Joseph Roark, Hamilton County, Tennessee," the letter–one of the very few pieces of correspondence maintained in the Joseph Roark papers–should be quoted in full:

> Mr. Roark
> I am informed by Mr. William B. Russell that he has succeeded in getting in a part of the muny owing to your ward from McKenzie. It would be regular for you to make a settlement with the County Clerk showing that you had the muny and then put the same out on interest, but you have in your power and you will be equally as safe to loan the muny taking note with sufficient security. When you settle with the Clerk of the County Court you can shew that the muny is loaned and where and who are the

Accounting of the Order of Property Sale by Meigs County Sheriff J.F. Zeiglar in Joseph Roark versus Harry McKensie and Benjamin McKensie. Land of the Leonard Brooks Estate was sold to provide Joseph with the estate settlement for Matilda and Juda Ann Brooks.

security. In loaning the muny you will either deduct the interest or make the note bear interest from date. If you was to go out of office if the muny was out on interest and on short credit, the Court would require your successor to take notes in place of the muny.

Respectfully yours,
Sam White

Joseph Roark
Hamilton County, Tennessee[36]

Why White would provide this helpful advice is not clear. Perhaps Judge Russell was impressed with the sincerity and dedication of Joseph Roark and asked White to write the letter to make suggestions that the judge himself was not in a position to make. We simply do not know the reason behind it. Nevertheless, Joseph did report receipt of the judgement to the Hamilton County Court and, as a "reward," was taxed by the County for the estate as "guardian of the Brooks heirs."[37]

With the Brooks girls and their new daughter, Susannah, James and Juda had a total of nine children living at home. It was during this period that Joseph added another room and loft to the homestead. This time using lumber from his sawmill instead of the planed logs used for the original cabin, Joseph constructed a 20-foot by 18 1/2-foot extension to the north side of the homestead. A second fireplace and chimney were constructed on the north wall of the new room, a doorway was cut in the north wall of the original front room to connect the two rooms, and a front porch was added along the west elevation of the house. The roof line of the original front room was extended for the addition, and the loft expanded to provide more sleeping area. More than likely the five girls slept in the loft, the three boys slept in the new north room, and Joseph, Juda, and the baby slept in the original front room.

What was life like in the Joseph Roark household in the early 1850s? Undoubtedly the routine of the home followed closely that of the pioneer home of Joseph in Claiborne County thirty years before. The boys were expected to rise early and build the fires each morning during the winter months, to feed and milk the cows, "slop" the hogs, and provide the necessary labor for the farming operations. The girls would support their mother in preparing the three large meals each day, churning the milk and molding the butter, washing, sewing, and mending for the family, collecting fruit from the orchard in the summer and fall, and maintaining to the best extent possible the cleanliness of the house. From later records we can conclude that the children of the household respected and loved their parents. To each of the children Joseph was "Pap," a true father figure to be obeyed yet emulated in good business practice and community involvement. Juda was "Mother" to the children and quickly responded to their needs. In return, the children bonded to her with love and affection. Of their own children and those whom they raised, only Matilda did not positively relate to the love and support provided by "Pap" and "Mother."[38] Evenings in the household were devoted to reading and family activities. While no record remains of religious training in the home, we can safely assume from Juda's participation in the Salem Baptist Church and the later religious faith of the children, that the Bible was regularly read.

It was in 1850 that Juda was to lose her oldest brother James Carr. The best evidence suggests that James Carr was seriously ill in early 1850, to the extent that his father Samuel Carr took the youngest son Alexander to live with his grandparents. Although James' wife was pregnant at the time, the other children had left the homestead or were of an age to provide help to their mother. James died in late 1850 or possibly in early 1851 and his last child, a son, was born in the spring of 1851. He was named James A. Carr after his father. James Carr was the father of several children, many of whom were grown by the time of his death. The widow apparently attempted to keep the remaining family together; however, she was unable to provide for the new baby. Sometime later, when he was between two and three years old, James A. Carr went to live with Joseph and Juda Roark. The other minor son, Alexander, who was eleven when his father died, remained with his grandparents.[39]

As he wrestled with the problem with the McKenzies, Joseph was also having difficulties with his son-in-law, Joel A. Talley. In January 1851, Joseph served as financial security for payment of three judgements against Talley by the local court system. At the time Joel and Elizabeth had been married five years–Elizabeth was then sixteen with two children, Amanda 3 and Elizabeth 2. The charges behind the judgements are unclear, but in late 1850 Talley was the loser in all three judgements, one in favor of John Nelson in the amount of $28.18 1/4, and two in favor of William F. McCormack, one for $35.55 and one for $64.16. Joel was thus faced with making a total payment of just over $127.89 to the local constable. Apparently he did not have the money and was faced with further court action and possible severe penalty if he did not make payment. One can imagine the scene as Elizabeth and Joel met together with her father seeking his help. The young mother was unfamiliar with the court system but was fearfully concerned about what might happen. Joseph obviously could have paid the judgements and relieved the anxiety of his young daughter; however, Joseph did not think in those terms. He clearly believed that every man should be responsible for his own actions and any penalties resulting therefrom. Joseph indicated to Talley that he would provide security for the judgements only if Joel would provide security to him in personal property of equal value. Thus, in a businesslike way, Joseph agreed to assist but only in a way that would keep the responsibility on Talley. Apparently Joel did not have personal property equal to the value of the judgements so he sought help from his cousin Jesse R. Talley, and on January 27, 1851, they jointly executed a mortgage to Joseph Roark surrendering a three-horse wagon, two mares–one "eight-year-old sorrel with a blaze face" and one "four-year-old bay"– four mules, one hundred bushels of corn, and one distillery.

So execution of the judgements was stayed. The personal property listed was to belong to Joseph if Joel Talley did not pay the judgements. Interestingly, the mortgage did not specify the deadline for payment of the judgements. It was executed by Joel Talley and J.R. Talley and witnessed by Hiram Cornwell and William C. Talley, brother of Joel.[40] It is unclear whether Joel reimbursed Joseph for payment of the judgements or surrendered the personal property. The mortgage, however, was maintained in the Joseph Roark papers. Would Joseph not have returned the executed mortgage if Talley had evidenced payment of the judgements? We can only speculate the outcome. Unfortunately, similar situations would again occur with Joel Talley.

Just over four years later Joel would again be faced with payments on another judgement against him. On May 17, 1855, local justice of the peace George Irwin issued a judgement against Talley in favor of Binyon and O'Conner for $13.00.[41] Again, Joel could not pay. Two weeks later, Joseph Roark made the payment and received the following receipt from Constable J.C. Roberts:

> Received of Joel A. Talley by the hand of Joseph Roark in full of a judgement and cost that Binon and Oconer obtained against the said Talley Befour George Irwin Esqr this the 2 of June 1855
>
> J.C. Roberts
> Const[42]

As he had done before with Talley, Joseph refused to accept responsibility for another man's mistakes or faults. In addition to the $13.00 judgement, Talley had other obligations for which he sought Joseph's financial assistance. He was then in debt to Joseph by more than $120 excluding the mortgage settlement four years earlier. This time to meet his current debts, Joel mortgaged 240 acres that he had purchased in the sale of the school section of the Third Fractional Township roughly five miles south of the Joseph Roark home place. Simultaneously, on May 19, 1855, two days after the Binyon and O'Conner judgement, Joel executed a promissory note to Joseph Roark in the amount of $129.22 ½ and a deed of trust to Byrd Irwin, trustee, for the 240 acres. If the promissory note from Talley to his father-in-law was not paid in full within one year, by May 19, 1856, Irwin, as trustee, was to sell the 240 acres to the highest bidder at an auction and, from the proceeds, provide payment to Joseph. The mortgage was placed of record in the Hamilton County courthouse.[43]

Joseph did not do business in a flippant or gratuitous manner. The mortgage was witnessed by Maise Blackburn and Joseph's other son-in-law, Robert B. Scott. More than likely, the debt was settled by Talley within the allotted year and the note returned to him as it was not maintained in the Joseph Roark papers. While Joseph's response to Talley may seem stern, he nevertheless sought to help and assist his son-in-law over the next few years and maintained a family relationship. Joel's name appears as a witness on several documents executed by Joseph indicating at least an acceptable relationship between the two.[44] Unfortunately their divergent personalities and work ethics would ultimately cause an irreparable separation.

Contrary to his relationship with Talley, Joseph Roark appears to have had a respect and admiration for his other son-in-law, Robert Beane Scott. In 1851, Robert and Mary Ann lived on the farm of Robert's father on Grasshopper Creek near the homes of M.H. Conner, Abner Smith, and Hiram Haney. Their first child, a daughter to whom they gave the name Jane, had been born November 1, 1850.

Joseph's father-in-law, eighty years old in 1850, continued to have problems in the local courts. On July 10, 1851, Samuel Carr was forced to pay William F. McCormack $19.00 under a judgement by Hiram Cornwell, justice of the peace. The cause for the judgement was not recorded; however, Carr paid the designated amount the day of the judgement and received a receipt from William Killian, who was serving in the office of constable.[45] Samuel and his son Alfred lived on Joseph Roark's land adjacent to the farm owned by McCormack. Since Carr owned no land, the dispute could not have been over property or crops. Carr had paid a similar judgement to McCormack four years earlier shortly after his move to Hamilton County. One wonders what an eighty-year-old man could do to warrant such a judgement against him. Nevertheless, the disagreement occurred. Disputes seemed to be characteristic of Samuel Carr. This dispute, however, was unique. It was to be his last.

In the early 1850s there is evidence that Joseph Roark continued a role of leadership in the Salem school on Grasshopper Creek. Strong local leadership was necessary in the absence of an equitable support effort by the State in public education. A school fund had been established by the State in the Constitution of 1834 with monies derived from land taxes, donations, taxes on licenses, and from the sale of public lands. From its inception, the school fund had been apportioned among counties of the state without restrictions or directions on its expenditure. In 1838, the legislature provided for the office of county school commissioner and local trustees for school districts coterminous with the civil districts within each county. Within the school districts, a school served each township with funds from the sale of lands from Section 16 of the township going to support that school. With no direction from the State and with little consistency in allocation of the state school fund, results from the common school system were disappointing. Even use of the school funds by the State was not sacred, and a portion of the earnings from the school fund was used by the legislature to pay the interest on State loans. The educational system in the state continued to languish. A report from the Common School Commissioner in 1847 stated that almost one-fourth of the 249,008 persons in Tennessee over twenty years of age could neither read nor write. The Commissioner recommended an annual tax levy in each county to support education. The recommendation was supported by the governor, who suggested legislation permitting counties, "in which the population agreed to do so," to levy and collect a school fund. No legislative action was taken. State funding was woefully insufficient in that in 1849, the state fund, if apportioned equitably, would have allocated an amount equal to 40 3/4 cents per child between the ages of six and twenty-one. The state was without a clear-cut program for education. Reports criticized the capabilities of teachers employed in the common schools as "young men equally destitute of education and experience as teachers." Little was done by the public to demand action by the legislature in support of public education. Petitions submitted by the public to the legislature in 1851-52 were heavily weighted to matters other than support for the common schools:

> Of one hundred and forty-three petitions submitted to the Senate direct, forty-six were on matters relating to intemperance, and only one on an educational topic, that single petition seeking relief for the trustee of Shelby County who had deposited school funds in a bank that had failed. If the number of petitions filed direct with the Senate be valid evidence as to what constituted matters of public interest, then there was as much interest in a sleight of hand performer, in a charter for a plank road through the Sequatchie Valley, or in Porter's self-loading rifle, as there was in the subject of public education. Each of the above was represented by just one petition, respectively.[46]

Initiative for local schools was left in the hands of whatever local leadership was available and Joseph Roark apparently had a strong role in this local leadership. While there is no record to suggest that he held an elective office such as trustee or commissioner, his role in financial support and administration of the school on Grasshopper Creek is evident. In 1851, Joseph developed a list of heads of households in the Salem Community with the number of their school-age children, ostensibly between the ages of six and twenty-one to match the State criteria. Undoubtedly this list was for the purpose of collecting a per-student assessment for operation of the school over and above what monies might be allocated by the State through Hamilton County. The list below is a general list of citizens of the Salem Community. If the Salem school should receive for the 107 prospective students tabulated the full allocation of 40 3/4 cents per student, the total amount would hardly pay a teacher's salary for a three-months term, leaving no funding for construction and maintenance of the school building, supplies, heat, etc.

M.H. Conner	8	James Roark	4
Hiram Haney	4	Joseph Roark	7
Maise Blackburn	4	Abner Smith	6
Joseph Guess	2	Richard Smith	2
Hambleton Guess	2	Sintha Swain	1
Jesse Killian	6	John Hickson	4
William Killian	5	John Roark	blank
Joseph Smith	3	Poly Bean	2
Henry Bare	4	Seamore Campbell	2
James Cameron	4	Hiram Cornwell	5
Archibald McCallie	8	Gilbert Hardin	3
George Cloise	6	George Wease	2
W.H. Stephenson	3	James Ballard	6[47]
W.M. Shipman	4		

In November 1851, Joseph took the lead in underwriting the cost of adding another brick chimney "to the school house on Grasshopper Creek." Writing in his own hand, Joseph developed a proposed subscription list for underwriting the cost of the chimney. In good organizational format, the lower portion of the document was subdivided into columns headed as "Names, Dollars and Cents." Five subscribers other than Joseph were listed with a total amount pledged of $19.50. Of the total amount, Joseph pledged $5.00. The document reads as follows:

> We whose names are hereunto subscribed promise to pay to Joseph Roark on his order the sum assigned to our names, which sum we subscribe for the special purpose of building a brick chimney to the school house on Grasshopper Creek and for no other purpose.
>
> this 14th day of November 1851

Names	Dollars	Cents
Joseph Roark	$5.00	
Hiram Cornwell	4.00	
Maise Blackburn	5.00	
W.H. Stephenson	2.00	
John Campbell	.50	
Wm. Killian	3.00[48]	

Special schools were sometimes held by those who could afford them. Teachers in the area solicited subscriptions to these special schools and conducted classes when sufficient students were available. These were schools of from one- to three-months duration, and costs generally ran about $3.00 per student for the duration of the class. In December 1854, Joseph subscribed to a writing school probably for two of his sons. A receipt was provided by the instructor:

> Dec. 27th/54
> Rec'd from Joseph Roark six dollars in full of his account for what his subscription was to a writing school
>
> Hugh A. McKibbins[49]

At another time, the date is unknown, Joseph was one of nine persons signed up at $3.40 per person for a special school of undesignated purpose. With Joseph were listed William Haney, Matilda Brooks, Elizabeth Talley, Mary Talley, Samuel Smith, John Campbell, Arnold Mangrum, and John Roark for a total subscription of $30.60. Joseph probably signed separately for Matilda Brooks to have a receipt record for the Leonard Brooks estate. His daughter Elizabeth more than likely participated for her children rather than for herself with Joseph paying the total subscription.[50] Although common schools were beginning to be available, such special private schools, somewhat spontaneous and unscheduled, were frequently supported.

Rev. Alfred King in the early 1850s was school trustee of Civil District 10 in which the Salem Community was located. King was a Baptist minister in the area, having served as pastor of the Salem Baptist Church at one time.[51] As trustee, King was responsible for allocating any monies available from the State school fund to townships within the district. On October 2, 1852, Joseph Roark submitted a certified statement that Hiram Cornwell had taught at the Salem school and requested payment to Cornwell in the amount of $20.00. The certification, signed by Joseph, appears to have been written by Cornwell. Apparently, from the certification, Joseph had some oversight position in regard to the Salem school:

> Mr. A. King trustee of Hamilton County
> Sir please to pay Hiram Cornwell twenty dollars out of the school funds belong[ing] to the Second Fractional Township North and Third Range West of the basis line Ocoee district and oblige yours   this 2nd day of October 1852
>
> I certify that Hiram Cornwell has taught school in the above named Township and that the above order is correct this 2nd day of October 1852
> Joseph Roark[52]

The success of the local common school was dependent on local initiative in each township. Unfortunately, any opportunity for even a rudimentary education was short-lived for the young people of the community–for the young men, since farm responsibilities became demanding as soon as a young man could do a good day's work and for the girls, who often married at a very early age and lost opportunity for schooling to childbearing and housework. Such would be the case when Joseph Roark was to lose another of his daughters to marriage. Margaret married Bill Swafford on January 22, 1853, just two months shy of her fifteenth birthday. William Linville Swafford was the son of John and Mary Fields Swafford and the grandson of William T. and Nancy Craig Swafford, who had come to Tennessee in 1805 from North Carolina.[53] The Swafford farm was located near the Hiwassee Campground in Meigs County.[54] Bill had attended the Georgetown Academy[55] in the Limestone Community and taught school briefly at the Salem school.[56] Quite probably it was at the school that he met Margaret.

The wedding was on a Saturday and was held in the front room of the Roark home with Rev. James Matthews performing the ceremony. As Margaret later remembered, she wore a red marina dress at the wedding. Another fond memory of Margaret was that her father, on being informed by Juda on Friday that they were without maple sugar for the wedding cake, walked–apparently the boys were using the horses–the five miles to Limestone to the store of Jonathan Wood for the sugar.[57] Following the wedding, the couple lived briefly with Bill's parents. After a very few months, they would return to Hamilton County where Bill would farm for three years.[58]

Shortly after Margaret's wedding, Joseph and Juda were to experience the loss of Juda's parents, Samuel and Margaret Carr. Although there are no firm records of when they died, Margaret Carr most likely preceded her husband in death. With the loss of her parents, Juda and Joseph took the responsibility for Carr's grandson,

Alexander. Joseph and Juda would raise Alexander to his adult years.[59]

As he would have been 83 sometime during 1853, it is possible that Samuel Carr was feeble during his later years and may have lived his last few days at the home of his son, Alfred. On Tuesday, March 8, Alfred took his father to Birchwood and at the store of B. Holman, Samuel Carr purchased two wool hats, one at $1.25 and the other at $1.00, both charged to the account of Joseph Roark.[60] More than likely it was the last trip outside the home for Samuel Carr. He died in late March or early April 1853.[61]

Following Carr's death, Joseph Roark was named by the county court as administrator of the Samuel Carr estate. Since Joseph was only a son-in-law and a son, Alfred, was close to his father, it may have been that Samuel, although he died intestate, had left a request that Joseph be named administrator. For whatever reason, Joseph was designated administrator in late April 1853 and began a laborious settlement of the estate that would extend over two years.[62]

Since Carr owned no land, the estate settlement primarily involved the identification of all heirs, the payment of all debts, collection of all accounts payable to Carr, the sale of all personal property, and distribution of proceeds to the heirs. The heirs were known to Joseph and were readily identified: John Carr, then living in Davidson County; Jane Carr Mahan in Meigs County; D.A. Medley, son of the Carr daughter that married Sanford Medley; Matilda and Juda Ann Brooks, daughters of Margaret Carr Brooks; Alfred Carr then living on the Joseph Roark farm in Hamilton County; the children of James Carr; and lastly Juda Carr Roark.

Records are available for neither the debts nor the accounts receivable of Samuel Carr. Similarly, a record of the sale of personal property and the amount received for each item was not maintained. Best evidence suggests that the sale of personal property was held the second week of May 1853, and cash was received for most items. Since there were no minor children to provide for, it is likely that some of the heirs asked for and received, in lieu of a cash distribution, particular items of personal property for which they had a sentimental attraction. One promissory note was received jointly from William Carr, probably a nephew of Samuel Carr, and W.C. Thatcher for items of personal property selected at the sale:

> Twelve months after date we or either of us promise to pay Joseph Roark administrator of the Estate of Samuel Carr dec'd four dollars and four cents value received.
>
> Witness our hands and seals this 14th May 1853
> his
> William X Carr
> mark
> W.C. Thatcher[63]

The settlement of the estate was nevertheless a laborious process consuming much of Joseph Roark's time over a two-year period. By April 1855, Joseph had completed the accounting for the estate and had submitted his final records to the Hamilton County Court in Harrison. After a review by the court, Joseph received a finding by the county clerk confirming that the final value of the estate was $97.98, which was the amount due the heirs:

> I find in the hands of Joseph Roark Administrator of Samuel Carr Deceased after settling with him $97.98 which is due the heirs of said Carr
>
> James Clift Clk
>
> By J.B. Peters DC[64]

A complete accounting of the estate distribution is impossible to establish but based on records available, it is clear that each of the seven children or their survivors was due $14.00. The following distribution of the estate can be safely assumed:

John Carr	$14.00	son
Jane Carr Mahan	14.00	daughter
Alfred Carr	14.00	son
Juda Ann Carr Roark	14.00	daughter
Matilda Brooks	7.00	granddaughter
Juda Ann Brooks	7.00	granddaughter
Francis M. Carr	2.50	grandson
D.A. Medley	2.50	grandson
Unnamed grandchildren	23.00	grandchildren

$98.00

Joseph made the first distribution payment to Jane Carr Mahan on May 16, 1855, and received a written receipt in return:

> $14 Received of Joseph Roark administrator of the Estat of my father Samuel Carr Deceast it being my distributive share of sed Estate after the debts and claims aganst said Estate by said administrator this 16th day of May 1855
>
> Jane Mahan[65]

Equal payments of $14.00 were made to John Carr and Alfred Carr on May 21, 1855, and written receipts were filed in the papers of Joseph Roark.[66] No receipt, of course, was necessary from Juda. Since no record is available of payments to Matilda and Juda Ann Brooks, it can be assumed that since they were minor children, their share of the estate was combined with their share of the Leonard Brooks estate and held until they were of age. The same is true of Alexander and James A. Carr, James Carr's sons whom Joseph and Juda would raise and to whom Joseph would later pay their share of the Samuel Carr estate. Payments to other grandchildren of Samuel Carr were also delayed probably due as well to their age. Only two records of payment to grandchildren are available: one to Francis M. Carr, assumed to be a son of

James Carr and a mature adult at the time, in the amount of $2.50 on March 3, 1859,[67] and one to D.A. Medley for $2.50 on September 7, 1855.[68] The receipt from Medley was signed by his father, Sanford Medley. No other grandchildren were identified.

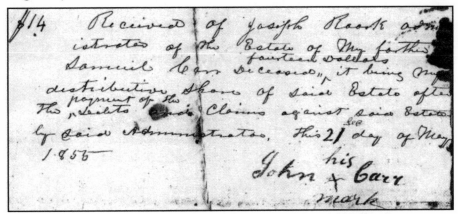

Receipt, May 21, 1855, from John Carr for $14.00 to Joseph Roark, Administrator of the Samuel Carr Estate, for John Carr's share of the estate.

Several questions remain in regard to the estate distribution. If D.A. Medley were the only son of the Carr daughter that married Sanford Medley, why did he not receive a full share of $14.00? Perhaps the amount paid to Medley was only a partial distribution with the remainder to be paid at a later date. This possibility is reinforced by a summons and promissory note by Joseph to Medley four years after the initial settlement. On September 28, 1859, Joseph Roark would receive the following summons from J.C. Roberts, local constable:

> To Joseph Roark I summons you as a garnyho [garnisher?] to appear befour Seamoor Campbell Esq at his one [own] home on the 30 of Sept 1857 and answer on an oath what you air in debted to one Sanford Medley whous property I hold in my hand & execution in favor of J.S. Lutteral obtained against him befour Seamoor Campbell & the said Medly has no property in my county to satisfy & also to state what effects of his you have in your hand or no of enny other person having to the best of your knowledge & beliaf this Sept the 28 1859
>
> J. C. Roberts Const[69]

Three weeks following the summons, Joseph wrote the following promissory note:

> One day after date I promise to pay Ivy Medley Seven dollars and eighty cents for value rec'd this the 19th day October 1859
>
> Joseph Roark[70]

The identity of "Ivy" Medley is unclear. Was this a nickname for D.A. Medley or Sanford Medley? Speculation would suggest that Joseph Roark had some concern about the financial stability of Sanford Medley and delayed full payment to the grandson until he was of a mature age. Even under the promissory note of October 19, 1859, a payment of only four dollars was delayed until a year later on October 10, 1860.[71]

Equally puzzling is the distribution to the children of James Carr. The payment of $2.50 to Francis M. Carr, if he were in fact the son of James, would indicate that there were six surviving children of James. Why were not these children identified and when was payment made to them? Simply, it cannot be confirmed that James had six surviving children and we do not know the answer. Questions also remain in regard to the estate of James Carr. In the Joseph Roark papers is the following claim against the estate of James Carr by his sister, Jane Mahan, indicating other questions on the settlement of that estate:

> State of Tennessee
> Meigs County
> This day comes Jane Mahan in her own proper person and makes oath in the form of law that the estate of James Kerr [Carr] dec'd is justly indebted to her the sum of ten dollars and fifty seven cents of money and interest that she paid to Isaiah Womack as the security of the said James Kerr dec'd on a note of hand and further avows and says that said note is destroyed so that she cannot produce it as claimant
> As sworn to and signed before me this 13th day of June 1856
> Witnys   her
> W.B. Russell   Jane X Mahan
> Justice of the Court   mark[72]

The W.B. Russell who witnessed the statement of Jane Mahan was, of course, the judge who had assisted Joseph in obtaining monies of the Leonard Brooks estate from Harvey McKenzie. It would appear that the estate of James Carr was not settled for several years following his death. The distribution from his estate to his heirs is not available to us today and remains a mystery similar to the distribution from his father's estate. One fact is clear: Joseph and Juda Roark assumed the responsibility of raising Alexander and James A. Carr, the two young sons of James Carr.

One other question remains in regard to the Samuel Carr estate. On April 19, 1855, Joseph Roark received a promissory note from William Carr in the amount of $10.00 "for value received."[73] Was this connected to the estate settlement or merely a business obligation? And was William truly a nephew of Samuel Carr as has been assumed?

Samuel and Margaret Carr were buried in the Old Salem Baptist Church Cemetery[74] and passed from the scene in the life of Joseph Roark. Joseph had known the Carrs for over twenty years and, as far as we can determine today, he enjoyed a good relationship with both. Joseph and Juda had provided for her parents in their last years and cared for their every need. They had fully met their responsibilities to Juda's parents.

Following the estate sale of personal property of Samuel and Margaret Carr, their home sat vacant for only a short period. In the early summer of 1853, as he had done for daughters Mary Ann and Elizabeth, Joseph gave his daughter, Margaret, and her husband, Bill Swafford, a farm that included the Samuel Carr home.[75] The size and location of the farm is difficult to determine, although the strong probability is that it was part of the Joseph Roark homestead that lay within Section 35, FT2N, R3W. Margaret and Bill were to maintain title to their farm and the old Carr home place until after her father's death. At that time she would return it to the estate for a cash settlement. The Swaffords were to live in the Carr home place for three years while Swafford was to make his living as a farmer.[76] Their first child was born in the old Carr house in 1854; however, the child lived only a short time and was buried at the Hiwassee Campground Cemetery near the home of Bill's parents.[77]

Joseph had been engrossed in the settlement of the Samuel Carr estate for six months when he unexpectedly was called upon to serve as administrator of a major estate more difficult than Carr's estate. Henry Bare, a neighbor and landowner in the Salem Community, died intestate in September 1853 at the age of forty-six, leaving a widow and six minor children. Probably at the request of the widow and the acquiescence of Joseph, the Hamilton County Court appointed Joseph as administrator of the estate.[78] Henry Bare had settled in the Cherokee territory before 1836[79] and was joined by his brother Andrew before the Ocoee District was formed in 1838. When entries were taken for the Ocoee District grants, Henry Bare had submitted eleven entries and received grants for a total of 660 acres.[80] In September 1841, Bare had added to his holdings when he purchased 80 acres in two tracts from Martha Smith. Joseph Roark had witnessed the deed.[81] In April 1838, when he was 31, Bare had married Malinda Fry, who was 21 at the time of her marriage. Malinda was born in Alabama and had been orphaned when she was nine years old. After the death of her parents, she was raised by her uncle, Samuel Fry, whose wife Nancy was a sister to William Blythe and Jerusha Blythe Roark.[82] Malinda was thirty-four when Henry Bare died and Joseph Roark was named administrator of the estate. The six children, three boys and three girls, ranged in age from four to fourteen at the death of their father. The two oldest children were both girls.[83] On her petition and to her credit, Malinda was named by the county court as guardian of her minor children.[84]

In spite of his workload in settling the Carr estate and in the management of his partnerships and farming operations, Joseph plunged immediately into the task at hand on the Bare estate. Notices were sent to the community requesting notification of any promissory notes against or due Henry Bare. Likely this was done by word of mouth or handwritten notice to residents within the community and particularly to merchants in the area. The promissory notes would be assembled over a period of twelve months and would be given due consideration in the settlement of the estate. Sensitive to her new status as a widow, Joseph worked closely with Malinda Bare to schedule the sale of personal property to provide her with funds needed to care for the children and for herself. The estate sale was scheduled at an early date in November 1853.[85]

The estate sale of personal property may have been conducted over a two- or three-day period since two undated records remain, each in a different handwriting. Over 105 items are listed with the purchaser's name and the amount paid for each item. The widow obviously was given a first choice at each item but was charged the market price for each item she chose to keep. One can only imagine the thoughts that went through the widow's mind during the estate sale, as she saw bids taken on the plow that her husband had used to break their land, the crosscut saw he had used to cut firewood and to remove the trees–remembering perhaps some special day that had been dear to both of them–and the tools he had used to build their cabin. What would take the place of the plans that she and her husband had made together? There was no government-certified insurance company to provide an annuity for her welfare and that of the children. The widow was now on her own and, as guardian of her children, she must provide for their welfare. Yet, here were her husband's prized possessions, tools that he had used in starting their married life together, being auctioned to the highest bidder and taken away. Life could be harsh.

The items taken by Malinda Bare at the estate sale provide a unique look at her personality and determination. At many similar estate sales, the widow took the furniture and personal family items such as tableware and the family Bible. Items taken by Malinda, however, identify a widow with determination to continue the family farm and to work her way through the immediate tragedy. The items she retained consisted of "one lot of tools, a reaping hook, a cotton wheel, one flax wheel, one spade and mattock, and one scythe and cradle." Clearly, Malinda kept the tools that she would need to work the farm and provide for her family.

Others of the community bought items at the estate sale that they could appropriately use and the purchase of which would provide some help to the widow. Buyers at the sale included M.H. Conner, who purchased "one lot of plows and irons" for $1.90, Jonathan Wood–"mill utensils" for $1.55, William Roark (most likely the son of James Roark, then at age 21)–one "yoke and bow" for $0.05, R.B. Scott–"kitchen utensils" for which the price is illegible, William Potter–a "grind stone" for $0.15, Archibald McCallie–"saws" for $7.00, William H. Stephenson–"hogs" for $52.08, James Roark–"hogs" for $28.15, and Joel A. Talley–"fishhooks" for $0.10.[86]

Many of the purchasers paid cash for the small items, netting a total of $27.16 1/4 for the estate. For the larger items and bulk purchases, the buyers used promissory notes payable to "Joseph Roark, administrator of the estate of Henry Bare, deceased" and payable "twelve months after date." Following the sale, Joseph made a list, in his own handwriting, of all promissory notes due the estate as a result of the sale. The list of promissory notes included:

G.W. Bottoms	$15.20
Joseph Lock	7.70
John Hixon	7.50
J.C. Lock	82.20
Francis Gross	0.30
Jesse Killian	5.00
William H. Stephenson	52.08
W.B. Riggs	37.87
James Roark and William Potter	37.75
T.J. Bottoms	66.00
John Gross	12.21
R.B. Scott	11.05
T.J. Matthews	78.10
Joseph Gass	27.00
Duke Kimbrough	35.50
Pleasant Doughty	8.55
James Finley	17.50[87]

The promissory notes would be collected during the following twelve months and a fund established to pay the debts of Henry Bare, debts that were to be identified during the same twelve-month period. Interestingly, one promissory note from the above list remained in the Joseph Roark papers:

> twelve months after date we or either of us promise to pay Joseph Roark administrator of Henry Bare decist thirty seven dollars and seventy five cents this twenty sixth day of November 1853
>
> James Roark
William Potter[88]

If the note from James Roark and Potter had been paid within the twelve months, why was not the note returned to them rather than being kept in the records of the estate settlement? One can only assume that return of the note was not demanded by either James Roark or Potter or its retention was an oversight on the part of the administrator. From what we know of Joseph Roark and his meticulous attention to detail and accuracy, we can safely conclude that the promissory note was paid and that the funds were duly provided to the Henry Bare estate.

In November 1854, Joseph made a list, again in his own handwriting, of all debts against the Bare estate. With a minimum of imagination, one can see Joseph in the late fall of the year sitting at the family table, using the fireplace for light, sorting through the stack of claims against the Bare estate and developing a final list for settlement. In his orderly fashion, Joseph made, on the single sheet of paper, two columns for claimants against the estate with vertical lines separating the dollars and cents for each claim amount. He headed the page:

Joseph Roark
  Against the Estate of Henry Bare

He listed each claim below. The list with spelling for each name exactly as he wrote it follows:

T.J. Walker	$17.66	
Johnathen Wood	2.75	[Jonathan Wood, merchant]
Jim Campbell	45.00	
Ma Wood	2.25	[M.A.Wood, son of Jonathan]
Ma Wood	13.14	
W.C. Hutcheson	5.70	[merchant]
1 taxe Receit	4.87 ½	[Tax statement or possibly receipt if paid by Joseph]
W.C. Hutcheson	3.10	
W.C. Hutcheson	13.10	
1 tacks Recpt	3.19	[tax statement or paid receipt]
Z. Martin	188.00	[merchant]
John Taylor	21.00	
Archibald Mcallie	5.32	[McCallie]
J.B. Eldridg	4.00	[Eldridge]
R.M. Adams	3.83 ¼	
Byrd Irwin	96.28	
T.H. Calaway	34.00	[Thomas H. Callaway, major Ocoee District landowner]
James Johnson	1.20	
Thomas Mils	50.00	[Mills?]
Joseph Gass	31.12 ¾	
P. Douty	6.00	[Pleasant Doughty]
Malinda Bar	46.00	[Malinda Bare–apparently settlement expenses]
Thomas Callaway	7.50	[Thomas H. Callaway]
B Holemon	33.02	[B. Holman, merchant]
Wm Potter	25.50	
B Holemon	49.06	[B. Holman, merchant][89]

At the bottom of the list Joseph had a total for the Bare debts of $787.60 ½ which is exactly $75.00 greater than the total of the debts listed. Apparently Joseph had an additional debt of $75.00 which was not listed, perhaps his own expense as administrator of the estate. No probable mistake in Joseph's addition could be identified.

In December 1854, Joseph Roark submitted his report as administrator of the Henry Bare estate to the county court of Hamilton County and received approval by the court.[90] Following court approval, funds remaining in the estate were turned over to Malinda Bare, and on January 1855, Joseph received a receipt from her. The receipt was not written by Joseph, indicating that someone else was assisting

Malinda in reviewing the records and recommending her acceptance:

> Received of Joseph Roark administrator of the Estate of Henry Bare deceased seventy five dollars and sixty four cents in full of said estate in his hands after settlement with the clerk of the county court of said state January the 7th 1855
>
>
>
> her
>
> Malinda X Bare
>
> mark
>
> Guardian of the Minor Heirs[91]
>
>

None of the land owned by Henry Bare was sold during the estate settlement. Malinda and her children continued to farm for a living and were able to provide for their own welfare without selling any of the farmstead or receiving help from the community. Later, Malinda was to marry again to a man by the name of Irvin. Unfortunately she was to become a widow again within a brief period. In 1864, Malinda Irvin was taxed on 925 acres[92] and was listed as the head of the household both on the tax list and in the 1870 census. Her second son, James P. Bare, upon his return from service in the Fifth Tennessee Infantry (Union) during the Civil War,[93] was to purchase 260 acres from the rest of the heirs for $400 in February 1867.[94] The second daughter of Malinda and Henry Bare, Eliza Jane, was to marry a son of M.H. Conner, James Madison, upon his return from Confederate service in the Civil War.

It was late in 1853, during his efforts in settling the estates of both Carr and Bare, that Joseph received sad news from Claiborne County. His mother, Sarah Bolen Roark, was dead. Sarah had been the one person at the home place who had consistently written to Joseph and his brothers keeping them informed on the family. It is unknown whether she was in bad health for an extended period or died suddenly. Had she written of her bad health or was her death a complete surprise to the three brothers in Hamilton County? Who wrote the letter to Joseph informing him of his mother's death? More than likely it was Timothy Jr., the youngest living son, who took on that responsibility as he appears to have been the most qualified writer of the family at home.

Sarah Bolen Roark died in October at the age of seventy-seven.[95] She was survived by ten of her twelve children, all of whom she had raised on the western frontier of Virginia and Tennessee. Sarah had been a widow for twenty years and, following her husband's death, had lived at the home place, continuing to manage the farm. When her youngest, Mary Ann, had married James Jefferson Lambert in 1843, Sarah had suggested that they live at the home place with her and take over the farm operation. She was living at the home place with her daughter and son-in-law when she died. Sarah Bolen Roark was buried next to her husband in the family cemetery southwest of the home place. There she rests in an unmarked grave.

Although she died without a will, Sarah doubtless had expressed a desire that Jeff Lambert and Mary Ann receive the homestead and buy the interest of the other heirs. After the first of the following year, Jeff Lambert approached the five heirs in Claiborne County about deeding their interest in the homestead to him. At the same time, Lambert doubtless wrote Joseph, James, and John with a similar enquiry. The five brothers and sisters in Claiborne County agreed to sell their undivided interest in the homestead, and on February 8, 1854, William, Jeremiah, Timothy Jr., Nancy and husband James Richardson, and Elizabeth and husband Martin B. Nunn signed a quit claim deed to Jeff Lambert. For their undivided interest in the homestead, the five were paid a total of $129.00, or $25.80 per heir. The deed transferring title contained field notes from a new survey of two tracts of 50 acres and 150 acres, matching, respectively, the Timothy Roark Entry Nos. 136 and 589.[96] We can only assume that the $129 was negotiated among the heirs and was not based on an appraisal or current market values.

Joseph and his brothers in Hamilton County did not immediately respond to Lambert's request for transfer of title. More than likely neither party wanted to handle the transaction by mail and a visit to Claiborne County would be necessary for the three brothers. At the time–late 1853 or early 1854–Joseph was engrossed in the estate settlements and other pressing business activities. Probably the same was true for both James and John. For what ever the reason, the three brothers made no immediate effort to surrender their title in the homestead, perhaps indicating to Jeff Lambert, whom James had never met and John and Joseph had known only as a small child, that the three would plan a trip to Claiborne County at some future date. Over two years would pass before the trip was made and the homestead title was transferred.

At the national level, the ugly specter of slavery again haunted the Union. The Compromise of 1850 had briefly stilled the waters of tumult and had settled the slavery issue in respect to New Mexico and California. By 1854, however, steps were underway to form two new states in the Nebraska territory west of the Missouri River. Were these two new states, Kansas and Nebraska, to be slave states or free states? The leading politician on the issue was Senator Stephen A. Douglas, Democrat, of Illinois. Shrewd, articulate, and ambitious, Douglas proposed the concept of "popular sovereignty" in the Kansas-Nebraska Bill in 1854 under which the people in each state would determine whether the state was to be slave or free. The bill was passed by the Congress in May 1854 and was signed shortly thereafter by President Franklin Pierce. The new law resulted in a split in the Democratic Party, with the free-soil advocates breaking away to form the Republican Party. The law also fostered violence in Kansas as both pro-slavery and anti-slavery elements sought to control the state–by the force of arms if necessary. "Bleeding Kansas" suffered as the issue of slavery became more and more divisive. The divisiveness of the issue was also present within the state of Tennessee, as illustrated by the vote of the Tennessee delegation to Congress–the Tennessee vote was almost equally split on the Kansas-Nebraska Bill.[97]

While the Tennessee congressional delegation was split on Kansas-Nebraska, there was unanimity toward progress in Tennessee. Railroads continued to be the primary topic in business conversation. The Nashville and Chattanooga Railroad (N&C) was completed and in operation by February 1854, connecting Chattanooga and Hamilton County to the northwest. To the north and east, the East Tennessee and Georgia Railroad (ET&G) between Dalton, Georgia, and Knoxville was opened in June 1855. Passenger service was then available between Chattanooga and Knoxville; however, all traffic had to take an indirect route through Dalton to make the connection. It would not be until 1858 that the connection between Cleveland and Chattanooga would be completed and a direct route between Chattanooga and Knoxville would be provided. Meanwhile the extension of rail service north of Knoxville by the East Tennessee and Virginia Railroad (ET&V) was under development and would be completed by 1858. With the ET&G and the ET&V, Chattanooga would be connected to Virginia, Washington, D.C., and the other east coast cities. By the end of the decade, Tennessee was to have over 1,200 miles of track and was eighth in the nation in total mileage.[98] Chattanooga and Hamilton County were thus to become a major focal point of river traffic, and a network of railroads that created new markets for raw materials of the south in the northeast factories. Unhappily, this same system of river and rail transportation that brought prosperity to Chattanooga in the 1850s would also make it a focal point in the coming Civil War and would attract armies from both North and South to the locale. North of Chattanooga, however, the Salem Community was miles away from the new railroads and remained within its agrarian isolation.

The prosperity of Hamilton County and the significant financial success of Joseph Roark in the Salem Community brought new opportunities of personal development to Joseph and his family. In addition to being able to take advantage of special schools for members of his family, other items of cultural and spiritual development could now be afforded. In response to the opportunity provided by P.B. Cate, traveling salesman and agent for William Garretson and Company, Joseph ordered a copy of the Life of Christ, bound in rich leather, for the family. Delivery was to be by August first and Cate left a printed certificate of agreement:

> Mr. Joseph Roark subscriber for the Work entitled "LIFE OF CHRIST" bound in rich leather price $ [left blank] agrees to take and promptly pay for the same when delivered (provided it proves as represented) which I expect to be by soon after the 1st of August.
>
> Subscribers are earnestly requested to be ready for me punctually at the above mentioned date, and will please leave the money at the house, for I expect to be here then; but should I fail to do so, on account of sickness, or delay in getting my books, you may expect me any day in the future.
>
> Very Respectfully,
>
> P.B. Cate, Agent[99]

In addition to some expenditures for family items, James and Juda also took advantage of a traveling photographer to have their portrait made. It was the era in which photography was becoming popular and affordable to middle-class families. The then-prevalent technology for portraits was to enlarge the photograph and add detail and contrast by artistically applied charcoal enhancement. So in their best clothes reserved for special events, Joseph and Juda sat patiently for the photographer. In the tradition of the time, both maintained a solemn composure for the benefit of posterity.

Joseph and Juda Carr Roark, Circa 1855

Joseph Roark's successful ventures also brought him some renown that made him susceptible to various sales gimmicks. Tragically, one such gimmick had to do with his daughter Jerusha, who continued to have seizures. Sometime in the early 1850s, Joseph received the following letter, folded and addressed to him on the outside of the fold with the notation "Please Forward" written before his name:

> Mr. Joseph Rowark
> Sir
> I have understood that you have a daughter that is subject to fits. I take this method to inform you that I can furnish you a medicine that will positively cure them, if not it shall cost you nothing only the medicine. Please to call down and see me.
>
> Respectfully yours
Gilbert L. Hemenway
>
> enquire at P. Mungers for me[100]

No record remains that would indicate Joseph and Juda took advantage of the "medicine" that Hemenway had to offer. Meanwhile, they continued their struggle with Jerusha, who was then in her mid teens. Joseph and Juda continued to do what they could for Jerusha and worked closely with Dr. Yarnell who graciously adjusted his bill to them to accommodate their situation:

> Mr. Joseph Rowark: James Rowark paid me $10.00 on your Bill. The balance amount would be $38. If it suits you and you will settle for $22.50 cash by Benjamin Webb I will mark your bill [paid] in full
>
> yours truly
>
> March 19, 1850 John L. Yarnell[101]

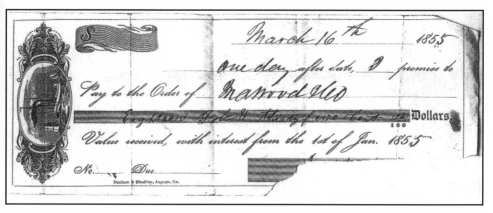

Promissory Note from Joseph Roark to Merchant M.A. Wood and Company for $18.35. This was the first promissory note written by Joseph Roark on a printed form, March 16, 1855.

In the first half of the 1850s, the promissory notes written by Joseph Roark were directed to real estate transactions and payments to merchants on accounts Joseph had set up for his family. Small debts and obligations could by then be paid in cash; promissory notes were used for larger purchases or payments and, in general, were written for significantly larger amounts. As he had done in the past, Joseph continued to periodically pay his merchant accounts by the use of the promissory note, albeit such notes were by then for larger sums. The merchants Joseph dealt with during this period and the amounts of the promissory notes or payments made to them in cash were Z. Martin, May 22, 1850, for $2.60;[102] W.C. Hutcheson, January 14, 1851–$49.87;[103] M.A. Wood, January 15, 1852–$28.78[104] and late 1853–$38.32;[105] John Taylor and Co., March 6, 1853–$15.00;[106] Jonathan Wood May 19, 1853–$20.07;[107] G.W. Housley, March 1, 1854–$19.98;[108] and Burton Holman, November 30, 1855–$33.00.[109] On March 16, 1855, Joseph signed, as far as we can determine, his first promissory note written on a printed form. The promissory note was written to "M.A. Wood & Co." for $18.35, with the usual wording but now in print–"Value received, with interest from the 1st of Jan. 1855." In using the printed format, Joseph neglected to enter the numerical amount of the note in the blank designated for that purpose but wrote out the amount of the note as he had customarily done over the past twenty-five years.[110]

In February 1852, Joseph also wrote a particular promissory note that was unique for him. It was for borrowed money rather than for value received. The recipient of the note, J.C. Wilson, apparently had cash available, and a loan to Joseph Roark was a reasonably safe way of putting the money to work:

> $44.00 One day after date I promise to pay J.C. Wilson on order Forty four
> Dollars for loned monney as witnes my hand and seal Feb the 5 1852
> Joseph Roark[111]

In another move that to Joseph was unique was the purchase of, or acceptance in lieu of cash payment, a promissory note to A.D. Meeks from Preston Biggs on which Meeks had been unable to collect. The note was written by Preston Biggs on January 26, 1854, for $6.85 with payment due on January 26, 1855. By April 1855, Meeks had been unable to collect from Biggs on the note so Meeks submitted it on May 2 to the local constable, William Killian, for collection. Killian had also been unable to collect on the note and since Meeks apparently did not want to pursue punitive action, he assigned or sold the note to Joseph Roark on September 5, 1855, for some discounted amount. Just over two months later, on November 20, 1855, Joseph was able to record on the reverse side of the note, "Received on the within note five dollars, this 20 day of November 1855." Using whatever pressure he could apply, Joseph was able to collect almost 75% of the value of the note and quite possibly collected the remaining principal and interest at a later date.[112]

Joseph continued to maintain his interest in land and stayed up to date on current ownership and availability of land within the local township. In the early 1850s, Joseph obtained in some fashion the right to purchase forty acres in the Salem Community or close by. Within the time limits for purchase under the acquisition agreement, Joseph received the following note from Jacob Roller:

> Mr Joseph Roark Sir please to keep the wright of them forty acres of land
> in your hands till I return home and I will stand good to you for the same. I
> do not now when the time is out of the order and you will greatly oblige me
> Jacob Roller[113]

Apparently Joseph relinquished the right to purchase the forty acres to Jacob Roller since deed records reflect no appropriate purchase of forty acres by Joseph.

Probably pertaining to land were two promissory notes, both written by Joseph Roark in his own handwriting, each in what was then a sizable amount in 1853 and 1855. The first was to William F. McCormack on April 21, 1853, in the amount of $250 "for value received."[114] No record is available that explains the purpose of the promissory note. The second promissory note was in favor of J.C. Wilson for $200 on January 16, 1855.[115] Joseph was to buy river-bottom land from Wilson two years later and the note could probably have been related to that purchase, maybe rental of the land until the purchase was recorded. No other clues are available to us today.

Duncan Colvin continued to rent land from Hiram Cornwell and a house from Joseph Roark. Under the rental agreement, Colvin was to pay the taxes on the house and the land. In early 1855, Colvin presented to Joseph a tax receipt from A. Selcer, tax collector, for $0.50 as the 1854 taxes on the house and the two acres on which the house was located.[116] The following year, Colvin and Roark were taken to court by G.W. Housley, probably for non-payment for materials purchased by Colvin for maintenance of the house. Although the expense was the responsibility of Colvin, Joseph, as landowner, was brought into the case before John Anderson, justice of the peace, to settle on what today would be termed a vendors lien. The receipt from Housley, following a judgement by the court, read as follows:

> Oct 30th 1856
> Received of Dunkin Colvin principle & Joseph Roark stay by J. Roark ten dollars and fifty six cts the full amount of a judgement that I received against the said Colvin before John Anderson Esq. day and date above ritten
> G.W. Housley[117]

The following day, Joseph Roark executed a promissory note to Housley in the amount of $19.94, apparently to cover the judgement plus other expenses related to the rental property.[118]

Joseph's state and county taxes were also paid annually; however, of interest is the fact that the tax amount varied considerably from year to year, possibly indicating that the value of the crop for each year was considered. In 1851, Joseph's taxes were $5.05; in 1852, $4.10; in 1853, $5.70; in 1854, $3.40, which was a reduction of 40% from the previous year; and in 1855 the tax amount was $5.62 ½.[119] Also in 1855, Joseph paid taxes for the first time on the Leonard Brooks estate for Matilda and Juda Ann Brooks. The amount of the taxes on the estate was $2.54.[120]

1852 Tax Receipt to Joseph Roark for State and County Taxes, Hamilton County, Tennessee.

To assist him in his farming operations, Joseph continued to employ his brother-in-law Alfred Carr, and in 1850, he also employed Benjamin Webb. Both men were allowed to make purchases from local merchants for farm items needed. Purchases were charged to Alfred Carr's account with Burton Holman which was paid and maintained by Joseph Roark. In 1854, Benjamin Webb charged the purchase of materials totaling $2.61 to the Alfred Carr account.[121] On June 2, 1855,

Joseph Roark paid Burton Holman the amount of $6.12 due on the Alfred Carr account to bring the account current.[122]

By 1854, Benjamin and Jane Webb were able to purchase land of their own. Both had worked hard since their marriage seven years before and, probably with appropriate help from Joseph, were in a position to buy the land of Hiram Cornwell when it became available. On March 17, 1854, Webb paid Cornwell $700 for 270 acres in Section 28, FT2N, R3W. The tract was adjacent to and northwest of the Joseph Roark homestead tract and immediately south of the 80 acres Joseph had given to Joel and Elizabeth Talley.[123] At the time of their land purchase, Benjamin and Jane Webb were the parents of three children: Sarah Elizabeth 5, John L. 3, and Merida, named for Benjamin's brother, nine months old.[124]

The prosperity of the country and of Hamilton County continued through 1856. Joseph used fewer promissory notes in 1856 than any other year (only one promissory note remains from 1856) as more cash was available through Chattanooga banks, and bank notes were more readily acceptable. Overall, the nation was expanding, railroads were being built to small communities on the frontier and even into unsettled areas hoping for rapid development. Land speculation along new rail lines increased land prices as speculators and investors bought land in anticipation of sizeable future returns. In Chattanooga, the iron industry was the foremost industrial enterprise as iron smelters took advantage of locally available ore to manufacture a

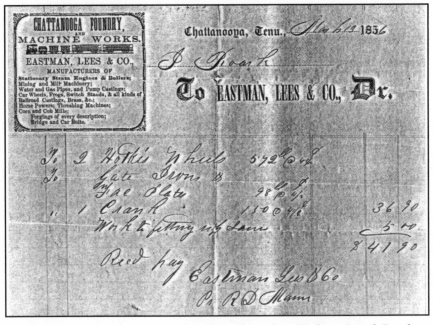

Receipt from the Chattanooga Foundry and Machine Works to Joseph Roark
for purchase of mill equipment, March 13, 1856.

variety of iron products. The Chattanooga Foundry and Machine Works, Eastman, Lees & Co. at the time employed forty-nine men and manufactured steam engines and boilers plus mining and mill machinery.[125] On Wednesday, March 12, 1856, Joseph Roark made a trip to the foundry in Chattanooga, most likely by steamer on the Tennessee, for the purpose of buying equipment for his sawmill and gristmill. The next day Joseph purchased two hotchkiss wheels, gate irons, face plates, and a crank, and had the parts fitted for proper operation. Confident of a booming economy, Joseph paid cash for the purchase and received a receipt for $41.90 signed by R.D. Mann from the foundry.[126]

While in Chattanooga, Joseph also visited the firm of A.D. Taylor, "Dealing in Dry Goods, Boots, Shoes, Hats, Caps, Bonnets, Paints and Dye Stuffs, Books, Fancy Goods and Groceries." Rather than shopping for "fancy goods," Joseph was there to purchase tools and equipment for his mill and farm operation. From Taylor he bought an anvil and hammer, a crow bar, bellows pipe, turning bar, bellows, and a screw plate. Again Joseph paid cash and received a receipt for $38.12 from Thomas Boydstum of the A.D. Taylor Company.[127] It is very likely that Joseph took with him to Chattanooga his oldest son James and maybe his middle son John to assist in transporting the tools and purchased equipment. If so, it probably was the first trip to Chattanooga for the boys. In any event, Joseph obtained the necessary equipment in a two-day trip and returned by steamer on Thursday afternoon, March 13.

In early summer, Margaret and Bill Swafford divulged their plans to move west with Bill's father to Middle Tennessee. Land was available in the middle of the state on both sides of the Tennessee where the river flows north to the Ohio. Bill and Margaret had farmed on Joseph's land for three years, had made a good living, and had maintained the taxes on that portion of Joseph's land that they farmed. But they had just started their family–their oldest daughter, Mary Ann, was one year old[128]–and, following his father's lead, Bill felt that this was the best time to seek land of their own. Then, too, Margaret was four months pregnant expecting their second child in January, and if they waited much later, it would be unwise for Margaret to travel. John Swafford, his wife and family, would make the trip with Bill and Margaret and both families would settle in Decatur County. Bill's grandfather, William Swafford, would remain in Meigs County.

It was a day of melancholia that Friday, August 8, 1856, when Margaret, Bill, and the baby daughter said goodbye to Joseph, Juda, and the rest of the family. Ahead of them lay a hard three-week trip by wagon over rough country roads. Joseph and Juda were not to see their daughter again.

As the crops were in by late summer and following Margaret's departure, Joseph and his brothers decided to make the trip to Claiborne County to accommodate brother-in-law Jeff Lambert in deeding to him their interest in the old Timothy Roark homestead. A letter doubtless was written to Timothy Jr. indicating their plans to arrive at the homestead the third week in August. The three brothers were to go by train for eighty percent of the trip. Some of the family would take them by wagon the twenty miles to Charleston to take the ET&G, the first train ride for the three brothers. One can imagine the childlike excitement of the brothers as they waited at the Charleston depot for the northbound train to arrive. James 58, John 56, and Joseph 43 had not seen the homestead or the family there in over a quarter of a century. It had been thirty-four years since James had left home and twenty-five years since Joseph had been at the home place. John had left in 1834 but had returned briefly in 1840 to sell his remaining land. So after a significant period of time, the three brothers, now middle-aged with large families, anxiously awaited the train's arrival and beyond that to see again the old home place where they had been raised.

They rode the ET&G to Knoxville and the ET&V to Morristown–the line would then have been extended only ten miles farther to Russellville[129]–and there they rented a horse and wagon at the local livery stable. Morristown was, at the time, a new community transformed rapidly by the advent of the railroad. From Morristown the brothers crossed the Holston, passed through Bean Station and over Clinch Mountain to the Clinch River and Tazewell beyond. From Tazewell they took the Kentucky Road toward Cumberland Gap, then north to the Powell River and the old home place. They were greeted by Mary Ann and Jeff Lambert and their three children. Mary Ann had only been a baby when Joseph left; James saw his youngest sister for the first time. Later they would visit with Elizabeth and her new husband, Martin B. Nunn, and Elizabeth's six children still at home. Some time would be spent with brothers William and Jeremiah, both of whom would speak of opportunities in Missouri and express thoughts of moving there. All of William's children were married and living outside the home. His younger daughter, Eliza, had married Daniel Friar in 1850, and his younger son, James, had married Sarah Friar, sister to Eliza's husband, only the year before. Jeremiah then had eight children still at home; the youngest, Eliza A., was only a baby. Brother Timothy Jr. by 1856 had acquired significant land north of Henderson Mill Hollow and was then living near Jeremiah just south of the Powell River. All nine of Timothy's children were then still at home; the youngest, Elizabeth, was just a baby. Living with Timothy and Mary was Mary's mother, Mary Williams. James Richardson and Nancy lived near the headwaters of Blair's Creek with five children still at home plus one grandson–their daughter Elizabeth Condray having died five years before. James Richardson was then a deacon in the Cave Springs Baptist Church.

On Saturday, August 23, 1856, James, John, and Joseph sat down with Jeff Lambert and Mary Ann to talk about the transfer of title to the old homestead. Jeff Lambert shared with them the quit claim deed executed by the rest of the family two years before. In anticipation of their coming, Lambert had prepared a similar quit claim deed for the three brothers to consider. The deed was different from the deed executed by the other family members in 1854 in that a complete survey with field notes was not included in this later deed. For a description of the property, the latest deed referred to Timothy Roark's Entry Number 136 for 50 acres and Entry

Number 589 for 150 acres, which were the two tracts still owned by Sarah Bolen Roark at her death. For their undivided interest in the estate, Lambert proposed to pay each of the three brothers the amount of $11.00. This was less than half the amount each of the other surviving family members had received two years before. The reason behind the difference is not clear; however, the proposed amount was apparently acceptable to the three brothers, who executed the deed in the order of John signing first, followed by James, and then Joseph. Timothy Jr. and George W. Richardson, son of Nancy and James, witnessed the deed.[130] Jeff Lambert and Mary Ann then had full title to the homestead.

This would be the last visit to the homestead and Claiborne County by the three brothers, and none of the three would ever see any of the local family members again. Unbeknownst to any of the family, a horrible civil war was less than five years away, a war that would pit many of their sons against each other in mortal combat. But there at the old home place, in August 1856, they were together as a family one last time.

Doubtless, while he was there, Joseph took a few minutes by himself to walk over the area of the homestead he had known as a boy. He visited the graves of his mother and father and from the family cemetery saw Cumberland Gap in the distance. What were his thoughts as he stood alone on the low hill overlooking the home place? Did he remember times of play with his younger brother Jeremiah? Did he live again that hot July day when at the age of thirteen he had helped Walter Evans survey his uncle James Eastridge's tract? He had come a long way in the twenty-five years since he had left home, but now he was again at the home place and the twenty-five years doubtless seemed to have passed so quickly. But time for reminiscing was limited; Joseph had work to do at home, and soon it was time to go. The three brothers said their goodbyes, probably at a farewell Sunday dinner spread on the shaded ground at the home place, and returned to Morristown and their train ride home.

Shortly after his return home, Joseph received a letter from Bill Swafford and Margaret. Addressed from Shady Hill, Tennessee, a community in Decatur County no longer identifiable, the letter was folded and sealed with no envelope and was addressed on the back side to "Mr. Joseph Roark, Birchwood, Tennessee." Affixed to the letter on the addressed side was a three-cent stamp, labeled "U.S. Postage" with a profile of George Washington. The letter, written by Swafford for both himself and Margaret, gave a report on their move west:

> Shady Hill, Tennessee   1st Sept 1856
> Dear father, Mother and family   I take my pen in hand to rite you a few
> lines to let you know that we are all well at this time, hoping that these
> few lines will find you all well. We landed hear the 27th and was 19 days
> on the road and stood our trip fine conciderin the seizin. Margaret stood
> the trip much better than I expected. she was a little sick twice. fathers
> family have had some sickness and have a little yet and there is some sick-
> ness. Janerly threw the country the corn crops are good. Oats and weat

[wheat] were good. Corn is worth $1 to 1.50 per bushel 4 new corn. Weat 50 to 75 cts per Bushel, Oats 20 to 30 cts per doz [bushel?], Bacon [illegible] cts per lb, horses No. 1 $1.50 to 2.00 work scarce, 50 to 100 [acres] land agreeable to what I have seen is reasonably low and but little improvements in this county. there is a heap of poor land in this country and some first quality of land. But I think is all subject to the [illegible] as is common in all the western countries [counties]. I wish to conduct this letter to grandfather and read it to him and her when you rite to us rite how he is. So no more at pres [present] but remain yours

W. L. Swafford

Margaret Swafford[131]

The grandfather mentioned in the letter was William Swafford in Meigs County. He was elderly at the time and was to die a year later, October 27, 1857.[132] Margaret's "seizin" would end January 5, 1857, with the birth of a healthy son, John L. Swafford.[133]

On December 16th, Joseph closed out a successful year by paying merchant W.R. Davis $8.78 in cash to close out his account for the year.[134] Joseph started the new year in the same fashion by paying William Haney in cash for a small debt of $7.50 with no need for a promissory note.[135] The year ahead looked favorable, the crop lands had been cultivated, and Joseph had accumulated a sufficient amount of cash on hand to see him through the coming year. On January 11, Joseph sent Lewis Patterson of Sale Creek a note acknowledging that Joseph owed him $3.83, probably for hides, an amount that would soon be paid to Patterson along with an additional $28.35, doubtless for leather, plus $0.18 interest.[136] On March 27, Joseph again made a cash payment, this time as guardian for the Brooks girls, for $2.80 to merchant Burton Holman. The cash payment was for shoes and apparel for Matilda and Juda Ann.[137] On April 27, he paid $28.37 cash to W.C. Hutcheson to settle his account with that store.[138]

The last week in April, Joseph received the following letter from George W. Arnette, County Clerk for Hamilton County, folded and addressed to "Joseph Roark Esq., at Home," for apparent personal delivery:

Harrison April 22nd 1857

Mr. Joseph Roark,

Dear Sir, I see on file in this office one or two guardian bonds given by you. Will you please come down and make settlements. It is verry essential that you attend to this as soon as convenient, say this week or next.

Very Respectfully, Your friend

Geo. W. Arnette[139]

Joseph had posted a bond, probably in the form of a promissory note, when he had been named by the court in 1848 as guardian of Matilda and Juda Ann Brooks. Apparently Hamilton County had some rule that limited the life of a promissory note and, since the note posted by Joseph was then over eight years old, Arnette requested that Roark update the promissory note for his guardian bonds. Although Arnette suggested some urgency in updating the bonds, no record is available that indicates Joseph responded immediately. It was not until March 22, 1858, that Joseph executed a promissory note to Arnette in the amount of $31.00 for value received.[140] It is unclear as to whether this was the "settlements" that Arnette requested. Perhaps some negotiation was possible since Matilda was almost sixteen and Juda Ann almost fourteen in 1858 and a guardian bond could be reduced in amount due to their ages.

During the summer of 1857, Joseph expanded his farming operation and simultaneously attempted to help his son-in-law Joel A. Talley. The records suggest that Joseph had leased 120 acres of river-bottom land belonging to J.C. Wilson for three years beginning in 1855 and had permitted Talley to do the farming and share the proceeds. Under the lease, there apparently was an agreement with Wilson that Joseph would buy the 120 acres after three years for $2,000. The equivalent price per acre of almost $17 indicates the inflation in land values that had occurred by the summer of 1857.

The active speculation in land in the Salem Community had also taken place throughout the country and had been related primarily to areas opened up by new railroad construction. Speculators throughout the U.S. bid up land prices with borrowed money. Profitable speculation could not last forever and, as had been the case before and certainly in boom times since, periods of high speculation end suddenly in a market panic. It happened that summer in what history refers to as the Panic of 1857. The panic started in August, far from Hamilton County, with the failure of the Ohio Life Insurance and Trust Company, and the cards began to fall. The situation was aggravated by the banking system and, in many instances, by the issuance of poorly secured bank notes, which fluctuated greatly in value. Panic seized the business community, particularly in the northeast. Reports of business failures spread and, with the new network of the electric telegraph, the bad news was spread quickly throughout the country. Railroad construction was brought to a halt, and the country entered a period of extended depression. The ET&V Railroad between Knoxville and the Virginia state line, so close to completion in mid 1857 could not be completed until late 1858 and then only with the involvement of slave labor. The depression aggravated the sectional differences already dividing the nation. Northern industrialists pointed a finger at the Southern influence in the Democratic administration which had resulted in a low tariff policy. While northern business was paralyzed, the world demand for cotton maintained a good business climate for the southern cotton farmer and the price of cotton remained high. The small farmer in East Tennessee, however, was to suffer from the depression as the eastern market for his farm products was seriously reduced.

Although far removed from the industrial northeast and within the isolation of the Salem Community, Joseph Roark personally felt the impact of the financial panic in late September. Suddenly bank notes were greatly reduced in value and the cash Joseph had accumulated no longer had its face value. What cash he had was committed to complete the purchase of the 120 acres from Wilson, the closing then set for October. The financial crisis deepened and, although the complete inter-workings are not totally clear, the local "panic" involved Joseph with his longtime neighbor Jesse Killian. Joseph had sold lumber from his mill to Killian during the summer, as well as wheat, bacon, and a quarter of beef, all for a total of $44.73. Killian's account with Joseph was "squared by settlement" on July 21, 1857.[141] It appears that sometime following the settlement of his account with Joseph, Killian became overextended and could not cover his outstanding promissory notes or other debts against him. What was the reason for Killian's precarious position? Had he invested in bank notes or perhaps railroad bonds that had seriously deteriorated in value? That possibility seems unlikely for a farmer in the Salem Community. Most likely Killian had poorly managed his money and debts, and when the word to that effect had spread in the wake of the national panic of 1857, a run of calls was made on his promissory notes. For some reason, whether it was a financial obligation or merely rescuing a friend, Joseph Roark stepped in to assist. It seems the first calls on the Killian notes were by the two merchants, W.R. Davis and Burton Holman, with Davis seeking payment on a debt of $17.76 before justice of the peace George Irwin.[142] Holman's claim was $14.30 to settle an account balance.[143] Apparently the situation was serious enough to warrant his help or perhaps he felt threatened finan-cially, but for whatever reason, Joseph took action on Monday, September 21. To reduce the panic, Joseph executed a promissory note to Maise Blackburn for $99.63 to cover two outstanding promissory notes by Killian. Written by Blackburn, or someone other than Joseph, the promissory note read:

> $99.63 One day after date I promise to pay Maise Blackburn ninety nine dollars and sixty three cents for value recevd it being the amount of two notes on Jesse Killian this the 21 first day of Sept 1857
> Joseph Roark[144]

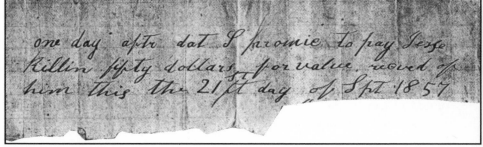

The first of three promissory notes written by Joseph Roark to Jesse Killian on September 21, 1857, to stabilize the financial position of Killian within the Salem Community.

On that same Monday, Joseph wrote three promissory notes to Jesse Killian, ostensibly to provide Killian with marketable securities to cover his immediate debts. All three notes, each written by Joseph in his handwriting, were the same except for the amount and due date. The first promissory note in the amount of $50 read:

> one day after dat I promie to pay Jesse Killin fifty dollars for value recved
> of him this the 21st of Spt 1857
>
> Joseph Roark[145]

The second note, also for $50 was, due "two days" after the date of the note[146] while the third for $200 was due "four days" after September 21.[147] Joseph spread the due dates to allow him time to maneuver if a "run" were to be made on his promissory notes. Also on that infamous Monday for Jesse Killian, Joseph wrote a promissory note to J.H. Locke for $50. While Killian's name is not mentioned on the Locke note, the date of the note was probably not just coincidental and the debt involved Killian in some way.[148]

Apparently the panic was quickly overcome by Roark's timely action and the crisis had passed by September 29. The first promissory note to Killian for $50 was returned to Joseph, and he removed his name by knife in his usual manner. The second note to Killian, also for $50, was returned to Joseph on the following Sunday. On the reverse side of the note, Joseph wrote, "Settled, September 27/57 By Note." He obviously accepted a promissory note from Killian, the man whose credit the community would not trust the week before, and then removed his name from his note to Killian. This time, however, Joseph tore–he did not neatly remove it with his knife, he tore–his name from the note. Was this an indication of frustration or a second alternative for a man who had left his knife at home?

On his debt to Burton Holman, Jesse Killian passed Joseph's third promissory note for $200 to Holman for settlement of the debt. Holman then returned the $200 note to Joseph in trade for a promissory note, dated September 29, in the amount of $14.30 "on Jesse Killian's account."[149] Joseph noted on the reverse side of the returned $200 promissory note:

> Rec'd $14.30 on the within note Fourteen dollars & 30 cts. Settled by B.
> Holman Sept 29th 1857. Rec'd on the within note in full to date Sept 29th
> 1857.[150]

Joseph was able to obtain from Killian the $14.30 paid to Holman and, of course, he had the $200 promissory note returned to him without having to make payment on the note. In the final settlement with Killian, Joseph received title to a tract of 40 acres located adjacent to the 120 acres under contract for purchase from J.C. Wilson. The 40 acres would be retained in the land holdings of Joseph and would be part of the estate settlement at his death.[151]

On the note to J.H. Locke, Joseph settled with Locke on some later date and received his promissory note back after a principal payment of $50.00 plus $1.57 in interest. With the court mandated judgement of $17.76 to W.R. Davis, Joseph was able, through the justice of the peace, to get Davis to settle for $15.50 and wrote a promissory note to Davis in that amount on September 29. The note was paid and returned to Joseph March 11, 1858.

No resolution remains in the Joseph Roark papers of the promissory note to Maise Blackburn. Ostensibly, Joseph accepted promissory notes from Killian in the total amount as the promissory note to Blackburn and helped Killian through the settlement of his debts.

The quick and decisive action by Joseph in regard to the Jesse Killian crisis did not seem to impact his business within the local community. Lumber orders were down, but the reduction was more a result of the national depression than local business decisions. In fact, just one month after the Killian settlement, Burton Holman placed a lumber order with Joseph to satisfy an order by Sanford Medley.[152] Likewise, Joseph returned to trade with Holman and maintained his account there. In bringing his account current for 1857 and early 1858, Joseph made payment on an itemized invoice for $35.44, which included a pair of boots, a wool hat, a neck tie, a silk handkerchief for Juda, and purchases by William Bean and Alfred Carr. An additional item, not identified, was in the coincidental amount of $14.30. Recognizing that this was the same amount as that on the note to satisfy Killian's debt the previous September, Holman had written next to the amount–"not Killian." Settlement on the invoice was made March 8, 1858.[153]

On October 8, Joseph made good on his obligation to buy the 120 acres of river-bottom land from J.C. Wilson. Roark and Joel A. Talley jointly purchased the tract for $2,000 which was doubtless an inflated price. Nevertheless, the deal had been made. To ensure that all taxes were current on the tract, Joseph required that Wilson submit a receipt for the taxes paid on the tract through 1858. Such receipt was submitted and filed in Roark's papers.[154] The deed was executed by Wilson on the date agreed to and was witnessed by Jonathan Wood and John Anderson. Recording in the deed records was accomplished by county clerk George Arnette on November 2, 1857.[155] It is unclear whether Joseph paid the full amount for the 120 acres or whether Joel Talley was able to pay his share of $1000. Either way, it appears clear that Joseph was attempting to help his daughter and son-in-law make a success with some of the best farm land available.

Following the Wilson purchase in the midst of a national depression, Joseph was forced again to rely on promissory notes for his business transactions. Before the year was out, Joseph executed a promissory note on December 5 to J.E. Eldridge for $100. The purpose of the note was not stated. Joseph paid $20 on the note June 27, 1858, and at some later date reclaimed the note.[156]

Joseph's return to the use of promissory notes continued into 1858, and many of the notes reflect a payout over an extended period of two to three years. Two promissory notes were written in 1858 to his brother John, the first on March 5 for $40,[157] and the second for $60 on September 2. On the second note to John, a payment record is noted on the reverse side indicating a payment in corn in 1860, and payments of $9.00 in June 1861 and $3.00 in September of the same year. Final payment came at even a later date.[158]

Promissory notes were written to pay for purchases from Hutcheson and Witt for $4.00 in January 1858[159] and to Curry Samples and Son for $4.93 in July.[160] In a somewhat different format, Joseph wrote a promissory note September 23, 1858, to W.G. West for $20.00 to be paid by December 25, 1859, bearing interest from Christmas Day 1858. The note was not paid by the due date; however, a payment of $4.00 was made on January 15, 1860. Interestingly, on the reverse side of the promissory note the location for Joseph's homestead is included, indicating that the note was probably written in one of the adjoining counties. The notation reads: "Joseph Roark Note for $20.00–3 miles south of Birchwood in Hamilton County."[161]

In October Joseph executed a printed promissory note to John N. Moore for $20.00 payable September 1, 1859. Moore assigned the note to R.G. Campbell "for value received" and Campbell further passed the promissory note to C.H. Wolman. No record is provided as to when the note worked its way back to Joseph for payment.[162] The note illustrates the acceptability of Joseph's promissory notes in the community. A person can objectively and safely conclude that Roark's promissory notes were equivalent to cash and were valued more highly than many bank notes.

In addition to writing more promissory notes, Joseph was also forced on one occasion to seek the help of the local constable in the collection of a promissory note in Joseph's possession. On October 23, 1858, Joseph submitted a promissory note from J.B. Eldridge written January 30, 1855, for $88.00 to constable J.C. Roberts for collection.[163] No record is available on the results of the collection efforts. The promissory note from Eldridge was most likely for lumber from Roark's sawmill as several orders were filled for lumber to be delivered to J.B. Eldridge and G. Curenton in the same time frame as the promissory note.[164]

Joseph's business ventures continued to be reasonably active in 1858 despite the serious depression gripping the country. In February, Joseph filled a lumber order for A.P DeFriese for sealing plank, studs, and weatherboarding.[165] Also in February, he supplied Maise Blackburn with an order of rafters, studs, and one-inch plank.[166] Later, an order by Dr. John L. Yarnell for 1,100 feet of planed plank was filled.[167] Also in 1858, Joseph sold six and one-half bushels of wheat to A.P. DeFriese plus nine bushels of corn, six bushels of which were "hauled by Conner," probably M.H. Conner.[168] In an assorted order from Rufus Friddle, Joseph delivered 70 pounds of bacon, 580 pounds of pork, two pounds of beef, 300 feet of plank, and one and one-half bushels of meal.[169] His farming operation expanded, and 1858 apparently yielded a good wheat crop, since for the first time Joseph contracted for thrashing the wheat.[170]

In March, Joel A. Talley informed his father-in-law that he did not want to farm the Wilson tract and asked Joseph to buy his undivided interest. Only six months after Roark and Talley had jointly purchased the 120-acre Wilson tract of good river-bottom land, Talley wanted out of the joint venture. A deed was drawn March 15, 1858, in which the tract was described using the same field notes from the previous deed, and Talley deeded his undivided interest to Joseph for $1,000. The deed was witnessed by William E. Bean and R.B. Scott.[171] One is mystified today by Talley's action. Why would Talley give up the opportunity to farm bottom land with his father-in-law's backing? Was it because Joseph was too aggressive and demanding as a partner? Did Talley initially have the $1,000 to invest or had he supplied Joseph with a promissory note for his share? Did he back out because he could not make payments on such a note, or was it because Talley simply did not want to put forth the effort to make the 120 acres a successful venture? We do not know the answer to these questions. Whatever the reason for Talley's decision, Joseph now had full title to the 120 acres to add to his total land holdings. If Talley did not have a desire to farm the tract, Joseph had other alternatives. His sons were now eighteen, sixteen, and fourteen, and they would be able to take on the responsibility of farming the additional acreage.

After buying Talley's interest in the Wilson tract and even during the economically depressed period of tight money, Joseph still continued to maintain an interest in acquiring additional land as it became available. On March 20, 1858, he purchased 160 acres from Thomas H. Callaway for $150. The tract, described as the SW4, Section 28, FT2N, R3W, was located west of and adjacent to Joseph's homestead tract. The deed was witnessed by Maise Blackburn and John W. Swafford, brother to Joseph's son-in-law.[172] Thomas Callaway was a large landowner in the Ocoee District, having submitted 220 entries for over 23,400 acres, much of it purchased at $0.01 per acre. Callaway had obtained grants for over 2,520 acres in Fractional Township 2 North alone. He had gained an advantage in the Ocoee District public land sale when, as son-in-law to Entry Taker Luke Lea, he had been named in 1836 as deputy surveyor on the survey team to lay out the Ocoee District.[173] Just one year older than Joseph, Callaway became wealthy through his sale of Ocoee District lands and later built a mansion for himself and his family in Cleveland. He was a large stockholder in the ET&G and the ET&V railroads and was one of the incorporators and the first president of the Ocoee Bank in Cleveland in 1850. He also served as first president of the Masonic Female Institute in Cleveland.[174]

Joseph continued to use promissory notes to cover purchases for himself and his family. In March 1858, he signed a $56 promissory note to Edmond Atley, payable in six months, to cover the cost of two saddles, a side saddle for Juda, stirrups, and two bridles. While the full amount was due in May 1859, Joseph did not make a first payment on the note until August 25, 1859, then for $25.[175] As was usually the case, when Joseph paid cash to merchants he did so only after an extended period. On June 1, 1858, Joseph bought tobacco, coffee, sugar, "two fine cap hats," and one pair

262

of ladies calf shoes from Coulter and Newman for $28.25.[176] An invoice was received on the account January 1, 1859, with an interest charge of $0.70.[177] No record exists as to when the invoice was finally paid.

Joseph was consistent in providing help and assistance to his family after they had left home. Bill and Margaret Swafford had been gone from home for two years when, on March 15, 1858, Joseph paid G.W. Housley $10.00 under a judgement by Maise Blackburn, justice of the peace, against Joseph and his son-in-law Bill Swafford.[178] Apparently Swafford had left unresolved an unpaid debt to Housley when he and Margaret left for Middle Tennessee in 1856, and Housley involved Joseph in the court action. No record remains of any correspondence with Swafford to obtain reimbursement from him.

In a move that cannot be explained today, Joseph executed on July 8, 1858, a promissory note to his son-in-law Robert Beane Scott in the amount of $585.[179] This was a significant amount for a promissory note at that time. It was equivalent to what one might pay for a half section–320 acres–of farm land in the Salem Community. Since no deed records remain that document Joseph's purchase of land from Scott, one can only wonder as to the purpose of the promissory note. Perhaps it was to provide Scott a financial asset as security for purchases or trades. Family tradition holds that Scott was a Baptist minister, and it would have been during this period in his life that time would have been devoted to study and preaching. Maybe this was the way that Joseph financially helped his son-in-law at a critical time in Scott's life. The promissory note was returned to the Joseph papers either unused or paid in full. A notation for neither probability remains with the note.

An unusual and interesting circumstance in the fall of 1858 illustrates Joseph's strict regimen in record keeping. In July of that year, Joseph had provided his nephew, James A. Carr, whom he and Juda were raising following the death of Juda's brother, with a promissory note in the amount of $29. The promissory note could well have been an estate settlement to Carr, who was then seven years old, from the estate of his father. Beyond that speculation we do not know its purpose. In the few months following the issuance of the note, Joseph made cash payments to his nephew for a total credit under the note of $14.60. Then, sometime in October or early November, James Carr lost the note. What did Joseph do? Did he simply pay the amount remaining on the note and excuse a seven- year-old boy for losing the note? That response did not fit Joseph's character. Rather, he took the matter to the local justice of the peace. In a statement before Justice Seamore Campbell, Carr swore that he had lost the $29 promissory note from Joseph, that credit had been given for $14.60, and that the note had not been bartered, sold, or conveyed. In documenting the sworn statement before the justice of the peace, Joseph signed James Carr's name for him on the document. Joseph paid the remaining $14.40 on the note but had insisted that Carr go through Justice Campbell to sufficiently void the lost promissory note and document its existence.[180]

Sworn Statement by James A. Carr before Seamore Campbell, justice of the peace, on Carr's loss of a promissory note from Joseph Roark for $29.00, July 21, 1858. Jim Carr was seven years old at the time.

Late in the year a letter came from Timothy Roark Jr. in Claiborne County with the news that brothers William and Jeremiah had moved their families to Missouri. Both had sold their land in Claiborne County and, with other families, had relocated to Dent County in central Missouri to take advantage of available land grants. The letter from Timothy was to be the last communication with the family in northern Tennessee until long after the Civil War.[181]

As 1858 came to a close, Joseph was hit with several tax bills totaling a significant amount. He was again taxed on the Brooks estate as guardian of Matilda and Juda Ann Brooks for $3.27. Since Bill Swafford had surrendered the portion of the Roark homestead that he was farming, Joseph was forced to pay $6.25 in taxes for 1857 and 1858 that Swafford no longer paid. In addition to his own taxes of $8.65 for 1858, Joseph also paid $2.44 for the 1857 and 1858 taxes of Jesse Killian, probably on the 40 acres obtained from Killian in 1857.[182]

Joseph devoted a large percentage of his time in early 1859 to his business ventures and his farming activities. He continued to do business with Lewis Patterson of Sale Creek, and in May purchased more leather from Patterson for his own use and to sell within the Salem Community. A promissory note in the amount of $32.35 was issued to Patterson May 5, 1859.[183] Improvements to his farm were also important. In

April, Joseph purchased grafts for almost a hundred fruit trees–apples, peaches, pears, and plums. On April 4, Joseph executed an agreement with Wheaton Allen under which P. Wilson would provide fruit tree grafts at $0.15 per graft. Under the agreement, final payment was to be made "for all found alive when counted after the first of May." Wilson was to be provided "board and horsefeed . . . while at work."[184] Under the agreement, Joseph paid $13.90 for the fruit tree grafts plus "three dollars for extra board" for which Joseph was given credit. Apparently Wilson was an especially heavy eater. The orchard that was begun that spring of 1859 was located on a hill north of the home place.[185] Joseph also used the orchard to cultivate honeybees. Honey was produced for both home consumption and sale through approximately twenty-five bee stands.[186] Also, in addition to the staple corn crop, evidence suggests that Joseph began to devote more of his farming to wheat, contracting with others to do the thrashing. At the 1859 harvest, Joseph paid G.W. Gardenhire for thrashing 202 bushels of wheat.[187]

Joseph did more business in 1859 with Burton Holman and G.W. Housley in Birchwood and less with Jonathan Wood in Limestone. He also opened an account with merchant J.P. Turbyfill, probably also located in Birchwood. To all three Birchwood merchants, Joseph, in his consistent practice, would make infrequent payments on his accounts and then, most likely, with a promissory note rather than cash. On February 26, 1859, Joseph wrote a promissory note to G.W. Housley for $54.65.[188] Less than two weeks later, March 8, Joseph wrote a promissory note to B. Holman for $23.84.[189] It appears that Turbyfill wanted to be paid more frequently than the other merchants, for just one month after his first promissory note to Turbyfill on July 27, 1859, for $7.00, Joseph wrote a second promissory note to Turbyfill for $30.60 on August 29.[190] Then, on November 3, Turbyfill wrote a request for cash payment under one of the notes:

Nov the 3, 1859

Mr. Roark Sir you will pleas to let [illegible] have an order to the stor for three dollars and oblige

J.P. Turbyfill[191]

Joseph continued to provide support to persons other than his immediate family. Beyond his own family of Jerusha, James, John, William, Susannah, and Nancy still at home, the household included Matilda Brooks, Juda Ann Brooks, Alexander Carr, and James A. Carr. On October 10, 1859, Joseph bought James Carr a pair of shoes and provided him with twenty-five cents in cash.[192] And, of course, there was Matilda and Juda Ann Brooks, now seventeen and fifteen, respectively. Joseph continued to maintain records of costs involved in raising the girls, and in June he received the following receipt from J.T. Witt and Company after a purchase for Matilda:

received of Joseph Roark two dollars and eighty five cents as guardian for Matilda Brooks this June 15th 1859

J.T. Witt & Co[193]

Outside the Salem Community, however, the political future of the U.S. was dark indeed. Moderates in both North and South were losing control to radicals whose opinions prevailed on both sides of the slavery issue. James Buchanan, a Democrat, was president, but his party was divided along sectional lines and lost congressional seats in the 1858 election. In Illinois, Democratic senator Stephen A. Douglas was challenged by Abraham Lincoln, a Republican. In his nomination acceptance speech prior to formal debates with Douglas, Lincoln quoted from the Gospel of Matthew, "A house divided against itself cannot stand." Although Lincoln was defeated in the senate race, his arguments split the Democratic party in 1858 and a Republican victory in the 1860 presidential election appeared to be a certainty. Talk in the South suggested secession from the Union if a Republican were elected president. Still, the vast majority of Tennesseans were Unionists and loathed the idea of secession. The tinderbox situation was intensified on October 16, 1859, when John Brown led a fanatical raid on the arsenal at Harpers Ferry, Virginia, to obtain arms and rally slaves to revolt. Stories were circulated in the South and Tennessee Senator Andrew Johnson charged that Brown had been encouraged in his raid by the Republican party leaders. Brown's ridiculous raid caused extremists in the South to begin talk of leaving the Union. Secession and war were at hand.[194]

By the time Joseph received his 1859 tax notice for $16.81 in the latter part of the year, he was the owner of 800 acres of good farm land in the Salem Community. After the brief downturn for him in 1857, his overall financial situation was quite good. His partnerships were providing income and his farm operations were continually expanding. Also, and most important, Joseph's three sons were now of an age to take a strong role on the farm. James was nineteen, John was eighteen, and William sixteen. The future for Joseph, who was now at the age of forty-six, looked bright. Within the next year, the picture would drastically change.

Chapter 9

Elections and Civil War
1860-1865

The prosperity of the 1850s continued into the first few months of the new decade. The advent of the railroad and the development of new markets to other southern states and the east coast in the mid 1850s had opened up new opportunities for Joseph Roark and other Hamilton County farmers. Wheat had become a new cash crop for Joseph, a product that could be shipped to meet market demands in the South. Since only five percent of cotton plantations in the Deep South met their own food needs, Hamilton County and much of east Tennessee began growing wheat to meet the South's food demands.[1] The railroads by the mid 1850s provided the required means of transportation, and new markets were developed for Hamilton County products. Between 1850 and 1860, the production of wheat in Hamilton County grew by over 700% from 11,000 bushels to almost 79,000 bushels each year.[2] Wheat grown by Joseph Roark was sold to commission merchants and found its way to Atlanta, Augusta, and Savannah as well as New Orleans and Charleston, South Carolina. Economically, Hamilton County and the Salem Community had developed strong ties with many of the neighboring southern states through the sale of the local farm products.

The growing of wheat was popular with Joseph and others in the Salem Community, not only for its marketability and profit but also because of the relative ease with which it could be raised. Compared with corn and other crops, the planting of wheat was a simple process. Fields were cultivated, seeds were sown, and then covered by harrowing. Little manure, if any, was needed for fertilizer. After planting, almost no cultivation was required and, as the crop matured during the winter months, and since little work was required, the farmer could attend to other chores. Joseph harvested his wheat crop in June of each year and, early on, used threshing machines (generally referred to as "thrashers") that were available by contract for the harvest. As noted in the previous chapter, Joseph first used a thrasher for the harvest in 1858. Although records are not available on his production of wheat, Joseph's yield probably was between ten and fifteen bushels per acre, with his devoting up to fifty acres of his cultivatable land to that crop.

Corn, however, remained the staple crop for Joseph and the other farmers of Hamilton County. Even with the growth in wheat production, Hamilton County increased its corn output between 1850 and 1860 from 520,000 bushels per year to over 606,000 bushels.[3] Joseph and other farmers of East Tennessee had discovered a way to turn large corn production into a cash crop–feed the corn to hogs and sell pork and bacon to the populations of the adjoining states. By 1850, East Tennessee had become a major source of pork for the plantations of Alabama, Georgia, and the Carolinas. Prior to the railroad, hogs were driven through the mountain passes to their market in adjoining states. With the availability of the railroad, the market was extended. So extensive was the raising of hogs in East Tennessee by 1860 that, during the Civil War, soldiers from the area were derisively referred to as "hog drivers."[4] A total of over 21,000 hogs were reported in Hamilton County in 1860–an average of almost two hogs for every man, woman, and child in the county, including those living in towns. It can be safely estimated that Joseph Roark, as part of his farming operation, had as many as two hundred hogs on his farm at any one time.

In addition to hogs, Hamilton County also reported in 1860 almost 2,700 horses, 2,800 milk cows, 4,600 "other cattle," and 5,100 sheep. Doubtless Joseph raised his share of each type of livestock.

In addition to his corn and wheat, Joseph also raised Irish potatoes and sweet potatoes, both for market and consumption by his family. Additionally, his orchard, which numbered over one hundred fruit trees, not only met his own family's consumption requirement but also provided an additional source of income at local markets. The same was true of his bee stands and the production of honey. He raised no cotton. Little cotton was produced in Hamilton County–only 61 ginned bales were produced in 1860.

While the Salem Community was located over twenty-five miles from the nearest depot on the ET&G railroad, Joseph Roark and his neighboring farmers had the benefit of the Tennessee River to move their products to the Chattanooga depot of the W&A Railroad. From there Joseph was paid good prices by the commission merchants who shipped his products to Alabama, Georgia, and South Carolina. Economic ties were thus forged and strengthened with the states of the Deep South. In 1857, the senior editor of the *Chattanooga Advertiser,* in reporting on his visit to Montgomery, Alabama, cited Chattanooga's advantages in river shipments to Mobile and then direct to New Orleans. His article concluded with the benefits of trade with Montgomery and with Alabama:

> These advantages make it a superior grocery market, to which we call the
> attention of our merchants and commission men. The cards of several of
> the reliable houses indicate that their energetic proprietors have a looking-
> forth eye to the trade and products of Tennessee; and wisdom on the part

of each section will be attracted with profitable results. May closer ties bind more strongly together the two States, and tend largely to promote their mutual prosperity.[5]

By the time of the census in the spring of 1860, Joseph's land ownership ranked him high among farmers in Hamilton County. With his 800 acres, his farm was listed as one of only eight in the county larger than 500 acres. Within the Salem Community, his ranking was even higher. In the 1860 Census for Hamilton County, Civil District No. 10, which covered the area on the south side of the Tennessee River from the Hamilton-Meigs county line southwest to present-day Gamble Road, a total of 165 families were listed. Of these, 75 families were landowners within the district–land holdings for which an appraised value was provided by the census taker. With a median farm value of $850 and an average farm value of $2,020 for the 75 landowners within the district, Joseph Roark's farm value was appraised at $10,000. His farm was valued second only to a farm value of $27,000 for George W. Gardenhire, who at 63 was seventeen years senior to Joseph. Unlike Joseph, who had started out in Hamilton County with only his brother's initial help, George Gardenhire had received the benefit of a significant inheritance from his father, William Gardenhire, and in 1858 had received transfer of other lands in his father's estate from James T. Gardenhire Jr.[6]

While the total acreage of Joseph's farm was used in calculating its value, the condition of his land contributed heavily to his net worth. Much of his land was in cultivation, pasture being maintained only as needed for the livestock, barns had been constructed, orchards begun and maintained, and rail fences had been built to enclose pastures, cultivated land, and orchards. Additionally, the sawmill and gristmill added to the total value of the estate. It had been but twenty years since Joseph filed his first entry for Ocoee District land. In that period Joseph had worked hard to make his land productive. The plateau of achievement that he had reached by 1860 speaks loudly to his hard work as a farmer and his significant acumen in business.

Of his children, six remained at home–Jerusha 22, James 20, John 18, William 16, Nancy 13, and Susannah 9. Also then living with the family were Juda Ann Brooks 16, William Carr 21, and James Carr 9. Matilda Brooks, almost eighteen in the spring of 1860, was living with the Merida Webb family and providing domestic help to the Webbs and their nine children.[7] Relations with Matilda had become strained in recent years, and problems beyond those normally encountered during the teenage years had frequently arisen. Both Joseph and Juda supported Matilda's desire to live outside the home and work for her room and board.

Problems also remained with Jerusha. Her seizures continued to occur, and by 1860 she required much more attention, plus her health had deteriorated and was not good. Medical help by Dr. Yarnell had resulted in little if any progress, and he had advised Joseph and Juda that Jerusha's life span would probably be limited. Her health was particularly bad during the spring of 1860. So difficult was her condition

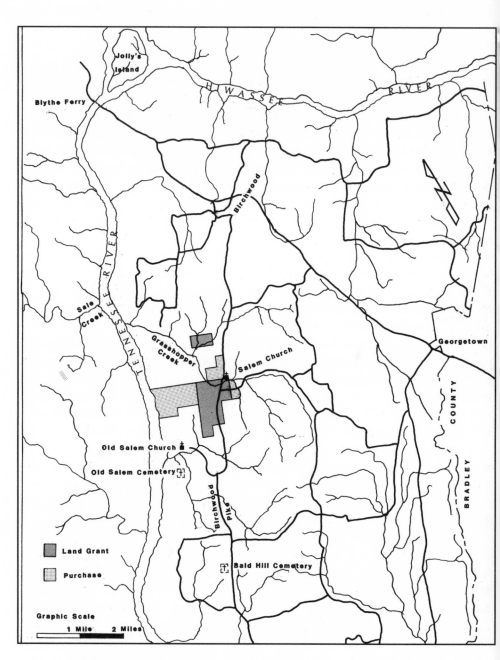

Land holdings of Joseph Roark prior to the beginning of the Civil War in 1861–a total of 840 acres.

that Dr. Yarnell was called for assistance on several occasions. Her condition resulted in many sleepless nights for Joseph and Juda. In late spring, Joseph wrote the following promissory note to Dr. Yarnell for his work with Jerusha:

> Three months after date I promise to pay J.L. Yarnell forty dollars for value rec'd of him. Witness my hand and seal April 20th 1860
>
> Joseph Roark[8]

Eldest son James A. Roark, or Jim as he was known by the family, by then worked full time on the farm. He had attended the math school conducted by Hiram Cornwell in 1852[9] and had received other schooling for brief periods of time. Beyond that his formal education was limited. Jim's love was farming and it was his plan to continue in his father's footsteps. He apparently was a good worker and could appropriately expect to take over a portion of his father's farming operation. Additional schooling was unnecessary to someone in his position and with his love of farming.

By contrast, his brother John Wesley had attended school at Salem and had been fortunate to have been in the school when Maise Blackburn relocated to the Salem Community. Blackburn purchased 390 acres from Samuel Gamble just north of the Salem school in January 1849[10] and brought to the school his four sons, who came as "studious boys, good to learn." The Blackburn boys had a positive impact on John and one, Jessie, taught at the Salem school while John was there. John later said that "Jessie Blackburn . . ., one of the best boys I ever knew, taught us a good school and was my first teacher to have devotional exercises. They [the Blackburn boys] had a great moralizing influence over the community and did much good. I count this a stepping stone in my life . . ." In 1853, when he was twelve, John, too, planned to be a farmer, but events intervened:

> That fall before the corn was gathered, Burket [M.H.B. Bourkett, head of the Georgetown Academy] came after me to go to Georgetown to school. Pap agreed for me to go. Wood Hale hooked up the big speckled yoke of oxen, loaded in my bed, some cooking utensils, and a quart bottle full of ground coffee, but they wouldn't let me make it when I got there, said I was healthier without it. I took plenty of flour and meal–everything was homemade then, there was no store-bought goods then. Nothing came out of the store to eat and very little to wear. I took a gallon jug full of molasses, a ham of meat and whatever mother said to take I took, but had no idea what it took to keep a house.[11]

John attended the Georgetown Academy, probably during the four winter months each year, and by the spring of 1860 was but a few short months from completing his work there at which time he would be authorized to teach school.

William, or Will, the third son at home, and the girls–Nancy, Susannah, and Juda Ann Brooks–were part of the household and were expected to do their part of the expanding farm operation of Joseph Roark.

Of Joseph and Juda's married daughters, Mary Ann and Elizabeth were close by. Mary Ann and Robert Scott farmed 200 acres in the Salem Community, and Robert preached in local churches on Sunday. By the spring of 1860, the Scotts had five children–four daughters and one son. The eldest, Jane, was ten. The youngest, Juda Ann, named for her grandmother, was two.[12] As Robert Scott continued his work in the ministry, he was forced to call upon his father-in-law for financial help from time to time. On Friday, February 10, 1860, Scott was approached at his house by a man with a payment request from M.H. Conner who was a leader in the local Salem Baptist Church. Respecting Scott's his position as a pastor by addressing him affectionately as "Brother Scott," Conner requested he pay the bearer of a five dollar note "in full of all demands that I have against you–yours with due respect, M.H. Conner." Scott apparently did not have the requested five dollars and so walked with the "bearer" to the home of his father-in-law who paid the five dollars. Upon making the payment as requested by his good friend Conner, Joseph Roark duly filed the satisfied payment request in his papers.[13]

Elizabeth and Joel Talley lived just south of her parents. She was then twenty-five and was the mother of five children–three daughters and two sons. Amanda was the eldest and was thirteen; Benjamin the youngest was just over a year old. Joel was listed in the census as a farmer.[14] During 1860 Joseph was called upon again to help his daughter and son-in-law. Apparently Talley had been involved with one William Bettis and had accepted two promissory notes from Bettis for a total of $150, due in December 1859. Additionally, Talley had received a judgement for $44 against Bettis, also in December, on a related matter, but had been unable to collect on either the promissory notes or the judgement. Even after receiving $40 from Bettis in March 1860, Talley continued to pursue the matter and submitted both the note and the judgement to Constable John McCallie for collection. After failure in collection attempts by McCallie, Talley approached Joseph Roark for help. In responding, Joseph purchased the note and judgement from him, probably at some discounted

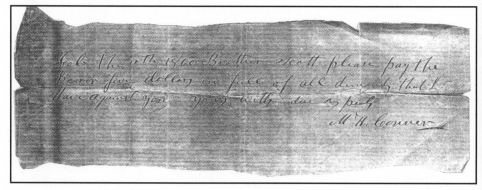

Respectful request for a $5.00 payment by Preacher Robert Beane Scott from M.H. Conner signed "yours with due respect." Payment of the $5.00 was made by Joseph Roark.

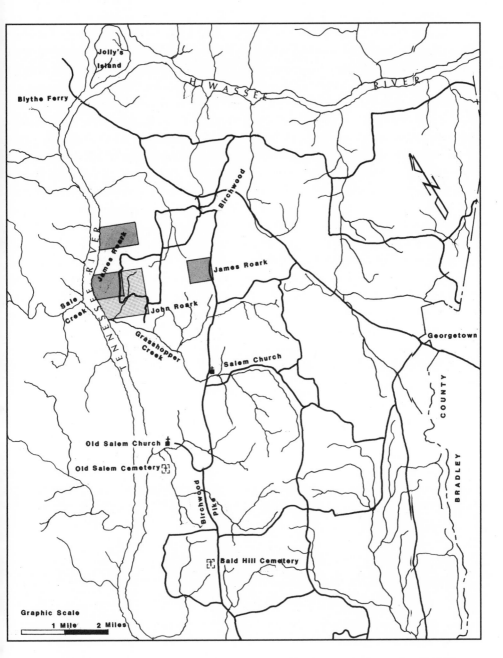

Land holdings of Joseph Roark's brothers, James and John, just prior to the Civil War.

price. No record is available as to the success of Joseph in collecting any monies from Bettis.[15]

Later, sometime after 1860, Joseph purchased a promissory note from Talley in favor of Georgetown merchant William H. Tibbs for $54.74, which Talley had been unable to pay. Joseph paid the amount due to Tibbs and filed the promissory note in his papers. No record remains of any further collection from Talley.[16]

In late April, Joseph received a message, delivered by one of his nephews, that his brother John's wife, Margaret, was seriously ill. Soon thereafter the message came that Margaret had died–April 27, 1860. Joseph and Juda attended the brief service at the home the following day and walked with John as the body was carried to the small family plot located on a small knoll across the road from the home. John, then sixty, would continue to live at home with the nine children still at the home place, the youngest of whom was John Lewis "Jack" at twelve years old.

From what we can determine today, Joseph was quick to help the family of his two brothers whenever possible. After James' daughter Martha married Granville Samples, a new store opened in Birchwood under the name of Carson and Samples with Joseph's nephew as proprietor. To help the newly established merchant, Joseph opened an account. On April 30, 1860, he received his first statement of items purchased that also acknowledged a credit of $8.00 for a beef cow in trade:

Aprile 30, 1860
Joseph Roark to Carson & Samples
        To Merchendising goods $31.23 ¾

                Cr. 1 Beaf Cow   8.00
                                                    _____
                                                    $23.23 ¾[17]

In 1860, Joseph maintained accounts with local merchants for his brother-in-law and employee, Alfred Carr. Apparently the accounts were open to the purchase of personal items by Carr over and above items purchased for the farm. In May 1860, Joseph received and paid a charge ticket from William H. Tibbs for the purchase of ladies apparel by Carr:

                                            Georgetown May 26th/60
Joe Roark per Carr bought Bot of Wm. H. Tibbs

        To 1 pr Shoes, Ladies   1.00
        "   1 "   do   "   1.40
        "   1 "   Vest,   "   1.50
        Charged to a/c $3.90[18]

James A. Carr, Joseph's nephew and the surviving son of James Carr, lived at the Roark home place during the 1860s and received financial assistance from Joseph and Juda. It appears that Joseph took an active interest in James A. Carr, or Jim as he was called, and provided him money through promissory notes, probably to assist Jim in learning financial transactions in the local economy. In May 1860, Joseph provided the following promissory note to Jim Carr:

> On or before the first of September I promise to pay James A. Car Thirty seven dollars and thirty cts for value receivd of him May the 20th 1860
>
> Joseph Roark[19]

While the local economy remained strong for Joseph during the first half of 1860, signs were evident that the economy was slowing as a result of the political turmoil nationally. Lumber orders slowed for the sawmill as the local farmers and merchants were cautious in considering home and business improvements that could be postponed.[20] Joseph himself extended the payout on his promissory notes that he wrote in 1860 and delayed payments on promissory notes that were still active. On a promissory note for $70.75 to J.T. Witt and Company written on January 2, 1860, Joseph did not make a payment until November 22, 1860, paying $49.50 on the note at that time. Final payment was made at some even later date.[21] On another note, made January 10, 1860, just a week after the Witt note, Joseph promised to pay Hiram Haney $200 for value received. He did not make a first payment of $50 until September 3, 1861, and a second payment, also of $50, was not made until December 24, 1862. Final payment was made on the note at an even later date.[22] Similarly, on a note dated February 3, 1860, to George W. Gardenhire for $83.50, Joseph did not make a payment until October 31, 1861, and then for only $4.50. A second payment soon followed, however, this time for $42. It appears that another two payments were made on the note, the first for $33, before the promissory note was finally redeemed in 1862.[23] Apparently bank notes were then not readily available to cash out or pay off promissory notes. Also, bank notes at the time fluctuated wildly in value and were often much less preferred than a debt, guaranteed by a promissory note from a trustworthy party. To keep the public informed in regard to the actual value of bank notes versus their face amount, lists with discounted values were frequently published in local newspapers.

In addition to the diminishing availability of cash, interest rates began to rise. By December 15, 1860, a promissory note from Joseph to Simeon Eldridge carried an interest rate of 10 percent from the date of the note. Previously, stated interest rates on promissory notes had never risen above 8 percent.[24]

Similarly payments made to settle judgements before the local justice of the peace were delayed longer than had previously been the case. Joseph lost a judgement in favor of W.R. Davis and H.B. Davis before Justice Seamore Campbell on April 21, 1860. The judgement, in the amount of $33.75 was not paid to Constable John McCallie until January 10, 1861.[25] Another case at the same time before Seamore Campbell, this one brought singularly by W.R. Davis, resulted in a judgement against Joseph for $47.39. Action by the justice of the peace notwithstanding,

Joseph did not pay the judgement until December 13, 1861, then to Deputy Sheriff John Kimbrough.[26]

The economic slowdown in Hamilton County and East Tennessee in general during the latter part of 1860 was principally due to the uncertainty in the political future of the U.S. as it was reflected in the major political parties. There dissension and confusion reined. The Democratic Party was split on the slavery issue, while the Republican Party, only four years old and sectionally located only in the north, was under the control of rabid abolitionists. The Whig Party had ceased to exist, and its former adherents struggled to find a place after its descendant Know-Nothing Party had faded into obscurity. Joseph Roark followed the progress of the major parties through the Chattanooga and Cleveland newspapers as presidential nominees were selected for what would be the most critical presidential election in U.S. history.

The Democrats met in convention at Charleston, South Carolina, on April 23, 1860. The issue of slavery dominated the meeting. Northern Democrats pushed for Stephen A. Douglas of Illinois for president, but Douglas was unacceptable to the southern states because of his equivocation on slavery in the territories west of the Mississippi. Tennessee Democrats supported Andrew Johnson, then U.S. senator from Tennessee, for the nomination. In a heated disagreement over the party platform, delegates from the lower South left the convention while the Tennessee delegates remained. After thirty-six ballots, no candidate was selected and the convention adjourned to meet again in Baltimore, Maryland, in June. Delegates from the lower South, after their walkout, decided to meet in Richmond two months later to select a Southern Democrat as their candidate.

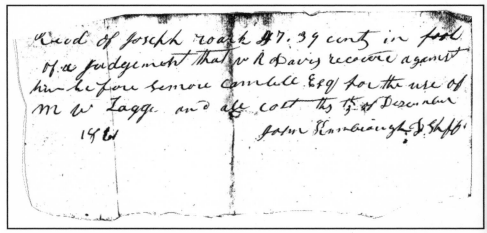

Receipt to Joseph Roark from Deputy Sheriff John Kimbrough for payment of $47.39 in a judgement against him in favor of W.R. Davis in December 1861. At the time of this payment by Joseph Roark, Davis had just been incarcerated by the Confederacy as being a "Unionist" and was in prison at Tuscaloosa, Alabama.

Concern about talk of secession by the southern states and the future of the Union was behind a meeting in February of former Whigs and Know-Nothing adherents, mostly from East Tennessee. From the meeting came the creation of the Union Party and its formation not only in Tennessee but in all the states. The party's guiding principle was the preservation of the Union and support of the U.S. Constitution. Organization of the new party progressed rapidly, and a national convention was scheduled in Baltimore for May 9. At the convention, John Bell of Tennessee and Sam Houston of Texas were the two leading candidates. Bell won the nomination on the second ballot.

The Republican Party met in Chicago in mid May for its convention. William H. Seward of New York, a noted abolitionist, was the leading contender but was rejected in favor of Abraham Lincoln of Illinois. The Republican platform rejected any approval of slavery by Congress in the territories and spoke of secession as treason. No representative from Tennessee was present in Chicago.

Several weeks later, the Democrats met in Baltimore to nominate Stephen A. Douglas. With adoption of a platform of popular sovereignty, nineteen of the delegates from Tennessee withdrew to meet with the Southern Democrats in Richmond. Only five delegates from Tennessee remained in Baltimore at the convention. In Richmond, the nomination for president went to John C. Breckinridge of Kentucky. Thus, with four presidential nominees, U.S. voters were faced in the November election with a choice among the Union Party with John Bell, the Democratic Party with Stephen A. Douglas, the Southern Democratic Party with John C. Breckinridge, and the Republican Party with Abraham Lincoln. In Tennessee and Hamilton County, with no Republican Party organization, Lincoln's name would not appear on the ballot.

Tennessee was divided among the other three candidates. Douglas was supported in West Tennessee while Bell and the Union Party were strong in East Tennessee among former Whigs. Breckinridge was supported by Senator Andrew Johnson and Democrats in Middle and East Tennessee. In the lower South, the states primarily supported Breckinridge and threatened secession if Lincoln were elected and the Republican abolition platform forced upon the South. Neither the Republicans nor the Northern Democrats considered secession by the southern states a serious threat. Even Breckinridge, the Southern Democrats own candidate, was known to be in favor of preserving the Union.

The election for president was held on Tuesday, November 6, and Joseph Roark cast his vote at the local polling place. His position and his vote are unknown. One can safely assume that he was a Democrat based on later family history. More than likely his choice was between Bell and Breckinridge, and quite possibly, he voted for the latter because of his party affiliation.

As the election returns were tabulated, the worst fears of the lower South were realized. Lincoln was elected carrying all the northern states except New Jersey;

however, he received only 40 percent of the popular vote and carried no state in the South. Bell and the Union Party carried Tennessee, Kentucky, and Virginia. In Hamilton County the vote was:

Bell (Union)	Breckinridge (Democrat)	Douglas (Democrat)
1,074	820	165[27]

With the election of Lincoln, the country was immediately thrown into a crisis. The extremists in the South screamed for immediate secession. The North, they argued, had yielded to the abolitionists, had honored the fireball irrational John Brown and his raid, and now had elected a minority president through a sectional party in the North with a plan to dominate the South by the abolitionists. In their minds, the time for action had come. Two days after the election, the South Carolina legislature called a convention for secession, and on December 20, the delegates unanimously voted an ordinance of secession. Tennessee moved slowly as its people tried to decide the best course of action:

> With relatively few exceptions, the people of Tennessee resented South Carolina's withdrawal from the Union. . . . Since they believed that several other states would follow it out of the Union, they felt it was precipitating a crisis in national affairs. They were convinced that anything which jeopardized the existence of the Union affected adversely the interests of Tennessee.[28]

The concern of Tennesseans was not misdirected. Within a matter of weeks, six other southern states–Georgia, Alabama, Florida, Mississippi, Louisiana, and Texas–had seceded, and in February, representatives of the seven states met in Montgomery to establish the Confederate States of America. In Washington, the Congress debated ways to resolve the crisis. Two days prior to the secession of South Carolina, Tennessee Senator Andrew Johnson had argued strongly in a speech before the Senate that "no state has the constitutional right to secede and withdraw from the Union."[29] "Parson" William G. Brownlow, in Knoxville, agreed for the first time with Johnson, who just previously had been his bitter enemy, in supporting preservation of the Union. The pro-Union *Chattanooga Gazette* wired Washington for 1,000 copies of Johnson's speech. Tennessee, particularly East Tennessee, clung tenaciously to the Union.[30]

In Nashville, however, the Democrats and Governor Isham Harris of Shelby County in West Tennessee controlled the state government. Harris was sensitive to the interests of the slave-holding, cotton-raising plantation owners of West and Middle Tennessee. In response to these interests, Governor Harris convened a special session of the Tennessee legislature on January 7, 1861, because "the political crisis needed legislative consideration."[31] At the special session, Harris addressed the legislature with his pro-southern argument and requested that body submit the question of secession to the people in a statewide vote. The legislature set the referendum for February 9, 1861.

In preparation for the vote, Union leaders and secessionists debated the issue. The vote to be taken was not directly on secession but rather the people were called upon to vote for "Convention" or for "No Convention" to consider secession. On the election day, the people of Tennessee rejected the convention by a substantial majority: 69,387 against and 56,232 for a convention. The vote, however, was significantly different by sections of the state:

	Convention	No Convention
East Tennessee	7,767	33,299
Middle Tennessee	25,842	28,224
West Tennessee	22,623	7,864

In Hamilton County, the vote was 455 in favor of a convention and 1,445 against. No breakdown of the vote within Hamilton County is available but, based on the results of the election four months later, it is clear that the citizens of Chattanooga favored secession and probably voted heavily in support of the convention. The rural areas of Hamilton County strongly rejected the call for a convention and favored delay to see what action Lincoln would take. In neighboring Bradley County, voters more heavily favored the "No Convention" option than in Hamilton County, with 1,443 voting against a convention and only 242 voting in favor.[32]

His neighbors thus voted heavily against a convention to consider secession, but how did Joseph Roark stand on the issue, and more importantly, how did he vote? While his political leanings were toward the Democratic Party of Governor Harris and West Tennessee, Joseph was a businessman and could see his successful farming operation and partnerships in jeopardy if the nation were divided by secession. True, the markets for his crops and livestock tied him closely to the neighboring states of Alabama, Georgia, and South Carolina; however, could not these markets be maintained even if Tennessee remained within the Union after their withdrawal? Like the majority in East Tennessee, Joseph doubtless did not want to be swept along as part of precipitous action by large plantation owners and slave-holders. In all probability, Joseph voted against the convention and was pleased with results of the election. But other hard choices were to be faced in the near future.

In Hamilton County, citizen interest was given more to the political crisis than to business, and as a result, business activity slowed. A Chattanooga business man writing to Andrew Johnson summarized: "Business of all sorts is at a stand still; dull times is the cry of every body. And all dread and fear the worst has not yet come."[33] In one of his last business transactions before the war, Joseph had Alfred Carr sell, just one week before the convention referendum, wheat and bacon to one of the local merchants. In exchange, Carr was to purchase large quantities of salt, soda, and copperas for the family plus two pair of shoes for Carr.[34] Did Joseph have the prescience to anticipate the shortages that would result from the coming conflict?

The week following the vote on a secession convention, Joseph settled his account with merchant B. Holman of Birchwood that included purchases from March 26, 1859, through February 13, 1861.[35] Joseph executed a promissory note for $38.43 to cover the full amount of the settlement.[36] On March 26, Joseph sent $5.00 by his son-in-law Robert Beane Scott to Holman for application to the note and on March 27, he received a note from Holman acknowledging receipt of the five dollars:

> Mr. Joseph Roark
> Sir, I place a credit on your note for five dollars by Bene Scott, March 27th 1861
>
> B. Holman[37]

In between the time of Joseph's promissory note to Holman and his first payment on March 27, events had moved rapidly in the South. Representatives of the seven seceded states had met in Montgomery, Alabama, and on February 8 had adopted a constitution for the Confederate States of America. On February 16, Jefferson Davis, until late a U.S. Senator from Mississippi, was sworn in as president of the Confederacy. In Washington, on March 4, Lincoln was inaugurated as president. William H. Seward, the radical abolitionist, was named secretary of state.

Lincoln and his cabinet faced an immediate crisis. Fort Sumter in the harbor of Charleston, South Carolina, was under siege by Confederate forces and its commander had requested supplies and reinforcements from Washington. With no supplies, he would be forced to comply with the Confederate demands to surrender the fort. When Lincoln ordered reinforcements to the fort on the morning of Friday, April 12, the Confederate forces saw it as an act of belligerence rather than surrender and immediately began artillery bombardment of the fort. Fort Sumter surrendered the following day. The Civil War had begun.

The week before the Fort Sumter bombardment, Joseph sold to a local merchant twenty-two and two-thirds bushels of wheat at $1.30 per bushel and 106 pounds of bacon at $0.10 per pound. At the same time, Joseph purchased thirty-eight gallons of molasses, forty-five dozen spools of threads, forty-five pounds of coffee, and one pair of shoes.[38] Two days following the surrender of Fort Sumter, President Lincoln issued a call to governors of all states, including Tennessee, for 75,000 volunteers to suppress the rebellious southern states.

Lincoln's call for troops significantly changed the attitude of Tennesseans toward the Union. It gave Governor Harris a reason for further action toward secession. Harris responded to the president by telegraph: "Tennessee will not furnish a single man for purposes of coercion but 50,000 if necessary for the defense of our rights and those of our southern brothers."[39] Additionally, Harris immediately called a special session of the legislature to convene in Nashville April 25. In Nashville,

Statement on Joseph Roark's account with merchant Burton Holman which was paid in full two months prior to the opening of the Civil War at Fort Sumter.

secession was discussed on every corner. Harris told the legislature in its special session that Lincoln had "inaugurated . . . war upon the people of the slave and non-slave-holding states" and called for dissolving the relations between the State of Tennessee and the United States. Accordingly, the legislature drafted a "declaration of independence" and called a referendum on June 8 for its acceptance or rejection by the people of Tennessee. Not waiting for results of the referendum, Governor Harris, as authorized by the legislature, entered Tennessee into a military agreement with the Confederacy and authorized the construction of an artillery battery by the Confederates at Memphis.

Many in East Tennessee, in fact a majority, had no desire to leave the Union and opposed secession. Despite the enthusiasm for separation expressed by local secessionists and the many Confederate flags raised on Tennessee courthouses, Unionists in East Tennessee took the lead against secession and launched a campaign to keep Tennessee in the Union. Unionists meetings were held in counties in East Tennessee, and conventions met in Knoxville and Greeneville in an attempt to develop a course of action to defeat the secession movement. Politically, East Tennessee had, since the creation of the state in 1796, exercised control of the state government. Only in recent years had leadership been shifted to the middle and western areas of the state. Leaders in East Tennessee, particularly those supporting the Union, resented the new domination of state politics by large slaveholders. Brownlow's *Knoxville Whig*, strongly against secession, carried reports of Union activity in East Tennessee and charged the governor and legislature of usurping power and overriding "the free will and real mind of the people."[40] Andrew Johnson, known for his hatred of the southern aristocracy of plantation owners, presented heated and emotional arguments for Unionist votes.[41]

Locally the *Chattanooga Gazette*, then published by Unionist James R. Hood, argued against secession and noted that Tennessee was "the home and resting place of [Andrew] Jackson, in his lifetime the terror of disunionists."[42] Contrary to the *Gazette*, the *Chattanooga Advertiser*, then four years old, argued for secession and against the "faithless Northern States, which have so frequently outraged the Constitution, and ruthlessly trampled right and justice under feet."[43]

The June 8 referendum to decide for or against secession was held as Confederate troops from the deep South moved through Chattanooga and as Tennessee units drilled at the fairgrounds in Knoxville. With a higher participation of voters than in the February 9 election, the referendum produced the following results:

	Separation	No Separation
East Tennessee	14,780	32,933
Middle Tennessee	58,265	8,198
West Tennessee	29,127	6,117
Military Camps (8 in TN, VA, FL)	2,742	-
State Total	104,913	47,238[44]

Only six of the twenty-nine counties in East Tennessee supported secession, five of which were in lower East Tennessee–Sequatchie, Rhea, Meigs, Polk, and Monroe. In Hamilton County, the vote was 854 for "Separation" and 1260 for "No Separation."[45] Of the 854 votes for separation, 421 were from Chattanooga, which favored secession by a vote of 421 to 51. The vote in Hamilton County was not unique. In fact, the three contiguous counties of Hamilton, Marion, and Bradley all voted against secession and thus became the most southern of all counties in the Confederacy in which a majority favored the Union over secession.[46]

How did Joseph Roark vote on secession in June 1861? Was he one of the 433 in the rural areas of Hamilton County who voted for secession or did he go with the majority of 1209 who supported the Union? It is a question for which we have no answer. Since his three sons later served in the Confederacy and Joseph later swore allegiance to the Confederate States in order to obtain permission of the provost marshal to visit his sons in Knoxville, we can only assume that he voted for secession or, even if voting for the Union, he later became a reluctant Confederate. If he did vote for separation, he joined 432 others in rural Hamilton County who supported secession. What motivated these men to support the Confederacy in opposition to the majority of their neighbors? One reason which has been put forth was the ties and allegiances to the Democratic Party. Of thirty-three Confederate leaders from East Tennessee identified in recent studies, twenty-eight identified with a political party and of that number twenty-two were Democrats.[47] A similar study of Union Leaders in East Tennessee during the period indicates that a large majority of Unionists were former Whigs.[48] Joseph's alignment with the Democratic party doubtless influenced his decision.

Another factor suggested for secession votes from East Tennessee was the possibility that each man saw himself more as a southerner than any other part of the country. This was particularly true of Hamilton County voters. Their business dealings were primarily with southerners located in adjacent states. The bank notes they traded were issued by Alabama, Georgia, and South Carolina banks. Joseph sold wheat and hogs to markets in Alabama, Georgia, and South Carolina. The railroads used for shipping his products to those markets– the ET&G, that ran south to Atlanta and then east to Charleston, and the Memphis and Charleston into Alabama–were vital. Economic reasons doubtless influenced the vote by many in Hamilton County. What would it do to Joseph economically if Tennessee remained in the Union and these rail lines were ruptured and/or the markets closed by a high tariff from the new Confederate government? Unfortunately, no record remains of Joseph's position or his vote in the most critical election in Tennessee's history.

Just over two weeks prior to the June 8 referendum, Joseph received a lumber order from J.B. Jett of Birchwood:

> Birchwood May 21st 1861
>
> Mr. Joseph Roark   Sir if you please send me 250 ft of sealing lumber 16 ft long. If you have not that length 12 ft long will do, 750 ft of fencing or weatherboarding. By so doing you will much oblige and I will settle with you when I see you.
>
> Yours with respect
> E.B. Jett[49]

It would be Roark's last lumber order for the duration of the war. Interestingly, Joseph wrote no promissory notes or made major purchases between April 4 and September 11, 1861. Business came to a standstill since his neighbors were then disinterested in business. War talk dominated all conversation.

Following Fort Sumter in April, all across Tennessee there was a rush to arms as young men volunteered and mobilized for war, primarily for the Confederacy. In some towns, elaborate ceremonies were planned as volunteer companies left for training and incorporation into the Confederate army. In Benton, county seat of Polk County to the east, volunteers were honored as a torch-light parade with bands and banners paraded through the streets until late in the evening. By late May, over twenty Confederate volunteer companies from the Tennessee Valley had arrived in Knoxville and were encamped at the fairgrounds. Local communities responded enthusiastically to the Governor's call for volunteers in May and organized companies bearing the name of the town of origin like the "Knoxville Grays," and the "Decatur Guards." Young men from lower East Tennessee, filled with war fervor, eagerly enlisted out of patriotism. Few, if any, were motivated by white supremacy or the defense of slavery.[50]

In May 1861, at the most active time of enlistments by Tennessee volunteers, Joseph Roark had three sons, all of the age desired by an army–Jim was 21, John was 19, and Will was 17. Yet none of the three enlisted in that early surge of patriotism and war fervor in the early summer of 1861. They were farm boys and felt no community pressure to join the army. There was no mass support in the Salem Community for war or for the Confederacy. Many, in fact, were strong Unionists, and there was little enthusiasm to volunteer for either army, Union or Confederate.

On July 21, the first major battle of the Civil War occurred at the railroad junction of Manassas, Virginia. Here Confederate forces under Gen. P.G.T. Beauregard defeated Gen. Irvin McDowell, whose Union troops retreated in panic toward Washington, D.C. The Battle of First Manassas or Bull Run was a victory for the South, and newspapers in Tennessee loudly proclaimed the success of Southern troops. The war was applauded with enthusiasm in the South. In Cleveland, southern supporters illuminated their houses in honor of the victory and heard rousing speeches for the Confederacy.[51] In Chattanooga, Unionist publisher James R. Hood, after a private visit by secessionists, left for the North and the *Chattanooga Gazette* ceased publication. Secessionists H.S. Hill and W.L. Scruggs of the *Chattanooga Advertiser* took over the presses of the *Gazette* and began publishing under the name of the *Chattanooga Gazette and Advertiser*.

The battle of First Manassas and the call by Governor Harris for an additional 20,000 troops resulted in new enlistments, although not with the enthusiasm that had been evidenced in the spring. Enlistments were arranged primarily through the forming of units from within a specific locale. In most cases an individual took the responsibility of forming a company of which he would be captain. Quite frequently, companies and even regiments were organized through ads run in the local newspaper.

The standard number of men for the organization of a company was one hundred, although companies were formed with less. Newly formed companies were designated cavalry units when the enlistees could furnish their own horses and were qualified riders. Such was the case when sometime in late July 1861, William Snow and James B. King began recruiting a cavalry company in Hamilton County and parts of Bradley County. Snow lived in the Snow Hill Community near the home of

Dr. Yarnell, just west of Whiteoak Mountain near the Hamilton-Bradley county line.[52] He was from an established family and was a successful farmer owning ten slaves in 1860.[53] Snow's political views and his interest in the Confederacy are unknown; however, his slave holdings may have caused him to support the Confederacy on the issue of slavery. Snow and King recruited heavily in the Salem Community and the Grasshopper Creek area. By August 7, they had completed their work as the recruits were registered in Cleveland on that date. Along with the two sons of Joseph Roark, Jim and John Roark, the group of recruits from the Salem Community also included John C.I. Smith and James Smith, sons of Abner Smith; Bill Webb, son of Merida Webb; William F. Conner and James Madison Conner, sons of M.H. Conner; Francis Gardenhire, son of George W. Gardenhire; and Billy Killian, son of William Killian.[54] Each enlistment was for a period of twelve months. After all, everyone knew it would be a short war. Apparently, Joseph's third son, Will, who was seventeen at the time, did not enlist at the same time as his brothers but enlisted in the same company at a later date.[55]

The enlistment of Joseph's middle son, John, provided an abrupt change in environment for the nineteen-year-old. On Tuesday, August 6, the very day before his enlistment and a week before his twentieth birthday, John completed his work at the Georgetown Academy and received the following certificate qualifying him as a school teacher:

> Georgetown, August 6th, 1861
> This is to certify that the bearer, Mr. John W. Roark, is qualified to take charge of a free school where Orthography, Reading, Writing, Oral and Written Arithmetic, Geography, and the elementary branches of Natural Philosophy, Algebra, and English Grammar are required.
> Given under my signature this date above written
> M.H.B. Bourkett
> Examiner Comm. of Hancock Co. Tenn.[56]

What were the motivations for the enlistment of Joseph's sons in the Tennessee cavalry unit of the Confederacy? Quite likely they reflected their father's thoughts toward the secession effort and the war. Whether Joseph encouraged their enlistment or counseled against it, we do not know. The Salem Community, like all of East Tennessee, was divided in its support of the Confederacy. Community pressure for enlistments that influenced the decisions of many volunteers in communities in both North and South was absent in Salem. There the decision to enlist, for either the Union or Confederate army, was an individual matter–a decision to be made not in the flurry of early emotional enlistments but after weeks of consideration. While many friends of Jim and John Roark were enlisting for Confederate service, a group influence probably had little effect on the two brothers since many of their local friends and even their cousins were not enlisting with the Confederacy and would later join the Union army. Without a doubt, Lincoln's call for troops and the strong possibility of an "invasion" by Union troops "to put down the rebellion" influenced the enlistments of many young men from East Tennessee. The defense of one's homeland from an invading army has always provided strong motivation for taking up arms. Perhaps in the late summer of 1861, it provided the impetus for the enlistment by Joseph's sons.[57]

As Captain Snow's company was formed the first week in August, recruits were quartered in a temporary camp in Cleveland. The camp, designated by a proclamation from the governor, served as an induction center for lower East Tennessee. There the companies were formed, men and horses registered, officers elected, and some similitude of basic military instruction provided. The induction camp was located on the Bradley County fairgrounds south of Cleveland, near the railroad junction of the ET&G and the Cleveland-Chattanooga line. Georgetown merchant W.H. Tibbs, who also had a store in Cleveland and with whom Joseph Roark had business dealings, was named by the governor as commissary for the Cleveland camp. Later Tibbs would be elected to the Confederate congress.[58]

After a month at the Cleveland camp, Snow's company was moved to Camp Cummings in Knoxville on September 17, 1861. There the company was assigned to the 3rd (Brazelton's) Tennessee Cavalry Battalion, Lt. Col. William Brazelton, Jr., commander,[59] and participated in cavalry drills. Camp Cummings had been hastily established on the fairgrounds at Knoxville and gave the appearance of a county fair rather than a camp for strict military training. As new troops arrived, they saw a camp with long rows of shelter tents and other varieties of shelter and lodging. No uniforms were available for issue, and clothing consisted of that brought by each recruit. Each man was responsible for washing his assorted clothing in a nearby creek.[60]

Local newspapers available to the Salem Community announced that on July 22, 1861, Tennessee had been formally admitted to the Confederate States of America. In East Tennessee, however, Unionists strongly challenged Confederate rule. In late June, Unionists had met at a convention in Greeneville, Tennessee, and, among other things, submitted a resolution to the state legislature requesting the organization of a separate state in East Tennessee, similar to the organization of West Virginia. The resolution was submitted to the legislature June 26, 1861, by a committee of three, one of whom was John Netherland, who had purchased the 150 acres in Claiborne County from Thomas Ellison in 1840. A joint committee of the Tennessee senate and house took no action on the request.

Violence flared in East Tennessee in the summer of 1861 as Unionists mobilized to resist Confederate takeover. Everywhere in Hamilton County, animosities began to develop among neighbors. Just across the Tennessee River from the Salem Community, Joseph heard of a gathering of local recruits for the Union army on the land of William Clift. Clift was a strong Unionist and recruited volunteers for the Union army, quartering them on his land on Sale Creek, some of which he had purchased from James Roark in 1838. Clift's camp of future Union soldiers in the heart of the Confederacy caused much anxiety for Confederate leaders and several steps were taken throughout the remainder of 1861 to disperse Clift's "army." It would be in the spring of 1862 before Clift would move his camp north. Throughout the war, Clift would provide means by which young men could volunteer for the Union army and be secretly moved to Kentucky for induction.

Almost all counties in East Tennessee suffered from violence during the last half of 1861. Both Unionists and secessionists were killed. Confederate troops moving northward on the ET&G and ET&V were ambushed by Union bushwhackers and, in turn, Confederate troops responded by harassing known Union leaders in the area. Confederate army units had to be assigned to East Tennessee to assist in putting down the Unionist rebellion. The situation in East Tennessee has been appropriately described as "a civil war within a civil war." The Confederate leadership expressed frustration at having to use troops to put down a rebellion against its authority. Brig. Gen. Felix Zolliecoffer from Nashville was assigned to Knoxville in July 1861 to break up the Unionist political organization and to suppress the treasonous activity.[61]

Rebellion by the Unionists was close at hand to the Salem Community. On Saturday night, July 6, a rumor spread among Unionists in Bradley County that a Confederate regiment was in Georgetown for the purpose of reprisal against the local Unionists. The rumor was false, but between 500 and 1,000 Unionists armed themselves and met north of Cleveland early Sunday in a rebellious mood. The pro-Confederate *Cleveland Banner* reported the event and warned such "Lincoln men" what to expect in the case of any similar treasonous acts:

> Armed Lincoln men are enemies to the Confederate States, whether they are found in Massachusetts, Virginia, or East Tennessee–and such armed men with hostile intentions, if persisted in, must as a matter of course in a state of war expect to be treated as enemies.[62]

In response to the troubles in East Tennessee, the Confederate Congress in August 1861 passed two pieces of legislation aimed at controlling rebellion there. The first, the Alien Act, called for the arrest and removal, as alien enemies, of all males over the age of fourteen who were identified as Unionists. All East Tennesseans were called upon to swear allegiance to the Confederacy or be subject to arrest. The second piece of legislation, the Sequestration Act, authorized the seizure of property belonging to men who did not swear the same allegiance. Almost simultaneous with the acts by the Confederate congress, Tennessee Governor Harris directed an order to all county clerks requiring local constables to make a house-by-house search and confiscate "muskets, bayonets, rifles, swords, and pistols." The order was taken to mean weapons currently possessed by Union supporters.[63]

As Joseph and Juda said goodbye to their sons in August 1861, they could see an attitude of hatred and bitterness beginning to infect their lives and their community.

The time marked the beginning of the bloody civil war within a civil war that would consume the Salem Community, Hamilton County, and East Tennessee over the next three and one-half years. It signaled for Joseph and his family the beginning of a new way of life that would be forever branded in their memories. Family, friends, and neighbors were then frequently grouped against each other as part of the struggle. Life itself became tense.

> Violence now became an integral part of everyday life for most people of the region. Long after the war, one East Tennessean warned those who read his memoirs if they were ever caught in a rebellion of citizen against citizen "to fly from it as a burning house. Tarry not . . . but fly at once. Leave all you have behind if you cannot escape with it rapidly, for it is of no value."[64]

By August 1861, it was clear that Lincoln and the North intended "to make war rather than let [the Nation] perish"[65] and planned to invade the seceding states. Decisions made far beyond the environs of the Salem Community would therefore determine the course of events for Joseph Roark and his family as never before. From Washington, the strategy was to invade Tennessee through its long and unprotected border with Kentucky, which had declared its neutrality in the conflict. Both North and South violated this neutrality as both armies positioned themselves—one to invade and the other to protect itself from invasion. Unfortunately, the Confederate defense of the Tennessee border with Kentucky was to be difficult since rivers and railroads, both primary means of transportation for armies, penetrated Tennessee from north to south. The Tennessee, Mississippi, and Cumberland Rivers provided direct access to Tennessee and the Federal staff, in its strategic planning, was quick to capitalize on the potential of the rivers. Similarly the Nashville-Chattanooga railroad and the ET&V with the ET&G were vital transportation links for both North and South in moving armies north and south. Because of its then heavy use to move Confederate units to Virginia and later its potential for reverse movement of Union troops, the ET&V and the ET&G was considered "the most significant railroad line in the South."[66] Throughout the war, railroads and rivers were to be the primary determinants of major battlefield locations. Unfortunately for Joseph Roark and others in the path of the maelstrom, Chattanooga was located at a vital intersection of the most significant railroad and, with the exception perhaps of the Mississippi, the most important river.

With two sons no longer at home, Joseph was required to spend much more time in hard labor on his farm than before. Besides the obvious labor shortage, finances were also difficult. Cash money was hard to come by, and promissory notes, when they were accepted by the receiver, were written to secure payment within a much more limited time frame. As sons Jim and John were in the process of moving from Cleveland to Camp Cummings in Knoxville, Joseph wrote the following promissory note to merchant J.P. Turbyfill, which required settlement within two weeks:

On or before the twenty fifth day of September next I promis to pay J.P. Turbyfill or bearer the sum of thirty two dollars for value recieved of him. September the 11, 1861

Joseph Roark[67]

Joseph was able to pay twenty dollars to Turbyfill on September 30, five days beyond the note due date, and received credit in that amount on the note. The balance was paid on some future date. Credit and good faith that had come easily in the past would, beginning in the first year of the war, be more difficult and, in the future, would be impossible to obtain.

Others in the Salem Community were experiencing equally difficult times. On November 4, Joseph received a summons from Constable John McCallie to appear before Justice John B. Brown in regard to the assets of E.J. Jett. Jett, for whom Joseph had filled a lumber order six months before, was in court in defense of a lawsuit by L.B. McNabb for twelve dollars. A judgement had been rendered by the justice of the peace and Jett's assets were to be seized to settle the judgement. As the economy tightened and war came even closer, business failures like that of Jett's became more prevalent.[68] Cash money became difficult to come by. Joseph was able to maintain a cash balance from the sale of his 1861 corn crop. On November 8, Joseph secured a cash payment from Dr. John L. Yarnell of $43.60 for one hundred bushels of corn at $0.45 per bushel to be delivered to Yarnell's farm between December 1 and December 10. The balance was to be paid upon delivery. The advance payment of almost 97% of the sale price might indicate the seriousness of the economy.[69]

The very night that Joseph received the advance payment from Yarnell for the corn, events occurred that would forever shatter the peace that remained in Hamilton County and the Salem Community. On that Friday night, bridges were burned on the ET&V and the ET&G railroads plus the Cleveland-Chattanooga connection. Included in the sabotage was the bridge over the Hiwassee at Charleston in Bradley County and two bridges over Chickamauga Creek near Chattanooga. The burning of the three bridges was part of what was revealed later as a massive plot by Unionists in East Tennessee to burn a total of nine bridges between Bristol, Tennessee, and Stevenson, Alabama. The subversive strike was preliminary to a promised Federal invasion of East Tennessee. A total of five bridges were destroyed and telegraph lines were cut. Anticipating the Union army moving through Cumberland Gap to their rescue, Unionists in East Tennessee openly defied Confederate rule and fought with Confederate units. Unbeknownst however to the Unionist bridge burners, the Federal invasion had been called off, leaving the subversives to their fate. While the bridge burning disrupted rail transportation for a brief period, it resulted in punishment of the Unionists to a degree far beyond the damage caused the Confederacy. Response by the State of Tennessee and Confederate officers in Richmond was swift and severe. Secretary of War Judah

Benjamin at Richmond immediately prepared to send troops "to crush the traitors" and ordered the guilty parties "to be tried summarily by drum-head court-martial, and if found guilty, executed on the spot by hanging." Additional Confederate troops were sent to East Tennessee and General Zolliecoffer reported, "I have ordered all posts and detachments to disarm Union men and seize leaders. Have made dispositions to cut off tories of Rhea, Hamilton, and Sevier [counties]." Confederate units fanned out into the countryside identifying Unionists and sus-pected bridge burners. Complete repression of the Unionists was ordered. Four men were hanged and over two hundred Unionists were arrested and imprisoned in Tuscaloosa, Alabama. A rein of terror prevailed.[70]

The most prominent figure arrested was "Parson" William G. Brownlow of the *Knoxville Whig*. After his attempt to escape to Kentucky failed, Brownlow surren-dered to the local Confederate commander. Brownlow was kept in jail for more than three weeks and then given safe passage out of the Confederacy. Brownlow's arrest and treatment increased his natural bitterness. His imprisonment etched into his memory a hatred for all who were affiliated with the Confederacy in any minor way and provided him a platform for his later revenge and vindictiveness.[71]

Arrested in Bradley County as a Unionist was Levi Trewhitt, a prominent judge in Bradley County with whom Samuel Carr had doubtless been acquainted and who was known by Joseph Roark. At the time of his arrest November 19, 1861, Judge Trewhitt was 65 and in poor health. He was sent with sixteen other prisoners from Bradley County to the Confederate prison in Tuscaloosa. Included in the group of prisoners was W.R. Davis, to whom Joseph had lost a judgement for $47.39 the year before. Trewhitt's arrest and sentencing was appealed before Judge T.J. Campbell but to no avail. Levi Trewhitt died in Alabama January 31, 1862.[72]

The violence in East Tennessee engendered by the bridge burning and the response by Confederate authorities would continue throughout the war and beyond. Union and Confederate armies would fight major battles in East Tennessee but, as the war progressed, both moved to other arenas. But the fight among neighbors would continue day by terrible day and would be fueled by grievances and animosities that would remain long after the war had ended and the armies disbanded. Unfortunately, the violence also attracted a bushwhacking criminal element. These often masquer-aded as guerrilla bands participating in "actions such as theft and assault that did not always possess a military or political significance but that were nonetheless a com-mon feature of guerrilla operations. Many bushwhacker bands lived partly or entire-ly by theft, and they routinely broke into houses, carried off horses and stock, and waylaid people on the roads."[73] This was the environment in which Joseph Roark and his family were to live during the war and for years after its close.

In October, the 3rd Tennessee Cavalry Battalion, with Jim and John Roark by then trained in cavalry tactics, was assigned to the army of Gen. Felix Zolliecoffer as it moved north into Kentucky. With the movement of Federal troops into

Kentucky, Zolliecoffer was ordered to move northwest through Cumberland Gap to monitor the Union threat. By the end of the year, Joseph's sons were in Kentucky north of the Cumberland River, across from Mill Spring, expecting battle with the Union army under Gen. George H. Thomas.[74]

In December 1861, Joseph, in a move that obviously was to provide him with needed cash, sold 50 acres from his homestead tract to Nancy M. Ford and her son, David H. Ford. The tract was located in Section 28 and was adjacent to the tract purchased by Benjamin Webb from Hiram Cornwell. For the tract, Joseph received $200 and, in return, submitted a bond in that amount, guaranteeing to provide the widow Ford a good and marketable title to the property. The bond was witnessed by J.P. Turbyfill and Joel A. Talley.[75]

The requirement for the bond probably reflects delays in deed registration as a result of county reorganization. With Tennessee then a part of the Confederacy, county officers, to remain in office, were required to swear an oath of allegiance to the Confederate States of America. In many cases this requirement resulted in resignations when office holders with Unionist sympathies refused to take the oath. When this occurred, election of new county officers was required. County offices continued to function but at a much slower pace than before. The Hamilton County Court continued to meet in Harrison on the first Monday of each month, and on January 11, 1862, the pro-southern editor of the *Chattanooga Gazette & Advertiser* printed what was perhaps an idealized view of unanimity in "the upper end" of Hamilton County:

Trip to Harrison

On Monday last (being County Court day) it was our good fortune to visit the quiet little town of Harrison, and though much has been said and written of the good people of that place, we can truthfully state, that never have we seen a more unified people in their opposition to the enthroned tyrant who disgraces the seat of Washington. Lincoln's recent usurpations and outrages have done the work, and we are more than gratified to state, that our county is now "one in earnest, one in heart." Volunteering is going on rapidly in the upper end of the county. Capt. Smith came into camps yesterday with as fine a body of men as ever kept step. Capt. Roddy of Harrison has nearly completed his company, and we heard of others who are engaged in raising companies for Col. Morgan's regiment. Capt. Clift's and Capt. Tankersley's men are mostly from the upper end of the county and are in camps. Three cheers for the upper end of Hamilton.[76]

To illustrate the divisiveness within families, it should be pointed out that the Captain Clift mentioned in the editorial was the son of adamant Unionist William Clift of the Sale Creek area.

In Joseph Roark's family, no correspondence remains in his papers from any of his sons during their time of service with the Confederate army. This is not necessarily an indication that Jim, John, or Will did not write home since few items of correspondence were collected and maintained by Joseph in his files. His sons were, however, in a cavalry regiment and cavalry units, to be the eyes and ears of the army itself, were constantly on the move. Such consistent movement allowed little time for writing, particularly when compared to infantry regiments that moved more slowly and spent more time in encampment. Also, in cavalry units, the horses had to be fed, groomed, and taken care of, leaving little time for the rider to maintain any degree of correspondence. It is a reasonable assumption, however, that some correspondence did take place and, if not extensive by the three Roark brothers, then by others in the company to their families at home in the Salem Community. Doubtless the parents in the community with sons in the same company shared what information was received from any soldier in the unit.

In early January 1862, rumors began to circulate that a major battle lay ahead for the Confederate forces in Kentucky. On Saturday, January 25, 1862, Joseph and Juda read with anxiety a dispatch in the *Chattanooga Gazette and Advertiser*:

TELEGRAPHIC
Great Battle in Kentucky!

The Confederates Defeated
Overwhelming Numbers of the Federals

GENERAL ZOLLIECOFFER KILLED

PARTICULARS OF THE ENGAGEMENT

Knoxville, Jan. 23.–Lieut. Jackson has just arrived from the scene of our late disaster and reports that the fight occurred on Sunday morning about daylight. It was reported that the enemy's force, about fourteen thousand strong, was divided by Fishing Creek, and that they could not be united in consequence of the swollen condition of the creek from the late rains. It was under this impression that Gen. Crittenden ordered our forces to move forward and attack the enemy, when they met the entire Federal force, and after fighting for more than two hours, our forces were repulsed and fell back to their entrenchments.

Late in the evening they were again attacked by the Federals, and after a short cannonading, night came on and the firing ceased. Then the order was given for our forces to retreat across the river.

Gen. Zolliecoffer was killed, Major Fogg wounded, Major Shields killed, Baillie Peyton Jr., killed, Col. Stanton wounded in the arm, and Col. Powell badly wounded.

Our loss is variously estimated, but it is undoubtedly large. The Mississippi regiment fought bravely, and was cut up badly. Battle's regiment also fought gallantly.

The enemy was reported crossing the river at Burkesville, to intercept the retreat of our forces.[77]

As Joseph and Juda would later learn, General Zolliecoffer had attacked the Union forces under Gen. George Thomas early that Sunday morning west of Somerset, Kentucky. Unfortunately for the Confederates, the attack had come after Thomas had been able to combine his forces in spite of the fact that Fishing Creek was out of its banks. Neither Jim nor John Roark had been wounded. John Roark had been assigned to a detail to accompany the body of General Zolliecoffer through the lines after the body had been prepared for burial at the command of General Thomas. The battle was the first major defeat for the Confederacy and Zolliecoffer was the first general officer to be killed in the western theater of the war. Following the battle, the Confederate army retreated across the Cumberland River and into Tennessee. Gen. George B. Crittenden replaced Zolliecoffer and as the army retreated further into Tennessee, the 3rd Tennessee Cavalry Battalion was moved to Cumberland Gap and assigned to picket duty from February to April 1862. On March 8, Gen. Edmund Kirby Smith assumed command of the Confederate forces in East Tennessee.[78]

With the Confederate defeat at Fishing Creek, the entire border between Kentucky and Tennessee was open to invasion by the North. Disastrous events awaited the South during the next few months. The Confederate States had labored during the last year to erect two forts on the Tennessee and Cumberland Rivers south of the Ohio–Fort Henry at the mouth of the Tennessee and Fort Donelson on the Cumberland. On February 6, Fort Henry surrendered to Federal gunboats, and just over a week later Fort Donelson was surrendered to forces under Brig. Gen. U.S. Grant. With the fall of the two forts, Union forces were in control of the Tennessee and Cumberland Rivers. Federal gunboats sailed up the Cumberland to Nashville and up the Tennessee as far as Florence, Alabama, spreading fear and anxiety among the civilian populations along the rivers. By March 13, Nashville had fallen to the Union army forcing Governor Isham Harris and the state government to move to Memphis. President Lincoln named Andrew Johnson as military governor of Tennessee and a complete new state government assumed control of state offices.

With almost all of Middle and West Tennessee under Union control, Gen. Albert Sidney Johnston, the commander of all Confederate forces in the west, concentrated his forces at Corinth, Mississippi, in an attempt to block further advance of Union forces down the Mississippi Valley. Beginning on April 6, 1862, in the first major battle in the west, Confederate forces swept the Union army from the field at Shiloh Church in southwest Tennessee, but they were forced to retreat the following day when Union forces were reinforced. During the first day of the battle, General Johnston, a brilliant tactician and leader, was killed, contributing to the subsequent retreat. Following the battle, the Confederate army was placed under the command of Gen. Braxton Bragg, who moved the army eastward by rail to Chattanooga via Mobile, Montgomery, and Atlanta. As Bragg moved eastward, the City of New Orleans fell to the fleet of Union Adm. David Farragut. The city formally surrendered

Joseph Roark

to Federal forces April 29, culminating a string of disasters for the Confederacy. Hopes of the South for an easy and quick victory were quickly vanishing and a much longer and more painful war was then expected. Over 20,000 men had been lost to the Confederacy at Shiloh and Fort Donelson. Manpower had become critical to the South and the twelve-month enlistments executed when a short war had been anticipated were quickly expiring.

As bad as things were for the Confederacy in the west, they were even worse in East Tennessee. Following the Confederate defeat at Fishing Creek, General Kirby Smith established his headquarters at Knoxville. A professional soldier, having served as a division commander in the Confederate Army of Northern Virginia, Kirby Smith* found conditions in East Tennessee much worse than he had anticipated. After his arrival in Knoxville, he wrote that "no one can conceive the actual condition of East Tennessee, disloyal to the core, it is more dangerous and difficult to operate in than the country of an acknowledged enemy." In a letter to General Bragg, Kirby Smith wrote that "East Tennessee is an Enemy's country . . . and in open rebellion."[79] At his recommendation, Confederate President Jefferson Davis proclaimed on April 8, 1862, that the Department of East Tennessee was under martial law. Joseph Roark read of the action in the April 25, 1826, issue of the *Cleveland Banner*:

PROCLAMATION
Adjutant and Inspector Gen. Office
Richmond, April 8, 1862

General Orders No. 21
   The following proclamation is published for the information of all concerned:
   By virtue of the power vested in me by law to declare the suspension of the privilege of the writ of *habeas corpus*, I, Jefferson Davis, President of the Confederate States of America, do proclaim that martial law is hereby extended over the Department of East Tennessee, under the command of Major General E.K. Smith; and I do proclaim the suspension of all civil jurisdiction . . . and the suspension of the writ of *habeas corpus* in the department aforesaid.
   In faith whereof I have hereunto signed my name and set my seal this 8th day of April, in the year one thousand eight hundred and sixty two.
                                          Jefferson Davis[80]

Kirby Smith requested and received additional troops for his command in East Tennessee. Thus troops that were desperately needed by the armies in Virginia and southwest Tennessee were instead used to keep order. He used the Confederate troops to enforce martial law and to reduce guerrilla activity and violence by the Unionists in East Tennessee. His enforcement marked a significant hardening of Confederate policy to Union rebellion. In turn, Confederate troops in East Tennessee were subject to attack from Unionist guerrillas at all times. Unionists lurked near

*Kirby was simply Smith's middle name, but to distinguish himself from other Smiths, he used "Kirby Smith" as his last name, signing that way without the hyphen.

294

Confederate camps hoping to ambush individual soldiers coming to or leaving the camp. In August 1862, a Tennessee soldier was bushwhacked just outside a Confederate camp near Chattanooga. Southern troops were called upon to be continually on the alert to Unionist guerrilla attacks and harassment against Confederate supporters, communities, and supply lines.[81]

The Southern shortage of manpower was severe by the spring of 1862 when volunteer enlistments had significantly decreased and the twelve-month enlistments of the year before were terminating. To address the problem, the Confederate congress on April 16, 1862, passed the Conscription Act "declaring every able-bodied white man between the ages of 18 and 35 to be subject to the military service of the Confederate States" for a period of three years. Additionally, the Act extended all twelve-month enlistments to three years from the date of their original enlistment "unless the war shall sooner terminate." The Act provided a thirty-day grace period in which local volunteer companies could be formed. It also provided, within the same grace period, the privilege of volunteering into units already in the field.[82]

The Conscription Act was to have a significant influence on the Salem Community. Its content was widely disseminated through local newspapers, and strict enforcement was promised by Confederate conscription officers. Young men of conscription age were forced to decide among three options: (1) to enlist in existing units, generally those that had been formed from the local area; (2) to wait and be conscripted into the Confederate army; or (3) to "escape" to Kentucky to enlist in the Union army. With the enforcement of the Conscription Act, they could not simply stay at home. It was probably at this time that Joseph's third son, Will, enlisted in the 3rd Tennessee Cavalry Battalion with his brothers. He had a horse which made him eligible for the cavalry, so after brief orientation and basic training at Knoxville, Will joined his brothers' unit in the vicinity of Cumberland Gap. Joseph and Juda thus saw their remaining son leave home for the army. Joseph alone was left to work the farm.

The Conscription Act also affected others in the Salem Community. Joseph's son-in-law Joel Talley was thirty-eight in the spring of 1862 and thus was not in the proscribed age for conscription; however, the rumor in East Tennessee was that the age for conscription would soon be raised to forty-five. (The conscription age was in fact changed to between 18 and 45 by the Confederate congress, October 11, 1862.) Subsequent to the Conscription Act in April, Talley enlisted in the Union army and was mustered into Company G, Fifth East Tennessee Infantry at Camp Pine Knot, Kentucky, on May 21, 1862.[83] When Talley left for Kentucky, Elizabeth was left at home with six children. Amanda, the oldest, was fifteen. Andrew Jackson, the youngest, was one year old. Elizabeth would be forced to look to her father for help and support during her husband's absence.

Joseph's other son-in-law in the Salem Community, Robert Beane Scott, was not forced to make the decision that faced others of conscription age. The Conscription Act specifically excluded "ministers in the regular discharge of their duties." Robert

Scott was thus able to remain in his pulpit and was permitted to work in the fields six days a week as most rural pastors did. There was little criticism on a minister's exclusion from conscription "for Southerners were as a rule very religious and public opinion would frown on any attempt to substitute the pulpit for the camp."[84]

The Conscription Act also affected the families of Joseph's two brothers. James Roark had two sons to enlist. The elder of the two, John B. Roark, 33, enlisted in Company E, Fifth Tennessee Infantry of the Union army and was mustered in at Barbourville, Kentucky, March 29, 1862.[85] Doubtless James Roark used his contact and friendship with Col. William Clift, who by then had organized the Seventh Tennessee Infantry (Union) Regiment and served as its commander, to obtain passage to Kentucky for his son as well as the sons of his brother John. When John B. left for Kentucky, his wife Nancy was left with two children, Martha 8, and Jacob 6.[86] James' other son, Joseph, age 19, probably contrary to the wishes of his father and brother, enlisted April 4, 1862, in the Confederate army at Chattanooga and was enrolled in Capt. R.L. Barry's Company, Tennessee "Lookout" Light Artillery.[87] To further divide the family politically, James' daughter Sarah would marry Bill Webb November 12, 1862, while he was home on leave from the 3rd Tennessee Cavalry Battalion.[88]

Joseph's other brother, John, had three sons plus two sons-in-law to enlist in the Union army following passage of the Confederate Conscription Act. John Roark's youngest son, John Lewis Roark, was the first of the family to enlist and did so with his cousin, John B. Roark, March 29, 1862. He was enrolled in Company E, Fifth Tennessee Infantry (Union) in Barbourville, Kentucky, when he was fifteen years old.[89] His older brothers, both still single, James W. Roark, 27, and William C. Roark, 22, enlisted September 17, 1862, and were enrolled by Col. William Clift at Huntsville in northern Tennessee in Company C, Seventh Tennessee Infantry (Union).[90] Future son-in-law Archibald McCallie, husband-to-be of Margaret Roark, also enlisted with John B. Roark and John Lewis Roark, March 29, 1862, in Company E, Fifth Tennessee Infantry (Union).[91] Future son-in-law David Gregory, husband-to-be of America Roark, enlisted June 14, 1863, in Company E, Eighth Tennessee Infantry (Union).[92]

With so many of the young men leaving for service, the farms in the community suffered. Cultivated acreage was reduced simply because of the lack of manpower to tend to the crops. With the reduced production of money crops, income was reduced and little cash money was in circulation. Bank notes were available but were risky because of their fluctuation in value. The *Chattanooga Gazette & Advertiser* periodically carried its Bank Note List that provided a ranking of notes from various banks. In its issue of January 4, 1862, the *Gazette & Advertiser* carried a list of bank notes from 39 Tennessee banks. The notes of twelve of the banks were classified as "Worthless and Broken," and fourteen were shown as trading at a discount of between two and five percent. Only thirteen were noted as trading at par value.[93] In addition to the banks, states in the Confederacy also issued their own paper money, further complicating the southern economy. The primary concern, however, in the economies of Hamilton and contiguous counties was the financial policy of the Confederacy. Early on, the Confederate congress decided to minimize the levy of taxes to pursue the war effort. Any taxes would initially be levied through the states as a strict recognition of the concept of states rights. Also, the Confederacy issued no coins, making it difficult for citizens to make change in business transactions. Coins from the United States were in circulation; however, these were hoarded as a hedge against the risky finances of the Confederacy. The primary source of monies for operating expenses of the Confederate government was from treasury notes, which bore no interest and had no backing in gold, silver, or other specie. The paper money was issued in amounts ranging initially for between $5 and $100. Each note was personally endorsed by the Register and by a representative of the treasurer and promised payment in dollars "two years after the ratification of a treaty of peace between the Confederate States and the United States of America." As the war continued, more and more treasury notes were issued, many in amounts as small as fifty cents, and the notes progressively were worth less and less. Acceptance of Confederate treasury notes became a patriotic issue and citizens were encouraged to use the Confederate money for all commercial transactions. In the *Cleveland Banner*, Joseph Roark read the following editorial:

CONFEDERATE MONEY

We learn that some of our citizens are refusing to take Confederate money, and are doing what they can to depreciate it in value. We regret that there are such men among us–they are the worst enemies the South has. They are pretended friends, and let no sly opportunity pass but what they are stabbing at our dearest institutions. . . .

Confederate money is the best money we have–it passes at par in all the States of the Confederacy. That is not the case with State money. Cotton cannot be purchased in Georgia with Tennessee money, without a shave.–In view of these facts we should like to know why certain men refuse to take it. . . . Don't trade with them. Let them dry out, and go to Lincolndom where their feelings have always been. We have no use for them.[94]

Early in the war, the Confederate government proposed the sale of its bonds and notes directly for farm produce in lieu of money. Farmers had the produce to sell but had no cash with which to buy Confederate bonds. By accepting such produce for direct purchase of bonds, the Confederacy accumulated stores of cotton, sugar, rice, tobacco, and wheat, only a small portion of which could be converted into cash or credit from European countries because of the Union naval blockade.

As the naval blockade by the North severely restricted Confederate imports and as more and more of the country's gross product went to the war effort, shortages among the population soon became evident. By mid 1862, Joseph and other farmers in the Salem Community were experiencing a shortage in salt–a product vital to the preservation of pork and other meats. In the summer of 1862, a 150-pound bag of salt sold for $20, whereas a year earlier the same bag sold for $0.65. Such shortages and the resulting inflation in price severely limited productive farm output. Combined with reduced manpower available for the farms, the prices and shortages limited Joseph's farming operations, requiring him to reduce the number of hogs and other livestock that he raised as well as the number of acres he had in cultivation.[95]

Joseph Roark's reduced output was reflected in the number of promissory notes that he executed and accepted for payment. Only two promissory notes were used for all of 1862. The first of the notes illustrates both the depressed economy and the almost obsessive determination of Joseph to pay all his debts. On February 8, 1862, Joseph executed a promissory note in the amount of $65.69 to merchants W.C. and C.L. Hutcheson, doubtless for goods that he purchased. As the financial depression resulting from the war deepened, Joseph could not make a payment. Nine and one-half years later–October 20, 1871– the interest was calculated to be $38.21 for a total amount due of $103.90. As a payment, Joseph provided a horse for which a credit of $80 was given on the note. Just over three years later, with an additional interest cost of $1.71, Joseph made a final payment of $33.64, and the promissory note was returned to him. Doubtless with some satisfaction, Joseph removed his name with his pocket knife and filed the thirteen-year-old note with his papers.[96] The note provides a character evaluation of Joseph Roark, in that when failed banks and even state and national governments were defaulting on notes and bonds, Joseph refused to take the easy route of default and, following difficult years, settled the account with a full payment of both principal and interest.

The only other promissory note in 1862 was written to G.F. Farris on April 25 just after East Tennessee was placed under martial law. The note was in the amount of $21.40 for value received and was due "twenty days after date" of the note. No indication remains on the note of any interest due, so the date of payment was doubtless within the twenty days or soon thereafter. As was most often the case, Joseph's name was neatly removed when the paid note was returned to him.[97]

As Joseph struggled to survive and provide for his family in the first half of 1862, Chattanooga took on new strategic importance in the war. Federal armies turned east following the Battle of Shiloh with the intent of capturing Chattanooga and cutting the railroad connecting Virginia with Georgia, Alabama, and Tennessee. As Bragg laboriously moved the Confederate army by rail through Montgomery and Atlanta, General Buell and the Union Army of the Ohio moved eastward along the Memphis and Charleston Railroad. While the two large armies both moved toward Chattanooga, the city was subjected to bombardment by a small Union reconnaissance force. Joseph Roark and the Salem Community heard the thunder-like rumble of distant artillery for the first time as the war moved ever closer. It was on the afternoon of June 7 that Gen. James F. Negley, commanding a Union force of 7,000 men arrived on the north bank of the Tennessee across from Chattanooga and began an artillery bombardment of the city. With no way to cross the river, Negley had no opportunity to occupy Chattanooga; however, the attack caused significant excitement among the citizens. General Kirby Smith arrived with reinforcements in the afternoon, and fire was returned by the Confederates. That night Joseph could see the campfires of the Union army. The bombardment continued the morning of June 8 until the Union forces withdrew in the afternoon and retreated over Walden Ridge. The assault had done little damage and no railroad traffic was interrupted. The brief battle did, however, bring war to Hamilton County for the first time.[98]

Sometime between February and the first bombardment of the city, the *Chattanooga Gazette & Advertiser* ceased publication. In July, the presses of the *Gazette & Advertiser* were leased by Franc M. Paul, a former clerk of the Tennessee senate, to publish a journal for circulation within the Confederate army. A consummate supporter of the Confederacy, Paul published the first issue of Chattanooga's successor newspaper on August 1, 1862. It was appropriately named *The Daily Rebel*. It was to continue as a daily paper until April 1865, with few and brief interruptions, continuing publication at other locations after the Federal occupation of Chattanooga. While it is doubtful that Joseph subscribed to Paul's newspaper, copies of it would be available in the Salem Community for his review along with the other local paper, the *Cleveland Banner*.[99]

By July 20, Buell's Union army had reached Stevenson, Alabama, thirty miles west of Chattanooga and had captured the junction with the Nashville and Chattanooga Railroad. Kirby Smith, faced with fighting an enemy both at Chattanooga and at Cumberland Gap 180 miles away, withdrew from Cumberland Gap and focused his army on lower East Tennessee. Simultaneously on July 27, advanced units of Bragg's Confederate army arrived in Chattanooga, and on July 29, Bragg arrived to establish his headquarters in the city. By the first of the following month, over 35,000 Confederate soldiers were within the environs of Chattanooga. Camps were established as far east as Harrison, and Joseph Roark saw for the first time the impact of the presence of large armies as the troops foraged for food in the countryside. Picket lines were established along the Tennessee and Hiwassee Rivers and picket campfires consumed wood from rail fences of Salem farms. War had come to the Salem Community.

By August 1, Generals Bragg and Kirby Smith were meeting in Chattanooga to plan an offensive northward into Kentucky to free Middle Tennessee of the Federal occupation. On August 13, Kirby Smith moved his army north out of Knoxville toward Barbourville, Kentucky.[100] In Chattanooga, Bragg prepared for the overland march of his army by confiscating all usable wagons, harness, and horses in the Hamilton County area.[101] He organized his army of 28,000 with the right wing under

Maj. Gen. Leonidas Polk and the left wing under Maj. Gen. William Hardee. On August 20, Polk began the movement of the right wing along the south side of the Tennessee with General Cheatham's division in the lead followed by Wither's division. As Cheatham's division moved north, Joseph Roark and the Salem Community saw for the first time a large army on the move. Polk moved his army across the Tennessee by flatboats at Harrison, Igou's Ferry and Blythe's Ferry.[102] As the troops moved north along the Birchwood Pike, foraging parties purchased corn for the horses and beef/pork for the soldiers from the local farms. Corn crops were appraised by the foraging officers and the appraised value was paid to the farmer. Payment was made by requisition orders redeemable in Confederate bonds. Since this was home country, foraging officers were careful to compensate each farmer in a fair and equitable manner. As Gen. Withers followed Cheatham's division north, Withers asked for a follow-up on foraging payments in a report to the Assistant Adjutant General under Bragg:

> Major Williamson
>   Assistant Adjutant General
>   . . . Moving forward has prevented my sending back officers to appraise and pay for that field of corn. Can the order not be given to the quartermaster at Chattanooga to attend to it?
>   Very respectfully, etc.
>
>   J.M. Withers
>   Major General[103]

Doubtless the crops of Joseph Roark and others in the Salem Community helped supply Bragg's army as it moved north into Kentucky.

When Kirby Smith's army moved out of Knoxville, Joseph and Juda were aware that their three sons were part of the march. In late April, the 3rd Cavalry Battalion had been assigned to Kirby Smith, and on May 12, it had been renamed the 14th Confederate Cavalry Battalion. Command of the battalion had been assigned to Lt. Col. James E. Carter. From May through the first of August, the battalion had operated in light cavalry action against Union forces in Greeneville, Tennessee, and at Cumberland Gap.[104]

In mid August, while the army of Kirby Smith was on its march to Kentucky, Joseph received a request signed by both sons Jim and John asking him to "let Mr. Webb have five dollars for value received of him." Written August 10, the note, without letter or explanation, was in the handwriting of John and it appears that both signatures were written by the same hand. Perhaps the note was hand carried by Mr. Webb to Joseph; nevertheless, the request represents the only correspondence to Joseph, from any of his sons, that has been preserved. The mystery of the request becomes more interesting when on September 29, Joseph was issued a pass from the Confederate provost marshal in Cleveland for Joseph to travel, probably by rail, to Knoxville:

Office Dept. Provost Marshal
No. 1219   Cleveland, Tennessee   Sept. 29, 1862

Permission is granted Joseph Roark to visit Knoxville and Back upon honor not to communicate in writing or otherwise any conditional fact ascertained which if known to the enemy might be injurious to the Confederate S. America

W.L. Loffish   D.P. Marshal

On the reverse side of the pass is a written and sworn statement of allegiance signed by Joseph, which had been necessary to obtain the pass:

I, Joseph Roark, do solemnly swear or affirm that I will bear true faith and yield obediance to the Confederate States of America and that I will serve them honestly and faithfully against their enemies.

Joseph Roark   Sept 29, 1862[105]

One might conclude from the slimmest of evidence that Jim and John had been in some kind of trouble in Knoxville that required financial help from Joseph. Not only did Joseph pay Webb the requested amount, but he also went through the trouble of a trip to Chattanooga to handle some situation while his sons were with Kirby Smith in Kentucky. Unfortunately, no other records shed any light on the issue.

Prior to his trip to Knoxville, Joseph and Juda tried to follow the progress of Kirby Smith's army in Kentucky. On August 28, the *Cleveland Banner* carried the following:

From Kentucky. — The Knoxville register of the 26th inst., says reliable information has been received here that our forces in Kentucky have captured some two hundred wagons. We hope it is so, and they will continue to pick them up, and likewise the Feds who are supplied by them.[106]

Kirby Smith's army in Kentucky defeated a Federal army in Richmond, occupied Frankfort, and frightened Cincinnati with a raid on Covington on the south bank of the Ohio. When Bragg's army arrived in Kentucky, he engaged the Union army at Perryville and won a decisive victory. Bragg hesitated, however, much to the disappointment of his army and especially to Kirby Smith, and withdrew with his army back to Tennessee. *The Daily Rebel* in Chattanooga carried a report on the Kentucky campaign on Sunday, October 19, 1862:

NEWS FROM KENTUCKY

We met on yesterday with Captain H.A. Rogers of the 9th Tennessee Regiment who was in the fight at Perryville last week. –From him we learn that our forces gained a decided victory. Our loss was about thirty-five hundred in killed and wounded and the enemy's about ten thousand in killed and wounded and about ten thousand prisoners. We lost no general officers. The enemy fell back to Lebanon and our forces concentrated at or near Camp Dick Robinson. The principal fight was on Wednesday. We captured a large quantity of artillery. Our army is in fine spirits and would soon be ready for another battle. He left there on Friday night.[107]

After Bragg's disappointing retreat from Kentucky, Kirby Smith returned with his army to Knoxville while Hardee's wing of Bragg's army went by train to Chattanooga and then north to Murfreesboro to face the Union army again moving south out of Nashville. Polk's wing of the army and the wagon trains moved south along the Tennessee to Smith's Cross Roads (Dayton) and then over Walden Ridge to Murfreesboro.

In late November, Joseph and Juda heard of changes in the military unit of their three sons. November 14, 1862, had been a big day for the 14th Battalion and its commander, Lieut. Col. James E. Carter. On that date, with the reorganization of Kirby Smith's army, the battalion was elevated to a regiment, to be known as the First Tennessee Cavalry, and Carter was promoted to colonel. Four companies were added to the regiment and the company of Joseph's sons, Company C, was redesignated as Company B. The First Tennessee Cavalry was in turn assigned, along with four other regiments, to Brig. Gen. John Pegram's Brigade. In early December, the brigade was moved to Murfreesboro and was placed under the command of Gen. Joseph Wheeler and would participate in the anticipated battle for Middle Tennessee.[108]

At Murfreesboro, Bragg established his headquarters and fanned his army out in a wide semicircle southeast of Nashville to block any advance by Gen. William S. Rosecrans who, having replaced Buell, then commanded the Union forces in Nashville. On December 26, Rosecrans started his army of 47,000 out of Nashville toward Chattanooga to face Bragg with an army of 38,000. As the two armies approached each other and prepared for battle, General Wheeler was assigned the responsibility of harassing and delaying the Federal army as much as possible in its move south. To do this, Wheeler began, very early on December 30, a raid with several regiments, including the First Tennessee Cavalry, which would take them on a daring raid completely around the flank and rear of the whole Federal army. In the circuitous route around the Union position, Wheeler's cavalry destroyed Union wagon trains, captured and paroled numerous Union troops, left a trail of devastation in its wake, and brought in enough captured guns to arm a brigade. After the raid, Wheeler's cavalry joined the left flank of Bragg's army which had, during the first day of the battle, driven the Union forces back three or four miles toward Nashville. Initially it appeared that the battle of Murfreesboro was to be an overwhelming victory for the South. Similar however to Shiloh, the second day belonged to the North as Rosecrans' army recovered to occupy the field as Bragg retreated to Tullahoma with Wheeler's cavalry covering his retreat.[109] Joseph and the Salem Community soon were to learn of the participation of the First Tennessee Cavalry in Wheeler's raid. But with the Federal army then south of Murfreesboro, the war was getting ever closer to Chattanooga and Hamilton County.

The first six months of 1863 were relatively quiet in Middle Tennessee as both armies rested, reorganized, and trained. In East Tennessee, however, guerrilla warfare increased. The number of guerrilla bands multiplied as deserters and men fleeing conscription formed bands for the purposes of escape, survival, and plunder. Both Union and Confederate deserters were involved when desertions increased as the war progressed. With no civil government to provide protection for families on widely separated farms, the civilian population was particularly susceptible to the guerrilla menace. Few households in the Salem Community escaped the terrifying raids by guerrillas both day and night. Robberies of helpless farm households were common as guerrillas sought valuables to increase their plunder:

> These crimes demonstrate the blurred distinctions in the partisan war, for theft could result from hardship, greed, revenge, political calculation, or all these motives at once. But regardless of their motives criminal attacks could be as ruthless and terrifying as other partisan operations. Robbers strung up men by their necks, whipped them, or threatened to burn their homes until they revealed where their money and other valuables were hidden. Sometimes they also shot their victims after finishing their robbery. Neither women nor children were immune from this violence, and a number of women were hanged or tortured by robbers.[110]

In addition to guerrilla bands, local farmers suffered under local raiders, bands made up of both Confederate and Union supporters, seeking retribution and harassing local opponents. The impacts of the internal civil war were devastating:

> It pitted family members against each other, split communities into factions, and erased former friendships. But perhaps no institution suffered more from the polarization of the population than the churches in East Tennessee.[111]

In the midst of the Salem Community stood the Salem Baptist Church, which continued to serve the community during the conflicts of "the civil war within a civil war." Church records are not available for the Civil War period to describe the resolution of the many conflicts which doubtless occurred within the church's membership. Church minutes and membership rolls for the years immediately following the war reflect a membership made up of former supporters of both the Union and Southern causes, as well as veterans of both armies. While the divisiveness during the war must have seriously tested the Christian faith of the church members, records of the church following the war indicate strong ties of faith that apparently carried the church through the storm. We can today, however, only imagine the emotions within the church as it met to worship during the years 1862 to 1865.

Doubtless the church provided support to individual members as sickness, sorrow, and death visited the homes represented in the church. Joseph and Juda doubtless felt the support of the church during this period when the health of their daughter Jerusha began to seriously fail. Never healthy and always to suffer from seizures, Jerusha responded poorly to treatment and sometime, during the early years of the war–we do not know exactly when–her life of suffering, both within herself and for her parents, ended. She was buried in the new Bald Hill Cemetery on Birchwood Pike three miles south of the homestead. No grave marker remains.

At the death of Jerusha, Joseph and Juda were to share the grief of their daughter, Elizabeth, whose oldest daughter, Amanda, died in 1863 at the age of sixteen. Elizabeth grieved without the support of her husband who was then with the Federal army. Both families sought and received the comfort of the Salem church in their loss and grief.

The church fellowship also provided consolation and help to Joseph's brother John when he received word in February 1863 that his son William had died while serving with the Seventh Tennessee Infantry (Union) in Kentucky. William had been in the Union army just over four months when he became ill. He died of pneumonia on January 29 at Nicholasville and was buried in the cemetery nearby.[112]

The financial condition of the South including Hamilton County and the Salem Community continued to deteriorate during the first half of 1863. Conditions resulting from the war destroyed the system of promissory notes that had been used by the Salem Community for almost thirty years. Farmers of reputation and sincere intent simply could not commit to making payments at some future date and, similarly, few would accept payment in the form of a promissory note–the risk was just too high. Joseph Roark accepted a promissory note for the last time in February 1863 and suffered the loss of its total value. Probably for the sale of corn or pork, Joseph, in his own hand, had written out the following promissory note:

> one day after date we or either one of us promise to pay Joseph Roark one hundred and ten dollars for value recieved of him   this 9th day of February 1863
>
>
>
> his
>
> Wilson X Hixon
>
> mark
>
> John W. Smith[113]
>
>

Joseph was unable to collect on the note and it was ultimately filed with his papers as an unpaid promissory note. It was the last promissory note Joseph was to accept for the duration of the war. It was not, however, the last time Joseph would be loser in dealing with Wilson Hixson.

During the summer of 1863, both the Confederate army under Bragg and the Union army under Rosecrans moved closer and closer to Chattanooga. The two armies together totaled 100,000 men that had to be fed by foraging through the countryside and through supply lines extending over hundreds of miles. It was during this period that the South and particularly Hamilton County, then in the path of two large armies, began to seriously suffer under shortages resulting from the war. The Confederate government, on March 26, 1863, passed an act of impressment to better supply and feed its army. Under the act, the seizure of livestock and forage was permitted by officers appointed by each state. Seizure was not permitted, however, until after an appraisal had been made by the impressment officer. A certificate of payment was to be provided to the owner. To meet the supply demands of the Confederate army, impressment became more severe as the war progressed. Crops and foodstuffs were taken in wholesale quantities along with horses, mules, and wagons.[114]

Joseph Roark and the rest of the Salem Community began to desperately feel the shortages in early 1863. After salt, one of the first items to be in short supply was coffee. Families in Hamilton County and throughout the South found substitutes for coffee including parched particles of sweet potatoes, peanuts, rye, corn, and okra. Sugar was also in short supply and sorghum molasses became an almost universal substitute. The shortage of salt continued to be a serious problem for farmers as large quantities were needed by the army for meat preservation. In trying to meet the shortage, many farmers scraped the dirt from smoke house floors to recover what little salt might be available. Before actual food shortages were to impact the Salem Community later in the war, fats of all kind were scarce in early 1863. These included butter, oil, lard, and mayonnaise. Both the armies in the field and the civilian population of the Confederacy had begun to suffer the deprivations of war.[115]

With Joseph's sons in the army, following the battle of Murfreesboro and a raid to Fort Donelson, the First Tennessee Cavalry and Pegram's brigade was transferred from Wheeler's cavalry and ordered to Knoxville. Through the spring and early summer of 1863, the First Tennessee Cavalry was involved in activities to harass the supply lines of Rosecrans' army north of Chattanooga. During the summer, Jim Roark returned home on furlough and, while on furlough, he married America Jane McGill, daughter of William J. McGill of the Sale Creek area north of the river. The McGills had settled on Sale Creek as early as 1807, and William McGill had done business with Joseph Roark on several occasions. McGill was a strong supporter of the Confederacy. The wedding, more than likely, took place in the home of the bride's parents and the vows were read by the local Sale Creek minister. Without a honeymoon, Jim moved his new wife to the Roark homestead and lived with her there until the end of his furlough. Shortly after Jim's return to the First Tennessee Cavalry at Loudon, Tennessee, Pegram's Brigade was reassigned to Wheeler's Cavalry in support of Bragg at Chattanooga.[116]

During the summer, Bragg's army continued to retreat in Middle Tennessee and surrendered large areas of rich farm land with abundant crops to the Federal army. By mid July, the Army of Tennessee had retreated across the Tennessee River and had returned to Chattanooga. The first week in July, Hamilton County received the news that Lee had been defeated at Gettysburg and that Pemberton had surrendered the Confederate garrison at Vicksburg. Bragg's retreat across the Tennessee, combined with the losses at Gettysburg and Vicksburg, signaled dark days ahead for the Confederacy.

As Bragg's army settled south of the Tennessee, Cleburne's division was assigned to the area between Harrison and the Hiwassee River. General Cleburne established his headquarters at Tyner's station on the railroad and distributed his forces to guard every ford and ferry from the mouth of Chickamauga Creek to the Hiwassee River. Joseph Roark saw troops continually move past the homestead as Cleburne moved to construct rifle pits and place artillery at Thatcher's Ferry, Gardenhire's Ferry, and Blythe's Ferry. Clayton's Brigade was placed on the north bank of the Hiwassee across from Jolly's Island. Maj. Gen. Pat Cleburne was an energetic and gifted soldier, a native of Ireland, and a successful lawyer from Arkansas. Ever enthusiastic about his assigned task, Cleburne was seen frequently on the Birchwood Pike as he moved to allocate his resources and to inspect the work being done. Cleburne's army was forced to forage for food, and the local farmers saw their corn fields, livestock, and poultry consumed by the army's foragers. Corn cribs were emptied to supply the horses and mules supporting the artillery. Soldiers camped on pasture land, and with the recent heavy rains, grasses were trodden under the feet of horses and men. Rail fences on Roark's land and others in the community were removed to feed the numerous campfires of platoons and companies. Even with the devastation naturally resulting from the camp of an army, Joseph Roark and the Salem Community gained from the army's presence and felt some relief from guerrilla raids and bushwhackers as Cleburne's division established, for a brief period, a rule of law and order. It was evident to all, however, that a major battle was in the making.[117]

On August 21, Union troops north of the Tennessee began shelling Chattanooga and, in the afternoon of the same day, Federal troops appeared on the north bank of the Tennessee at Blythe's Ferry. On Saturday, August 22, Union guns shelled Harrison, and the following Wednesday, the Confederate company commander at Gardenhire's Ferry reported that his company had been shelled in their camp by Federal units from across the river. Joseph and Juda with the rest of the Salem Community heard close at hand the thunder of artillery and the rattle of musketry.[118]

The activity by the Federal units across the Tennessee from the Salem Community was actually a diversionary tactic of Rosecrans as his main army crossed the Tennessee southwest of Chattanooga. After Rosecrans' surprise crossing of the river, Bragg was forced to abandon Chattanooga. He moved his army through Rossville toward Rome, Georgia, recalling Cleburne's division from the Harrison area. Confederate cavalry screened the move of Cleburne's division south of Chickamauga Creek. As the Tenth Confederate Cavalry moved past the Roark homestead, the unit commander noticed a bay horse in the barn. Always in need of horses, the acquisition agent for the regiment approached Joseph and left him with an acquisition receipt for "one bay horse worth two hundred & fifty dollars for the use of the CSA."[119]

For a brief period, Joseph and the Salem Community were in "no man's land" between the two armies. As a result, the bushwhacker menace returned. Marauding bands–civilians, deserters, and dodgers of conscription–scoured the countryside. Bushwhacking gangsters and ragtag groups of men on horseback, who often maliciously claimed military status, swarmed through the area, burning, looting, and killing.[120]

In Chattanooga, almost totally abandoned by August 30, *The Daily Rebel* issued its Sunday paper from the safety of the basement of the Bank of Tennessee:

> Sat. 6 o'clock P.M.
> The enemies batteries opened on the town at 10 o'clock this morning, from works nearly opposite Cameron Hill. The firing continued for about an hour. The balls did little damage to men or houses. Quite a dust from Main street was the cause. All quiet at this hour. No news of consequence.
>
> ---
>
> At this writing, 12 o'clock midnight, the enemy are shelling the town vigorously. Our sanctum and our solitary printer, with his "case" and composing stick, are removed to the basement of the Bank of Tennessee.[121]

In the first few days of September, Rosecrans split his command after crossing the Tennessee, sending McCook's Corps through Winston Gap and Thomas' Corps through Steven's Gap in Lookout Mountain. Bragg, with his Confederate army moving out of Chattanooga, saw the opportunity of attacking the individual segments of Rosecrans army before they could be consolidated east of the mountains. Bragg had an advantage in that he was personally familiar with the local topography since he had served under Gen. Winfield Scott in the Cherokee removal twenty-five years before. Meanwhile at Richmond, it was decided to send Gen. James Longstreet with two divisions from Lee's army to assist Bragg. In what was the first major strategic deployment of an army by rail, Longstreet moved his two divisions south from Richmond to Charleston and Savannah and then north through Atlanta to Chickamauga Creek south of Rossville, Tennessee. To the northeast, General Burnside had moved his Union army out of Kentucky into East Tennessee and south to Knoxville. By September 2, Burnside occupied Knoxville and was in control of the northern half of East Tennessee. Along Chickamauga Creek, Bragg was delayed in beginning his attack against the two corps of Rosecrans and, as a result, the battle of Chickamauga did not begin until Saturday, September 19. It was to be the bloodiest battle in the western theater of the Civil War.

By late Sunday, the Union forces had been routed except for a heroic stand by Thomas' Corps. The Federal army retreated into Chattanooga and Confederate forces took up siege positions on Missionary Ridge and Lookout Mountain. The large majority of Confederate wounded in the battle of Chickamauga were taken by train to Atlanta. Some, however, were taken to a field hospital at the Salem Baptist Church. There Joseph Roark was to see firsthand the tragic results from the horrors of war.[122]

Rather than follow up on his victory and pursue the Union army as his subordinates suggested, Bragg decided to cut the supply lines for Rosecrans' army and to starve the Union troops into surrender. Inside Chattanooga, the Federal army attended its wounded and prepared for a siege. Bragg distributed his army south and east of the city and in the surrounding countryside. Confederate soldiers again occupied the Salem Community and took up defensive positions along the Hiwassee against a possible move south by Burnside.

Again Joseph saw the movement of large bodies of soldiers as the Confederate army sought to recover from the battle and to establish the right flank of Bragg's army along the Hiwassee. A movement of cavalry north along Birchwood Pike was particularly noticeable early on the morning of Tuesday, September 29. Strung out along the road for several miles was Wheeler's Cavalry, made up of Wharton's and Martin's divisions. Included in the march was the First Tennessee Cavalry and Joseph's three sons. Wheeler was on a raid to destroy wagon trains in Sequatchie Valley attempting to supply the Union army in Chattanooga. Riding through enemy-occupied country and hoping to also attack McMinnville and Murfreesboro, Wheeler had to guard against stragglers or Union supporters that would give away his objective. Hence there would be no time for the First Tennessee troopers from the Salem Community to visit their families. Only a brief wave or acknowledgment could have occurred as the First Tennessee Cavalry forded Grasshopper Creek at the Joseph Roark homestead.[123]

In the midst of the confusion of combating armies, the movement of troops, and unstable conditions of war, Joseph was approached by his son-in-law Robert Beane Scott on Tuesday, October 27, with a note from R.A. Sloan:

> Mr. Joseph Roark
> Please send by Mr. Scott six dollars the full of my medical claim against you.
> Oct. 27, 1863
>
> R.A. Sloan[124]

Obviously, Scott was only a messenger. The medical services had been for Joseph's family, and Sloan was used because of the unavailability of Dr. Yarnell. Little comfort was derived from knowing that invoices could be received even during war and under the most difficult circumstances. Doubtless Joseph struggled to accumulate the six dollars to keep medical bills current.

In Chattanooga, Rosecrans was replaced by Thomas as commander of the army following the designation of Gen. Ulysses S. Grant as commander of all Union forces between the Appalachian chain and the Mississippi.[125] Grant immediately took steps to gain reinforcements and to provide a supply line to the Union soldiers in Chattanooga living on short rations. In the headquarters of the Army of Tennessee, Bragg conceived an idea to hurriedly move Longstreet's two divisions north to Knoxville to defeat Burnside and then return to Chattanooga to oppose any attempted breakout by the Union army. Longstreet began the move with 15,000 troops on

November 4 and entrained his two divisions at Tyner's station for Knoxville. Assigned to him were Alexander's artillery and Wheeler's cavalry, both of whom were to travel by road west of the ET&G railroad used by Longstreet. Again Confederate troops moved northward along the Birchwood Pike past Joseph Roark's homestead.[126]

As both Union and Confederate armies were now living almost entirely "off the land," Joseph Roark and the Salem Community began to experience an extreme shortage of food. Soldiers in Longstreet's army noted that civilians suffered from the army's foraging and many "poor defenseless Southern women and many poor helpless children" faced starvation.[127] A Federal leader of a foraging party in the Chattanooga area noted that:

> The thieves who accompany our forage and supply trains are . . . no respecters of persons. When they discover a hen roost, sheep, or hogs, they do not stop to inquire the sentiments of the owners; neither does it concern them if they are about to take the last sheep or hog belonging to the family . . . almost every garden is found stripped and one will hardly discover a chicken or hog.[128]

On November 23, Joseph Roark could hear the thunder of artillery from Chattanooga as the Union army began its breakout. Federal troops moved against Lookout Mountain and Missionary Ridge on November 24, and by nightfall the following day, Union forces occupied both locations. Bragg's army again retreated into Georgia, and the Salem Community was occupied by Federal soldiers. The first Union troops to enter the Salem Community were those of the Fourth Ohio Cavalry and the Second Cavalry Brigade under Col. Eli Long. As Federal troops occupied Missionary Ridge and the Confederates retreated, Long's cavalry moved east out of Chattanooga on the road to Cleveland, destroying freight cars at Ooltewah and driving the Confederate cavalry out of Cleveland. From Cleveland, Long moved north to Charleston on the Hiwassee destroying the railroad and rail cars. After an attack by Confederate cavalry at Charleston, Long moved west across Candies Creek, through Birchwood, and south on Birchwood Pike past the Roark homestead to Harrison and Chattanooga. Long's men were the first Federal soldiers Joseph saw. Doubtless, with his knowledge and experience with the Confederate cavalry in their homespun butternut and makeshift equipment, Joseph was overwhelmed by the well-clothed and well-armed Union troopers.[129]

Joseph was soon to see other Federal troops on the move. On November 27, Grant ordered General Sherman to move his Union army north to Knoxville to relieve Burnside who was then under siege by Longstreet. Sherman moved two corps from Ringgold through Cleveland to Charleston, where he waited on repair of the railroad bridge over the Hiwassee. He also moved two divisions under Granger's command north along Birchwood Pike, crossing the Hiwassee at Kincannon's Ferry east of Sugar Creek.[130] It was a day of bitter cold November 29 when Joseph and Juda watched from the homestead as Granger's soldiers forded Grasshopper Creek. What were Joseph's thoughts as he watched the passage of the Union army and heard it splashing the waters of Grasshopper Creek? Did he wonder how long the war was to continue? Did his mind's eye see again the peaceful and prosperous days before the war when his whole family was together? Did he not wonder about the welfare of his sons–whether they were alive and, if so, were they in good health or was one or perhaps all three sick, cold, and miserable in some field hospital? Would they survive the war? Doubtless he could see that the South was defeated. What did the future hold? Could he and Juda live through the hard days that obviously lay ahead? Nearby, in Cleveland, Myra Inman noted in her diary for November 29:

> The Yanks came in town this evening about 3 o'clock. Gen. Sherman's Co. camped all around us tonight, robbing us of our corn, potatoes, and taking all our chickens, left only two . . . The soldiers are in Uncle Ned's house and in the kitchen stealing and taking everything they can get. Took Aunt P's quilt off her bed . . . We sit in the house with bowed-down heads while the victorious army passes along with waving banners.[131]

By December 11, Sherman had relieved Knoxville as Longstreet moved further north in East Tennessee to make his winter encampment at Rogersville. Sherman returned south, establishing his army along the south bank of the Hiwassee. Joseph Roark was again to see Federal troops on the move, this time to the south. The Fourth Army Corps, under General Granger, returned from the Knoxville campaign, crossing the Hiwassee at Kincannon's Ferry. The First Division of the Fourth Corps, under Maj. Gen. D.S. Stanley, was ordered to take a position for the winter between Chickamauga Depot and the Hiwassee River. While the area was locked in a period of bitter cold with temperatures well below zero, Joseph was to see Stanley's division establish its winter quarters all along the Birchwood Pike between Harrison and the Hiwassee. During this period, Sherman had his engineers prepare a map of the area south of the Hiwassee and west of the ET&G railroad, identifying the occupant of each farmhouse. Obviously the purpose was to locate both Confederate and Union supporters.[132]

Confederate cavalry raids through the various passes in Whiteoak Mountain harassed the Federal garrisons throughout the winter. Bushwhacking raids tormented all households, Union and Confederate supporters alike. It was a time of great suffering by all the civilian population. During the past twelve months, both armies had traversed eastern Hamilton County four times, living off the land. In late 1863, William Clift, now back in Chattanooga, expressed the opinion that scarcely an acre of corn was left from Chattanooga to Rhea County–"The army is consuming everything in the shape of substanance[sic] in lower East Tennessee."[133]

In January 1864, with almost all of Tennessee cleared of Confederate forces, radical politicians plotted the takeover of the state government. In October, "Parson" William Brownlow had returned to Knoxville from the North where he had traveled extensively on speaking engagements. As a result of his speaking in support of Lincoln's conduct of the war, Brownlow had been named by the Federal government as special treasury agent for East Tennessee, a post that made him a virtual dictator over commercial affairs. No one might sell goods, buy goods, or import goods without his consent. He also had control over any property abandoned by Confederate supporters. Brownlow energetically used his office as treasury agent to reward his friends, punish his enemies, and increase his political power.[134] The Federal government also supplied Brownlow with a printing press, paper, and supplies plus $1,500 to start again his printing operations in Knoxville.[135] In November, Brownlow began publication of the *Knoxville Whig and Rebel Ventilator* and began to spew forth his vitriolic hatred of all who had supported the Confederacy. In speaking of those who supported the Confederacy, Brownlow wrote, "Let the Imps of Hell die the death of traitors and upon the shortest possible notice."[136]

In December, President Lincoln had proclaimed the policy by which states could be readmitted to the Union–if ten percent of the state's voters in 1860 took a loyalty or amnesty oath, a new state government could be established and the state readmitted. Steps to that end were begun in Tennessee. On January 26, 1864, Andrew Johnson, as military governor, ordered an election for March 5 of all county officers in the state, promulgated an amnesty oath much more severe than the one by Lincoln, and ordered that only "loyal" persons would be allowed to vote.[137] In the election held in Hamilton County on Saturday, March 5, only seventy-five persons voted.[138] A county court was elected along with the county clerk, sheriff, and other officers. In a meeting of the elected officials April 12, Peter Mounger was elected chairman of the county court, and the new county government organized itself. George W. Rider was sworn in as sheriff, John Kimbrough as deputy sheriff, and James P. Talley and Joseph Cookston as justice of the peace and constable, respectively, for District 10 which included the Salem Community. In one of its first actions the County Court appointed William Clift as one of a committee of five "to regulate and levy a tax upon property and polls for 1864."[139]

Unionists were in control in East Tennessee after March 1864. Brownlow repeatedly stated in his *Whig and Rebel Ventilator* that Unionists and secessionists could not live together in East Tennessee, and he called on all Confederate supporters to leave the state altogether. In regard to local Confederate leaders, Brownlow suggested that Union people would be "justified in shooting them down on sight, and we shall regard hundreds of them as wanting in courage and in resentment if they do not dispatch them whenever they meet their rotten carcasses."[140]

In Hamilton County, the winter of early 1864 was the most punishing period in the war years.[141] Conditions were described as extremely difficult:

> During the winter of 1864, ten thousand army animals died in East Tennessee for lack of feed and forage. Many civilians were forced to let

their horses and cattle die for the same reason. Travelers in the spring of 1864 commented on the scarcity of the stock and the emaciated condition of the few seen. Barns looked empty, almost no fences were still standing, and hogs and poultry were rare sights.[142]

In Chattanooga, rations accumulated to support Sherman's army when it was to move south toward Atlanta were distributed to destitute citizens. In eastern Hamilton County where both armies had stripped the area clean, "a siege atmosphere" seemed to exist.[143] Joseph and Juda Roark and others in the Salem Community survived on what had been hidden and preserved. Many families lived solely on boiled corn and sweet potatoes. Clothing was scarce and none was available for purchase. Old clothes were made over several times until they fell into shreds. Women returned to knitting, cording, spinning, and weaving as arts learned during the pioneer days of the Ocoee district were again put into practice. Juda Roark took up again the spinning wheel and loom for her family. Additionally, she apparently provided material for her neighbors. On May 24, 1864, Juda received a note from W.C. Thatcher asking her to provide to Mrs. McCormack three and one-half yards of cotton frocking and "I will settle with you for it," adding, "If not that amount two and one-half will much oblige."[144]

The shortage of shoes was a particular problem. During the shortage, shoes were made from leather tanned at home. When sole leather was unavailable, wood was used for the sole and the upper leather was tacked to the wood sole. Carpets, too, were cut up and used for shoes; however, many carpets found their way into suits and coats. By 1864, bedding had been worn out in most homes and could not be replaced. It was the usual thing to find ragged sheets and pillow cases in even the finest homes. The scarcest commodity, however, was soap. When soap was no longer available for purchase, oil from corn shucks and chinaberries was used in the home manufacture of "poor man's soap."[145]

The situation in East Tennessee became so desperate in 1864 that relief societies were formed in northern states to provide money and quantities of needed materials. Donors contributed a sum exceeding $250,000. Organizations like the Sanitary Commission, the Pennsylvania Relief Society, and the East Tennessee Relief Society distributed clothes and food to East Tennessee citizens. Distribution was, however, selective. Union families were assisted first, followed by those who had taken the amnesty oath, and, lastly, distribution was made to persons like Juda and Joseph who had immediate family members in the Confederate army. All relief distribution agencies employed a common specification–no Confederate supporter of "fighting age" would be given consideration.[146]

To assist in relief distribution, the Hamilton County Court, in some of its first actions as a newly formed body, approved, on April 5, 1864, a motion that included:

> it appearing . . . that a large sum of money has been donated by the good people of the Northern States . . . that in no portion of Tennessee, or any other part of the Government has the suffering of the people been greater,

than in Hamilton County . . . [that] Rev. Hiram Douglas is appointed as an agent for the County of Hamilton, with full power and authority to receive any and all contributions . . . and distribute such supplies . . . and employ such aid and assistance as he may think necessary and proper.[147]

It is highly unlikely that Joseph Roark either was offered or accepted such relief assistance.

Cash money was practically nonexistent in the Salem Community. If per chance a family had saved some Confederate notes, they were unusable within the Federal area of occupation. Gold and silver had passed completely out of circulation by 1864, and bank notes, even in a depreciated value, gradually disappeared. Any bank notes saved or held back had to be carefully hidden from robbers, marauders, and pillagers.[148]

Joseph and Juda had a particularly difficult time in early 1864. It was, more than likely, during this period that their two young daughters failed to survive the terrible conditions and poor diet of the times. The payment for medical services requested by R.A. Sloan could very well have been for medical help for Nancy and Susannah. Nancy would have been sixteen and Susannah thirteen in early 1864. We know nothing of their deaths nor the order in which they died; however, the tragedy and deep sorrow felt by both parents can be imagined. Doubtless both Nancy and Susannah were buried next to Jerusha in the Bald Hill Cemetery in unmarked graves. Remaining at home with Joseph and Juda after the loss of their two daughters were Jim's wife America, then pregnant with her first child, Juda Ann Brooks, and Jim Carr. In late spring, America's baby was born, a girl. She was named Nancy after her maternal grandmother.

In January, Joseph and Juda had a visit from their daughter Elizabeth who had walked from her nearby home. She was distressed–her husband Joel had deserted from the Union army the last of December and was determined not to go back. Joel Talley had not related well to military service. He had returned home in February 1863 without leave and, as a result, had been court-martialed, sentenced to hard labor for thirty days and to forfeit a month's pay. Talley's daughter, Amanda, had died in 1863, possibly near the time of Joel's absence without leave, and, if the two events were related, Talley's AWOL status would, at least partially, be excusable. This time, however, Joel was to remain at home for the duration of the war, probably without incident since the Union army did not pursue deserters in the latter stages of the war.[149]

In early February 1864, during that terrible winter of Federal military occupation, Joseph made a trip to Chattanooga. Why he made the trip is unknown, but doubtless he considered the trip of utmost importance since travel at that particular time was extremely difficult. Steamboats were not running on the river and he probably walked the entire distance, either not having a horse available to him or not wanting to risk the loss of a horse to Union army confiscation. As he walked the 30 miles to his destination, Joseph would have been stopped and interrogated many times. With the Federal army in control, all travel by civilians was restricted and any movement required a pass from the office of the Federal Provost Marshal. In spite of the difficultly in travel, Joseph made the trip. Was it related to the death of his daughters and was it an attempt to get medicine for them in their final illnesses? We can only wonder. Prior to leaving Chattanooga, Joseph applied for and received a "pass" for his return trip. Issued on a printed form of the Provost Marshal General's Office, Headquarters Department of the Cumberland, the pass was written by R. Colt, who signed for William M. Wiley, Provost Marshal General, "By the Order of Major General Geo. H. Thomas." The handwritten pass by Colt read as follows:

No. 2056   Chattanooga, Feb. 6, 1864
Pass Joseph Roark to his home ten (10) miles above Harrison on south side of the Tenn. River.[150]

Joseph and Juda knew little about the location or health of their three sons. Mail delivery had ceased with the Federal occupation and little news arrived from any of the Confederate units.[151] If word was received from the First Tennessee Cavalry by someone in the Salem Community, it doubtless was shared. Perhaps Joseph and Juda were aware that the First Tennessee Cavalry, by then dismounted and fighting as infantry, was in Bristol assigned to Vaughn's Brigade for action in Virginia's Shenandoah Valley.[152] Some flow of information increased with the renewed publication of a Chattanooga newspaper. Following the occupation of the city by Federal troops in the fall of 1863 and the move south by *The Daily Rebel*, James R. Hood returned to Chattanooga to again publish his paper. His first issue appeared February 29, 1864, under the banner of the *Chattanooga Daily Gazette*.[153]

In Chattanooga, General Sherman prepared his army for the campaign in Georgia. His army was made up of 100,000 men under Generals Thomas, McPherson, and Schofield. Sherman had accumulated mass stores of supplies in Chattanooga for a hard-driving campaign against Gen. Joseph E. Johnston, then commanding the Confederate Army of Tennessee. Throughout the first four months of 1864, Sherman's army was encamped along a line from Chattanooga through Cleveland to Charleston on the Hiwassee. The large number of Federal troops in the area significantly reduced the guerrilla and bushwhacker activity. For that the Salem Community was thankful. On May 7, Sherman started his army forward, personally taking command in the field. Soon the Chattanooga area was practically empty of soldiers, with only the local commands remaining for supply and provost martial duty. As soon as the army had departed, guerrilla activity and marauder raids started in earnest.[154]

At the first of the war guerrillas had restricted their activities to mainly military targets, but in Hamilton County in the late spring of 1864, civilians became fair game–marauding parties of guerrillas pillaged and persecuted. "Men were taken from their homes at night and whipped, beaten, and sometimes murdered. Food was stolen, citizens robbed, barns burned, cattle driven off, and crops trampled by men on horseback." Confederate deserters and parolees made up some bands of pillagers; vengeful Unionists retaliating against Confederate treatment early in the war made up others. With no army, Union or Confederate, of sufficient size to preserve order nor with a local government capable of enforcing the law, the sparsely populated rural areas of Hamilton County suffered.[155]

Joseph Roark personally felt the brutality of marauders. In one instance he was threatened with hanging if he did not reveal the location of valuables that ostensibly were hidden. At another time, a pistol was placed at his temple as a similar threat. He was robbed on several occasions and bullet holes exist today in his home place from random shootings by marauding raiders. Juda Roark had her fingers broken as she fought with pillagers attempting to steal what little remained in the corn crib. Unionists and southern supporters alike throughout East Tennessee pleaded with the military governor for assistance.[156]

In spite of the harassment and unsettled times, Joseph remained at the homestead and cultivated at least a portion of his land. Having saved back and preserved some seed corn, Joseph began a corn crop in April. We know little about what Joseph was able to retain in the way of livestock following the foraging of the armies and the raids of marauders; however, he apparently had oxen or mules for plowing in the raising of his corn crop. Later events indicate that he also had protected and retained the beginnings of a new beef cattle herd and a drove of hogs. Doubtless the plowing for the corn crop was done by Joseph himself. At the time he had not quite reached his fifty-first birthday.

It was a warm day in July 1864 when a ray of hope brightened the lives of Joseph and Juda. By then, most recognized that the South was defeated. Still the war dragged on and the final end of the conflict could not be foreseen. Long days of struggle for survival and recovery lay ahead and Joseph and Juda could only pray for the safe return of their three sons. It was on that day in July that their prayers were partially answered–their son John, tired and sore, appeared at the home place. John had been wounded and captured at the battle of Piedmont, Virginia, in early June, and after a brief period of treatment and recovery at a Union hospital in Staunton, had been paroled. With a joyous welcome and following a brief reunion with the family and a welcome home by neighbors, John related how in early June the First Tennessee Cavalry, then without horses, had been sent by train from Bristol to Lynchburg and then to Staunton. The regiment under Vaughn's Brigade was assigned to the army of Brig. Gen. William E. "Grumble" Jones, who was attempting, at General Lee's direction, to make a stand against the Federal army moving up the Shenandoah Valley. In a battle on June 5 at the small village of Piedmont northeast of Staunton, the First Tennessee had been in the thick of the fighting as the Confederate army was defeated. John related that General Jones had been shot from his horse and killed; Maj. John B. King, one of the recruiters of Company B, was killed; and many of the First Tennessee were killed, wounded, or captured. John did not know what had happened to his brothers during the battle. John told of his wound and his treatment in Staunton. He said that, oddly, he felt fortunate that he had been wounded in that following his treatment he had been paroled. Those captured without being wounded had been marched off to a Federal prison in Indiana. Bill Conner, son of M.H. Conner, was one of those sent to Indiana.[157]

John provided a big assistance to Joseph at a time when few men were available to work the farms. John assisted in cultivating the corn crop and in January 1865, he and Joseph sold thirty bushels to the U.S. Army in Chattanooga for one dollar per bushel, receiving a voucher in payment. John tried to collect on the voucher for almost two months, using the help of Union Capt. J.J. Wright. Wright wrote a letter of support, with a personal recommendation for John, to Capt. H.H. Manning of the 124th Ohio Voluntary Infantry, Subsistence Officer for the Chattanooga area. The voucher was forwarded to the Subsistence Department in Nashville and on September 11, 1865, to the Office of the Commissary General in Washington, D.C. In typical bureaucratic fashion, the voucher was returned to Nashville with this reply:

> The within property not having been accounted for, these vouchers are respectfully returned and attention is called to the enclosed Circular No. 9.
>
> A.E. Shires
> Assistant Commissary of Subsistence[158]

Joseph and John were never paid for the corn.

By late 1864, the newly established county government for Hamilton County had begun to function. With the assistance of the Federal government, the county tax committee had developed an assessment of property within the county. Under the ponderous heading of "State of Tennessee, under the act of Congress entitled 'An Act for the Collection of District Taxes in insurrectionary districts,' approved June 7, 1862, and on the act amendatory thereto," the county was provided a list of property assessments for all land within the county. On the list, Joseph Roark was to be taxed on a total of 752 acres.[159] Taxes were particularly onerous to former supporters of the Confederacy since payment was required in U.S. dollars or bank notes, few of either of which were then in their possession. The penalty for delinquent taxes was serious. Unpaid taxes provided vengeful Unionists, on the order of "Parson" Brownlow, a reason to confiscate "rebel land." No record is available that documents the payment of 1864 taxes by Joseph Roark. It might be concluded that the tax statements for 1864 were not ready for distribution by the county for that year and the first tax statements following the war were those for 1865. No taxes had been collected in 1863.[160]

The 1865 taxes for lands of Joseph Roark combined with those of his son-in-law Robert Beane Scott amounted to $1.95. The tax amount obviously indicates that the

THE UNITED STATES,

To *Joseph Roark* Dr.

186		Dolls.	Cents.
Jany 3d	For Thirty bushells of Corn at one Dollar per bushell	30	00
	I Certify that the above accts is Correct and just and that it was necessary for the public Service and that it has not been paid by me for want of funds		
	H.H. Manning Capt 124th Ohd Ifantry $	30	00

RECEIVED at _____ this _____ day of _____, 186 , from

Lieut. _____ Reg't of _____ A. C. S., United States Army,

_____ Dollars and _____ Cents, in full of the above account.

(SIGNED IN DUPLICATE.)   *Joseph Roark*

NOTE.—"Disbursing officers, when they have the money, shall pay for public supplies purchased by them. When they are not in funds, they will furnish the seller with a certified account of the purchase. Public supplies purchased by an Officer or Agent, *whether paid for or not*, must be taken up by him on the proper Return, and accounted for." (Subsistence Regulations of 1862.)

Voucher from the U.S. Army, signed by Capt. H.H. Manning, 124th Ohio Voluntary Infantry, for purchase of 30 bushels of corn from Joseph Roark at $1.00 per bushel in January 1865.

tax appraisal considered the value of crops quite low as crop land was slow to recover in the last year of the war. Still, the tax was a particular burden at the time. Scott had an idea for a possible solution for the tax payment and, with his father-in-law, approached Deputy Sheriff John Kimbrough who at the time also served the county as tax collector until a tax collector would be elected. Kimbrough had been deputy sheriff before the war and Joseph had known him for several years. Scott proposed that he work for the county in manual labor for however many days were required to satisfy the tax payments. Apparently as a special favor to Joseph, Kimbrough agreed to the arrangement and, following Scott's service with the county, wrote a receipt to Joseph. The crisis of immediate tax payments, through the unselfish effort by Scott, passed with the handwritten receipt provided by Kimbrough:

> Recieved of Joseph Roark one dollar & 95 cents for the use of Bean Scott in full of their tax for the year 1865
>
> John Kimbrough[161]

As the war dragged on in early 1865, Tennessee Unionists met in Nashville in January to begin the formation of a new state government. Without following constitutional requirements, and with the support of Military Governor Andrew Johnson, who was also the vice president elect with President Lincoln, the radical Unionists scheduled elections for state offices. "Parson" William G. Brownlow, as the most noted Unionist in Tennessee, was elected governor, along with a legislature dominated by

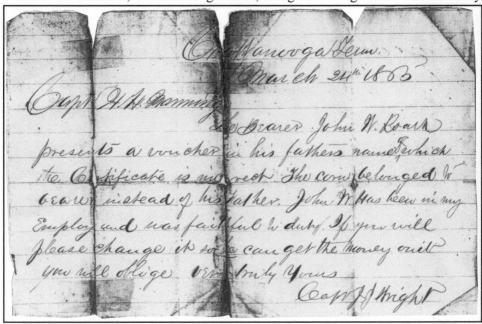

Letter, March 24, 1865, from Capt. J.J. Wright to Capt. H.H. Manning in support of John W. Roark for payment of the $30 for the corn purchased by Manning from Joseph Roark. Neither John nor his father received payment for the corn.

radical Unionists. Brownlow became governor "with the stated intention of punishing Confederate supporters . . . by vindictiveness and increasingly desperate measures to bar Confederates from politics."[162] Brownlow was, as governor, to rule over a million people. His supportive biographer described his election as governor as "a strange and dangerous act" and:

> For the promoting of the orderly progress of peace, it would have been impossible to make a worse choice; for carrying out a war of vengeance of a minority against a majority, Brownlow was incomparably the best selection that could have been made throughout the land. As a master in whipping up hate and revenge, he had no peer.[163]

News of the war in late 1864 and the first few months of 1865 was slow to come to the Salem Community. Men traveling from Chattanooga and Cleveland brought news of Confederate Gen. John Bell Hood's defeat at Franklin, south of Nashville, of Gen. Jubal Early's Confederate raid on Washington, D.C., and later of the Union siege at Richmond and Petersburg. In early April, however, news came in rapid-fire order. Lee surrendered to Grant April 9 at Appomattox Courthouse in Virginia. By Sunday morning, April 16, word reached the Salem Community that President Lincoln had been shot Friday evening and had died early Saturday morning. In its Sunday issue, the *Chattanooga Daily Gazette*, published the telegraphic dispatches that it had received on the tragedy. The paper would be circulated, read, and reread in the Salem Community:

BY TELEGRAPH
For *Chattanooga Daily Gazette*
DEATH OF PRESIDENT LINCOLN
Washington, 12:30 A.M. April 15

The President was shot in the theatre tonight. He is perhaps mortally wounded.

SECOND DISPATCH

The President is not expected to live through the night. He was shot at the theatre.

Official Account
War Department, 4 A.M. April 15

Major General Dix:

The President continues insensible and is sinking. Secretary Seward remains without change. . . . It is now ascertained with reasonable certainty that two associates were engaged in the horrible affair. Wilkes Booth being the one that shot the President and the other, a companion of his whose name is not known, but whose description is so clear that he cannot escape. It appears from letters found in Booth's trunk that the murder was planned before the fourth of March, but fell through then because the accomplice backed out until Richmond could be heard from.

Booth and his accomplice were at the Livery Stable at 6 o'clock last evening and left there with their horses about 10 o'clock, or shortly before that hour. It would seem that they had for several days been seeking their chances, but for some unknown reason, it was not carried into effect until last night. One of them has evidently made his way to Baltimore, the other has not yet been traced.

(Signed)   E.M. STANTON

War Department, Wash.   April 15.

To Major General Dix:
   Abraham Lincoln died this morning at twenty-two minutes after seven o'clock.

E.M. STANTON

SUNDAY MORNING, APRIL 16, 1865

No Pardon for Traitors — No Terms with Rebels.

APRIL 13th, 1861 — APRIL 15th, 1865

Again have traitors and assassins aroused the indignation of a generous people. Like a thunder clap in a clear sky, came yesterday the announcement that "Abraham Lincoln is dead, killed by an assassin!" Our voluminous dispatches, this morning, gives all the particulars in regard to the parricidal deed, and leave nothing further to be told. . . . The blood of thousands of Union soldiers, spilled on a hundred battlefields, and the groans of thousands of men starved to death in rebel prisons, cry out for vengeance. Where now are the professions of peace, and mercy, and love, with which the columns or certain journals were loaded? Cast to the winds, shattered by the report of the firearm which closed the well-spent life of Abraham Lincoln. Talk not to us in terms with traitors. Never, never, shall we give our acquiescence in any truckling which looks to the restoration of citizenship to those who have been leaders in this unholy crusade against a nation's liberties. . . [164]

Receipt for the 1865 State and County Taxes of Joseph Roark and his son-in-law Robert Beane Scott. Scott had worked for Deputy Sheriff John Kimborough to work out the amount due for taxes from both himself and his father-in-law.

So the long war was ended. Unfortunately its end had been followed by the act of a madman–an act that killed "the best friend that [the South] had" and one that would engender hatred and bitterness for years to come.[165] Joseph and Juda Roark had lived through the war in an area of the country that had suffered as much as any other and had experienced deep suffering in the sorrowful loss of three daughters. Now that the war was over, hopefully they would soon learn something of sons Jim and Will. In the interim, nothing lay ahead but the hard work of recovery and a lingering concern as to how former supporters of the Confederacy would be treated by a radical state government.

Chapter 10

Reconstruction
1865-1869

Jim and Will arrived home just over two weeks following Lee's surrender at Appomattox. At the time of the surrender, the First Tennessee Cavalry and Vaughn's Brigade were assigned to Echol's Division in the Shenandoah Valley. Jim and Will received news of the surrender during their encampment at Christiansburg, Virginia, and were advised by General Echols to return home and attempt to peacefully reconstruct their lives. There had been no formal surrender and no final ceremony or conclusion to their war. The First Tennessee Cavalry had simply been disbanded and the soldiers dismissed. The men from the Salem Community had then begun their long walk home.

Jim greeted his wife and daughter, Nancy, then just over a year old. Both Jim and Will were gratified to see their brother John alive and well–they had not known of his status or condition since his wound and capture at Piedmont. With the three sons now safely returned, the family at home included Juda Ann Brooks and Jim Carr–Matilda Brooks still worked at the home of Merida Webb. One can imagine the family dinners the first few days of Jim and Will's return and the stories shared by the returned soldiers. Jim and Will told of their experiences since the battle at Piedmont in June the year before. Jim had been slightly wounded in that battle and had been treated at a Confederate field hospital following the encounter. The battle at Piedmont had been one of the most fiercely fought battles of the war and was a horrendous experience for members of the First Tennessee Cavalry. The regiment had lost over half its strength in those killed, wounded, or captured.[1]

Following Piedmont, the First Tennessee Cavalry had been assigned to Echol's Division under Gen. Jubal A. Early's Second Corps and had been in Early's march north down the Shenandoah Valley, through Maryland, to the outskirts of Washington, D.C. Jim related that they saw the major buildings of the nation's Capitol from its northern outskirts, as Early's Corps threatened Washington before retreating back to the Shenandoah Valley. At and following the battle at Piedmont, the First Tennessee Cavalry had fought as infantry and had seen its strength continually diminish. Losses in killed, wounded, and captured had decimated the unit. By the end, the once-proud regiment was the size of a company. Doubtless Jim and Will told of their discouragement as the war ground to a close and they recognized that total defeat was to be the final result. But now the family was together again, saddened by their loss of Jerusha, Nancy, and Susannah, but determined to face with resolve the difficult task of rebuilding and reconstructing their lives.

Other vererans, Union and Confederate, returned home to the Salem Community at different times during the summer of 1865. John B. Roark, the son of Joseph's bother James, arrived home the middle of April, having been mustered out at Nashville on April 4 as a corporal in Company E, Fifth Tennessee Infantry (Union). He had been sick during the last few months of the war and had been in the hospital at Nashville since February 1865.[2] James Roark's other son, Joseph, did not arrive home until September. He had served in Capt. R.L. Barry's Tennessee "Lookout" Light Artillery of the Confederacy and had been seriously wounded in the left arm, hip, and knee in the Battle of Kenesaw Mountain in Georgia. After recovery, he had been sent to Mobile, Alabama, where he was captured in August 1865, then released.[3]

James W. Roark, the son of Joseph's brother John, had arrived home on a hospital furlough in October 1864 after having been assigned to the hospital in Knoxville since August 1863. He had been transferred to the First Tennessee Infantry (Union) on August 6, 1863, at the time of his debilitating illness. He was officially discharged on October 20, 1864, by a certificate from the War Department dated May 20, 1890.* The other son of John Roark, John Lewis Roark, was discharged at Nashville April 4, 1865, and arrived home with his cousin, John B. Roark, and his brother-in-law, Archibald McCallie, in mid April 1865. Archibald McCallie had received a bullet wound in the foot on May 14, 1864, at the Battle of Resaca, Georgia, and, after treatment in the hospital for two months, had been given a furlough for sixty days. It had been during his time at home on furlough that McCallie married John Roark's daughter Margaret Ann.

So it was that veterans of opposing armies, who until recently had considered the other army their mortal enemy, then returned home to the small community of their youth. Most had but one thought in mind–to forget the war and obtain a small plot of farm land on which to build and raise a family. Joseph Roark was determined to help his sons with their common objective. As he had done with his daughters, Joseph allocated land to Jim and gave him a portion of the 120 acres that Joseph had purchased from J.C. Wilson in 1857. Referred to as the "river farm," the tract was good bottom land that had lain dormant during the war. Jim was to farm the south half of the river farm and on it he would build a home on the higher ground above the river bottom. Here he would live with his family for the next thirteen years. John and Will, as they were still unmarried, would temporarily live at the home place, but they, too, would be given land to farm by their father. John was allotted the north half

---

*During his stay in various hospitals, the records of James W. Roark were lost. As a result, he was carried on the records as a deserter for several years. His record was ultimately corrected and he was officially and honorably discharged by a certificate from the War Department dated May 20, 1890, with an effective date of October 20, 1864.

of the river farm. Will was assigned an unidentified portion of the homestead tract. If deeds were given to each of the three sons for their land, the deeds were not recorded. Title was established, however, in the name of each son at the county tax office and all three sons were to pay the taxes on land assigned to them.[4]

In Nashville, the radical general assembly had been in office since April 1865. Responding to the direction of the ultraradical governor, "Parson" Brownlow, it moved to enact punitive legislation against former Confederate supporters. Samuel R. Rodgers, Brownlow's speaker of the senate, defined the major aim of the assembly as being that of keeping the loyal people from ever again being "governed by rebels."

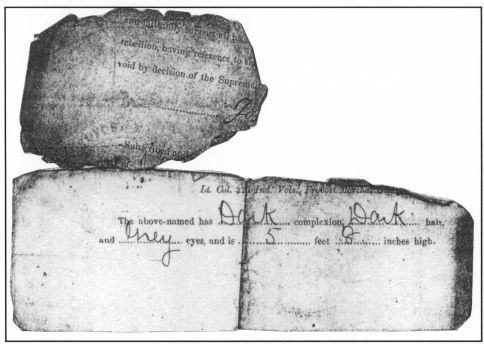

The fragmented remains of the Loyalty Oath to the U.S. Government sworn to by Joseph Roark in the early summer of 1865.

The assembly enacted sedition laws that made a mockery of the Bill of Rights and passed a franchise law that restricted voting by Confederate veterans. The underlying purpose of the franchise law, in addition to its punitive measures directed at former Confederates, was to restrict voting in a manner to perpetuate the control of state government by the radicals. Brownlow and the rest of the radicals recognized that they were in the minority in the state and could only preserve their position of power by controlling the ballot box.[5]

The Tennessee General Assembly on April 7, 1865, ratified the Thirteenth amendment to the U.S. Constitution emancipating all slaves. In May, it passed an act making it unlawful for any person except returned Federal soldiers and citizens "who

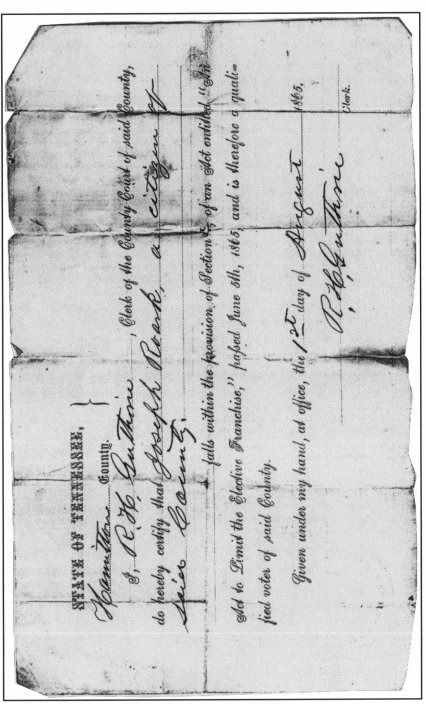

Voter Registration Certificate issued to Joseph Roark on August 1, 1865, by R.H. Guthrie, County Clerk of Hamilton County, under the 1865 Tennessee Franchise Law. The voter registration was revoked when more restrictive franchise legislation was passed to prohibit voting by former supporters of the Confederate States.

have always been loyal" to carry "any and all necessary side arms." Also in May, the assembly passed the "sedition act," which made it unlawful and punishable by fine and imprisonment for anyone to utter "seditious words or speeches, spreading abroad false news or utter false libels against the state." And in June, the general assembly passed the franchise law, which disenfranchised all Tennesseans except those who had been "publicly known to have entertained unconditional Union sentiments from the outbreak of the rebellion until the present time."[6] Brownlow and his radical legislature clearly planned to punish all "rebel" supporters and restrict voting to maintain radical control in the state. In his Knoxville paper, which he continued to publish while governor, Brownlow strongly proposed banishment of all "rebels" from East Tennessee. In August, Brownlow offered his "most religious advice" to all "rebels" in East Tennessee–"*sell out and go to a new country.*"[7]

In Washington, President Andrew Johnson continued the positive and lenient policies begun by Lincoln in restoring local government in the South, and in readmitting states to the Union. The loyalty oath directed by Lincoln was promulgated through the army's local offices of provost marshal, and former Confederate supporters were encouraged to take the oath. On the controversial issue of how former Confederate states were to be readmitted to the Union, Lincoln had already recognized Tennessee in 1864 as having met the requirements for readmission. President Johnson, as the former military governor of Tennessee, supported that effort and worked to minimize the punitive requirements sought to be imposed by Congress on all southern states. He was to face, however, as would have Lincoln had he lived, a radical congress that was intent on controlling the reconstruction process and in punishing the former states of the Confederacy.[8]

Joseph Roark took the loyalty oath to the U.S. government in June or July, 1865. Only a fragment of the executed oath remains in the Joseph Roark papers and the date of the oath is obliterated. The oath was taken before the provost marshal, a lieutenant colonel in the 22nd Indiana Volunteer Infantry Regiment. The preserved fragment shows the wear from being folded in the wallet of Joseph Roark and carried during the hard work and sweat of restoring his farm.[9]

On August 1, 1865, following his execution of the loyalty oath, Joseph approached County Clerk R.H. Guthrie in Harrison to obtain a voter's certificate. Guthrie knew Joseph and obviously had respect for his reputation. Although Joseph's qualifications for voter registration were questionable under the strict interpretation of the June 5 franchise law, Guthrie issued a certificate to vote in Hamilton County to "Joseph Roark, a citizen of said county."[10] Joseph was then able to vote in the congressional election held in August 1865. The leniency of Guthrie and other county clerks would, however, become a major issue with Governor Brownlow following the August election. In that election, a total of 61,783 Tennesseans went to the polls to elect eight congressmen, half of which were conservative Unionists opposed to the Brownlow regime. The radical governor immediately saw the crack that had appeared in the foundation of his tightly controlled governmental structure. Obviously voter registration must be more restrictive and more rigidly policed–Brownlow immediately called upon the county clerks and sheriffs for a report on the methods used in issuing voter registration certificates. The reports would be used to guide legislation during the next session of the general assembly.[11]

In the fall of 1865, Joseph's daughter, Mary Ann Scott, broke the news to Joseph and Juda that she and Robert had made the decision to move west. Their youngest son, Joseph, named after his maternal grandfather, had been born September 25, and both Mary Ann and Robert felt that the time was opportune to seek a more stable environment than East Tennessee. Since Robert was a minister, he no doubt felt God's leadership in the decision to move. At the time of their move, Mary Ann and Robert were the parents of eight children: Jane almost 15, Tennessee (Tennie) 13, James A. 11, Florence Bethena 9, Juda Ann 7, Lizzie 4, Noah 2, and Joseph, the baby. Mary Ann and Robert would first move to Warren County, Tennessee, near McMinnville, with the idea of a later move to Arkansas and the Indian Territory (later Oklahoma).[12] It appears that Joseph had been particularly close to Robert Scott and respected him as a son-in-law. His help to Joseph and Juda throughout the war and during reconstruction, both physically and spiritually, had been a godsend. Doubtless Robert had provided comfort and solace during sorrowful times when Joseph and Juda had lost their three daughters within a brief period. Robert had also probably spoken at length with Joseph about religion and Joseph's own personal faith and trust in God. Obviously there had been a closeness between parents and daughter/son-in-law that now was to be separated by distance. As the Scotts left that fall, Joseph and Juda saw their eldest daughter leave the Salem Community, their second daughter to do so. Joseph and Juda were not to see Mary Ann, Robert, or their family again.

Since Joseph's son John had returned home earlier than brothers Jim and Will, he was able to start a crop in the spring in the first year following the war. In the fall of 1865, John was able to sell his first corn crop. For it he received $50 in cash and took a promissory note in the amount of $213.12 ½, which basically represented his year's work. Since John had expenses that could not be covered by the $50 he received in cash, he approached his father about purchasing the balance of the note. To help his son, Joseph accepted the assigned note and provided John with scarce cash money, probably in increments as needed. On the reverse side of the note, John provided the assignment:

> I do sign the within note to Mr. Joseph Roark for value received of him.
> Dec 11, 1865
>
> J.W. Roark[13]

Joseph also sold a corn crop at the same time. Apparently Joseph had contracted with V.C. Walker to farm Walker's land on the river with rent to be paid as a share of the harvested crop. Most likely, Walker was an absentee landlord, his fertile land being on the river, and it was to his advantage to have Joseph farm his land. The crop was sold in early November, Joseph paid Walker $60 for Walker's share of the crop sale as rent, and received a receipt from Walker, dated November 4, 1865. It is of interest that Walker received the $60 "by the hand of Joseph Cookston" indicating perhaps that Cookston was a partner with Joseph in rental of the farm. Another possibility, however, should be considered. Joseph Cookston, at the time of the receipt, was serving as constable in the Salem Community for the Tenth Civil District of Hamilton County and would remain in that office until March 6, 1866. He could have been making the collection from Joseph and the subsequent payment to Walker as constable under the orders of the local justice of the peace. In almost all cases, however, when the constable made a collection under orders from the justice of the peace, he issued a receipt to the contributor carefully referencing the judgement of the court. The receipt for the $60 was direct from Walker to Roark for the rent, simply acknowledging that it was received through Cookston's hands. Understanding Joseph's diligence in paying his just obligations, court action was probably not involved and Cookston made the payment, either as a partner with Joseph or as a friend assisting by making delivery of a cash payment.[14] Besides being a neighbor and friend to Joseph Roark, Joseph Cookston was also soon to be related to Roark by marriage. On May 20, 1870, Elizabeth Talley, daughter of Elizabeth and granddaughter of Joseph and Juda, was to marry Francis Marion Cookston, son of Joseph and Sarah Cookston.[15]

Although the government of Hamilton County had been established under Federal mandates and local officers were in place, the county had insufficient funds for adequate police protection and officers for enforcement of law and order. Doubtless the county government attempted to maintain order as Federal troops were withdrawn; however, the state's legislative program was a hindrance to local law and order. Working against a peaceful transition from military rule to responsible local civil government was the policy of retribution emanating from Governor Brownlow's office in Nashville. In support of his official policies, Brownlow's Knoxville newspaper published descriptions of "Rebel Atrocities" that had been committed against Unionists from 1861-1863. The governor's intense hatred of all who had supported the Confederacy spread throughout the state and discouraged attempts at healing and reconciliation. Under such discouragement, law and order almost ceased to exist in East Tennessee.[16]

The violence in East Tennessee was reported and properly criticized by newspapers and condemned by people north and south. Responding by letter to critical comments by the *Cincinnati Gazette* in November 1865, Governor Brownlow stated his venomous position:

> I am one of those at the South who believe that this war was closed out two years too soon! The rebels have been whipped but not whipped enough. For saying these things I expect to be abused by all rebel papers South, and by all traitorous sheets North.[17]

Following the governor's lead, radicals were determined to control East Tennessee, and the best way to do it was to expel as many former Confederate supporters as possible. The "civil war within a civil war" continued long after the cessation of hostilities between the armies and became a political fight for control of the area. Most of the radical Unionists were former Whigs who saw the situation as an opportunity to punish the Democrats in a move to gain political dominance. Letters from East Tennessee Democrats to President Andrew Johnson suggested that the punitive measures taken by the governor and other former Whigs were part of a plan "to rid East Tennessee of Democrats."[18]

Former Confederate supporters faced another challenge in the court system. Brownlow had encouraged the Federal courts to file indictments against "rebels" for treason and for providing "aid and comfort to the enemy." He also actively encouraged damage suits against "rebels" in state courts by Unionists who had suffered loss of property during the war. After some success in the state courts, Brownlow urged other damage awards by the courts–"Imprison the villains . . . take all they have . . . give their effects to the Union men they have crippled and imprisoned . . . let them have their 'Southern rights.'" By late 1865, Brownlow's newspaper, indeed most newspapers in East Tennessee, carried numerous notices from county courts in East Tennessee of attachments, sheriff's sales, and other legal actions.[19] The docket of the Hamilton County court system in 1865-1866 was filled with suits against former Confederate supporters and it was reported from Chattanooga in January that "every rebel of prominence and property is sued for damages and the dockets of the courts are groaning under this class of suit."[20] The Brownlow followers exhibited a fixation to bring suit against any former Confederate supporter with any property or status. Among the many sheriff's sales that were held, one had a particular interest to Joseph's son Jim and his father-in-law William McGill. In February 1866, McGill had sold a tract of almost 200 acres to D.C. Howell for $1,995.[21] In early 1867, Howell was to lose the tract through a sheriff's sale following a judgement against him in favor of Thomas Smalley. The notice of the sheriff's sale was typical of the many that were served as a result of radical vengeance:

SHERIFF'S SALE

By virtue of an order of sale to me directed by the Circuit Court of Hamilton County, Tennessee, I will on the 12th day of January, 1867, sell at the courthouse door for cash in hand the following lands to wit: One hundred and ninety-nine acres, more or less, in the 12th District of Hamilton County, Tennessee, adjoining the lands of widow Wallace and others, the lands formerly owned by William McGill, to satisfy a judgement that Thomas Smalley recovered against D.C. Howell on the 18th of July, 1866, before John D. Blackford, Esqr., and the same will be sold unless said judgement and cost are previously satisfied, this Dec 4th, 1866

A.B. Conner, Sheriff [22]

Returning veterans of the Confederate army in East Tennessee faced threats and intimidation from Unionists bands, which were a greater menace to peace in the area than bushwhackers. At the end of the war, both Union and Confederate veterans returned to their homes in East Tennessee in a situation different from any other locale in the states of the former Confederacy. As both Union and Confederate veterans returned home together, the proximity of such men, who until recently had fought a bitter war in hand-to-hand combat, inevitably increased tension. Many Federal veterans returned home to avenge wrongs that they and their families had suffered during the war. With the collapse of the Confederacy, Unionists no longer had to be concerned about Confederate retribution and many took a more belligerent attitude toward their former adversaries.[23] In East Tennessee, conditions went from bad to worse in 1865, and Confederate veterans returning home immediately experienced hostility and felt a spirit of animosity from Unionists. "Brownlow, through his *Knoxville Whig* and his public utterances, made it a policy to encourage that spirit for many months after the end of hostilities."[24]

Under the vengeful policy of Brownlow, the climate in Hamilton County was tense. Violence could break out at any time and location. In February 1866, at the opening of the Hamilton County Circuit Court in Harrison, fights broke out and "several poor rebels–most of them old men, were severely beaten" by a Unionist mob.[25] This was the environment of intimidation for all supporters of the Confederacy who were struggling to remain in the area and regain their position in the community. The Salem Community was not immune to violence. Billy Killian, formerly of the First Tennessee Cavalry and son of William Killian, adjacent landowner to Joseph Roark, defended himself at home against raiders from Savannah Valley. Killian barricaded himself in his home and shot one of the raiders as he was trying to enter through the barricade. Conditions were so severe in the Salem Community in 1865-66 that Joseph Roark's son John and Maise Blackburn were sent by the community to Harrison to seek protection of law enforcement officers and to Chattanooga to request help from the provost marshal.[26] Other former Confederates in Hamilton County filed for relief through the court system and petitioned that Unionists be "legally ordered to discontinue whipping and driving them out of the region."[27]

Hostilities and violence continued in Hamilton County and the rest of East Tennessee through all of 1866. Many former Confederate supporters left the area, but most of those in the Salem Community remained and worked through the problems that followed the war. The night raids to "punish the rebels" continued, however, and not until the late 1860s was peace fully restored in East Tennessee.[28]

Some degree of civil normality began to return in mid 1866 as mail delivery began again in southeast Tennessee. Bids were received by the Federal government, following advertisement in the local newspapers, for mail service to begin July 1,

1866. In the bid specifications for the service, mail to the Salem Community through the post office at Birchwood was to be provided:

> From Cleveland, by Potter's Branch, Limestone, and Birch Wood [sic], mouth of Hiawassee [sic], 20 miles and back once a week.
>> Leave Cleveland Thursday at 5 a.m.
>> Arrive at Mouth of Hiawassee [sic] by 12 n.
>> Leave Mouth of Hiawassee [sic] at 1 p.m.
>> Arrive Cleveland by 8 p.m.[29]

Other governmental services, however, particularly those normally provided by the county, continued to languish. The few improved roads in Hamilton County were those within Chattanooga. "No improved roads extended into the hinterland, and such dirt roads as existed became impassable in bad weather. When Chattanoogans went to the county seat at Harrison, about 14 miles away, they preferred to go by steamer on the river."[30] County roads were still maintained by the abutting property owners with one landowner designated overseer by the county court for each segment of roadway. On February 16, 1867, John McCallie was appointed by the Hamilton County Court as "overseer on the public road of the 2nd class from Joseph Roarks to the Blythe Ferry Road near Todds farm."[31] Such was the source of maintenance for the Birchwood Pike.

In late fall 1865, Juda Ann Brooks told Joseph and Juda that she planned to marry Noah Atchley of Meigs County. Atchley had served as a private in Company A, Twenty-Sixth Tennessee Infantry Regiment (Confederate) during the war, and since had been courting Juda Ann for several months. A marriage license was obtained October 25, 1865, with the wedding planned for some time after the first of the year. The wedding ceremony was conducted Friday, January 5, 1866, more than likely at the Roark home place since Joseph and Juda had been the only parents that the bride had known.[32] The couple was to live in Meigs County near the parents of the groom. With Matilda Brooks working for and living with the Merida Webbs, Joseph and Juda then only had sons John and Will at home plus Jim Carr, then 14.

John was not long to remain at home. By March 1866, he was in Warren County near McMinnville, doubtless living for a period of time with his older sister Mary Ann Scott and her family. It could have been that John went with them to McMinnville to assist in the move as he was in McMinnville the spring after their move either on a visit or in an extended stay following their move. Why John left home at the time, other than perhaps to assist Mary Ann and Robert in their move west, is unknown. It was after the fall harvest and before the spring plowing that he left, so farm work was the slowest of the year. Much work, however, remained at the homestead–fences to replace, repairs to be made, and livestock attended. Obviously it was not a time in which John had nothing to do and a "vacation" was warranted. Did John leave because of the East Tennessee violence or did he leave to escape the demands of a romantic episode in his life? There is strong evidence to suggest that

John did not plan to return to the Salem Community and intended to remain in Warren County, for there on March 3, 1866, he applied to the county clerk for voter registration under the 1865 franchise act. Apparently John had earlier taken the required amnesty oath and was thus found to "fall within the provisions of Section 1" of the franchise act. On that Saturday in March, Warren County Clerk Sam Henderson issued John Roark his voter certification. Whatever the reason for John's visit to Warren County, he returned home by mid summer 1866.

The first half of 1866 did not provide much evidence of a financial recovery for Joseph Roark. In April he was taken before justice of the peace J.P. Talley on a charge by John Eldridge, the details of which are unknown. The judgement went against Joseph and on April 14, 1866, he was ordered to pay $101.88 to Eldridge. A week later, Joseph paid the judgement to the local constable and received a receipt dated April 21, 1866. The constable was Archibald McCallie, son-in-law to Joseph's brother, John.[33]

The month following, Joseph joined with John Burton to execute a promissory note, dated May 5, 1866, to William L. Hutcheson in the amount of $12 for value received. Hutcheson was the son of merchant W.C. Hutcheson; however, it is unclear as to whether or not the promissory note was for a purchase made at the Hutcheson store. Since it was a joint promissory note, it probably was not for items purchased. While there is no evidence as to the date of payment of the promissory note, it is abundantly clear as to the person making the payment. Joseph's signature has been neatly removed while the signature of Burton still remains on the preserved copy of the note.[34]

By October, Governor Brownlow had received and evaluated his report from the county clerks and sheriffs on those citizens who had been authorized to vote in the August congressional elections. Brownlow knew that many who voted did not vote the radical ticket and, from the report, he concluded that most county clerks, occupying an office that was local in character, had registered voters under the franchise law that were not totally supportive of the governor. Such probably had been the case when Hamilton County Clerk R.H. Guthrie issued Joseph Roark his voter's certificate. Brownlow recognized that his was a minority party and could only perpetuate itself in office by strictly limiting who could vote. Therefore, when the legislature met in October, the governor proposed a new franchise law, one that would disenfranchise all who had supported the Confederacy in any way. The new franchise law, passed May 3, 1867, took the responsibility of voter registration away from the county clerk and gave it to governor-appointed, special election commissioners–men who were totally loyal to Brownlow. Under the new law, Joseph Roark was again disenfranchised and was not permitted to vote in an election until 1869. Radical control of the state was complete.[35]

Brownlow's control of the state was a major factor in the readmission of Tennessee to the Union. By July 1866, the radicals in the U.S. Congress were at war with President Johnson for control of the reconstruction process. Recognizing Brownlow as a fellow radical, Congress required that Tennessee, for readmission to the Union, had only to ratify the Fourteenth Amendment, authorizing citizenship for all former slaves. Following the ratification by the Tennessee legislature, Brownlow, who by then considered President Andrew Johnson a traitor for implementing Lincoln's lenient policies, notified the clerk of the U.S. Senate by telegram of the ratification, closing with typical Brownlow venom, "Give my respects to the dead dog in the White House." Tennessee was readmitted to the Union July 23, 1866, the first of the former Confederate states to be so recognized. The early readmission of Tennessee as a state saved it from the military occupation that was so punitive to the other states of the former Confederacy.[36]

By the summer of 1866, John W. Roark had returned from Warren County and was courting Permelia Britannia Conner, the daughter of Maximilian Haney and Martha Palmer Conner. The Conners lived on the Birchwood Pike less than a mile north of the Roarks and had been friends of the family for a number of years. Conner had settled in the Cherokee territory before the creation of the public lands district[37] and had received grants in the district for 160 acres, which he had been farming since 1836.[38] Conner had been one of the founders of the Salem Baptist Church, and he and his wife had been staunch members through the years. Conner's father-in-law, Thomas Palmer, was a Revolutionary War veteran who also had received grants in the Ocoee District and owned land adjacent to the Conners. On Palmer's death in 1852, he had been buried on Conner's place–on a small knoll a mile west of the Birchwood Pike.

The wedding between John W. Roark and Permelia Conner was held Saturday, September 8, 1866, probably in the home of the Conners.[39] At the time of their marriage, John was 25, Permelia was 19. For their home, John rented the log cabin owned by Nancy Ford on the 50 acres purchased from Joseph Roark in 1861. The cabin was located across the road from the Roark river farm–the north half then being farmed by John. The first child of John and Permelia was born in the fall of 1867. They named their new daughter Lorena. Unfortunately she was to live only a few months.[40]

Joseph continued to face suits in the local courts throughout 1866. In November, he was again loser in a case before J.P. Talley in favor of J.N. Witt. The judgement was paid November 10, 1866, and Joseph obtained a receipt from Constable Archibald McCallie:

> Received of Joseph Roark fifty one dollars and sixty cents in full of a judgement, costs and commissions that J.N. Witt obtained against him befor J.P. Talley, Esqr., on the 10th Nov 1866
>
> A. McCallie[41]

The reference to payment of a commission as part of the judgement would indicate that a third party was involved in the case, possibly a bill collector or a lawyer. The commission would also serve to suggest that the case may have been one of those brought against former Confederate supporters.

At the end of the year, Joseph paid $5.00 as his state and county taxes for 1866 and received in return a tax receipt from W.B. Pearson in the Department of Tax Collection of Hamilton County. Interestingly, the receipt was made to "Joseph Roark Senior," doubtless to differentiate him from his nephew Joseph, son of James P. Roark, who was then farming on his father's land in the Salem Community[42] Similarly, when Joseph's nephew was designated as an overseer of a public road by the county court in 1869, the court minutes referred to him as "Joseph Roark Jr."[43]

The greatest tax load for Joseph in 1866 was not, however, altogether for his own land. His son-in-law Joel Talley had not paid his taxes for the previous four or five years and was in a position to lose his land to a tax lien. Elizabeth and Joel approached Joseph for help in paying the $30.15 delinquent tax bill. Joseph agreed to pay $21.85 if Joel could pay $8.50. His gracious help was accepted and Joseph received a receipt from W.B. Pearson–"Received of Joel A. Talley by the hand of Joseph Roark Twenty-one Dollars & eighty-five cts in part of his tax." Elizabeth and Joel would require more help and support in the next few years.[44]

Joseph's financial position, while not great, was considerably better as 1867 began. Crops had been raised and sold in the two previous years, and the homestead farm was in much better condition. His improved financial condition is evidenced by a promissory note written by Joseph on January 15, 1867, to James McCormack for the unusually large amount of $318.17 "for value received." Nothing is available to suggest what the "value received" was nor the purpose of the note. James McCormack, 22, was the eldest son of William F. McCormack, with whom Joseph had done considerable business in the past. Joseph made the first payment on the note December 26, 1868, in an amount of $100 with the note being paid in full at some later date.[45]

Joseph was also able to provide Juda Ann and Noah Atchley a partial cash payment of Juda Ann's share of the Leonard Brooks estate. Noah and Juda Ann had been married a year when they requested that the Brooks estate be divided and Juda Ann's share be provided to them. On February 18, 1867, Joseph paid the young couple $133.00 and obtained a receipt from Atchley:

> $133.00 Received of Joseph Roark one hundred and thirty three dollars it being a portion of my father-in-law Leonard Brooks estate. This February the 18th 1867
>
> > his
> > Noah X Atchley
> > mark[46]

At the same time, Joseph supplied to Juda Ann and Noah a promissory note in the amount of $267.00 for the balance of her share of the estate. The promissory note was formal in its tone and content and obviously was written by someone other than

Joseph. Strangely, it was signed jointly with another party whose name was removed when the note was paid. Most likely, the cosigner was an advisor, an attorney familiar with the estate, or possibly an individual with whom Joseph had placed funds of the estate to gain a proper return on the investment. Joseph obviously took careful precautions to complete the estate settlement with Juda Ann in the proper manner:

> $267.00
> One day after date we or either of us promise to pay Noah Atchley Two
> Hundred and Sixty Seven Dollars it being the balanc of the Lenard Brooks
> estate for value received this the 18th of February 1867
> Attest   Joseph Roark
> W.C. Campbell   [Unknown Co-Signer]
> James P. Roark[47]

Later in the year, July 22, Joseph made a payment of $18.00 on the note and subsequently made a second payment of $50.00 on September 16. Two weeks later Joseph paid the note in full and received a receipt, written in Joseph's handwriting, this time executed by Juda Ann with her husband:

> Received of Joseph Roark Gardien of Juda An Brooks my ful shur of
> Lenard Brooks estat this 30th day of September 1867
>   Juda Ann Atchley
>   Noah Atchley[48]

Joseph's responsibilities as guardian of Juda Ann and the settlement with her of her father's estate were complete. Joseph and Juda had raised Juda Ann since she was three and had cared for her for over nineteen years. From all available evidence, it appears that Juda Ann had a strong affection for Joseph and Juda, felt a sincere appreciation for their help and guidance, and was satisfied with the estate settlement. Unfortunately, this satisfaction would later diminish.

In Nashville, Governor Brownlow continued to take steps to perpetuate his regime. Although the next gubernatorial election would not be held until August, Brownlow had concluded that the votes of former slaves would be needed to maintain his position in office. Such a step to franchise the blacks was totally contrary to his previously off-stated bias and prejudice. Nevertheless, at his insistence that the black population be used in this way, the general assembly enacted the necessary legislation on February 26, 1867.[49]

Still the vengeful governor was not through. On February 20, the general assembly, at his bidding, passed legislation creating an armed force to be known as the Tennessee State Guard with one or more regiments to be organized in each Congressional District. On March 6, Brownlow set about to create his army and sought enlistments for a three-year period. Blacks were encouraged to enlist and at least one black captain was commissioned in each regiment. The first company of the Tennessee State Guard was organized in Jonesboro in May, where they were issued guns and paraded through the streets.[50]

The week following the creation of the Tennessee State Guard as Brownlow's private army, The *Weekly American Union* in Chattanooga carried his proclamation citing violence in the state as the justification for the state guard. It also carried an editorial on "Tennessee Radicalism":

> It is a noticeable fact that nowhere in the whole country has radicalism arrived at such an extravagant development as in Tennessee. . . . If such disturbances [as stated in the Proclamation] as one complained of are real, it is right that it should be suppressed as every good citizen is interested in the preservation of law and order. But with almost dictatorial powers thus in the hands of an Executive whose prejudices are so strong that he can see no sin beneath a cloak of loyalty, and nothing but villainy where participation in the rebellion has been imputed, we can see nothing but imminent danger to the state.[51]

Still Brownlow felt he had insufficient power. Five days after the creation of the state guard, the legislature passed an act giving the governor the power to reject voter registration in any county. With almost dictatorial power, Brownlow was then ready for the gubernatorial campaign and election. Not surprisingly, "Parson" Brownlow was re-elected in an almost complete sweep of the state.[52] As he had been denied the privilege of registering to vote, Joseph Roark did not cast a vote in the August elections. The radicals would continue in power for at least another two years.

Irrespective of the despotic government in Nashville and the radical congress in Washington, Joseph Roark's fortunes continued to improve as the lower portion of East Tennessee struggled to recover. In addition to the sale of his corn and wheat crops, Joseph also dealt in livestock. In September, Joseph executed an agreement to deliver beef cattle to J.W. Smith and a colt to W.C. Hutcheson:

> Joseph Roark agrees to let J.W. Smith have 3 beef cattle for which 30 dollars is to be paid. Also 1 colt to W.C. Hutcheson to be delivered sound in one month, on this thirty seven dollars & fifty cents. The colt and cattle being pointed out and agreed upon this 4th Sept 1867.
>
> Joseph Roark[53]

Later the same month Joseph joined with another party, unknown since his name was removed from the preserved document, in two promissory notes: one to John Eldridge for $53.00 and one to William Haile for $50.00. Both promissory notes were written by the same hand on September 27, 1867, for "value received." More than likely Joseph was a cosigner on the notes with one or two of his sons.[54]

A promissory note to merchant W.C. Hutcheson gives an indication that Joseph was financially able to settle promissory notes within a reasonable time. The note to Hutcheson was written October 17, 1867, for $9.50, obviously for items purchased from Hutcheson. The note was paid in full April 4, 1868.[55]

In December1867, Joseph's friend and neighbor, Merida Webb, died. Webb's wife, Betsy Jane, was named administratrix of the estate. On December 9, 1867, Joseph Roark, G.W. Gardenhire, and W.C. Thatcher were appointed commissioners by the Hamilton County Court "to lay off and set apart one year's support to Betsy Jane Webb, widow of M.W. Webb, Dec'd, out of the effects of said estate."[56] By the following summer, M.H. Conner had replaced both Gardenhire and Thatcher as commissioner. On June 24, he and Joseph Roark, with county surveyor R.L. McNabb, submitted to the court a survey plat of 207 acres lying in Sections 26 and 27, FT2N, R3W, as a dower for Betsy Jane Webb. The dower was estimated to be one third of the real estate owned by Merida Webb at his death. The report was accepted by the heirs and approved by court. The widow was thus given a life estate in 207 acres lying adjacent to the farms of Joseph Roark and William Killian.[57] Betsy Jane Webb remained a close friend of the Roark family for years following the death of her husband and was present to assist members of Joseph's family when needed. In 1874, for example, she was present with Dr. Lee when John W. Roark's third daughter, Julia, was born February 3, 1874, at the old Nancy Ford place.[58]

Joseph's taxes for 1867 were assessed at $6.40, which Joseph paid in late 1867 and received a receipt from Peter Bolton, deputy tax collector for Hamilton County.[59] The tax rate had been set in January 1865 as $0.25 per $100 property valuation and remained the same in 1867.[60] One has to conclude that Joseph received favorable appraisals for his taxes in the first three years following the war. True, his lands were recovering and were not yet in full production, his fences were being rebuilt, and his livestock herd was much less than it had been before the war. Also, his three sons were paying the taxes on that portion of the homestead they were farming, although their taxes, individually, were less than three dollars for any of the years after the war. In 1868, however, Joseph's taxes were assessed for $30.60, which would indicate that Joseph's lands were again in crop production. Joseph paid his 1868 taxes on Monday, November 30, 1868, and was provided a printed receipt from R.A. Hunter, Tax Collector, signed by Peter Bolton, Deputy. Interestingly, the receipt was printed for payment in Chattanooga rather than the county seat of Harrison, indicating that the tax offices were then located in the larger town. The receipt also provides a clue that steps were being taken behind the scenes to move the county seat from Harrison to Chattanooga, a move that would portend less than favorable consequences for Joseph and his descendants.[61]

Joseph continued to bear the tax burden for his son-in-law Joel A. Talley. Again in 1867, Joseph paid $24.00 for the state and county taxes for Talley.[62] The amount of Talley's taxes cannot be explained when compared to Joseph's. Doubtless Talley's tax bill had significant penalties for past-due amounts. This assumption seems reasonable when the receipt for Talley's 1869 taxes (which Joseph again paid in full) is analyzed. The receipt for Talley's 1869 taxes was issued to Joseph on January 11, 1871, by D.J. Alexander, Deputy Sheriff in Hamilton County, indicating that the delinquent tax bill had been forwarded to the sheriff's office for collection.[63]

It appears that Joseph's patience was quickly reaching its limit in dealing with his son-in-law. Joseph had exercised more patience than normal in dealing with Talley, obviously out of consideration for Elizabeth and her children. Joseph was not generally tolerant with persons who did not meet their obligations and, even with family, his endurance had a limit. In 1869, Joseph took steps to document before the local justice of the peace some of Talley's debts to him during 1868:

Hamilton County, Tennessee

Joel Talley in Account with Joseph Roark   1868
    for house Bought of Wm. Hany $ 10.00
    for thirty six (36) Bushels Corn at $1.00 per Bushel   36.00

        46.00

This day personally appeared before me Joseph Roark and made oath in due form of law that the above account is just and true to the best of his knowledge and that he has no way to prove only by his oath and book account Given under my hand and seal this 25th day of August 1869
    A.P. Defriese
    Justice of the Peace
    For Hamilton County, Tennessee[64]

Two months later, Talley acknowledged the debt and Joseph accepted a promissory note from him for the $46.00. Apparently a third party was involved since the promissory note signed by Talley was in the handwriting of neither Talley nor Joseph.[65]

Talley's problems impacted the rest of the family as well. In September 1870, Joseph's son Will, obviously to collect a debt, accepted from A. Mangram the assignment of a judgement against Talley for $53.50:

I this day sign over my right to William Roark for a judgement that I obtained against Joel A. Talley on the 5th of February 1869 for $53.50 before A.P. Defriese, J.P.
This Sept 1, 1870

        his
        A. X Mangram
        mark

Over a year later, Will had been unable to collect the judgement from his brother-in-law, and he further assigned the obligation to his father who probably knew the judgement was uncollectible. On the reverse side of the original assignment, the following was written in Will's handwriting:

I sine the within Judgement over to Joseph Roark for value received of him
    This the 23rd Sept 1871
    William Roark[66]

Doubtless Joseph paid Will for the assignment to help him financially without any expectation of receiving reimbursement from Talley. By the summer of 1871, Joseph had taken steps to protect himself from Talley's insolvency and no longer anticipated that Talley would meet his financial obligations.

With Talley's debts continuing to mount, Joseph Roark took action to place a lien on and take possession of the 80-acre tract given to Elizabeth and Joel some years before. Debts had accumulated for Talley to the extent that his land holdings were subject to a sheriff's sale for delinquent taxes or a lien foreclosure by other parties if Joseph did not act on behalf of his daughter. In March 1870, Joseph paid the costs for a sheriff's sale of the Talley lands for debts against the property. He received a receipt from Deputy Sheriff J.W. Watkins:

> $11.95   Received of Joseph Roark Eleven Dollars and ninety five cents in full of the amount of Cost that is against Joseph Roark in the Case where the conditions of Joel A. Talley's land was sold and bid off by Joseph Roark, the said Cost had to be paid before said Sale could be confirmed. This the 10th day of March 1870
>
> J.W. Watkins
Deputy Sheriff[67]

At the time of the sheriff's sale, Talley owned only the 80 acres, so no other property could have been taken by his debtors to satisfy their claims against him. At the sale, Joseph bid for and received title to the tract. By his court action, Joseph was able to keep the tract in the family and again place title to the tract in his name. Joseph paid the 1870 taxes for the 80 acres on December 5, 1870.[68]

In September 1869, Joseph received a letter from his brother-in-law John Carr in Nashville. Carr was concerned about a deed for land in Kentucky that his father had apparently maintained in his papers. While no record of other correspondence between the two brothers-in-law remain, it appears that Carr had previously urged Joseph, as administrator of the Samuel Carr estate, to pursue the deed and obtain title for the heirs. As one of the few letters saved by Joseph in his papers, Carr's letter is included below as it was written:

> Nashville, Sept 6th, 1869
>
> Joe   I want you to write me fourthwith whether you have or have not seed anything about that land up in Kentucky which father had a deed too at his death.
>
> if you have not I wish you would come out here & bring the deed with you.
>
> we can have the deed tested in a few days after you come. There is an old land agent an experienced land deed and rite tester who also has binn vary successful in that buisness. he live in franklin 50 miles from Nashville.
>
> he says that it don't make any difference how far back this deed may be he can raise it. I have talked to several about it men of buisness all says that

we cant be kept out of it. I am confident that we can get it. if the land lays near the place where I have considered it does it is worth $150 per acre

less not delay this thing no longer but start the thing to mooveing fourthwith. I have no idea but what we will be successful. it wont take long to come and you can only make it a visit out here to see us all and tend to this buisness at the same time.

don't delay a day after you get this. if you can not possible come yourself write immediately what you can do or what can be done about it. it is ours if we try to get it. that is all we hafto do.

respectfuly your brother
John Carr

To Joseph Roark[69]

No record remains that would indicate Joseph made the requested trip to Nashville nor that he mailed the deed to his brother-in-law. The deed itself did not survive in the preservation of the Samuel Carr papers, indicating the possibility that it was forwarded to John Carr.

In Washington, the radical congress, after their new majority took office in March 1867, began proceedings to impeach President Johnson and thereby gain full control of the reconstruction process. After impeachment by the House, the Senate vote was

Second Voter Registration Certificate issued to Joseph Roark on July 19, 1869, by S.F. Towne, Commissioner of Registration for Hamilton County, appointed by the governor under the 1867 Tennessee Franchise Law. Registration required proof of qualifications by two competent witnesses—"unconditional Union men."

taken May 16, 1868, by which the president kept his office by a single vote. In Nashville, Governor Brownlow was overjoyed at Johnson's impeachment but disappointed that he was able to remain in office. The big political event in Tennessee, however, was the resignation of Brownlow as governor in 1869. The U.S. Senate seat of David Patterson was to be vacant in March and Brownlow resigned as governor February 25, 1869, to accept his election by the Tennessee Legislature to replace Patterson. As soon as Brownlow left the state, radical control in Tennessee began to diminish. Even the attitudes of his appointed voter registration commissioners began to improve. On July 19, 1869, Joseph Roark appeared before S.F. Towne, Brownlow's appointed Commissioner of Registration for Hamilton County, to again request registration as a qualified voter. After submitting sworn statements by two competent witnesses, "known . . . to have been at all times unconditional Union men," Joseph was provided his second voter registration certificate. The "unconditional Union" witnesses were not named on the certificate. Joseph again was referred to as "Joseph Roark Sr." to differentiate him from his nephew.[70]

Joseph was then able to vote in the August elections for governor and the legislature. When the votes were counted, the results indicated the end of Brownlow's control. Dewitt Senter, a former state senator who proposed universal suffrage, was elected governor by a wide majority, and conservatives won a strong majority over the radicals in both houses of the legislature. Reconstruction was over in Tennessee, and the dictatorship of the radicals was broken. Joseph Roark and his family would once again be permitted to participate in and enjoy the benefits of representative government. The government of Tennessee was once again in the hands of the majority.[71]

As state political conditions thus stabilized, communities could focus on civic and church activities. The Salem Baptist Church was the center of activity in October when the Ocoee Association of Baptist Churches met at Salem on Saturday, October 2. Twenty-three churches were represented at the annual meeting of the association at which C.B. Martin of Ooltewah was elected moderator. The churches, which were from communities as far away as Cleveland, Ooltewah, Chickamauga, and Chattanooga, reported on membership, additions, meeting days per month, and contributions to the association. Of the twenty-three churches, the Salem Church was the fourth largest with 114 members, led only by the White Plain Church with 144, the New Prospect Church with 123, and the Macedonia Church at Cleveland with 117 members. The smallest church was the New Friendship Church with seventeen members. Representing the Salem Church were I.Z. Kimbrough, pastor, and A.L. Stulce, supply pastor.[72] With the Salem Church just across Grasshopper Creek from the Joseph Roark homestead, Joseph and Juda doubtless provided much of the food and refreshments for the delegates. Since the meeting was held in the afternoon and extended through dinner, Joseph and Juda opened their home for overnight guests for those who desired to spend the night.

On the first of the following month, Joseph's son John purchased the fifty acres and the log cabin in which he and his family had been living from Nancy M. Ford. The widow Ford had purchased the tract from Joseph in 1861 and lived there during the war. She had been identified on the map prepared at the direction of General Sherman in 1863. Since she no longer lived there and had rented to John W. Roark and his family, she agreed to sell the property for $250 in "good and lawful money of the U.S." John and his family would live on the Ford place for the next seven years.

With stability and normalcy returning to Tennessee and Hamilton County, action was taken by the county court to improve the county's road network and to locate needed roadways. On September 4, 1869, the court named a "jury of view" consisting of D.A. Wilson, M.H. Conner, Benjamin Webb, William Killian, and William Haney "to view and layoff a public road of third class leading from Joseph Roark's to the Tennessee River so as to run on a line on the lands of Joseph Roark." The jury, or committee, completed its work and the road was established along the north property line of Joseph's homestead tract from the Birchwood Pike to the river.[73]

Similarly, on July 7, 1869, a jury of view had been named by the court "to view, mark, and layoff a road from the Tennessee River to Georgetown through the lands of Mrs. Betsy Jane Webb." The jury named by the court consisted of Joseph Roark, Jim Roark, John Campbell, A.L. Stulce, and A.P. Defriese.[74] The jury of view completed its work by October and submitted a report to the county court. The court, however, rejected the report and the work "was not confirmed as damages were claimed by John McCallie." The road was never built and an opportunity was lost for a major access route to the river.[75]

New overseers were also named by the court to maintain the road system then existing. It was interesting to Joseph, who was 56 in 1869, to note that the torch was being passed to the new generation in the Salem Community. Joseph Roark "Jr.," son of James P. Roark, had been named by the county court as a road overseer on February 8, 1869; John Lewis Roark, youngest son of John Roark, was named an overseer June 9, 1869; and Joseph's son William was to be named overseer on the Birchwood Pike in January 1870.[76]

As 1869 came to a close, Joseph would note with some degree of sadness that many of his friends and coworkers in the community were passing from the scene. Hirem Haney had died in February 1867; Merida Webb in December of the same year; Lewis Patterson, Joseph's partner from the Sale Creek area, had died June 16, 1869; and William Killian, his neighbor and associate for over 30 years since the Ocoee District opened, had just died in December.[77] Even Joseph's brother John was severely ill and not expected to live much longer. The suffering through the war and the struggle during the violent times of reconstruction had taken their toll. Yet good days remained, and Joseph looked forward to a new decade and more prosperous times.

Chapter 11

The Last Years
1870-1876

The new decade began on a sad note for Joseph. The health of his brother John continued to deteriorate in January, and on Wednesday, February 2, word came to Joseph that his brother had died. John was just three months shy of his seventieth birthday. He was buried next to his wife in the family cemetery on a knoll above their home place. John Roark had been preceded in death by his wife Margaret, his daughter Mary Ann Cross, who had died in June almost two years before, and son William who had died in 1863 while in the Union army. Still living at home when their father died were son James W. 35, and daughters Nancy 41, Juda Ann 38, and America 26. Other surviving children were Sarah Shelton 43, Elizabeth Campbell 41, Margaret McCallie 28, and John Lewis Roark 24.[1] Since their father died intestate, the youngest son, John Lewis, was named administrator of the estate and worked for an extended period in that capacity. The estate was settled April 10, 1871, and the Chancery Court of Hamilton County provided title to parcels of the estate as distributed among the appropriate heirs. John Lewis Roark was assisted in the estate land distribution by Commissioners William Johnson and A.L. Stulce, who were named by the Court along with County Surveyor R.L. McNabb for that purpose.[2]

The early 1870s provided the dawn of recovery for the South, but it followed the deep darkness of reconstruction. Gen. U.S. Grant had been elected president in 1868 and, upon his election, gave full support to the radicals in the Congress on the matter of reconstruction. No longer faced with the opposition of President Andrew Johnson, the Congress initiated a "more thorough" plan of reconstruction which wiped out nearly all Lincoln and Johnson had done. Military rule was imposed on all states of the former Confederacy except Tennessee, and a carpetbag government was established in each state house. Slowly the other states of the old South were readmitted to the Union–first, Arkansas in June 1868, and last, Georgia in July 1870. With "alien rule" in the South, corruption was widespread in each of the states as taxes were punitive and property rights disdained. In Washington, under the weak

Grant administration, corruption was even more astounding. The "gold conspiracy" by Gould and Fisk resulted in a violent panic in the stock market during the fall of 1869.[3] The combined impact of reconstruction, corruption, and market manipulation devastated the economies of the southern states and severely limited the market for farm products of the Salem Community. But by 1870, punishment of the South had become boring to the radicals, and the country turned its interest to the west where expansion seemed limitless. On May 10, 1869, the golden spike was driven at Promontory Point in Utah, and the nation was connected by rail from coast to coast. The "gilded age" in America had begun.

Like the rest of the South, Tennessee struggled to rehabilitate its economy. The trading partners in Alabama, Georgia, and South Carolina, which had fueled the market for Hamilton County farm products in the 1850s, had yet to recover from military occupation and punitive reconstruction.[4] The demand for corn, pork, and bacon, which had previously been the "money products" for Joseph Roark and the Salem Community, was limited in the adjoining states and farm prices remained low. Corn was no longer a "cash crop" as prices declined. As a result, corn production in Hamilton County in 1870 was almost half of what it had been in 1860. Similarly, the number of hogs in the county was 30% lower in 1870 than ten years before. Other crops showed significant reduction in output. Irish potato production in 1870 was only 20% of what it had been in 1860. The most significant drop in production was that of sweet potatoes which in 1870 was only 5% of what it had been a decade before. So many people in the South had survived on yams during the dark days of the war that, perhaps given a choice even five years later, sweet potatoes were not in demand and production responded accordingly. The farm product that showed an increase in 1870 was wheat, of which over 103,000 bushels were produced in Hamilton County in 1870, an increase of over 30% from 1860.[5]

Joseph Roark had previously shown significant acumen in responding to market trends and doubtless did so again in 1870. He devoted a considerable amount of his cultivated land to wheat. Less work was required and, with his sons all farming on their own, it was a crop that more nearly fit his capabilities. Similarly, with his drove of hogs still being developed from the few that remained after the war, Joseph needed less corn and reduced his production accordingly. In time, the market for farm products of the Salem Community would recover, but full demand would have to wait on the economic resurrection of the South.

In 1870, the city of Chattanooga, with a population of 6,093, had shown a growth in population of almost 250% since 1860. The primary source of growth, however, was in former slaves then crowding urban areas in search of jobs. Over 36% of Chattanooga's population in 1870 was black. Hamilton County grew in population from 13,258 in 1860 to 17,241 in 1870; however, all of the county population growth came in Chattanooga, none in the rural areas. Hamilton County's Civil District 10, in which the Salem Community was located, dropped in population from 960 to 898 during the decade of the 1860s.

The concentration of population in Chattanooga gave rise to a political effort that could have been anticipated. Why should the largest city in the county not be designated as the county seat? Although Harrison was centrally located within the county, its population in 1870 was less than 500 persons. The only paved roads in the county were within the city of Chattanooga, and beyond its city limits the roads were unpaved and impossible to travel during inclement weather. Chattanooga was not slow to use the new political muscle it derived from the 1870 Census. The General Assembly in Nashville was petitioned, and on June 24, 1870, an act was passed providing for a referendum to decide between Harrison and Chattanooga as county seat. The election was held in early November and, as one might expect, Chattanooga won overwhelming approval of the voters. By December 5, county records were being removed from Harrison for deposit in a temporary courthouse in Chattanooga.

The people of eastern Hamilton County, particularly those residing in Harrison, resented the outcome of the election and bemoaned the fact that a long trip was then necessary to reach the courthouse. From Joseph Roark's perspective, however, the location of the court seat at Chattanooga made little difference. Most of his commercial business, primarily the acquisition of farm equipment and parts, was done in Chattanooga, not Harrison, and by river it was just as easy to reach Chattanooga as Harrison, particularly when the weather was bad and the roads were in very poor condition. The citizens of Harrison, however, were slow to accept defeat and, with support from other locations south of the Tennessee River, they petitioned the General Assembly to permit the creation of a new county. An act was passed and signed January 30, 1871, and the new James County was created from the eastern portion of Hamilton County and a small portion of Bradley County. As the new county organized itself, an election was held in late April to locate the county seat in either Harrison on the Tennessee River or Ooltewah on the railroad between Chattanooga and Cleveland. Again Harrison lost as Ooltewah was chosen, indicating perhaps the importance then given to railroad travel as opposed to river transportation. Now Joseph Roark had a reason to complain. Ooltewah was at the far south end of the new county and a trip of two days was often needed to reach the courthouse and return. But travel to the new county seat was the least of negative impacts from the creation of James County.[6]

With a population of 5,000, almost all of which was rural, James County had no industry, and the burden of taxes to support roads and schools was thrust heavily upon the individual farmer. Taxpayers were to suffer and tax revenue was inadequate, resulting in poor roads and lower quality schools that were to keep the descendants of Joseph at a disadvantage. In pulling back the curtain of the future in 1870, one would see results of the precipitous action in creating James County. During its fifty-year life, James County only increased in population from 5,000 to only 5,467, while during the same period, Hamilton County grew from 12,241 (after the population within the area of James County was removed) to over 110,000.[7]

The impact of the new county on Joseph Roark was significant. His last tax bill from Hamilton County for 1870 state and county taxes was paid November 25, 1870, and amounted to $12.00.[8] Ten months later, Joseph's state and county taxes in James County were almost doubled at $22.50. Joseph paid the taxes but protested the significant increase. On Joseph's receipt for the 1871 taxes issued by J.C. Heaton in Ooltewah, September 29, 1871, Heaton had written in the lower left–"Under Protest."[9] The date of the receipt would indicate that Joseph did not delay after receiving his tax notice but went immediately to the courthouse to question the amount.

In late March 1870, Joseph's granddaughter, Mary C. Talley, daughter of Joel and Elizabeth, married William M. Smith in the Salem Community. A.L. Stulce, pastor of the Salem Baptist Church, performed the ceremony.[10] Shortly after the marriage, Smith announced his plans to move with his new bride to Yell County, Arkansas. He had relatives there and had received word that land suitable for raising cotton was available and the economy was booming. Smith encouraged his father-in-law to join him in the trek to Arkansas and improve his fortunes there. Joel Talley needed a new start, so in April or May, he left for Arkansas with his daughter and son-in-law and took sons Joseph 13, Benjamin 11, and Andrew 9, with him, leaving Elizabeth in Tennessee with their two youngest children, Margaret 5, and James 3. Joel arrived in Yell County in the Dardanelle Township on the Arkansas River in time to be enumerated in the 1870 Census. He and son Joseph were listed as "farm laborers" by the census taker.[11] Talley's move apparently was to find better opportunities than his reputation permitted him in the Salem Community and to leave behind him there his hardships, debts, and obligations. Doubtless his plan with Elizabeth was to send for her when he found farm land and a home in Arkansas.

By mid 1870, Matilda Brooks was again living with Joseph and Juda. Matilda was then twenty-eight years old and was listed on the census as a "domestic servant," a title which was not suggested by her but one that she might have sarcastically put forth. Matilda was unhappy with her lot in life. She had been unable to marry and doubtless was ready to leave the care of the Roarks. Joseph and Juda probably felt the same, as Matilda was sensitive about her lack of suitors and easily became abrasive. It was a difficult situation. Matilda had no job skills other than as domestic help and no doubt felt locked within her circumstances. Feelings were on edge and the household felt the animosity.

At the time, the household included Will Roark 23, who was living at home assisting his father and farming his own assigned acreage on the homestead farm. Also, the household in 1870 included four others who were not immediate family members. Harry McCrerre was a thirty-year-old school teacher who was rooming and boarding with Joseph and Juda during the five-month school term. Since the home place was adjacent to the Salem school, it was a convenient place for the teachers to live. Also at the home place was Jim Carr, then nineteen, listed on the census with no occupation. Doubtless he assisted Joseph in the operation of the farm. Two others lived at the home place: Caroline Irwin and her daughter, Nancy. Caroline was listed by the census taker as assisting in keeping house, while Nancy was noted as being "at school." Their reason for being with the Roarks is unclear.[12]

With all of his children married except Will and the reduced size of his household in 1870, Joseph's financial activities reflected fewer promissory notes to merchants and a reduction in the number of promissory notes in general. He appears to have made a focused effort as the decade began to collect obligations due him, probably as an attempt to maintain a stronger cash position. In February 1870, Joseph apparently asked G.R. Poter for payment of $20 on a note due him. Poter, about whom we know very little, immediately wrote out four payment requests to persons who were indebted to him: first to Thomas Conner for $4.00, second to Abner McCallie for $4.00, third to Miss Hixon for $4.00 and, fourth to John Roark (obviously John L. Roark) for $8.00. The order in which Poter wrote out the payment requests is quite clear. All were strips torn from the same sheet of paper–all match perfectly–beginning with Thomas Conner at the top and continuing to the bottom of the page. The text of each request was basically the same with only the amount changed for the one:

> Mr. Thomas Conner
>
> You will please pay Joseph Roark $4.00 and oblige yours, this February 10th 1870
>
> G.R. Poter[13]

On April 11, 1870, Joseph cosigned a note with Philip Rains to William F. McCormack "for value received," in the amount of $10.00. Since it was not a sum sufficiently large enough to require a cosigner, it apparently was an attempt by Joseph to help Rains by using Joseph's credit with McCormack. It was considered a note from Rains, not Joseph, inasmuch as McCormack had labeled it on the reverse side as "Philip Rains note–$10.00." Although it was Rains' note, it is quite obvious that Joseph Roark made the last payment, as his name was the only one removed when he filed it away with his papers. On the reverse side, McCormack had recorded payments, probably by Rains, of $2.50 on February 10, 1870, $3.00 on July 29, 1871, $5.00 on September 21, 1871, and a final payment of $1.23 some time shortly thereafter. With each payment, McCormack had calculated the interest due, apparently at 10%. The total interest paid by Rains and Joseph on the promissory note during its two-year life was $1.73. No record remains that would indicate any reimbursement by Rains.[14]

Promissory notes and payment requests during 1870 remained small in number and amount when compared to other years. On September 9, 1870, Joseph received a payment request from his nephew:

> Mr. Joseph Roark
>
> You will please pay C.P. Gamble four dollars and 75 cts for me.
>
> September 9, 1870   John L. Roark[15]

The requirement for the payment request or any reference to the obligation to make the payment is not stated and is unknown. Joseph obviously came up with the cash to make the payment, which may have been related to the settlement of the John Roark estate for which John L. had the responsibility.

Joseph's largest promissory note for 1870 was written November 13, 1870, to his eldest son, Jim, for $100. The purpose of the note was not stated but perhaps it was for payment for James' corn crop which had been sold jointly with Joseph's to the commission merchant.[16]

In October 1870, in a move that cannot be explained, Joseph purchased the assignment of an obligation payable to Dr. Thomas J. Defriese. The obligation lay with Wilson Hixson* of the Salem Community in response to an invoice from Dr. Defriese for medical assistance and prescriptions beginning December 29, 1868, and extending through April 28, 1869. Dr. Thomas J. Defriese served the medical needs of the Salem Community after he had opened his practice in Birchwood in 1860. He had served as a surgeon in the Confederate army during the middle years of the war and had suffered severe damage to his health before he resumed his private practice in 1864.[17] On October 10, 1870, Defriese, having been unable to collect from Hixson, appeared before Justice of the Peace Silas Witt to submit the delinquent account for a judgement against Hixson. In the accounting submitted to Justice Witt, Defriese listed seventeen occasions on which he had provided medical advice to Hixson for a total charge of $25.00. The accounting also listed three payments on the account: one on February 12, 1869, for six pounds of tobacco at $0.35 per pound for $2.10; another on March 23 in cash for $2.00; and a subsequent payment in June 1869 for "6 bushels corn at 75 cts by Webb–$4.50." The balance due on the account was then $16.40. A judgement was rendered, which recognized the accounting by Defriese as true and just, in the form of a certification by Justice Witt:

> State of Tennessee, Hamilton County
>
> Personally appeared Thos. J. Defriese before the undersigned, an acting justice of the peace for said county and makes oath in the form of Law that the above accpt of sixteen dollars & fourty cents against William Hickson as it stands charged is just and true to the best of his knowledge and that he knows of no other means of proving this accpt except by his oath & Book of which the above is a true coppy.
>
> Sworn to and subscribed before me this 10th Oct 1870
>
> Silas Witt, J.P. for Hamilton County   Thos. J. Defriese[18]

At the time of his appearance before Justice Witt, Dr. Defriese was in bad health–he was to die less than a month later, November 8, 1870–so on the date of the

---

*Referred to by Defriese as "William Hickson." The name was actually "Wilson Hixson."

certification he assigned the judgement to his son, Henry C. Defriese:

> I assign the above accpt over to Henry C. Defriese waiving all demands back on me for the same whatever
>
> this 10th Oct 1870   Thos. J. Defriese[19]

Also on the same date, October 10, 1870, Henry Defriese, who also was to be a doctor in the Birchwood area, assigned the judgement to Joseph Roark:

> I assign the above accpt over to Joseph Roark, Sen. For value received waiving all demands back on me for the same whatever
>
> this 10th Oct 1870   Henry C. Defriese[20]

To accept the assignment, Roark clearly had to settle the account with Defriese either in payment of the full judgement or in some discounted amount. Since Joseph accepted the assignment on the same date as the judgement itself, it would appear that the assignment had been prearranged–that both Thomas and Henry Defriese knew of some obligation of Joseph Roark to pay the medical bills of Wilson Hixson.

What was this obligation or commitment by Joseph Roark to Wilson Hixson? Or was it purely a business decision by Joseph–did he have a sufficient "hold" on Wilson to make him comfortable that he would be reimbursed? Strangely, it was not the first time Joseph had dealt with Wilson Hixson. In 1863, Joseph had accepted a promissory note from Hixson and John W. Smith for $110, only to have both Hixson and Smith default on the note. Only a few clues remain to guide our analysis. First, a previous sworn statement by Dr. Thomas Defriese in 1864 on charges against Hixson remains in the Joseph Roark papers. This previous statement was made November 20, 1864, before Justice of the Peace Pleasant L. Matthews:

> 1862 Wilson Hickson Due to Thos. J. Defriese
>
> | Dec 15 | To visit self , med & pres at Fathers | 4.00 |
> | Dec 16 | To med & prescription | 1.50 |
> | Dec 19 | To med & prescription | 1.50 |
> | | | $7.00 |
>
> State of Tennessee, Hamilton County
> Personally appeared Thos. J. Defriese before the undersigned an acting justice of the peace of said county and makes oath in the form of law that the above accpt of seven dollars against Wilson Hickson as it stands charged is just and true to the best of his knowledge and that he knows of no other means of proving this accpt except by his oath & book of which the above is a true copy.
>
> Sworn to & subscribed before me this Nov 20, 1864
>
> Attest: P.L. Matthews   T.J. Defriese
>   J. P.

On the reverse side of the judgement, the following notes appear:

Wilson Hickson
Accpt
$7.00
Credit April 16, 1872
to $9.30[21]

Had Joseph also accepted responsibility for the medical bills of Hixson in 1862 and settled the account by paying $9.30 in 1872 to settle the original bill and the interest charged against it? If so, one must again ask why.

A second clue is provided in a group of seven promissory notes to Joseph Roark that were unpaid at the time of his death and which were submitted to Constable J.C. Smith on October 28, 1876, for collection. First on the list of notes was "Wilson Hixson for $50.00 Due Jan 7, 1874." This note appears to document that Joseph had obtained a commitment from Hixson in the form of a promissory note for some indebtedness which could have included his 1864 medical bills.

A last clue appears in 1932 in a letter to Mrs. W.M. Roark, widow of Joseph's son Will, from the War Department in Washington, D.C. At the time Mrs. Roark was seeking a pension for the Will's Confederate service and had had significant correspondence with Nashville in trying to establish the service record of Will in the First Tennessee Cavalry. She had been told that consideration could be given to her request if sworn statements by at least two Confederate veterans who had served with Will could be provided. Mrs. Roark had apparently written to the War Department for Will's service record plus that of Wilson Hixson who ostensibly had served with Will. The response was as follows:

War Department
The Adjutant General's Office
Washington   February 5, 1932

Mrs. W.M. Roark
Birchwood, Tennessee

The name William M. Roark has not been found on the muster-in roll on file in this office of Company B, 1st (Carter's) Tennessee Cavalry, Confederate States Army, dated August 7, 1861, only roll on file, nor has any record been found of his service, capture or parole as a member of that organization. . . .

The name *Wilson Hixson* has not been found on the muster-in roll on file in this office of Company B, 1st (Carter's) Tennessee Cavalry, Confederate States Army, dated August 7, 1861, only roll on file, nor has any record been found of his service, capture or parole as a member of that organization.

Union prisoner of war records show that *Wilson Hixson*, private, company not shown, 1st Regiment Tennessee Cavalry, Confederate States Army, was captured in Hamilton County, Tennessee, date not shown, and took the oath of allegiance to the United States December 23, 1863, at Louisville, Kentucky, a deserter from the rebel army, and was sent north of the Ohio River. . . .

C.H. Bridges
Major General
The Adjutant General[22]

It would appear that Wilson Hixson served in the First Tennessee Cavalry, probably in Company B, but was captured in Hamilton County sometime before December 23, 1863. This would coincide with the Battle of Chattanooga and the activities of the First Tennessee Cavalry. So Hixson's capture in Hamilton County was quite possible, although from the War department letter, it could be concluded that he deserted rather than having been captured. The dates of Hixson's medical treatment by Dr. Defriese raise questions in regard to Hixson's Confederate service. Dr. Defriese provided medical help December 15-19, 1862. Was this not during the period that Hixson was serving with the First Tennessee Cavalry or had Hixson enlisted subsequent to that date? Defriese's invoice for his services to Hixson in 1862 was dated March 20, 1864, the time Hixson was a prisoner of war north of the Ohio River, although the probability is good that Hixson might have been paroled to return home by November 1864. While these questions cannot be completely answered, the bigger questions are—who was Wilson Hixson and why did Joseph assume the responsibility for payment of Hixson's medical bills from Dr. Defriese?

The question cannot be satisfactorily answered. By 1870, Wilson Hixson was living with his father in the Salem Community,[23] although marriage records indicate that he married Ann Killian, daughter of William and Elizabeth Killian, on January 5, 1865.[24] Quite likely, Ann Hixson died soon after their marriage and Wilson was back at home by 1870. Ten years later, he was forty years old, married, wife's name was Donie, with five children, and living in the Salem Community.[25] He was not on any of the church rolls of the Salem Baptist Church from 1872 and later. These later facts on Hixson provide little additional insight into his relationship with Joseph Roark. One possibility is that Joseph doubtless would have been quick to help the son-in-law of William and Elizabeth Killian and for that reason took on his medical bills. We can also conclude that possibly Joseph felt some obligation to help Hixson and Defriese, perhaps because of their service in the Confederacy, Defriese's poor health resulting from his military service, and Hixson's time in a Union prison. Beyond these two possibilities, the reason for Joseph's assumption of the debt for Hixson's medical bills remains a mystery. While he may have assisted Hixson at the time, Joseph's sense of responsibility would not let him absolve Hixson of the debt—Hixson was required to furnish the promissory note in 1873 or 1874.

Following the sale of his wheat crop in May 1871, Joseph was in a better financial position than he had been since the war. For the first time in over ten years he began to feel some comfort about his finances, his farm operation, and the general recovery in the community. New products for the home and farm were again being produced and sold, and Joseph could now consider purchases that would make life easier for Juda in household duties. One of the new products that was being demonstrated by salesmen from Chattanooga and Cleveland was the home sewing machine. In 1846, Elias Howe of Massachusetts had received a patent on a mechanical sewing machine of a double thread and lock-stitch design. By the late 1860s, the sewing machine had been fitted with a foot-operated treadle and presser foot for holding the fabric down, both as designed by Isaac Singer. Juda had always enjoyed sewing and apparently was quite talented as a seamstress. The new sewing machine attracted her attention, and on June 2, 1871, Joseph made the purchase in Birchwood. He executed a printed promissory note in the amount of $21.25 to "Darwin & Owen, General Agents for Elias Howe Jr., Inventor and Maker, New York, USA." The note was to be payable upon delivery of the sewing machine on June 12. Doubtless Juda enjoyed and appreciated the sewing machine and Joseph felt a husband's pride in being able to provide his wife with a new product from the U.S. economy.[26]

Although he had reduced his overall use of promissory notes, Joseph continued to use the promissory note as a cash equivalent in doing business in the community. On October 13, 1871, Joseph wrote out a promissory note to William F. McCormack for $110. In writing such promissory notes over the years, Joseph was consistent in the misspelling of two words: "promise" was always written without the "e" as "promis" and "received" was consistently written in an abbreviated form as "recivd." He followed the same practice in writing the McCormack note; however, no indication was given as to the purpose of the note. Almost a year after the note was written, McCormack recorded on the reversed side of the note that he received $50 on August 2, 1872.[27]

In late September 1871, Joseph wrote a promissory note to his son Will in the amount of $351.47. The specific amount in odd cents would indicate that the promissory note was probably payment to Will for his share of a corn crop that was sold jointly or for some other division of profits:

$351.47
One day after date I promis to pay W.M. Roark three hundred dollars and fifty one dollars and 47 centes for value recivd of him

This the 23 of September 1871
Joseph Roark[28]

At the time, Will was twenty-eight and yet unmarried, although family records indicate that he was involved in various amorous adventures with young ladies in the community. Following his years in the Confederate cavalry, he had perhaps developed a wanderlust, and was not ready to settle down at the home place. It seems as if he were hesitant to take responsibility. The County Court on January 10, 1870, had appointed Will as overseer for a segment of the Birchwood Pike:

> William Roark (Son of Joseph Roark) is appointed overseer of the public road of the 2nd class from the center of the creek at Joseph Roark to McCormack's Mill Race including the Bridge across said Mill race and to have all the hands that formerly worked on Said road under his predecessor.[29]

Yet just over a month later, whether at his request or for other reasons justifiable to the court, Will was replaced as overseer by James McCormack in action by the County Court.[30]

In February 1872, Will decided to leave home for a period and requested his father provide some cash settlement for the promissory note written the past September. In an attempt to accommodate his son, Joseph raised what was a significant amount of cash and made a payment to Will under the note. On the reverse side of the September promissory note, Will recorded the payment:

> $187.25 Received on the within note one hundred and eighty seven [dollars]
> & 25 sentes
>   this the 27 of february 1872[31]

Will left home soon thereafter and visited a lady friend in Douglas County, Missouri for a brief period.[32] By May 1872, he was visiting his sister Mary Ann in Crawford County, Arkansas, and helped her family plant their cotton. In August, Will was back home to stay, much to the relief of his mother.[33] Will maintained a correspondence with his lady friend in Missouri, whom he had apparently known in the Salem Community, writing her in January 1873 that he planned to return soon to Missouri. In a return letter to Will in April, his lady friend, whom we know only as "A" from the salutation on her letter, indicated that she did not believe he was coming to her and that she suspicioned that he was making a crop there on the home place and planned to stay in Tennessee. Interestingly, Will had her address her letters to him in Georgetown, Meigs County, rather that at the home place in Birchwood, obviously with privacy in mind. No evidence remains that Will traveled again to Missouri and, after his return in August, he remained at the homestead throughout his adult years.

Sometime in early 1872 or before, Joseph's other son John was elected church clerk of the Salem Baptist Church. Both John and his brother Jim were active in the church at Salem and, with their mother, probably encouraged their father toward a profession of faith. While Joseph appears to have regularly attended church with Juda and his family, he had not made a profession of faith and thus had not become a member of the church. True, he had given the land for the church and doubtless had supported the church financially, but until 1872 or 1873, he had not taken seriously the need for a personal religion. From the church records available after 1872, it appears that Joseph began to consider his need for a personal faith and a stronger involvement in the church.

The Salem Baptist Church was fundamental in its basic Baptist beliefs and in the authority of the Holy Bible. Baptisms for the church were conducted in Grasshopper Creek and at Moon's Landing on the Tennessee River. "Extended meetings" were held when a visiting preacher would conduct revival services that lasted three days to two weeks. "Foot washings," following the scriptural example of Jesus, were conducted approximately every other month; communion or the "Lord's Supper" was commemorated as decided by the church body or at least twice each year. Sunday School was held in the church each Sunday morning; however, preaching was limited to the last Saturday and Sunday of each month. Religious instruction and evangelism were not the only objectives of the church as it was also diligent in disciplining its members for various "offenses." The church minutes reflect the withdrawing of fellowship or "exclusion from membership" for members guilty of nonattendance at scheduled church services, fighting, using bad language, fornication, and "swearing and drunkenness." The church was apparently quick to forgive and restore to membership any member so disciplined after the member publicly asked the church for forgiveness. One can only imagine the emotions shared within the church as it strove to provide the moral leadership for the community and, in the judgement of the faithful, to mete out punishment to violators of the moral code.

In September 1872, John W. Roark, as church clerk, suggested that, for the benefit of the church, his father formalize the gift of the land to the church and execute a deed for that purpose. On the fourth Saturday of September, at the regular monthly business meeting of the church, Joseph executed a deed for the land occupied by the church since 1856:

> State of Tennessee, James County
>
> I Joseph Roark for and in consideration of respect that I have for the cause of religion and education, do give and bequeath to the Trustees of the Salem Baptist Church a certain tract or parcel of land containing by estimation one acre, be the same more or less, situated in the Third Civil District of James County and bounded as follows: Embracing the land where the meeting house now stands running in every direction from the house so as to include an acre outside my fence which land the said Trustees and their successors are to have and to hold as long as the same is used for Church and Education purposes but for no other then the same returns back to me as giver or donor of the same.
>
> This the 28th day of Sept. 1872.
>
> Joseph Roark
>
> Attest:
> A.L. Stulce
> John W. Roark[34]

A.L. Stulce was pastor of the Salem Baptist Church at the time and also was a special deputy of the James County Court Clerk. On March 23, 1873, as special deputy of the Clerk, he took and witnessed the acknowledgment from Joseph in the execution of the deed:

> State of Tennessee
> James County
>
> Personally appeared before me A.L. Stulce, special Deputy County Clerk of said County of James, Joseph Roark the maker of the within Deed, a man with whom I am personally acquainted, and acknowledge the within Instrument for the purposes therein contained.
> Witness my hand at office in Ooltewah the 22nd day of March 1873
>
> > A.L. Stulce
> > Special Deputy County Court Clerk[35]

Subsequently the deed was recorded in the courthouse at Ooltewah over the signature of J.G. Ruston, Register:

> State of Tennessee   Register's Office
> James County   April 1st 1873
>
> Then was the foregoing deed received for registration with certificate and is now of record in Book 1, Page 136.
> Witness my hand at office the day and date last above written
>
> > J.G. Ruston
> > Register[36]

The economy of the Salem Community and Hamilton County continued to improve in 1872. Documents seem to indicate, however, that although crops were good, cash remained in short supply. The interest rate remained at ten percent, and promissory notes continued to be the primary means of conducting business. On March 4, 1872, Joseph executed a promissory note, neatly written by the recipient, to J.A. Doughty at the ten percent interest rate:

> One day after date I promise to pay J.A. Doughty $75.00 Seventy five dollars for value received of him, this March the 4 1872, with ten percent interest from the above date
>
> > Joseph Roark[37]

Six weeks later, with the shortage of cash in evidence, Doughty sent Joseph a neatly written letter requesting payment of $25 under the note:

> Birchwood, Tenn. April the 26 1872
>
> Mr. Joseph Rowark Esq.
> Dear Sir: I am standing in kneed of a little money at present. If you could come or send & pay me $25.00 you would oblige me by so doing. The sooner you could send it or bring it the better it would suit me. As to the remainder, I am not kneeding it know.
>
> > Yours with Respect
> > J.A. Doughty[38]

Two days after the date of Doughty's letter, on April 28, 1872, Joseph made the requested payment of $25 in cash. Doughty noted the payment, in the presence of Joseph, on the reverse side of the original $75 promissory note: "Received on the within, $25 twenty five dollars, April the 28, 1872."

Just over five months later, Doughty again requested payment under the note, this time for $12, in a letter hand-delivered to Joseph:

Birchwood, Jas. Co. Tenn. Oct the 3 1872

Mr. Joseph Rowark

Dear Sir: if you have any money on hand you will pleas send me 12.00 twelve dollars by the bearer as I am needing that amount very bad at present. I need it against twelve oclock tomorrow. If you send it this shal be your receipt for the same.

Yours with Respect
J.A. Doughty[39]

This time Joseph was able to pay only $10.00 but made the payment within the requested deadline. Credit was duly given by Doughty on the reverse side of the promissory note. No information is available on when Joseph paid the note in full; however, final payment on other notes were, at that time, delayed as long as two to three years. On a promissory note to James Cross dated March 1, 1872, for $100, Joseph did not make a payment until November 16, 1874, then for $60. A second payment was not made until March 25, 1875, with the final payment made later the same year.[40]

As the financial recovery for the Salem Community continued, Joseph did not hesitate to to use credit and promissory notes to make purchases when, in his mind, he felt it appropriate. On May 24, 1872, following the death of John S. Moon, an estate sale was conducted by Sarah C. Moon, ostensibly the widow and guardian of the minor heirs. Following the sale, Joseph wrote a promissory note to Sarah Moon in the amount of $115 for undisclosed items purchased at the sale.[41]

Similarly, on August 2, 1872, Joseph executed a promissory note to John Eldridge in the amount of $100 for the typical "value received." No clue remains that would indicate the purpose of the promissory note.

By mid-summer 1872, Joseph's daughter, Elizabeth Talley, had letters from her husband, Joel, and her family in Arkansas. Her daughter Mary Smith and husband William had settled in Yell County just west of Chickalah near the community of Sulphur Springs. In Sulphur Springs a new hotel had just been completed and the warm sulphur waters were being advertised as a cure for many ailments.[42] Joel Talley and sons Joseph, Benjamin, and Andrew were working as farm laborers close to the Smiths, and Joel was seeking to acquire good farm land for the family. Doubtless the letters encouraged Elizabeth to bring the two young children—Margaret Ellen 8, and James William 5—and join the family in Arkansas. While Elizabeth hated to leave her parents and her daughter Elizabeth Cookston in the Salem Community, she nevertheless wanted to be with her husband and have their family together. So in mid

September, doubtless following long conversations with her parents, she requested a letter from the Salem Baptist Church by which she could transfer her membership to a church in Arkansas. Meeting in conference on Saturday, September 28, 1872, the church voted to grant Elizabeth her letter. The minutes on the third item of business read: "Upon application, the church granted Sister Sarah E. Talley a letter of recommendation."[43] The actual letter supplied by the church would read as follows:

> State of Tennessee   James County
>
> The Salem Baptist Church of Christ at Salem do certify that our beloved Sister Sarah E. Talley is a member in good fellowship with us and is hereby released from us at such time as she joins another church of the same faith and beliefs.
>
> Done and signed by order of the church in conference the 4th Saturday in September 1872.
>
> Rev. A.L. Stulce, Moderator
>
> John W. Roark CClk[44]

Prior to asking the church for her letter, Elizabeth had sent a letter to her sister Mary Ann Scott in Crawford County, Arkansas, seeking her advice about a possible move to nearby Yell County. Mary Ann answered in August in a letter addressed to their brother Will, who probably had written Elizabeth's letter for her. In her letter, Mary Ann sent encouraging words to Elizabeth of prospects in Arkansas and evidenced her concern about Will. She could only begin her letter by expressing her happiness that Will had returned home to his parents. A beautiful and sincere letter, and one which probably required much labor on the part of Mary Ann to write, is given below with spelling and major grammatical errors corrected for readability:

> Mr. William Roark   August 2, 1872
> Dear Brother
>
> I seat myself this good Sabbath evening to answer your most kind and welcomed letter which came to hand. All well and well satisfied, hoping this may find you the same.
>
> Will, you don't know how glad I was to hear from you and to hear that you was at home with Mother for I know that it is satisfaction to her.
>
> Will, tell Liz if she is coming west this is the fall to come. Corn [there] won't bring more than two bits. She can make more in one year than she can there in five. I think that I will make two thousand dollars worth of cotton this year. Tell pap and mother that I am coming to see them as soon as we get our land paid for.
>
> Will, I am so proud of your likeness that I would not take any thing for it. Will, don't fret for that pup that is not a lie about you bringing [five words illegible].
>
> So I must close for the present. Hoping to hear from you soon.
>
> R.B. and Mary A. Scott to Will Roark[45]

Included in the letter to Will were letters from Tennessee Scott and Martha Jane Scott, both daughters of Mary Ann, to their "Gramma" Juda Roark. Both Tennessee and Martha Jane were enthusiastic about the crops that year. Tennessee wrote "I think we will make 20 bales of cotton and plenty of corn and more vegetables than we can use." Martha Jane wrote that "prospects for our crops are fine, fine, fine," and commented on the health of Jane Clingan Webb and Benjamin Webb who had recently arrived in Crawford County from Tennessee. Martha Jane also had advice for young Jim Carr, then 22, about marriage: "Tell Jim Carr I said for him to not marry yet and to wait until he was old enough to make a good choice—one he will not regret."[46]

For Mary Ann, the letter was written at a time that would later be considered critical in her life. The month before, on July 7, her youngest daughter was born, yet Mary Ann makes no mention of her in her letter to Will. Her daughter Tennessee mentions in her letter that "Ma's babe is named Mary Ellen." Mary Ann had no way of knowing and had no indication when she wrote her letter to Will that her husband would die within a matter of weeks—Robert Beane Scott died suddenly September 7, 1872. Mary Ann was left with baby Mary Ellen and six girls still at home plus three young sons to raise. She was never able to make that trip home that she spoke about in her letter.[47]

Life soon presented a bitter turn for Elizabeth as well. Some time in the late fall 1872 or early in 1873, as she was preparing to make the move to Arkansas, she received word that Joel and their oldest son Joseph had died suddenly. Both had eaten green corn and had been stricken with food poisoning. Mary and William Smith had helped with the burials and would assist the two younger sons, Benjamin and Andrew, to return to Tennessee.[48] In June 1873, Elizabeth asked the Salem Church to withdraw her letter of recommendation and to restore her to membership. The church minutes of June 28, 1873, reflect action by the church:

> On motion and second, the Church agreed to rescind the act of granting . . .
> Sary E. Talley [a] letter of recommendation and restore her [to membership]."[49]

By the end of 1873, Benjamin and Andrew Talley were back at home with their mother and, by early 1874, both were members of the Salem Baptist Church.[50]

Without a doubt, Joseph and Juda felt a deep parental love for Elizabeth and an empathy for her troubled and difficult home life. By 1874, Elizabeth was only thirty-nine but had been the mother of eight, was a grandmother, and by then was a single parent with four young children living at home. After the death of her husband, she was to raise her family alone and remain in the Salem Community. During that period she would have the love and support of her father and mother.

In November 1872, Ulysses S. Grant was re-elected president during a period of economic boom. Railroad expansion continued and a transcontinental system was developed. Telegraph networks across the country provided rapid communication. Plans were begun for the country to celebrate its one-hundredth anniversary in 1876 in a centennial exposition at Philadelphia. Unfortunately, during 1873, the numerous scandals within the Grant administration and Congress would come to light and an economic depression would end the prosperity enjoyed by the country since the end of the Civil war.

Joseph Roark began the year 1873 by bringing his account current with merchant W.C. Hutcheson. On January 1, 1873, Joseph executed a promissory note to Hutcheson in the amount of $33.64. With fewer of his family at home, Joseph maintained fewer accounts with merchants and paid for more of his purchases in cash. The account with Hutcheson was one of the last accounts to be closed with a promissory note.[51]

The year also brought serious problems with Matilda Brooks. In early 1873, Matilda had developed inflated estimates of the amount of money she was to receive from her father's estate. The care and love that she had received from Joseph and Juda for over twenty-five years was forgotten and discord became an almost daily visitor to the home. Matilda apparently employed an attorney to represent her in getting the most money she could from the Brooks estate, thus requiring Joseph to also get an attorney and to make overnight trips to Ooltewah in an attempt to settle the disagreement. By late summer, the issue was drawn. Matilda was ready to move from home and terminate all relationships with the two people who had provided for her following the death of her parents.

As the issue moved forward through the court, Joseph developed with his attorney a list of expenses in raising Matilda for ten years until she was able to work as a domestic helper for a self-supporting income. As an expense, Joseph listed his attorney fees and out-of-pocket expenses in the lawsuit, state and county taxes on the estate, costs "for raising and schooling [for] ten years at $60.00 per year," doctor bills, county clerk fees, and cash payments for a saddle and clothes for Matilda.[52] It is unclear whether the court rendered a judgement or whether compromise was reached between Joseph and Matilda. In any event, Joseph executed on September 26, 1873, a promissory note to Matilda for $750 and, in turn, received a receipt from her indicating that all issues between them were resolved. Joseph sought help from two of his neighbors and friends, W.C. Thatcher and M.H. Conner, in witnessing the receipt from Matilda and attesting its validity. Thatcher and Conner may have also played a role in negotiating a settlement between the two parties. The receipt was originally written for $700; however, an additional $50 was later added, indicating that negotiation continued up until the final agreement was reached and the receipt executed.

The receipt from Matilda, written by neither Joseph or Matilda, appears to have been dictated by Matilda and written by either Thatcher or Conner. It obviously was not written by an attorney which probably says that the issued was settled out of court and without immediate legal assistance. Whoever its scribe, the receipt reflects a total absence of appreciation and affection:

> Recd of Joseph Roark his promissory note for Seven Hundred ["& fifty" was added] Dollars in full satisfaction of the Money due me from my father's estate, Lenard Brooks. This settlement is to include [conclude?] all matters between us on account of my living at his house. He is to deliver up to hur all hur waring aparals & beding
>
> September 26, 1873
>
> Attest:
> W.C. Thatcher   Matilda H. Brooks
> M.H. Conner[53]

The depth of the discord can be detected in the reference by Matilda that she lived at "his house" rather than noting that it had been her "home" for over twenty-five years. Also her demand that Joseph deliver her clothes and bedding carried an implication that would appear to be cutting and totally unfair. The episode must have been a significant disappointment for Joseph and particularly for Juda since Matilda was her niece and blood relative. It was a hurt that would remain with the family for years.

As Joseph was attempting to settle the issues with Matilda Brooks, the economy of the U.S. was in a free fall that would become known as the Panic of 1873. With the failure of the banking firm of Jay Cooke and Company, bankruptcies became

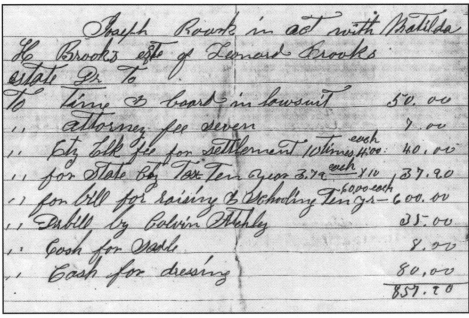

List of expenses in raising Matilda Brooks–Developed by Joseph Roark in anticipation of legal actions by Matilda.

numerous and the New York Stock Exchange dropped so precipitously that the market was closed for ten days. Factories were shut down, business came to a standstill, and the depression that was to last for six long years was underway.[54] The depression was particularly difficult for farmers in southeast Tennessee as the prices for farm produce fell lower and lower. Fortunately, Joseph had maintained a strong cash position with little outstanding debt. He would weather the storm. For many others in the Salem Community, however, including Joseph's son Jim, the depression was reason to look westward toward available land in Texas.

While the county was in a state of financial turmoil, the Salem Church continued to be a mainstay in the community. With John Roark's resignation as church clerk in September 1874, Jim Roark was elected by the church to serve in his place. Joseph's other son, Will, had yet not affiliated with the church. By mid 1873, the church had a total of 162 members on the church rolls, almost twenty percent of the total population of Civil District 3 in James County which included the Salem Community and Birchwood. The church roll included Juda Roark, John W. Roark, Jim Roark and his wife America, Elizabeth Talley with her daughter Elizabeth Cookston and husband Marion Cookston; Joseph's brother James and wife Jerusha with their daughters Martha Jane Sample and Sarah Webb, and their son John B. Roark, his wife Nancy and daughter Martha Jane; and Joseph's nephew John Lewis Roark and his wife

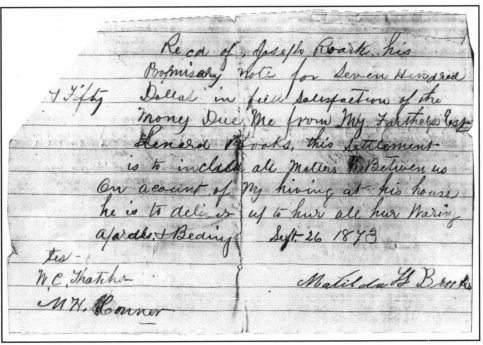

Receipt from Matilda Brooks in "concluding all matters" with Joseph Roark and receiving $750 as settlement with her for her father's estate, September 26, 1873.

Victoria. Others on the roll included M.H. Conner and wife Martha; Joseph Cookston and wife Sally; Betsy Jane Webb, widow of Merida Webb; Silas Witt and wife Martha Jane Conner Witt; merchant Burton Holman and wife Sarah; Malinda Irvin, formerly Malinda Bare; and William F. McCormack and wife Mary.[55]

On Saturday, November 22, 1873, the Salem Church began an extended meeting with the pastor A.L. Stulce doing the preaching. After the service on the following Sunday, Nancy Cross made a profession of faith, and during the afternoon the church met at Moon's Landing on the Tennessee River where she was baptized. The meeting continued from day to day the following week, and by the following Sunday, five others had made a profession of faith. Again the baptismal service was held Sunday afternoon at Moon's Landing. The services continued the following week and at one of the daily services, Joseph Roark made a profession of faith and was received into the Christian fellowship of the church. The following Sunday, December 7, 1873, Joseph, along with ten other candidates for baptism, was baptized in the Tennessee River at Moon's Landing. Among those baptized that Sunday afternoon in December were Joseph's son Will, John's wife Permelia, and Calvin Witt, son of Silas and Martha Jane Conner Witt.[56]

Doubtless Juda was pleased with the results of the extended meeting. Now her husband, all three sons, and their daughter Elizabeth were professing Christians and members of the Salem Baptist Church. Both John and Jim had served as church clerk. Soon Will would be active, and on August 22, 1874, he was named as one of four messengers to the Ocoee Baptist Association with instructions to petition the Association to conduct the next meeting at the Salem Church.[57] With Joseph now participating as a member in its fellowship, the church continued its effort to strengthen the moral fiber of its members by the strict enforcement of a code of conduct. In October 1874, for example, the church in conference voted on the application by William F. McCormack, long time business associate of Joseph, to grant him a new hearing on the discipline previously imposed on him. In September 1872, the church had heard a charge against McCormack for "disorderly and immoral conduct" and, by a vote of the congregation, had decided that the "church declare she cannot fellowship with him." By October 1874, McCormack had apparently asked for forgiveness by the church and requested a new hearing. The hearing was held Monday morning, December 14, 1874. The minutes reflect the discussion and final decision by the church:

> Monday Morning   Dec. the 14th 1874
>
> The church met according to appointment and after prayer proceeded to business by appointing Elder R.T. Howard moderator for the day.
>
> First, took up the case of Brother Wm. F. McCormack for reconsideration which was debated at some length and, upon motion, the Church agreed to sustain her record of September 1872 and upon the acknowledgment of Brother Wm. F. McCormack, the Church forgave and restored him.[58]

The church apparently recognized the weakness of the flesh and in most cases was quick to forgive and restore the estranged party to membership when guilt was admitted and forgiveness requested. Numerous members were identified in the church minutes over a ten-year period as failing to maintain the moral code and detracting from the fellowship of the church body. When a charge was brought against a member, a committee was appointed to visit with the offending party to determine the truth of the allegation and, if it were true, to invite the member to meet with the church and seek its forgiveness. Such was the case in April 1873, when Mac Conner, son of M.H. Conner, confessed to the charge of "fighting" and begged forgiveness. The church voted to forgive him following a motion and a second.[59] Contrary to that of many others of the community, the name of Joseph Roark, during his time as a member of the church, does not appear in the minutes as a person charged with a violation of the code of conduct nor with disturbing the fellowship of the church.

Much of Joseph's Christian character was tested, however, by the taxes rendered by James County. His 1873 taxes had climbed to $36.00 which he paid April 2, 1874. By the next year, his state and county taxes were assessed at $43.20, an increase of almost 100% over his taxes for the first year of James County and 400% greater than his last taxes paid to Hamilton County in 1870. Nevertheless, Joseph paid his 1874 taxes on January 5, 1875.[60]

The business activity for Joseph in late 1874 and 1875 clearly indicates that Joseph was not in good health. No business transactions were recorded and very few bills were paid. No promissory notes were written after 1873. Joseph had been very active on his farm and in the community during his lifetime and a cessation of such activity could only indicate declining health. Joseph previously had stomach problems and trouble with his digestive system but by late 1874 the problems were severe. In October he had made a trip to Chattanooga, presumably his last, and while records do not indicate as much, probably consulted a doctor about his health.[61] In December, Joseph made five trips to Old Washington in Rhea County to consult with the elderly and respected Dr. Darius Waterhouse. Waterhouse was the son of merchant Richard Waterhouse from whom Joseph and his brother James had made purchases in the early 1830s. Dr. Waterhouse had lived in Old Washington most of his life, having remained there after his father had left for Texas in 1850. He had studied medicine at Transylvania College in Lexington, Kentucky, and had confined his practice to Old Washington and the surrounding area. At the time he treated Joseph, Waterhouse was sixty years old. Following his examination of Joseph, Dr. Waterhouse shared his diagnosis–it was cancer.[62] At each subsequent visit, the doctor labored with Joseph and prescribed medicine and treatment. Dr. Waterhouse recommended no solid foods be eaten and prescribed a diet of milk, tapioca, broths, and cooked pulp of ripe fruit. Following the medical practice of the day, Waterhouse probably prescribed pills of combined chloride of gold and soda, and extract of conium, to be taken three times a day with the results closely observed. The frequency of the visits to Dr. Waterhouse–three to four days between visits–would indicate the severity of Joseph's problems and the rapid evaluation of prescribed treatment. It is doubtful that the medicine did much good and probably the conclusion of both Waterhouse and Joseph was that the stomach cancer had developed to such an extent that successful treatment could not be expected. Joseph doubtless was somewhat discouraged after his final visit with Dr. Waterhouse. Six weeks later, Joseph received word that the doctor himself had died.[63]

Joseph's condition grew worse in 1875, and he was apparently in some pain much of the time. His condition became acute in the latter part of 1875, and a bland diet and careful attention to the foods he ate no longer provided relief. Doubtless the last six months was a time of suffering and pain.

As Joseph struggled with his health in 1875, two of his contemporaries who had significantly influenced the political environment following the Civil War, also were suffering reverses in fortunes. Andrew Johnson, after surviving his impeachment,

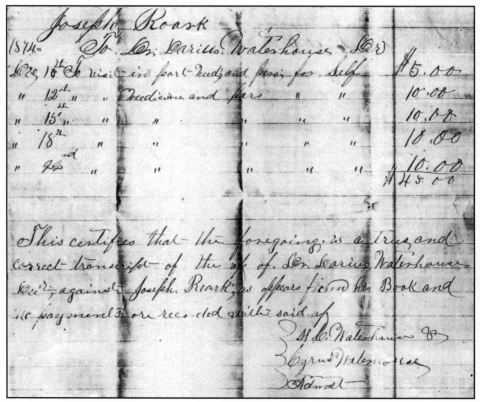

Invoice from Dr. Darius Waterhouse, Old Washington, Rhea County, to Joseph Roark for treatment of stomach cancer in December 1874. The invoice was sent over the signatures of H.C. Waterhouse and Cyrus Waterhouse, administrators of the estate of Darius Waterhouse, who died six weeks following his treatment of Joseph.

left the White House in 1869 and had returned to his home in Tennessee. The Tennessee General Assembly elected him to fill the U.S. Senate seat in early 1875 and Johnson returned to Washington to gather with those who had decided his fate in 1868. He died shortly thereafter in Washington on July 31, 1875. Meanwhile, at his home in Knoxville, former governor William G. Brownlow lay sick and paralyzed in 1875, unable to speak above a whisper, his vituperative voice thus silenced. He died on April 29, 1877.

Still, as one might expect of a person who had been orderly in his business, Joseph Roark moved to get all of his affairs in order. He spoke to Juda, his three sons, and Elizabeth in what would have been a sad and somber meeting, of the manner in which the estate was to be divided. On May 3, 1875, Joseph sent a registered letter to his daughter Mary Ann Scott in Arkansas. The contents of the letter are unknown but only estate matters would warrant the additional expense of a registered letter.[64]

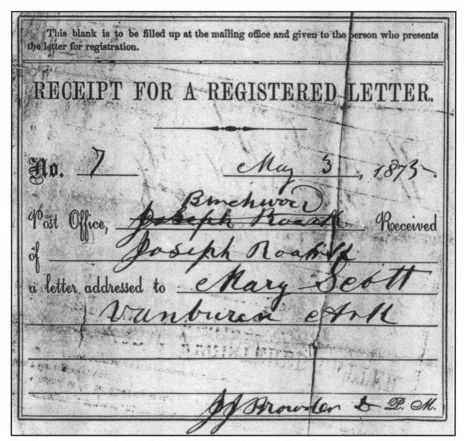

Receipt to Joseph Roark for a registered letter to his daughter, Mary Ann Scott, May 3, 1875, doubtless dealing with estate issues.

In the first part of August, Joseph received a letter from Noah Atchley, written for his wife Juda Ann, asking for additional monies thought to be due her from the Leonard Brooks estate:

Elk Creek, Texas County, Mo.
August 1, 1875

Mr. Joe Roark

dear sir, after my compliments to you and family I will simply ask you if you are willing to pay the interest on the money that you paid my wife. She has as much right to her part as Matilda had or any one else. The principle is all she ever received and the interest I want because it is just. So will you please write to me immediately and let me know what you will do whether you will pay it or not. So write soon direct to Elk Creek, Texas County, Mo.

Noah Atchley[65]

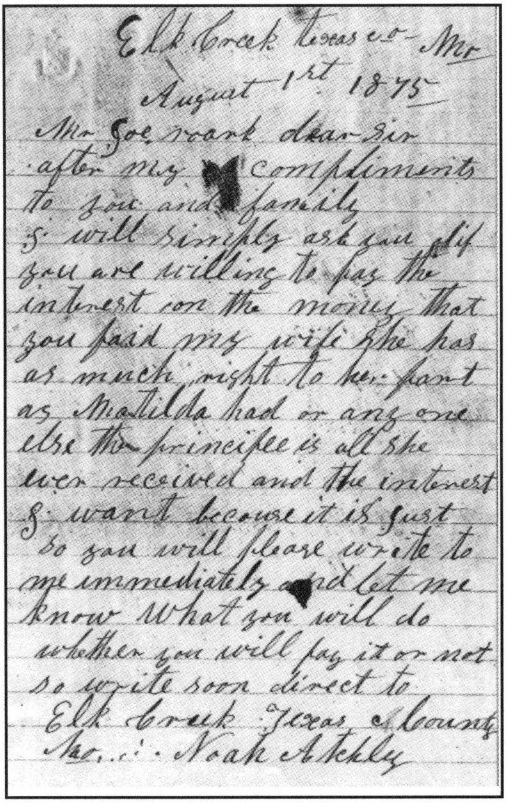

Letter dated August 1, 1875, from Noah Atchley, Texas County, Missouri, seeking additional monies for his wife, Juda Ann Brooks Atchley, from Joseph Roark and the Leonard Brooks estate.

No record of a response to Atchley remains. Under the circumstances, one can easily imagine the response of Joseph, even if he answered the letter at all.

By late November, Joseph undoubtedly knew the end was near. In his organized way, he wanted to have all personal matters taken care of and all bills paid. His 1875 taxes were not due until late January but Joseph wanted to pay the taxes early and clear all debts. So he asked Davis Priddy to make the tax payment for him on Priddy's next trip to Ooltewah. Priddy was a local farmer, four years older than Joseph, and a member of the Salem Church. Priddy made the trip to Ooltewah on November 19 and returned to Joseph a receipt from S.J. Lewis, Tax Collector for James County, for $41.00.[66] Priddy was to remain supportive of Joseph's family until Priddy's death in February 1882.

Christmas came and went and Joseph was doubtless visited by his children and grandchildren that lived in the area. Joseph and Juda then had eighteen grandchildren living in the Salem Community ranging in age from Elizabeth Cookston, Elizabeth's daughter at 25, to Julia, the daughter of John and Permelia, who was almost two. No doubt Joseph and Juda enjoyed the family and delighted at being together.

Joseph's health continued to decline after the first of the year. On January 19, 1876, he felt well enough to transact business by paying his account in full with Georgetown merchant W.F. Francisco and Company. It was to be his last known business transaction.[67]

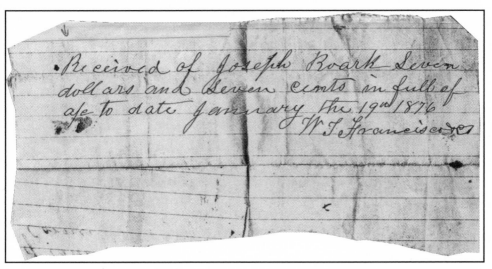

Receipt from W.F. Francisco, Georgetown merchant, evidencing the last business transaction of Joseph Roark on January 19, 1876, twenty-seven days before his death.

By the first of February, Joseph had become very weak and it became clear that the end was now in sight. He suffered more as each day passed. The pain was intense as he struggled to survive. The excessive pain, nervous irritability, and wakefulness required the sedatives that the doctor had prescribed for pain when it became unbearable in the last days. Sedatives and narcotics such as conium, belladonna, and mild combinations of opium and extract of scullcap were given to him in order to provide some relief from the pain.[68] During Joseph's days of suffering, the local papers in Cleveland and Chattanooga told of plans for the centennial celebration to be held in both cities on July 4–Joseph's birthday–and described the facilities under construction in Philadelphia for the Centennial Exposition. The *Cleveland Banner* wrote that Edwin Booth, brother of John Wilkes Booth, would play in Chattanooga on February 26 and concluded, "it will be a treat to hear him."[69]

By Monday, February 14, Joseph was decidedly weaker and by now he could only take liquids. He had lost considerable weight and was confined to his bed. The strong mind and indomitable spirit faded in and out as the sedatives and drugs took their effect. Tuesday morning, February 15, 1876, Joseph Roark breathed his last–five months shy of his sixty-third birthday. The *Chattanooga Daily Times* that day carried an editorial entitled, "Tennessee and the Centennial" in which the paper strongly supported the Centennial Exposition in Philadelphia for "the grandeur and importance of our international exhibition on the occasion of a century of American progress."[70] The progress of the United States, during its first century, that would be so enthusiastically exhibited in Philadelphia that summer would be missed by Joseph Roark, a man who had witnessed and participated in so much of that progress.

He had been born during the War of 1812 at a time when the new nation was struggling to establish its personality and its position in the family of nations. During his formative years, the nation's population was generally centered between the Atlantic coast and the western slopes of the Appalachians but was enamored with the possibilities of western expansion. He was a man of that western expansion and a man of the frontier, born in the path of Daniel Boone, and had grown up with the self-sufficiency required of frontier living. He knew little of culture or the finery of east coast society. Yet he had been able to observe and participate in the expansion and growth of the country far beyond the vicarious experiences of many of those in that society. He followed the events of the war with Mexico and saw its results in the nation's "Manifest Destiny" and expansion to the west coast. Prior to his death, he had been able to envision, with others of that time, the final boundaries of the continental United States.

He had been able to observe and participate in the expansion and growth of the country as it utilized the products of the industrial revolution. From the days when farm production resulted solely from a man's own labor plus that of his horse or oxen, he saw the development and effective utilization of mechanical farm equipment that greatly expanded the production of the individual farmer. He saw the development of the steamboat and then saw its use surpassed by the nation's system of railroads. He saw the development of the telegraph system for rapid communication and, after growing up in the isolation of the ridges of Claiborne County, was able to receive the news of Lincoln's assassination early morning of the next day.

He lived throughout the Civil War and survived the most divisive period in the nation's history. Tragically, he had lived during the war in East Tennessee where not only the nation was divided but where neighborhoods and communities were equally divided. He saw his hard-earned fortunes wane and the daily objective become one of simply finding enough to eat. He came through that divisive and savage period with self-respect and respect from his neighbors. He saw his sons mature beyond their years in the brutality of combat, yet return after the war to take up the plow and become respected citizens of the community. With his family, he survived the hard years of reconstruction and, without bitterness, rebuilt his fences, restored his crop lands, completely rebuilt his mill, reestablished his herds, regrew his orchards, and left for his children a significant estate.

He was a man with business acumen and possessed the drive to succeed against overwhelming odds. He thrived on free enterprise and the American system. He was intense in his business ventures, hard-nosed in his negotiations, and organized in a level of detail far beyond what might be expected of a frontier farmer. He kept detailed records of his business activities and used his innate ability of organization to assist others in estate settlements in a fair and equitable manner.

His demeanor was serious, for life for him had not been an easy road to travel. He met his responsibilities and obligations and he expected others to do the same, having little patience with those who did not.

He was involved in the local community and provided meaningful support to the community school and church. While his brothers served terms as constable and as the local justice of the peace, he sought no elective office or public recognition. Community service to him was behind the scenes in day-to-day work in mundane tasks. Personal popularity had little meaning to him.

Nevertheless, the respect in which he was held by the local community was obvious. Without distinctive family inheritance, he developed, on his own, a reputation of honesty and reliability. His promissory notes were preferred over most bank notes, and he could do more on his credit than many could do with cash. His advice was sought on financial matters and he had little trouble forming partnerships to expand his business opportunities. He was both courageous and tenacious in taking action against any adversary to obtain what he considered fair settlement. Matilda and Juda Ann Brooks could never really appreciate his bulldog tenacity in securing their inheritance for them.

In sharp contrast to his often harsh approach to business was his compassion. He was always ready to help those who needed a home and could not provide for themselves, particularly minor children. He raised six children of his own to maturity and marriage, yet in addition he brought five other young children into a home that was already much too small and welcomed them as part of his family. Jane Clingan, Matilda and Juda Ann Brooks, and Alexander and Jim Carr were loved, cared for, raised as family, and were recipients of his compassion. His compassion quite naturally extended to hospitality, and he provided board and lodging for ministers at the Salem Church and teachers at the local school. He reached out to the local community and it, in turn, responded with respect and admiration.

Family was important to him and, with Juda, he was able to provide an environment that encouraged his children to become mature adults. While he was able to provide each of his children with an inheritance, love for his children went far beyond financial assistance. The precious memory by his daughter Margaret of his walking to Georgetown to buy sugar for her wedding cake, in itself, speaks volumes.

But lastly and most of all, he was courageous. He had the courage to daily look life in the face and to act responsibly. Not only was he courageous in facing the problems of daily living, he was also unafraid to step out in confidence and faith to face new challenges and opportunities. This courage enabled him to establish a new home with a young family in the frontier environment of the Ocoee District. He was truly a man of character, with the strength to do, the will to dare, and the courage to find his place.

> *In the fell clutch of circumstance*
> *I have not winced nor cried aloud.*
> *Under the bludgeonings of chance*
> *My head is bloody, but unbowed.*

William Ernest Henley

Chapter 12

Epilogue

On Wednesday, February 16, 1876, friends and relatives of Joseph Roark gathered at the home place and followed the wagon carrying the wood coffin to Bald Hill Cemetery. Moving slowly in wagons along the Birchwood Pike that cold winter day were Joseph's family and that of his brother James, plus his nieces and nephews from his brother John's family. Included in the procession were close friends and members of the Salem Church with whom Joseph had been associated throughout the years in the old Ocoee District–M.H. and Martha Conner, Davis and Eliza Priddy, Betsy Jane Webb, Silas and Martha Jane Witt, William and Nancy Thatcher, Joseph

Cookston, and others. Arriving at the Bald Hill Cemetery, A.L.Stulce, then pastor of the Salem Church, conducted the brief graveside service. Joseph Roark was laid to rest on the prominent hill overlooking the valley of the Tennessee River.

Following the funeral, Juda Roark returned to the home place with her family. She would continue to keep house for herself and her son, Will, who would live at the home place and run the farm. Will would provide strong support for his mother in the days immediately following Joseph's death. Other family members would keep her company and help her in the necessary adjustment.

Grave Marker

By 1885, two years after the death of Juda, a stone marker was placed at the head of Joseph's grave. Unfortunately,

Original grave marker placed at the head of Joseph Roark's grave sometime after 1785. Data on the marker gives incorrect information on Joseph's life span.

371

with the passing of his wife and his older brother James, the exact birth date of Joseph was not available to the family. The grave marker, with its hand-carved data, is thus in error in regard to Joseph's age at his death. Nevertheless, the original marker reads:

Joseph Roark
Died
Feb 15 1876
Age
62 Yrs 10 Mos 18 Days

Years later, a new marker was placed to mark the graves of both Joseph and Juda Roark. The new marker is also in error in that it gives his birth simply as 1814 rather than the correct date, July 4, 1813.

Estate Settlement

At the time of his death, Joseph was the owner of 840 acres, gener-ally located along the Tennessee River and Grasshopper Creek. In the conversation with his fami-ly just prior to his death, Joseph had made it clear just how he wanted his estate to be divided. Although he left no will, his intent and desire was apparently clear to all the

Later grave marker at the graves of Joseph Roark and Juda Carr Roark. The birth date of Joseph is incorrectly given as 1814.

family. In the custom of the time, Juda was not provided a life estate in the home place by a written document, but doubtless it was clearly understood that the home place was to be her home as long as she might choose or until her death. The youngest son, Will, who still lived at the home place, had the primary responsibility of providing for his mother's welfare.

It is reasonably clear that Joseph had given farms to each of his children as they married and began their family. What is unclear, however, is the manner in which title to each farm was actually transferred from Joseph to his children. One fact is clear—no deed for land given to any of his children was ever recorded in the court-houses of either Hamilton or James Counties. More than likely a deed of sorts was written or given to the son or daughter who then took the "deed" to the courthouse to establish title for the purpose of taxation, since that was the condition of the gift—the son or daughter was to be responsible for paying the taxes but also, of course, was to receive all revenue the farm was to produce. For what ever reason,

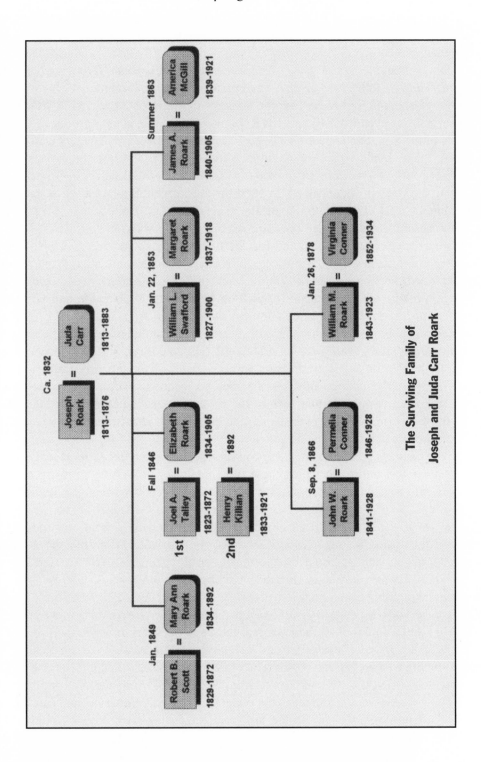

**The Surviving Family of
Joseph and Juda Carr Roark**

whether on instruction from Joseph or neglect on the part of the recipients, the deeds were never recorded.

As an example, Joseph's first daughter to marry, Elizabeth, following her marriage to Joel A. Talley, was given a small tract south of the Joseph Roark home place on which she and Joel lived, plus the 80 acres of Grants 2131 and 3176 which her father had received in 1840 and 1841. The two forty-acre tracts were the NE4 and NW4 of the SE4, Section 21, FT2N, R3W, and were located immediately west of the M.H. Conner land. No deed to the 80 acres was recorded, but Joel Talley was taxed on the specific 80 acres under the direct assessment by the Federal government following the war.[1] In a land survey in 1868 for the adjacent Benjamin Webb tract, the field notes refer to the south line of the 80 acres as "J.A. Talley's line."[2] Regardless of the absence of a recorded deed, tax assessors and surveyors considered the 80-acre tract the property of Joel and Elizabeth Talley. As noted earlier, Joseph Roark had been forced in early 1870 to take possession of the 80-acre tract, through loan default and sheriff's sale, to protect the tract from claims against unpaid taxes.

Simililarly, Margaret and Bill Swafford lived on, paid taxes for, and farmed a portion of Joseph's land prior to their move west in 1856. As in the case of Elizabeth, a deed probably was given to the Swaffords but not recorded. It appears that the title still rested with the Swaffords in 1876 at the time of Joseph's death. The same was true for Mary Ann and Robert Beane Scott. They, too, had unrecorded title to some part of Joseph's holdings although the specific location of their tract is unknown today. It is quite possible that each of the three sons also had unrecorded deeds in 1876 for specific portions of Joseph's land, although it is least likely in the case of Will, since he was the youngest and was yet unmarried.

The primary question that had to be addressed in settlement of the Joseph Roark estate was the manner in which these individually owned tracts, with unrecorded title, would be handled in conjunction with the division of the remaining land owned by Joseph. Would, for example, the tract that Margaret owned be her sole share of the estate or would it be combined with an additional portion? Joseph apparently had shared the answer to this question; however, the mechanism for equitably dealing among all the siblings could lead to thorny issues yet unresolved. Obviously, the three brothers met very soon after their father's death and began to address the sensitive and possibly contentious issues to be resolved. Of course, the sensitivity in settling the estate was increased by the fact that both Elizabeth and Mary Ann were now widows and would look to their share of the estate for their future support.

Whether it was because he was the eldest son, or because Joseph Roark had specifically so directed, Jim Roark took on the responsibility as administrator of the estate. In his first task as administrator, Jim developed a list of accounts payable and accounts receivable. Undoubtedly, his father had carefully preserved and catalogued all of his promissory notes so the task involved listing from Joseph's records all appropriate promissory notes. By the first of the month following Joseph's death, Jim had developed a list of debts and receivables of the estate and had begun some collection of debts as might be expected. The list Jim developed included 40 promissory notes or accounts of unsecured cash debt. The last nine notes on the list were euphemistically labeled by Jim as "Notes that not good." Also on the list were ten unsecured accounts that apparently were receivables. As best that could be determined today, since Jim was not real clear as to which notes were payable and which were receivable, the total amount of promissory notes payable to the estate amounted to $1,558.13, unsecured accounts totaled $59.25, while the notes regarded by Jim as non-collectible amounted to $171.02. Notes payable, brought in from individuals in the community when notified that the estate was being settled, were apparently insignificant, indicating that Joseph had made a special effort to clear all debts before he died.[3]

The largest promissory note on Jim's accounts receivable list was from R.B. Friddle for $400, the smallest from I.L. Fuis for $1.00. The "not good" notes were from:

Joseph Gooden	$5.00
Wilson Hixson	40.00
James Smith	16.32
Calif Johnson	3.75
John Bare	3.75
John Campbell	2.20
Cleaver Shelton	50.00
B. McClanahan	30.00
Jonathan Smith	20.00

Interestingly, the three sons of Joseph Roark were on the list of persons with outstanding promissory notes payable to him. Jim was listed with a promissory note of $180, John had a note of $154.98 due, and Will had a note payable in the amount of $19.60. Upon completion of the list, Jim reviewed it with his brothers in an informal status report. Will settled his promissory note to his father by writing another to Jim, as administrator of the estate, for the same amount, payable in twelve months:

Amt $19.60
Twelve months after date I promise to pay James A. Roark, Admr of Joseph
Roark, Deceased, Nineteen Dollars and sixty cts to draw ten per [cent]
interest when [?] for value recieved of him. This mar the 18th 1876
William M. Roark[4]

One of the three brothers, probably Will, had written sisters Mary Ann Scott and Margaret Swafford shortly after the funeral advising them of their father's death. In the middle of March, Margaret and Bill Swafford arrived from Decatur County to visit Margaret's mother. Bill still had family in the area so it was a trip home for both of them. At the time, Bill was a county magistrate in Decatur County and served on the county court. Probably coming by train through Nashville and Chattanooga, they were met by Will at the train station in Ooltewah and taken to the home place where they would stay. Whether they brought with them any of their children, who ranged in age from Mary Ann 21, to Azelea, just six months, is unknown. In the first few days after their arrival, Margaret and Bill met with Jim, John, Will, and Elizabeth to discuss the procedure for settling the estate.

Jim explained the wishes of their father, as they had heard them, for an equitable distribution of the estate among the six children. It seems apparent that just prior to his death, Joseph had estimated the total value of the estate and had indicated that the two daughters that still had unrecorded title to land in the estate, Mary Ann and Margaret, should receive $800 for their portion. In turn, they would destroy the deed given to them previously by their father (if in fact such an instrument had been written) and quit claim their undivided interest in the homestead either to the estate or to their three brothers jointly. What then about Elizabeth? The 80-acre tract that she and Joel Talley had previously owned had gone back to the estate when Joseph had gained title through the sheriff's sale. Apparently Joseph had specified a reduced amount be provided to Elizabeth for that reason plus the fact that she continued to live on a small tract of the estate south of the home place. With her expression that she was in need of money, Jim responsively provided her with three promissory notes and a cash payment of $39.65. A receipt was in turn provided by Elizabeth:

March 23rd 1876

Recievd of James A. Roark, Admr of Joseph Roark, Deceased

One note for	$400.00
One note	60.00
One note	5.00
Act for	39.65

Attest

W.L. Swafford   Sarah E. Roark[5]

The purpose of the individual notes is unclear. It is interesting to see that the receipt was witnessed by Bill Swafford. He probably was requested to witness the receipt since he was outside the immediate family. Also of interest is the fact that Elizabeth signed with her maiden name rather than her married name. Probably little should be read into this. Since it was an estate settlement and her maiden name that related her to the estate should appear in her signature, she signed as "Roark" and simply omitted her married name.

The next item on the agenda for settlement of the estate was the sale of personal property. This undesirable task was scheduled the last week in March and a list remains of each item sold, the purchaser, and the amount paid. The handwriting on the list indicates that John kept the records at the sale while Jim and Will managed the event. The list records that Joseph's widow, Juda, took several items to maintain her household: two beds with furniture, one desk, one clock, two cans of lard, three bee stands, and one heifer, all at a cost of $3.00. The most expensive items sold were,

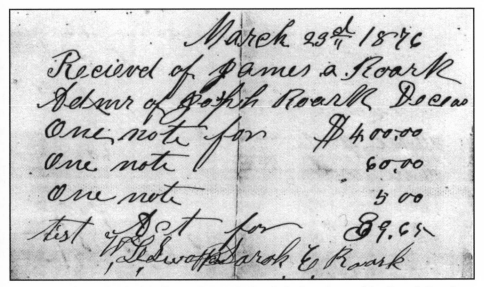

*Receipt from Elizabeth Talley to James A. Roark for her share of the Joseph Roark
estate. Elizabeth signed her name as Sarah E. Roark. Her husband, Joel A. Talley,
had died in Arkansas three years before. The receipt was witnessed by
her brother-in-law, William L. Swafford.*

of course, horses. Four horses were sold for a total of $292.50–Elizabeth Talley took
one for $60.00, and John took one for $99.75. Those taking part in the sale and purchasing other items were W.W. Lillard, J. Aslinger, W.F. Rains, James Campbell, Ben
Davis, John Eldridge, Robert Armor, A.G. Irwin, W.F. Conner, T.J. Leonard, A.L.
Stulce, Pleasant Doughty, Bill Gardenhire, J.C. Norman, and Jacob Baker. Items
sold include a turning plow and various other plows, a shovel, a scythe, a grindstone,
bacon, fifteen bee stands, a wagon, a harrow, a mule, two cows, and two heifers. The
item sold which most clearly touched the emotions was the sewing machine that
Joseph had bought for Juda five years before. It was purchased by John Roark for
$20, hopefully to return it to his mother as a cherished possession.

Sometime after the personal property sale, the three brothers were confronted
with a crisis in the estate settlement. Perhaps it resulted from a disagreement within
the family, perhaps not. Most likely, it came from the realization that significant
money was involved in the estate, that they had no written will to guide them, that
severe family disagreements could occur, that a cash infusion would be needed from
each of the brothers if they were to keep all the land in the estate and settle in cash
with their sisters, and that final settlement of the estate could not be achieved for
many months. Simultaneously, Jim expressed a distaste for being administrator. He
did not feel qualified and, second, he and America had made plans to relocate to Texas
within the year–he did not want the estate settlement to delay his move. Jim had
purchased nothing at the personal property sale for a specific reason–he would soon

have to dispose of many of his own possessions when he relocated. Doubtless he suggested Will be the administrator since he lived at the home place, did not have a family to look after, and was more centrally located to deal with estate matters. A change in the administrator of the estate added to the compounding issues. The crisis forced corrective action. The brothers agreed to seek assistance from and employ J.P. Talley, a family friend and member of the Salem Church, who was on the county court of James County and was familiar with estate settlements. Talley agreed to help and the brothers reviewed with him the instructions that had come from their father. Talley suggested he draft a written agreement that would guide the further settlement of the estate. He also suggested that Will, as administrator, would need to obtain Letters of Administration from the county clerk before the estate could be finally settled.[6]

Even after the personal property sale, the estate had insufficient cash to settle with the three daughters of Joseph. It appears that sufficient cash was available to pay only Margaret for her share, and since she and Bill had made the long trip to the home place, it was agreed that she should receive her share immediately. On April 5, Margaret and Bill received $800 and executed the following quit claim deed, probably drafted by J.P. Talley, in accordance with her father's wishes:

> This indenture made the 5th day of April the year one thousand eight hundred and seventy six between W.L. Swafford and wife Margaret Swafford of the County of Decatur and State of Tennessee of the first part and James A. Roark, John W. Roark and William Roark of the County of James and State of Tennessee of the second part:
>
> Witnesseth that the said parties of the first part for and in consideration of the sum of eight hundred dollars to them in hand paid the receipt whereof is hereby acknowledged have remised, released and quit claimed and by these presents do remise, release and quit claim unto the parties of the second part and to their heirs and assigns forever all their right, title, claim and undivided interest and heirship in the estate of Joseph Roark, deceased, consisting of real and personal effects and interest in dower to have and to hold the above premises mentioned together unto the said parties of the second part their heirs and assigns forever.
>
> In witness whereof we have hereunto set our hands and seals the day and year first above written.
>
> W.L. Swafford (Seal)
her
Margaret J. X Swafford (Seal)
mark
>
> Sealed and delivered in the presence of
> John Swafford
> John Campbell
> A.R. Irwin[7]

By the first week in April, Talley had drafted an agreement to assist in settling

Left page of the agreement, executed by Jim, John, and Will Roark, for settlement of the estate of their father, Joseph Roark.

Right page of the estate settlement agreement, executed by Jim, John, and Will Roark on April 11, 1876. The agreement was witnessed by Davis Priddy.

the estate. After detailed review, Jim, John, and Will executed the agreement and posted bonds with Talley to guarantee its execution. The document remains and consists of a folded page written book-style on facing pages. Portions of the agreement have been frayed and lost and the remainder is quite fragile. The text remaining, as best as can be determined, reads as follows:

> . . . and the contract [approximately three words missing] James A. Roark and John W. Roark is to have the land that belong to the Estate of Joseph Roark deceased known as the river farm and William Roark is to give them a quit title to his interest in said farm and one third interest of Margaret Swafford that he has bough[t] of her and William also to give a quit claim of one third parte of said land that did belong to Sary E. Roark [Talley] and is to buy that portion that belongs to Mary A. Scott and make the title of the same to the above named James A. Roark and John W. Roark and James A. Roark and John W. Roark is to pay each to William M. Roark [one word missing] hundred [one or two words missing] dollars . . . [end of left side of document] . . . be entitled to said estate and James A. Roark and John W. Roark is to have 40 acres that joins the River farm known as the Jesse Killian forty and William M. Roark is to give a quit claim to that in the same manner that he does the River farm. Where unto we subscribe our names this 11 day of April 1876
>
> Attest: Davis Priddy   James A. Roark
>   John W. Roark
>   William M. Roark[8]

From the agreement it is clear that Joseph intended for Will to have the home place and surrounding lands and that Jim and John were to pay some amount, probably several hundred dollars, to receive the river-bottom land. The monies paid by Jim and John were to be used by the estate to pay Mary Ann, Elizabeth, and Margaret in cash for their share of the estate.

In the week following execution of the agreement, Will, now administrator of the estate, wrote Mary Ann in Arkansas asking her to execute an enclosed quit claim deed for her portion of the estate lands. Will stated in his letter that Mary Ann's share of the estate was $800 which would be sent when the quit claim deed was received. Mary Ann responded in a letter written for her but obviously expressing her ideas. The letter shows the sage wisdom of one who had experienced the hard knocks of life:

> Van Buren Ark May the 6th
> Wm. Roark
>
> Will you must not think hard of me for not singing [signing] the deed before the money come. I was not afraid to trust to your honer about it but life [is] uncertain and deth [death] sure and if I was to sign the deed and send it and you should drop of sudent [sudden] and say nothing about it I would be out forever. So I just send a bond binding my self to make the deed when you sent [send] the money. I only give you to the 1st of July to

Letters of Administration, issued to Will Roark, administrator of the Joseph Roark estate, by James County Clerk, J.C. Heaton, on October 1, 1877.

Receipt to Will Roark, administrator of the Joseph Roark estate, issued by J.C. Heaton for $13.00 as the full amount of court costs "for winding up said Estate," September 23, 1878.

send it. I suposed that would be as much time as you would want.

This leaves us all well hoping [it] will find you all injoying the same blessing.

Will, write soon let me know how Mother is getting along. I will have to close hoping to here from you soon. I remain as ever your sister

M.A. Scott[9]

Mary Ann enclosed a handwritten bond in the amount of $1,600 signed by her and attested by Josiah Hanui and George W. Webb.[10] Will sent the $800 as requested and received the quit claim deed, identical to that executed by Margaret, signed by Mary Ann on June 2, 1876.[11]

In the interim, Will continued to pursue collection of the "not good" notes. In June he was able to obtain $15.00 from James Smith on his promissory note of $16.32. Two weeks later, June 28, 1876, Will compromised slightly and accepted a new promissory note from Smith for $1.21 to settle the account.[12]

To settle with J.P. Talley for his services, John paid his one-third in cash to Jim and Will, and on July 24, Jim and Will executed jointly a promissory note to Talley for $100.[13]

On July 27, 1876, John and Will quit claimed their interest to Jim in sixty acres as the south one-half of the river farm and in fifteen acres as the east one-half of the Killian tract.[14] The deed records are not conclusive, but it can be safely assumed that Jim and Will executed a similar quit claim deed to John for the north one-half and the west one-half, respectively, of the above tracts. On the same date in July, Jim and John executed a quit claim deed to Will for their interest in "three hundred and fifteen acres be the same more or less known as the

The three sons of Joseph Roark, taken in Chattanooga following the settlement of their father's estate and prior to Jim's departure for Texas. Left to right: Jim, John (standing), and Will.

home farm lying on the waters of grass hopper creek."[15]

Following significant effort on his part to collect on the "not good" notes, Will delivered them to Constable John C.I. Smith for collection. Smith was an old friend who had served with the Roark brothers in Company B, First Tennessee Cavalry, during the war. No record remains on Smith's success at collecting on the notes.[16]

The following year, as work on the estate settlement pointed to completion, Will applied for and received, on October 1, 1877, Letters of Administration from James County Clerk J.C. Heaton.[17] Settlement of the estate was finally concluded when Will, on September 23, 1878, paid $13.00 as final court costs "for winding up said Estate."[18]

It is difficult to determine from the estate settlement and the quit claim deeds executed just how much land Jim, John, and Will each received from the estate. This is primarily because land previously deeded to each son by their father was not included in the transactions. Assuming that each son had previously been given 125 acres by Joseph and had a deed to that acreage going into the estate settlement, one can calculate that Will ended up with 440 acres near and including the "home farm" and Jim and John each received 200 acres of river bottom land on the Tennessee. From the estate settlement agreement, one will note that some cash was exchanged to obtain an equitable distribution.

Following the successful settlement of the estate and prior to Jim's departure for Texas, the three brothers visited a photographer's studio in Chattanooga to have a picture made. It is the earliest picture of any of the three that survives.

Juda Carr Roark

Juda outlived her husband by almost eight years. She continued to live at the home place during those years and was homemaker for her son, Will, until January 1878, when Will married Virginia Conner, daughter of M.H. and Martha Conner. Will was living at the home place with his wife and family when Juda Roark died there on Tuesday, August 28, 1883, at the age of seventy. Juda was buried next to her husband in Bald Hill Cemetery.[19]

Mary Ann Scott

Mary Ann Scott was forty-two when her father died in 1876 and had been a widow for almost four years. When her husband, Robert Beane Scott, died in September 1872, her nine children were still at home. The five oldest children were all girls, between the ages of eleven and twenty-one. The youngest, Mary Ellen, had been just two months old when her father died. The family had then been living on and purchasing the Williams' farm in Jasper Township, Crawford County, Arkansas. She had written her parents in 1872 that she and Robert planned a visit to the Salem Community "as soon as we get our land paid for." Unfortunately, with the death of her husband and with her oldest son only ten, Mary Ann had been unable to continue farming and had lost the opportunity to purchase the farm.

When she received word of the death of her father in late February 1876, Mary

Ann had three girls and three boys still at home. One daughter, Juda Ann, obviously named for her maternal grand-mother, was married the very next day following Joseph's death–February 16, 1876, her eighteenth birthday–to Charles M. Thompson.

Mary Ann received the $800 check from Will Roark as her share of her father's estate in late May 1876 and on June 2, 1876, she executed a quit claim deed to Will as promised.[20] On November 1 the same year, Mary Ann purchased a nearby farm from Alexander and Susan Thompson for $800. The farm was described as the W2, NW4, Section 20, T10N, R32W in Crawford County, and had originally been a land grant signed by U.S. President James Buchanan, March 1, 1860.[21] Within six years, Mary Ann was able to buy an adjoining 40-acre tract from the Little Rock and Fort Smith Railway (NE4, NE4, Section 19, T10N, R32W) for $200.[22] It was necessary for her, however, to mortgage her farm on December 31, 1886, for $175, probably to meet farm and household expenses. The mortgage was satisfied in full on December 24, 1891.[23]

Mary Ann Roark Scott, Crawford County, Arkansas, Ca. 1890.

Mary Ann Scott died on her farm on Sunday, October 9, 1892, at the age of fifty-eight. At the time of her death, she was a member of the local Apostolic Church of the New Testament. She was buried next to her husband in Dripping Springs Cemetery in Crawford County. The year following their mother's death, the heirs deeded all interest in the Scott farm to Florence Bethena and husband Thomas Cicero Thompson.[24]

The children of Mary Ann Roark and Robert Beane Scott were:

(1) Martha Jane Scott, born November 1, 1850, married James E. Slover in 1873. Died February 7, 1912, buried in Dripping Springs Cemetery.

(2) Tennessee Scott, born August 17, 1852, never married. Died September 17, 1892, buried in Dripping Springs Cemetery.

(3) Florence Bethena Scott, born January 15, 1856, married Thomas Cicero Thompson in 1875. Died June 7, 1925, buried in the Thompson Family Cemetery, Crawford County.

(4) Juda Ann Scott, born February 16, 1858, married Charles M. Thompson on

February 16, 1876. Died February 15, 1930, buried in Dripping Springs Cemetery.
(5) Elizabeth (Lizzie) Scott, born January 20, 1861, married James A. Thompson on December 4, 1878. Died October 22, 1910, buried in the Thompson Family Cemetery.
(6) Noah Scott, born March 7, 1863, married Phoebe Duty on September 17, 1882. Died November 2, 1928, buried in Peevyhouse Cemetery, Crawford County.
(7) Joseph Scott, born September 25, 1865, married Emma Bell Slover on March 5, 1890. Died January 23, 1899, buried in Dripping Springs Cemetery.
(8) Mary Ellen Scott, born July 7, 1872, married Stonewall Kirkes on September 25, 1890. Died March 1947.[25]

Dripping Springs Cemetery, Crawford County, Arkansas, burial location of Mary Ann Roark Scott and Robert Beane Scott. Unidentifiable graves are marked only by field stones.

Sarah Elizabeth Talley

Elizabeth had seen more than her share of sorrow in the months and years before her father died. She and her husband, Joel, had lost their daughter Amanda at age sixteen in 1863, and in 1870 Joel, daughter Mary and husband William Smith, and sons Joseph, Benjamin, and Andrew had left for Arkansas to seek a new start. Then the word had come that both Joel and her son Joseph were dead. Just a short three years later, she lost her father and with him, the strength and support on which she had leaned many times.

After her father's death, Elizabeth continued to live on the small tract south of the Joseph Roark home place that she and Joel had received from her father. At home with her were Benjamin 17, Andrew 15, Margaret Ellen 12, and James William 9. As a single parent, still at the young age of only forty-one, she had work ahead in raising her family. Still, time moved rapidly, and in June 1883, both Benjamin and Andrew left again for Arkansas to pursue the opportunities they knew existed there. Two months after their departure, Elizabeth's mother died and Elizabeth had then lost both supportive parents. Five years later, in the summer of 1888, daughter Margaret Ellen married Thomas Palmer Chambers and moved to Cleveland, Bradley County. Late in the same year, Elizabeth's last child, Bill, married Elsie Jane Smith and they set up house-keeping on their own. Elizabeth, then at fifty-three, was alone.

Henry Killian and Sarah Elizabeth Roark Killian, Erath County, Texas, Ca. 1892.

She would live alone for just over three years. Events in the life of Elizabeth during that period are not clear to us today but somehow, someway, contact was made with an old childhood friend who then lived a thousand miles to the west. The roll of the Salem Baptist Church indicates that on April 9, 1892, Sarah E. Talley was again "lettered off" to transfer to another church.[26] Some time later that year, after her children were grown and departed, Elizabeth married Henry Killian of Erath County, Texas.

Henry Killian was born on September 27, 1833, in Tennessee, the second child and eldest son of William and Elizabeth Killian, neighbors to and good friends of the Joseph Roarks. A year older than Elizabeth, Henry doubtless had known Elizabeth through church and community activities. On how close they were in their early childhoods we can only speculate, but after Elizabeth's early marriage they probably had little contact. Henry Killian married his first wife, Lizzie, in 1853, and their first son, William, was born in Tennessee in 1854. Henry later had children born in Arkansas in 1865, 1867, 1869, and 1872 and records indicate that he served in the Confederate army during the Civil War. Some time in the mid 1870s, he left

Arkansas and relocated his family to Texas, choosing for his home the open range country southwest of Fort Worth. On August 27, 1878, Henry purchased 160 acres from J.B.L. Duval and R.H. Kingsbury in the cattle ranch country of northeast Erath County near the community of Morgan Mill.[27]

On March 10, 1890, Lizzie Killian died, leaving Henry a widower at age fifty-seven.[28] Some time in 1892, Henry married Elizabeth and the new Mrs. Killian was taken on her first visit to Texas. The exact date and place of their marriage has thus far been impossible to determine. Also unknown is how Henry and Elizabeth got reacquainted after having been separated for almost forty years. Did they communicate over the years? If so, some support would have been necessary since, although both were able to read, neither could write.[29]

The most likely scenario for the linking of Henry Killian and Elizabeth Talley involved the coincidental sale of a small tract adjacent to the southeast corner of the old Joseph Roark homestead tract. Sarah Killian, sister to Henry and seven years junior to him, had married E.P. Smith and, with her husband, had relocated to Erath County, Texas, following her brother there after several years. At the death of her father, William Killian, in December 1869, Sarah inherited a 31-acre tract adjacent to the Joseph Roark homestead. In late 1890, shortly after Lizzie Killian had died, Sarah had correspondence from D.A. Smith, possibly her brother-in-law, expressing an interest in buying her inherited tract. On February 17, 1891, Sarah Killian Smith sold the 31-acre tract for $15.00 to D.A. Smith and executed a deed with the signatures of E.P. and Sarah being witnessed by a justice of the peace in Erath County.[30] Coincidently, Elizabeth Talley's home was near the tract purchased by D.A. Smith and, with little imagination, one can envision a chance visit by D.A. Smith to the widow Talley, perhaps for some reason so insignificant as to ask for a drink of water or to explain his purchase of the 31 acres. Conversation turned to Sarah Smith and Henry Killian in Texas and the recent death of Henry's wife. Smith later sent the $15 to Sarah Smith in Texas and, as an aside, mentioned his visit with Elizabeth Talley. Sarah read the letter to Henry Killian and,

Grave marker for Elizabeth Roark Killian, Hightower Cemetery, Erath County, Texas.

with the work of Providence complete, Henry did the rest. Shortly thereafter, Elizabeth was on her way to the Texas cattle ranch country.

In her move to Texas in 1892, did Elizabeth make an opportunity to visit her two sons, Benjamin and Andrew, who had returned to Yell County, Arkansas, in 1883? Both sons had married in 1885 and had families by the time of her trip. Benjamin most likely married in Yell County, although the location of the marriage and the last name of his bride are both unknown. History knows her only as "Mary E."[31] By September 1886, Benjamin and Mary E. were in Delta County, Texas, where their first son was born.[32] Unfortunately, Mary E. died in 1890 or 1891, and, prior to his mother's marriage and trip to Texas, Benjamin married, a second time, to Mrs. M.J. Curry on February 24, 1892.[33] If Elizabeth were to have visited Benjamin on her train trip between Texarkana and Fort Worth, she would have met his new wife and his son John, who was then six years old. In July 1886, when his wife was expecting a child within weeks, Benjamin would settle in the town of Klondike in Delta County, purchasing that month 40 acres eight miles southwest of the county seat of Cooper.[34] Shortly after their move, Benjamin and his wife would be blessed with the birth of Benjamin's second son, Robert.[35] Tragedy, however, would seem to follow Benjamin and, in 1898, his wife, M.J., died in Klondike, leaving him a widower the second time but then with two young sons. Benjamin would marry a third time, on May 20, 1900, to Mary Alice Harper.[36] At the time of Benjamin's third marriage, John was fourteen and Robert was three. Unhappily, misfortune would strike again on March 23, 1905, when Mary Alice would die in their home at Klondike.[37] Benjamin was not to marry again. He would sell his land holdings in Delta County by 1907, the last sale occurring October 8, 1907, to J.R. Rainey Jr.,[38] and the next month, Benjamin would purchase 160 acres in Baylor County, Texas, 100 miles northwest of Fort Worth.[39] There Benjamin would raise his younger son, Robert, and would live alone after Robert left home. Benjamin Franklin Talley died of pellagra in Seymour, Texas, on March 29, 1931.[40]

Elizabeth's other son in Arkansas, Andrew Jackson Talley, or "Jack" as he was known locally, married Rebecca Smith in Yell County on January 1, 1885.[41] If Jack's mother had an opportunity to visit her son on her travel through Arkansas in 1892, she would have met Rebecca and their five sons, ages two through seven. After his mother's visit, Jack would homestead on 158 acres of rich farm land along the Petit Jean River and on January 26, 1898, would receive a land grant signed by U.S. President William McKinley.[42] Jack and Rebecca were to raise a family of twelve children, all of whom would remain in Yell County.[43] Jack and Rebecca would live until 1948 and 1950, respectively.[44]

After her move to Texas, Elizabeth was able to visit her brother, Jim, in the summer of 1894 and spend two weeks with him and his family at his home in Johnson Station in Tarrant County.[45] There is no record of Elizabeth visiting her other brother, John, who was in southeast Texas in 1901 in Milam County.

Elizabeth died on September 10, 1905, and was buried in the Hightower Cemetery just north of the Killian ranch and overlooking the rolling hills of the Texas ranch country. Henry Killian died on May 1, 1921, and was buried between his two wives in Hightower Cemetery.[46]

Grave markers for Henry Killian and his two wives in the Hightower Cemetery, Erath County, Texas. Henry's marker is the taller, flat marker in the center; Lizzie is to the left, Elizabeth is to the right.

The children of Sarah Elizabeth Roark and Joel A. Talley were:

(1) Amanda Talley, born in 1847, never married. Died in 1863, place of burial is unknown.

(2) Elizabeth Talley, born in 1850, married Francis Marion Cookston on May 20, 1870. Buried in the Cookston Cemetery, Hamilton County, Tennessee.[47]

(3) Mary C. Talley, born in 1852, married William C. Smith on March 27, 1870. Died in 1932, buried in Sulphur Springs Cemetery in Yell County, Arkansas.[48]

(4) Joseph Talley, born in 1856, never married. Died ca.1872, buried somewhere in Yell County, Arkansas.

(5) Benjamin Franklin Talley, born April 9, 1859, married, first, Mary E., probably in Yell County, Arkansas. He married, second, Mrs. M.J. Curry on February 24, 1892, in Delta County, Texas, and, third, Mary Alice Harper on May 20, 1900, in Klondike, Delta County. Died March 29, 1931, in Seymour, Texas, buried in the Old Seymour Cemetery, Baylor County, Texas.[49]

(6) Andrew Jackson Talley, born October 11, 1861, married Rebecca Smith on January 1, 1885. Died April 30, 1948, buried in Riley Creek Cemetery, Yell County, Arkansas.[50]

(7) Margaret Ellen Talley, born December 24, 1864, married Thomas Palmer Chambers in 1888. Died December 27, 1935, buried in Hillcrest Cemetery, Cleveland, Bradley County, Tennessee.[51]

(8) James William (Bill) Talley, born February 17, 1869, married Elsie Jane Smith on December 9, 1888. Bill and Elsie Jane raised a family of twelve children on a farm one mile south of the Joseph Roark homestead. He died May 18, 1955, and was buried in Bald Hill Cemetery, Hamilton County.[52]

Margaret Jane Swafford

Margaret Swafford and husband Bill returned home to Parsons in Decatur County, Tennessee, after their visit to the Salem Community following her father's death. She was thirty-eight when Joseph Roark died. During her visit to the home place, Margaret had celebrated her thirty-ninth birthday. Bill Swafford had been recently elected a magistrate in Decatur County as a Republican and was to serve in that office until 1882. He had served in the army during the Civil War with the Third Tennessee Cavalry (Union) and spent some six months with Margaret and his family in Indiana during the war.[53]

Margaret Jane Roark Swafford, Decatur County, Tennessee, Ca. 1900

In their original move to Decatur County in the mid 1850s, Bill Swafford had located near the community of Parsons. Although he made his living as a farmer, Swafford was involved in elective offices in the county and was a strong supporter of public schools and "all educational affairs." He and Margaret were members of the Missionary Baptist Church in Parsons.[54]

Bill Swafford died August 5, 1900, and was buried in the Bear Creek Cemetery west of Parsons. Following his death, Margaret moved with her oldest son, John L. Swafford, and his family near Perryville, just west of the Tennessee River in Decatur County, where she lived in her own home. Following the death of her son John in 1908, Margaret and her daughter-in-law, Dora, became particularly close. Margaret died February 13, 1918, and was buried in the Hopewell Missionary Baptist Church Cemetery west of Perryville.

The children of Margaret Jane Roark and William L. Swafford were:

(1) Mary Ann Swafford, born 1855, married T.J. Moore on November 23, 1879.[55]

(2) John Lee Swafford, born January 15, 1857, married Margaret Glendora "Dora" Moore on

Margaret Jane Roark Swafford, Decatur County, Tennessee, Ca. 1915

390

September 15, 1878.[56] Died December 16, 1908, buried in the Sardis Ridge Cemetery, Decatur County, Tennessee.[57]

(3) Julia "Judy" Swafford, born 1859. Died 1885, buried in Perryville, Decatur County.

(4) Joseph Asberry Swafford, born May 1860, married, first, Inda Bussell on December 19, 1880, and,

Grave marker of Margaret Roark Swafford with erroneous data. The marker should read: "March 27, 1837- February 13, 1918."

second, Melvina V. Bussell on April 4, 1889.[58]

(5) Isaac David Swafford, born September 28, 1861, married Tilda Dosha Rosson on November 14, 1880.[59] Died December 21, 1941, buried in Doak's Cemetery, Clarksville, Red River County, Texas.

(6) Henry Jasper Swafford, born September 23, 1863, married Sarah Rachel Jones. Died April 5, 1947, buried in Mt. Pleasant Cemetery, Graves County, Kentucky.

(7) James William Swafford, born 1864, married Sadie Boone, ca. 1888. Died and buried in Oklahoma.

Hopewell Missionary Baptist Church Cemetery, Perryville, Tennessee, burial location of Margaret Jane Roark Swafford.

(8) Sarah Callie Swafford, born 1866, married Benjamin Moore on January 5, 1885.[60]

(9) Horace M. Swafford, born 1868. Died ca. 1878.

(10) Thomas A. Swafford, born August 1870, married Emma Houston on August 27, 1899.[61] Died and buried in Arkansas.

(11) Margaret Jane "Maggie" Swafford, born June 23, 1872, married, first, John Wesley Garrett on December 18, 1890, and, second, John Henry Wright on June 23, 1900. Died May 19, 1941, buried in the Bemis Cemetery, Madison County, Tennessee.[62]

(12) America Asilee "Azelea" Swafford, born August 1875, married, first, Mat Mathison on September 11, 1888,[63] and, second, Logan Stanfield, ca. 1901. Buried in East Lawn Cemetery, Jackson, Tennessee.

(13) Louise Francis (Francis is the traditional family spelling) Swafford, born September 15, 1877, married Jerry Jerome Burton. Died July 22, 1958, buried in the Bunches Chapel Cemetery, Parsons, Decatur County, Tennessee.

James A. Roark

Jim Roark was thirty-six years old on the day his father died in 1876. His family at the time consisted of his wife, America, and seven children, ranging in ages from Nancy Jane, who was eleven, to Walter, almost two. Jim was farming the river farm of his father in 1876, but he and America were planning on a move to Texas to take advantage of available land opportunities. The move to Texas was originally planned for mid 1877, but was postponed when America became pregnant with their eighth child. Following the birth of son, Johnny, on Christmas day 1877, Jim and America set the date on their move for March 4, 1878. They requested and received their membership letter from the Salem Baptist Church in February 1878, and left the Salem Community for Texas the following month.[64]

James A. Roark and America McGill Roark, Mansfield, Texas, 1900.

Jim purchased 210 acres south of the community of Johnson Station in Tarrant County in September 1778 and settled his family ten miles southeast of Fort Worth. He and America became members of the Rehoboth Baptist Church located a mile south of their farm. In April 1889, the youngest child, Johnny, just over two years old, died and was buried in the church cemetery. The following year, October 31, 1881, their last child, Mary Maud, was born. The year 1891 was a difficult time for Jim and his wife. On January 12, Jim and America lost their son, Mitchell

Leonidas, who died at age twenty-four. In August, their eldest daughter, Nancy Jane, died seventeen months after her marriage to H.W. Smith and four months after the birth in February of twin girls, both of whom died in May 1891. It was only four years after Nancy died that Jim and America lost another daughter, Belle, a school teacher in Italy, Texas, who died in December 1894 of pneumonia.

In 1900, Jim retired from farming and purchased a home in Mansfield, Texas. He and America lived in Mansfield for less than three years when Jim's love for farming led him to buy another farm, 154 acres, in northeast Tarrant County. There Jim lived for just over a year before he died on Saturday, May 6, 1905. America survived Jim by sixteen years and died in her Fort Worth home on June 26, 1921. Both Jim and America were buried in the Rehoboth Church Cemetery.

The children of James A. Roark were:

(1) Nancy Jane "Nannie" Roark, born 1864, married H.W. "Wat" Smith on March 25, 1890, in Johnson Station, Texas. Died August 20, 1891, in Alvarado, Texas. Place of burial is unknown.

(2) Joseph William Roark, born May 21, 1866, married Dorcas Annie Turner on December 24, 1890, in Gainesville, Texas. Died July 14, 1953, and buried in Evergreen Cemetery, Colorado Springs, Colorado.

(3) Mitchell Leonidas Roark, born 1867, never married. Died January 12, 1891. Location of death and place of burial is unknown.

Grave marker of James A. and America Roark, Rehoboth Baptist Church Cemetery, Arlington, Texas.

(4) Ameda Belva "Belle" Roark, born July 20, 1869, never married. Died December 22, 1894, in Italy, Texas, and buried in the Rehoboth Church Cemetery, Tarrant County, Texas.

(5) Laura Alice Roark, born November 24, 1870, married John T. Honea on April 17, 1898, divorced March 7, 1921. Died April 26, 1954, and buried in the Rehoboth Church Cemetery.

(6) James Frank Roark, born October 15, 1872, married Rosa Dunwoody on February 15, 1903. Died June 1, 1943, buried in the Crowley Cemetery, Crowley, Texas.

(7) Walter H. Roark, born 1874, married Oda Roy in December 1898. Died February 5, 1910, buried in the Rehoboth Church Cemetery.

(8) Johnny Roark, born December 25, 1877, in James County, Tennessee. Died April 1, 1880, buried in the Rehoboth Church Cemetery.

(9) Mary Maud Roark, born October 31, 1881, in Johnson Station, Texas, married C.E. Millar in 1914 in Boulder, Colorado. Died May 31, 1959, buried in the Mountain View Mausoleum in Altadena, California.[65]

John W. Roark

John Roark was living with his family in the log cabin purchased in 1869 from Nancy Ford and was thirty-four when his father died. He and Permelia were then parents of four children: Mary Ellen 7, Martha Jane 5, Daniel 3½, and Julia 2. They had just lost a child, a son whom they had named John. He was born in January but had lived only a few days.

After his father died and the estate had been settled, John built a new frame house across the road from his log cabin on what would be his portion of the river farm. There he lived with his family for four years, and there, twins Haney and Joe were born followed by daughter Maude Virginia. In 1881, John sold his river farm

John W. Roark and Permelia Conner Roark, Rockdale, Milam County, Texas, Ca. 1907.

to his brother Will with the intent of following his brother Jim to Texas.[66] Unfortunately, illness of the children and poor health of Permelia prevented the move, so John located land in Meigs County, lived there two years, and moved to Birchwood. In 1886, John moved his family to Jolly's Island at the confluence of the Hiwassee and Tennessee Rivers and lived there as a tenant farmer until December 1897. Children added to the family prior to or during the time on Jolly's Island were

Grave marker of John W. and Permelia Roark, Edgewood Cemetery,
Lancaster, Dallas County, Texas

Caria Victoria, born in Birchwood, twins James Oscar and Benjamin Arthur, daughter Jessie May, and adopted granddaughter Dora. During the time on the Island, Benjamin Arthur died at age eight and was buried in the Conner Cemetery located on the land of his maternal grandfather.

In December 1897, John again moved his family, this time to Hixson, Tennessee, north of the Tennessee River across from Chattanooga, where he again lived as a tenant farmer on the Caldwell place. There his daughter Martha married John Plumlee, but died suddenly on June 8, 1899. Martha was buried in the Hixson Cemetery.[67]

In January 1901, John made the long-planned trip to Texas with all of his family except Ellen, then married to Jacob C. Gross, Daniel, and Julia, both of whom had teaching positions in the Chattanooga area. In Texas, John and Permelia settled first with Permelia's nephew, Jacob Haney Conner, at Davilla in Milam County. In 1904, John bought 90 acres north of Rockdale in Milam County and purchased 72 additional acres in 1907.[68] During John's first two years in Texas, Daniel, Julia, and Ellen Gross and family joined the rest of the John Roark family in Milam County.

In 1921, John and Permelia retired from farming and moved with their daughter, Maude Virginia, to Lancaster, Dallas County. Their daughter, Caria Victoria, died at Lancaster in November 1927 and was buried there in the Edgewood Cemetery. John Roark died six months later on June 7, 1928, at age 86, and was followed in death later that year by Permelia on November 30, 1928. Both were buried in the Edgewood Cemetery, Lancaster, Texas.

The children of John Wesley Roark were:

(1) Mary Ellen Roark, born March 28, 1869, married Jacob C. Gross on November 21, 1894. Died November 7, 1958, buried in the Rockdale Cemetery, Rockdale, Texas.

(2) Martha Jane Roark, born January 11, 1871, married John K. Plumlee on January 11, 1899. Died June 8, 1899, buried in the Hixson Cemetery, Hixson, Hamilton County, Tennessee.

(3) Daniel Blythe Roark, born August 10, 1872, married, first, Iva Elizabeth Crouch on June 20, 1917, and married, second, Myrtle Mae McKinney on July 5, 1930. Died April 13, 1956, buried in the Laurel Land Cemetery, Dallas, Texas.

(4) Julia Roark, born February 3, 1874, married Oscar F. Robinett on September 28, 1909. Died December 2, 1969, buried in Murray Cemetery, Milam County, Texas.

(5) Joseph David Roark, born August 16, 1879, married Bertha Weldon on May 8, 1925. Died February 16, 1957, buried in the Ferris Cemetery, Ferris, Texas.

(6) Haney Maximilian Roark, born August 16, 1879, married Belle Christian on August 18, 1911. Died March 12, 1967, buried in Bellwood Memorial Park, Temple, Texas.

(7) Maude Virginia Roark, born September 10, 1881, never married. Died March 26, 1969, buried in Edgewood Cemetery, Lancaster, Texas.

(8) Caria Victoria Roark, born April 14, 1885, never married. Died November 7, 1927, buried in Edgewood Cemetery, Lancaster, Texas.

(9) James Oscar Roark, born March 29, 1888, married Julia Wykes on September 6, 1913. Died October 12, 1974, buried in Moore Memorial Gardens, Arlington, Texas.

(10) Benjamin Arthur Roark, born March 29, 1888. Died May 4, 1896, buried in the Conner Cemetery, Hamilton County, Tennessee.

(11) Jessie May Roark, born May 5, 1890, married John N. Luce on February 7, 1920. Died December 16, 1970, buried in Woodside Cemetery, Grand Saline, Texas.

(12) Dora Roark (adopted), born July 7, 1890, never married. Died January 20, 1914, buried in Murray Cemetery, Milam County, Texas.[69]

William M. Roark

Will was still single and living at home when his father died. He would remain at home with his mother for less than two years before he married Virginia Conner on Saturday, January 26, 1878. Virginia was the daughter of Maximilian Haney Conner and Martha Palmer Conner and was the sister of John's wife, Permelia, and John L. Roark's wife, Victoria. At the time of their marriage, Will was thirty-four and Virginia was twenty-five. They would make their home at the Joseph Roark homestead and farm the land he had inherited from his father. He and Virginia cared for Will's mother during her declining years and were with her when she died in August 1883.

Will and Virginia began their family the year of their marriage and their first child, a daughter, was born November 17, 1878. They named her Laura Belle. Over the next eighteen years of their

William M. Roark, Hamilton County, Tennessee, Ca. 1900.

marriage, Will and Virginia were to be the parents of nine other children. Sadness and loss came their way in January 1897, when their youngest, Rosalie Vivian, died at the age of three months, and again in September 1898, when their son, John Mark, died at the age of ten. Eight of their children lived to maturity.

In 1878 and in 1881, Will purchased from his brothers James and John, respectively, the river-bottom lands inherited from their father.[70] He then owned roughly 700 acres of the estate that had been accumulated by his father. Will lived at the Joseph Roark home place throughout his life and made his living by farming. He remained a strong supporter and longtime member of the Salem Baptist Church.

Virginia Conner Roark, Hamilton County, Tennessee, Ca. 1900.

Both of their daughters were the first of the family to marry. The eldest daughter, Laura Belle, married J.A. Shropshire in November 1902, and Lilly Victoria married Ben Moon in November 1904. The entire family suffered and grieved in 1906-07 when the eldest son, Luther, contacted tuberculosis and died in May 1907 after a protracted and torturous illness.

In 1914, Will and Virginia began a process by which land from the homestead tract was given to each of the children. On January 27, 1914, a portion of the river farm of the old Joseph Roark

Grave marker of William M. and Virginia Roark, Bald Hill Cemetery, Hamilton County, Tennessee.

estate was given to each of five of their children: Laura, Luke, Lilly, Berry, and Tom. The deeds to the children were identical except in the field notes for description. The deed to Tom is quoted:

> For and in consideration of the sum of $50.00 . . . we, W.M. and V.A. Roark have love for our son Thomas Jefferson and his heirs do hereby sell . . . the following described real estate . . . . It is hereby agreed that the said Thomas Jefferson shall on the 1st day of January each year pay fifty dollars $50.00 to said W.M. and V.A. Roark during their natural lives otherwise the deed is null and void. . . .[71]

At the same time, the two other sons, Joseph Walter and William Grover, were jointly given the remainder of the homestead with the youngest, William Grover Roark, to occupy the home place itself. In 1937, the five Roark heirs who had acquired farms along the Tennessee River would be forced to surrender their lands to the Tennessee Valley Authority for construction of the Chickamauga Dam and Lake.

Will Roark lived at the home place until his death on December 6, 1923, at the age of eighty. Virginia survived her husband by almost eleven years. She died at the home place on October 23, 1934. Both Will and Virginia are buried at Bald Hill Cemetery.

The children of William Marion Roark were:

(1) Laura Belle Roark, born November 17, 1878, married J.A. Shropshire on November 20, 1902. Died July 29, 1968, buried at Bald Hill Cemetery.

(2) Martin Luther Roark, born December 31, 1879, never married. Died May 19, 1907, buried at Bald Hill Cemetery.

(3) Joseph Walter Roark, born January 8, 1882, married Mary M. Millard on January 3, 1915. Died May 3, 1973, buried at Bald Hill Cemetery.

(4) Lucas Haney Roark, born March 21, 1883, married Nora Stinnett on December 1, 1947. Died September 20, 1954, buried at Thomaston, Georgia.

(5) Lilly Victoria Roark, born August 29, 1884, married Benjamin F. Moon on November 30, 1904. Died July 10, 1957, buried in Valhermosa Springs, Morgan County, Alabama.[72]

(6) Frank Scott, born September 14, 1884, married Cora Jenkins on August 10, 1925. Died September 21, 1955, buried at the Moore Chapel Cemetery, Bradley County, Tennessee.

(7) Franklin Asbury Roark, born May 21, 1886, married, first, Mattie White on March 5, 1916, and, second, Isabelle Pina in 1958. Died May 19, 1974, buried with Mattie White Roark in the Chapel Hill Cemetery, Elmhurst, Illinois.

(8) John Mark Roark, born February 23, 1888. Died September 7, 1898, buried at Bald Hill Cemetery.

(9) Thomas Jefferson Roark, born November 7, 1889, married Minnie B. Price on January 1, 1922. Died June 2, 1984, buried at Foley, Alabama.

(10) William Grover Roark, born June 26, 1892, married Willie Myrtle Roark on January 25, 1918. Died December 7, 1972, and buried in Hamilton Memorial Gardens, Chattanooga, Tennessee.[73]

(11) Rosalie Vivian Roark, born October 15, 1896. Died January 8, 1897, buried in the Conner Cemetery, Hamilton County, Tennessee.[74]

Jeanette Clingan Webb

Jane and Benjamin Webb farmed a large tract adjacent to the Joseph Roark homestead and raised their family in the Salem Community. Following the sale of their land in 1868,[75] the Webbs left the Salem Community in 1870 to assist their daughter, Sarah Elizabeth Campbell, in West Plains, Howell County, Missouri, in the very serious illness of her husband. Sarah Elizabeth, the Webb's eldest daughter, had married William C. Campbell, son of Seymour Campbell, a justice of the peace in Hamilton County and a business associate of Joseph Roark, and had lived in Missouri only a short time. After they left the Salem Community, the Webbs lived one year in Missouri, during which time William Campbell died, leaving Sarah a widow with two small children. In 1872, the Webbs, with their daughter Sarah and her two children, left Missouri to settle in Arkansas. The family arrived in Crawford County shortly before the death of Robert Beane Scott in September 1872, and were reunited again with Mary Ann Scott, whom Jane had known almost as a blood sister in her years at the Joseph Roark home. The Webbs established their permanent home on Cedar Creek near the Figure Five Store, northwest of Van Buren.[76]

Jeanette "Jane" Clingan Webb, Crawford County, Arkansas, Ca. 1873. Jane was raised by Joseph and Juda from age seven until her marriage in 1847 at age twenty.

Jane and Benjamin Webb were the parents of eleven children, eight of whom were living when Benjamin died on July 22, 1881. Following the death of her husband,

Jane and her daughter, Sarah, continued farming on their place on Cedar Creek. Jane was recognized in the local community as "a lady of more than ordinary business ability" and was an active member in the Missionary Baptist Church until her death in 1923.[77] Jane and Benjamin were buried in the Oliver Springs Cemetery, Crawford County, Arkansas.[78]

The children of Jeanette Clingan and Benjamin Webb were:

(1) Sarah Elizabeth Webb, born October 6, 1849, married William C. Campbell in Hamilton County in 1867. Died June 1935, buried in the Canfield Cemetery, Idabel, Oklahoma.

(2) John L. Webb, born July 25, 1851, married Mary E. Winfrey on December 25, 1878.

Benjamin Webb, husband of Jane Clingan Webb, Crawford County, Arkansas, Ca. 1873.

Died October 8, 1898, buried Oliver Springs Cemetery, Figure Five, Arkansas.

(3) Merida Webb, born June 1, 1853. Died before 1889.

(4) George Washington Webb, born June 2, 1855, married Matilda Odelia Carney on January 29, 1880. Died October 11, 1939, buried Oliver Springs Cemetery, Figure Five, Arkansas.

(5) Jerusha Evaline Webb, born October 9, 1857. Married John L. Toney.

(6) Nancy A. Webb, born in 1859. Died young.

(7) Mary Ellen Webb, born February 19, 1861. Married Thomas Phillips.

(8) William J. Webb, born May 9, 1863. Nothing further is known.

(9) Joseph Thomas Webb, born October 7, 1865. Married Elizabeth Phillips.

(10) Samuel Zachary Webb, born February 21, 1869. Married Minnie Mae Henderson.[79]

Matilda Brooks

Matilda Brooks left the home of Joseph Roark in late 1873. Efforts to locate her after her move have been unsuccessful.

Juda Ann Brooks

Juda Ann left the Joseph Roark home when she married Noah Atchley in January 1865. She had received her share of her father's estate in February 1867, and shortly thereafter, the Atchleys began their family–daughter Nancy J. was born later that same year. During their early married years, Juda Ann and Noah apparently lived with his family in Meigs County, during which time another daughter, Lydia, was born in 1869. In 1870, the Atchleys moved to the Elk Creek Community in Texas County, Missouri. There two children were born, Leonard in 1871 and a daughter, Tennessee, in 1875. Juda Ann and Noah were in Missouri until after 1875, at which time they relocated to Sebastian County, Arkansas. By 1880, Noah and Juda Ann had a family of five children. Nancy J., the eldest, was thirteen; James F., the youngest, was just over six months.

Some time before 1900, the Atchleys moved to the Earlboro Township in Pottawatome County, Indian Territory (Oklahoma) and were there in 1900. Their youngest, James F., was still living at home. Their location in their later years is unknown.

James P. Roark

James Roark outlived his younger brother Joseph by eighteen months. His wife, Jerusha, died on May 6, 1876, just three months after Joseph's death. James died August 29, 1877, and was buried with his wife in the cemetery established by M.H. Conner on his farm west of the Birchwood Pike, later known as the Conner Cemetery.

James and Jerusha were the parents of six children. The eldest, Timothy, was born October 23, 1826, and the youngest, Sarah Blythe, was born April 16,1845. Of the six, only Sarah was born in the Salem Community after her father had moved there from the Sale Creek area.

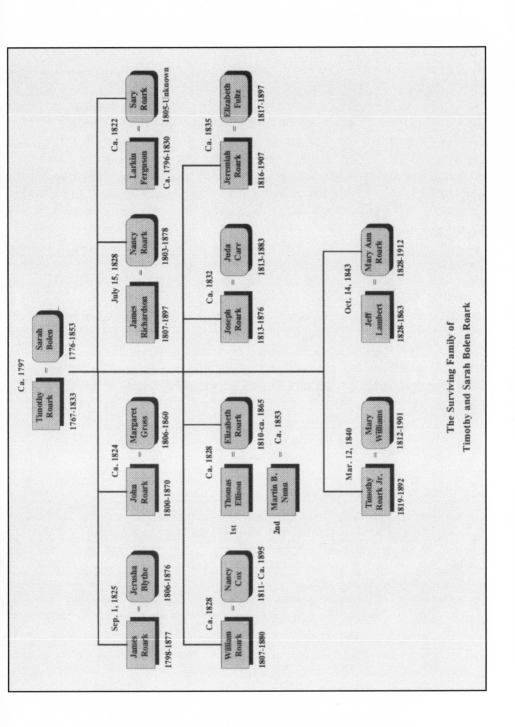

The Surviving Family of
Timothy and Sarah Bolen Roark

Nothing is known about Timothy other than his birth date that was recorded by James in his copy book. Perhaps Timothy died young; however, no certain information has been discovered to date.

The second son of James and Jerusha, John B., was born January 19, 1829. He married Nancy Cameron before 1850, and together they were the parents of seven children. Of the seven, five remained in the Birchwood area after marriage and raised their families there. One son, James Thomas Roark, relocated to the Indian Territory after his marriage and raised his family in Oklahoma. Another son, Alfred Thaddeus, known as "Alf" to his cousins, moved to California in 1913, married there and remained. The surviving daughter of John B., Martha Jane, married John Eldridge and together made their home in Soddy, Tennessee. She was buried in the Soddy Presbyterian Cemetery. John B. Roark remained at the James Roark home place during his lifetime and, at his death, was buried in the Birchwood Baptist Cemetery.

The third son of James and Jerusha was William, born January 21, 1832. William lived to maturity–he was still at home in 1850 at age eighteen–but apparently died soon after beginning his family. He does not appear in the 1860 census; however, a Caroline Roark with a daughter by the name of Jerusha was living on a tract adjacent to his father. One might conclude that William had died before 1860 and this was his widow and daughter.[80] Apparently William had another daughter, for in the meeting of the Hamilton County Court on June 4, 1866, James Roark was appointed guardian of "Emaline Roark, minor heir of William Roark deceased."[81] Oddly, two and one-half years later, in the County Court minutes of January 9, 1869, this record appears:

> Clerk presented Affidavit of James Roark, Guardian of Emaline Roark, stating that he had received no effects for or belonging to his said ward, and asked to be discharged from further liability which was granted.[82]

One would speculate that William's widow had remarried and desired to raise her children without the help of James and Jerusha.

The fourth child of James and Jerusha Roark was Martha Jane, born December 4, 1834. She married David Granville Samples and raised a family of five children in the Birchwood area. Martha Jane died December 23, 1923, and was buried with her husband in Birchwood Baptist Cemetery.

Joseph Roark (referred to in the community as "Junior" to differentiate him from his uncle) was the fifth child of James and Jerusha. Born September 18, 1842, Joseph married Elizabeth Smith prior to his service in the Confederate army. They were the parents of twelve children, seven of whom lived to maturity–one daughter and six sons. One son, James, was listed in the 1870 Census as an eight-year-old; however, no subsequent record could be found. It must be assumed that he died soon after 1870. Joseph and Elizabeth left the Salem Community in November 1883[83] and relocated to Marion County, Tennessee, until 1907, at which time they moved with their family to Parker County, Texas. Three of their family–Jerusha, John, and

Two-story log house of James and Jerusha Roark, west of the Birchwood Pike and southwest of Birchwood, Hamilton County, Tennessee, Ca. 1877.

Robert–settled with them in Parker County. Of the others in the family, Judge F. settled in Dallas, J.J. located in Oklahoma City, William remained in Cowan, Tennessee, and George J. in Chattanooga.[84] Joseph died August 27, 1916, and is buried with his wife in the Baker Schoolhouse Cemetery in southern Parker County.[85]

The youngest child of James and Jerusha, Sarah Blythe, was born April 16, 1845. Sarah married Bill Webb November 12, 1862, when he was home on furlough from Confederate army service. William Webb was born March 27, 1848, the son of Merida and Betsy Jane Webb. Sarah and Bill were parents of eleven children–five boys and six girls–most of whom married and raised their families in the Hamilton County area. For name continuity, the marriages of the six daughters of Sarah and Bill Webb are provided below:

1. Martha Jane Webb married Sam Farris.
2. Lodema Webb married James Smith.
3. Emma Webb married Frank Conner.
4. Ida Angeline Webb married James Marion Poe.
5. Laura Webb married Jesse Burgess.
6. Kathryn Lillian Webb married John R. Anderson.

The children of James P. Roark were:

(1) Timothy Roark, born October 23, 1826. Neither a synopsis of his life nor a record

of his death has been discovered.

(2) John B. Roark, born January 19,1829, married Nancy Cameron before 1850. Died June 19, 1909, buried in Birchwood Baptist Cemetery. John B. Roark served in Company E, Fifth Tennessee Infantry (Union) during the Civil War. He applied for and received on February 8, 1884, a pension for his military service.

(3) William Roark, born January 21, 1832. His marriage, death, and burial are unrecorded.

(4) Martha Jane Roark, born December 4, 1834, married David Granville Samples. Died December 23, 1923, buried in Birchwood Baptist Cemetery.

(5) Joseph Roark, born September 18, 1842, married Elizabeth Smith in 1861. Died August 27, 1916, buried at Baker Schoolhouse Cemetery, Parker County, Texas. He served in Capt. Barry's Company, Tennessee Light Artillery (Confederate) and was seriously wounded at the Battle of Kennesaw Mountain in Georgia. He applied for a pension from the State of Tennessee for his service in the Confederacy on April 24, 1901. The pension application was approved June 1, 1907.[86]

(6) Sarah Blythe Roark, born April 16, 1845, married William W. Webb on November 12, 1862. Died September 26, 1908, buried in the Sivley Cemetery, Hamilton County, Tennessee, with her husband, William Webb, who died March 15, 1900.[87] William Webb served in Company B, First Tennessee Cavalry (Confederate).

Grave marker of Jerusha Blythe Roark, wife of James Roark, Conner Cemetery, Hamilton County, Tennessee.

Grave marker of James Roark, brother of Joseph, Conner Cemetery, Hamilton County, Tennessee.

John Roark

Both John Roark and his wife, Margaret, died before his brother Joseph. Many of their children married and raised their families in the Hamilton County area; however, son James W. and daughters Nancy and Juda Ann did not marry, and together lived their lives in the John Roark home place. All three are buried in the Roark Cemetery with their father and mother. The other five daughters had all married prior to the death of their father and all five remained in the area with their families. The youngest son, John Lewis Roark, married Victoria Conner and raised a family of fourteen children.[88] He died July 14, 1941, and, at his death, was recognized as the "last surviving Union veteran of the Chattanooga area."[89] His funeral was the last service held at the Salem Baptist Church.

John Roark, brother of Joseph, Hamilton County, Tennessee, Ca. 1859.

The children of John Roark were:

(1) Mary Ann "Molly" Roark, born February 1, 1825, in Claiborne County, Tennessee, married John Cross ca. 1846, in Hamilton County, Tennessee. Died June 28, 1868, buried in the Roark Cemetery near Birchwood, Hamilton County, Tennessee.

(2) Sarah Roark, born ca. 1827, married Cleaver Shelton ca. 1846. Died January 3, 1897, buried in the Roark Cemetery.

(3) Elizabeth Roark, born ca. 1828, married George Campbell.[90] Nothing further is known.

(4) Nancy Roark, born December 19, 1830, never married. Died September 27, 1907, buried in the Roark Cemetery.[91]

5) Eliza Roark, born June 9, 1833, married James A. Pendergrass ca. 1852. Died September 19, 1909, buried in the Roark Cemetery.

(6) James W. Roark, born September 13, 1835, never married. Died September 16, 1905, buried in the Roark Cemetery.[92] He served in

Margaret Gross Roark, wife of John Roark, Hamilton County, Tennessee, Ca. 1859.

Company C, Seventh Tennessee Infantry (Union). He applied for and received on June 13, 1890, a pension for his military service.

(7) Juda Ann Roark, born September 10, 1837, never married. Died June 19, 1915, buried in the Roark Cemetery.[93]

(8) William C. Roark, born ca. 1840, never married. Died January 29, 1863, of pneumonia at Nicholasville,

Grave markers of John and Margaret Roark, Roark Cemetery, Hamilton County, Tennessee. John Roark marker is in left foreground, Margaret Roark marker is in right foreground.

Kentucky, while serving in Company C, Seventh Tennessee Infantry (Union). Burial assumed to be at Nicholasville.[94]

(9) Margaret Roark, born May 11, 1842, married Archibald L. McCallie on July 22, 1864. Died February 13, 1927, buried in the McCallie Cemetery near Birchwood, Hamilton County, Tennessee. Archibald McCallie served in Company E, Fifth Tennessee Infantry (Union). He applied for and received on September 6, 1879, a pension for his military service. After his death, his widow received a pension beginning November 4, 1920.

(10) America Roark, born April 4, 1844, married David Gregory ca. 1866. America died August 23, 1940, buried in the Roark Cemetery.[95] David Gregory served in Company E, Eighth Tennessee Infantry (Union). He applied for and received on August 13, 1889, a pension for his military service. After his death, his widow received a pension beginning May 21, 1915.

(11) John Lewis Roark, born July 4, 1846, married Victoria Conner on September 19, 1866. Died July 14, 1941, buried in the Roark Cemetery.[96] He served in Company E, Fifth Tennessee Infantry (Union). He applied for and received on July 21, 1891, a pension for his military service.

Nancy Roark

Joseph Roark last saw his sister Nancy when he was in Claiborne County in August 1856 to execute a quit claim deed on the Timothy Roark homestead. Following that meeting at the homestead, the Civil War interrupted all communication with the Claiborne County families and, quite possibly, political differences in regard to the national conflict weakened family loyalties. After Joseph and his brothers returned home from their visit to Claiborne County in 1856, war clouds gathered and skies darkened. Old family ties were severed and each went their own way. The members of the Timothy Roark family aged and their children grew, married, and had families of their own.

Nancy and husband James Richardson lived in Claiborne County near the Timothy Roark homestead all their lives. Both were active in church. James and Nancy first joined the Baptist church at Cedar Fork in September 1834, and James was instrumental in organizing the Cave Springs Baptist Church in July 1845. He was ordained a deacon on July 9, 1849, and, with Nancy, were members of that church for thirty years. As they settled in their final homestead on Blair's Creek, James again was part of a group to form Blair's Creek Baptist Church on July 20, 1877, which, by 1885, had a membership of 40 persons.[97] James remained active in the church during his later years and often represented the Blair's Creek Church at meetings of the Cumberland Gap Baptist Association.[98]

When Joseph was at the home place in 1856, Nancy had five of her children still living at home: John 21, Mary 19, William N. 17, Nancy 14, and James T. 11.[99] Three years before, Nancy's daughter Elizabeth Condray had died, and Nancy and James had taken her baby son, James Condray, to raise. Nancy and James lost another daughter, Sarah Jane Large, in 1857, and, again, took the grandchild, Nancy J., to raise.[100]

Two sons of Nancy and James who were still at home in 1856 became Baptist preachers in the area. John Richardson was pastor of local churches and at one time was pastor of Blair's Creek Baptist Church in which his father was active.[101] William N. Richardson also became a minister and pastored local churches.

Two of Nancy's family were in military service during the Civil War. Her eldest son, George W. Richardson, who had assisted in the estate settlement with Jeff Lambert in 1856 by witnessing the deed executed by Joseph and his brothers, served in Company E, Second Tennessee Infantry (Union).[102] Nancy's son-in-law, Calvin James Cunningham, husband to her daughter Mary Ann, served in Company G, First Tennessee Cavalry (Union).[103] Interestingly, Cunningham was with his regiment in southeast Tennessee in September and October 1863 and was involved in the pursuit of Gen. Joseph Wheeler's Confederate Cavalry during its raid to

Grave marker of Nancy Roark Richardson, Cave Springs Cemetery, Claiborne County, Tennessee.

interrupt the supply lines to the Federal army in Chattanooga. Accompanying Wheeler on that raid were the cousins of Cunningham–Jim, John, and Will Roark of the First Tennessee Cavalry (Confederate).[104]

The homestead of James and Nancy Richardson was 115 acres on Old Blair's Creek Road near the farm of Nancy's brother, Timothy Roark Jr., and near the final home of her aunt and uncle, Lucy and James Eastridge. While the 1870 census lists James and Nancy together with their two grandchildren, Nancy Large and James Condray, certain events were recorded in 1870 and later which cast doubts in regard to the closeness of their marriage. On October 25, 1870, Nancy bought 100 acres in her own name from her brother, Timothy Jr.[105] In both 1871 and 1872, Nancy, in her name, was assessed and paid taxes on the homestead 115 acres.[106] No divorce records are available from Claiborne County for this period to evidence a separation between James and Nancy; so, it is quite possible that they were not separated and the land assessments were an estate move they made jointly.

In the early 1870s, Nancy began to have serious problems with skin cancer, and by 1877, the cancer, most likely melanoma, had spread to the lymph nodes.[107] Nancy died April 20, 1878, and was buried in Cave Springs Cemetery. Later that same year, James Richardson married Mary F. Lambert.[108] James Richardson died October 11, 1897, and was buried very near Nancy in Cave Springs Cemetery.[109] No grave marker for the second Mrs. Richardson could be found in Cave Springs Cemetery or other cemeteries in Claiborne County.

Children of Nancy Roark and James Richardson were:

(1) George W. Richardson, born April 10, 1829, married Mary J. Weirman. Died March 21, 1908, buried with his wife in the Richardson Cemetery on Old Blair's Creek Road near the home of Nancy and James Richardson.[110] George served in Company E, Second Tennessee Cavalry (Union). He applied for and received a pension for his military service on March 22, 1883.

(2) Sarah Jane Richardson, born May 31, 1831, married James C. Large on November 28, 1851. Died May 1, 1857, buried in the Cave Springs Cemetery.[111]

(3) Elizabeth Richardson, born May 31, 1833, married Thomas Condray on January 10, 1852. Died July 10, 1853, buried in the Cave Springs Cemetery.[112]

(4) John Richardson, born November 16, 1835, married Louiza Jane Ferguson on December 24, 1852. Died August 6, 1871, buried in the Ferguson Cemetery, Claiborne County.[113]

(5) Mary Ann Richardson, born June 15, 1838, married Calvin James Cunningham on August 30, 1859. Died February 7, 1911, buried in the Richardson Cemetery.[114] Calvin James Cunningham served in Company G, First Tennessee Cavalry (Union). He applied for and received a pension for his military service on May 18, 1883. His widow, Mary Ann, began receiving a widow's pension on March 13, 1907.

(6) William N. Richardson, born 1839, married a Morrison. Death and burial are unknown.[115]

(7) Nancy Richardson, born 1842, married, first, Liberty Ferguson, and, second, Robert Alex Brooks on March 27, 1867. Death and burial are unknown.[116]

(8) James Thomas Richardson, born October 4, 1845, married Catherine Williams on October 10, 1867. Died May 9, 1927, buried in the Richardson Cemetery.[117]

William Roark

Joseph's brother William was forty-eight when Joseph last saw him in 1856. William had married Nancy Cox, daughter of Aaron Cox, in 1827, and by 1856, William had four children. John had married in 1846 and by 1856, he and his wife Jane had two sons, James 6 and Frederick 1.[118] William's daughter, Cynthia, had married William Williams at the age of fifteen in 1845; and by 1856, when she was twenty-five, she had three children, Louisa 10, Nancy 5, and Mary Jane 3.[119] William's second son, James, had married Sarah Friar on July 28, 1855.[120] Eliza, the second daughter and fourth child of William and Nancy, was born in 1835 and had married Daniel Friar, brother to James' wife, on October 23, 1850.[121]

Doubtless William discussed with Joseph at their last meeting the opportunities in Missouri and William's plans to relocate. Shortly after his visit with Joseph, William sold a 25-acre tract adjacent to the Timothy Roark homestead to his brother-in-law Jeff Lambert, then owner of the old Roark homestead. William and Nancy had been given the 25 acres as a wedding gift from her father in 1827.[122] Just over two years later, with his plans to move crystalized, William sold his homestead tract of 150 acres to his brother Timothy for $475.[123] His homestead tract was part of a 415-acre tract that William had purchased in 1841 from Thomas McBroom. The 415 acres lay south of the old Timothy Roark homestead and consisted of steep ridges and deep hollows with little area suitable for cultivation. William had earlier sold a large portion of the 415 acres to Bailey Sutton in 1846.[124]

With his land liquidation complete, William and Nancy began the move to Missouri with other families from Claiborne County–the Whitakers, the Rices, the Mundays, the Friars, William's brother Jeremiah and his family–plus William's son, James, and his family, and William's daughter Eliza and her husband, Daniel Friar. The rest of William's family did not move; John Roark and William Williams remained with their families in Claiborne County. The group of relocating families settled in Dent County, Missouri, and in early January 1860, William purchased 80 acres with his son-in-law, Daniel Friar, from David Simmons for $240. The tract was described as the S2, SE4, Section 11, T34N, R5W, and apparently most of the tract was suitable for cultivation.[125] Subsequently, Roark and Friar added another 40 acres to their farm by acquiring the adjacent SE4, SW4, of Section 11. Lands were fertile in Dent County and opportunities in farming looked good; however, the year following William's relocation, the Civil War came to Missouri.

With the war's coming, William's son James enlisted September 8, 1862, in Company D, Thirty-second Missouri Infantry. William's nephew, son of Jeremiah, who was also named James, had enlisted in the same unit the month before. Both men were mustered in at the same time on October 18, 1862, and since William's son James was the older at 29, he was enrolled as James Roark "Senior." Jeremiah's son was enlisted as James Roark "Junior." Both men served in the Vicksburg campaign; however, both were taken seriously ill during the siege, probably with malaria. William received word in March 1863 that his son had died February 15 on a hospital ship on the Mississippi north of Vicksburg. In sad irony, William's nephew died May 20, also on a hospital ship.[126]

During the time between the death of his son and the end of the war, an estrangement occurred between William and his son-in-law, Daniel Friar. The circumstances surrounding the relationship with Friar are unclear and perhaps centered more on marital problems between Eliza and Daniel than on business and farming disagreements between William and his son-in-law. Although Daniel was of the age to participate in the war, no military service record could be located. One must assume that Daniel remained at home during the war and the estrangement was not because of his absence in military service. Divorce records are unavailable but later circumstances strongly suggest that Daniel and Eliza separated sometime before late 1865 and Eliza returned home to live with her parents.[127]

After the death of their son and problems with their son-in-law, William and Nancy no longer could see the allure in Missouri. In 1864 and early 1865, they tried to sell their portion of the 120-acre homestead to return to Claiborne County. After harvesting their crop in 1865, they left Missouri having not sold their land and, upon arriving back in Claiborne County, sought first to buy a new homestead. On September 5, William paid J.A. Hamilton $600 for 250 acres in Claiborne County near his daughter Cynthia and adjacent to the tract they had sold just six years before.[128] By late 1865, William and Nancy were back in Claiborne County to stay. Daughter Eliza was with them.

Two years later, still owning his land in Missouri, William executed a power of attorney, in favor of his brother Jeremiah, to sell William's land in Dent County.[129] It is significant that he did not give the power of attorney to Daniel Friar. In November, six months later, Jeremiah sold James' half interest in the 120-acre tract to John F. Angle for $70–significantly less than his investment seven years before.[130]

William lived on his 250 acres in Claiborne County and farmed the small portion suitable for cultivation until his death in 1880.[131] The location of William's burial is unknown. After William died, Nancy lived with her daughter Cynthia Williams, then located in Lee County, Virginia. On July 28, 1881, Nancy sold the 250-acre homestead tract to Timothy Roark Jr. for $200–the same tract for which William had paid $600 sixteen years before. The money received from the sale was distributed $100 to Nancy, $50 to her son John and wife Jane, and $50 to her daughter Cynthia and husband William Williams.[132] Since Nancy's daughter Eliza is not mentioned in the distribution of monies, it has to be assumed that she died earlier than 1881. Nancy later made her home in Clay County, Kentucky with her son, John, until her death.[133]

The children of William Roark were:

(1) John Roark, born 1828, married Martha Jane "Kissy" Massengill on March 5, 1846.[134] By 1900, John and Martha Jane were living in Clay County, Kentucky. Death and place of burial are unknown. He served in Company F, Eighth Tennessee Cavalry (Union) during the Civil War.

(2) Cynthia Roark, born 1830, married William Williams in 1845.[135] Death and place of burial are unknown. William Williams served as a sergeant in Company E, Sixth Tennessee Infantry (Union). On September 11, 1890, he applied for and received in Indiana a pension for his military service.

(3) James Roark, born 1833, married Sarah Friar on July 28, 1855.[136] Died in military service, February 15, 1863, with Company D, Thirty-second Missouri Infantry (Union). Place of burial is unknown. No application for a widow's pension is on record.

(4) Eliza Jane Roark, born 1835, married Daniel Friar on October 23, 1850.[137] Lived in Dent County, Missouri, in 1860 on the farm Daniel Friar purchased with William Roark. The circumstances surrounding Daniel Friar are unclear. Eliza last appears in the 1870 Census under her maiden name with her parents in Claiborne County. Death and place of burial are unknown.

Elizabeth Roark

Elizabeth Roark was two and a half years older than her brother Joseph and was next oldest to him in the Timothy Roark family. Doubtless he was closer to Elizabeth than others in the family for that reason. Joseph saw her for the last time in 1856 and, at the same time, met her new husband, Martin Nunn. Unfortunately, we know little of Elizabeth after 1856 and even her death and place of burial are obscure. The best estimate is that she died in 1865, nine years after Joseph's last visit with her.

The children of Elizabeth Roark and Thomas Ellison were:

(1) Timothy Ellison, born 1829, married Jane Ferguson. Best information suggests that Timothy moved west to Missouri.

(2) John Ellison, born 1830, married Nancy M. Whitaker, and raised his family in Claiborne County.

(3) Jeremiah Ellison, born May 16, 1832, married, first, Sousan (Sousan is traditional family spelling) Lambert on November 23, 1859, and, second, Eliza Augusta Sandifer on March 4, 1872.[138] Died August 13, 1927, buried with wife Eliza in the Sandefur Cemetery on the old Rev. Joseph Lambert farm, Claiborne County.[139]

(4) Nancy Ellison, born December 10, 1834, married Joseph Lambert Jr. (brother to Jeremiah Ellison's wife, Sousan, and brother to Jeff Lambert, husband of Mary Ann Roark) on December 27, 1855.[140] Joseph Lambert Jr. served in the Eighth Tennessee Cavalry (Union). Nancy died September 28, 1915. Place of burial is unknown. Joseph Lambert Jr. applied for and received a pension for his military service on August 14, 1888.

(5) George W. Ellison, born 1838, married, first, Sarah Black, in Illinois; married,

second, Cynthia A. Farrow in Williamson County, Illinois, on November 17, 1877. Later moved to Douglas County, Missouri.

(6) William M. Ellison, born September 15, 1840, married Sarah Elizabeth Carroll on September 30, 1861. Died September 22, 1903, buried with his wife in the Ellison Cemetery on Johnson Road, one mile northeast of Pine Hill Road, Claiborne County.[141]

(7) Wiley Ellison, born 1842, married, first, Nancy Carroll on August 24, 1867,[142] and, second, Viola Campbell. Enlisted in Company I, Third Tennessee Infantry (Union) on February 10, 1862. Mustered- out at Nashville February 23, 1865.[143] Death and place of burial are unknown. On July 24, 1890, he applied for and received in Missouri a pension for his military service.

(8) Elizabeth Ellison, born February 20, 1844, twin to Thomas Ellison Jr., married first, F. Fletcher, second, Ledford, and third, Benjamin Lambert.

(9) Thomas Ellison Jr., born February 20, 1844, twin to Elizabeth Ellison, married Mary Elizabeth Kibert on July 15, 1869. Died July 15, 1929, buried in Cave Springs Cemetery.[144]

(10) Joseph Ellison, born 1849, married Elizabeth Lambert on February 7, 1880. Died 1921, buried in the Hazelwood Cemetery near Old Little Creek School, Claiborne County.[145]

Jeremiah Roark

Joseph's younger brother, Jerry, already had eight children when Joseph saw him last in 1856. Jerry had married Elizabeth Fultz,* daughter of John and Martha Fultz, in 1835. The year following their marriage, Jerry bought 160 acres from his father-in-law for $300. The farm was located on the Powell River opposite Island Creek, three miles east of the old Timothy Roark homestead.

In late 1857, Jerry made the decision to go west to Missouri with his brother William and the other families making the move. Of his own family, his son John was the only one married, having just wed Turresay Murphy that November. As Jerry planned the move to Missouri, it was agreed that John and Turresay would join them along with all the rest of Jerry's family. Jerry sold his farm to Robert Patterson on September 6, 1858, for $700[146] and in 1859, with the other families from Claiborne County, the move to Missouri was under way.

In Dent County, Jerry purchased a 40-acre farm on December 23, 1859, from G.S. Duckworth, the land described as the E2, E2, NW4, Section 4, T34N, R5W.[147] Here Jerry established his homestead.

The year after his move to Missouri, Jerry gave two of his daughters in marriage. In April 1860, daughter Martha married Joshua Munday, who had also come with his parents from Tennessee.[148] Four months later in August, Jerry's daughter Sarah married William H. Moore.[149]

Jerry's family continued to increase in number after his arrival in Missouri. A son, Joseph R., was born in 1861 and on December 29, 1862, his last son, James

---

*Also spelled Fults and Fulse in deeds and land surveys. Fultz is the most common and also the traditional family spelling.

Ervin, was born, just as the Civil War expanded to its full fury and devastation.[150]

Jerry's son James, still unmarried, enlisted in the Union army with his cousin by the same name, who was designated by the army as James Roark "Senior," and assumed his new name, also assigned by the army, James Roark "Junior." Both were mustered in October 18, 1862, and were assigned to Company D, Thirty-second Missouri Infantry (Union). The day following James' enlistment, Jerry's son-in-law William Moore enlisted in Company F of the same regiment and was mustered in October 18 at Benton Barracks in Missouri. Jerry's son John did not enlist until August 16, 1864, probably because of his wife and family. He reported in at Rolla, Missouri, September 16, 1864, and was assigned to Company D, in the same regiment as his brother.

The Civil War was not kind to Jerry Roark, just as it was unkind to so many other families. In March 1863, Jerry grieved with his brother William on the death of James Roark Sr. only to receive a notice three months later that his own son had died of illness in the Vicksburg Campaign. But sorrow hovered over Jerry in a special way. His son-in-law, William Moore, was lost—records only reflect a discharge in St. Louis, October 6, 1863—and disappears from history, probably dying in his young manhood. Family tradition tells of his wife's struggle to return home to her father and of her death, probably of malnutrition, before reaching her destination. On February 4, 1865, Jerry was officially designated by the county court as the guardian of his grandson, Douglas Moore, son of Sarah and William. Jerry would raise Douglas as a son.[151] Jerry's son John returned home without incident after his separation from the army in the latter months of the war.

In 1868, Jerry and Elizabeth sold their land in Dent County to their son John and moved southwest to the adjoining Texas County.[152] In November 1873, Jerry bought 200 acres in southeast Texas County and, on November 16, 1875, he bought an additional 240 acres in the adjoining township near Summersville. Jerry was successful as a farmer and continued to add land—80 acres in 1876, another 80 acres in January 1883, 120 acres in March 1883, and 160 acres in May 1884.[153]

Grave markers of Jeremiah and Elizabeth Fultz Roark, Cold Springs Cemetery, south of Summersville, Texas County, Missouri. Jeremiah's marker is to the right.

Jerry and Elizabeth were active in and faithful to their church. As his land holdings increased, Jerry gave land for the Cold Springs Church of United Brethren and was instrumental in its organization on June 15, 1872. Elizabeth died July 15, 1897, and was buried in the Cold Springs Cemetery.[154] Jerry lived with his daughter Martha Munday until his death in 1907.[155] He was buried in Cold Springs Cemetery, next to his wife.[156]

The children of Jeremiah Roark were:

(1) John Roark, born 1836, married, first, Martha J. Jones on March 6, 1854,[157] and married, second, Turresay Murphy in Claiborne County, Tennessee, on November 10, 1857.[158] He served in Company D, Thirty-second Missouri Infantry (Union).

(2) Sarah Roark, born 1839, married William H. Moore on August 20, 1860. Died ca. 1864. Place of burial is unknown. William H. Moore served in Company F, Thirty-second Missouri Infantry (Union).

(3) James Roark, born 1840, did not marry. Died May 20, 1863, while serving in Company D, Thirty-second Missouri Infantry (Union). Buried in the Vicksburg National Cemetery.[159]

(4) Martha Roark, born April 1842, married Joshua Munday in Dent County, Missouri, on April 29, 1860. Died 1905, buried in the Lay Cemetery, Dent County, Missouri. Joshua Munday served in Company D, Forty-eighth Missouri Infantry (Union).

(5) Mary Josephine Roark, born 1845. Died young. No further information is available.

(6) Elizabeth Roark, born 1847, married John B. Rutledge in Dent County, Missouri, on February 1, 1870.[160] Date of death and place of burial are unknown.

(7) Jeremiah M. Roark, born July 1849, married Hester J. Waddell in Texas County, Missouri, on November 12, 1882.[161] Date of death is unknown, burial was with his wife in Cold Springs Cemetery, Texas County, Missouri.[162]

(8) Timothy Roark, born July 5, 1851, married Samantha Dutton in Texas County, Missouri, on October 26, 1874. Died November 7, 1927, buried in the Summersville Cemetery, Summersville, Missouri.[163]

(9) Eliza A. Roark, born 1856, married Sanford S. Cope in Texas County, Missouri, on April 6, 1873. Died June 13 1930, buried in Eakly Cemetery, Caddo County, Oklahoma.

(10) David Roark, born 1858, married Emma McClary in Texas County, Missouri, March 22, 1885.[164] Died September 27, 1941. Place of burial is unknown.

(11) Joseph R. Roark, born July 25, 1861, married Martha Crabtree on January 18, 1880. Died September 25, 1936, buried in Contra Costa County, California.

(12) James Ervin Roark, born December 29, 1862, married, first, Eliza Hunt[165] and, second, Cora Melvina Bell.[166] Died January 2, 1898.[167] Place of burial is unknown.

(13) Douglas P. Moore (grandson), born 1862, married Leona Ford on July 3, 1884, in Henry County, Missouri. Died November 29, 1950, in Springfield, Missouri, and

buried with his wife in the Greenlawn Cemetery, Springfield, Greene County, Missouri.

Timothy Roark Jr.

Timothy Roark Jr. was thirty-seven when his older brothers made the trip from the Salem Community to Claiborne County to quit claim title to the Timothy Roark homestead. He had married Mary Williams on March 12, 1840, when he was twenty-one, and by 1856, his family consisted of nine children, six boys and three girls. His eldest, James, was sixteen; the youngest, Elizabeth, was just one year old.[168]

In 1856, Timothy Jr. owned 450 acres on the south side of the Powell River and north of Henderson Mill Hollow. He had purchased his first tract of 100 acres in 1848 from Thomas J. Johnston, who at the time was clerk of the county court.[169] In 1850, he had purchased an additional 200 acres from John Fultz, father-in-law to Timothy's brother Jeremiah,[170]

Timothy Roark Jr., brother of Joseph, Claiborne County, Tennessee, Ca. 1880.

and in 1853, he had purchased an additional 100 acres from Samuel Day, south of the farm then owned by John Fultz.[171] Timothy located his home place not far from his brother Jeremiah and built his home north of Henderson Mill Hollow near the road providing access to his farm. The road today is still known as Roark Road in Claiborne County.

In 1858, Timothy Jr. began purchasing land on the headwaters of Blair's Creek just north of the Kentucky Road (now U.S. Highway 25E) and southeast of the old Timothy Roark homestead. On September 14 of that year, he purchased 100 acres from his cousin, Timothy Eastridge.[172] The following year, 1859, Timothy Roark bought seven tracts of land in the area of his purchase from Eastridge, thus adding 212 acres to his land holdings.[173] Some of the purchases in 1859 were from people, including his brother William, who were making the move to Missouri. Timothy purchased three additional tracts between 1859 and 1863, so that by the early fall of 1863, his land holdings amounted to more than 1040 acres.

In September 1863, Timothy sold all of his land north of Henderson Mill Hollow to Robert Patterson and moved his home to Blair's Creek Road (now Old Mulberry Road) along the upper reaches of Blair's Creek. The location of his new home place was very close to his sister Nancy Richardson and her husband James. Also nearby were Timothy's aunt and uncle, Lucy and James Eastridge, who had moved from the north side of the Powell River to the Blair's Creek area. A community developed around the families gathered on Blair's Creek that was known as the Bacchus Community, for which a post office was established in 1883.

The Civil War came to Claiborne County in the summer of 1861 as both Union and Confederate armies sought to occupy and defend the important Cumberland Gap. As the war developed, there was no rush by young men in Claiborne County to join either army, and not until threatened enforcement of the Confederate conscription laws in 1862 did men enlist in the Union army. Timothy Roark Jr. had three sons of conscription age in 1862–James 22, John 20, and William 19. All three enlisted February 10, 1862, in Company I, Third Tennessee Infantry (Union) at Flat Lick, Kentucky. James Roark was soon elected corporal and a year later, April 18, 1863, he was appointed sergeant in the company.[174]

Home of Timothy Roark Jr. in the Bacchus Community, Claiborne County, Tennessee.

The Third Tennessee Infantry served under Brig. Gen. George W. Morgan's 7th Division in the occupation of Cumberland Gap in July 1862. The regiment fought at Richmond, Kentucky, against the Confederate drive into Kentucky in the fall of 1862 and, on January 2, 1863, was engaged in escorting wagon trains south from Nashville to supply the Union Army at Murfreesboro. It was at this time that the wagon trains were raided and destroyed by Gen. Joseph Wheeler's Confederate Cavalry raid around the Union army between Murfreesboro and Nashville. With Wheeler's Cavalry rode the First Tennessee Cavalry (Confederate), the roster of which included the Hamilton County cousins of Timothy's sons–James, John, and Will Roark–ironically with names identical to those of their three Claiborne County cousins.

Following the Battle of Murfreesboro, the Third Tennessee Infantry remained in the town for several months and then moved with General Rosecrans in the occupation of Chattanooga on September 24, 1863. During October and November, the regiment performed picket duty along the north side of the Tennessee River between Sale Creek and Blythe's Ferry. Just across the river in the Salem Community, the relatives of Timothy's sons suffered through their coldest and most miserable winter of the war. Following the Battle of Chattanooga, the Third Infantry was moved up the Tennessee Valley and by late February 1864 was in Knoxville.[175]

In was in March that Timothy and Mary received word that their son William had been sick in Knoxville and, on February 28, had died of typhoid fever. Their other two sons remained with the regiment and were discharged at Nashville on February 23, 1865.

Beginning in 1881, Timothy and Mary, by then well established in the Bacchus Community, began to pass portions of their land to their family. In May 1881, Timothy sold 15 acres to his nephew James T. Richardson.[176] On November 22, 1883, Timothy sold 50 acres to son Jeremiah, gave 44 acres to son Timothy (who was by

then known in the community as "Timothy Jr."), sold 125 acres to son-in-law Levi Campbell, husband to daughter Nancy, and sold 68 acres to son Joseph. It is obvious that Timothy and Mary worked carefully to give each child an equitable share in the estate. For example, the "sale" to Joseph calls for the 68 acres to be sold for $300; however, of that amount, $150 was given to Joseph and the remaining $150 was covered by a promissory note from Joseph with a long-term payout. In each of the other transactions, a similar effort was made to balance the gifts made to the family.[177]

On March 11, 1885, Timothy sold 75 acres to son Timothy with no gift included. On July 22, he gave 45 acres to son-in-law James J. Richardson, husband of daughter Margaret, and on December 24, he sold 20 acres to son John.[178]

His estate generally settled, Timothy lived his last years at his home place in the Bacchus

Grave marker of Timothy Roark Jr., Cave Springs Cemetery, Claiborne County, Tennesse.

Community. He died there on Monday, May 23, 1892. Mary survived her husband by nine years. She died on April 19, 1901. Both were buried in the Cave Springs Cemetery, Claiborne County, Tennessee.

Children of Timothy Roark Jr. were:

(1) James Roark, born September 22, 1840,[179] married Mary A. Morrison on May 1, 1865.[180] Died ca. 1890, buried in Cave Springs Cemetery. He served in Company I, Third Tennessee Infantry (Union).

(2) John T. Roark, born July 12, 1842, married Mary A. Patterson on July 11, 1867.[181] After Mary's death on January 14, 1902, he married Harriet Colyer. John Roark died on March 25, 1920. Harriet died July 25, 1935. John and both his wives were buried in the Irish Cemetery in Tazewell.[182] Harriet applied for and received a pension from John's service during the war in Company I, Third Tennessee Infantry (Union).

(3) William Roark, born June 23, 1843, never married. Died in service with Company I, Third Tennessee Infantry (Union) at Knoxville, Tennessee. Buried in the National Cemetery in Knoxville.[183]

(4) Joseph Roark, born February 4, 1845, married Eliza E. Friar on November 3, 1868.[184] Died in California on October 24, 1937.[185]

(5) Jeremiah Roark, born November 24, 1846, married Nancy E. Patterson on November 28, 1871.[186] Jeremiah was ordained in the ministry at Blair's Creek Baptist Church on April 10, 1886. He died February 12, 1895. Burial location is unknown.[187]

(6) Louisa (Eliza) Roark, born December 17, 1848, married William P. Whitaker on December 22, 1874.[188] Died January 7, 1946, buried with her daughter in the England Cemetery, Claiborne County.[189]

(7) Sarah Roark, born March 19, 1851, married George W. Whitaker on December 19, 1869. Died August 28, 1903, buried at Cave Springs Cemetery next to her mother and father.[190]

(8) Timothy Roark, born February 27, 1853, married Elizabeth Vaughn on August 24, 1877.[191] No record of death was discovered.

(9) Elizabeth Roark, born July 22, 1855. Died 1884. No record of marriage or burial was discovered.[192]

(10) Mary Roark, born December 31, 1857, married Gilbert (Elbert) Williams on January 15, 1875.[193] Died May 9, 1946, buried in Cave Springs Cemetery.[194]

(11) Margaret Roark, born February 29, 1860, married James J. Richardson on October 3, 1880.[195] Died October 28, 1946, buried in the Ferguson Cemetery, Claiborne County.[196]

(12) Nancy Jane Roark, born July 26, 1862, married Levi Campbell on June 15, 1879. Died June 10, 1963, buried in Hurst Cemetery, Middlesboro, Kentucky.[197]

Mary Ann Roark

Mary Ann, known by the family and local community as "Polly," was twenty-eight when she met with her brother Joseph in 1856 to gain full title to the Timothy

Roark homestead. She had only been a baby when Joseph left home, having been born three years before on May 11, 1828. Mary Ann had married James Jefferson Lambert on October 14, 1843, when she was fifteen.[198] Jeff Lambert was the son of Joseph and Mary Lambert and brother to Sousan Lambert Ellison and Joseph Lambert Jr., both of whom were also niece and nephew by marriage to Mary Ann. After their marriage, Mary Ann and Jeff lived with her mother at the old Timothy Roark home place. Their first child, Nancy, was born in 1844, and by the time of Joseph's visit in 1856, their family consisted of two boys and three girls. Mary Ann and Jeff raised their family at the old home place, with their last daughter Susan born there on December 13, 1857.

Mary Ann Roark Lambert, Claiborne County, Tennessee, Ca. 1880.

Jeff Lambert was apparently successful as a farmer as he was able to acquire additional land and expand his farm. Unfortunately, the C i v i l War interrupted, as it did for many others, both his farming and his family life. Early in the war, at age thirty-six, Jeff enlisted in Company I, Third Tennessee Infantry (Union) with his nephews, the three sons of Mary Ann's brother Timothy Jr., and was mustered in at Flat Lick, Kentucky, on February 10, 1862. The probable reason for Jeff's enlistment was patriotism. Although he would have later been subject to Confederate conscription under the laws passed that year, he nevertheless had a wife and six dependent children that should have at least delayed conscription. Then, too, the first conscription act was not passed until three months after his voluntary enlistment and then was only applicable to men between the ages of 18 and 35. The conscription law that would include Jeff's age bracket would not be passed until October 1862, and rigid enforcement was begun even later.

James Jefferson Lambert, husband of Mary Ann Roark, Claiborne County, Tennessee, Ca. 1861.

Jeff's army service would, regretfully, be short-lived. When the Third Tennessee Infantry Regiment occupied Cumberland

Grave marker of James Jefferson Lambert in the Lexington National Cemetery, Lexington, Kentucky.

Gap in July 1862, Jeff Lambert became seriously ill and was ordered to report to the hospital on September 12. When the regiment withdrew into Kentucky on September 17 before the Confederate advance on Cumberland Gap, Jeff was captured by Confederate forces. Two weeks later, October 2, he was paroled in what was the usual practice on both sides during the war. The paroled sick and wounded were returned to the Union lines and transported by Union forces to Lexington, Kentucky. There Jeff Lambert, seriously ill, was hospitalized and, in typical army fashion, given a number–Hospital No. 1346. His illness was diagnosed as erysipelas–a bacterial infection of the skin with which high fever was associated. Jeff Lambert suffered for months in the Lexington hospital but the infection could not be controlled. He died Sunday, April 12, 1863, and, according to the record, was buried at 5:00 p.m. the next day in what would become the Lexington National Cemetery.[199]

Mary Ann received notice of Jeff's death sometime in late April 1863. She was left to raise alone a family of six children. The three oldest were girls, ages 15 to 19, and the youngest was a girl, age 4. The boys, ages 8 and 11, were required to quickly assume a man's role on the farm.

Mary Ann did not remarry but remained at the home place with her family. Her youngest, Susan, remained single and lived with her mother after the others married and left home. The two women managed the farm and made their living on the homestead for almost fifty years. Mary Ann died at the home place on January 11, 1912, and was buried with her parents in the old homestead cemetery overlooking Cumberland Gap.

The children of Mary Ann Roark and James Jefferson Lambert were:

(1) Nancy Lambert, born 1844, married Patrick Leonard on November 28, 1867.[200] Buried in the family plot on the old Timothy Roark homestead. The cemetery near the Timothy Roark home place, following the burial there of Mary Ann Lambert's family, became known in the local community as the Lambert Cemetery.[201]

(2) Sarah Lambert, born May 24, 1847, married Lafayette Evans on January 18,

1865.[202] Died November 10, 1881, buried in the Lambert Cemetery, Claiborne County.[203]

(3) Elizabeth Lambert, born November 23, 1848, married Pleasant Eastridge on March 23, 1872.[204] Died June 21, 1912, buried in the Scott Cemetery, Claiborne County.[205]

(4) Joseph Lambert, born June 2, 1851, married Mary J. Cosby on December 16, 1875.[206] Died February 5, 1936, buried in the Lambert Cemetery, Claiborne County.[207]

(5) George W. Lambert, born February 22, 1856, married Mahalah Hatfield. Died April 1, 1922, buried in the Lambert Cemetery.[208]

(6) Susan Lambert, born December 13, 1858, never married. Died November 30, 1930, buried in the Lambert Cemetery.[209]

Lambert Cemetery, formerly family plot of Timothy Roark southwest of the Timothy Roark home place, and burial place of Mary Ann Roark Lambert. The grave of Mary Ann Lambert is in the upper left.

The Timothy Roark Family and the Civil War

The single event that most seriously impacted the surviving family of Timothy and Sarah Bolen Roark was the Civil War. The children of Timothy and Sarah had all married by 1845 and all had families at the beginning of the war. Many of their young sons and sons-in-law were of the prime military age, between eighteen and thirty-five, when the war began. An exception was Mary Ann Roark Lambert, whose children would be too young throughout the war for military service. However, her husband, Jeff Lambert, served in the Union Army and did not survive the war. Timothy and Sarah Roark had seventy-four grandchildren that grew to maturity. They had a total of twenty-eight family members serve in the two competing armies during the war. Of these, twenty-three fought for the Union and five for the Confederacy. Six died in military service, one was seriously wounded, and two others suffered minor battle-related injuries.

Fifteen of the twenty-eight that served in the military had the surname of Roark. Of those fifteen, there were six with the name John Roark, five with the name James Roark, and two with the name William Roark. Of the six family members that did not survive the war, three were single and three were married with dependent children.

Those serving in the military during the Civil War, listed under each family head, were:

James P. Roark
>   John B. Roark, Fifth Tennessee Infantry (Union)
>   Joseph Roark, Captain Barry's Company, Tennessee Light Artillery (Confederate)
>   William Webb, First Tennessee Cavalry (Confederate)

John Roark
>   James W. Roark, Seventh Tennessee Infantry (Union)
>   William C. Roark, Seventh Tennessee Infantry (Union)   **Died in Service**
>   Archibald L. McCallie, Fifth Tennessee Infantry (Union)
>   David Gregory, Eighth Tennessee Infantry (Union)
>   John Lewis Roark, Fifth Tennessee Infantry (Union)

Nancy Roark Richardson
>   George W. Richardson, Second Tennessee Infantry (Union)
>   Calvin James Cunningham, First Tennessee Cavalry (Union)

William Roark
>   John Roark, Eighth Tennessee Cavalry (Union)
>   William Williams, Sixth Tennessee Infantry (Union)
>   James Roark, Thirty-Second Missouri Infantry (Union)   **Died in Service**

Elizabeth Roark Ellison
>   Wiley Ellison, Third Tennessee Infantry (Union)
>   Joseph Lambert Jr., Eighth Tennessee Cavalry (Union)

Joseph Roark
>   James A. Roark, First Tennessee Cavalry (Confederate)
>   John W. Roark, First Tennessee Cavalry (Confederate)
>   William M. Roark, First Tennessee Cavalry (Confederate)
>   Joel A. Talley, Fifth Tennessee Infantry (Union)
>   William L. Swafford, Third West Tennessee Cavalry (Union)

Jeremiah Roark
>   John Roark, Thirty-Second Missouri Infantry (Union)
>   James Roark, Thirty-Second Missouri Infantry (Union)   **Died in Service**
>   Joshua Munday, Forty-Eighth Missouri Infantry (Union)
>   William P. Moore, Thirty-Second Missouri Infantry (Union) **Died in Service**

Timothy Roark Jr.
    James Roark, Third Tennessee Infantry (Union)
    John T. Roark, Third Tennessee Infantry (Union)
    William Roark, Third Tennessee Infantry (Union) **Died in Service**
Mary Ann Roark Lambert
    James Jefferson Lambert, Third Tennessee Infantry (Union) **Died in Service**

Timothy Roark Homestead

At the death of Timothy Roark in 1833, his widow, Sarah Bolen Roark, retained title to the homestead, which at the time consisted of 350 acres. Sarah Roark sold 150 acres to her son-in-law Thomas Ellison in 1840 and, at her death in 1853, Sarah informally left the remaining acreage to her daughter Mary Ann and son-in-law James Jefferson Lambert. Both Mary Ann and Jeff Lambert had lived with Sarah at the home place since their marriage in 1843.

Jeff Lambert obtained clear title to the 200 acres through quit claim deeds from the other heirs in 1854 and 1856. By the time of his death in 1863, Jeff Lambert had increased the size of his holdings to 225 acres, acquiring a 25-acre tract from William Roark in December 1856.

Mary Ann Lambert did not remarry after her husband's death, and she lived at the homestead with her daughter, Susan. In 1904, Mary Ann subdivided the Jeff Lambert estate among her sons Joseph and George and her daughter Susan in which the three heirs each received title to an equitable portion of the estate. Mary Ann died at the home place in 1912.

Susan Lambert, having never married, lived at the home place alone until her death in 1930. Prior to her death, Susan sold her share of the Jeff Lambert estate to her two brothers, Joseph and George Lambert.

Title to the Timothy Roark homestead left the family in early 1933, when Joseph and George Lambert sold the tract to Minerva Woodard. Interestingly, the deed to Woodard was signed by eighteen additional heirs, principally children of Joseph and George Lambert and four by the name of Ellison, obviously for the purpose of transferring a clear title to the tract.[210] The homestead tract, or the portion thereof containing the old home place site, was subsequently sold to Noal Day, and then later to Preston Smith, the current owner in late 2000.

Joseph Roark Homestead

After the death of Joseph Roark in 1876, and in accordance with the estate settlement, Will Roark was recipient of title to the homestead and lived there until his death in 1923. His widow, Virginia, continued to live at the home place until her death in 1934. In 1914, Will and Virginia had given portions of the homestead along the river to five of their children and had given equal and undivided interest in the remaining 308 acres, including the home place, to Joe and Grover, the eldest and youngest sons, respectively. After the death of their father and in accordance with his wishes, Grover moved into the home place with his family in 1932 and helped in the support of his mother.

In 1939, Joe responded to the request of Grover to divide their interest in the homestead tract and, by a quit claim deed, surrendered full title to Grover in 154 acres including the home place.[211] Simultaneously with his receiving clear title to the home place, Grover sold the 154 acres to Margaret Adlaid McCallie and Sarah Jane McCallie, unmarried daughters of Archibald L. McCallie and Margaret Roark McCallie, and second cousins to Grover.[212]

Joseph Roark home place, Ca. 1986, prior to restoration.

The McCallie sisters lived at the home place with their brother during their remaining years. In September 1953, they sold the 154 acres to Thomas J. Johnson and Mary McCallie Johnson, retaining a life estate in the home place.[213] After the death of Sarah McCallie, Thomas and Mary Johnson sold the homestead to Lucille Boyd, retaining a life estate for themselves and honoring the life estate that still remained with Margaret Adlaid McCallie.[214]

The home place was unoccupied and vacant for seventeen years following the death of the Johnsons. Title to the homestead remained outside the immediate descendants of Joseph Roark until the home place was purchased by Margene Roark Higham, daughter of Franklin Asbury Roark, and Gertrude Roark Davenport, daughter of William Grover Roark, both great-granddaughters of Joseph.[215] In 1992, Marleita Roark Carmichael, also a daughter of William Grover Roark and great-granddaughter

*Joseph Roark home place in 2000 after restoration by Ms. Marleita
Carmichael. Original planed-log structure is located at the chimney in the
southwest corner of the home place.*

Interior of Joseph Roark home place showing original planed-log construction.

of Joseph, purchased the home place and restored it to its 1920s condition. Ms. Carmichael is the current owner as of December 2000.

The Salem Community

The Salem Community began to decline shortly after the Civil War. With all merchants located in Birchwood and Georgetown, the Salem Community was centered only around its church and school. Its people and its sense of community were its reason for being, but after the war and during Reconstruction, the people began to leave–slowly at first and then at an accelerating rate. There were many reasons why people left: higher taxes for support of the new James County government, punitive state legislation as part of Reconstruction, the lack of jobs other than farm labor for those who owned no land, and, most likely, the same reason that had motivated their ancestors for several generations–opportunity of cheap land and better opportunity in other areas of the country. Land opportunities were being advertised in Texas, Arkansas, Missouri, and even in the Indian Territory that would be Oklahoma. Railroads had land to sell and networks of tracks to provide access–both of which had been heavily advertised. Many of the young men saw little reason to stay in the home community. The large families that had been required to provide adequate farm labor over the last half-century worked to the detriment of the individual family member. Land offered the family members an opportunity of wealth and well-being, but in almost all cases the family farm was too small after the estate was settled to provide adequate land to but a few in the large family. Opportunity lay elsewhere and many families were similar to the Joseph Roark family. There the family was separated geographically when five of the six family members sought opportunity outside the community.

The migration started in earnest in the 1870s. Joseph's son, James A. Roark, left for Texas in 1878; the Benjamin Webbs left for Arkansas in 1871; and the James Madison Conners left for Missouri in the early 1880s. The migration was not confined to single families. Larger groups formed, jointly planned, and made the move to the southwest. One such group moved to Parker County, Texas, in December 1881. Included in the group were the families of William L. Hutcheson, Alfred L. Hutcheson, and James C. Hutcheson, all sons of W.C. Hutcheson, the merchant with whom Joseph Roark had done business for many years; Pleasant Doughty and family, brother-in-law to the Hutchesons and operator of the Doughty Ferry on the Tennessee; the family of Silas Witt and Martha Jane Conner Witt, sister to three Conner girls who married Roarks; the William Haney family; and the Josh Baker family.[216]

The Salem Community continued to dwindle in population during the first quarter of the twentieth century. By the time the TVA took the river farms in 1937 for the Chickamauga Lake, the Salem Community was known by name by only a few. The Salem Baptist Church was the last bulwark against the inevitable.

The Salem Baptist Church

The church had been organized in 1835 before the Ocoee District was created and when the land was still in the possession of the Cherokees. By 1856, the church had constructed its "meeting house" on land donated by Joseph Roark across Grasshopper Creek from the home place. In 1872, probably at its largest membership, the church had 162 members, meeting for preaching the fourth Saturday of every month, with Sunday School held each Sunday morning.

As the population of the Salem Community declined, the local citizens clung tenaciously to the church. By 1898, membership in the Salem Baptist Church had declined to 108 members, and by 1916, it had dropped to 59 members. Unhappily for the church, membership and attendance continued to dwindle. Volunteer preachers and a few dedicated members kept the church alive into the 1930s. In 1935, a cer-

Salem Baptist Church, Ca. 1915.

emony to celebrate the one-hundredth anniversary of the church was held on Sunday, May 26. Lunch was served and many former members attended. The principal address was given by T.J. Campbell.

The last known service in the church building was the funeral of John Lewis Roark on July 15, 1941. Afterward, the building was not maintained and its condition steadily deteriorated. By 1960, only the collapsed ruins of the once-proud meeting house remained. The church site is currently identified by a historical marker.

> *What though the radiance which was once so bright*
> *Be now forever taken from my sight, . . .*
> *We will grieve not, rather find*
> *Strength in what remains behind . . .*

> William Wordsworth
> "Ode on Intimations of Immortality"

Joseph Roark

Endnotes

Chapter 1: Independence Day 1813

1. Cunliffe, Marcus, The Nation Takes Shape: 1789-1837, The University of Chicago Press, 1969, p. 181.

2. Ibid., p. 88.

3. Larkin, Jack, The Reshaping of Everyday Life, 1790-1840, Harper & Row, 1988, p. 11.

4. Matthews, Jean V., Toward a New Society, American Thought and Culture, 1800-1830, Twayne Publishers, Boston, 1991, p. 105.

5. U.S. Bureau of the Census, 1810 Federal Census, Microfilm Roll Number 1, Population of the United States, 1800-1830.

6. Bailyn, Bernard, Voyagers to the West, Vintage Books, 1988, p. 65.

7. Ibid., pp. 245-265.

8. Op. cit., Cunliffe, Nation Takes Shape, pp. 70-82.

9. Krout, John Allen and Dixon Ryan Fox, The Completion of Independence, 1790-1830, Quadrangle Books, Chicago, 1971, p. 139.

10. Op. cit., Cunliffe, Nation Takes Shape, p. 111.

11. Op. cit., Krout and Fox, Completion of Independence, p. 233.

12. Ibid., p. 86.

13. Op. cit., Matthews, Toward a New Society, p. 26.

14. Ibid., p. 29.

15. Op. cit., Krout and Fox, Completion of Independence, p. 176.

16. Op. cit., Larkin, Reshaping of Everyday Life, p. 35.

17. Op. cit., Matthews, Toward a New Society, p. 56.

18. Op. cit., Larkin, Reshaping of Everyday Life, p. 3.

19. Ibid., p. 271.

20. Ibid., p. 274.

21. Op. cit., Cunliffe, Nation Takes Shape, p. 123.

22. Op. cit., Matthews, Toward a New Society, p. 22.

23. Brant, Irving, <u>James Madison, Commander in Chief, 1812-1836</u>, The Bobbs-Merrill Company, Inc., 1961, p. 188.

24. Allison, John Murray, <u>Adams and Jefferson, The Story of a Friendship</u>, University of Oklahoma Press, 1966, p. 254.

25. Randall, Henry S., <u>The Life of Thomas Jefferson</u>, Books for Libraries Press, 1970, p. 390.

26. Op. cit., Brant, <u>James Madison</u>, p. 188.

27. Smith, Page, <u>John Adams</u>, Volume II, 1784-1826, Doubleday & Company, Inc., 1962, p. 1113.

28. Bassett, John Spencer, <u>The Life of Andrew Jackson, Volume 1</u>, Doubleday, Page & Company, 1911, p. 85.

29. Remini, Robert V., <u>Andrew Jackson and the Course of American Empire, 1767-1821</u>, Harper & Row, 1977, p. 180.

30. Heiskell, S.G., <u>Andrew Jackson and Early Tennessee History</u>, Ambrose Printing Company, 1918, pp. 389-400.

31. Sellers, Charles Grier, Jr., <u>James K. Polk, Jacksonian, 1795-1843</u>, Princeton University Press, 1957, pp. 39-42.

32. Thomas, Lately, <u>The First President Johnson</u>, William Morrow & Company, Inc., 1968, pp. 7-17.

33. Coulter, E. Merton, <u>William G. Brownlow, Fighting Parson of the Southern Highlands</u>, The University of Tennessee Press, Knoxville, Tennessee, 1971.

34. Faragher, John Mack, <u>Daniel Boone, The Life and Legend of an American Pioneer</u>, Henry Holt and Company, 1992, pp. 303-307.

35. Deed Records, Rhea County, Dayton, Tennessee, July 10, 1813, Deed Book C, Page 137.

Chapter 2: Ancestry–James Roark

1. The author uses the term "Scotch-Irish" with a full appreciation that there exists no unanimity in its meaning or its applicability. The term "Scotch-Irish" appears to have been first coined in 1730 in Pennsylvania and was used in a derogatory way to refer to the newly arrived emigrants from Ulster. Some have offered the opinion that "Scots-Irish" is a more appropriate reference. Accepting the more widely used "Scotch-Irish," the term refers to those who emigrated from the Ulster plantation in northern Ireland between 1717 and 1775 and their descendants in America. It is consistently used herein as so defined.

2. Leyburn, James G., <u>The Scotch-Irish, A Social History</u>, The University of North Carolina Press, 1962, pp. 83-139.

3. Ford, Henry Jones, The Scotch-Irish in America, Princeton University Press, 1915, pp. 188-194.

4. Schweitzer, George K., The Scots-Irish: Aggravation, Emigration, Immigration, Migration, Assimilation, distributed notes from the Dallas Genealogical Society 1997 Lecture Series, June 14, 1997, p. 3.

5. Dickson, R.J., Ulster Emigration to Colonial America, 1718-1775, Routledge and Kegan Paul, London, 1966, pp. 201-220.

6. Paxson, Frederic L., History of the American Frontier, 1763-1893, Houghton Mifflin Company, p. 4.

7. Op. cit., Leyburn, The Scotch-Irish, pp. 190-191.

8. Op. cit., Ford, The Scotch-Irish in America, pp. 265-268.

9. Kercheval, Samuel, A History of the Valley of Virginia, C.J. Carrier Company, Harrisonburg, Virginia, 1994, pp. 49-54.

10. Summers, Lewis Preston, History of Southwest Virginia, 1746-1786, Washington County, 1777-1870, The Overmountain Press, Johnson City, Tennessee, 1989, p. 117.

11. The conclusions on the ancestry of Joseph during the period between 1730 and 1770 are based on an extensive review of court records in the Virginia counties in the Northern Neck and the Shenandoah Valley as the counties existed and others were later organized. The distinction between the families of Bryan Roark and Timothy Ororke Sr. and the conclusion that Joseph Roark descended from Bryan Roark is based primarily on the spelling of the name prior to 1770 and the fact that the "Junior" used with Timothy Roark Jr. referred more to a differentiation by age rather than a father-son relationship. In a practice common to the time, the older of two men with the same name was referred to as "Senior" while the younger was "Junior" without indicating a father-son relationship. No records indicate that Timothy Ororke Sr. had a son by the name of Timothy. While more than the noted Roark and Ororke families could have existed in Frederick County, Virginia, between 1738 and 1755, only Bryan Roark and Timothy Ororke Sr. are mentioned in the court records. Evidence suggests that both lived in the southern portion of Frederick County that would later be part of Shenandoah County.

Timothy Ororke Sr. died in 1768 with his wife, Sarah, being named as administratrix of the estate. Court Records, Frederick County, Virginia, Court Order Book 14, Page 300, August 2, 1768, 4-1-1-3354. An appraisal of the personal property of the Ororke estate was conducted September 17, 1768. Court Records, Frederick County, Virginia, Will Book 3, Pages 476-477, April 21, 1769, 4-1-1-3332. Timothy Ororke Sr. apparently wished his land holdings of 443 acres to go to his son Philemon with Timothy's widow to maintain a life estate in one-third of the tract.

Following her death, Philemon was to have full title in the tract. Northern Neck of Virginia Grants Book O, Page 281, May 17, 1770; Gray, Gertrude E., <u>Virginia Northern Neck Land Grants</u>, Volume II, 1742-1775, Genealogical Publishing Co., Inc., Baltimore, 1988, p. 204, 4-1-1-3326. Children of Timothy and Sarah Ororke Sr. were Philemon, Michael, Ann, George, Rebecca, Jesse, and David. Armentrout, Georgie Carrier Early, <u>Carrier - Carryer and Allied Lines</u>, Gateway Press, Inc., Baltimore, 1985, p. 179, 4-1-1-3346. Philemon, Michael, and David Ororke remained in the Northern Neck after their father's death and they are later mentioned in deed records for Rockingham County. Court Records, Rockingham County, Virginia, Deed Book, Page 25, February 11, 1783, and Page 71, April 13, 1787; Kaylor, Peter Cline, <u>Abstract of Land Grant Surveys, 1761-1791</u>, Genealogical Publishing Co., Inc., Baltimore, 1984, pp. 105, 121, 4-1-1-3339.

Bryan Roark is mentioned in the court records of Frederick County, Virginia, seven times between May 1743 and August 1748, in cases primarily involving suits for damages. In most instances Bryan Roark was the plaintiff. His name was consistently spelled "Roark." Court Records, Frederick County, Virginia, Court Order Book 1, Pages 115, 282, 295, 426, May 14, 1743, March 8 and 9, 1744, October 5, 1745; Court Order Book 2, Pages 136, 341, 470, August 7, 1746, October 9, 1747, August 4, 1748; Library of Virginia Microfilm Reel Frederick County No. 66. No deed record could be found of land owned by Bryan Roark nor was any record discovered which documented his death.

The conclusion that Timothy Roark, ostensibly the son of Bryan Roark, was in Frederick County with his father between 1750 and 1757 is based on three records. First, Timothy Roark was identified in court records as a debtor to John Hite in 1750. Chalkley, Lyman, <u>Chronicles of the Scotch-Irish Settlement in Virginia</u>, Volume I, Genealogical Publishing Co., Baltimore, 1965, p. 464. Second, Timothy was identified in the militia of Frederick County, Virginia, September 2, 1755, which, at that time, places him between the ages of 18 and 50. On the militia record he is referred to as "Junior." Gilreath, Amelia C., <u>Frederick County, Virginia, Early Troop Records, 1755-1761</u>, privately published, Nokesville, Virginia, p. 149. Third, Timothy Roark was in court in Frederick County in 1757 as a plaintiff in a suit against John O'Neal. Court Records, Frederick County, Virginia, Court Order Book 7, Page 226, April 6, 1757; Library of Virginia Microfilm Reel Frederick County No. 69. That Timothy Roark was in Botetourt County by 1770 is based on court records from Christiansburg. Timothy was in what would be Fincastle County near present day Christiansburg in 1770 and was involved in court action against a Samuel Simpson. In seven court sessions between 1770 and 1775, all of which would be recorded in records of Fincastle County, Timothy pursued legal action against Simpson, finally winning a judgement against Simpson and his "goods and chattles" on August 1, 1775. Hackler, Sarah Katherine Smith and Mary B. Kegley, Rowark/Roark and Related Families of Elk Creek, Grayson County, Virginia, privately published, Galax, Virginia, 1995, pp. 143-150.

12. Op. cit., Leyburn, The Scotch-Irish, pp. 319-321.

13. Op. cit., Chalkley, Chronicles of the Scotch-Irish, p. 465.

14. Op. cit., Leyburn, The Scotch-Irish, p. 274.

15. Heyrman, Christine Leigh, Southern Cross, The Beginnings of the Bible Belt, Alfred A. Knopf, 1997, pp.77-116.

16. Weis, Frederick Lewis, The Colonial Churches and the Colonial Clergy of the Middle and Southern Colonies, 1607-1776, Lancaster, Mass., 1938, p. 17.

17. Letter of James Reed, an S.P.G. minister, to the Secretary of the Colony, June 26, 1760. Colonial Records of North Carolina, VI, p. 265.

18. In 1773, James Roark, grandfather to Joseph, was located in the "Baptist Valley" of the upper Clinch River in southwest Virginia. "Baptist Valley was so named from the number of persons belonging to the Baptist denomination of Christians who settled in it." Bickley, George W., History of Tazewell County, Virginia, 1852, reproduced in Harman, John Newton, Sr., Annals of Tazewell County, Virginia, Volume 1, W.C. Hill Printing Company, 1922, p. 354.

19. Op. cit., Summers, Southwest Virginia, pp. 43-45.

20. Ibid., pp. 50-52.

21. The conclusion that there were three brothers is based primarily on the three land grants from the Loyal Land Company in 1774, with James Roark and John Roark receiving the surveys on the same date, with Timothy Roark receiving his grant only months later. Reference: Library of Virginia, Microfilm Records, Land Office, File 123, Loyal Land Company, Fincastle County, 1774, 4-1-1-3492, 3493, 3494. The names of James Roark's sons, i.e., John and Timothy, add credibility to the conclusion that he had brothers by those names. A Joseph Roark is mentioned on the militia list for the Elk Creek District of Montgomery County on September 6, 1782, Captain Charles Morgan's Company, along with James and Timothy Roark. This Joseph Roark, however, does not appear again in tax records or other militia records. He may or may not have been a brother.

22. Joyner, Peggy Shomo, Abstracts of Virginia's Northern Neck Warrants & Surveys, Frederick County, 1747-1780, Volume II, privately published, p. 115, 4-1-1-3329.

23. Court Records, Augusta County, Virginia, Court Order Book 4, Page 135, March 25, 1754, Library of Virginia Microfilm Reel Augusta No. 63. Court Records, Augusta County, Virginia, Court Order Book 6, Page 332, November 23, 1759, Library of Virginia Microfilm Reel Augusta No. 63.

24. Hicks, John D., George E. Mowry, and Robert E. Burke, The Federal Union, Houghton Mifflin Company, Boston, 1964, p. 150.

25. The Library of Virginia, Land Records, Archival and Library Collection, Grants 123, Loyal Land Company, Survey for James Roark, 63 acres, Fincastle County, February 19, 1774, 4-1-1-3493.

26. The Library of Virginia, Land Records, Archival and Library Collection, Grants 123, Loyal Land Company, Survey of 110 acres to Timothy Roark, Fincastle County, December 12, 1774, 4-1-1-3492.

27. The Library of Virginia, Land Records, Archival and Library Collection, Grants 123, Loyal Land Company, Survey of 93 acres to John Roark, Fincastle County, February 20, 1774, 4-1-1-3494.

28. Op. cit., Summers, Southwest Virginia, pp. 84-85.

29. Van Every, Dale, Forth to the Wilderness, The First American Frontier, 1754-1774, Quill William Morrow, New York, 1961, pp. 21-22.

30. Op. cit., Bickley, Tazewell County, in Harman, p. 342.

31. Op. cit., Summers, Southwest Virginia, pp. 85-90.

32. Faragher, John Mack, Daniel Boone, The Life and Legend of an American Pioneer, Henry Holt and Company, New York, 1992, pp. 53-71.

33. Court Records, Botetourt County, Virginia, Court Order Book for 1772, Page 29, April 18, 1772, Library of Virginia Reel Botetourt No. 27.

34. Schreiner-Yantis, Netti, Montgomery County, Virginia – Circa 1790, privately published, Springfield, Virginia, 1972, p. 101.

35. Op. cit., Summers, Southwest Virginia, pp. 106-107.

36. Kegley, Mary B., Militia of Montgomery County, Virginia, 1777-1790, Kegley Books, Wytheville, Virginia, 1990, Preface.

37. Hening, Statutes at Large, An Act Concerning Tithables, 1748, Colony of Virginia.

38. Kegley, Mary B., Glimpses of Wythe County, Virginia, Volume 2, Pictorial Histories Publishing Co., Charleston, West Virginia, pp. 151-154.

39. Op. cit., Faragher, Daniel Boone, pp. 88-89.

40. Op. cit., Summers, Southwest Virginia, p. 831.

41. Ibid., p. 256.

42. Pendleton, William C., History of Tazewell County and Southwest Virginia, 1748-1920, The Overmountain Press, Johnson City, Tennessee, 1989, pp. 257-258.

43. Kegley, Mary B., Early Adventurers on the Western Waters, Volume II, Green Publishers, Inc., Orange, Virginia, pp. 276-277, 4-1-1-3485.

44. Op. cit., Summers, Southwest Virginia, p. 791.

45. Op. cit., Pendleton, Tazewell County, pp. 233, 418.

46. Ibid., pp. 233, 541.

47. Ibid., pp. 233, 439-443.

48. Ibid., pp. 471, 541.

49. Court Order Book, Wythe County, Virginia, August 13, 1799. Also, see Kegley, Mary B., Abstracts of Court Orders of Wythe County, Virginia, 1790-1791; 1795-1810, 1996, p. 50, 4-1-1-3337.

50. Op. cit., Summers, Southwest Virginia, p. 115.

51. Op. cit., Pendleton, Tazewell County, pp. 207-217.

52. Deed Records, Washington County, Abingdon, Virginia, April 30, 1783, Land Grant Book 1, 1753-1797, Page 201, 4-1-1-3475.

53. Op. cit., Pendleton, Tazewell County, pp. 422-423.

54. Ibid., pp. 237-241.

55. Op. cit., Bickley, Tazewell County, in Harman, pp. 353-356.

56. Op. cit., Pendleton, Tazewell County, pp. 434-440.

57. Op. cit., Bickley, Tazewell County, in Harman, pp. 344-345.

58. Op. cit., Pendleton, Tazewell County, p. 406.

59. Ibid., p. 405.

60. Op. cit., Bickley, Tazewell County, in Harman, p. 344.

61. Brancrofts History of United States, Volume X, p. 77.

62. Op. Cit., Dickson, Ulster Emigration, p. 176.

63. Op. cit., Pendleton, Tazewell County, p. 231.

64. Augusta County Chancery Court Records, Staunton, Virginia, Successors of the Loyal Land Company versus David French, 1832, 4-1-1-3491. This court record provides an excellent history of the Loyal Land Company.

65. The Library of Virginia, Land Records, Archival and Library Collection, Grants 123, Loyal Land Company, Survey for James Roark, 63 acres, February 19, 1774, 4-1-1-3493.

66. Washington County Historical Society, Abingdon, Virginia, Microfilm Reel No. 68, Land Tax and Personal Property Tax Lists, Page 003. John Rorke [sic] was listed on the Personal Property Tax List for 1787 as one tithable.

67. Timothy Roark appeared on John Montgomery's list of Tithables for 1773 for Captain Herbert's Company in Fincastle County. The exact location for Herbert's Company is unknown; however, names also on the list such as Enoch Osborn and others known to have been in the Elk Creek area indicate Timothy was probably on his 110 acres at that time. Op. cit., Kegley, Glimpses of Wythe County, Volume 2, pp. 160-170.

68. Will Book 1, Grayson County, Independence, Virginia, pp. 75-77, Will of Timothy Roark, June 15, 1811.

69. Nuckolls, Benjamin Floyd, Pioneer Settlers of Grayson County, Virginia, Genealogical Publishing Co., Inc., 1975, p. 6. Nuckolls quotes from the Grayson County court records of June 10, 1793: ". . . different ways petitioned for by the inhabitants of Elk Creek . . . say there may a waggon Road be made from Jeremiah Stones to Hale's Meeting house, from thence to the Widow *Roarch* Cabin . . .," 4-1-1-3335.

70. Op. cit., Bickley, Tazewell County, in Harman, p. 408.

71. Op. cit., Faragher, Daniel Boone, p. 92.

72. Ibid., pp. 89-98.

73. Roosevelt, Theodore, The Winning of the West, Volume One, P.F. Collier & Son, New York, The Works of Theodore Roosevelt in Fourteen Volumes, 1889, p. 229.

74. Op. cit., Pendleton, Tazewell County, p. 264.

75. Op. cit., Van Every, Forth to the Wilderness, p. 195.

76. Ibid., p. 284.

77. Ibid., pp. 293-295.

78. Op. cit., Summers, Southwest Virginia, p. 149.

79. Op..cit., Pendleton, Tazewell County, p. 334.

80. Op. cit., Summers, Southwest Virginia, p. 203.

81. Roosevelt, Theodore, The Winning of the West, Volume Two, P.F. Collier & Son, New York, The Works of Theodore Roosevelt in Fourteen Volumes, 1889, pp. 29-30.

82. Op. cit., Pendleton, Tazewell County, p. 365.

83. Op. cit., Summers, Southwest Virginia, p. 233.

84. Op. cit., Pendleton, Tazewell County, pp. 356, 389.

85. Op. cit., Summers, Southwest Virginia, p. 249.

86. Van Every, Dale, Men of the Western Waters, Houghton Mifflin Company, Boston, 1956, pp. 43-44.

87. Op. cit., Pendleton, Tazewell County, pp. 390-391.

88. The conclusion that James Roark served in the capacity as a spy is based on the following facts:

> 1. Roark served in the militia under Capt. (later Major) Thomas Mastin and was later listed in Mastin's precinct in Washington County in 1782. Library of Virginia, Personal Property Tax List, Washington County, Virginia, 1782, Microfilm Page 002.

> 2. Mastin's Company of militia belonged to the regiment of the Virginia State Line commanded by Col. William Preston and was used for Indian spy duty for six months each year from 1776 until the close of the Revolutionary War. Harman, John Newton, Sr., Annals of Tazewell County, Virginia, W.C. Hill Printing Company, Richmond, Virginia, 1922, p. 224.

3. Associates and neighbors of James Roark–Thomas Witten, William Cecil, and Joseph Oney–supplied sworn statements that they served as spies in Mastin's company during the war; ibid., pp. 221-229.

4. Lt. James Maxwell, second in command of Mastin's company during the war, lived only one mile south of James Roark and would have been a leader in selecting local settlers and militia for spy duty; ibid., pp. 221-222.

89. Op. cit., Bickley, Tazewell County, in Harman, p. 411.

90. Doddridge, Rev. Dr. Joseph, Notes on the Settlement and Indian Wars of Virginia and Pennsylvania, reprint of the 1824 edition by Garland Publishing, Inc., New York, 1977, pp. 118-119.

91. Op. cit., Pendleton, Tazewell County, pp. 437-440.

92. In his history of Tazewell County, Bickley in 1852 names only John as one of the two sons who escaped the tragedy. We learn from later family history that the other son was Timothy. Harman, John Newton, Sr., Annals of Tazewell County, Virginia, Volume 1, W.C. Hill Printing Company, 1922, pp. 435-436; quote from Bickley, George W., History of Tazewell County, Virginia, 1852.

93. Op. cit., Pendleton, Tazewell County, pp. 441-442. A copy of Taylor's report is in the files of the author.

94. Library of Virginia, Washington County, Virginia, Personal Property Tax List, 1782, Microfilm Page 002, 4-1-1-3533.

95. Deed Records, Tazewell County, Tazewell, Virginia, October 20, 1824, Volume 3, Page 430, 4-1-1-2825. This deed furnishes evidence that the cabin lay on the north side of the river.

96. Land records are clear that James Roark owned the 130-acre Baptist Valley farm and the 100-acre Clinch River farm; however, his other land holdings have proven impossible to trace. After his death in 1792, attorney John Greenup (actually attorney-in-fact) was listed on the land tax list for Russell County as the administrator of the James Roark estate that was taxed for 194 acres. Quite possibly this 194 acres included the 100-acre river farm but the remaining 94 acres has neither been identified nor located. Title may have passed to the attorney for his settlement of the estate which dragged on for nine years. Albert, Anne Roberts and Ethel Evans Albert, Russell County, Virginia, Personal Property and Land Tax List, 1973, pp. 178 and 195, 4-1-1-3344.

97. Library of Virginia, Washington County Land Tax Records, 1782, Microfilm, 4-1-1-3552.

98. Op. cit., Bickley, Tazewell County, in Harman, p. 436.

99. Fulkerson, P.G., "Early Settlers of Claiborne County," Tazewell-New Tazewell Observer, August 13, 1980. Shropshire, Mrs. Laura Roark, Pioneer

Days–Stories of the Roark-Conner Ancestry, locally published, Revised Edition, 1992, p. 26. ____, History of Texas Together with a Biographical History of Tarrant and Parker Counties, The Lewis Publishing Company, 1895, p. 58. This last reference includes a biography of James A. Roark (1840-1905), grandson of Timothy, to which he no doubt provided the information that states Timothy "was a prisoner among the Indians for about twelve years." Although James A. Roark may have over estimated the duration of his grandfather's captivity, his recollection, only two generations removed from the capture, has to be respected.

100. Schreiner-Yantis, Netti and Florene Speakman Love, The 1787 Census of Virginia, Volume 1, Genealogical Books in Print, Springfield, Virginia, p. 484, 4-1-1-3106.

101. Washington County, Virginia, Land Grant Book 1, 1753-1797, Page 201.

102. Op. cit., Summers, Southwest Virginia, pp. 420-447.

103. Op. cit., Pendleton, Tazewell County, p. 365.

104. Deed Records, Wythe County, Wytheville, Virginia, Deed Book 2, Pages 3 and 4, 4-1-1- 3345.

105. An argument can be made that the mother of James Roark lived on Elk Creek in southern Montgomery County (now Grayson County) near Timothy, that she outlived James, and that she was alive in June 1793. Please refer to op. cit. Nuckolls, Pioneer Settlers of Grayson County.

106. Montgomery County, Virginia, Court Records, "A List of the Militia, Elk Creek District, Montgomery County," September 6, 1782, 4-1-1-3479. Also, Crush, Judge C.W., Montgomery Virginia, The First Hundred Years, Iberian Publishing Company, p. 102.

107. Washington County, Virginia, Land Grant Book 1, 1753-1797, Page 201.

108. James Roark was listed for the 100-acre river farm on tax rolls of Washington County for 1782 and 1786. Reference: Library of Virginia, Washington County, Virginia, Personal Property Tax List, 1786, Microfilm Pages 0097-0098, 4-1-1-3538. With the creation of Russell County in 1786, James Roark was taxed for the 100-acre river farm beginning in 1788 and continuing through 1791; however, he never appeared on the personal property tax lists of Russell County and was not a resident of Russell County or Washington County after 1786.

109. Summers, Lewis Preston, Annals of Southwest Virginia, 1769-1800, Genealogical Publishing Co., Inc., 1996, pp. 791-793.

110. Op. cit., Albert and Albert, Russell County, p. 56.

111. Op. cit., Pendleton, Tazewell County, pp. 391-392.

112. Kegley, Mary B., Early Adventurers on the Western Waters, Volume II, Green Publishers, Inc., Orange, Virginia, p. 56. "Timothy Roark, assignee of Moses Poore, 400 acres on both sides of Beaver Dam Fork of waters of Elk Creek, 100 acres surveyed 1774 for Roark, settled 1772."

113. Op. cit., Schreiner-Yantis and Love, The 1787 Census of Virginia, p. 434.

114. Will Book 1, Grayson County, Independence, Virginia, June 15, 1811, pp. 75-77, 4-1-1- 3099.

115. Op. cit., Schreiner-Yantis and Love, 1787 Census of Virginia, p. 434. The personal property tax list used by Schreiner-Yantis and Love does not list James Roark as even having a horse; however, the personal property tax list for Montgomery County in 1790 does list James with a horse. Reference: Schreiner-Yantis, Netti, Montgomery County, Virginia–Circa 1790, 1972, p. 25. It can be safely assumed that James had a horse in 1787.

116. Ibid., pp. 24 and 91. The exact location of Timothy Roark in 1787 cannot definitely be determined. Schreiner-Yantis places him in Baptist Valley and ten years later he was to buy the 130-acre home place from David Crouch. Crouch is never shown, on any tax list, to have resided in Baptist Valley so it can be concluded that he rented the farm to someone, most likely Timothy Roark.

117. Montgomery County, Virginia, Court Order Book, October 3, 1787, 4-1-1-3477.

118. Some effort should be made to explain the conclusion that this James Roark in the Elk Creek area was the same James Roark of the 1780 massacre in Baptist Valley. It would first appear unlikely, with the eighty miles separating Baptist Valley from Elk Creek and the difficult means of direct travel (even today) between the two locations, that James Roark would have been at his brother's (and possibly his mother's) place on so many different occasions. Could it have been another James Roark in the Elk Creek area? To answer this question, one must investigate available tax records each year between 1782 and 1792 for Montgomery and Washington Counties, for Russell County after 1786, for Wythe County after 1790, and for Grayson County after 1793. The following summarizes the results of such an effort:

    1. In early 1782, James Roark was listed on the Land Tax List (4-1-1-3552) and on the Personal Property Tax List for Washington County (4-1-1-3533). No James Roark was listed on either the Land Tax List or Personal Property Tax List for Montgomery County in 1782.

    2. On September 6, 1782, James Roark appears on a militia list for the Elk Creek District of Montgomery County. This was the area of residence of his brother Timothy (4-1-1- 3479); however, no James Roark was named on militia lists for Montgomery County for the following year, 1783, indicating James' visit to his brother was of short duration.

    3. On April 30, 1783, James Roark was in Washington County to assign the certificate for his 130 acres in Baptist Valley to David Crouch (4-1-1-3475); however, he was not listed on the Personal Property Tax List for Washington

County although the list did include his neighbors Moses Skaggs, John Deskins, Richard Oney, and John Hankins (4-1-1-3534).

4. In 1784, no James Roark was included on personal property tax lists for either Washington or Montgomery Counties (4-1-1-3535).

5. On July 26, 1785, James Roark served on a jury in Montgomery County (op. cit., Summers, Annals of Southwest Virginia, p. 789). Serving on the same jury was David Crouch, indicating the jury was selected from northern Montgomery County residents. In the Court Records for Montgomery County of the same date, neighbors of James Roark–William Cecil, John Greenup, and Thomas Peary (Peery)–were named to locate a wagon road. For 1785, James Roark was not listed on the Washington County Personal Property Tax List (4-1-1-3536), placing him in Montgomery County during at least a portion of 1785.

6. In 1786, James Roark was named on the Personal Property Tax List for Washington County (4-1-1-3538) thereby placing him on his 100-acre river farm.

7. In 1787, with the formation of Russell County, one would expect James Roark to be listed for the land tax list for his 100-acre river farm and also on the personal property tax list. He was listed on neither. He was listed on the Russell County Tax List for his 100 acres in 1788 and from 1790 through his death in 1792; however, he was not listed on any Personal Property Tax List for Russell County for 1787 through 1792 (4-1-1-3344). This would indicate he lived elsewhere, probably in Montgomery County. In the Court Order Book of Montgomery County for October 3, 1787, James Roark was listed as a constable in Captain Ozburn's (Enoch Osborne) Company of Militia (4-1-1-3477) indicating a location in the Elk Creek District of Montgomery County. This was supported in the excellent work by Schreiner-Yantis and Love in The 1787 Census of Virginia, in which James Roark was included in List A (for the southern portion of Montgomery County). No James Roark was included in Lists B or C for the remainder of Montgomery County nor for any portion of Russell County.

8. Fields in Grayson County: A History in Words and Pictures states that December 2, 1788, James Roark was replaced as constable by Joseph Fields. James Roark apparently had returned to the northern area of Montgomery County.

9. No tax records have been located for Montgomery County for 1789.

10. For 1790, Schreiner-Yantis in Montgomery County, Virginia–Circa 1790 lists James Roark in Baptist Valley on February 23, 1790 (Personal Property Tax List B) with neighbors John Greenup, James Maxwell, and Thomas

Witten. Another James Roark was, however, listed by Schreiner-Yantis for March 7, 1790, on Personal Property Tax List A (southern Montgomery County); however, this James Roark (referred herein as the "other James Roark") was apparently some distance from the Timothy Roark on Elk Creek as Timothy was listed on October 19, 1789.

11. With the creation of Wythe County in 1790, tax records for the western portion of Montgomery County from which Wythe County was taken have been difficult to locate. The first available Wythe County tax lists are for 1793 (Murphy and Douthat, Wythe County, VA, Tax List 1793-1800) do not list a James Roark, probably as a result of his death in 1792. Timothy Roark of Elk Creek was listed for only 1793 since Grayson County (including the Elk Creek area) was formed in 1793. It is interesting to note, however, that the "other James Roark" was not listed in Wythe County tax records between 1793 and 1800.

12. Finally, the first Personal Property Tax List for Grayson County in 1795 (4-1-1-3540) lists a James Roark; however, no James Roark was named on the Grayson County Personal Property Tax List for 1796, 1797, 1798, and 1799 (4-1-1-3541, 3542, 3543, 3545). (A James Roach was listed on the various tax lists and should not confuse the researcher.) Thus, the "other James Roark" in 1790 was either an erroneous carryover in the tax list or was in Grayson County for a later brief period.

It would appear therefore that the James Roark of the 1780 massacre and the James Roark mentioned in the tax lists for the Elk Creek area on several occasions were, in fact, one and the same. The later relocation of two daughters of Timothy Roark of Elk Creek to the Clinch Valley near the James Roark river farm gives additional credibility to the conclusion.

119. Op. cit., Schreiner-Yantis and Love, The 1787 Census of Virginia, p. 484.

120. Fields, Bettye-Lou, Grayson County: A History in Words and Pictures, Grayson County Historical Society, 1976, p. 37.

121. Law Order Book Number 1, Russell County, Lebanon, Virginia, p. 160, 4-1-1-3480.

122. Op. cit., Albert and Albert, Russell County, Virginia, pp. 42, 51, 60, 69; 4-1-1-3344.

123. Will Book Number 1, Russell County, Lebanon, Virginia, Page 199, 4-1-1-3480.

124. Op. cit., Albert and Albert, Russell County, p. 42, 51, 60; 4-1-1-3344.

125. Op. cit., Russell County Order Book Number 1, p. 213, 4-1-1-3480.

126. Op. cit., Schreiner-Yantis, Montgomery County, p. 25.

127. Will Book 1, Wythe County, Wytheville, Virginia, Page 76, 4-1-1-3341.

128. Op. cit., Albert and Albert, <u>Russell County</u>, p. 98, 4-1-1-3344.

129. This conclusion is based on the fact that Green (Greenup) is listed in the 1796 Land Tax List for Russell County (Albert and Albert, p. 178) as "att. for Rourke [Roark]." Later in the Albert lists, Greenup is listed as the "admn. of Rourke [Roark]." In Wythe County Will Book Number 1, Greenup is identified as the administrator of the estate.

130. Will Book Number 1, Wythe County, Wytheville, Virginia, p. 59, 4-1-1-3341.

131. Ibid., pp. 76-77, 4-1-1-3341.

132. Ibid., p. 189, 4-1-1-3341.

133. Deed Records, Wythe County, Wytheville, Virginia, Deed Book 2, January 16, 1797, Pages 3 and 4, 4-1-1-3345.

Chapter 3: Ancestry–Timothy Roark

1. No record has been found to firmly establish the date of birth of Timothy Roark. The estimate of his birth in 1767 is based on two records listed below in order of reliability:

> (a) Timothy was listed in the 1787 Personal Property Tax List for Area B of Montgomery County which was "an accounting of the Name of Every White Male Tithable over 21 years." Schreiner-Yantis, Netti and Florene Speakman Love, <u>The 1787 Census of Virginia</u>, Volume 1, Genealogical Books in Print, Springfield, Virginia, 1976, p. 442. The latest he could have been born is 1767.

> (b) The "right of passage" for a young man on the Virginia frontier was at the age of twelve years at which time he was given a rifle and hunted with the men. One must conclude that he was hunting with his father and his brother John at the time of the massacre in March 1780. Bickley states that there were *two* sons with James Roark that fateful day; however, only John is named. Bickley, George W., <u>History of Tazewell County, Virginia</u>, 1852, reproduced in Harman, John Newton, Sr., <u>Annals of Tazewell County, Virginia</u>, Volume 1, W.C. Hill Printing Company, 1922, p. 436. It is most likely that Timothy was the second son with his father and that he was at least twelve years old, making his birth in 1767 or very early in 1768. If another son was with James that day, no record or name has surfaced.

A safe conclusion is that Timothy was born at the earliest in 1766 or, at the latest, 1767.

2. Doddridge, Joseph, <u>Notes on the Settlement and Indian Wars of the Western Parts of Virginia & Pennsylvania</u>, Garland Publishing, Inc., New York, 1977, Reprint of the 1824 original publication, p. 158.

3. Ibid., pp. 113-115.

4. Van Every, Dale, <u>A Company of Heroes, The American Frontier, 1775-1783</u>, Quill, William Morrow, New York, 1962, p. 4.

5. Ibid., pp. 3-4.

6. Van Every, Dale, <u>Men of the Western Waters</u>, Houghton Mifflin Company, Boston, 1956, p. 1.

7. Ibid., p. 27.

8. Faragher, John Mack, <u>Daniel Boone, The Life and Legend of an American Pioneer</u>, Henry Holt and Company, New York, 1992, p. 35.

9. O'Neill, Laurie A., <u>The Shawnees, People of the Eastern Woodlands</u>, The Millbrook Press, Brookfield, Connecticut, 1995.

10. Fulkerson, P.G., "Early Settlers of Claiborne County," <u>Tazewell-New Tazewell Observer</u>, August 13, 1980. Shropshire, Mrs. Laura Roark, <u>Pioneer Days–Stories of the Roark-Conner Ancestry</u>, Locally published, Revised Edition, 1992, p. 26. ___, <u>History of Texas Together with a Biographical History of Tarrant and Parker Counties</u>, The Lewis Publishing Company, 1895, p. 58. Fulkerson states that Timothy Roark was captured "on the headwaters of the Clinch and taken to the Great Lakes."

11. Op. cit., Van Every, <u>Men of the Western Waters</u>, pp. 44-45.

12. Drake, Samuel G., <u>Indian Captivities or Life in the Wigwam</u>, *Narrative of . . . the Capture of . . . Mrs Clendenin . . .*, Auburn, Derby and Miller, 1851, Reprint by Heritage Books, Inc., 1995, pp. 284-286.

13. Severance, Frank H., <u>The Captivity and Sufferings of Benjamin Gilbert and his Family, 1780- 1783</u>, The Burrows Brothers Company, Cleveland, 1904, Reprint by Heritage Books, Inc., 1997, pp. 34-35.

14. Ibid., pp. 40-41.

15. Ibid., p. 37.

16. Op. cit., Drake, <u>Indian Captivities</u>, *Narrative of the Captivity of Frederick Manheim*, p. 333.

17. Op. cit., Drake, <u>Indian Captivities</u>, *A True and Wonderful Narrative of the Surprising Captivity and Remarkable Deliverance of Mrs. Francis Scott*, pp. 338-342.

18. Op. cit., Van Every, <u>Men of the Western Waters</u>, pp. 48-49.

19. Op. cit., Severance, <u>Captivity and Sufferings</u>, pp. 55-56.

20. Ibid., p. 59.

21. Ibid., p. 87.

22. Ibid., p. 95.

23. Ibid., p. 98.

24. Ibid., p. 132.

25. Ibid., p. 51.

26. Ibid., pp. 125-127.

27. Ibid., pp. 132-134.

28. Shropshire, Pioneer Days, pp. 26-27. Ms. Shropshire states: "Meantime he [Timothy] was planning his escape . . . He secretly arranged with the two white women the Indians were holding captive, to be prepared to leave with him. One dark night he and the women secretly escaped, running for their lives to the canoe on the river, and paddling furiously until they were for [sic] down the river. He took the women to their homes and made his way to his own home. Later, he married one of these escaped women–Sarah Bolen." It is highly unlikely that one of the "women" would have been Sarah Bolen. Sarah Bolen was born in 1776 and would have been less than ten years old at the latest probable date for Timothy's escape or release. Her formal education and training at the time of her marriage in 1796 would appear to allow little time as a captive of the Indians. While it would have been possible, it nevertheless appears unlikely that Sarah Bolen was one of the women who escaped with Timothy.

29. Op. cit., Severance, Captivity and Sufferings, p. 178.

30. Ibid., p. 187.

31. The period and length of Timothy Roark's captivity by the Shawnees is based on the known dates of his whereabouts. Records establish two alternative time periods for his captivity: either (1) between 1780 and 1786 or (2) between 1790 and 1796. Records place Timothy at four locations during the period: he was at or near the massacre in March 1780; he was on the personal property tax list of Area B in northern Montgomery County in February 1787; he was on the same personal property tax list in 1790 (which would indicate that he was in Baptist Valley by late 1789); and he was in Baptist Valley to purchase the 130 acres from David Crouch in January 1797 (which also places him in Baptist Valley in late 1796). Since there probably was insufficient time for his captivity between 1787 and 1790, the most probable times are those listed above. Given the two possible time periods, it would appear most logical for the captivity to have occurred between 1782 and 1786 rather than between 1790 and 1796 since he paid 100 pounds cash for the farm in January 1797, no small task for a farmer in that period let alone a recently returned captive. The question, however, remains: Was Timothy captured at the time of the massacre rather than two years later? Since he was on the personal property tax list in 1787, he had to be at least twenty-one years old, which makes him at least twelve at the time of the massacre. If he had been at home on that fatal day, rather than hunting with his father and brother(s)(?), he would have been old enough to have fought intensely for the survival of the family and, more than likely, would not have been spared by the Shawnee raiders.

32. Op. cit., Severance, Captivity and Sufferings, p. 8.

33. Op. cit., Van Every, <u>Men of the Western Waters</u>, p. 49.

34. Op. Cit., Schreiner-Yantis, <u>The 1787 Census of Virginia</u>, p. 442.

35. Schreiner-Yantis, Netti, <u>Montgomery County, Virginia–Circa 1790</u>, privately printed, Netti Schreiner-Yantis, Springfield, Virginia, 1972, pp. 24, 91.

36. Ibid., p. 91. Both James and Timothy Roark were recorded in Baptist Valley in Montgomery County; however, James was listed on February 23, 1790, while Timothy was listed on February 25, indicating a separate location. See *Explanation* by Schreiner-Yantis for conclusions on location of individual residents.

37. Microfilm Records, Library of Virginia, Richmond, Virginia, 1782 Land Tax Records, Montgomery County, Virginia.

38. Microfilm Records, Library of Virginia, Richmond, Virginia, 1786 Personal Property Tax Records, Washington County, Virginia, Microfilm Page 0085-0086. For field notes and property description, see deed from James Ramey to David Hansen, Deed Records, Russell County, Lebanon, Virginia, February 27, 1798, Deed Book 2, Pages 315-316 and 410-411.

39. Library of Virginia, Virginia Land Grants, Book 27, Pages 370-371, Russell County, December 13, 1792.

40. Schreiner-Yantis, Netti, <u>Archives of the Pioneers of Tazewell County, Virginia</u>, privately printed by Schreiner-Yantis, Springfield, Virginia, 1973, reprinted 1992, p. 242. The author quotes a Deskins descendant that Sarah Roark found the baby, John Deskins, on her doorstep and raised him. No explanation is given as to how the baby acquired the surname of Deskins.

41. The name Bolen had many variant spellings in the county records and tax lists of Virginia and Tennessee. The most common were *Bowling* and *Bolling*. The traditional spelling of Bolen is used herein. Sarah Bolen Roark was educated and probably had a great deal to do with establishing the traditional spelling.

42. Microfilm Records, Library of Virginia, Richmond, Virginia, <u>1782 Personal Property Tax List, Montgomery County, Virginia</u>, Microfilm Page 015. Also, the <u>1782 Land Tax List, Montgomery County, Virginia</u> includes a listing entitled "The Enumerated Articles," which is obviously a personal property tax list in which the *Bowlings* are also listed.

43. Op. cit., Schreiner-Yantis, <u>Tazewell County</u>, p. 292.

44. Microfilm Records, Tennessee State Library and Archives, Nashville, Tennessee, Marriage Bonds, Grainger County, 1796-1809, Microfilm Roll No. 20A. This record confirms that Lucy was the daughter of Joseph Bolen.

45. The marriage date for Timothy Roark and Sarah Bolen is based on the birth date of their first child, October 9, 1798. Late 1796 would seem to be the most probable date of the wedding.

46. Deed Records, Wythe County, Wytheville, Virginia, Deed Book 2, Pages 3-4.

47. Pendleton, William C., <u>History of Tazewell County and Southwest Virginia, 1748-1920</u>, The Overmountain Press, Johnson City, Tennessee, 1920, Reprint 1989, pp. 401-405.

48. Albert, Anne Roberts and Ethel Evans Albert, <u>Russell County, Virginia, Personal Property and Land Tax List, 1787 through 1800, 1802, 1810</u>, privately printed by Albert and Albert, 1973, pp. 197, 213; 4-1-1-3344.

49. Microfilm Records, Library of Virginia, Land Tax Records for Wythe County, Virginia, 1798, 1799, and 1800, Area B, Microfilm Roll 343, pp. 122, 147, 178.

50. Op. cit., Schreiner-Yantis, <u>Tazewell County</u>, pp. 296-298.

51. Op. cit., Pendleton, <u>Tazewell County</u>, p. 396.

52. Marriage Records, Tazewell County, Tazewell, Virginia, October 7, 1800.

53. Microfilm Records, Library of Virginia, 1798 Grayson County Land Tax List, Microfilm Page 36, 4-1-1-3556; and 1799 Grayson County Personal Property Tax List, 4-1-1-3544.

54. James Roark Copy Book which provides birth dates for most of the Timothy Roark family, copy provided by Ms. Janis Ragar, Sedalia, Missouri, 4-1-1-2818.

55. Bickley, George W., <u>History of Tazewell County, Virginia</u>, 1852, reproduced in Harman, John Newton, Sr., <u>Annals of Tazewell County, Virginia</u>, Volume 1, W.C. Hill Printing Company, 1922, p. 436.

56. Tazewell County Court Records, Tazewell, Virginia, Tazewell County Court Order Book No. 1, Page 16.

57. Op. cit., Pendleton, <u>Tazewell County</u>, pp. 471-475.

58. Tazewell County Court Records, Tazewell, Virginia, Tazewell County Court Order Book No. 1, Page 6.

59. Tazewell County Court Records, Tazewell, Virginia, Tazewell County Court Order Book No. 1, Page 10.

60. Tazewell County Court Records, Tazewell, Virginia, Tazewell County Court Order Book No. 1, Page 79.

61. Tazewell County Court Records, Tazewell, Virginia, Tazewell County Court Order Book No. 1, Page 82.

62. Tazewell County Court Records, Tazewell, Virginia, Tazewell County Court Order Book No. 1, Page 89.

63. Op. cit., Albert and Albert, <u>Russell County Tax Records</u>, pp. 197 and 213.

64. Op. cit., Schreiner-Yantis, <u>Tazewell County</u>, p. 299.

65. The date for the move of Joseph Bolen to Tennessee is based on his purchase of a farm in Grainger County (now Claiborne County), Tennessee, May 25, 1801. Deed Records, Grainger County, Rutledge, Tennessee, Deed Book A, Page 206.

66. Op. cit., Pendleton, <u>Tazewell County</u>, p. 406.

67. Microfilm Records, Library of Virginia, Richmond, Virginia, 1801 Tazewell County Personal Property Tax List.

68. Microfilm Records, Library of Virginia, Richmond, Virginia, 1802 Tazewell County Personal Property Tax List.

69. Microfilm Records, Library of Virginia, Richmond, Virginia, 1802 Tazewell County Land Tax List.

70. Tazewell County Court Records, Tazewell, Virginia, Tazewell County Survey Book No. 1, Page 55, 4-1-1-3338.

71. Deed Records, Grainger County, Rutledge, Tennessee, May 25, 1801, Deed Book A, Page 206.

72. Microfilm Records, Tennessee State Library and Archives, Nashville, Tennessee, <u>Minutes, County Clerk, Grainger County, Tennessee, December 1797 Term</u>, Microfilm Roll No. 39.

73. 1850 Federal Census, Claiborne County, Tennessee.

74. Microfilm Records, Tennessee State Library and Archives, Nashville, Tennessee, Marriage Bonds, Grainger County, 1796-1809, Microfilm Roll No. 20A. The note from Joseph Bolen to Ambros Yancey reads as follows: *September 13, 1801 Sir, this is to certify that I am agreed for James Eastrich [sic] for to have my Daughter Lucy and I Desire you for to issue licence [sic] on this as if I was there present. Joseph Boling [sic]   Attest: William McKee*

75. Microfilm Records, Tennessee State Library and Archives, Nashville, Tennessee, Marriage Bonds, Grainger County, 1796-1809, Microfilm Roll No. 20A.

76. Claiborne County Court Records, Tazewell, Tennessee, County Court Order Book, Volume 1, 1801-1803, Pages 48-52.

77. Claiborne County Court Records, Tazewell, Tennessee, County Court Order Book, Volume 1, 1801-1803, Page 75.

78. Grainger County Court Records, Rutledge, Tennessee, County Court Order Book No. 1, Pages 86 and 96; Claiborne County Court Records, Tazewell, Tennessee, County Court Order Book, Volume 1, Pages 75 and 81; Volume 3, Page 207; Volume 6, Page 100.

79. Claiborne County Court Records, Tazewell, Tennessee, County Court Order Book, Volume 1, 1801-1803, Page 81.

80. Deed Records, Tazewell County, Tazewell, Virginia, Volume 1, Page 119, Roark to Bruster, 4-1-1-2822, and Volume 1, Page 121, Roark to Witten, 4-1-1-2823. The deed to Bruster did not contain the acreage within the tract. For the 66.5 acres, see Microfilm Records, Library of Virginia, Richmond, Virginia, 1806 Tazewell County Land Tax List, for Thomas Bruster.

81. Harman, John Newton, Sr., <u>Annals of Tazewell County, Virginia</u>, W.C. Hill Printing Company, Richmond, Virginia, 1922, Volume 1, p. 171.

82. Op. cit., Schreiner-Yantis, <u>Tazewell County</u>, p. 287.

83. Op. cit., Pendleton, <u>Tazewell County</u>, p. 402.

84. Leslie, Louise, <u>Tazewell County</u>, The Overmountain Press, Johnson City, Tennessee, 1982, Reprint 1995, p. 558.

85. Op. cit., Pendleton, <u>Tazewell County</u>, p. 402.

86. Deed Records, Tazewell County, Tazewell, Virginia, Volume 1, Page 122, 4-1-1-2824.

87. Op. cit., Faragher, <u>Daniel Boone</u>, p. 41.

88. Holt, Edgar A., <u>Claiborne County</u>, Memphis State University Press, 1981, p. 19.

89. Grainger County Court Records, Rutledge, Tennessee, Grainger County Court Order Book, March 14, 1797.

90. The location of the Joseph Bolen tract along the river can be documented through a careful trace of deed records involving thirteen land transactions from 1797 through 1839. Location of the tract was particularly difficult as a result of the then current practice of duplicating survey calls from one survey to the next without an updated field survey, thus limiting identifiable landmarks. For example, the first survey in 1797 began at "a bunch of Lyns" and in the sale May 4, 1839, the survey began at "a bunch of Lynn trees." The abstract of land titles to locate the Joseph Bolen tract is as follows:

> 1. From a larger land grant from the State of North Carolina, Robert King sold on September 26, 1797, 250 acres to David Hodgson. Deed Records, Grainger County, Rutledge, Tennessee, Deed Book A, Page 47. In subsequent deeds, "Hodgson" is spelled "Hudson, Hutson, and Hodson." In Deed Book A, referenced above, Page 45, Hodgson witnessed a deed and signed his name as "Hodgson" as the correct spelling.
>
> 2. David Hodgson sold, on May 25, 1801, the south 123 acres from his 250-acre tract to Joseph Bolen. Deed Records, Grainger County, Rutledge, Tennessee, Deed Book A, Page 206. The deed references "the conditional line between Hodgson and Bolen."
>
> 3. David Hodgson sold, on September 6, 1802, the remaining 130 acres from his original purchase to Amos Johnson. Deed Records, Claiborne County, Tazewell, Tennessee, Deed Book A, Page 41.
>
> 4. Joseph Bolen sold, on June 15, 1803, the 123-acre tract to Timothy Roark. Deed Records, Claiborne County, Tazewell, Tennessee, Deed Book A, Page 80.
>
> 5. Timothy Roark sold, on July 4, 1809, the 123-acre tract to Amos Johnson. Deed Records, Claiborne County, Tazewell, Tennessee, Deed Book C, Pages 30 and 31.

6. Amos Johnson sold, on August 24, 1812, the north 130 acres to Andrew Hunter. Deed Records, Claiborne County, Tazewell, Tennessee, Deed Book D, Page 127. Deed refers to "Joseph Bowling's corner" and "Joseph Bowling's line."

7. Amos Johnson sold, on August 19, 1813, the 123-acre tract to John Henderson. Deed Records, Claiborne County, Tazewell, Tennessee, Deed Book D, Page 163. Deed refers to "the conditional line made between Hudson and Bowlen."

8. John Henderson sold, on March 4, 1817, the 123 acres to John Whiteaker. Deed Records, Claiborne County, Tazewell, Tennessee, Deed Book E, Page 138. Deed refers to "the conditional line made between Hutson and Bolin."

9. John Whiteaker sold, on March 20, 1819, the 123 acres to Squire Hunter. Deed Records, Claiborne County, Tazewell, Tennessee, Deed Book G, Page 56. Deed refers to "the conditional line made between Hudson and Bolin."

10. Squire Hunter sold, on February 23, 1821, the 123-acre tract to Andrew Hunter. Deed Records, Claiborne County, Tazewell, Tennessee, Deed Book S, Page 96. Deed still refers to the lynn trees and the conditional line.

11. Andrew Hunter sold, on February 1, 1822, the 130-acre north tract to David Burk. Deed Records, Claiborne County, Tazewell, Tennessee, Deed Book N, Page 89.

12. Andrew Hunter sold, on February 1, 1822, the 123-acre tract to James Burk. Deed Records, Claiborne County, Tazewell, Tennessee, Deed Book N, Page 90. Lynn trees and conditional line are again referenced.

13. James Burk sold, on July 29, 1839, the 123-acre tract to David Burk. Deed Records, Claiborne County, Tazewell, Tennessee, Deed Book O, Page 170. Deed refers again to the lynn trees and "the conditional line made by Hudson and Boling."

14. A survey made under a grant for John Roark (son of Timothy and Sarah Roark) on 150 acres on the Powell River at Ellison Bend includes a sketch which clearly identifies the 150 acres and a description in the first call in the field notes of "a small elm and Spanish oak in Burk's line." The location of the Burk tract provides the location of the Joseph Bolen tract. Deed Records, Claiborne County, Tazewell, Tennessee, Surveyor Book B, Page 243, Survey of Entry No. 350, April 26.

91. Abernethy, Thomas Perkins, From Frontier to Plantation in Tennessee, University of Alabama Press, 1967, p. 223.

92. Ibid., pp. 157-158.

93. Deed Records, Claiborne County, Tazewell, Tennessee, June 15, 1803, Deed Book A, Page 80, 4-1-1-3342.

94. Op. cit., Holt, <u>Claiborne County</u>, p. 17.

95. Claiborne County Court Records, Tazewell, Tennessee, <u>Claiborne County Court Order Book, Volume 1</u>, 1801-1803, Page 141, 4-1-1-3442.

96. Claiborne County Court Records, Tazewell, Tennessee, <u>Claiborne County Court Order Book, Volume 1</u>, 1801-1803, Page 88, 4-1-1-3442.

97. Claiborne County Court Records, Tazewell, Tennessee, <u>Claiborne County Court of Pleas, Volume 2</u>, 1803-1806, Page 167 and Page 250, 4-1-1-2814.

98. Claiborne County Court Records, Tazewell, Tennessee, <u>Claiborne County Court of Pleas, Volume 2</u>, 1803-1806, Page 22, 4-1-1-3442.

99. James Roark Copy Book in which family births are recorded, 4-1-1-2818.

100. Russell County Court Records, Lebanon, Virginia, <u>Russell County Law Order Book 3</u>, March 1806, Page 490, 4-1-1-3497.

101. Russell County Court Records, Lebanon, Virginia, <u>Russell County Law Order Book 3</u>, June 1806, Page 619, September 1806, Page 626, December 1806, Pages 724 and 737, 4-1-1-3497.

102. Claiborne County Court Records, Tazewell, Tennessee, <u>Claiborne County Court of Pleas, Volume 3</u>, 1803-1806, November 24, 1806, Page 18, 4-1-1-2814.

103. Bamman, Gale Williams, *This Land is Our Land! Tennessee's Disputes with North Carolina*, <u>Genealogical Journal</u>, Volume 24, Number 3, 1996.

104. Op. cit., Holt, <u>Claiborne County</u>, p. 14.

105. Whitney, Henry D., <u>The Land Laws of Tennessee</u>, W.H. Anderson & Co., Law Book Publishers, Cincinnati, Ohio, 1793, Microfilm Records, Tennessee State Library and Archives, Nashville, Tennessee, Microfilm Roll No. L 49, p. 136.

106. Ibid., p. 123.

107. Ibid., pp. 123-129.

108. The access road in 1998 is not much improved from that in Timothy Roark's day. On current county maps the road is designated as Vancel Road.

109. Op. cit., James Roark Copy Book, 4-1-1-2818.

110. Claiborne County Court Records, Tazewell, Tennessee, <u>Claiborne County Court of Pleas, Volume 3</u>, August Term 1808, Page 207, 4-1-1-3442.

111. Deed Records, Claiborne County, Tazewell, Tennessee, Deed Book C, Pages 30 and 31, 4-1-1-3343.

112. The deed from Robert King to David Hodgson for the 250 acres records the last call as a straight line as follows: "thence South forty-three degrees West down the river three hundred and forty-eight poles to the Beginning." Deed Records, Grainger County, Rutledge, Tennessee, Deed Book A, Page 47. The subsequent deed to Joseph Bolen recorded the same call "from a poplar and beech on the north side of the river bank" as "thence to the Beginning." Deed Records, Grainger County, Rutledge, Tennessee, Deed Book A, Page 206. Joseph Bolen thus purchased and sold

on a straight line for the last call in the legal description but properly claimed a line that followed the meanders of the Powell River. This area between the straight line and the river meanders amounted to approximately twenty acres. Following the sheriff's sale of the twenty acres to satisfy the debts of Joseph Bolen, the tract was apparently declared a part of the public lands and thus was eligible to be claimed as an entry under the public land statutes. James and David Burk obviously saw what had happened over a twenty-five year period and David Burk filed Entry No. 183 for the twenty acres. The tract was surveyed on October 10, 1825 and David Burk received Grant No. 16618, July 6, 1831, to gain title to the river frontage. David Burk ultimately sold, July 29, 1839, all of his holding in four tracts, three of which include all of the 250 acres originally purchased by David Hodgson. Deed Records, Claiborne County, Tazewell, Tennessee, Deed Book T, Page 575.

113. Russell County Court Records, Lebanon, Virginia, Russell County Law Order Book 4, March 6, 1810, Page 125; March 7, 1810, Page 132, 4-1-1-3497.

114. Op. cit., Timothy Roark Family Bible, 4-1-1-2818.

115. Deed Records, Russell County, Lebanon, Virginia, February 27, 1798, Deed Book 2, Pages 315-316 and 410-411, 4-1-1-3503 and 4-1-1-3504.

116. Court Records, Grayson County, Independence, Virginia, Will Book 1, Pages 75-76, 4-1-1- 3099.

117. Court Records, Grayson County, Independence, Virginia, Grayson Chancery File 64, *Roark vs Roark*.

118. Claiborne County Court Records, Tazewell, Tennessee, Claiborne County Court of Pleas, Volume 6, May Term 1813, Page 100, 4-1-1-3442.

119. Op. cit., James Roark Copy Book, 4-1-1-2818.

Chapter 4: The East Tennessee Frontier Farm

1. Holt, Edgar A., Claiborne County, Memphis State University Press, 1981, pp. 1-8.

2. Faragher, John Mack, Daniel Boone, The Life and Legend of an American Pioneer, Henry Holt and Company, 1992. pp. 9-23.

3. Krout, John Allen and Dixon Ryan Fox, The Completion of Independence, 1790-1830, Quadrangle Books, Chicago, 1971, p. 92.

4. Ibid., p. 104.

5. Cunliffe, Marcus, The Nation Takes Shape: 1789-1837, The University of Chicago Press, 1969, p. 81.

6. Rogers, William Flinn, "Life in East Tennessee Near the End of Eighteenth Century," East Tennessee Historical Society Publications, Volume 1, 1929, p. 28.

7. Robinson, Raymond H., The Growing of America: 1789-1848, Forum Press, Inc., 2nd Edition, 1973, 1991, p. 165.

8. Op. cit., Krout and Fox, <u>Completion of Independence</u>, p. 94.

9. Ibid., p. 94.

10. Op. cit., Cunliffe, <u>The Nation Takes Shape</u>, p. 82.

11. Ibid., p. 33.

12. Op. cit., Krout and Fox, <u>Completion of Independence</u>, pp. 95-96.

13. Ibid., p. 99.

14. Larkin, Jack, <u>The Reshaping of Everyday Life, 1790-1840</u>, Harper and Row, 1988, p. 107.

15. Ibid., p. 122.

16. Ibid., p. 123.

17. Op. cit., Krout and Fox, <u>Completion of Independence</u>, p. 141.

18. Op. cit., Larkin, <u>Reshaping of Everyday Life</u>, p. 138.

19. Ibid., p. 144.

20. Ibid. p. 128.

21. Op. cit., Rogers, "Life in East Tennessee," p. 29.

22. Op. cit., Larkin, <u>Reshaping of Everyday Life</u>, p. 30.

23. Op. cit., Rogers, "Life in East Tennessee," p. 41.

24. Op. cit., Krout and Fox, <u>Completion of Independence</u>, p. 175.

25. Fish, Carl Russell, <u>The Rise of the Common Man, 1830-1850</u>, Quadrangle Books, Chicago, 1971, p. 202.

26. Op. cit., Krout and Fox, <u>Completion of Independence</u>, p. 179.

27. Op. cit., Holt, <u>Claiborne County</u>, p. 42.

28. McLoughlin, William G., <u>Revivals, Awakenings, and Reform</u>, The University of Chicago Press, 1978, pp. 45-97.

29. Ibid., pp. 98-140.

30. Cleveland, Catherine C., <u>The Great Revival in the West, 1797-1805</u>, The University of Chicago Press, 1916.

31. Bruce, Dickson D., Jr., <u>And They All Sang Hallelujah: Plain-Folk Camp-Meeting Religion, 1800-1845</u>, The University of Tennessee Press, Knoxville, 1974, p. 4.

32. Op. cit., Cleveland, <u>The Great Revival</u>, pp. 10-14.

33. Ibid., pp. 34-49.

34. Ibid., p. 36.

35. Op. cit., Bruce, <u>And They All Sang Hallelujah</u>, pp. 42-43.

36. Sweet, William Warren, <u>Religion in the Development of American Culture, 1765-1840</u>, Scribner's, 1952, p. 137.

37. Op. cit., Bruce, <u>And They All Sang Hallelujah</u>, pp. 48-49.

38. Op. cit., Larkin, <u>Reshaping of Everyday Life</u>, p. 275.

39. Ibid., p. 279.
40. Op. cit., Cleveland, <u>The Great Revival</u>, pp. 55-56.
41. Op. cit., Larkin, <u>Reshaping of Everyday Life</u>, pp. 252-253.
42. Ibid., p. 35.
43. Ibid., p. 64.
44. Ibid., p. 72.
45. Ibid., p. 79.
46. Ibid., p. 87.
47. Ibid., p. 98.

Chapter 5: Early Years and Adolescence

1. Typed copy of the James Roark Copy Book by Mrs. C.P. Kelley, 2 North Crest Road, Chattanooga, Tennessee, May 4, 1969. Notes by Mrs. Kelley state that the original of the copy book is "in the possession of the descendants of Mr. Frank Conner of Dayton, Tennessee," 9-1-1-3622. The author has in his possession a photocopy of the copy book obtained from Mrs. Janis Ragar of Sedalia, Missouri, a descendant of Jeremiah Roark.

2. The death date for David Roark is unknown. His birth is recorded in the Copy Book of James Roark; however, he does not appear in the 1830 Census nor in any subsequent family records. His death prior to age nine is assumed.

3. Family Bible of James and Lucy Eastridge, copy provided by Linzey W. Estridge, Big Stone Gap, Virginia, great-great grandson of James and Lucy Eastridge. The children of James and Lucy Eastridge listed in the Family Bible are as follows:

Mary "Polly" Eastridge	Born April 27, 1801
Ezekiah "Squire" Eastridge	Born August 28, 1803
Lawson Eastridge	Born March 5, 1806
Aleon Eastridge	Born September 21, 1809
Jeremiah Eastridge	Born June 8, 1812
John Eastridge	Born April 14, 1814
Isaac Eastridge	Born April 20, 1817
Elizabeth Eastridge	Born June 8, 1820
James Eastridge Jr.	Born June 19, 1821
Nancy Eastridge	Born October 7, 1824
Louisay Jane Eastridge	Born March 1, 1828

The author and Linzey Estridge discussed at length the correct first name of Squire Eastridge. In the Family Bible, the name could be read either Ezekial or

Ezekiah, Mr. Estridge favoring Ezekial. With apologies to Linzey and appreciation for his significant help, I have used the name Ezekiah throughout this work. This is based on the name as written in County Court Records which is clearly "Ezekiah." Re: County Court Records, Claiborne County, Tazewell, Tennessee, June 18, 1832, 4-1-1-3524.

4. Op. cit., James Roark Copy Book.

5. Deed Records, Claiborne County, Tazewell, Tennessee, Volume N, Page 116, October 21, 1834.

6. The conclusion that Sary was the wife of Larkin Ferguson is based on circumstantial evidence which should be summarized. Sary Roark is not mentioned in any of the available historical records of Claiborne County or the family there. Larkin Ferguson is mentioned frequently in the James Roark Copy Book and was in Rhea County, Tennessee, at the same time as James Roark, James helping Larkin "raise" his house (Copy Book). At Larkin's death in early 1830, James Roark joined with Jeremiah Bowling (Bolen?) to furnish a bond for Larkin's wife "Sarah" as administratrix of the estate. When the 1830 Census was taken later that year, the household of James Roark, beyond that of his own family, included one female at an age between twenty and thirty, one male under five, and two females between five and ten and under five. This would match the age of Sary and logically those of her children. Sary, in all probability, married again after Larkin's death; however no marriage record has surfaced and Sary cannot be traced further. She apparently died before 1854 since she was not included when all the surviving children of Sarah Bolen Roark began a process to quit claim all title interest in the Timothy Roark homestead to the youngest son-in-law, James Jefferson Lambert. Unfortunately, Sary is never mentioned in the extensive records preserved in the Joseph Roark papers; however, Juda Ann Roark purchased a scarf and other accessories for a "Miss Elander Ferguson" in October 1840 (1-1-1-422). Could this have been a daughter of Sary and Larkin Ferguson? For the death of Larkin Ferguson, see County Court of Rhea County, Court of Pleas and Quarter Sessions, Dayton, Tennessee, Minutes, February 1, 1830 Session, p. 57. Another consideration for the marriage of Sary Roark resulted from the work of Mary A. Hansard in which she stated that Andy Whitaker "married a Miss Rorark, daughter of Timothy Rorark." Re: Hansard, Mary A., Old Time Tazewell, Published by Mary Lorena Hansard Wilson, Sweetwater, Tennessee, 1979, p. 252. Some have concluded that the "Miss Rorark" was Sary Roark since the marriages of all other daughters of Timothy had been recorded. After some research, the author concluded that Ms. Hansard was in error. Andy Whitaker married Fannie Williams. Re. Fulkerson, P.G., *The Tazewell Observer*, October 22, 1980, "Early Settlers of Claiborne County."

7. Deed Records, Claiborne County, Tazewell, Tennessee, 1816, Deed Book G, Page 256.

8. Deed Records, Claiborne County, Tazewell, Tennessee, 1820, Deed Book H, Page 62. This record provides the sale of Ferguson's tract in 1820. Unfortunately, Deed Book H was destroyed in the courthouse fire at Tazewell and the actual purchase of the Ferguson tract could not be traced. The estimated size of eighty acres is based on the sale price of $320 in 1820.

9. Deed Records, Claiborne County, Tazewell, Tennessee, Surveyor's Book A, Page 71.

10. Op. cit., James Roark Copy Book.

11. Ibid.

12. Grave Marker, Margaret Gross Roark, Roark Cemetery located southwest of Birchwood, Tennessee.

13. Will of William Gross, December 22, 1827, Messick, Eugenia L., Hawkins County Tennessee Wills, Volume 1, 1786-1864, pp. 151-152.

14. Deed Records, Claiborne County, Tazewell, Tennessee, Surveyor's Book B, Page 243, Microfilm Records, Tennessee State Library and Archives, Nashville, Tennessee. This is the record of John Roark's filing for his homestead tract in 1826 which he would have occupied in 1824 shortly after his marriage to Margaret Gross.

15. Shropshire, Mrs. Laura Roark, Pioneer Days–Stories of the Roark-Conner Ancestry, locally published, Revised Edition, 1992, p. 54.

16. Whitney, Henry D., The Land Laws of Tennessee, W.H. Anderson & Co., Cincinnati, Ohio, 1893, Microfilm Records, Tennessee State Library and Archives, Microfilm Roll No. L49, p. 225.

17. Ibid.

18. Deed Records, Claiborne County, Tazewell, Tennessee, Surveyor's Book A, Page 13, Microfilm Records, Tennessee State Library and Archives, Roll No. 35.

19. Deed Records, Claiborne County, Tazewell, Tennessee, Surveyor's Book B, Page 113, Microfilm Records, Tennessee State Library and Archives, Roll No. 35, 4-1-1-2808.

20. Deed Records, Claiborne County, Tazewell, Tennessee, Surveyor's Book B, Page 196, Microfilm Records, Tennessee State Library and Archives, Roll No. 35.

21. Deed Records, Claiborne County, Tazewell, Tennessee, Surveyor's Book B, Page 205, Microfilm Records, Tennessee State Library and Archives, Roll No. 35, 4-1-1-2809.

22. Microfilm Records, Tennessee State Library and Archives, State of Tennessee Land Grant for Entry Number 203 in Claiborne County, signed February 10, 1827, by Governor William Carroll, 4-1-1-2810.

23. Little is known of Rebecca and the cause of her death. Her birth is recorded in the Copy Book of James Roark but no death date is available. She is not listed in the 1830 Census nor is she mentioned in any subsequent family documents. Her death at a very early age or prior to her sixth birthday is assumed.

24. Op. cit., Whitney, Land Laws, p. 120.

25. Deed Records, Claiborne County, Tazewell, Tennessee, Surveyor's Book B, Page 211, Microfilm Records, Tennessee State Library and Archives, Roll No. 35.

26. Deed Records, Claiborne County, Tazewell, Tennessee, Surveyor's Book B, Pages 253-255, Microfilm Records, Tennessee State Library and Archives, Roll No. 35.

27. Deed Records, Tazewell County, Tazewell, Virginia, August 14, 1826, Volume 4, Pages 99-100, 4-1-1-2826.

28. Chancery Court Records of Tazewell County, Tazewell, Virginia, February Term 1830, Pages 236-239, Timothy Roark versus William Deskins, 4-1-1-3505. See also July Term 1830, Page 247, Timothy Roark, Heir-at-Law of James Roark versus William Deskins, 4-1-1-3506.

29. United States Postal Service, History of the U.S. Postal Service, 1775-1993, 1997.

30. Op. cit., James Roark Copy Book.

31. Brigance, Pat Hicks, Blythe, Volume 1, Maryville, Tennessee, 1995, pp. 23-29.

32. Holmes, Tony, "Early Cherokee Ferry Crossings of the Eastern Tennessee River Basin," The Journal of East Tennessee History, East Tennessee Historical Society, Volume 62, 1990, pp. 54-79.

33. Broyles, Bettye J., Rhea County, Tennessee Tax Lists, 1819 through 1829, Rhea County Historical and Genealogical Society, 1989, pp. 72-73.

34. Op. cit., James Roark Copy Book.

35. Marriage Records, Rhea County, Tennessee, p. 366.

36. Deed Records, Claiborne County, Tazewell, Tennessee, Surveyor's Book B, Page 243, Microfilm Records, Tennessee State Library and Archives, Roll No. 35.

37. Op. cit., James Roark Copy Book.

38. Op. cit., Broyles, Rhea County Tax Lists, Taxables in Captain Russell's Company for 1827, p. 132.

39. Ibid., Taxables in Captain Roark's Company for 1828, p. 145. James Roark is listed as being taxed on 184 acres.

40. Minutes, Cumberland Gap Baptist Association, August 19, 1897, as reproduced in Reflections, Claiborne County Historical Association, Summer Edition 1999. The minutes include an obituary of James Richardson that gives the date of his marriage to Nancy Roark as July 15, 1828. This conflicts with the marriage date

provided by Dr. Jesse Vancel, grandson of James Richardson, who gives the year as 1826. Vancel, Dr. Jesse, <u>Reflections</u>, The Quarterly Newsletter of the Claiborne County Historical Society, Volume 4, Number 1, Winter Edition 1986. I have chosen to use the date from the obituary.

41. Grave Marker, Cave Springs Cemetery, Claiborne County, Tennessee.

42. Op. cit., Vancel, <u>Reflections</u>.

43. Sandefur, Ina Mae, Kokomo, Indiana, <u>Family Group Record</u>, Thomas Ellison and Elizabeth Roark Ellison, February 2, 1996.

44. 1833 Tax Records, Claiborne County, Tennessee, Microfilm Records, Tennessee State Library and Archives, Roll No. 2.

45. Claiborne County Historical Society, <u>The People's History of Claiborne County, Tennessee, 1801-1988</u>, Walsworth Press, 1988, p. 70.

46. Op. cit., Sandefur, <u>Family Group Record</u>.

47. Op. cit., James Eastridge Family Bible.

48. County Court Records, Claiborne County, Tazewell, Tennessee, June 15, 1829, 4-1-1-3454.

49. Hicks, John D., George E. Mowry, and Robert E. Burke, <u>The Federal Union</u>, Houghton Mifflin Company, Boston, 1964, p. 394.

50. Ibid., p. 520.

51. No copy remains of Timothy Roark's Entry Number 589 nor its survey by the county surveyor. The entry is identified with field notes from a survey in a quit-claim deed from heirs of Timothy Roark to their brother-in-law James Jefferson Lambert in 1854. Deed Records, Claiborne County, Tazewell, Tennessee, Volume W, Pages 303-305, February 8, 1854, 4-1-1-2819.

52. Chancery Court Records, Tazewell County, Tazewell, Virginia, February Term 1830, pp. 237-239, 4-1-1-3505.

53. Chancery Court Records, Tazewell County, Tazewell, Virginia, July Term 1830, p. 247, 4-1-1-3506.

54. Chancery Court Records, Tazewell County, Tazewell, Virginia, September Term 1831, p. 257, 4-1-1-3507.

55. <u>Black's Law Dictionary</u>.

56. Chancery Court Records, Tazewell County, Tazewell, Virginia, <u>Chancery Court Execution Book, 1832-1847</u>, p. 3, 4-1-1-3507.

57. Op. cit., James Roark Copy Book.

58. Op. cit., Broyles, <u>Rhea County Tax Lists</u>, *Taxables in Captain Roark's Company for 1829*, p. 169.

59. Court of Pleas and Quarter Sessions, Rhea County, Dayton, Tennessee, August Session, 1828, 4-1-1-2754.

60. Op. cit., Broyles, Rhea County Tax List, *Taxables in Captain Jackson's Company for 1824*, pp. 72-73.

61. County Court of Rhea County, Court of Pleas and Quarter Sessions, Dayton, Tennessee, Minutes, February 1, 1830 Session, p. 57. It is interesting speculation that Sarah was, in fact, James' sister Sarah (or "Sary") since no other record on Sary has been uncovered. The assistance James provided at the death of Larkin would be quite natural for a man to provide to a close relative such as a sister, but only to someone that close.

62. 1830 Census, Rhea County, Tennessee.

63. Court Order Book, Claiborne County Court of Pleas, Tazewell, Tennessee, 1827, Page 114, June 19, 1827, 4-1-1-3446.

64. Hansard, Mary A., Old Time Tazewell, published by Mary Lorena Hansard Wilson, Sweetwater, Tennessee, 1979, p. 262.

65. Deed Records, Claiborne County, Tazewell, Tennessee, December 1, 1856, Volume Z, Page 564. This deed describes the twenty-five acres when William Roark sold it to James Jefferson Lambert. No deed of record could be found for transfer of title from Aaron Cox to William Roark.

66. Deed Records, Claiborne County, Tazewell, Tennessee, Deed Book K-2, Page 401. This deed is for the sale of the land owned by William Roark after his death and identifies his first two children as John and Cynthia. The birth date of Cynthia, who was to marry William Williams, was determined from the 1850 Census, Claiborne County, Tennessee. The birth date of John was assumed based on the birth dates of the other children of William Roark and from the 1900 Census, Clay County, Kentucky.

67. That Squire Eastridge went to southeast Tennessee with Joseph Roark is based on a promissory note executed by Ezekiah Eastridge in 1832 in Rhea County. Re: Promissory Note from Ezekiah Eastridge to Francis Rievily, April 22, 1832, 1-1-1-813. Rievily [or Revily] was on the tax rolls of Rhea County, Tennessee, during this period. The promissory note was maintained by Joseph Roark in his papers, indicating that he was close to Eastridge at that time and made have paid the $1.50 due on the promissory note.

68. Goodspeed's History of Tennessee, Containing Historical and Biographical Sketches of Thirty East Tennessee Counties, Reprinted from Goodspeed's History of Tennessee 1887, Charles and Randy Elder Booksellers, Nashville, 1972, p. 818.

69. Campbell, T.J., Records of Rhea, A Condensed County History, Rhea Publishing Company, Dayton, Tennessee, 1940, pp. 27-28.

70. State of Tennessee Historical Marker, Sale Creek, 2A-7.

71. Deed Records, Hamilton County, Chattanooga, Tennessee, November 11, 1834, Volume 2, Page 168, 4-1-1-2738. This record identifies the James Roark tract

when it was sold in 1834. The deed record for the acquisition of the tract has not been found.

72. Records do not reveal the exact date and record of James Roark's purchase. The 1827 purchase date is based on tax records. Re: Op. cit., Broyles, <u>Rhea County Tax List</u>, 1828.

73. 1830 Census, Hamilton County, Tennessee.

74. Ibid.

75. Op. cit., Shropshire, <u>Pioneer Days</u>, p. 47.

76. 1850 Census, Bradley County, Tennessee. Samuel Carr's wife is incorrectly listed as "Mary" in this census. Her correct name as it appears in all family records was "Margaret."

77. Promissory Note from James Carr to Samuel Carr for $100.00, August 20, 1795, 1-1-1-335.

78. Coleman, Kenneth, Gen. Ed., <u>A History of Georgia</u>, The University of Georgia Press, Athens, Georgia, Second Edition, 1991, pp. 101-115.

79. Promissory note from Samuel Carr to George Keith, January 15, 1805, 1-1-1-780.

80. Op. cit., Coleman, <u>A History of Georgia</u>, p. 113.

81. That Samuel Carr was in Augusta, Georgia, during this period is supported by family tradition researched by Dr. Leonard Diehl, Oklahoma City. See Diehl, Leonard, unpublished paper, *Scott's, My Wife's Family*, Presented at the Roark-Conner Reunion, Chattanooga, Tennessee, July 16, 1994, 4-1-1-3061.

82. Op. cit., Coleman, <u>A History of Georgia</u>, pp. 108-110.

83. The logic for the estimated order and birth dates of the Samuel Carr family is as follows: The 1850 and 1860 U.S. Census for Tennessee provide with some certainty the birth years for John Carr, Alfred Carr, and Juda Ann Carr Roark as 1802, 1806, and 1813, respectively. These dates were accepted as correct. Jane Carr Mahan was identified in the estate settlement of the Samuel Carr estate by Joseph Roark in a receipt from Jane Mahan, May 16, 1855, 1-1-1-341 and was between 30 and 40 in the 1840 Census (Meigs County, Tennessee). Placing her between John Carr and Alfred Carr followed the placement of Margaret and the daughter who married a Medley. Margaret Carr married Leonard Brooks December 23, 1841 (Meigs County Marriages, Microfilm Records of the Tennessee State Library and Archives, Roll No. 16). This was the second marriage for Brooks who was between 50 and 60 at the time of his marriage to Margaret. They had two children in the next four years, Matilda, and Juda Ann, before Margaret died. Another minor child of Leonard Brooks at the time of his death was Zachariah, who was Leonard's last child with his first wife. This would probably mean that Margaret had married late but was still in her child-bearing years. Assuming she was living with her sister Jane Carr Mahan in 1840 and was the

female between 20 and 30 with Jane Mahan in the 1840 Census would place her birth in 1810 just before Juda Ann. The daughter of Samuel Carr that married a Medley is obscured by history. The only reference is to a grandson of Samuel Carr, D.A. Medley, who received from Joseph Roark a portion of the estate and returned to Roark a receipt September 7, 1855, 1-1-1-342. D.A. Medley, however, did not sign the receipt. It was signed by Sanford Medley, indicating that D.A. was quite young at the time. Also, since D.A. was the only Medley to receive an estate distribution, one can conclude that Samuel's daughter was no longer living and, if D.A. were a maximum of twelve, Carr's daughter would have probably been not over forty-six or forty-seven in 1855. Therefore, she was placed in the hypothetical Carr family before Margaret and Juda Ann with a birth year of 1808. James Carr cannot be positively identified in either the 1830 or the 1840 Census since two appropriate James Carrs are listed in each census. He apparently was dead by the time of the 1850 Census. The number of children of the more likely James Carr in the 1840 Census and their absence in the estate settlement is particularly troublesome. The census listings for 1830 and 1840 both have James Carr born between 1800 and 1810. With John born in 1802, Jane Carr Mahan in 1804, and Alfred in 1806, all with some degree of certainty, roll the dice and place James Carr's birth in 1800.

84. Receipt to Samuel Carr from Colleen Campbell, 1807, 1-1-1-786.

85. Promissory Note to Samuel Carr, October 18, 1807, 1-1-1-756.

86. Court of Pleas and Quarter Sessions, Rhea County, Dayton, Tennessee, Minute Book B, January 1810-April 1813, p. 19.

87. Ibid., Minute Book B, pp. 54, 56, 60, 61, 72, and 73.

88. Promissory Note from Irby Holt to David Gilbreath in the amount of $3.00, June 9, 1809, 1- 1-1-773. The promissory note, typical of three-way transactions during that period, reads as follows:

> Mr. David Gilbreath
> Sir, you will please to pay Mr. Samuel Carr three dollars for the season
> of your mare put last spring and this shall be your receipt for the same.
> Irby Holt
> 9th June 1809

Holt and Carr would continue to be associated as Holt was to remain in Rhea County until 1821 after which he was no longer on the tax lists of Rhea County.

89. Receipt from Abner Witt, Constable, to Samuel Carr for $2.50, November 23, 1811, 1-1-1- 345.

90. Microfilm Records, Tennessee State Library and Archives, Tax Lists Roll Number 7, Rhea County Tax List 1819.

91. Receipt from M. Francis to Samuel Carr for "my cost in the suit by Thomas Clark," January 12, 1813, 1-1-1-761. For evidence that Miller Francis was sheriff of

Rhea County in 1813, see op. cit., <u>Goodspeed's History of Tennessee</u>, p. 819.

92. The birth date of Juda Ann Carr is based on data from the 1860 Census, Hamilton County, Tennessee.

93. Meigs County Tax Records, Decatur, Tennessee, July 10, 1813, Book C, Page 137.

94. Handwritten receipt from Samuel Carr to William Low for expenses at Atlanta, Georgia, in the amount of $39.10, April 18, 1816, 1-1-1-330.

95. Op. cit., Broyles, <u>Rhea County Tax Lists</u>, *Taxables in Captain W. McGill's Company for 1820*, p. 13.

96. Handwritten receipt from Samuel Carr to William Smith for hauling a load from Augusta, Georgia, to Rhea County, Tennessee, in the amount of $75.00, 1-1-1-338.

97. Deed Records, Rhea County, Dayton, Tennessee, August 5, 1814, Deed Book C, Page 212.

98. Op. cit., Broyles, <u>Rhea County Tax Lists</u>, *Taxables in Captain John Lewis' District for 1819*, p. 5.

99. Handwritten note from Limeen Geren to Samuel Carr, January 27, 1819, 1-1-1-781.

100. Manuscript, *Record Book of the Supreme Court of the Cherokee Nation, 1823-1835*, in Allen Collection, October 16, 1823.

101. Letter from William Blythe to Boon Mays, March 10, 1818, 1-1-1-767.

102. Public Sale Order by Charles Gamble, Sheriff of Hamilton County, Tennessee, July 18, 1820, 1-1-1-328.

103. Receipt to Samuel Carr from Spelsby Dyer for damages paid by Carr in settlement of a court judgement against Carr in favor of Jacob Schultz, October 4, 1814, 1-1-1-770.

104. Op. cit., Broyles, <u>Rhea County Tax Lists</u>, *Taxables in Captain W.S. Bradley's Company for 1820*.

105. Receipt from M. Francis, Rhea County Sheriff, to Samuel Carr for payment of the full amount of a judgement against Carr, May 3, 1819, 1-1-1-759.

106. Receipt to Samuel Carr from Hardy Hughs for court costs in Samuel Carr's suit against William Carr, June 10, 1830, 1-1-1-789.

107. This description of Joseph Roark was available, years later, from his Oath of Allegiance to the United States following or near the end of the Civil War, 1-1-1-1621.

108. Charge Ticket to Joseph Roark from the store of Jonathan Wood, Washington, Tennessee, August 28, 1832, 1-1-1-406.

Chapter 6: Homestead and Family

1. Armstrong, Zella, <u>The History of Hamilton County and Chattanooga Tennessee</u>, Volume 1, The Overmountain Press, Johnson City, Tennessee, 1993 Reprint, pp. 194-195.

2. Ibid., pp. 90, 97.

3. Deed Records, Hamilton County, Chattanooga, Tennessee, August 4, 1834, Volume 1, Book 2, Pages 169-170, 4-1-1-2737.

4. Deed Records, Hamilton County, Chattanooga, Tennessee, August 4, 1834, Volume 1, Book 2, Pages 171-172, 4-1-1-2737.

5. Deed Records, Hamilton County, Chattanooga, Tennessee, November 11, 1834, Volume 1, Book 2, Pages 168-169, 4-1-1-2738.

6. Promissory Note from Joseph Roark to William Hutcheson, January 1, 1833, 1-1-1-437.

7. The Tennessee River through Hamilton County flows in the general direction of south twenty degrees west. In most cases, this would suggest the use of "east" or "west" when referring to one bank of the river or the other; however, it appears to be quite traditional in Hamilton County to refer only to the "north" or "south" banks of the Tennessee. The author has tried to consistently follow this tradition.

8. Livingood, James W., <u>A History of Hamilton County Tennessee</u>, Memphis State University Press, 1981, pp. 43-54.

9. Ibid., pp. 89-90.

10. Ibid., p. 87.

11. Davidson, Donald, <u>The Tennessee, Volume 1, The Old River: Frontier to Secession</u>, J.S. Sanders & Company, Nashville, Tennessee, 1991 printing, p. 6.

12. Livingood, James T., "The Tennessee Valley in American History," <u>The Journal of East Tennessee History</u>, East Tennessee Historical Society, Volume 21, 1949, pp. 19-32.

13. Op. cit., Davidson, <u>The Tennessee</u>, p. 40.

14. Ibid., p. 244.

15. Malone, Henry Thompson, <u>Cherokees of the Old South</u>, The University of Georgia Press, Athens, Georgia, 1956, pp. 6-11.

16. Jackson, Helen Hunt, <u>A Century of Dishonor</u>, Corner House Publishers, Williamstown, Massachusetts, 1973, pp. 264-278.

17. Folmsbee, Stanley J., Robert E. Corlew, and Enoch L. Mitchell, <u>Tennessee A Short History</u>, The University of Tennessee Press, Knoxville, Tennessee, Second Edition, 1981, p. 150.

18. Op. cit., <u>Cherokees of the Old South</u>, pp. 74-170.

19. Folmsbee, <u>History of Tennessee</u>, pp. 277-279.

20. Op. cit., Livingood, <u>History of Hamilton County</u>, p. 10.

21. Davis, Kenneth Penn, "Chaos in the Indian Country: The Cherokee Nation, 1828-35," The Cherokee Indian Nation, Duane H. King, Ed., The University of Tennessee Press, Knoxville, Tennessee, p. 130.

22. Deed Records, Tazewell County, Tazewell, Virginia, March 18, 1833, Volume 6, Page 72-73.

23. The exact date for the death of Timothy Roark cannot be firmly established. The month of his death has been estimated from the date the will was probated before the commissioners court–June 17, 1833.

24. The grave of Timothy Roark is unmarked in the family cemetery that is now known in Claiborne County as the Lambert Cemetery through burials of descendants of Timothy's daughter, Mary Ann Roark Lambert. The fact that Timothy Roark is buried there is based on Vancel, Dr. Jesse, Reflections, The Quarterly Newsletter of the Claiborne County Historical Society, Tazewell, Tennessee, Vol. 4, No. 1, Winter 1986.

25. This birth order for the children of John Roark and Margaret Gross Roark differs slightly from that work done previously by Mrs. Laura Roark Shropshire, Re: Pioneer Days–Stories of the Roark-Conner Ancestry, locally published, Revised Edition, 1992, pp. 54-55; and Lat Roark, Re: Roark, Cal Latimore, locally published paper on descendants of John Roark and John Lewis Roark. From later census records, it can be confirmed that Sarah was the second child rather than Elizabeth.

26. Op. cit., Vancel, Reflections.

27. The Timothy Roark will was lost when the Will Book of Claiborne County for that period was destroyed in a courthouse fire in 1932.

28. County Court Records, Claiborne County, Tazewell, Tennessee, June 17, 1833, 4-1-1-3525.

29. County Court Records, Claiborne County, Tazewell, Tennessee, September 17, 1833, 4-1-1-3527.

30. County Court Records, Claiborne County, Tazewell, Tennessee, April 16, 1833, 4-1-1-3526.

31. Deed Records, Claiborne County, Tazewell, Tennessee, Surveyor's Book C, Page 106, Microfilm Records, Tennessee State Library and Archives, Nashville, Tennessee.

32. County Court Records, Claiborne County, Tazewell, Tennessee, March 16, 1830, 4-1-1-3515.

33. County Court Records, Claiborne County, Tazewell, Tennessee, December 17, 1833, 4-1-1-3528.

34. County Court Records, Claiborne County, Tazewell, Tennessee, June 18, 1832, 4-1-1-3524.

35. Deed Records, Hamilton County, Chattanooga, Tennessee, November 11, 1834, Volume 2, Pages 168-169, 4-1-1-2738.

36. Hansard, Mary A., Old Time Tazewell, published by Mary Lorena Hansard Wilson, Sweetwater, Tennessee, 1979, p. 142.

37. Deed Records, Claiborne County, Tazewell, Tennessee, December, 1834, Volume M, Page 459.

38. Op. cit., Handard, Old Time Tazewell, pp. 251-252.

39. Op. cit., Armstrong, History of Hamilton County, pp. 99, 180.

40. Receipt from Richard Waterhouse to James and Joseph Roark, February 3, 1835, 1-1-1-376.

41. Receipt from James W. Smith to Joseph Roark, July 16, 1835, 1-1-1-438.

42. Op. cit., Armstrong, History of Hamilton County, pp. 106, 242-244, 578.

43. Promissory Note from Joseph Roark to Lewis Patterson, November 2, 1835, 1-1-1-439.

44. Promissory Note from Joseph Roark to William and H. Hutcheson, January 1, 1836, 1-1-1-440.

45. Receipt from J. Kelly to Joseph Roark for making a coat, March 23, 1836, 1-1-1-441.

46. Op. cit., Armstrong, History of Hamilton County, pp. 183, 203, 247.

47. Receipt from Thomas McCallie to Joseph Roark, January 5, 1836, 1-1-1-442.

48. Op. cit., Shropshire, Pioneer Days, p. 55.

49. Roark, John J., A Short Biography of Sarah Elizabeth Roark Talley Killian, unpublished paper, February 11, 1995, pp. 4-5.

50. 1830 Census, Hamilton County, Tennessee.

51. History of Benton, Washington, Carroll, Madison, Crawford, Franklin, and Sebastian Counties, Arkansas, The Goodspeed Publishing Co., Chicago, 1889, p. 1211.

52. Court Records, Rhea County, Dayton, Tennessee, Will Book A, Page 416.

53. Broyles, Bettye J., A Compendium of Rhea and Meigs Counties Tennessee 1808 through 1850, Rhea County Historical and Genealogical Society, 1991, p. 66.

54. Allen, Penelope Johnson, Leaves from the Family Tree, Southern Historical Press, Easley, South Carolina, 1982, p. 45.

55. Op. cit., Shropshire, Pioneer Days, p. 50.

56. Typed copy of the James Roark Copy Book by Mrs. C.P. Kelley, 2 North Crest Road, Chattanooga, Tennessee, May 4, 1969, 9-1-1-3622.

57. Receipt from Clingen Fain to Samuel Carr for two payments of $6.00 and $11.25, March 23, 1831, 1-1-1-415.

58. Promissory note from John Mahan to John Carr for $15.00, February 3, 1830, 1-1-1-779.

59. Promissory Note from James Carr to William Powers for $1.50, February 8, 1831, 1-1-1-337.

60. Payment Request from Gibson Witt to Samuel Carr for $0.75., December 31, 1831, 1-1-1-784.

61. Holmes, Tony, "Early Cherokee Ferry Crossings of the Eastern Tennessee River Basin," The Journal of East Tennessee History, East Tennessee Historical Society, Volume 62, 1990, pp. 54-79.

62. Op. cit., Livingood, History of Hamilton County, pp. 43-54.

63. United States War Department, Surveys of the Tennessee River, March 17, 1846, Institute of Historic Research, Signal Mountain, Tennessee, p. 51.

64. Malone, Henry T., "Return Jonathan Meigs–Indian Agent Extraordinary," The Journal of East Tennessee History, East Tennessee Historical Society, Volume 28, 1956, pp. 3-22.

65. Op. cit., Livingood, History of Hamilton County, pp. 59-61.

66. Hicks, John D., George E. Mowry, and Robert E. Burke, The Federal Union, Houghton Mifflin Company, Boston, 1964, p. 580.

67. Op. cit., Armstrong, History of Hamilton County, p. 118.

68. Op. cit., Hicks, The Federal Union, p. 521.

69. Hamilton County Tax List, 1836, Microfilm Records, Tennessee State Library and Archives, Nashville, Tennessee.

70. Royce, Charles C., The Cherokee Nation of Indians, A Smithsonian Institution Press Book, Aldine Publishing Company, Chicago, 1975, p. 167.

71. Op. cit., Davis, "Chaos in the Indian Country", p. 130.

72. Ibid., pp. 132-133.

73. Ibid., p. 138.

74. Ibid., p. 141.

75. Ehle, John, Trail of Tears, The Rise and Fall of the Cherokee Nation, Anchor Books/ Doubleday, 1988, pp. 271-272.

76. Op. cit., Royce, The Cherokee Nation, pp. 156-158.

77. Op. cit., Royce, The Cherokee Nation, pp. 158-160.

78. Op. cit., Ehle, Trail of Tears, pp. 276-278.

79. Murray, Melba Lee, Bradley Divided, Bradley County, Tennessee During the Civil War, The College Press, Collegedale, Tennessee, 1992, p. 6.

80. Op. cit., Royce, The Cherokee Nation, p. 255.

81. 1836 Tax List for Hamilton County, Tennessee, Tennessee State Library and Archives, Microfilm Tax Records by County, Roll Number 4.

82. Op. cit., Ehle, Trail of Tears, p. 279.

83. Op. cit., Royce, The Cherokee Nation, p. 161.

84. Op. cit., Shropshire, Pioneer Days, p. 55. Ms. Shropshire is slightly in error as to the year of birth of some of Joseph's children. A good estimate of the year of Timothy's birth is late 1835 or early 1836. The fourth child, Margaret, was born

March 27, 1837 (Grave Marker, Decatur County, Tennessee), and a fifth child was born in 1838.

85. The timing of the move of Samuel Carr to what would be Bradley County is based primarily on the fact that he was not included in the 1836 Hamilton County Tax List. Also, Carr documents in the Joseph Roark papers clearly put Samuel Carr in Bradley County as early as 1837.

86. Whitney, Henry D., The Land Laws of Tennessee, W.H. Anderson & Co., Cincinnati, Ohio, 1893, Microfilm Copy from the Tennessee State Library and Archives, pp. 436-451.

87. Campbell, T.J., "The Centennial of Salem–Reminiscence," printed address at the One Hundredth Anniversary of the Salem Baptist Church, May 26, 1935, 1-1-1-1457, 1-1-1-409.

88. Shropshire, Laura Roark, unpublished notes, 2-1-1-1002.

89. Tennessee Historical Records Survey, Inventory of the Church Archives of Tennessee, Tennessee State Planning Commission, February 1942, pp. 22-23, 4-1-1-2636.

90. Deed Records, Hamilton County, Chattanooga, Tennessee, October 25, 1836, Volume 4, Pages 93-94, 4-1-1-2736.

91. Two years following Blythe's sale to Clift, James Roark was to sell, also to Clift, the 200 acres that Blythe and Roark had purchased jointly. In that transaction, Roark executes the deed and no mention is made of Blythe's part ownership. Deed Records, Hamilton County, Chattanooga, Tennessee, March 7, 1838, Volume 4, Page 92-93, 4-1-1-2736.

92. Broyles, Bettye J., History of Rhea County, Tennessee, Rhea County Historical and Genealogical Society, 1991, pp. 124, 170.

93. Promissory Note from Joseph Roark to Isaac Benson, July 11, 1836, 1-1-1-445.

94. Promissory Note from Joseph Roark to Thomas McCallie, March 1, 1837, 1-1-1-446.

95. The author is indebted to Mrs. Reba Wilson, through her memories as a young girl, for a description of the arrangement and the construction of Joseph Roark's cabin.

96. 1850 Census, Hamilton County, Tennessee.

97. Promissory Note from Joseph Roark to Lewis Patterson, September 7, 1837, 1-1-1-443.

98. 1837 Hamilton County Tax List, Tennessee State Library and Archives, Microfilm Tax Records by County, Roll Number 4.

99. Payment Request from Mortimer Sams to Joseph Roark, November 17, 1837, 1-1-1-444.

100. McClure, Lucille, <u>Abstracts of Ocoee District Early Land Records–Entries</u>, privately published, 1990.

101. Op. cit., Whitney, <u>Land Laws</u>, pp. 440-447.

102. Op. cit., Armstrong, <u>History of Hamilton County</u>, p. 112.

103. Ocoee Plat Book, Microfilm Records, Tennessee State Library and Archives, Nashville, Tennessee, Roll Number 204.

104. Op. cit., Allen, <u>Leaves from the Family Tree</u>, p. 141.

105. Flyer as reprinted in the *Hamilton Gazette*, Ross's Landing, Tennessee, July 26, 1838, Tennessee State Library and Archives, Nashville, Tennessee, Microfilm Records of Newspapers, Chattanooga (Miscellaneous), 1838-1894, Roll Number 101.

106. Op. cit., Royce, <u>The Cherokee Nation</u>, p. 169.

107. Op. cit., Ehle, <u>Trail of Tears</u>, p. 326.

108. Op. cit., Royce, <u>The Cherokee Nation</u>, p. 161.

109. Op. cit., Ehle, <u>Trail of Tears</u>, p. 328.

110. *Hamilton Gazette*, Ross's Landing, Tennessee, July 26, 1838, Page 3, Column 1.

111. Ibid., Page 3, Column 4.

112. Annual Report of Commissioner of Indian Affairs, November 25, 1838, as quoted in Royce, <u>The Cherokee Nation</u>, p. 170.

113. Ibid., p. 170.

114. Bond from Samuel Carr and James R. Finley, October 11, 1837, 1-1-1-787.

115. Receipt to Samuel Carr for payment to settle a judgement against John Carr by William Hickman, October 18, 1837, 1-1-1-790.

116. Invoice to Samuel Carr from Stuart and Carmichael, October 23, 1838, 1-1-1-788.

117. Deed Records, Hamilton County, Chattanooga, Tennessee, March 7, 1838, Volume 4, Page 92-93, 4-1-1-2736.

118. Op. cit., Armstrong, <u>History of Hamilton County</u>, pp. 107-108, 398.

119. Deed Records, Hamilton County, Chattanooga, Tennessee, Volume 4, Page 92, August 27, 1838, 4-1-1-2736.

120. Hoskins, Shirley Coats, <u>Cherokee Property Valuations in Tennessee 1836</u>, privately published by Hoskins, April 6, 1984, pp. 184-186, 238. Page numbers refer to the copies of the individual appraisals included in the valuation report.

121. Op. cit., Holmes, "Early Cherokee Ferry Crossings," pp. 78-79.

122. The location of James Roark's major tract in the Second Fractional Township has been impossible to document. The fact that he owned a major tract not mentioned in the deed records or the Ocoee Grant Records is documented by tax rolls of the U.S. Government following occupation in 1864 of that portion of

Hamilton County by Federal troops. At that time, James Roark was assessed taxes on 600 acres of land which was between 300 to 500 acres greater than that which can be accounted for through the deed records of both Hamilton and Meigs counties. Re: U.S Tax Commission Report for the state of Tennessee "under the act of Congress entitled `An act for the Collection of Direct Taxes in insurrectionary districts approved June 7, 1862, and the act amendatory thereto,'" District No. 10, Hamilton County, Tennessee, Tennessee Reel T277 No. 3, 4-1-1-3751. James Roark apparently lived on this large tract and left a major portion of it to his son, John B. Roark, although neither deed records nor estate records have been located. In 1908, John B. Roark sold 134 acres in Section 8 to his son, Jacob L. Roark. Since no record can be found of the purchase of any land in the area by John B., one can only assume that it was inherited from his father. Re: Deed Records, Hamilton County, Chattanooga, Tennessee, February 14, 1908, Volume 682, Page 695. (Recorded originally in James County, transferred to Hamilton County records after 1920.) James Roark's land holdings in Sections 10 and 15 are evidenced by a deed from James Roark to W.M. Smith for 60 acres on April 18, 1861. Re: Deed Records, Hamilton County, Chattanooga, Tennessee, April 18, 1861, Volume 14, Page 379.

123. The timing of the move of both James Roark and John Roark is based primarily on the 1840 census in Hamilton County. In that census, James is listed near known landowners north of Grasshopper Creek on the south side of the river: Thomas Palmer, Hezekiah Haney, Henry Bare, Andrew Bare, Jacob Roller, and his brother Joseph. John Roark, on the other hand, was listed among property owners in the Sale Creek area: Edward F. Wiley, Elizabeth McGill, and Robert Patterson.

124. Receipt from Isaac Benson to Joseph Roark, January 15, 1838, 1-1-1-451.

125. Promissory Note from Joseph Roark to Thomas McCallie, January 26, 1838, 1-1-1-448.

126. Op. cit., *Gazette*, July 26, 1838, Page 3, Column 5.

127. Invoice and receipt from Joseph Roark to Lewis Patterson, 1838, 1-1-1-450.

128. Promissory Note from Joseph Roark to Lewis Patterson, July 30, 1838, 1-1-1-449.

129. The assumption that the Killians were brothers is based on the 1840 Census for Hamilton County, Tennessee, in which the listings for Jesse and William are adjacent. Jesse was the older, being between 30 and 40 in the 1840 Census, while William was listed as being between 20 and 30.

130. Op. cit., Whitney, Land Laws of Tennessee, Section 6, p. 442.

131. Performance Bond from Jesse Killian to Joseph Roark, July 3, 1838, 1-1-1-458.

132. Op. cit., Roark, Short Biography of Sarah Elizabeth Roark.

133. Poll Tax Receipt to Joseph Roark issued by A.W. Rogers, Sheriff, Hamilton County, Tennessee, 1838, 1-1-1-661.

134. Op. cit., Livingood, Hamilton County, Tennessee, p. 82.

135. Op. cit., *Hamilton Gazette*, July 26, 1838, Page 3, Column 4.

136. Recorded Mortgage of One Sorrel Mare from Samuel Carr to J.D. Traynor, January 15, 1839, 1-1-1-792.

137. Op. cit., Murray, Bradley Divided, pp. 34, 61.

138. Receipt from William W. Mitchell to Joseph Roark, January 9, 1839, 1-1-1-466.

139. Invoice from Isaac Benson to Joseph Roark, February 11, 1839, 1-1-1-447.

140. Promissory Note from Joseph Roark to Benson and French, February 12, 1839, 1-1-1-457.

141. Letter to Joseph Roark from Wiley B. Skillern requesting the passing of a particular promissory note, October 2, 1839, 1-1-1-453.

142. Promissory Note and Record of Payments therefor from Joseph Roark to Jesse Killian, July 3, 1839, 1-1-1-452.

143. Promissory Note from Joseph Roark to Jesse Killian, July 3, 1839, 1-1-1-455.

144. Promissory Note from Joseph Roark to John Conner, August 21, 1839, 1-1-1-527. The identity of John Conner could not be determined but he probably was unrelated to Maximilian Haney Conner who was in the Cherokee land in 1836 and who would later be related to Joseph Roark through marriage of their children. John Conner was listed in the 1840 Census for Hamilton County, Tennessee, age between 60 and 70 years old. He probably was the merchant partner with Weir and Conner.

145. Promissory Note from Joseph Roark to Lewis Patterson, November 1, 1839, 1-1-1-454.

146. Op. cit., Whitney, Land Laws of Tennessee, Sec. 2, p. 450.

147. Payment Request from David McGill to Joseph Roark, December 3, 1839, 1-1-1-465.

148. Op. cit., Ehle, Trail of Tears, pp. 374-379.

Chapter 7: Land Acquisition and Expansion

1. Ocoee Land Grant Records, Entry 1654, Grant No. 1751, SW4, NW4, Section 21, FT2N, R3W, January 22, 1840.

2. Ocoee Land Grant Records, Entry No. 1656, Grant No. 1619, SE4, NW4, SW4, Section 27, FT2N, R3W, January 22, 1840.

3. Ocoee Land Grant Records, Entry No. 1657, Grant No. 1618, FSW4, Section 8, FT2N, R3W, January 22, 1840.

4. Ocoee Land Grant Records, Entry No. 1900, Grant No. 2131, NE4, SE4, Section 21, FT2N, R3W, January 30, 1840.

5. Tennessee State Library and Archives, Microfilm Records, Roll No. 204, Ocoee District Plat Book.

6. Livingood, James W., A History of Hamilton County Tennessee, Memphis State University Press, 1981, p. 92.

7. 1840 Census, Hamilton County, Tennessee, tabulation by the author.

8. Op. cit., Livingood, History of Hamilton County, p. 91.

9. Donnelly, Polly W., Ed., James County, A Lost County of Tennessee, Old James County Chapter, East Tennessee Historical Society, Ooltewah, Tennessee, 1983, pp. 10-12.

10. Op. cit., Livingood, History of Hamilton County, p. 115.

11. Allen, Penelope Johnson, Leaves from the Family Tree, Southern Historical Press, Easley, South Carolina, 1982, p. 126.

12. Op. cit., Livingood, History of Hamilton County, p. 116.

13. Ibid., p. 94.

14. Deed Records, Hamilton County, Chattanooga, Tennessee, September 23, 1845, Volume F, Pages 185-186. This document in the deed records is for the sheriff's sale of the Jacob Roler 140 acres to Samuel Wilson to satisfy debt of Roler. A judgement for a portion of the debt was rendered "on the 2nd day of October 1841 before James Roark Esquire, a Justice of the Peace for Hamilton County."

15. Summons from James Roark, constable, for testimony before Hiram Cornwell, justice of the peace, in regard to the assets of Jacob Roler, May 31, 1842, 1-1-1-472.

16. Deed Records, Claiborne County, Tazewell, Tennessee, March 25, 1840, Deed Book R, Page 303-304.

17. Deed Records, Claiborne County, Tazewell, Tennessee, August 1, 1838, Deed Book P, Page 247.

18. Deed Records, Claiborne County, Tazewell, Tennessee, Deed Book P. Page 247. The tract was originally owned by James Eastridge and was given to his son-in-law and daughter by the above referenced deed.

19. Deed Records, Claiborne County, Tazewell, Tennessee, 1840, Deed Book Q, Page 65. Details of this purchase by William Roark are not available inasmuch as Deed Book Q was destroyed in the Tazewell courthouse fire. Information on the transaction is documented in the deed records index.

20. Family Group Sheet of Jeremiah Roark, graciously provided by Ms. Sondra Martin, Kansas City, Missouri. Elizabeth Fults was the daughter of John Fults and Martha (Patsy) Fullington Fults.

21. Deed Records, Claiborne County, Tazewell, Tennessee, Surveyor's Book C, Page 87, Microfilm Copy from the Tennessee State Library and Archives, Nashville, Tennessee.

22. Op. cit., Jeremiah Roark Family Group Sheet.

23. Timothy Roark Jr. Family Bible, a copy of which was graciously provided by Ms. Rebecca A. Campbell, Crofton, Maryland.

24. Promissory Note from Joseph Roark to Dearson and McGill, January 25, 1840, 1-1-1-467. That Dearson and McGill were located in the Sale Creek area is based on the fact that the McGills were a Sale Creek family. Joseph Roark's son, James A. Roark, was to marry America McGill, ca. 1863. America was the daughter of William and Nancy McGill of Sale Creek, Hamilton County.

25. Receipt from Hardy Clifton to Joseph Roark, February 29, 1840, 1-1-1-468.

26. Handwritten note from Hiram Haney to Joseph Roark, March 13, 1840, 1-1-1-469.

27. Promissory Note from Joseph Roark to William Killian, April 29, 1840, 1-1-1-460.

28. Killian signed the Promissory Note, dated March 28, 1840, to Joseph Roark with an "X." Also the 1850 Census, Hamilton County, Tennessee, lists him as being able to neither read nor write.

29. Abernethey, Thomas P., "The Early Development of Commerce and Banking in Tennessee," *Mississippi Valley Historical Review*, XIV, December 1927, pp. 311-317.

30. Schweikart, Larry, "Tennessee Banks in the Antebellum Period, Part I," *Tennessee Historical Quarterly*, XLV, Summer 1986, Number 2, pp. 119-129.

31. Promissory Note from Joseph Roark to A.A. Clingan, June 24, 1840, 1-1-1-461.

32. The deed to Ellison does not reference Timothy Roark's Entry No. 203 and the field notes describe but do not reference Timothy Roark's Entry No. 589. Both Entry No. 203 and Entry No. 589 were for 150 acres. It doubtless was the intent of Sarah Bolen Roark to sell the 150 acres of Entry No. 203 since much later, following her death in 1853, her children quit claimed their interest in what was Entry No. 589 to James Jefferson Lambert, son-in-law of Sarah Bolen Roark, indicating that Entry No. 589 had remained in the ownership of Sarah Bolen Roark until her death (Deed Records, Claiborne County, Tazewell, Tennessee, Volume W, Pages 303-305, February 8, 1854, 4-1-1-2819, and Volume Z, Page 566, August 23, 1856, 4-1-1-2806). Tax records for Claiborne County in 1850 verify that Sarah Bolen Roark owned 200 acres of the 350-acre homestead tract of Timothy Roark. What could have happened to cause this confusion? Sarah probably told the person handling the sale

to Ellison that she wanted to sell the southwest 150 acres of the homestead to Thomas Ellison. The person handling the sale secured the three grant deeds, found one for 150 acres and, copied verbatim, obviously without a field survey, the field notes of Entry No. 589 instead of the intended 150 acres of Entry No. 203. Regretfully, when the sale was made by Ellison to Smith and Netherland, the same mistake was made and the field notes were again copied verbatim from the deed from Sarah Bolen Roark to Ellison. So, Ellison, and later Smith and Netherland, bought a tract different from that described in the deed. How was the mistake ultimately corrected? This question cannot be answered conclusively. Apparently it did not cause a problem for the heirs of Sarah Bolen Roark in the title to the 150 acres of Entry No. 589 since James Jefferson Lambert and wife, Mary Roark Lambert, had clear title as late as 1930 when the tract was sold by their daughter Susan Lambert. The author checked the Claiborne County Deed Records for eleven tracts sold by John Netherland (obviously the money partner with C.C. Smith) between 1848 and 1880. None were applicable except a tract of unspecified area sold by Netherland and Smith to Joseph Lambert in 1880. Field notes in the deed refer to the tract as "Ellison land conveyed to us by Lafayette Goin," locates the tract in Civil District 9 (same as the Timothy Roark homestead), but describes the tract as being near the "Cave Springs Meeting House" and "McHenry Ferry." Thus it is not clear whether this is the applicable tract. So the mystery continues, probably not worth the lifetime of research (beyond the one-tenth lifetime already spent) it would take to solve it.

33. Deed Records, Claiborne County, Tazewell, Tennessee, April 7, 1848, Deed Book T, Pages 410-413, 4-1-1-3458.

34. Land Assignment from Josiah Goforth to Joseph Roark for the NE4, Section 33, FT2N, R3W, of the Basis Line for the Ocoee District. Prepared and witnessed by William F. McCormack, justice of the peace, Hamilton County, Tennessee, December 31, 1840, 1-1-1-720.

35. Payment Request from Thomas Gregory to Joseph Roark, 1-1-1-420.

36. Armstrong, Zella, The History of Hamilton County and Chattanooga Tennessee, Volume 1, The Overmountain Press, Johnson City, Tennessee, 1993 Reprint, p. 201.

37. McClure, Lucille, Abstracts of Ocoee District Early Land Records–Entries, privately published, 1990.

38. Receipt from Britain Freeman to John W. Gamble, May 16, 1841, as part payment on a promissory note from Gamble to Freeman, later surrendered to Joseph Roark, 1-1-1-462.

39. Op. cit., Armstrong, History of Hamilton County, p. 106.

40. Receipt from James Gothard, constable, Hamilton County, to Joseph Roark, November 3, 1841, for two uncollected promissory notes, 1-1-1-463.

41. *Chattanooga Gazette*, Chattanooga, Tennessee, May 11, 1844, from Microfilm Records of the Tennessee State Library and Archives, Roll Number 102.

42. Receipt from Alphard Hutcheson to Joseph Roark on behalf of Margaret Carr, May 31, 1841, 1-1-1-754.

43. Receipt from M.F. Carle to Samuel Carr by A.A. Clingan, Sheriff of Bradley County, December 29, 1841, 1-1-1-774.

44. Circuit Court Records, Bradley County, Cleveland, Tennessee, Minute Book B, Pages 361- 363, WPA Microfilm Records of Bradley County, Roll No. 6.

45. Ocoee Land Grant Records, Land Grant Nos. 1618, 1619, 1751, and 1751, each dated March 11, 1841.

46. Ocoee Land Grant Records, Entry No. 2675, Grant No. 2750, N2, SE4, Section 28, FT2N, R3W, April 14, 1841. The times for the entries submitted by Joseph Roark and the prices paid do not follow the schedule of price reductions in the creating statutes. Apparently there had been a moratorium declared on entries for a brief period although such moratorium has not been documented.

47. Ocoee Land Grant Records, Entry No. 2927, Grant No. 3176, NE4, SE4, Section 21, FT2N, R3W, May 29, 1841.

48. Ocoee Land Grant Records, Entry No. 3470, Grant No. 3455, NW4, SE4, Section 33, FT2N, R3W, August 6, 1841.

49. Promissory Note from Joseph Roark to Hiram Haney, September 24, 1841, 1-1-1-804.

50. Promissory Note from Joseph Roark to West Freeman, September 25, 1841, 1-1-1-479.

51. Promissory Note from Joseph Roark to Thompson Crews and Company, October 31, 1841, 1-1-1-520.

52. 1840 Census, Meigs County, Tennessee; Records of Hiwassee District, Grant No. 11830, September 7, 1825, Book 4, Page 126.

53. Lillard, Stewart, <u>Meigs County Tennessee</u>, The Book Shelf, Cleveland, Tennessee, 1982, p. 52.

54. Ibid., p. 60.

55. Meigs County Heritage Book Committee, <u>The History of Meigs County, Tennessee and Its People, 1836-1997</u>, Walsworth Publishing, Waynesville, North Carolina, 1997, p. 19.

56. County Court Records, Rhea County, Dayton, Tennessee, Volume B, pp. 167-168, WPA Microfilm Records.

57. County Court Records, Meigs County, Decatur, Tennessee, County Court Minutes, 1836-1841, p. 37b.

58. Marriage Records, Meigs County, Decatur, Tennessee, December 23, 1841, p. 63, Microfilm Records of the Tennessee State Library and Archives, Roll No. 16.

59. Op. cit., Donnelly, James County, pp. 184-185.

60. Op. cit., Armstrong, History of Hamilton County, p. 115.

61. Invoice from Jonathan Wood to Joseph Roark, December 30, 1841, 1-1-1-422.

62. Letter from Jonathan Wood to Joseph Roark, February 23, 1842, 1-1-1-429.

63. Promissory Note from Joseph Roark to Jonathan Wood, February 23, 1842, with a credit notation on the reverse side by Jonathan Wood, August 2, 1842, 1-1-1-464.

64. Receipt from Jonathan Wood to Joseph Roark, August 2, 1842, 1-1-1-476.

65. Deed Records, Hamilton County, Chattanooga, Tennessee, November 22, 1841, Deed Book 5, Page 212.

66. Deed Records, Hamilton County, Chattanooga, Tennessee, February 16, 1842, Deed Book 5, Page 213.

67. Payment Request from Brittain Freeman to Joseph Roark, March 18, 1842, 1-1-1-471.

68. Receipt from William C. Dyche to Joseph Roark, December 15, 1842, 1-1-1-478.

69. Charge Ticket from William H. Tibbs to Joseph Roark, January 16, 1842, 1-1-1-817

70. Murray, Melba Lee, Bradley Divided, Bradley County Tennessee During the Civil War, The College Press, Collegedale, Tennessee, 1992, p. 247.

71. Payment Request from Anderson Campbell to Joseph Roark, February 25, 1842, 1-1-1-470.

72. Official Summons from James Roark, Constable, to Joseph Roark in regard to Colvin versus Roler, May 31, 1842, 1-1-1-472.

73. Payment Request from John Hoyal to Joseph Roark, July 21, 1842, 1-1-1-477.

74. Ocoee Land Grant Records, Entry No. 6476, Grant No. 6247, NE4, Section 33, FT2N, R3W, April 5, 1842.

75. Ocoee Land Grant Records, Entry No. 6555, Grant No. 6248, SW4, SW4, Section 27, FT2N, R3W, April 5, 1842.

76. Ocoee Land Grant Records, Entry No. 7564, Grant No. 7190, S2, SE4, Section 28, FT2N, R3W, May 19, 1842.

77. Receipt from Jacob Goodner to Joseph Roark, June 7, 1842, 1-1-1-474.

78. Ocoee Land Grant Records, Entry No. 3141, Grant No. 2876, SE4, SE4, Section 2, T2N, R1E, June 4, 1841.

79. Receipt from P.J.R. Edwards, Ocoee District Register, to Samuel Carr, Cleveland, Tennessee, April 27, 1842, 1-1-1-333.

80. Receipt from James Donohoe, Deputy Sheriff for Bradley County, Tennessee, to Samuel Carr, February 4, 1843, 1-1-1-757.

81. The evidence of Alfred Carr's location on land of Joseph Roark is based on (1) the judgement against him November 10, 1842, before Hiram Haney, who was justice of the peace in the Salem Community, (2) the 1850 Census for Hamilton County and Carr's location on the census taker's route, particularly his location relative to William F. McCormack and Joseph Roark's tracts, (3) the fact that he was not a landowner in the 1850 Census, and (4) the adjacent location of Samuel Carr in the 1850 Census who almost for certain was living on land and in a home owned by Joseph Roark.

82. Receipt from Samuel Dunn, constable, Hamilton County, Tennessee, to Alfred Carr, November 10, 1842, 1-1-1-772.

83. The name of Jane Carr Mahan's husband has been difficult to determine. It could have been either Isaac Mahan or John Mahan. The probability favors John Mahan although Isaac Mahan sold 165 acres to Leonard Brooks in 1837 and thus was more closely associated with that area of Meigs County. The estimate of the date of his death is based on Jane Mahan's listing in the 1840 Meigs County Tax Roll (Tax Rolls, Meigs County, Tennessee, 1839-1883, Microfilm Records, Tennessee State Library and Archives, Roll No. 74) and the 1840 Census for Meigs County.

84. Payment Request from E.M. Hall to Joseph Roark, December 27, 1842, 1-1-1-519.

85. Payment Request from E.M. Hall to Joseph Roark, January 9, 1843, 1-1-1-518.

86. Promissory Note from Mitchell R. Norman to Joseph Roark, January 16, 1843, 1-1-1-517.

87. Shropshire, Mrs. Laura Roark, Pioneer Days–Stories of the Roark-Conner Ancestry, locally published, Revised Edition, 1992, p. 52.

88. 1850 Census, Claiborne County, Tennessee.

89. Promissory Note from Joseph Roark to John Roark, February 11, 1843, 1-1-1-516.

90. Itemized Purchase List and Charge Ticket from Jonathan Wood to Joseph Roark, July 8, 1843, 1-1-1-513.

91. Receipt of Payment of Judgement from Samuel Dunn, constable, to Joseph Roark, December 24, 1843, 1-1-1-512.

92. Receipt from Blair & Matthews to Joseph Roark, March 31, 1843, 1-1-1-514.

93. Receipt for Payment of a Judgement from Jonathan Belim, constable, to Joseph Roark, December 14, 1844, 1-1-1-833.

94. White, Robert Hiram, Ph. D., Development of the Tennessee State Educational Organization, 1796-1929, Southern Publishers, Inc., Kingsport, Tennessee, 1929, pp. 39-49.

95. Receipt from William Killian to Joseph Roark "in part pay of his improvement," March 28, 1840, 1-1-1-459.

96. Payment Request from J.A. Freeman to Joseph Roark for return of public monies, March 13, 1844, 1-1-1-509.

97. Receipt from William Rogers, Trustee, to Joseph Roark, July 27, 1847, 1-1-1-877.

98. Promissory Note from Joseph Roark and unknown signatory to William Hayes for payment in corn, June 13, 1844, 1-1-1-511.

99. Payment Request from Morgan Potter to Joseph Roark for payment in corn, June 14, 1844, 1-1-1-508.

100. Payment Request of D.L. Colvin to Joseph Roark for payment in corn, August 28, 1846, 1-1-1-505.

101. Deed Records, Hamilton County, Chattanooga, Tennessee, March 29, 1844, Volume 6, Pages 154-155, 4-1-1-2739.

102. Deed Records, Hamilton County, Chattanooga, Tennessee, FSW4, Section 17, FT2N, R3W, September 15, 1845, Volume F, Page 188.

103. A confirmation of the date of Leonard Brooks' death is based on county court minutes. On July 7, 1845, Brooks had been named "inspector for the forthcoming county elections." The next mention of Brooks in the minutes is on the date an administrator of the estate was named, October 6, 1845. No other record of the death of Leonard Brooks nor his wife Margaret Carr Brooks has been found other than that reported in Meigs County histories.

104. Op. cit., Meigs County Heritage Book Committee, History of Meigs County, p. 19.

105. Meigs County Court Minutes, Microfilm Records, Tennessee State Library and Archives, Roll No. 19, October 6, 1845, p. 375.

106. Broyles, Bettye J., A Compendium of Rhea and Meigs Counties Tennessee 1808 through 1850, Rhea County Historical and Genealogical Society, 1991, p. 50.

107. Meigs County, Tennessee, Wills and Inventory Sales, Volume 1, 1836-1850, Pages 136-140.

108. Ibid., Pages 159-160.

109. 1845 Tax Rolls, Meigs County, Tennessee, Microfilm Records, Tennessee State Library and Archives, Roll No. 74.

110. Meigs County Court Minutes, Book 3, 1846-1852, February 1, 1847, p. 32.

111. Bradley County, Tennessee, Chancery Court Minutes, 1840-1859, March 1848 Session, p. 157.

112. Meigs County, Tennessee, WPA Microfilm Records of Guardian Settlements, March 1848- March 1850.

113. Meigs County, Tennessee, County Court Minutes, 1852-1857, October 4, 1852, p. 55.

114. Receipt from A.A. Clingan, Sheriff of Bradley County, Tennessee, to Samuel Carr, March 10, 1845, 1-1-1-782.

115. Receipt from A.A. Clingan, Sheriff of Bradley County, Tennessee, to Samuel Carr, July 5, 1845, 1-1-1-414.

116. Two Receipts from A.A. Clingan, Sheriff of Bradley County, to Samuel Carr for payment of judgements rendered by James E. Walker, J.P., January 13, 1846, 1-1-1-791.

117. Receipt from A.A. Clingan, Sheriff of Bradley County, to Samuel Carr for payment of a judgement rendered by the circuit court of Hamilton County, June 12, 1844, 1-1-1-763.

118. Receipt from James Grigsby, constable in Bradley County, to Samuel Carr for payment of a judgement rendered by James E. Walker, J.P., July 1, 1845, 1-1-1-760.

119. Receipt from F.A. Carter, constable in Bradley County, to Samuel Carr for payment of a judgement rendered by James E. Walker, J.P., September 19, 1-1-1-776.

120. Promissory Note from John Carr and Joseph Roark to E. Bates, attest by James Grigsby, Constable in Bradley County, May 5, 1845, 1-1-1-778.

121. The timing of the Carr's move to the Salem Community is based primarily on two receipts issued to Carr for payment on judgements. The last known receipt issued to Carr in Bradley County was executed by A.A. Clingan, Sheriff of Bradley County, January 12, 1846 (1-1-1-791). The first known receipt issued to Carr in Hamilton County was executed by William F. McCormack of the Salem Community, November 22, 1847, for a judgement against Carr by Hiram Cornwell, justice of the peace for Hamilton County in the Salem Community (1-1-1-777). Therefore sometime between January 1846 and November 1847, the Carrs relocated to Hamilton County where they were listed in the 1850 Census. Also, John Carr was still in Bradley County until late 1845 and probably 1846 (1-1-1-778). It would appear most likely that Samuel and Margaret Carr would not have left Bradley County until John departed for Nashville, suggesting their departure for the Salem Community in late 1846 or early 1847. This estimate would allow Carr sufficient time to develop an argument and bring it before Hiram Cornwell by November 22, 1847.

122. Receipt from William F. McCormack to Samuel Carr for payment of a judgement, November 22, 1847, 1-1-1-777.

123. *Chattanooga Gazette*, July 6, 1844, Microfilm Records, Tennessee State Library and Archives.

124. Op. cit., Armstrong, History of Hamilton County, p. 190.

125. Martin, Albro, Railroads Triumphant, Oxford University Press, New York, 1992, p. 14.

126. Folmsbee, Stanley J., Robert E. Corlew, and Enoch L. Mitchell, History of Tennessee, Lewis Historical Publishing Company, Inc., New York, 1960, Volume I, p. 388.

127. Op. cit., Livingood, History of Hamilton County, p. 117.

128. *Chattanooga Gazette*, May 18, 1844, Microfilm Records of the Tennessee State Library and Archives.

129. Receipt from Yarnell and Edens to Joseph Roark, January 14, 1846, 1-1-1-506.

130. Op. cit., Allen, Leaves, p. 295.

131. Request for purchase of corn from John L. Yarnell to Joseph Roark, undated, 1-1-1-431.

132. Promissory Note from James Roark to John L. Yarnell, December 26, 1846, 1-1-1-367.

133. Deed Records, Hamilton County, Chattanooga, Tennessee, November 10, 1847, FNW4, Section 17, FT2N, R3W, Volume 7, Page 415, 4-1-1-2742.

134. It is practically impossible to document the land holdings of James Roark since acquisition records do not appear in the deed records of Hamilton County. Similarly, recorded tract sales by James Roark are limited to those already referenced herein and one of 60 acres to W.M. Smith on April 18, 1861, for what appears to be James' total land holdings in Section 10. (Re: Deed Records, Hamilton County, Chattanooga, Tennessee, April 18, 1862, Deed Book N, Page 379.) The tax record, following the Federal occupation of the area in 1863, indicates James Roark owned a total of 600 acres which does not include the 60 acres in Section 10 since that tract was sold in 1861. (Re: Tennessee State Library and Archives, Microfilm Roll T277, No. 3, Direct Tax Assessment List of Lands and Lots, District 10, Hamilton County, entitled, "State of Tennessee, under the act of Congress entitled 'An Act for the Collection of District Taxes in insurrectionary districts,' approved June 7, 1862, and on the act amendatory thereto," 4-1-1-3751.) Based generally on subsequent land ownership of later descendants of James Roark but with no heirship records, the land holdings of James Roark in the Salem Community are estimated as follows:

140 acres of the NW4, Section 17, purchased from Yarnell, Wilson, and Roler,

160 acres of the NE4, Section 8, based on descendant ownership in 1936,

140 acres of the FNW4, Section 8, based on descendant ownership in 1936,

160 acres of the NW4, Section 15, based on the home place location.

The location of the James Roark home place is based on its location shown on the map prepared in November 1863, for Gen. William T. Sherman. (Re: Library of Congress, Sherman's Map No. 163, Information Map by the Topographical Engineer's Office, Chattanooga, November 26,

135. Deed Records, Hamilton County, Chattanooga, Tennessee, December 6, 1844, Volume F, Pages 99-100.

136. Deed Records, Hamilton County, Chattanooga, Tennessee, March 17, 1846, Volume F, Page 274.

137. Op. cit., Shropshire, <u>Pioneer Days</u>, p. 56.

138. Boles, Oscar Ray, Talley descendant, unpublished Talley Family Group Sheet, May 25, 1994.

139. Locating the farms given by Joseph Roark to his children without recorded deeds is difficult but not impossible. That a deed or similar instrument was given to the Talleys for land under Ocoee District Grant Nos. 2131 and 3176 is based on at least four documents: (1) The field notes for a deed from Benjamin Webb to A.L. Stulce for 324 acres clearly identifies the 80-acre tract given to the Talleys and refers to it as the "J.A. Talley tract." Deed Records, Hamilton County, Chattanooga, Tennessee, March 12, 1868, Deed Book R, Page 189; (2) the Direct Tax Assessment List developed immediately after the war lists Joel A. Talley with 85 acres (probably estimated in the absence of a recorded deed or survey; (3) Joseph repossessed the tract through a sheriff's sale in 1870 when it was in danger of being repossessed for delinquent taxes, Receipt from Deputy Sheriff J.W. Watkins to Joseph Roark, March 10, 1870, 1-1-1-543; (4) the estate settlement agreement following Joseph's death mentions the "said land that did belong to Sary E. Roark." Estate Settlement Agreement and Bonds executed by James A. Roark, John W. Roark, and William M. Roark, April 11, 1876, 1-1-1-848.

140. Roark, John J., <u>A Short Biography of Sarah Elizabeth Roark Talley Killian</u>, unpublished paper, February 11, 1995, p. 1.

141. Receipt from Hiram Cornwell to H.L.D. and Joseph Roark, November 3, 1857, 1-1-1-831.

142. Lease Contract between Hiram Cornwell and Duncan L. Colvin, May 10, 1847, 1-1-1-823.

143. Op. cit., Shropshire, <u>Pioneer Days</u>, p. 41.

144. Promissory Note from Joseph Roark to Caswell Luttrell, April 5, 1847, 1-1-1-828.

145. Delivery Request from Archibald McCallie to Joseph Roark, July 13, 1848, 1-1-1-876.

146. Receipt for Leather from Joseph Roark to Lewis Patterson, October 4, 1848, 1-1-1-875.

147. Receipt from Weir and Conner to Joseph Roark, February 22, 1847, 1-1-1-643. The relationship between the Conner, of Weir and Conner, and M.H. Conner, friend of Joseph Roark is unknown.

148. Payment Request from John Cross to Joseph Roark, December 28, 1847, 1-1-1-867.

149. The assumption that Benjamin was the son of John Webb and brother of Merida is based primarily on the 1840 Census, Hamilton County, Tennessee.

150. For the date of the marriage, see <u>History of Benton, Washington, Carroll, Madison, Crawford, Franklin and Sebastian Counties, Arkansas</u>, The Goodspeed Publishing Co., Chicago, 1889, p. 1211.

151. Receipt of purchases by Benjamin Webb under the account of Joseph Roark with merchant Burton Holman, 1854, 1-1-1-432.

152. Account Purchase Record from W.H. Tibbs to Joseph Roark, August 16, 1847, 1-1-1-826.

153. Op. cit., Shropshire, <u>Pioneer Days</u>, p. 56; 1860 Census, Hamilton County, Tennessee.

154. Tracing the guardianship of the three children of Leonard and Margaret Carr Brooks is difficult at best. Chancery Court Minutes, Bradley County, 1840-1859, Microfilm of WPA Transcription, p.157, March 1848, indicates that Joshua Guinn was appointed guardian of Zachariah, Matilda, and Juda Ann. Guardian Settlement Records, Meigs County, March 8, 1848, Pages 120-121, speak of Harvey McKenzie as guardian. County Court Minutes, Meigs County, Book 3, 1846-1852, June 2, 1851, Page 600, indicates that McKenzie guardianship of Matilda and Juda Ann Brooks was removed to Hamilton County. Hamilton County records for the period are not available due to a courthouse fire. County Court Minutes, Meigs County, Book 4, 1852-1857, October 4, 1852, Page 55, states that William Fairbanks was appointed guardian of Zachariah Brooks on January 21, 1851, and had petitioned Harvey McKenzie to turn over funds of the estate.

155. Op. cit., Shropshire, <u>Pioneer Days</u>, p. 57.

156. Diehl, Leonard R., <u>Scotts–My Wife's Family</u>, unpublished paper, July 1994.

157. Ocoee Plat Book, Microfilm Records, Tennessee State Library and Archives, Roll No. 204, S2, SE4, Section 21, FT2N, R3W.

158. Payment Request from Jesse Killian to Joseph Roark, January 1, 1849, 1-1-1-874.

159. Sales Ticket from Z. Martin to Joseph Roark, May 22, 1850, 1-1-1-1804.

160. Receipt from Jesse Killian to Joseph Roark, January 4, 1849, 1-1-1-873.

161. Hamilton County Deed Records, Chattanooga, Tennessee, April 13, 1849, Volume H, Page 222.

162. Promissory Note from Joseph Roark to Jonathan Wood with a noted receipt of monies by Wood, April 10, 1849, 1-1-1-870.

163. Promissory Note from Joseph Roark to Merida Webb with noted payment credit by Webb, March 20, 1849, 1-1-1-872.

164. Receipt from Dr. John L. Yarnell to Joseph Roark, August 24, 1849, 1-1-1-868.

165. Record of Account Purchase from W.C. Hutcheson by Joseph Roark, September 11, 1849, 1-1-1-836.

166. Hamilton County tax receipts to Joseph Roark for years 1838, 1839, 1842, 1843-44, 1845, 1846, 1847, and 1849, 1-1-1-661 through 1-1-1-668.

167. Op. cit., Livingood, History of Hamilton County, p. 117.

168. *Chattanooga Gazette*, February 16, 1849.

169. *Chattanooga Gazette*, February 19, 1849.

170. Coulter, E. Merton, William G. Brownlow, Fighting Parson of the Southern Highlands, The University of Tennessee Press, Knoxville, Tennessee, 1971, pp. 1-83.

171. Trefousse, Hans L., Andrew Johnson, W.W. Norton & Company, New York, 1989, pp. 1-83.

Chapter 8: Prosperity With Dark Clouds

1. 1850 U.S. Census, Hamilton County, Tennessee, Slave Schedule.

2. Folmsbee, Stanley J., Robert E. Corlew, and Enoch L. Mitchell, History of Tennessee, Volume I, Lewis Historical Publishing Company, Inc., New York, 1960, pp. 513-516.

3. Hicks, John D., George E. Mowry, and Robert E. Burke, The Federal Union, A History of the United States to 1877, Houghton Mifflin Company, Boston, Fourth Edition, 1964, p. 531.

4. Op. cit., Folmsbee, History of Tennessee, Volume I, p. 521.

5. *Chattanooga Gazette*, June 14, 1850.

6. Ibid.

7. Trager, James, The People's Chronology, Henry Holt and Company, New York, First Revised Edition, 1994, p. 453.

8. Livingood, James W., A History of Hamilton County Tennessee, Memphis State University Press, Memphis, Tennessee, 1981, p. 123.

9. *Chattanooga Gazette*, June 14, 1850.

10. Op. cit., Livingood, History of Hamilton County, pp. 122-123.

11. Ibid., pp. 121-128.

12. Shropshire, Mrs. Laura Roark, Pioneer Days–Stories of the Roark-Conner Ancestry, locally published, Revised Edition, 1992, pp. 48-49.

13. Op. cit., 1850 Census. Estimated population of the Salem Community was developed from the 1850 Census based on the identification of known residents of the Salem Community.

14. Receipt from Joseph Roark to Lewis Patterson, August 26, 1851, 1-1-1-486.

15. Receipt from Lewis Patterson to Joseph Roark, May 5, 1852, 1-1-1-503.

16. List of leather sales by Joseph Roark to five listed customers, date not recorded, 1-1-1-838.

17. Lumber order to Joseph Roark, not dated, 1-1-1-1801.

18. Lumber order from Jesse Eldridge to Joseph Roark, not dated, 1-1-1-801.

19. Lumber order to Joseph Roark, not dated, 1-1-1-1802.

20. Deed Records, Hamilton County, Chattanooga, Tennessee, October 24, 1850, Deed Book 10, Page 249.

21. Deed Records, Hamilton County, Chattanooga, Tennessee, January 4, 1851, Deed Book 10, Page 267.

22. Promissory Note from Joseph Roark to George W. Gardenhire, June 27, 1851, 1-1-1-839.

23. Promissory Note from Joseph Roark to William F. McCormack, February 27, 1850, 1-1-1-863.

24. Promissory Note from Joseph Roark to T. Rayl. January 1, 1850, 1-1-1-866.

25. Payment Request from Joseph Roark to Pleasant Doughty, October 17, 1850, 1-1-1-871.

26. 1839 Tax Records, Claiborne County, Tazewell, Tennessee, Microfilm Records, Tennessee State Library and Archives, Nashville, Tennessee, Roll No. 2.

27. Deed Records, Claiborne County, Tazewell, Tennessee, mortgage of the corn crop anticipated by James McVey from ten acres, "the rent corn excepted," and live-stock to satisfy a debt of $60.71 to William Houston, July 17, 1838, Deed Book M, Page 391.

28. Hansard, Mary A., Old Time Tazewell, published by Mary Lorena Hansard Wilson, Sweetwater, Tennessee, 1979, p. 228.

29. Tennessee State Penitentiary, Nashville, Tennessee, Ledger 87, p. 4; Sandefur, Ms. Ina Mae, "Things I Remember," locally published paper, Kokomo, Indiana, not dated. Also see op. cit., Hansard, Old Time Tazewell, p. 228.

30. Claiborne County Historical Society, The People's History of Claiborne County Tennessee, 1801-1988, Walsworth Press, Waynesville, North Carolina, Second Printing, 1990, p. 99.

31. 1850 Census, Claiborne County, Tennessee.

32. Neither the exact date of Elizabeth's divorce from Ellison nor that of her marriage to Nunn is known. In February 1854, she executed a deed as the wife of Martin B. Nunn, thus establishing an outside date for her marriage to Nunn. Deed Records, Claiborne County, Tazewell, Tennessee, February 8, 1854, Volume W, Pages 303-305, 4-1-1-2819.

33. Tennessee State Statutes, Title 30, Administration of Estates, TnCode, 1999.

34. Meigs County Tax Records 1839-1855, Meigs County, Decatur, Tennessee, Microfilm Records, Tennessee State Library and Archives, Nashville, Tennessee, Roll No. 74.

35. Meigs County Circuit Court Records, Decatur, Tennessee, Order of Sheriff's Sale to satisfy judgement against Harvey McKenzie and Benjamin F. McKenzie, December 27, 1852, 1-1-1-421.

36. Letter from Sam White to Joseph Roark, letter not dated, ca. January 1853, 1-1-1-849.

37. Tax Receipt from James Rogers, tax collector for Hamilton County, Tennessee, to Joseph Roark as "guardian of Brooks heirs" for calendar year 1855, 1-1-1-674.

38. Letter dated August 12, 1872, from Mary Ann Roark Scott to William M. Roark, 1-1-1-797; Roark, John W., "Autobiographical Sketch of the Life of John Wesley Roark," Roark-Conner Family News, Issue Seven, June 1994, Chuck Gross, editor.

39. The family of James Carr is difficult to trace. He is identifiable in the 1830 Census for Hamilton County, Tennessee, and in the 1840 Census in Bradley County. Neither he nor his family can be located in the 1850 Census. Alexander Carr was with Samuel and Margaret Carr in the 1850 Census for Hamilton County and was with Joseph and Juda Roark in the 1860 Census as a twenty-one-year-old. James A. Carr received support from Joseph Roark in 1858 (1-1-1-327) and in 1859 (1-1-1-1623) but for some reason was not included with the Joseph Roark household in the 1860 Census. He was included with Joseph and Juda Roark in the 1870 Census as a nineteen-year-old. Available evidence suggests that Joseph and Juda played a strong role in raising both Alexander and James A. Carr.

40. Mortgage from Joel A. Talley and Jesse R. Talley to Joseph Roark, January 27, 1851, 1-1-1- 879.

41. Letter from George Irwin, as justice of the peace, to Constable J.C. Roberts in regard to a judgement against Joel A. Talley in favor of Binyon and O'Conner, 1-1-1-602.

42. Receipt from Constable J.C. Roberts to Joel A. Talley for payment of a judgement by the hand of Joseph Roark, June 2, 1855, 1-1-1-601.

43. Deed Records, Hamilton County, Chattanooga, Tennessee, May 19, 1855, Deed Book K, Page 204.

44. Deed from Joseph Roark to Nancy M. Ford and son David H. Ford for 50 acres in District 10, Hamilton County, Tennessee, witnessed by Joel A. Talley, December 1, 1861, 1-1-1-532.

45. Receipt from William Killian, Constable, to Samuel Carr, July 10, 1851, 1-1-1-764.

46. White, Robert Hiram, Ph.D., Development of the Tennessee State Educational Organization, 1796-1929, Southern Publishers, Inc., Kingsport, Tennessee, 1929, p. 67.

47. List of Salem Community heads of households with number of school-age children, 1851, 1-1-1-820. Neither heading nor date is provided on the document. The fact that school-age children were numbered was verified against the families for which the number of school-age children were known for 1851, i.e., Joseph

Roark, James Roark, Henry Bare, and M.H. Conner. The date of the document was estimated considering that Henry Bare died in 1853 and that, of his six children, four would have been school age only in 1851 or 1852.

48. Subscription list for school chimney, November 14, 1851, 1-1-1-649.

49. Receipt from Hugh McKibbins to Joseph Roark for subscriptions to a writing school, December 27, 1854, 1-1-1-485.

50. List of special school subscribers, 1-1-1-529.

51. Donnelly, Polly W., Ed., James County, A Lost County of Tennessee, Old James County Chapter, East Tennessee Historical Society, Ooltewah, Tennessee, 1983, pp. 131-132.

52. Payment Request from Joseph Roark to A. King for payment of Hiram Cornwell, 1-1-1-712.

53. History of Tennessee, Decatur County, The Goodspeed Publishing Co., Nashville, Tennessee, 1886, p. 893.

54. Op. cit., Shropshire, Pioneer Days, p. 41.

55. Op. cit., History of Tennessee, Decatur County, Goodspeed, p. 893.

56. Op. cit., Donnelly, James County, p. 85.

57. Op. cit., Shropshire, Pioneer Days, p. 41.

58. Op. cit., History of Tennessee, Decatur County, Goodspeed, p. 893.

59. 1860 Census, Hamilton County, Tennessee.

60. Receipt from B. Holman to Alfred and Samuel Carr, March 8, 1853, 1-1-1-499.

61. The date of the death of Samuel Carr is based on the earliest mention of Joseph Roark as administrator of the Samuel Carr estate in a document dated May 14, 1853, 1-1-1-762.

62. Court records from Hamilton County are not available that would document the court action naming Joseph Roark as the administrator of the Carr estate. Later evidence in the form of a receipt from the county clerk is the only verification of his designation by the court.

63. Promissory Note from William Carr to W.C. Thatcher to Joseph Roark, administrator of the Samuel Carr estate, May 14, 1853, 1-1-1-762.

64. Finding by the Hamilton County (Tennessee) Clerk on the settlement of the Samuel Carr estate, undated, 1-1-1-783. The date of the finding was probably the second week of May 1855, inasmuch as the first payment to the heirs was made May 16, 1855.

65. Receipt from Jane Mahan to Joseph Roark for her share of the Samuel Carr estate, May 16, 1855, 1-1-1-341.

66. Receipt from John Carr to Joseph Roark for his share of the estate of Samuel Carr, 1-1-1-340, and receipt from Alfred Carr to Joseph Roark for his share of the estate of Samuel Carr, 1-1-1- 343.

67. Receipt from Francis M. Carr to Joseph Roark for his share of the Samuel Carr estate, March 7, 1859, 1-1-1-753.

68. Receipt from D.A. Medley, signed by Sanford Medley, to Joseph Roark for his share of the Samuel Carr estate, September 7, 1855, 1-1-1-342.

69. Summons from Constable J.C. Roberts to Joseph Roark in regard to debts payable to Sanford Medley, September 28, 1859, 1-1-1-530.

70. Promissory Note from Joseph Roark to Ivy Medley, October 19, 1859, 1-1-1-582.

71. Ibid., the reverse side of the promissory note has the following payment notation: "Received on the within note fore dollars, Oct the 10th 1860."

72. Sworn statement by Jane Carr Mahan before Judge W.B. Russell in regard to a claim against the estate of James Carr, June 13, 1856, 1-1-1-752.

73. Promissory Note from William Carr to Joseph Roark, April 19, 1855, 1-1-1-334.

74. Op. cit., Shropshire, Pioneer Days, p. 17.

75. Ibid., p. 41.

76. Op. cit., History of Tennessee, Decatur County, Goodspeed, p. 893.

77. Op. cit., Shropshire, Pioneer Days, p. 41.

78. Documentation is not available from the court records of that era. Confirmation of Joseph Roark's appointment as administrator of the estate is provided by subsequent documents.

79. 1836 Tax List for Hamilton County, Tennessee, Tennessee State Library and Archives, Microfilm Tax Records by County, Roll Number 4.

80. Ocoee Plat Book, Microfilm Records, Tennessee State Library and Archives, Roll Number 204.

81. Deed Records, Hamilton County, Chattanooga, Tennessee, September 27, 1841, Deed Book E, Pages 56 and 57.

82. Novak, V. Stewart, J.P. Dick, Henington Publishing Company, Wolfe City, Texas, 1966, p. 230, with additional handwritten notes by Zava Kenison, Oklahoma City, Oklahoma, January 12, 1978, 1-1-1-3721.

83. 1850 Census, Hamilton County, Tennessee.

84. Court records from Hamilton County are unavailable for this era. For confirmation of Malinda Bare as guardian of her minor children, see the receipt from Malinda Bare to Joseph Roark, January 7, 1855, 1-1-1-495.

85. The date of the estate sale is based on the date of a promissory note to Joseph Roark for items purchased at the sale, 1-1-1-493. The note is dated November 26, 1853.

86. Lists from the estate sale of personal property of the estate of Henry Bare, 1853, 1-1-1-821 and 1-1-1-822.

87. List of promissory notes from the estate sale of personal property of the estate of Henry Bare, 1-1-1-708.

88. Promissory Note from James Roark and William Potter to Joseph Roark, administrator of the Henry Bare estate, November 26, 1853, 1-1-1-493.

89. List of claims against the Henry Bare estate by Joseph Roark, November 1854, 1-1-1-819. The list is actually dated November 1855 which had to be an error since the estate was finally settled in January 1855.

90. No court records remain from that era of the court. Court approval is indicated in the receipt from Malinda Bare, 1-1-1-495.

91. Receipt from Malinda Bare to Joseph Roark for the balance of funds in the Henry Bare estate after settlement, January 7, 1855, 1-1-1-495.

92. Tennessee Tax Commission, Direct Taxes in Insurrectionary Districts, 1864, District No. 10, Hamilton County, Tennessee, Tennessee Microfilm Reel T277, No. 3.

93. Civil War Centennial Commission, Tennesseans in the Civil War, Part 1, Nashville, Tennessee.

94. Deed Records, Hamilton County, Chattanooga, Tennessee, February 1867, Volume R, Pages 246-249.

95. The exact date of the death of Sarah Bolen Roark is unknown. The estimate of October 1853 is based on (1) tax records of Claiborne County in which she is listed as the owner of the homestead through 1853 but James Jefferson Lambert is taxed on the property for 1854; Tax Records, Claiborne County, Tennessee, Microfilm Records, Tennessee State Library and Archives, Roll No. 36; and (2) deed from Jeremiah Roark et al surrendering undivided interest in the homestead to James Jefferson Lambert, February 8, 1854; Deed Records, Claiborne County, Tazewell, Tennessee, Volume W, Pages 303-305.

96. Deed Records, Claiborne County, Tazewell, Tennessee, February 8, 1854, Volume W, Pages 303-305, 4-1-1-2819.

97. Op. cit., Folmsbee, History of Tennessee, Vol. II, pp. 5-11.

98. Jones, James B. Jr., Study Unit No. 4, Early Railroad Development in Tennessee, 1820s - 1865, Tennessee Historical Commission, State Historic Preservation Office, December 1986, pp. 12-15.

99. Certificate of Agreement with William Garretson and Company, Nashville, Tennessee, P.B. Cate, Agent, 1-1-1-598.

100. Letter from Gilbert L. Hemenway to Joseph Roark, 1-1-1-528.

101. Invoice from Dr. John L. Yarnell to Joseph Roark, March 19, 1850, 1-1-1-498.

102. Charge Ticket from Z. Martin to Joseph Roark, May 22, 1850, 1-1-1-1804.

103. Promissory Note from Joseph Roark to W.C. Hutcheson, January 14, 1851, 1-1-1-864.

104. Promissory Note from Joseph Roark to M.A. Wood, January 15, 18.52, 1-1-1-861.

105. Receipt from M.A. Wood to Joseph Roark, for 1853 account, 1-1-1-599.

106. Promissory Note from Joseph Roark to John Taylor and Co., March 6, 1853, 1-1-1-500.

107. Promissory Note from Joseph Roark to Jonathan Wood, May 19, 1853, 1-1-1-501.

108. Receipt from G.W. Housley to Joseph Roark, March 1, 1854, 1-1-1-489.

109. Promissory Note from Joseph Roark to B. Holman, November 30, 1855, 1-1-1-496.

110. Promissory Note from Joseph Roark to M.A. Wood and Co., March 16, 1855, 1-1-1-488.

111. Promissory Note from Joseph Roark to J.C. Wilson, February 5, 1852, 1-1-1-816.

112. Promissory Note from Preston Biggs to A.D. Meeks, January 26, 1854, transferred to Joseph Roark September 5, 1855, 1-1-1-487.

113. Handwritten message from Jacob Roller to Joseph Roark, undated, 1-1-1-703. Date of the "early 1850s" is assumed based on other activities of Joseph Roark and Jacob Roller.

114. Promissory Note from Joseph Roark to William F. McCormack, April 21, 1853, 1-1-1-492.

115. Promissory Note from Joseph Roark to J.C. Wilson, January 16, 1855, 1-1-1-600.

116. Tax Receipt from A. Selcer, Tax Collector, to Duncan Colvin for 1854 taxes, 1-1-1-497.

117. Receipt from G.W. Housley to Joseph Roark and Duncan Colvin, October 30, 1856, 1-1-1-606.

118. Promissory Note from Joseph Roark to G.W. Housley, October 31, 1856, 1-1-1-605.

119. Tax Receipts from Hamilton County, Tennessee, to Joseph Roark for calendar years 1851, 1852, 1853, 1854, and 1855, 1-1-1-669 through 1-1-1-673.

120. Tax Receipt from James Rogers, Tax Collector for Hamilton County, Tennessee, to Joseph Roark as "guardian of Brooks heirs" for calendar year 1855, 1-1-1-674.

121. Charge Ticket from B. Holman, merchant, to Benjamin Webb for purchases made on the A. Carr account, 1854, 1-1-1-432.

122. Receipt from B. Holman to Joseph Roark for credit on the "A.Carr store account," June 1, 1855, 1-1-1-802.

123. Deed Records, Hamilton County, Chattanooga, Tennessee, March 17, 1854, Deed Book J, Pages 327-328.

124. Family Group Sheet for Benjamin and Jane Webb, November 20, 2000, provided by R.V. and Faye Thompson, descendants.

125. Op. cit., Livingood, History of Hamilton County, p. 136.

126. Purchase Receipt from Chattanooga Foundry and Machine Works, Eastman, Lees & Co. to Joseph Roark, March 13, 1856, 1-1-1-3584.

127. Purchase Receipt from A.D. Taylor Company to Joseph Roark, March 13, 1856, 1-1-1-408.

128. 1870 Census, Decatur County, Tennessee.

129. Op. cit., Jones, Early Railroad Development, p. 14.

130. Deed Records, Claiborne County, Tazewell, Tennessee, August 23, 1856, Volume Z, Page 566, 4-1-1-2806. The question should be discussed as to whether James, John, and Joseph Roark went to Claiborne County or rather perhaps Jeff Lambert, Timothy Roark Jr., and George Richardson traveled to Hamilton County to get the deed signed. No definite answer can be provided; however, it appears logical to think that if Lambert had to go to Hamilton County to get the signatures, there would have been little reason to take Timothy Jr. and George Richardson along as witnesses. Their trip would have been expensive and witnesses before a justice of the peace could have been arranged in Hamilton County. Also, if Lambert had needed moral support for a trip south, he would have taken William or Jeremiah Roark rather than a nephew such as George Richardson. True, there would have been little motivation for the three brothers to return to Claiborne County if signing the deed were the only purpose for the trip. But Claiborne County had been their home and a trip to the old home place would have provided sufficient incentive for the trip.

131. Letter from William L. Swafford and Margaret Swafford to Joseph Roark, September 1, 1856, 1-1-1-2145.

132. Op. cit., History of Tennessee, Decatur County, Goodspeed, p. 41.

133. Grave Marker, Sardis Ridge Cemetery, Perryville, Decatur County, Tennessee.

134. Receipt from W.R. Davis to Joseph Roark, December 16, 1856, 1-1-1-604.

135. Receipt from William Haney to Joseph Roark, January 1857, 1-1-1-616.

136. Debt Acknowledgement Letter from Joseph Roark to Lewis Patterson, January 11, 1857, 1-1-1-865.

137. Receipt from B. Holman to Joseph Roark, March 27, 1857, 1-1-1-609.

138. Receipt from J.T. Witt and W.C. Hutcheson to Joseph Roark, April 27, 1857, 1-1-1-607.

139. Letter from George W. Arnette, County Clerk, Hamilton County, Tennessee, to Joseph Roark, April 22, 1857, 1-1-1-523.

140. Promissory Note from Joseph Roark to George W. Arnette, "Clerk of the County Court of Hamilton County, Tennessee," March 22, 1858, 1-1-1-575.

141. Itemized Invoice from Joseph Roark to Jesse Killian, July 21, 1857, 1-1-1-851.

142. Sworn Statement by W.R. Davis before Justice of the Peace George Irwin in regard to the indebtedness of Jesse Killian, September 29, 1857, 1-1-1-642.

143. Promissory Note in the amount of $14.30 from Joseph Roark to B. Holman "on Jesse Killian's account," September 29, 1857, 1-1-1-608. Receipt from B. Holman to Joseph Roark for $14.30, September 29, 1857, 1-1-1-571.

144. Promissory Note from Joseph Roark to Maise Blackburn, September 21, 1857, 1-1-1-627.

145. Promissory Note For $50.00 from Joseph Roark to Jesse Killian, September 21, 1857, 1-1-1-618.

146. Promissory Note for $50.00 from Joseph Roark to Jesse Killian, September 21, 1857, 1-1-1-614.

147. Promissory Note for $200.00 from Joseph Roark to Jesse Killian, September 21, 1857, 1-1-1-571.

148. Promissory Note from Joseph Roark to J.H. Locke, September 21, 1857, 1-1-1-615.

149. Op. cit., Promissory Note in the amount of $14.30 from Joseph Roark to B. Holman "on Jesse Killian's account," September 29, 1857, 1-1-1-608.

150. Op. cit., Promissory Note for $200.00 from Joseph Roark to Jesse Killian, September 21, 1857, 1-1-1-571.

151. Joseph Roark's ownership of the 40-acre tract is based on statements in the estate settlement agreement executed by Jim, John, and Will Roark following their father's death. No deed for the transfer of title from Killian to Joseph Roark was placed of record. Title finally rested with Will Roark and was placed of record in 1925 following Will's death and the settlement of his estate. Deed Records, Hamilton County, Chattanooga, Tennessee, recording date of January 21, 1925, Volume 465, Pages 250-252.

152. Lumber Order from Burton Holman to Joseph Roark, October 27, 1857, 1-1-1-565.

153. Invoice from B. Holman to Joseph Roark, March 8, 1858, 1-1-1-426.

154. Receipt from James Rogers, Tax Collector of Hamilton County, to J.C. Wilson for 1858 taxes, 1-1-1-678.

155. Deed Records, Hamilton County, Chattanooga, Tennessee, October 8, 1857, Deed Book 13, Pages 101 and 102 (Original Records, Volume M, Pages 116 and 117.)

156. Promissory Note from Joseph Roark to J.E. Eldridge, December 5, 1857, 1-1-1-611.

157. Promissory Note from Joseph Roark to John Roark, March 5, 1858, 1-1-1-573.

158. Promissory Note from Joseph Roark to John Roark, September 2, 1858, 1-1-1-619.

159. Promissory Note from Joseph Roark to Hutcheson and Witt, January 1, 1858, 1-1-1-620.

160. Promissory Note from Joseph Roark to Curry Samples and Son, July 16, 1858, 1-1-1-628.

161. Promissory Note from Joseph Roark to W.G. West, September 23, 1858, 1-1-1-581.

162. Promissory Note from Joseph Roark to John N. Moore, October 8, 1858, 1-1-1-630.

163. Receipt from Constable J.C. Roberts to Joseph Roark for a promissory note by J.B. Eldridge in the amount of $88.00, October 27, 1858, 1-1-1-569.

164. Lumber Order from J.B. Eldridge and G. Curenton to Joseph Roark, February 1858, 1-1-1-819.

165. Lumber Order from A.P. DeFriese to Joseph Roark, February, 1858, 1-1-1-819.

166. Lumber Order from Maise Blackburn to Joseph Roark, February 17, 1858, 1-1-1-1803.

167. Lumber Order from John L. Yarnell to Joseph Roark, February 1858, 1-1-1-1803.

168. Farm Produce Order from A.P. DeFriese to Joseph Roark, February 1858, 1-1-1-1803.

169. Farm Produce Order from Rufus Friddle to Joseph Roark, February 1858, 1-1-1-1803.

170. Payment Request from W.C. Thatcher to Joseph Roark for payment to "Mr. Campbell . . . for thrashing," November 18, 1858, 1-1-1-563.

171. Deed Records, Hamilton County, Chattanooga, Tennessee, March 15, 1858, Volume 13, Pages 384-385 (Original Records, Deed Book M, Page 417).

172. Deed Records, Hamilton County, Chattanooga, Tennessee, March 20, 1858, Volume 13, Page 200 (Original Records, Deed Book M, Page 225).

173. Allen, Penelope Johnson, Leaves from the Family Tree, Southern Historical Press, Easley, South Carolina, 1892, p. 24; McClure, Lucille, Abstracts of Ocoee District Early Land Records- Entries, privately published, 1990.

174. Lillard, Roy G., ed., The History of Bradley County, Bradley County Chapter, East Tennessee Historical Society, 1976, pp. 76-77, 256-257.

175. Promissory Note from Joseph Roark to Edmond Atley, November 7, 1858, 1-1-1-622.

176. Charge Record from Coulter and Newman to Joseph Roark, June 1, 1858, 1-1-1-562.

177. Invoice from Coulter and Newman to Joseph Roark, January 1, 1859, 1-1-1-568.

178. Receipt from Constable J.C. Roberts to Joseph Roark for payment of a judgement against William L. Swafford, March 15, 1858, 1-1-1-621.

179. Promissory Note from Joseph Roark to Robert Beane Scott, July 8, 1858, 1-1-1-625.

180. Sworn Statement by James A. Carr before Seamore Campbell, justice of the peace, November 16, 1858, 1-1-1-327.

181. No copy of the last communication with the family in Claiborne County remains. The communication in the form of a letter is assumed.

182. Combined tax receipts from James Rodgers, tax collector for Hamilton County, to Joseph Roark for 1857 and 1858 taxes, 1-1-1-677.

183. Promissory Note from Joseph Roark to Lewis Patterson, May 5, 1859, 1-1-1-617.

184. Printed agreement between Joseph Roark and Wheaton Allen for tree grafts, April 4, 1859, 1-1-1-561.

185. Op. cit., Shropshire, Pioneer Days, p. 48.

186. Evidence of the honey production is found in the sale of the bee stands during the settlement of the Joseph Roark estate.

187. Promissory Note from Joseph Roark to G.W. Gardenhire, August 26, 1859, 1-1-1-574.

188. Promissory Note from Joseph Roark to G.W. Housley, February 26, 1859, 1-1-1-433.

189. Promissory Note from Joseph Roark to B. Holman, March 8, 1859, 1-1-1-626.

190. Promissory Notes from Joseph Roark to J.P. Turbyfill, July 27, 1859, and August 29, 1859, 1-1-1-623, 1-1-1-624.

191. Payment Request from J.P. Turbyfill to Joseph Roark, November 3, 1859, 1-1-1-564.

192. Record of James A. Carr "account of articles" provided by Joseph Roark, October 10, 1859, 1-1-1-1623.

193. Receipt from J.T. Witt and Company to Joseph Roark, June 15, 1859, 1-1-1-526.

194. Op. cit., Folmsbee, History of Tennessee, Volume II, p. 22.

Chapter 9: Elections and Civil War

1. Groce, W. Todd, "Mountain Rebels: East Tennessee Confederates and the Civil War, 1860- 1870," Ph.D. diss., University of Tennessee, 1993, p. 3.

2. The Seventh Census of the United States, 1850, J.D.B. DeBow, Superintendent of the U.S. Census, Washington, Robert Armstrong, Public Printer, 1853, Tennessee, pp. 563-597; Agriculture of the United States in 1860, Compiled from Original Returns of the Eighth Census, Washington, D.C., Government Printing Office, 1864, Tennessee, Hamilton County.

3. Op. cit., 1850 Census, Tennessee, pp. 563-597; 1860 Agriculture Census, Tennessee, Hamilton County.

4. Op. cit., Groce, "Mountain Rebels," p. 4.

5. *Chattanooga Advertiser*, January 8, 1857.

6. Deed Records, Hamilton County, Chattanooga, Tennessee, December 17, 1858, Deed Book M, Pages 456-457.

7. 1860 Census, Hamilton County, Tennessee.

8. Promissory Note from Joseph Roark to Dr. John L. Yarnell, April 20, 1860, 1-1-1-572.

9. Roark, John W., "Autobiographical Sketch of the Life of John Wesley Roark," Roark-Conner Family News, Issue Seven, June 1994, Chuck Gross, editor.

10. Deed Records, Hamilton County, Chattanooga, Tennessee, January 19, 1849, Deed Book M, Pages 449-451.

11. Op. cit., Roark, John W., "Autobiographical Sketch."

12. The Scotts were not listed in the 1860 Census. The source of information on their family at that time was Diehl, Leonard R., Scotts–My Wife's Family, unpublished paper, July 1994, 4-1-1-3061.

13. Payment Request from M.H. Conner to Robert Beane Scott, February 10, 1860, 1-1-1-1444.

14. 1860 Census, Hamilton County, Tennessee.

15. Receipt from Constable John McCallie to Joel A. Talley for two promissory notes on William Bettis and one judgement against Bettis, September 21, 1860, 1-1-1-579.

16. Promissory Note from Joel A. Talley to William H. Tibbs, December 28, 1860, 1-1-1-416.

17. Statement from Carson and Samples to Joseph Roark, April 30, 1860, 1-1-1-589.

18. Charge Account Statement from William H. Tibbs to Joseph Roark, May 26, 1860, 1-1-1-766.

19. Promissory Note from Joseph Roark to James A. Carr, May 20, 1860, 1-1-1-583.

20. Only one order for lumber during 1860 remains in the Joseph Roark papers: Lumber Order from McCallie to Joseph Roark, October 27, 1860, 1-1-1-1624.

21. Promissory Note from Joseph Roark to J.T. Witt and Company, January 2, 1860, 1-1-1-584.

22. Promissory Note from Joseph Roark to Hiram Haney, January 10, 1860, 1-1-1-482.

23. Promissory Note from Joseph Roark to George W. Gardenhire, February 3, 1860, 1-1-1-586.

24. Promissory Note from Joseph Roark to Simeon Eldridge, December 15, 1860, 1-1-1-587.

25. Receipt from Constable John McCallie to Joseph Roark, January 10, 1861, 1-1-1-819.

26. Receipt from Deputy Sheriff John Kimbrough to Joseph Roark, December 13, 1861, 1-1-1-578.

27. Campbell, Mary Emily Robertson, The Attitude of Tennesseans toward the Union, 1847-61, Vantage Press, New York, 1961, pp. 284-287.

28. Ibid., p. 153.

29. *Congressional Globe*, 36 Cong., 2 Session, Pt. I, pp. 117-120, 134-143, as quoted in op. cit., Campbell, The Attitude of Tennesseans, pp. 151-153.

30. Livingood, James W., The Chattanooga Country; Gateway to History, Chattanooga Area Historical Association, 1995, p. 38.

31. Folmsbee, Stanley J., Robert E. Corlew, and Enoch L. Mitchell, History of Tennessee, Volume II, Lewis Historical Publishing Company, Inc., New York, 1960, p. 29.

32. Op. cit., Campbell, The Attitudes of Tennesseans, pp. 284-287.

33. As quoted in op. cit., Livingood, Chattanooga Country, p. 30.

34. Purchase and Sales Receipt to Alfred Carr and Joseph Roark, February 1, 1861, 1-1-1-818.

35. Account statement of items purchased from B. Holman to Joseph Roark, February 13, 1861, 1-1-1-805.

36. Promissory Note from Joseph Roark to B. Holman, February 13, 1861, 1-1-1-629.

37. Credit Note from B. Holman to Joseph Roark, March 27, 1861, 1-1-1-576.

38. Purchase Receipt from an unnamed merchant to Joseph Roark, April 4, 1861, 1-1-1-595.

39. Op. cit., Folmsbee, History of Tennessee, Volume II, pp. 32-33.

40. Bryan, Charles Faulkner, "The Civil War in East Tennessee: A Social, Political, and Economic Study," Ph.D. diss., University of Tennessee, 1978, p. 39.

41. Op. cit., Groce, "Mountain Rebels," pp. 68-77; op. cit., Folmbee, History of Tennessee, Volume II, pp. 32-34.

42. *Chattanooga Gazette*, January 24, 1861.

43. *Chattanooga Advertiser*, January 24, 1861.

44. Op. cit., Campbell, The Attitudes of Tennesseans, pp. 291-294.

45. Ibid., p. 291.

46. Op. cit., Livingood, Chattanooga Country, p. 58.

47. Op. cit., Groce, "Mountain Rebels," pp. 43-45.

48. Op. cit., Bryan, "Civil War in East Tennessee," p. 44.

49. Lumber Order from E.B. Jett to Joseph Roark, May 21, 1861, 1-1-1-596.

50. Op. cit., Groce, "Mountain Rebels," p. 97.

51. Murray, Melba Lee, Bradley Divided, Bradley County, Tennessee, During the Civil War, The College Press, Collegedale, Tennessee, 1992, p. 47.

52. Donnelly, Polly W., ed., James County, A Lost County of Tennessee, Old James County Chapter, East Tennessee Historical Society, Ooltewah, Tennessee, 1983, p. 75.

53. 1860 Census, Slave Schedule, Hamilton County, Tennessee.

54. Military Records, Company B, First Tennessee Cavalry Regiment (Confederate).

55. Unfortunately, the Civil War record of William M. Roark does not exist and, in response to a pension application by his widow in the 1930s, a pension was denied for that reason. This was not unusual for Confederate veterans. The service of Will Roark is confirmed by an inquiry in the *Confederate Veteran*, Volume XXXVIII, 1920, page 42, seeking information on a George W. Campbell. The article states about Campbell that "Some of his comrades were William and John Roark."

56. Teacher's Certificate for John W. Roark issued by M.H.B. Bourkett, August 6, 1861.

57. Op. cit., Groce, "Mountain Rebels," pp. 95-100.

58. Op. cit., Murray, Bradley Divided, pp. 65-66.

59. Civil War Centennial Commission, Tennesseans in the Civil War, Part 1, 1996, p. 49.

60. Op. cit., Murray, Bradley Divided, p. 49.

61. Fisher, Noel C., War at Every Door, Partisan Politics and Guerrilla Violence in East Tennessee, 1860-1869, The University of North Carolina Press, Chapel Hill, 1997, p. 45.

62. Hurlbut, J.S., History of the Rebellion in Bradley County–East Tennessee, Indianapolis, 1866, p. 63.

63. Op. cit., Murray, Bradley Divided, pp. 46-50; op. cit., Hurlbut, History of Rebellion, p. 97.

64. Op. cit., Bryan, "Civil War in East Tennessee," p. 73; Samuel Milligan Memoirs, Tennessee State Library and Archives, quoted by Bryan.

65. Second Inaugural Address of President Abraham Lincoln, March 4, 1865.

66. Catton, Bruce, Terrible Swift Sword, Doubleday & Company, Inc., Garden City, New York, 1963, p. 59.

67. Promissory Note from Joseph Roark to J.P. Turbyfill, September 11, 1861, 1-1-1-588.

68. Summons from Constable John McCallie to Joseph Roark, November 4, 1861, 1-1-1-425.

69. Purchase Order from Dr. John L. Yarnell to Joseph Roark, November 8, 1861, 1-1-1-631.

70. Op. cit., Livingood, Chattanooga Country, pp. 81-83; op. cit., Fisher, War at Every Door, pp. 53-58; op. cit., Murray, Bradley Divided, p. 55; op. cit., Bryan, "Civil War in Tennessee," p. 87.

71. Coulter, E. Merton, William G. Brownlow, Fighting Parson of the Southern Highlands, University of Tennessee, Knoxville, 1971, pp. 172-206; op. cit., Fisher, War at Every Door, pp. 58-59.

72. Op. cit., Hurlbut, History of Rebellion, pp. 113-115.

73. Op. cit., Fisher, War at Every Door, pp. 62-63.

74. Roark, John J., Hardtack and Hardship, The Life and Times of Confederate Veteran James A. Roark and His Family, Personal Profiles Publishing Company, Dallas, Texas, 1996, pp. 55-56.

75. Bond from Joseph Roark to Nancy M. Ford and David H. Ford, December 1, 1861, 1-1-1-532.

76. Chattanooga Gazette & Advertiser, January 11, 1862.

77. Ibid., January 25, 1862.

78. Op. cit., Roark, Hardtack, p. 57.

79. Kirby Smith, Gen. Edmund, quoted in op. cit., Fisher, War at Every Door, p. 103.

80. Cleveland Banner, April 25, 1862.

81. Op. cit., Fisher, War at Every Door, p. 70.

82. Moore, Albert Burton, Ph.D, Conscription and Conflict in the Confederacy, The MacMillan Company, New York, 1924, pp. 12-26.

83. Military Record, Joel A. Talley, Company G, Fifth Tennessee Volunteer Infantry Regiment (Union).

84. Op. cit., Moore, <u>Conscription</u>, pp. 53-59.

85. Military Record, John B. Roark, Company E, Fifth Tennessee Volunteer Infantry Regiment (Union).

86. 1860 Federal Census, Hamilton County, Tennessee.

87. Military Record, Joseph Roark, Captain Barry's Tennessee Light Artillery Company (Confederate).

88. Roark, David, <u>3022 Descendants of James Roark</u>, privately published, October 7, 1998, p. 13.

89. Military Record, John Lewis Roark, Company E, Fifth Tennessee Volunteer Infantry Regiment (Union).

90. Military Records, James W. Roark and William C. Roark, Seventh Tennessee Volunteer Infantry Regiment (Union).

91. Military Record, Archibald McCallie, Company E, Fifth Tennessee Volunteer Infantry Regiment (Union).

92. Military Record, David Gregory, Company E, Eighth Tennessee Volunteer Infantry Regiment (Union).

93. *Chattanooga Gazette & Advertiser*, January 4, 1862.

94. *Cleveland Banner*, March 19, 1862.

95. Coulter, E. Merton, <u>The Confederate States of America, 1861-1865</u>, Louisiana State University Press, 1950, pp. 149-182; Eaton, Clement, <u>A History of the Southern Confederacy</u>, The MacMillan Company, New York, 1954, pp. 233-259; Wiley, Bell Irvin, <u>The Plain People of the Confederacy</u>, Peter Smith, Gloucester, Mass., 1971, pp. 36-43.

96. Promissory Note from Joseph Roark to W.C. and C.L. Hutcheson, February 8, 1862, 1-1-1-590.

97. Promissory Note from Joseph Roark to G.F. Farris, April 25, 1862, 1-1-1-594.

98. Op. cit., Murray, <u>Bradley Divided</u>, p. 83; <u>War of the Rebellion: A Compilation of the Official Records of the Union and Confederate Armies</u>, 127 volumes., Washington, D.C., 1901, Series One, X, Part I, pp. 919-922. Hereafter these records will be referred to as <u>O.R.</u>

99. Livingood, James W., "The Chattanooga Rebel," <u>East Tennessee Historical Society Publications</u>, No. 39, 1967, pp. 42-55.

100. <u>O.R.</u>, Series One, XVI, Part II, p. 755.

101. Ibid., p. 787.

102. Ibid., p. 767.

103. Ibid., pp. 787-788.

104. Op. cit., Roark, <u>Hardtack</u>, p. 58.

105. Provost Marshal Pass to Joseph Roark and Loyalty Oath by Joseph Roark to the Confederate States of America, September 29, 1862, 1-1-1-1445.

106. *Cleveland Banner*, August 28, 1862.

107. *The Daily Rebel*, Chattanooga, Tennessee, October 19, 1862.

108. Op. cit., Roark, Hardtack, p. 61.

109. Ibid., pp.61-65.

110. Op. cit., Fisher, War at Every Door, pp. 88-89.

111. Ibid., p. 85.

112. Military Record, William C. Roark, Company E, Seventh Tennessee Volunteer Infantry (Union).

113. Promissory Note from Wilson Hickson and John W. Smith to Joseph Roark, February 9, 1863, 1-1-1-591.

114. Massey, Mary Elizabeth, Ersatz in the Confederacy, University of South Carolina Press, Columbia, 1952, pp. 36-37.

115. Op. cit., Wiley, Plain People, pp. 36-41; op. cit., Massey, Ersatz, pp. 63-65.

116. Op. cit., Roark, Hardtack, pp. 66-68.

117. Buck, Capt. Irving A., Cleburne and His Command and Hay, Thomas Robson, Pat Cleburne, Stonewall Jackson of the West, Broadfoot Publishing Company, Wilmington, North Carolina, 1987, pp. 134-136; Cozzens, Peter, This Terrible Sound, The Battle of Chickamauga, University of Illinois Press, Urbana, 1992, p. 42; Purdue, Howell and Elizabeth, Pat Cleburne Confederate General, Hill Junior College Press, Hillsboro, Texas, 1973, pp. 206-207.

118. Ibid., p. 206; O.R., Series One, XXX, Part I, pp. 445-446.

119. Acquisition Receipt from R.H. Longley, Acquisition Agent for the Tenth Confederate Cavalry, to Joseph Roark, September 1, 1863, 1-1-1-707.

120. Op. cit., Livingood, Chattanooga Country, p. 262.

121. *The Daily Rebel*, August 30, 1863.

122. Op. cit., Donnelly, James County, p. 3.

123. Dyer, John P., "Fighting" Joe Wheeler, Louisiana State University Press, 1941, pp. 122-135.

124. Request for Payment from R.A. Sloan to Joseph Roark, October 27, 1863, 1-1-1-806.

125. O.R., Series One, XXX, Part IV, pp. 450-51.

126. McDonough, James Lee, Chattanooga–A Death Grip on the Confederacy, The University of Tennessee Press, Knoxville, 1984, pp. 101-02; op. cit., Livingood, Chattanooga Country, pp. 462-464.

127. Robert Rutledge, April 8, 1864, quoted in op. cit., Bryan, "The Civil War in East Tennessee," p. 136.

128. Op. cit., McDonough, Chattanooga, p. 68.

129. O.R., Series One, XXXI, Part II, pp. 561-563.

130. Sherman, Gen. William T., Memoirs, Vol. I, pp. 379-380; O.R., Series One, XXXI, Part I, p. 431.

131. Myra Inman quoted in op. cit., Livingood, Chattanooga Country, pp. 471-472.

132. O.R., Series One, XXXII, Part II, p. 183; Atlas to Accompany the Official Records of the Union and Confederate Armies, Plate CXVII; O.R., Series One, XXXII, Part II, p. 198.

133. Op. cit., Livingood, Chattanooga Country, pp. 478-488; William Clift as quoted op. cit., Bryan, "The Civil War in East Tennessee," p. 133.

134. Op. cit., Fisher, War at Every Door, p. 135.

135. Op. cit., Coulter, Brownlow, pp. 250-254.

136. Knoxville Whig and Rebel Ventilator, April 1, 1864, as quoted in Campbell, James B., "East Tennessee During the Federal Occupation, 1863-1865," East Tennessee Historical Society Publications, No. 19, 1947, p. 67.

137. Op. cit., Murray, Bradley Divided, p. 227.

138. Govan, Gilbert E., and James W. Livingood, "Chattanooga under Military Occupation, 1863-1865," Journal of Southern History, XVII, February 1951, p. 37.

139. County Court Records, Hamilton County, Tennessee, 1864-1870, WPA Microfilm Records, Roll No. 29, Original Records, Pages 1-12.

140. Op. cit., Fisher, War at Every Door, p. 144; Knoxville Whig and Rebel Ventilator, January 9, 1864, as quoted op. cit., Bryan, "The Civil War in East Tennessee," p. 122.

141. Govan, Gilbert E. and James W. Livingood, The Chattanooga Country, 1540-1976: From Tomahawks to TVA, University of Tennessee Press, Knoxville, 1977, p. 265.

142. Op. cit., Campbell, "East Tennessee During the Federal Occupation," p. 73.

143. Op. cit., Livingood, Chattanooga Country, p. 503.

144. Request for Clothing Material from W.C. Thatcher to Mrs. Joseph Roark, May 24, 1864, 1-1-1-483.

145. Op. cit., Massey, Ersatz, pp. 79-113.

146. Op. cit., Livingood, Chattanooga Country, pp. 505-506; op. cit., Bryan, "The Civil War in East Tennessee," p. 144.

147. Op. cit., Court Records, Hamilton County, Chattanooga, Tennessee, 1864-1870, Original Records, Page 8.

148. Patton, J.W., Unionism and Reconstruction in Tennessee, 1860-1869, University of North Carolina Press, 1934, p. 71, quoted in op. cit., Murray, Bradley Divided, p.188.

149. Military Record, Joel A. Talley, Company E, Fifth Tennessee Volunteer Infantry (Union).

150. Pass No. 2056 to Joseph Roark, issued February 6, 1864, by the Provost Marshal General's Office, Headquarters, Department of the Cumberland, Chattanooga, Tennessee, 1-1-1-3966.

151. Op. cit., Murray, Bradley Divided, p. 225.

152. Op. cit., Roark, Hardtack, pp. 72-75.

153. Op. cit., Livingood, Chattanooga Country, p. 515.

154. Op. cit., Sherman, Memoirs, Volume II, pp. 14-33.

155. Op. cit., Livingood, Chattanooga Country, p. 504; op. cit., Bryan, "The Civil War in East Tennessee," pp. 146-150.

156. Shropshire, Mrs. Laura Roark, Pioneer Days–Stories of the Roark-Conner Ancestry, locally published, Revised Edition, 1992, p. 44.

157. Op. cit., Roark, Hardtack, pp. 75-81; The capture and imprisonment of William Franklin "Bill" Conner was documented in a brief biographical sketch written by his son, Haney Berlin Conner, and provided to the author by letter, dated November 12, 1993, from Mrs. Martha Helen Conner Byrd, daughter of Haney Berlin Conner.

158. Voucher for Abstract of Purchase from the United States to Joseph Roark, January 3, 1865, with return notation from the Office of the Commissary General for Subsistence, September 11, 1865, 4-1-1-2400.

159. Tennessee State Library and Archives, Microfilm Roll T277, No. 3, Direct Tax Assessment List of Lands and Lots, District 10, Hamilton County, entitled, "State of Tennessee, under the act of Congress entitled 'An Act for the Collection of District Taxes in insurrectionary districts,' approved June 7, 1862, and on the act amendatory thereto," 4-1-1-3751.

160. The non-collection of taxes for 1864 was confirmed by the records of Thomas Conner of Hamilton County which includes tax receipts for 1862 and 1865 only; 9-1-1-3669 and 9-1-1- 3670.

161. Tax Receipt from John Kimbrough to Joseph Roark, 1865 taxes, 1-1-1-684.

162. Op. cit., Fisher, War at Every Door, p. 167.

163. Op. cit., Coulter, Brownlow, p. 262.

164. Chattanooga Daily Gazette, Sunday morning, April 16, 1865.

165. Sandburg, Carl, Abraham Lincoln, the War Years, Volume Four, Harcourt, Brace & World, Inc., 1939, p. 343. Confederate Gen. Joseph E. Johnston was at a conference with Union Gen. William T. Sherman to surrender his army when Sherman received the telegram of Lincoln's death, which he passed to Johnston. With an aggrieved look of shock, Johnston said, "Mr. Lincoln was the best friend [the South] had."

Chapter 10: Reconstruction

1. Brice, Marshall Moore, <u>Conquest of a Valley</u>, The University Press of Virginia, Charlottesville, 1967, p. 85; Henry, J.L., "First Tennessee Cavalry at Piedmont," *Confederate Veteran*, Volume XXII, 1914, p. 397.

2. Military Record, John B. Roark, Company E, Fifth Tennessee Infantry Regiment (Union).

3. Military Record, Joseph Roark, Captain Barry's Tennessee Light Artillery Company (Confederate); Joseph Roark Confederate Pension Application to the State of Tennessee, Application No. 3291.

4. Receipt from W.B. Pearson, Tax Collector, Hamilton County, Tennessee, to William Roark for State and County Taxes for 1866, 1-1-1-721.

5. Folmsbee, Stanley J., Robert E. Corlew, and Enoch L. Mitchell, <u>History of Tennessee</u>, Volume II, Lewis Historical Publishing Company, Inc., New York, 1960, pp. 99-100.

6. Coulter, E. Merton, <u>William G. Brownlow, Fighting Parson of the Southern Highlands</u>, The University of Tennessee Press, Knoxville, 1971, pp. 268-270; op. cit., Folmsbee, <u>History of Tennessee</u>, Volume II, pp. 98-102.

7. *Knoxville Whig and Rebel Ventilator*, August 30, 1865. Italics are by this author.

8. Hicks, John D., George E. Mowry, and Robert E. Burke, <u>The American Nation</u>, Houghton Mifflin Company, Boston, Fourth Edition, 1963, pp. 15-20.

9. Loyalty Oath of Joseph Roark to the Government of the United States, 1865, 1-1-1-1621.

10. Voter Certificate, Hamilton County, Tennessee, issued to Joseph Roark, August 1, 1865, 1-1-1-706.

11. Op. cit., Coulter, <u>Brownlow</u>, pp. 280-281.

12. Diehl, Leonard R., <u>Scotts–My Wife's Family</u>, unpublished paper, July 1994, 4-1-1-3061.

13. Promissory Note to John W. Roark assigned to Joseph Roark, November 6, 1865, 1-1-1-593.

14. Receipt from V.C. Walker to Joseph Roark, November 4, 1865, 1-1-1-592.

15. Boles, Oscar Ray, "Joel A. Talley Family Group Sheet," unpublished research, May 25, 1994, 4-1-1-2052.

16. Op. cit., Coulter, <u>Brownlow</u>, pp. 272-273.

17. *New York Times*, November 18, 1865, as quoted in op. cit., Coulter, <u>Brownlow</u>, p. 274.

18. Fisher, Noel C., <u>War at Every Door, Partisan Politics and Guerrilla Violence in East Tennessee, 1860-1869</u>, The University of North Carolina Press, Chapel Hill,

1997, p.156. Groce, W. Todd, "Mountain Rebels: East Tennessee Confederates and the Civil War, 1860-1870," Ph.D. diss., University of Tennessee, 1993, p. 210, quote from letter from William Henry Maxwell to Andrew Johnson, November 2, 1865.

19. Bryan, Charles Faulkner, "The Civil War in East Tennessee: A Social, Political, and Economic Study," Ph.D. diss., University of Tennessee, 1978, pp. 168-169, quote from the *Knoxville Whig*, March 1, 1865.

20. Op. cit., Fisher, War at Every Door, p. 160, quote from David Key of Chattanooga.

21. Deed Records, Hamilton County, Chattanooga, Tennessee, February 14, 1866, Deed Book P, Page 260.

22. *Weekly American Union*, Chattanooga, Tennessee, December 26, 1866.

23. Op. cit., Fisher, War at Every Door, p. 156.

24. Alexander, Thomas B., "Neither Peace Nor War: Conditions in Tennessee in 1865," East Tennessee Historical Society Publications, No. 21, 1949, p. 41.

25. Op. cit., Bryan, "Civil War in East Tennessee," p. 172; op. cit., Fisher, War at Every Door, p. 157.

26. Shropshire, Mrs. Laura Roark, Pioneer Days–Stories of the Roark-Conner Ancestry, locally published, Revised Edition, 1992, pp. 126-127.

27. Op. cit., Groce, "Mountain Rebels," pp. 214-215.

28. Op. cit., Bryan, "Civil War in East Tennessee," pp. 184-186.

29. *Daily American Union*, Chattanooga, Tennessee, February 22, 1866.

30. Campbell, James B., "East Tennessee During the Radical Regime, 1865-1869," East Tennessee Historical Society Publications, No. 20, 1948, p. 88.

31. County Court Records, Hamilton County, Tennessee, 1864-1870, WPA Microfilm Records, Roll No. 29, Original Records, Page 274.

32. Sistler, Byron and Barbara Sistler, Meigs County, Tennessee, Marriages, privately published, 1988, p. 1.

33. Receipt from Constable Archibald McCallie to Joseph Roark, April 21, 1866, 1-1-1-536.

34. Promissory Note from Joseph Roark and John Burton to William L. Hutcheson, May 5, 1866, 1-1-1-533.

35. Op. cit., Folmsbee, History of Tennessee, Volume II, pp. 102-103.

36. Ibid., pp. 103-106.

37. Tennessee State Library and Archives, Microfilm Records, Hamilton County, Tennessee, 1836 Tax Lists by Civil Districts.

38. Tennessee State Library and Archives, Microfilm Records, Roll No. 204, Ocoee District Plat Book.

39. The date of September 8, 1866, for the marriage of John W. Roark and Permelia B. Conner comes from the Family Bible of the John W. Roark family, 4-1-1-

2058. Court Records of Hamilton County indicate a marriage license was issued September 7, 1867. Court Records, Hamilton County, Chattanooga, Tennessee, Marriage Records, Page 100, License No. 426, 4-1-1-2115.

40. Todd, Dora Maye, "My Legacy and My Memoirs from the J.W. Roark Family," unpublished paper, June 26, 1992.

41. Receipt from Constable Archibald McCallie to Joseph Roark, November 10, 1866, 1-1-1-577.

42. Tax Receipt from W.B. Pearson to Joseph Roark for 1866 State and County Taxes, 1-1-1-685.

43. County Court Records, Hamilton County, Tennessee, 1864-1870, WPA Microfilm Records, Roll No. 29, Original Records, Page 547, February 8, 1869.

44. Tax receipt from W.B. Pearson to Joel A. Talley for payment in part of 1866 state and county taxes, 1-1-1-686.

45. Promissory Note from Joseph Roark to James McCormack, January 15, 1867, 1-1-1-597.

46. Receipt from Noah Atchley to Joseph Roark, February 18, 1867, 1-1-1-537.

47. Promissory Note from Joseph Roark and an unknown co-signer to Noah Atchley, February 18, 1867, 1-1-1-418.

48. Receipt from Juda Ann Atchley and Noah Atchley to Joseph Roark, September 30, 1867, 1-1-1-375.

49. Op. cit., Folmsbee, History of Tennessee, Volume II, pp. 106-107.

50. Op. cit., Coulter, Brownlow, pp.332-333; op. cit., Folmsbee, History of Tennessee, Volume II, p. 109.

51. *Weekly American Union*, Chattanooga, Tennessee, February 27, 1867.

52. Ibid., p. 109.

53. Agreement between Joseph Roark and J.W. Smith/W.C. Hutcheson, September 4, 1867, 1-1-1-542.

54. Promissory Note from Joseph Roark and another party to John Eldridge, September 28, 1867, 1-1-1-539; Promissory Note from Joseph Roark and another party to W.C. Hutcheson, September 28, 1867, 1-1-1-538.

55. Promissory Note from Joseph Roark to W.C. Hutcheson, October 17, 1867, 1-1-1-906.

56. County Court Records, Hamilton County, Tennessee, 1864-1870, WPA Microfilm Records, Roll No. 29, December 9, 1867, Original Records, Pages 370-371.

57. County Court Records, Hamilton County, Tennessee, 1864-1870, WPA Microfilm Records, Roll No. 29, June 24, 1868, Original Records, Pages 472-475.

58. Letter from John W. Roark to Julia Roark Robinett, February 3, 1919, 5-1-1-3018.

59. Tax Receipt from Peter Bolton to Joseph Roark for 1867 state and county taxes, 1-1-1-689.

60. County Court Records, Hamilton County, Tennessee, 1864-1870, WPA Microfilm Records, Roll No. 29, January 3, 1865, Original Records, Page 49.

61. Tax Receipt from Peter Bolton to Joseph Roark for 1868 state and county taxes, 1-1-1-690.

62. Tax Receipt from Peter Bolton to J. A. Talley, by the hand of Joseph Roark, for 1867 State and County Taxes, 1-1-1-688.

63. Tax Receipt from D.J. Alexander, Deputy Sheriff to J. A. Talley, by the hand of Joseph Roark, for 1869 state and county taxes, 1-1-1-691.

64. Sworn Statement by Joseph Roark before A.P. Defriese, Justice of the Peace, August 25, 1869, 1-1-1-541.

65. Promissory Note from Joel Talley to Joseph Roark, October 28, 1869, 1-1-1-545.

66. Assignment of a judgement against Joel A. Talley from A. Mangram to William Roark and from William Roark to Joseph Roark, September 23, 1871, 1-1-1-841.

67. Receipt from Deputy Sheriff J.W. Watkins to Joseph Roark, March 10, 1870, 1-1-1-543.

68. Tax Receipt from Alex McNabb to Joel Talley, by the hand of Joseph Roark, for the 1870 state and county taxes, December 5, 1870, 1-1-1-693.

69. Letter from John Carr to Joseph Roark, September 6, 1869, 1-1-1-3891.

70. State of Tennessee Voter Registration Certificate for Joseph Roark Sr., July 19, 1869, 1-1-1-3577.

71. Op. cit., Folmsbee, History of Tennessee, Volume II, pp. 122-124.

72. Minutes, Annual Meeting of the Ocoee Association of Baptists at Salem Church, Hamilton County, Tennessee, October 2, 1869, 1-1-1-3742.

73. County Court Records, Hamilton County, Tennessee, 1864-1870, WPA Microfilm Records, Roll No. 29, September 4, 1869, Original Records, Page 561.

74. Ibid., WPA Microfilm Records, Roll No. 29, July 7, 1869, Original Records, Page 587.

75. Ibid., WPA Microfilm Records, Roll No. 29, October 4, 1869, Original Records, Page 590.

76. Ibid., WPA Microfilm Records, Roll No. 29, February 8, 1869, Original Records, Page 548; June 9, 1869, Page 581; January 10, 1870, Page 652.

77. The death dates of Joseph's associates were taken from County Court Records, Hamilton County, Tennessee, 1864-1870, WPA Microfilm Records, Roll No. 29, 1867-1869, Original Records, Pages 260 through 670; for information on

Lewis Patterson, see Allen, Penelope Johnson, <u>Leaves from the Family Tree</u>, Southern Historical Press, Easley, South Carolina, 1982, p. 188.

Chapter 11: The Last Years

1. 1840, 1850, and 1860 Census for Hamilton County, Tennessee; Roark, David, <u>3022 Descendants of James Roark</u>, privately printed, Birchwood, Tennessee, October 7, 1998, pp. 6-8; Roark, Cal Latimore, Unpublished paper on John Roark (1800-1870); with some reconciliation among sources.

2. Deed Records, Hamilton County, Chattanooga, Tennessee, April 11, 1871, Volume U, Pages 579-587.

3. Hicks, John D., George E. Mowry, and Robert E. Burke, <u>The American Nation</u>, Houghton Mifflin Company, Boston, Fourth Edition, 1963, pp. 20-40.

4. Folmsbee, Stanley J., Robert E. Corlew, and Enoch L. Mitchell, <u>History of Tennessee</u>, Volume II, Lewis Historical Publishing Company, Inc., New Yprk, 1960, p. 129.

5. <u>Wealth and Industry of the United States in 1870</u>, Compiled from Original Returns of the Eighth Census, Washington, D.C., Government Printing Office, 1872.

6. Livingood, James W., <u>A History of Hamilton County, Tennessee</u>, Memphis State University Press, 1981, p. 235; Armstrong, Zella, <u>The History of Hamilton County and Chattanooga, Tennessee</u>, Volume II, The Overmountain Press, Johnson City, Tennessee, 1933, p. 75; Doub, Chester J., "A History of Education in the James County Area," Master's thesis, University of Tennessee, 1946, pp. 51-56.

7. Ibid., p. 56.

8. Tax receipt from Hamilton County, Alex McNabb, for 1870 State and County Taxes, 1-1-1-556.

9. Tax receipt from James County, J.C. Heaton, for 1871 State and County Taxes, 1-1-1-695.

10. Marriage Records, Hamilton County, Chattanooga, Tennessee, Marriage Book 2, 1864-1874, Page 150.

11. 1870 Census, Yell County, Arkansas.

12. 1870 Census, Hamilton County, Tennessee.

13. Payment Request, February 10, 1870, from G.R. Poter to Thomas Conner, 1-1-1-378; to Abner McCallie, 1-1-1-546; to Miss Hixon, 1-1-1-547; and to John Roark, 1-1-1-548.

14. Promissory Note from Philip Rains and Joseph Roark to William F. McCormack, April 11, 1870, 1-1-1-549.

15. Payment Request from John L. Roark to Joseph Roark, September 9, 1870, 1-1-1-544.

16. Promissory Note from Joseph Roark to James A. Roark, November 13, 1870, 1-1-1-1850.

17. Donnelly, Polly W., ed., <u>James County, A Lost County of Tennessee</u>, Old James County Chapter, East Tennessee Historical Society, Ooltewah, Tennessee, 1983, pp. 95, 126.

18. Sworn Statement of account balance for Wilson Hixson by Dr. Thomas J. Defriese before Justice of the Peace Silas Witt, October 10, 1870, 1-1-1-858.

19. Ibid.

20. Ibid.

21. Sworn Statement of account balance for Wilson Hixson by Dr. Thomas J. Defriese before Justice of the Peace P.L. Matthews, November 20, 1864, 1-1-1-1251.

22. Letter dated February 5, 1932, from the War Department, Washington, D.C., to Mrs. W.M. Roark, Birchwood, Tennessee, 1-1-1-1206. Italics have been added by this author.

23. 1870 Census, Hamilton County, Tennessee.

24. Records of Hamilton County, Tennessee, Marriage Book 2, 1864-1874, Page 10, January 5, 1865. Marriage was solemnized by A.L. Stulce, M.G.

25. 1880 Census, Hamilton County, Tennessee.

26. Promissory Note from Joseph Roark to Dorris & Owen, June 2, 1871, 1-1-1-191.

27. Promissory Note from Joseph Roark to William F. McCormack, October 13, 1871, 1-1-1-842.

28. Promissory Note from Joseph Roark to William M. Roark, September 23, 1871, 1-1-1-715.

29. Hamilton County Court Records, Volumes 1 and 3, 1864-1878, January 10, 1870, Page 652, Tennessee State Library and Archives, Microfilm Roll No. 45 for Hamilton County.

30. Ibid., February 14, 1870, Page 657.

31. Op. cit., Joseph Roark to William Roark, 1-1-1-715.

32. Letter dated April 20, 1873, from "A" in Vera Cruze, Douglas County, Missouri, to Will Roark, Georgetown, Meigs County, Tennessee, 1-1-1-160.

33. Letter dated August 2, 1872, from Mary Ann Scott, Crawford County, Arkansas, to Will Roark, Birchwood, James County, Tennessee, 1-1-1-797.

34. Deed for One Acre of Land from Joseph Roark to the Trustees of the Salem Baptist Church, James County, Tennessee, September 28, 1872, 1-1-1-1455.

35. Ibid.

36. Ibid.

37. Promissory Note from Joseph Roark to J.A. Doughty, March 4, 1872, 1-1-1-419.

38. Payment Request from J.A. Doughty to Joseph Roark, April 26, 1872, 1-1-1-559.

39. Payment Request from J.A. Doughty to Joseph Roark, October 3, 1872, 1-1-1-525.

40. Promissory Note from Joseph Roark to James Cross, March 1, 1872, 1-1-1-552.

41. Promissory Note from Joseph Roark to Sarah C. Moon, May 24, 1872, 1-1-1-844.

42. Yell County Historical & Genealogical Association, Yell County Heritage, History of Yell County, Arkansas, 1997, p. 121.

43. Minutes, Salem Baptist Church, Saturday, September 28, 1872, 1-1-1-1052.

44. The actual letter to Elizabeth Talley was not preserved. The letter quoted follows the exact text of a similar letter from the Salem Baptist Church to Jane Alexander, 1878, with only the name changed, 1-1-1-1346.

45. Letter dated August 2, 1872, from Mary Ann Scott, Crawford County, Arkansas, to William Roark, Birchwood, Tennessee, 1-1-1-797.

46. Letters dated August 2, 1872, from Tennessee Scott and Martha Jane Scott, Crawford County, Arkansas, to William Roark, Birchwood, Tennessee, 1-1-1-797.

47. Diehl, Leonard R, Scotts–My Wife's Family, unpublished paper, July 1994, 4-1-1-3061.

48. Information on the cause of death of Joel and Joseph Talley and the help of Mary and William Smith in their burial was graciously furnished by Ms. Anne Moore, Danville, Arkansas, a grand-daughter of Andrew Jackson Talley.

49. Minutes, Salem Baptist Church, James County, Tennessee, June 28, 1873, 1-1-1-1052.

50. Church Roll, Salem Baptist Church, James County, Tennessee, 1874-1875, 1-1-1-1045.

51. Promissory Note from Joseph Roark to W.C. Hutcheson, January 1, 1873, 1-1-1-553.

52. Joseph Roark Account with Matilda Brooks, a list of expenses chargeable to her share of the Leonard Brooks Estate, Ca.1873, 1-1-1-319.

53. Receipt from Matilda H. Brooks to Joseph Roark for the receipt of $750 as her share of the Leonard Brooks Estate, September 26, 1873, 1-1-1-318.

54. Op. cit., Hicks, The American Nation, pp. 113-115.

55. Church Roll, Salem Baptist Church, James County, Tennessee, 1872-1873, 1-1-1-1044.

56. Minutes, Salem Baptist Church, James County, Tennessee, December 7, 1873, 1-1-1-1052.

57. Minutes, Salem Baptist Church, James County, Tennessee, August 29, 1874, 1-1-1-1053.

58. Minutes, Salem Baptist Church, James County, Tennessee, December 14, 1874, 1-1-1-1053.

59. Minutes, Salem Baptist Church, James County, Tennessee, April 26, 1873, 1-1-1-1052.

60. Tax Receipt for State and County Taxes for James County, Tennessee, 1873, 1-1-1-698; and 1874, 1-1-1-699.

61. Receipt from Truce & Rose, Chattanooga, Tennessee, to Joseph Roark, October 10, 1874, 1- 1-1-854.

62. Shropshire, Mrs. Laura Roark, <u>Pioneer Days–Stories of the Roark-Conner Ancestry</u>, locally published, Revised Edition, 1992, p. 41.

63. Invoice from Dr. Darius Waterhouse to Joseph Roark for medical service on five occasions between December 10 and December 22, 1874, 1-1-1-427; Allen, Penelope Johnson, <u>Leaves from the Family Tree</u>, Southern Historical Press, Easley, South Carolina, 1982, p. 282; King, John M.D., <u>The Causes, Symptoms, Diagnosis, Pathology, and Treatment of Chronic Diseases</u>, John M. Scudder, Cincinnati, 1866, pp. 722-724.

64. Receipt for a Registered Letter from J.J. Prowder, Birchwood, Tennessee Deputy Post Master, to Joseph Roark, May 3, 1875, 1-1-1-743.

65. Letter dated August 1, 1875, from Noah Atchley to Joseph Roark, 1-1-1-716.

66. Tax Receipt for 1875 State and County Taxes for James County, Tennessee, November 19, 1875, 1-1-1-1443.

67. Receipt from W.F. Francisco and Company to Joseph Roark, January 19, 1876, 1-1-1-555.

68. Medication from the period that probably was prescribed can be found in King, John M.D., <u>The Causes, Symptoms, Diagnosis, Pathology, and Treatment of Chronic Diseases</u>, John M. Scudder, Cincinnati, 1866, p. 724.

69. *The Cleveland Banner*, February 11, 1876.

70. *The Chattanooga Daily Times*, February 15, 1876.

Chapter 12: Epilogue

1. Tennessee State Library and Archives, Microfilm Roll T277, No. 3, Direct Tax Assessment List of Lands and Lots, District 10, Hamilton County, entitled, "State of Tennessee, under the act of Congress entitled 'An Act for the Collection of District Taxes in insurrectionary districts,' approved June 7, 1862, and on the act amendatory thereto," 4-1-1-3751.

2. Deed Records, Hamilton County, Chattanooga, Tennessee, Benjamin Webb to A.L. Stulce, March 12, 1868, Deed Book R, Page 189.

3. List of accounts payable and receivable in the estate of Joseph Roark, developed by James A. Roark, administrator of the estate, ca. March 15, 1876, 1-1-1-321.

4. Promissory Note from William M. Roark to James A. Roark, Administrator of Joseph Roark, Deceased, March 18, 1876, 1-1-1-1246.

5. Receipt from Sarah E. Roark to James A. Roark, Administrator of Joseph Roark, Deceased, March 23, 1876, 1-1-1-428.

6. The conclusion that the three brothers sought the assistance of Talley is based primarily on a promissory note to Talley by both Jim and Will, July 24, 1876, 1-1-1-366, plus the fact that the estate agreement is in the handwriting of someone else other than Jim, John, or Will. Someone also assisted the brothers in writing the quit claim deeds from Mary Ann and Margaret. No other payment or note was made by the brothers except the promissory note to Talley.

7. Deed Records, Hamilton County, Chattanooga, Tennessee, April 5, 1876, Volume 465, Pages 252-253, 4-1-1-2649. The reader will be interested to note that the above deed was not recorded at the Hamilton County Courthouse until January 21, 1925.

8. Estate Settlement Agreement executed by James A. Roark, John W. Roark, and William M. Roark, April 11, 1876, 1-1-1-848.

9. Letter dated May 6, 1876, from Mary Ann Scott to William M. Roark, 1-1-1-739.

10. Bond in the amount of $1,600 from Mary Ann Scott to William M. Roark, May 6, 1876, 1-1-1-738.

11. Deed Records, Hamilton County, Chattanooga, Tennessee, June 2, 1876, Volume 465, Pages 253-254.

12. Promissory Note from James Smith to William Roark, Administrator, June 28, 1876, 1-1-1-902.

13. Promissory Note from James A. Roark and William M. Roark to J.P. Talley, July 24, 1876, 1-1-1-366.

14. Deed Records, Hamilton County, Chattanooga, Tennessee, July 27, 1876, Volume 465, Page 251. The deed was not recorded until January 21, 1925.

15. Deed Records, Hamilton County, Chattanooga, Tennessee, July 27, 1876, Volume 465, Pages 251-252. The deed was not recorded until January 21, 1925.

16. Receipt from Constable John C. Smith to William Roark for six promissory notes for collection, October 28, 1876, 1-1-1-1247.

17. Letters of Administration to William M. Roark for the Joseph Roark Estate executed by J.C. Heaton, County Clerk of James County, Tennessee, October 1, 1877, 1-1-1-323.

18. Receipt from J.C. Heaton, County Clerk of James County, to William M. Roark, September 23, 1878, 1-1-1-326.

19. Grave Marker, Juda Carr Roark, Bald Hill Cemetery, Hamilton County, Tennessee.

20. Deed Records, Hamilton County, Chattanooga, Tennessee, June 2, 1876, Volume 465, Pages 253-254. The deed was not recorded until January 21, 1925.

21. Deed Records, Crawford County, Van Buren, Arkansas, November 1, 1876, Deed Book D, Page 62. The author is indebted to Mr. Don Thompson, Tulsa, Oklahoma, a descendant of Mary Ann Scott and current owner of the Scott farm, for information on the land transactions of Mary Ann Scott from his abstract.

22. Deed Records, Crawford County, Van Buren, Arkansas, November 18, 1882, Deed Book 40, Page 179.

23. Deed Records, Crawford County, Van Buren, Arkansas, December 31, 1886, Deed Book O, Page 368.

24. Deed Records, Crawford County, Van Buren, Arkansas, October 7, 1893, Deed Book 41, Page 282.

25. Names and dates on the children of Mary Ann Scott are from Diehl, Leonard R., Scotts–My Wife's Family, unpublished paper, July 1994, 4-1-1-3061; Crawford County Historical Society, *The Heritage*, Volume IX, April 1966, No. 4, 4-1-1-3063; Swinburn, Susan Stevenson and Doris Stevenson West, History in Headstones, A Complete Listing of All Marked Graves in Known Cemeteries of Crawford County, Arkansas, Press Argus Printers, Van Buren, Arkansas, August 1970, p. 97.

26. Church Roll, Salem Baptist Church, James County, Tennessee, 1874-1875 and later, 1-1-1-1045.

27. Deed Records, Erath County, Stephenville, Texas, August 27, 1878, Deed Book I, Pages 608-610.

28. Grave Marker, Lizzie Killian, Hightower Cemetery, Erath County, Texas.

29. 1900 Census, Erath County, Texas.

30. Deed Records, Hamilton County, Chattanooga, Tennessee, February 2, 1891, Volume 465, Page 254

31. The source of the name of Benjamin Talley's first wife was taken from a deed in which they sold community property. Deed Records, Delta County, Cooper, Texas, June 18, 1890, Deed Book P, Page 493.

32. 1900 Census, Delta County, Texas.

33. Allie, Linda Brown, Delta County, Texas, Marriage Records, 1871-1892, privately published, Fort Worth, Texas, undated, p. 52.

34. Deed Records, Delta County, Cooper, Texas, July 6, 1896, Deed Book U, Page 637.

35. 1900 Census, Delta County, Texas.

36. Marriages in Delta County, July 1892 to September 1928, published by Friends of the Delta County Public Library, Cooper, Texas, undated, p. 114.

37. *Cooper Review*, Cooper, Texas, March 29, 1905.

38. Deed Records, Delta County, Cooper, Texas, October 8, 1907, Volume 19, Page 451.

39. Deed Records, Baylor County, Seymour, Texas, November 25, 1907, Volume 36, Page 421.

40. Texas Death Certificate No. 10917, Benjamin Franklin Talley.

41. Marriage Records, Yell County, Danville, Arkansas, Volume E, Page 188.

42. United States of America, Andrew J. Talley, Dardanelle, Arkansas, Application No. 18289, Homestead Certificate No. 6073, Washington, D.C., January 26, 1898, Volume 207, Page 285.

43. Moore, Anne, "Family Group Sheet, Andrew Jackson Talley," Danville, Arkansas.

44. Grave Marker, Riley Creek Cemetery, Yell County, Arkansas.

45. Letter dated February 3, 1897, from Laura Roark Honea to Laura Roark Shropshire, 1-1-1-308; letter dated March 22, 1897, from Laura Roark Honea to Laura Roark Shropshire, 1-1-1-310.

46. Grave Markers, Elizabeth Killian and Henry Killian, Hightower Cemetery.

47. Family Group Sheet, Joel A. Talley and Sarah Elizabeth Roark, by Oscar Ray Boles, June 30, 1994, 4-1-1-2052.

48. Op. cit., Family Group Sheet by Boles; Marriage Records, Hamilton County, Chattanooga, Tennessee, Marriage Book 2, 1864-1874, Page 150. Death date was graciously provided by Ms. Anne Moore, Danville, Arkansas, a descendant of Andrew Jackson Talley.

49. Grave Marker, Benjamin F. Talley, Old Seymour Cemetery, Baylor County, Texas.

50. Marriage Records, Yell County, Danville, Arkansas, Volume E, Page 188; Grave Marker, Andrew Jackson Talley, Riley Creek Cemetery, Yell County, Arkansas.

51. Op. cit., Family Group Sheet by Boles; Grave Marker, Margaret E. Chambers, Fort Hill Cemetery, Cleveland, Bradley County, Tennessee.

52. Op. cit., Family Group Sheet by Boles.

53. History of Tennessee and a Biographical Sketch of Decatur County, The Goodspeed Publishing Co., Nashville, 1886, p. 893, 4-1-1-3081. This is the only reference to military service by William L. Swafford during the Civil War. No military service record could be located.

54. Ibid.

55. Alexander, Fred, and Margie Alexander, Early Marriage Records (1869-1921) of Decatur County, Tennessee, privately published, Decaturville, Tennessee, undated, p. 65.

56. Ibid., p. 87.

57. Grave Marker, Sardis Ridge Cemetery, Decatur County, Tennessee.

58. Op. cit., Alexander, Early Marriages, pp. 86-87.

59. Ibid., p. 87.

60. Ibid., p. 66.

61. Ibid., p. 86.

62. Information on Margaret Jane "Maggie" Swafford and Louise Francis Swafford and many of the other children of William and Margaret Swafford was graciously provided by Ms. Fran Marlow, Citrus Heights, California, a granddaughter of Louise Francis Swafford and Jerry Jerome Burton.

63. Op. cit., Alexander, Early Marriages, p. 61.

64. Church Minutes, Salem Baptist Church, James County, Tennessee, February 23, 1878, 1-1-1-1055.

65. Roark, John J., Hardtack and Hardship, The Life and Times of Confederate Veteran James A. Roark and His Family, Personal Profiles Publishing Company, 1996.

66. Deed Records, Hamilton County, Chattanooga, Tennessee, December 8, 1881, Volume 472, Pages 684-685, 4-1-1-2061.

67. Events in the life of John W. Roark to this point were taken from Robinett, Julia Roark, Brief Autobiography, 1874-1899, 5-1-1-3049.

68. Deed Records, Milam County, Cameron, Texas, August 19, 1904, Volume 68, Page 480; April 4, 1907, Volume 79, Page 311.

69. All dates in the John W. Roark family listing were taken from the John W. Roark Family Bible, 4-1-1-2058.

70. No deed was ever placed of record transferring title from Jim to Will on Jim's river farm. We know that Will gained title in some manner since he much later gave portions of the farm to his children. More than likely Jim had neither deed nor title, and he received a cash settlement from Will when he left for Texas in 1878. Will was comfortable in his title after 1878 by actual possession, strengthened by the quit claim deed from Jim in 1876. John, on the other hand, had title and sold his river farm to Will for $2,250. Ref: Deed Records, Hamilton County, Chattanooga, Tennessee, September 8, 1881, Volume 472, Page 684. John's deed to Will included sworn statement from Permelia before the James County Clerk, J.C. Heaton; however, the deed was not recorded until April 7, 1925.

71. Deed Records, Hamilton County, Chattanooga, Tennessee, January 27, 1914, Volume 662, Page 404.

72. Burial location provided verbally by Willa Eslick, daughter of Lilly Roark Moon.

73. *Chattanooga Times*, Obituary of William Grover Roark, December 8, 1972, 1-1-1-1693.

74. Records for the William M. Roark family were taken primarily (except as noted elsewhere) from Shropshire, Mrs. Laura Roark, "Recorded Dates of the Family of William M. Roark and Virginia Conner Roark," unpublished manuscript, 1-1-1-3595; *Chattanooga Daily Times*, Obituary of William Grover Roark, December 8, 1972, 1-1-1-1693.

75. Deed Records, Hamilton County, Chattanooga, Tennessee, March 12, 1868, Deed Book R, Page 189.

76. Jackson, Frances Nietta Campbell, "The House of Campbell," unpublished paper, 1965, 4-1-1-3079.

77. History of Benton, Washington, Carroll, Madison, Crawford, Franklin, and Sebastian Counties, Arkansas, The Goodspeed Publishing Co., Chicago, 1889, p. 1211. Reference includes a biographical sketch of Jeanette Webb.

78. Op. cit., Swinburn, History in Headstones, pp. 352-355.

79. Information on the family of Jeanette Clingan Webb and Benjamin Webb was graciously provided by Faye and R.V. Thompson. R.V. Thompson is a great-grandson of Sarah Webb Campbell and a great-great-grandson of Benjamin and Jeanette Webb.

80. 1860 Census, Hamilton County, Tennessee.

81. County Court Records, Hamilton County, Tennessee, 1864-1870, WPA Microfilm Records, Roll No. 29, June 4, 1866, Original Records, Page 197.

82. Ibid., January 9, 1869, Original Records, Page 533.

83. Church Minutes, Salem Baptist Church, James County, Tennessee, November 23, 1883, 1-1-1-1057.

84. *The Daily Herald*, Weatherford, Texas, Obituary for Elizabeth Roark, February 20, 1918, 4-1-1-2727.

85. *The Daily Herald*, Weatherford, Texas, Obituary for Joseph Roark, August 28, 1916, 4-1-1-2728.

86. Soldier's Application for Pension, State of Tennessee, Application No. 3291.

87. Information on Sarah Roark Webb and William Webb was graciously provided by Ms. Kathryn Conner, a descendant of Sarah and William Webb and also of Maximilian Haney Conner. Information on the James P. Roark family is taken from: Roark, David C., 3022 Descendants of James Roark, privately published, October 7, 1998.

88. Roark, Cal Latimore, "John Roark and John Lewis Roark," unpublished paper, undated, 4-1-1-3323.

89. *Chattanooga Daily Times*, Obituary for John Lewis Roark, July 15, 1941, 1-1-1-3038.

90. Shropshire, Mrs. Laura Roark, <u>Pioneer Days–Stories of the Roark-Conner Ancestry</u>, locally published, Revised Edition, 1992, p. 54. Mrs. Shropshire is the only source for the marriage to George Campbell. Elizabeth was identified in the 1850 Census as a twenty-two-year-old daughter of John and Margaret Roark; therefore, her marriage to Campbell probably occurred soon thereafter. No George Campbell can be identified in the census for 1860 or for subsequent years.

91. Ibid., p. 54.

92. Ibid., p. 54.

93. Ibid., p. 54.

94. Military Record, William C. Roark, Company C, Seventh Tennessee Infantry (Union).

95. *Chattanooga Daily Times,* Obituary for America Gregory, August 24, 1940, 1-1-1-1360.

96. The order of birth and estimated dates on the children of John Roark was based on a careful comparison and analysis of the work done by Mrs. Laura Roark Shropshire, Cal Latimore Roark, and David C. Roark, plus a comparison with information in the census of 1850, 1860, 1870, and 1880.

97. Vancel, Mary, "Memorial to James Richardson," unpublished paper, undated, copy provided by Ina Mae Sandefur, Kokomo, Indiana.

98. "Minutes of the Cumberland Gap Baptist Association, October 9, 1886," <u>Reflections</u>, The Quarterly Newsletter on the Claiborne County Historical Society, Volume 14, No. 3, Summer Edition 1996.

99. 1860 Census and 1870 Census, Claiborne County, Tennessee.

100. Vancel, Dr. Jesse, <u>Reflections</u>, The Quarterly Newsletter of the Claiborne County Historical Society, Volume 4, No. 1, Winter Edition 1986.

101. Ibid.

102. Military Record, George W. Richardson, Company E, Second Tennessee Cavalry (Union).

103. Military Record, Calvin James Cunningham, Company G, First Tennessee Cavalry (Union).

104. Civil War Centennial Commission of Tennessee, <u>Tennesseans in the Civil War, A Military History of Confederate and Union Units, Part I</u>, 1964, First Tennessee Infantry (Union), pp. 375- 378.

105. Deed Records, Claiborne County, Tazewell, Tennessee, October 25, 1870, Deed Book F-2, Page 274.

106. Microfilm Tax Records, Claiborne County, Tennessee, Microfilm Records of the Tennessee State Library and Archives, Nashville, Roll No. 36.

107. Hansard, Mary A., <u>Old Time Tazewell</u>, published by Mary Lorena Hansard Wilson, Sweetwater, Tennessee, 1979, p. 255.

108. Op. cit., Vancel, <u>Reflections</u>, 1886.

109. Grave Markers, James Richardson and Nancy Roark Richardson, Cave Springs Cemetery, Claiborne County, Tennessee.

110. Op. cit., Vancel, <u>Reflections</u>, 1886; Grave Markers, George W. Richardson and Mary J. Richardson, Richardson Cemetery, on Old Blair's Creek Road. It should be noted that on current highway maps of Claiborne County, what was Old Blair's Creek Road is now shown as Old Mulberry Road.

111. Op. cit., Vancel, <u>Reflections</u>, 1886; Malone, Georgeann, and Mary E. Parkey, <u>Claiborne County, Tennessee, Marriage Records, Book III, 1850-1868</u>, privately published, 1978, p. 3.

112. Ibid.; Dr. Vancel gives her death date as July 10, 1851, earlier than her marriage. The date herein of July 10, 1853, corrects an obvious typographical error, given the marriage date and time for birth of her first child.

113. Op. cit., Malone, <u>Claiborne County Marriages, Book III</u>, p. 32; Grave Marker, John Richardson, Ferguson Cemetery on Old Ferguson Road in Cave Springs Community, Claiborne County, Tennessee.

114. Op. cit., Malone, <u>Claiborne County Marriages, Book III</u>, p. 21; Grave Markers, C.J. Cunningham and Mary Ann Cunningham, Richardson Cemetery.

115. Op. cit., Vancel, <u>Reflections</u>, 1886.

116. Ibid.

117. Op. cit., Malone, <u>Claiborne County Marriages, Book III</u>, p. 30; Grave Markers, James T. Richardson and Catherine Williams Richardson, Richardson Cemetery.

118. 1860 Census, Claiborne County, Tennessee.

119. 1850, 1860, and 1870 Censuses, Claiborne County, Tennessee. The first daughter is listed as Eliza in the 1850 Census but as Louisa in the 1860 Census. Louisa is assumed to be the correct name.

120. Sistler, Byron and Barbara Sistler, <u>Early East Tennessee Marriages</u>, Byron Sistler & Associates, Inc., Nashville, 1987, Volume 1, Grooms, p. 310, 4-1-1-2789. Friar is given in various documents as Freyor, Fryor, etc. Friar is used consistently herein.

121. Ibid., Volume 2, Brides, p. 309. There is a possibility that William and Nancy had a third son by the name of William. In the 1860 Census for Dent County, Missouri, a William, age 11, was listed with William and Nancy Roark. Was this their third son? No definitive answer can be given as no other record can be found on this William. He does not appear on the 1850 Census nor the 1870 Census, nor is he mentioned when the estate of his father is settled. He is not mentioned in the text of this work since no satisfactory explanation is available.

122. Deed Records, Claiborne County, Tazewell, Tennessee, December 1, 1856, Deed Book Z, Page 564.

123. Deed Records, Claiborne County, Tazewell, Tennessee, September 17, 1859, Deed Book Z, Page 112.

124. Deed Records, Claiborne County, Tazewell, Tennessee, July 8, 1846, Deed Book S, Page 681.

125. Deed Records, Dent County, Salem, Missouri, January 7, 1860, Deed Book A, Page 345.

126. Military Record, James Roark Sr., Company D, Thirty-second Missouri Infantry (Union). Military Record, James Roark Jr., Company D, Thirty-second Missouri Infantry (Union).

127. This conclusion is based on two facts: first, when William sold his land in Dent County in 1867, he sold his "undivided one-half" ownership in the 120 acres he and Friar owned jointly to John F. Angle and Daniel Friar is not mentioned in the conveyance; second, in the census for Claiborne County in 1870, Eliza is listed with her parents, using her maiden name.

128. Deed Records, Claiborne County, Tazewell, Tennessee, September 9, 1865, Deed Book C-2, Page 44.

129. Deed Records, Dent County, Salem, Missouri, April 4, 1867, Deed Book F, Page 533.

130. Deed Records, Dent County, Salem, Missouri, April 4, 1867, Deed Book F, Page 620.

131. The exact date of William's death is unknown. The assumption that he died in 1880 is based on the fact that Nancy Roark paid the taxes on their land in 1881. Microfilm Tax Records, Claiborne County, Tennessee, Microfilm Records of the Tennessee State Library and Archives, Nashville, Roll No. 36.

132. Deed Records, Claiborne County, Tazewell, Tennessee, July 28, 1881, Deed Book K-2, Page 401.

133. Op. cit., Hansard, Old Time Tazewell, Mrs. Hansard indicates that Nancy's children lived in Kentucky, while the deed for the sale of the homestead tract gives the location for Nancy and her two children as Lee County, Virginia. Nancy's son John was identified in the 1900 Census, Clay County, Kentucky. Doubtless Nancy lived with her son in her later years.

134. Op. cit., Sistler, Early East Tennessee Marriages, Volume 1, Grooms, p. 310.

135. See Note 119.

136. Op. cit., Malone, Claiborne County Marriages, Book III, p. 12.

137. Sistler, Byron and Barbara Sistler, Early East Tennessee Marriages, Byron Sistler & Associates, Inc., Nashville, Tennessee, 1987, Volume 2, Brides, p. 309.

138. Op. cit., Malone, Claiborne County Marriages, Book III, p. 21.

139. Johnson, Paul, <u>Cemeteries of Claiborne County, Tennessee</u>, published by Paul Johnson, printed by Jostens, Clarksville, Tennessee,1992, p. 238.

140. Op. cit., Malone, <u>Claiborne County Marriages, Book III</u>, p. 13.

141. Op. cit., Johnson, <u>Cemeteries</u>, p. 69.

142. Op. cit., Malone, <u>Claiborne County Marriages, Book III</u>, p. 30.

143. Military Record, Wiley Ellison, Company I, Third Tennessee Infantry (Union).

144. Op. cit., Johnson, <u>Cemeteries</u>, p. 36.

145. All information on the family of Elizabeth Ellison, except that otherwise noted, was graciously provided by Mrs. Ina Mae Sandefur, Kokomo, Indiana, a descendant of Jeremiah Ellison and a storehouse of knowledge on the Ellisons and related families in Claiborne County. For death date and burial location of Joseph Ellison see ibid., p. 234.

146. Deed Records, Claiborne County, Tazewell, Tennessee, September 6, 1858, Deed Book Z, Page 41.

147. Deed Records, Dent County, Salem, Missouri, December 23, 1859, Deed Book A, Page 447.

148. Woodruff, Mrs. Howard W., <u>Dent County, Missouri, Marriages, Marriage Book A 1851- 1879</u>, published by Mrs. Howard W. Woodruff, 1972, p. 11.

149. Ibid., p. 12. The marriage of Sarah to William H. Moore is questioned by family descendants as possibly being incorrect. Family tradition is that Sarah Roark married a "Peyton" Moore.

150. Jeremiah A. Roark Family Group Sheet prepared by Ms. Janis Ragar, Sedalia, Missouri, a descendant of Jeremiah Roark.

151. County Court Records, Dent County, Salem, Missouri, February 4, 1865, Page 333.

152. Deed Records, Dent County, Salem, Missouri, January 1, 1868, Deed Book F, Page 626.

153. Deed Records, Texas County, Houston, Missouri, November 10, 1873, SW4, SE4, Section 11 and NW4, Section 14, T28N, R7W, Deed Book H, Page 324; November 6, 1875, NE4, SE4, Section 27, T29N, R7W, Deed Book I, Page 305; March 14, 1876, Entry Application No. 4999 for SW4, SW4, Section 11, and NE4, NE4, Section 15, T28N, R7W, Homestead Grant Certificate No. 2421; January 1, 1883, NW4, SW4, Section 14, and NE4, SE4, Section 15, T28N, R7W, Deed Book N, Page 72; March 1, 1883, SW4, SE4, and SE4, SW4, Section 27, and NW4, NE4, Section 34, T29N, R7W, Deed Book M, Page 631; May 22, 1884, N2, NE4, and SW4, NE4, and SE4, NW4, Section 23, T28N, R7W, Deed Book Q, Page 51.

154. Grave Marker, Elizabeth Roark, Cold Springs Cemetery, Texas County, Missouri.

155. 1900 Census, Texas County, Missouri.

156. Grave Marker, Jeremiah Roark, Cold Springs Cemetery, Texas County, Missouri. The date of death is not included on the marker.

157. Op. cit., Sistler, Early East Tennessee Marriages, Volume 1, Grooms, p. 310.

158. Op. cit., Malone, Claiborne County Marriages, Book III, p. 17.

159. Roll of Honor, Government Printing Office, Washington, D.C., 1868, Reprinted by Genealogical Publishing Co., Inc., 1994, James Roark, Company D, Thirty-second Missouri Infantry, Vicksburg National Cemetery, Section H, Grave 121, p. 69.

160. Op. cit., Woodruff, Dent County Marriages, p. 30.

161. Melton, Mildred F. and Neva N. Bryant, Texas County Missouri Marriage Records, 1876- 1888, privately published, undated, Houston, Missouri.

162. Texas County, Missouri, Genealogical and Historical Society, Texas County Cemeteries, Volume 3, Clinton, Burdine Sargent, Pierce, and Date Townships, privately published, 1983.

163. Grave Marker, Timothy Roark, Summersville Cemetery, Summersville, Missouri.

164. Op. cit., Melton, Texas County Marriages.

165. Ibid.

166. Melton, Mildred F. and Neva N. Bryant, Texas County Missouri Marriage Records, 1888-1893, privately published, undated, Houston, Missouri.

167. Information on the family of Jeremiah Roark, except as otherwise noted, was graciously provided by Ms. Janis Ragar, Sedalia, Missouri, Ms. Sondra Martin and Ms. Merriam White, Kansas City, Missouri, and Ms. Thelma Johnson, Clarksville, Tennessee, all descendants of Jeremiah Roark.

168. Op. cit., Sistler, Early East Tennessee Marriages, p. 310.

169. Deed Records, Claiborne County, Tazewell, Tennessee, August 4, 1848, Deed Book T, Page 482, 4-1-1-3769.

170. Deed Records, Claiborne County, Tazewell, Tennessee, March 9, 1850, Deed Book U, Page 334.

171. Deed Records, Claiborne County, Tazewell, Tennessee, May 12, 1853, Deed Book W, Page 89, 4-1-1-3771.

172. Deed Records, Claiborne County, Tazewell, Tennessee, September 14, 1858, Deed Book Y, Page 489, 4-1-1-3766.

173. Deed Records, Claiborne County, Tazewell, Tennessee, May 16, 1859, Deed Book Z, Page 58; May 27, 1859, Deed Book Z, Page 56; June 16, 1859, Deed Book Z, Page 57; June 22, 1859, Deed Book Z, Page 117; August 16, 1859, Deed book Z, Page 92; September 17, 1859, Deed Book Z, Page 112; September 23, 1859, Deed Book Z, Page 118.

174. Military Records, James Roark, John Roark, and William Roark, Company I, Third Tennessee Infantry (Union).

175. Civil War Centennial Commission of Tennessee, Tennesseans in the Civil War, A Military History of Confederate and Union Units, Part I, 1964, Third Tennessee Infantry (Union), pp. 380- 383.

176. Deed Records, Claiborne County, Tazewell, Tennessee, May 28, 1881, Deed Book K-2, Page 194.

177. Deed Records, Claiborne County, Tazewell, Tennessee, November 22, 1883, Deed Book L- 2, Page 474; Deed Book M-2, Page 149; Deed Book P-2, Page 518; Deed Book Q-2, Page 606.

178. Deed Records, Claiborne County, Tazewell, Tennessee, March 11, 1885, Deed Book O-2, Page 518; July 22, 1885, Deed Book Q-2, Page 151; December 24, 1886, Page O-2, Page 70.

179. Birth date of James Roark, as well as that for all other children of Timothy Roark Jr. was taken from a copy of the family Bible. This biblical record was graciously furnished by Ms. Becky Campbell, Crofton, Maryland, a descendant of Timothy Roark Jr. through Nancy Jane Roark Campbell. The date of death for James Roark was estimated from dates on deeds which he witnessed, and did not witness, for his father.

180. Op. cit., Malone, Claiborne County Marriages, Book III, p. 23.

181. Ibid., p. 29.

182. Op. cit., Johnson, Cemeteries, p. 115.

183. Roll of Honor, Government Printing Office, Washington, D.C., 1868, Reprinted by Genealogical Publishing Co., Inc., 1994, William Roark, Company I, Third Tennessee Infantry, Knoxville National Cemetery, Section 5, Grave 131, p. 425.

184. Op. cit., Malone, Claiborne County Marriages, Book IV, p. 1.

185. Death date for Joseph Roark was written in the family Bible.

186. Op. cit., Malone, Claiborne County Marriages, Book IV, p. 9.

187. "Minutes of the Cumberland Baptist Association," August 19, 1897, Reflections, The Quarterly Newsletter of the Claiborne County Historical Society, Volume 17, No. 3, Summer Edition 1999.

188. Op. cit., Malone, Claiborne County Marriages, Book IV, p. 17.

189. Op. Cit., Johnson, Cemeteries, p. 71.

190. Op. cit., Malone, Claiborne County Marriages, Book IV, p. 4; Grave Marker, Sarah Roark Whitaker, Cave Springs Cemetery, Claiborne County, Tennessee.

191. Op. cit., Malone, Claiborne County Marriages, Book IV, p. 23.

192. Death year for Elizabeth Roark was written in the family Bible.

193. Op. cit., Malone, Claiborne County Marriages, Book IV, p. 18.

194. Grave Marker, Mary Williams, Cave Springs Cemetery.

195. Marriage Records, Claiborne County, Tazewell, Tennessee.

196. Grave Marker, Mary Roark Richardson, Ferguson Cemetery, Claiborne County, Tennessee.

197. Campbell, Ms. Becky, Crofton, Maryland, Family Group Sheet, not dated.

198. Op. cit., Sistler, Early East Tennessee Marriages, Volume 2, p. 309. In providing information for the marriage license, Mary Ann gave her name as "Polly." Her birth date was the only one of the family not listed in the James Roark Copy Book. Its source was: Grave Marker, Mary Lambert, Lambert Cemetery, Claiborne County, Tennessee.

199. Military Record, James Jefferson Lambert, Company I, Third Tennessee Infantry (Union); Roll of Honor, Government Printing Office, Washington, D.C., 1868, Reprinted by Genealogical Publishing Co., Inc., 1994, Jefferson Lambert, Company I, Third Tennessee Infantry, Lexington National Cemetery, Circle 8, Grave 355, p. 253.

200. Op. cit., Malone, Claiborne County Marriages, Book III, p. 31. Much information on the Lambert family was graciously provided by Ina Mae Sandefur, Kokomo, Indiana.

201. Op. cit., Johnson, Cemeteries, p. 133.

202. Op. cit., Malone, Claiborne County Marriages, Book III, p. 23.

203. Op. cit., Johnson, Cemeteries, p. 133.

204. Op. cit., Malone, Claiborne County Marriages, Book IV, p. 10.

205. Op. cit., Johnson, Cemeteries, p. 190.

206. Ibid., p. 19.

207. Grave Marker, Joseph Lambert, Lambert Cemetery, Claiborne County, Tennessee.

208. Grave Marker, George W. Lambert, Lambert Cemetery.

209. Grave Marker, Susan Lambert, Lambert Cemetery.

210. Deed Records, Claiborne County, Tazewell, Tennessee, Volume 55, Pages 552 and 553, 4- 1-1-3773.

211. Deed Records, Hamilton County, Chattanooga, Tennessee, Volume 787, Pages 511-514.

212. Deed Records, Hamilton County, Chattanooga, Tennessee, Volume 787, Pages 510-511.

213. Deed Records, Hamilton County, Chattanooga, Tennessee, Volume 1657, Pages 254-255.

214. Deed Records, Hamilton County, Chattanooga, Tennessee, Volume 1657, Page 256.

215. Deed Records, Hamilton County, Chattanooga, Tennessee, Volume 3181, Pages 443-444.

216. Witt, Woodrow W., <u>From Tennessee to Texas</u>, unpublished paper, ca.1985.

Index

A

D

I

Johnston, Gen. Albert Sidney, 293
Johnston, Gen. Joseph E., 314
Johnston, Thomas J., 415
Jolly's Island, 158, 221
Jones, Jeremiah H., 137
Jones, Martha J., 414
Jones, Sarah Rachel, 391
Jones, Brig. Gen. William E. "Grumble," 315

K
keelboats, 140
Kegley, Mary B., 30
Keith, George, 129
Kelly, J., 146
Kennedy, John C., 157
Kennedy, Sam, 207
Key, Francis Scott, 11, 108
Kibert, Mary Elizabeth, 412
Killian, Ann, 351
Killian, Billy, 285, 330
Killian, Elizabeth, 386
Killian, Henry, 373, 386-389
Killian, Jesse, 166-167, 171-172, 213, 234, 243, 258-260, 264
Killian, Lizzie, 386, 387, 389
Killian, Sarah, 387
Killian, Sarah Elizabeth Roark, 386-389
Killian, William, 166-167, 182, 185, 201, 208, 233, 234, 235, 250, 342, 386, 387
Killian, William (son of Henry), 386
Killion, Nancy, 226
Kimbrough, Duke, 243
Kimbrough, I. Z., 341
Kimbrough, John, 276, 311, 318, 320
Kincannon's Ferry, 309, 310
King, Rev. Alfred, 235-236
King, James B., 284-285
King, Maj. John B., 315
King, Robert, 69
Kingsbury, R. H., 387

M

Y

Z